A SAGA OF SMITHS
(AN <u>EPIC</u> FAMILY HISTORY)

2

Produced by Richard John Smith
Details of his other publications are listed at the back of the Bibliography
Storefront: http://www.lulu.com/spotlight/R1Publications

Softcover and Kindle editions are also available through Amazon and other
International Book Distributors.

Notices

In *'A Saga of Smiths,'* the spelling and punctuation have been used as originally seen in a specific document or inscription, thereby explaining the apparent grammatical inconsistencies found throughout much of this work. My own inserts are enclosed in quotations and denoted by square brackets.

It should be noted that before the mid-eighteenth century, there was no conformity in the spelling of English in the British Isles. Consequently, the spelling of words varied from region to region, from person to person and even from the same person at various times! Thick local accents often hindered the accurate transcribing of personal names on Parish Records. Also, the varied abilities of Parish Clerks were often very telling with some writing in beautiful hand script and others being barely legible.

The place names (given at the end of each Census Information) always refer to a person's place of birth, unless otherwise stated. These were sometimes misspelt. Variations in the spelling of forenames like *'Betsy'* (or *'Betsey'*) can be attributed to the original sources and have been retained just as they were.

To make Census Returns and other old documents more readable I ran them through both Spellcheck and Grammarly. This led to a few minor modifications, in wording but great care was taken to ensure there was no change in meaning.

In this work, the names of male ancestors on census lists will be underlined while in names female ancestors will be *'italicised'* as well. In both cases, the lettering will be in bold font.

Any views or opinions given in this work are my own and do not necessarily reflect or concur with the beliefs, views or opinions of living family members, the sources listed here, or any other party connected to this work.

A SAGA OF SMITHS
(AN <u>EPIC</u> FAMILY HISTORY)

RICHARD JOHN SMITH

A Family History, tracing the varied fortunes of the Smiths of West Yorkshire and their relationship to other families, i.e.: -

- The Absaloms of Hampshire and London
- The Cardens of Brighton
- The Cloughs of Sutton and Crosshills
- The Fareys of Skipton
- The Fosters of Birmingham and Waterford in Ireland
- The Gillinsons of Leeds
- The Hastings of Holderness
- The Myersons of London and Eastern Europe
- The Stamfords of East Yorkshire
- The Wilsons of Colne, Sutton and Crosshills

It is dedicated to my parents Fred and Cynthia Smith. Also, to my Great Grand Father Edmund Smith *'who made it possible.'*

4

The Moral Right of the author has been asserted First Released for limited Distribution by Lulu Publishing, August 2018

ISBN: 978-1-910871-89-8

Published Works

Under my own name (or the pen names of **Leo Arland** or **Raymond Creed**) my own published works include: -

Arland Leo (2012) *The Exit Machine: A Dark Comedy Concerning the Office Romances and Internal Politics of a Euthanasia Centre and Set in a World where Assisted Suicide and Euthanasia is No Longer a Matter of Choice*

Arland Leo (2014) *Hoofbeats of the Apocalypse: Creative Works Exploring the Relationship between the Decay of Western Civilization, the Impact of Social Darwinism and the Growing Turmoil in the Middle East*

Arland Leo (2014) *Restless Ashes: Creative Pieces Exploring the Horrors of Auschwitz-Birkenau And Its Connection with Present Day Events*

Arland Leo (2017) *U.S. Redux: Exploring the Madness of a Nation: Some reflections on the Rise of Donald Trump to the U.S. Presidency*

Creed Raymond (2010) *Facing the Unthinkable: What the Jewish People May Feel When They Find their True Messiah*

Creed Raymond (2011) *The 52 Attributes of God: A Bible-Based Analysis of the Attributes of God – With Particular Reference to the Relationship between Divine Holiness and Divine Love*

Creed Raymond (2010) *The Leeds Liturgy: A Prayer Book Enabling Christians to 'Worship God in Spirit and in Truth'*

Creed Raymond (2010) *The Phantom Conflict: Bible Teaching on the Relationship between Divine Holiness and Divine Love in connection with Christian Idolatry and the Need for a Balanced Christian life*

Smith Richard (2013) *Advantage Study Skills: A Manual Designed to Assist Teachers and Students*

Smith Richard (2013) *At 47: Poems on 'This or That'*

All these titles are available in both hard and soft cover form on **Amazon** and **Lulu Publishing** except for *'U.S. Redux'* which is only available on **Amazon** and *'Restless Ashes'* which is only available on **Amazon Kindle.**

Contents

10

Each of the above chapters (plus the **Bibliography**) can be found in electronic form on **Amazon Kindle**. To locate them, go to **Google** and in the '*space bar*' key in the main title **'A Saga of Smiths'** followed by the chapter title and my name **'Richard Smith.'**

Readers are expected to conduct their own virus checks when visiting any sources cited in this work. The author is <u>not</u> legally, morally or financially responsible for any damage incurred by such an activity.

Introduction: A Preoccupation with Respectability

Begun as a labour of love (and first drafted from **April 1999** until **August 2002**) a *'Saga of Smiths'* was finally completed in **2018** in a vastly expanded version. It originated as a tribute to that truly remarkable man – my late father **Fred Gordon Smith** – who lived from **February 1914** until **April 1999**. My intention was always to convey something of the character of this man, ensuring that his influence would be passed down the generations to those who would never have known him. It was also a way of coping with the strong feelings of grief I had at the time of his death. Preparing it required the use of my entire intellectual and creative powers, along with an absolute determination to give my late father the very best I could offer. Emotionally, it was extremely taxing, but the high points were many – including the discovery of the family tomb at **Sutton-in-Craven** and the old **Vernon Road** address. These more than made up for any personal pressures. A particularly frustrating period included the time spent in the **Leeds Archive Centre** sifting through what I'd originally thought to be pertinent documents – only to find them yielding nothing at all in the way of useful information. There was also the persistent grind of scrutinising endless reels of microfiche and handling bulky Trade Directories. Furthermore, when information <u>was</u> eventually uncovered, it seemed to offer a myriad of interpretations, or at the very least one or two others. I was heartily thankful that I had been trained in certain ancient **Jewish** methods of Bible interpretation. To be honest, one needed the wisdom of a rabbi to try and wrestle with some of the unexpected material that came my way! One of the **Jewish** methods I used was the *'story format'* which helped convey certain aspects of truth concerning my father (set within his own socio-economic background). Although historically accurate, these *'stories'* are readily distinguishable from the factual material comprising the bulk of this work.

In the end, I feel I have made only a very small return for the compassion my father showed to his family members over the course of his lifetime. This was indeed a story worth telling. Within months of his decease, I grasped that, to better understand his life and the influences that shaped its development, it was necessary to step back two generations, to own **Fred's** Grandfather, **Edmund Smith**. This latter's life was pivotal to the whole subsequent **Smith** clan and without him, the **Smiths** would not be where (or who) they are today. Much attention was paid to this very complex man and to his background in the woollen trade.

By the end of **1999,** I quickly realised that this work was rapidly taking on a *'life of its own.'* I not only felt that I knew my own father better than I had done during his long life, I was also beginning to comprehend something of **Edmund's** life too. However, at this early stage, many gaps were still apparent. Through careful research and documentary evidence, many gaps were gradually filled. Even so, major new discoveries were <u>still</u> being made – even as late as **July 2018.** One can never claim to finish a Family History. Instead, all one can say is, *'I've given all I can to it.'* That has certainly been true in my case and that of my wife **June** who merits a *'proof-reader of the century award.'* Without her tireless editing, this work would never have begun. The *'Saintly Patience'* she displayed throughout this enterprise was commendable.

In **September 2006** (following the prompting of my mother **Cynthia**) I not only explored <u>her</u> side of the family but went deeper into the lives of my father's sisters – who proved to be a rather colourful lot! In **June 2017** (just before a major collapse in her health) my mother was still providing invaluable sources of information about them. In **March** the following year, despite being extremely frail, she disclosed that **Fred** had always viewed a certain nephew of his as being *'dishonest.'* This certainly turned out to be the case as his fraudulent malpractices were exposed on Television! Not for the only time, his view of certain people was confirmed by subsequent events. **Fred** was a shrewd judge of character.

During this research, the realization gradually dawned that similar patterns of behaviour were re-occurring – not only across the generations but across the centuries – in widely different social contexts. This suggested a significant genetic component underlying each of these patterns. This is not to advocate a crude determinism but does imply that an awareness of these patterns could prove helpful in providing examples of character traits – some to emulate <u>and</u> others to avoid. History is as much about learning how to live in the present as it is about studying the past. I really did find that to better understand a person, it is sometimes necessary to go back generations. This was certainly true of both my parents.

Of indispensable help to this *'History'* were the relatives (and even strangers) who provided many useful leads, as did professional Librarians and Registrar Officers in many diverse locations. (These sources are gratefully acknowledged in the Bibliography – although not always by name to preserve confidentiality.) Overall, I was amazed at what could be uncovered. For instance, I had never thought it possible to discern the likely motivations governing the actions of my nineteenth-century forebears. But now – if I were to meet some of my ancestors, I feel that I would already know some of their innate characteristics; they would strike me as being old acquaintances. Also, throughout this research, I was suddenly made privy to what had hitherto been tightly-held family secrets. Mysteries hidden for decades were being revealed and I felt that, because they were being brought out into the open, some old family wounds were being healed. There was a marked sense that a large-scale *'settling of old accounts'* was taking place. I felt, almost tangibly, that a musty old volume had been closed as I penned the final words of this *'Family History'* and a new and fresh volume (marking a new phase in the **Smith** family saga) was about to be opened.

Furthermore, it has always been my deliberate intention to guide the reader through the intricacies of compiling a Family History. My sincere wish is that they gain a *'feel'* of what this process is like and the various challenges it can bring. To some extent, this work is a *'mini-history'* of how (and why) this Family History came into being. It began as a simple tribute to my late father, a story of his life alone, then quickly became a record of the **Smith** line itself. Finally, over a period of nineteen years **(1999-2018),** it grew and grew into the *'monster'* epic you now hold in your hands! This *'incremental'* approach should benefit those wishing to write their own Family History or who are engaged in degree level historical research. Specialists in subject areas like **The Yorkshire Textile Trade, Nineteenth Century Baptist Chapels** and the **Leeds Jewish** and **Asian Communities** can also benefit. It may also prove of interest to those who have anything to do with the *'family unit,'* the psychological elements of which influence every family life. As this study makes clear, the **Smiths** have been endowed with more than their fair share of *'larger than life'* characters!

Through a mixture of imagination and detailed research, I have tried to *'bring to life'* those historical epochs in which earlier generations of **Smiths** lived. These often differed from one generation to the next and all were a huge contrast from the world in which we live today. Even a small settlement like **Sutton-in-Craven** would, under the impact of industrialisation, have undergone enormous changes within the space of one generation. This same point could also be said – but even more so – of large commercial centres like **Leeds.** Complicating matters still further was the fact that, even within one epoch (like the early **Victorian** period) wide-ranging differences existed between various geographical locations and classes of people in terms of both cultural and economic development. More recent and far-reaching changes took place under the impact of the two World Wars and the cultural upheavals of the **1960s.** These also had a major impact on the development of my family.

To place certain family members into a wider context, I have sometimes referred to an epoch-making event of their own day, *e.g.* **The Battle of Trafalgar.** Moreover, I have endeavoured to reconstruct some of the social circles in which they mixed. This explains why other connected families (*e.g.* the **Stamford** family of **Burton Pidsea**) received a great deal of coverage. Without this type of *'extra information'* key family members could well have been viewed in isolation, cut off from the rest of their community and the wider world. Such isolation may have led to incorrect conclusions about them. The previous generations of my family lived through (and died amidst) profound changes. This is exactly the point I have tried to convey – hopefully, with some degree of success.

This *'History'* has itself *'lived through'* a vast revolution in *'Information Technology'* (I.T.) – which directly opened-up new avenues of research. It became ever more challenging to keep abreast of the vast changes within the I.T. field itself. Until the rise of *'print on demand'* technology (in **2004**) placing this *'History'* into book form would simply not have been financially viable. Publishing things electronically would have seemed inconceivable when this work was first begun in **1999.** All I was vaguely aware of then was that relevant technology was generally *'moving in my favour'* but that a prolonged *'waiting game'* would be involved. As a *'History'* writer I have lived through changes as radical as those produced by the first Printing Presses! Its completion demonstrates that I as a **Smith,** have attempted to <u>fully exploit</u> those changes which would enhance my business and personal life. The **Smith** *'clan'* have always been opportunists!

When undertaking research, I found some periods, *i.e.* the **1830s,** contained a huge amount of documentation whilst, disappointingly, other later periods were only sparsely furnished. The latter necessitated a greater reliance upon the use of verbal testimonies. Sadly, *'knowledge gaps'* still occurred; *e.g.* no account at all could be given of my Great Grandfather – **Edmund Smith's** – Church connections during the late **Victorian** era. Also, only a sketchy outline could be provided of the courtship between my Grandparents **Frank Smith** and **Elizabeth Foster** during the **1890s.** When it came to the *'availability of information'* it really was a case of *'feast or famine!'* On several occasions, I was almost overwhelmed by the amount of data flooding my way, yet at others, I spent weeks or months chasing up just one bare fact, only to find that, in the end, it was frustratingly of no direct relevance! Furthermore, out of respect for living relatives, some of the most sensitive information has been deliberately omitted.

Amassing the vast amount of information and gathering it into one coherent whole was another challenge, resolved only in **June 2015.** It was at this point that I opted to follow a loose chronological order. Firstly, I divided this work into four *'Parts,'* each consisting of four *'Chapters.'* Each chapter was then further sub-divided into *'Sections,'* each one exploring an individual development, subject or personality. All Parts, Chapters and Sections are best compared to tributaries flowing into a wider flowing river – representing the **Smith** line. Closing this work is a Bibliography which places each source into an individual category. All contributing archive centres, libraries and organizational bodies are also referenced.

If there's one theme holding this vast work together it's that of *'respectability.'* Down the centuries (amidst very different socio-economic conditions) the **Smiths** continually displayed two types of *'respectability;'* <u>reactive</u> – preoccupied with <u>preserving</u> one's place in society and <u>proactive</u> striving for the <u>improvement</u> of the family's social standing. Woe to any family member who strayed from this tradition of *'respectability!'* In the case of the **Smiths,** their *'respectability'* was upheld via a whole mix of strategies. These included business transactions *e.g.* land deals in the eighteenth century, the careful handling of money, social networking and the making of advantageous marriages. They tended also to be active participators in the community *e.g.* a deep involvement in the local church or chapel and along with the determination to strive hard to obtain whatever education was available. Later evidence would confirm that my ancestors constantly aspired to *'better themselves.'* They seemed obsessed with achievement and were sometimes willing to *'cut off'* family members who were perceived to have failed. Generally, the **Smiths** were opportunistic social climbers. If the chance arose to move up the social ladder, they would take it and not be too bothered about those left behind. This ethos of self-improvement and striving for respectability is still very much in evidence in my own family and is even noticeable amongst all four of my children. To be viewed as *'respectable'* was of huge general and social importance. Possessing it immediately created a positive image wherein a craftsman or businessman could maintain customer loyalty and stand a better chance of flourishing in their chosen trade. The **Smiths'** obsession with respectability was understandable – often the only alternative would have been starvation or the eking out of an existence as an ill-paid labourer. My remote ancestors would have been all too aware of this – as would their immediate descendants (of the eighteenth and nineteenth centuries). Successive generations of **Smiths** have endlessly striven to maintain their respectability; they knew that to be respectable was to be recognized as being of *'sound'* character and of good social standing and reputation in the community. It also helped guarantee survival.

At the close of this Introduction, it's sincerely hoped that this History will have provided a fitting tribute to some of my forebears. Despite a few negative aspects their story has been of great interest, humour and pathos. To hear (almost) long-forgotten ancestors *'speak'* in their own words was an amazing experience. So much became clearer – what once had been vaguely remembered traditions became precisely documented events. Also, my engagement with this History on a truly personal level has resulted in me feeling firmly rooted! I now know for sure from *'whence I've come,'* I've also learned which familial character traits to encourage and which to be more cautious. Somewhat humorously, I like to ponder that I too have fully displayed this family trait of perseverance and dogged determination through the compiling of this history. It will be my own equivalent of my Great Grandfather's headstone in **Sutton-in-Craven, Yorkshire** – that it too will be a *'monument'* – keeping the tongues of my descendants wagging for generations to come! It is my personal legacy to the **Smith** family. They needn't provide a plaque in remembrance of me at some municipal crematorium; instead, this book will be my joyous memorial!

Richard John Smith
Sunday, 31st March 2019
(Exactly twenty years after this work was first conceived in a promise made during my last visit to my Father)

CHAPTER 1: A PENNINE SETTING

Section 1: Geography and Climate

Concerning the Geography and Climate of Calderdale

To help describe the four settlements where successive generations of my ancestors lived it will be necessary to begin at **Cowling** where the **Smiths** originated. A descent is then made to **Sutton** and onto **Crosshills** and **Glasburn.** The latter lies outside **Sutton** like the top bar of a 'T' and lines each side of the **Colne Road** (now known as the **A6068**) which runs through **Cowling.** Located to the North of **Crosshills** is the small hillside village of **Kildwick** which lies behind both the **River Aire** and the **Leeds-Liverpool Canal**. Besides the canal is the Parish Church which played a significant role in the lives of my forebears.

The **Pennine** location of these settlements means that they are sited below a natural meeting point of different air currents. This feature causes extremely variable weather that can alter in minutes. The relatively high altitude makes for the bleak weather during winter, especially in **Cowling** where swirls of windblown snow can sweep down the **Calder Valley**. In summer, it can be oppressively hot; my wife and I came near to suffering from heat stroke in **August 2003** near **Cowling Pinnacle** where we had to take shelter under a large rock. However, the locality is more noted for its heavy rainfalls which largely preclude all but the hardiest crops. All the townships in this area can be classified as valley settlements (although sections of **Cowling** are located on a moorland slope). They each lie tucked between the **Pennines** (a range of hills commonly referred to as *'the spine of England'*). This often-bleak **Pennine** setting would explain why much of the development that did take place related directly to sheep farming and the worsted trade. It still offers spectacular moorland scenery.

Both the **River Aire** and the adjacent **Leeds-Liverpool Canal** (lying immediately to the north) flow between **Kildwick** and **Crosshills** before heading northwards away from **Sutton** and **Cowling**. (The canal touches **Kildwick**.) Flowing at the bottom of **Cowling** is **Ickornshaw Beck** which joins the wider **Leys Beck** that divides **Glasburn** from **Sutton**. The latter is an elongated settlement lying immediately to the South. Eventually, this waterway joins the **River Aire,** well east of the **Crosshills-Kildwick** locality.

Having outlined the general topography of the above settlements (in which my ancestors lived and struggled to maintain some sort of respectability) I will now review each one, adding something of the *'flavour'* of each community.

Section 2: Cowling

Concerning the Pennine Settlement of Cowling

Sited high in the **Pennines** (on the road to **Colne** and near the **Yorkshire-Lancashire** border) was the village of **Cowling** where the early **Smiths** appear to have originated. It's now **(2016)** a settlement of **1-2,000** people and is characterised by thick-walled, grey stone houses. Details of its origins and history are provided by the following extracts, taken from **Wood's** extremely helpful and highly informative **'A Moorland Parish,'** that is found on http://www.bazzasoft.net/cowling.htm **(retrieved Tuesday, 30th June 2015)**.

Unfortunately, when first proof-reading this section my wife spotted severe grammatical and spelling errors in this source (and in other sources quoted in this chapter) which required many corrections to make it meaningful to the reader. Insertions also had to be added for the same reason and these will be denoted by square brackets.

"COWLING" - *this word has different meanings for different people. If you are a born and bred* [a] *'COWINHEEADER' the name is synonymous with home and will be pronounced with a long '0' (as in coal). If, however, you are what the indigenous population term an 'off-cumd-un' then this name will be pronounced as 'Cow' (the animal) ling.*

*The name lies deep in antiquity and is attributed to the **Angles** who invaded the **North** around **560 AD**. A family named **Coil** settled in the area and **Inge** is the 'home' or 'settlement' hence **COLLINGE** – **Coil's** settlement. Another brother [to this **Coil** family] settled at **Cull-ing-worth** [or] **Coils-home-by-the-river**.*

*However, the **Angles** were <u>not</u> the first inhabitants as traces of prehistoric man have been found on **Ickornshaw Moor**. A **Mesolithic** [Stone Age] site has been excavated and dated to **6000 BC**. Small chest triangles [a Stone Age tool] and rod-like implements were formed in association with burnt hazelnut shells, flint tools, arrowheads and a tranchet axe. These are on display at **Cliffe Castle**. There is also a **Trilithon** on **Earl's Crag*** [through] *which the Midsummer Day sunrise shines - whether this is man-made, or a natural rock formation is purely conjectural.*

It is suggested that the nearby **Hitchin stone** *was the venue of Druidical worship or a place where tribal laws were formulated. The hole hewn in this giant boulder is called the* **'Druid's Chair'.** *It is the largest detached boulder in* **Yorkshire,** *weighing approximately* **1,200** *tons, and is* **28 ft** *long,* **25 ft** *wide and* **21 ft** *high.*

Very little evidence has remained of how **Cowling** *developed between* [the] *period* [before] *the* **Norman** *Conquest; all that remains of the* [earlier] **Danish** *occupation appears to be in our place names: -* **Ickornshaw - 'Squirrel Copse', Knarrs End - 'Rugged Rock', Royds - 'Scarrs', Stubbin -** *'clearing in the trees' with many more names coming from the* **Danish** *language.*

The **Norman** *regime influenced the area sometime after the* **Norman Conquest.** *Land was given to the* **Emmott** *brothers as a reward for military support to* **William the Conqueror.** *One* [owned] *land from* **Laneshawbridge** *to* **Haworth,** [another from] **Laneshawbridge** *to* **Black Lane Ends;** *hence the* **Emmott Halls** *at* **Haworth** *and* **Laneshawbridge.**

The younger brother [owned] *the land in* **Cowling** *– around* **Beckfoot** *and* **Cowling Hill;** *the* **Emmott** *family living at* **Becksfoot** *for* **400** *years. All the* **Emmotts** *in and around the village were descended from this branch, the younger brother being* 'Lord of the Manor.'

The population was sparse [as far back as] **1385** [when] *this manor had* **18** *couples,* [this figure suggests a population of around one hundred and perhaps shows the after effects of the Black Death which may have killed up to one-quarter of the local inhabitants around the year **1348**] *expanding to* **35** *couples in* **1534.** *These figures are thought to be from an inventory of men eligible for military service for the* **Emmotts.** *This settlement developed with* **Cowling Hill** *as its centre, but there was little arable land in* **1086,** *only* **21/4** *carucates* [an old measure of land]. *In view of the high land – probably covered in trees, scrub and moorland, this is not surprising. The settlements (or farms) were widely dispersed with* **Owlcotes, Cowlaughton, Warleywise, Norwood** *and* **Holeyns** *all dated between* **1280-1580.**

In the **14th** *century,* **John-de-Tong** *(***Tong** *near* **Bradford***) held a third of the* **Manor of Collinge** *so it appears that the division into the three parts we now call* **Cowlin** *had*

20

[already] *taken place. No records have* [as] *yet been found as to when this division* [occurred].

*During the **15th** century accounts of the manors become confused. In the reign of **Henry VIII,** it belonged to **Thomas Blakay** who was hanged, and his estates forfeited to the Crown. (**Thomas Blakay** is thought to have lived near **New Hall Farm**). The lands were then granted to **Henry,** the **1st Earl of Cumberland** of **Skipton Castle.** [It then passed] by inheritance to **Earl George III**, who was notorious for gambling. [He most] probably sold it or used it to settle a gambling debt. In **Whitakers History of Craven,** we learn* [that] *the Manor was in possession of **Robert Parker Esq.,** with **Collinge** and **Ickornshaw** held by the **Freeholders.** It was* [then] *acquired by the **Copley Family** who held lands in **Craven,** then sold* [on] *to the **Laycocks.*** [It was then] *inherited by the **Wainmans** who inter-married with the **Laycocks.***

***Alvery Copley** defended the boundaries of the **Manor of Collinge** and **Ickornshaw** in the enquiry conducted by the **Duchy of Lancaster** in **1592**. This determined the boundaries between the **Manor of Colne** and the adjacent moors of **Yorkshire** as we know them today."*

Wikipedia (accessed on **Monday, 18th May 2015**) revealed some extra details. *"The village is **Saxon** in origin and is recorded in the **Domesday Book** as **'Collinge'**. The name means **Coll's** 'people' or 'tribe.' At the time of the **Norman Conquest,** the main landowner was **Gamel** [son of **Karli**] who had very large land holdings in **Yorkshire**. His name survives in **Gamsgill** on the northern edge of the village.*

Originally the village [had] *comprised* [of] *three separate hamlets – namely **Ickornshaw, Middleton Gill** and **Cowling Hill*** [where the **Smiths** appear to have owned some property by the eighteenth century]. *It was only following the construction of the main **Keighley** to **Colne Road*** [now the **A6068**] *and the building of large mills alongside the road that what is now regarded* [as the] *main village was constructed.* [It provided] *terraced cottage homes for the mill workers. The older parts of the village* [based around the stream, **Lothersdale Beck**] *faded in importance. As a result, the **parish church** and village school are located on what appears to be the outskirts of the village between **Ickornshaw** and **Middleton**. The centre of the village 'moved.'* [Its location is now in line with the newly constructed mills and terraced homes of the **1840s.**]

The mills continued to operate – providing the main source of local employment until the end of the 20th century. [They] *are now* [c.2015] *all closed-down and their sites largely redeveloped for housing and the village hall. The village is now very much a dormitory* [suburb] *village for those working in the surrounding towns* [within] **West Yorkshire** *and* **East Lancashire.**"

Incidentally, *"The name* **Gamel** [son of **Karli**] *was associated with* **86** [mainly **Yorkshire** – based] *places before the Conquest;* **0** *after the Conquest".* (http://opendomesday.org/name/208670/gamal-son-of-karli/**retrieved Tuesday, 30th June 2015.**) **Gamel** appears to have been one of the old **Anglo-Saxon** landowning class – almost eliminated by the **Normans.**

In **1086 The Domesday Book** suggested that **Cowling** was a poor area. This is underlined by the following entry: -
Hundred (A large sub-division of land): Craven
Area: West Riding
County: Yorkshire
Total tax assessed: 2.3 geld units (quite small).
Taxable units: Taxable value 2.3 geld units.
Value:
Lord in 1066: Arnketil
Lord in 1086: Roger of Poitou
Tenant-in-chief in 1086: Roger of Poitou

Cowling's local community website added the following details: -
"The village as it stands today is very different to the way it was years ago. Many people who are not from **Cowling** *(known locally as 'off cum'd uns') fail to understand why* **Holy Trinity Church** *and the Primary School were built so far from the main part of the village. The answer is that* **Cowling** *village of modern day was once very sparsely populated. The bulk of the population* [had lived] *in* **Ickornshaw** *and* **Middleton**, *and before that on* **Cowling Hill,** *close to water sources* [which would have been helpful to a blacksmith] *and the main roads of that time.* [The latter is] *now used as back roads by locals* [wishing to] *avoid modern day traffic.*

In the early days, agriculture was the main occupation, with corn being grown and [then] *ground within the village. When canal transport boomed corn became cheaper to buy from elsewhere and so the mills in* **Cowling** *turned from grinding corn to weaving.*

During the Industrial Revolution **[c.1760-1850]** *population in nearby* **Lancashire,** *towns grew rapidly.* [This increased the] *demand for farming produce, ensuring that less demand for crop growing* [in the locality] *did not see the end of the farms. Even so, there was only a* *meagre living to be earned; so many farmers or their families also took on weaving work, whether in the mill or at home on a hand loom. The number of mill workers also increased due to a trend towards keeping animals out to pasture rather than using the land to grow crops. [The latter] was more time consuming and expensive.*

*As workloads grew cottages were built close to the mills which used the local water sources, firstly around **Middleton** and **Ickornshaw**. The main road from **Keighley** to **Colne** (which now runs through the centre of the village) did not arrive until the early **1800's,** and even then, houses were only added very gradually. The Village Inn was once part of a farmhouse on **Cowling Hill** but was sold as changes to the structure of the village began. The son of the landlord later opened the **Bay Horse Hotel** on the new road, which still stands as a main feature of village life."*

One thing (clearly revealed by direct observation) was that, for the original **Anglo-Saxon** settlers, **Cowling** was sited in a very strategic location. It really was an open the door to **Western England** with its plentiful water supply and fields capable of supporting a variety of crops and animals. It had its fair share of hills and woods – useful to hide should any trouble arise. From about the seventh to the eighth century it would have been an **Anglo-Saxon** frontier village, bordering on the nearby **Celtic** territory. As skilled blacksmiths, my early ancestors would have occupied a respectable place in the village. They may have forged the weapons of war used to defeat the **Celts** and drive them into **Wales.** Up to the fourteenth century, if not later, the surname *'Smith'* would also have denoted their occupation as Blacksmiths. In terms of rank, they belonged to the upper peasantry – equivalent in status to other skilled craftspeople like the local Corn Miller.

By the eighteenth century, the **Smiths** appear to have been based around **Stott Hill,** leading-up toward **Cowling Pinnacle.** They were on the moor-side (rather than the valley end of the settlement). Meeting a present-day inhabitant of **Cowling** (when visiting the **York Family History Fair** on **Saturday 27th June 2015**) confirmed that there were still some **Smiths** around. Old photographs of **Cowling** confirmed that the prominent **Smith** nose (obvious on my own father) originated from there.

Section 3: Glasburn and Crosshills

Concerning Glasburn and Crosshills

A descent from **Cowling** takes one to the conjoined settlements of **Glasburn** and **Crosshills**. They lie a few hundred yards due **North** of **Sutton** as if they were the crossbar of a *'T.'* The boundary with **Sutton** is marked by **Holme Beck.** Of the two settlements, **Glasburn** is the oldest. **Wikipedia** provided the following details, all of which appear to concur with my own observations and those provided by other sources.

*"The village most likely dates to the **8th** century. The site on which **Glusburn** is situated is just above **Glus Beck,** which means the 'shining stream'. The site would have been rough uncultivated land, moorland and forest, with wolves, wild boar and deer around at the time*

*Before **1066,** most of the area was held by **Earl Edwin,** a **Saxon** nobleman. However, he broke his oath of loyalty to **King William I** and consequently the king took the land as revenge. Therefore, in the **Domesday Book,** the site is described as "Terra Regis" or 'Lands of the King'. Another part records that in **Gluseburn** and **Chelchis** were c. **360 acres** (c. **150** hectares) of ploughland of which **"Gamal Bern** had them; **Gilbert Tison** has them".* For in the 'Harrying of the North' lands were taken from **Anglo-Scandinavians** and given to **Norman** Lords*

*In **1369, John Scarborough** was **Lord of the Manor** and is believed to have lived at **Glusburn Old Hall**. In the 16th century, the estate was sold partly to **John Currer** of **Kildwick Hall,** but also to **William Garforth** of **Steeton.***

*In **1379,** it was recorded that **23** people in **Glusburn** paid a poll tax to **Richard II.** However, in **1587,** smallpox ravaged the village's population.*

*At the end of the **17th** century, 'vestry rule' came to **Glusburn** and it was placed under the parish of **Kildwick.***

*In **1700,** most villagers were farmers, with spinning and weaving as a secondary income. During the latter part of the **18th** century, there were major improvements in the transport infrastructure. In **1773** the **Leeds and Liverpool Canal** was opened and then in **1786,** the **Keighley** to **Kendall Turnpike Road** was opened. This was followed in **1823** by the **Blackburn** [to] **Addingham, Cocking End Road**. The improvements brought* *large numbers of people to the area and many more houses and workplaces were built. Six stagecoaches a day took advantage of these new roads. In **1847, Kildwick** and **Crosshills Railway Station** were opened, which had perhaps the greatest effect on the village and marked the end of the stagecoach era. During the early **19th** century, trade suffered* [because of **Napoleon's** blockade on **Britain** from **1807** to **1814**] *and many people became destitute. In **1850, Glusburn** had around **600** inhabitants; many were engaged in textile work, with farming as a secondary income."*

A visit to the site (made on **Saturday, 5th September 2015** with my wife and second cousin once removed) confirmed the centre of the village had indeed moved downwards into the valley and the former green was on a quiet hilltop location.

Crosshills was where most of the shops were located and it seemed to attract a slightly better class of people. (The shops still take advantage of their location on the main Road to **Colne,** running through **Glasburn** and **Cowling.**) In **1838,** it formed part of the **Glasburn Township** and (along with **Glasburn** itself) comprised of **987** inhabitants spread over **1,513** acres. As Wikipedia rightly observes, *"Geographically, **Crosshills** is in **Airedale** at a point where the **River Aire** bends east from its north-south course. The village lies on the south bank of the river just above the floodplain, which is wholly agricultural. As its name implies, **Crosshills** is surrounded by the hills of the **eastern Pennines, Steeton Moor** (south-east), **Cowling Moor** (south-west), **White Hill** (north-west) and **Kildwick Moor** (north-east).* **Crosshills** is located on the southern edge of the bend and is five miles **West North West** of **Keighley.**

Wikipedia again correctly notes that, geographically, **Crosshills** *"is overlooked by two monuments called **'The Pinnacles'** which stand above crags on the **Cowling Moor** skyline. These are small towers: **Sutton Pinnacle** is a square with an internal staircase and topped by a crenulated parapet; **Cowling Pinnacle** is an obelisk. They are known locally as the **Salt** and **Pepper Pot** [respectively]. **Sutton pinnacle,** called **Lund's Tower** was built in **1896** by **James Lund** of **Malsis Hall** (now **Malsis School)** to commemorate **Queen Victoria's** Diamond Jubilee. **Cowling pinnacle** (or **Wainman's Pinnacle)** was built in **1816** by **Richard Wainman** to commemorate the victory at the battle of **Waterloo** the previous year (in which his son was killed).*

*The village is adjacent to **Glusburn** which lies immediately to the west. **Kildwick** is due north of **Crosshills** on the other side of the **River Aire. Sutton-in-Craven** is less than a mile to the south-west and **Eastburn** less than a mile to the south-east. Crosshills is* *separated from **Sutton-in-Craven** and **Eastburn** by the beck which flows into the **Aire** just east of **Crosshills**. The beck is known by various names: **Surgill Beck, Holme Beck** and **Eastburn Beck**. It forms part of the county boundary between **North** and **West Yorkshire** as it approaches the **Aire; Eastburn** being in **West Yorkshire**.*

*Crosshills is split by the **Airedale Line** (the former **Midland Railway**)".*

My Great, Great, Great Grandfather **William Smith** and his father **Edward** lived in **Glasburn** from at least the late eighteenth until the mid-nineteenth century. At one point, they appear to have inhabited **Glasburn Hall** which itself appears to have been sub-divided into three family living spaces at an unknown date.

One social problem was that of *'illegitimacy.'* A lecture given by the local historian **Linda Croft** to **the Family History Section** of the **Yorkshire Archaeological Society** (on **Wednesday evening, June 14th, 2000**) revealed that the illegitimacy rate was in the order of **10-12%**. However, this figure relied upon incomplete Church Registers, so the real percentage may well have been higher (around **15-20%**). Many marriages took place because the partner was already *'with child'*. In **Burnley (15 miles southwest** of Sutton), the parents of one girl who worked in a mill sued the man who made her pregnant for loss of earnings. After awarding the girl's parents £50.00 the magistrate warned that he was not setting a legal precedent. During his *'summing up'* he remarked that the *'weaving class people'* appeared to *"enjoy their gravy first and say grace afterwards."* However, in accord with ancient custom some men felt it right to bring about a pregnancy before a marriage, thus ensuring the woman was fertile and could provide children who would care for them in their old age.

Like **Sutton, Glasburn Township** belonged to the Parish of **Kildwick.** Most of the inhabitants of this parish would have spoken in thick **Yorkshire** accents with such expressions as *"ayup lad,"* often used. A tough labouring life would have created a practical, realistic disposition – one which valued challenging work and disliked emotional displays. Drunkenness and wife beating may well have comprised the most common social problems. The presence of two Inns (in **1822**) **'The Black Bull'** and **'The Bay Horse'** provided evidence of a significant market for alcoholic beverages. A third Inn **'The Kings Arms'** had also been established by **1837**. Evidently, the local demand for *'the demon drink'* had been growing. Each Inn will once have had stone flagged floors, spittoons, benches and tables, with a landlady on hand to act as the local *'agony aunt.'*

Innkeepers often brewed their own ale. During the **1850s, Richard Laycock** (landlord of the **Bay Horse,** was reputed to have cooled his barrels of beer in **Clough Beck.**) The formation (in **1869**) of a **Sutton Branch** of the **Temperance Society** suggested that drunkenness was a major vice needing to be contained. In those days, people had little else to do with their evening leisure time except to get *'drunk on beer'* or to get *'drunk on religion!'* Both pub and chapel were catering for the same need to escape from a hard *'daily grind.'* They were places where a keen sense of community could be generated.

Section 4: Kildwick Village

Concerning Kildwick Village

Kildwick is a small village adjacent to the **Leeds-Liverpool Canal.** It lies **north** of the **River Aire** and directly **North** of **Crosshills.** It was originally a crossing point for the **Keighley** to **Skipton Road.** Unlike **Sutton** (which was an **Anglo-Saxon** settlement) **Kildwick** appears to have been of *Viking origin.* In **Norse,** the original name **Celdewic** meant *'a dwelling place* [or farm] *beside a spring of water,'* **(Wood p.4)**. It seems that at this period **(c.850-1050)** the **Anglo-Saxons** and their **Viking** neighbours lived in separate locations **Norse Crosses** (found built into the chancel wall of the local parish church) dated from around **875-925AD**. They perhaps reflected a time when **Christianity** was beginning to make itself felt, **(Wood p.5)**. Before then the religion would have been **Nordic Pagan**. In **1086** the Domesday book mentioned a church that appears to have been established for some time. From **1152-1539** the *'Manor of* ***Kildwick'*** was under the jurisdiction of the priors of **Bolton** who played a key role in developing the local sheep-rearing industry. My ancestor's involvement in woollen textiles can perhaps be traced back to this era.

Kildwick itself never reached a population of greater than **216.** (In **2001,** it was **191** and in **2011** it had risen slightly to **194**). However, the parish it served was large – with poverty being a continual problem, as shown by the following entries in Wikipedia: -
1379: Poll Tax recorded **Kildwick Township** as having only **10** households, all paying the minimum tax
1672: Hearth Tax counted **25** households in the township with mostly but one fireplace, but also the **14**-hearthed Manor House.
1821: parish registered **8,605** inhabitants.
1831: parish was **9,926,** however, the township only **190.**

Given the large numbers, it's hard to see how even a well-meaning vicar could fulfil the needs of more than a handful of the local population residing in its parish. Here surely was a space for religious dissenters to fill.

At the centre of **Kildwick** lay the very distinguished-looking fifteenth century Church of **Saint Andrew**. Thanks to its copious records it was possible to gain some idea of the population structure and religious loyalties of the parish. During the early eighteenth century, **Archbishop Herring** of **York** was so concerned about the perceived slackness of church life and the absenteeism of clergy from their parishes that he sent a list of eleven questions. Here is the reply sent from **Kildwick:**

1. Concerning Dissenters: *I believe there are upwards of **760** families in the parish. Out of these are (as I am told) **100** Dissenting Families, chiefly Anabaptists.*

2. Concerning Dissenting Meeting Houses: *There are **3** Licensed Meeting Houses in the Parish **2** Anabaptist, **1** Quaker. Anabaptists meet every Sunday about **50** assemble. Quaker Speaker **David Hall,** Anabaptist Teachers **David Horsley, Wm. Jackson.***

3. Concerning Educational Facilities: *School in **Kildwick** is not endowed. The Master has about **30** Scholars. He teaches them the Church Catechism and brings them to Church on Sundays and other Prayer Days.*

4. Concerning Endowments: *There is no Alms Houses or Hospital in the Parish, nor any Land left for the repair of the Church, but for the pious use of preaching a sermon on **Good Friday** there is left **10sh** by **Christopher Brown** which is duly paid.*

5. Concerning Absenteeism: *I reside in the Vicarage House.*

6. Concerning Salary: *The Vicar allows me for supplying the Vicarage together with the curacy of **Silsden** at a rate of £**30** per annum.*

7. Concerning Confirmation: *I know of none that come to Church that have not been Baptised, but I believe there are many who come to Church that are not confirmed.*

8. Concerning Services: *The Public service is read twice every Lord's Day*

9. Concerning Residence: *Having resided here only about **1** month I have only catechised twice publicly*

10. Concerning the Sacraments: *The Sacrament is administered here **4** times a year. There are at least **3,000** Communicants, a **100** of which usually receive*

11. Concerning Celebration of Communion: *Due notice was given of the celebration of the Communion the **Sunday** before Whitsunday. There were only **16** Communicants so that I did not refuse the Sacrament to anyone present.*

B. WAINMAN
*Curate of **Kildwick***
(Quoted in **Wood p.21**)

The Communicant figures highlight the limited impact of the Church at the time. Only **3.3%** of the population were participating in this rite. Through the sources used by **Wood** (an excellent local historian), it was possible to step into the world of the pre-industrial **Smiths** and to gain some understanding of its hardships and tensions.

Section 5: Sutton-in-Craven

Concerning Sutton-in-Craven

As this was the settlement where my Great Grandfather **Edmund Smith** was born in **January 1832** and the place he chose to be buried in **July 1915,** this settlement will be examined in far greater detail. Strong family connections with this locality not only existed through him but also with his own ancestors.

Wood p.1 suggested that the name **Sutton** was derived from the **Anglo-Saxon** word *'Sun-tun,'* meaning *'South Town.'* It had been settled by the **Angles** during the early to mid-Dark Ages **(C.500 –700AD).** This meant that, originally, the **Smiths** had come from **Southern Denmark** or the **Northern Rhineland** of **Germany.** The surname **'*Smith*'** implied that those of my remote ancestors who had been blacksmiths may well have forged some of the weapons used to destroy the power of **Rome.** In turn, the use of **Norse** words like *'Ellers'* (meaning *'Alder'* tree which was common in the locality) to describe a locality besides **Sutton** indicated a **Viking** influence. For much of the late Dark Ages, **(C.800-1000 AD)** **Sutton** lay in the **Danish**-held territory, known as the **Danelaw.** Consequently, some **Viking** blood in the **Smiths** could not be ruled out. However, the first documented evidence for an early settlement was provided by a **Domesday Book** entry. This revealed that, excluding woodland, **Sutton** (and other surrounding villages) were assessed on a value basis of **200 acres.** This suggested that **Sutton** had been a settled agricultural community sometime before the **Norman Conquest.** Generous supplies of spring water, woodland and game would have provided an incentive to settle in the area. Even so, life must have been hard, with a diet confined mainly to porridge and bread. At best **Sutton** was in a marginal area for arable crops, with farming at a subsistence level and famine an ever-present threat. Hardly surprisingly, there was a tendency to diversify into sheep farming at a very early stage and this would explain why the woollen trade began to develop during the Later Middle Ages.

During this period **Sutton** would have consisted of daub and wattle cottages strung along a dirt track, later to become the high street. Behind each cottage would have been a vegetable patch and behind these the open fields. Most people would have been short in stature, with well-defined jaws to chew the rough bread, having unwashed hair, probably infested with head lice. Diseases stemming from malnutrition will have been rife, with the bow-shaped legs of rickets being all too common. The little amount of leisure time would have been spent on drink and on activities connected to the Parish Church at **Kildwick.** A visit to the market at **Skipton** (five miles to the **North West**) would have constituted a rare treat. From perhaps **Tudor** times **(1485-1603).** The importance of **Sutton** would have tried to supplement a meagre agricultural living by spinning and weaving textiles. A document of **1558** provided the earliest record of the domestic system of weaving. It mentioned, *"a payre of loomes with a shear borde,"* **(Wood p.34).** By **1700** textile spinning and weaving were becoming an important secondary occupation for many hard-pressed farmers. Significantly, two entries from the **Sutton Township Account Book** (quoted in **Wood p.34**) recorded the costs involved in repairing two pieces of weaving equipment:

1760: *'Paid for wool for lumes for* **Richard Petty** *and two times going a brought it* **18/-.'**
1790: *'To two spinning wheels for* **Berry Shackleton 3/8d.'**

By the time the last of these entries were made the textile trade was beginning to become the major source of employment in **Sutton.** As will be shown shortly, farming became the *'supplementary'* activity – with work available on a seasonal basis *i.e.* at harvest time.

The technical difficulties involved in calculating population figures before the **1801** Census were partly resolved by employing other sources *e.g.* Poll Tax Returns, Militia Muster Rolls and Baptismal Registers. To follow accepted historical practice, the first two of these sources were multiplied between six and seven times to provide an estimated population range. (With Baptismal Registers, the calculations were more complex with a multiple of **31** being used (for mathematical reasons.) Particularly in remote areas like **Sutton** large-scale tax evasion may well have distorted some estimated population figures downwards. After adding an extra **5%** to estimated population totals (to allow for any tax evasion) it was possible to establish (with a reasonable amount of confidence) that the approximate pre-Census population of **Sutton** stood in the range of: -
115-150 in **1379**
180-220 in **1539**

300-350 in **1648**
380-420 in **1744**

Beyond periods of famine, outbreaks of contagious diseases (*i.e.* the epidemics of **1587** and **1604**) provided another major *'stop'* to population expansion. A tomb inscription next to **Kildwick Parish Church** revealed that two teenage boys had been buried on the same day in **January 1732.** Such closely connected deaths could easily have been due to an infectious illness. The names of these youths were **Robert** and **John Smith.** A more thoroughly documented case (mentioned in **Wood p.84**) was that of a **Benjamin Clough** who had married **Mary Emmott** in **1744.** They'd produced four children; **Robert, John, Elizabeth** and a baby born on **13/1/1749.** Five months later the whole family had been wiped out by some unknown infection. For many in those days, life was truly *'nasty, brutish and short.'*

By **1801** the population of **Sutton** had grown to **809** (probably an underestimate). Given what was known about the conditions in which the inhabitants lived it seemed unlikely that an improvement in health had played more than a minor role in creating this doubling of the population in just over half a century. The real reason lay in that massive shift from a rural to a manufacturing economy, known as *'The Industrial Revolution.'* The construction of the **Leeds-Liverpool Canal** at **Kildwick** in **1786** and the completion of the **Keighley** to **Kendal Turnpike Road** in **1798** opened the locality to new industries and to migrant labour. Most of the migrants would have travelled from within a ten-mile radius, but names like **McCoben** suggested that some of them had indeed come from much further afield. **Wood p. 12** revealed that most migrant workers lodged in **Sutton Mill** or **Ellers;** although a few were spread out on outlying farms, including **Long House** and **Valley Farm** (where two branches of the **Clough** family lived.) Such a sustained migration would indicate that very few people had retained much (if any) sentimental attachment to the land. To such migrants, agriculture was an occupation to escape from rather than to cherish. It was in textiles where new opportunities beckoned. **Sutton** itself possessed both the sheep and the waterpower to support a large-scale move into textiles. At this stage, most of the weaving and garment-making will have been done in people's homes. Soon water mills and larger workshops were to provide a foretaste of the large textile mills which would dominate the locality from **1830** until their closure in the **1980s.** At the beginning of the nineteenth century, most manufacturers would have had to make do with knocking a few cottages together to make a workshop. Throughout the nineteenth century, the major occupational trend was to move from agriculturally-based pursuits to cotton and then (following a major banking crash in the mid-**1820s)** to worsted (woollen) manufacture. However, some bypassed the cotton stage altogether and went straight into worsteds. Even where agricultural pursuits continued, they were often in conjunction with weaving and spinning. If times were hard the farm would be on hand to provide the food needed for survival. There was a marked trend toward diversification, although, in many cases, textile work alone would gradually take precedence.

During the nineteenth century, the main local pastoral agriculture would have been that of sheep farming. In most places, the soil was simply too poor to have grown much in the way of crops, except for oats in a few sheltered locations. These at least would have provided fodder for the horses, but it would have been difficult to have made a full time living as a Corn-Miller. This activity would, of necessity, have taken place in conjunction with other work. A **1799** *"Survey of Agriculture in the **West Riding**"* provided supporting evidence for this point. One part of this survey was quoted by **Wood pp. 27-8** and stated that: *"very little corn is now grown, grazing being the main farming occupation and sheep farming very common. The whole **Vale of Skipton** is under grass, a wet climate making it unfit for corn and small farms."* An **1841** Tithe Map of the **Vale of Skipton** showed that only **178** acres were given over to arable farming as compared to **1,974** acres for meadow and (mainly sheep) pasture. What fruit and vegetables there were, were often grown in small back gardens. **Sutton** itself enjoyed a reputation for producing superior quality strawberries.

Forming part of the Parish of **Kildwick, Sutton-in-Craven** had once contained three textile mills (all operating power looms.). The first of these mills had been constructed in **1830.** Prior to this year, the mechanisation of cotton and woollen yarn production was to cause sub-contracting to handloom weavers. This allowed handloom weaving to become the third largest occupation in the early nineteenth century – ranked only behind domestic service and agricultural labour. Both men and women moved into this occupation because there was money to be made. However, in late **1825** technological changes and a major banking crash caused a collapse in the domestic cotton-weaving sector. Nevertheless, woollen hand weaving continued to prosper for up to thirty years. Even after that, a handloom weaver could still make a living if he (or she) specialised in the production of high-quality cloth.

A typical handloom weaver's house tended to be sparsely furnished, with any spare room given over to weaving equipment. A pig would often be kept in the garden where vegetables were also grown. Sometimes, a handloom weaver would work flat-out for fifteen hours to earn **2s (shillings)** and **6d (pence)** for thirty yards of cloth. (On other occasions, the hours were less arduous.) In tough times, they were known to undertake an assortment of *'odd jobs'* to earn the extra penny. *'Friendly Societies'* such as the *"Odd Fellows,"* (still active today), provided financial support in the event of illness or death. To avoid the cost of a barber, the men in **Todmorden** (fifteen miles to the **South** of **Sutton**) were on record for cutting one another's hair. A special treat took place when the *"pig killer"* called round to slaughter the pig, after which extended family members would be invited round for a pig's supper where the perishable parts were eaten first. Pig suppers were something of a local custom and bacon was considered a delicacy. Sometimes a pig was kept for a lengthy period to be fattened up, to gain in value, and then to be sold on for profit.

Already well established in the village by the early nineteenth century was a **Baptist Chapel, (Sutton Baptist Church).** It stood beside the **Crosshills Road,** just above a small stream and sited behind it was the **Baptist Cemetery.** The Chapel had been founded in **1711** by the **Rev. Isaac Dewhurst** and had long been a very important centre of village life. At the time of **Edmund's** birth, this mill-like building will have been a substantial and imposing structure. The high degree of courtesy shown by **Sutton Baptist Chapel** in correspondence (conducted during late **1999**) pointed it out as being a Chapel having retained many good values. (This impression was strongly reinforced by an encounter with its very helpful pastor in **September 2015.**)

Prevalent throughout the Eighteenth and Nineteenth Centuries were the dreadful housing conditions which will have compounded any social problems like alcoholism. By **1840,** with the rise in population leading to severe overcrowding, such conditions may well have been at their worst. An **1840** map of **Sutton Village** (and its outlying farms) showed it a little to the south of (what was then called) **Glusburn Beck.** The village itself was an elongated settlement, straddling the **Kendal** to **Keighley Turnpike Road.** Up a very steep hill (at the very **Southern** tip of the settlement) lay a tiny hamlet called **Ellers,** (spelt *'Hellers'* in the **1851** and *'Owelers'* in the **1861** Census Returns). Flowing from an oblong alcove chiselled out of a sandstone wall was a spring known as **Dow Well,** which an old photograph (taken around **1900**) confirmed was still in use during the early part of the Twentieth Century. **Ellers** had three rows of cottages, <u>two</u> on the **East** and <u>one</u> on the **West Side** of the **Turnpike Road.** This tiny hamlet had strong associations with the **Smiths of Sutton.** A first-hand visit made to **Ellers** on **Monday, 19th March 2001** confirmed that some of the houses were indeed very old but a little more spacious than the cottages in **Sutton Mill.** I also found **Dow Well** sited near to a busy hillside road. It looked remarkably unchanged from the previously mentioned photograph. The only alteration was that the small gateway, once leading to it, was now blocked in by a drystone wall. The road climbing out of **Ellers** afforded a breath-taking view of **Sutton,** lying just inside the modern township boundary. (Incidentally, a Township consisted of isolated settlements grouped together under one local authority known as *'The Parish'* – their boundaries often being very indistinct. Hence, the *'Township of **Sutton'*** existed <u>within</u> *'the Parish of **Kildwick'** alongside other Townships *i.e.* **Glasburn.** The system of local government during the first half of the nineteenth century was often very confused.)

To the **North** of **Ellers** straddled the **High Street** of **Sutton,** which itself formed part of the **Turnpike Road.** In **1840** most of the buildings were sited on the **West Side** of the road, rarely more than two rows deep. It was on the **High Street** that most of the shops and small craft trades were located. Two Public Houses**, *'The Bay Horse'*** (nearest to **Ellers**) and *'The Kings Arms'* (more neatly tucked into the centre of **Sutton**) were still functioning in the early twenty-first century. No shops remain along the **High Street** now (in contrast to **Crosshills** which still has a busy main street) and the centre of **Sutton** is commercially dead. During my visit in **March 2001,** I saw an old butcher's shop, being converted into a private residence. I noticed no other retail outlets.

However, in **1822** things could not have been more different, with the Township of **Sutton** enjoying a very active commercial life. One of the shopkeepers in that same year was a grocer and draper with the name of **Rowland Wilson.** Joining the **Turnpike Road** (at the **northern** tip of **Sutton**) was the **Eastburn Road.** Before turning into **Sutton,** it ran parallel to the nearby **Glasburn Beck,** which lay a little to the **North.** Standing by this road and to the **east** of **Sutton** was the then isolated village of **Sutton Mill.** Like **Ellers,** it too had strong connections with the early **Smiths.** However, the fact that **John Smith** was a millwright suggested he lived at **Sutton Mill** (where two nearby corn mills were present – one in **Sutton** itself and the other on the boundary of **Crosshills** and **Glasburn**). It was possibly here at **Sutton Mill** that my Great Grandfather, **Edmund** was born. Nevertheless, the presence of **Smiths** living in **Ellers** would suggest that, as a boy, **Edmund** had experienced some contact with that locality too.

Sutton Mill was a compact settlement, consisting of some of the oldest houses in the locality: -

- **Tetley Row** – about **11** terraced cottages stretching along the **South Side** of the **Eastburn Road**. (This would later be known as **the Main Street** when new building work (in the **1850s** and **1860s**) joined **Sutton Mill** to the main Village of **Sutton**.) This row was sited due **north** of **Salt Pie Farm** where a family of Tenant Farmers called the **Roes** lived. A visit made there on **Monday, 19th March 2001** confirmed that **Tetley Row** had long since been demolished to make way for a small park and seating area.
- **Harker** and **Wells Street** – which ran directly onto the **Eastburn Road** from the **North. Harker Street** consisted of two facing rows of several back-to-back terraced houses. By **1868,** at the bottom left of **Harker Street** stood a slaughterhouse – whether it had been present at an earlier date could not be confirmed.
- On a back lane (behind the above-cited streets) in the nineteenth century, had once stood ten privies and two ash pits. In contrast to **Harker Street,** the houses on **Wells Street** had some small gardens. Like the cottages in **Tetley Row,** the houses in these streets had slanting slate roofs.
- A rather large house called **Garden Place** flanked the **East Side** of **Wells Street**. It may well have been constructed at an earlier period although exactly when couldn't be pinpointed.
- A row of four Corn Mill houses – each possessing a small garden. An old photograph on **p.16** of **Doris Riley's** booklet *'Owd Settings,'* showed that these houses had narrow oblong windows and tall chimney stacks. The large complex of **Bairstow's Mill** overshadowed them. Whether **Edmund** was born in one of these (now demolished) houses would depend upon whether his father had worked at this mill. These dwellings appear to have been rented out by the **Bairstow's** to their mill workers. Whether **John Smith** was one of them can't be ascertained, but later cited evidence confirms that **John's** father **(William)** had formerly enjoyed commercial links with **Bairstow's Mill.** He certainly lived in a community where everyone appeared to know everyone else.

The growing industrial plant of **Bairstow's Mill** lay wedged between these mill houses and **Glasburn Beck**. By **1840** a reservoir flowed **northwest** into the Beck itself. Until about **1838, Bairstow's** had been a corn rather than a textile mill. Two brothers of that family, **Thomas** and **Matthew** (who owned the mill) were responsible for its conversion to textile milling. (Once the financial capital had become available it would have been easy for the **Bairstow's** to have replaced corn mill machinery with power looms – both would have been driven by water power, generated by a large water wheel.)

A large dwelling with the name of **Royds Hill** stood a little way to the **North Side** of the **Eastburn Road**. It stood grandly in its own grounds to the **East** of the previously named streets and it was obviously the dwelling place of a very rich family. The latter could have only been the **Bairstow's** themselves. The **1841** Census confirmed that **Thomas Bairstow** with his wife **Elizabeth** (and two servants) inhabited **Royds Hill**.

Although documentary evidence was lacking, it seemed that the **Bairstow's** had hurriedly built most of these streets for their expanding workforce during the **1820s** and **1830s**. The now demolished Corn Mill Houses were perhaps the oldest dwelling places – having been constructed at a time when the **Bairstow's** had purchased the old Corn Mill. Despite having a keen sense of community, the impression remains that **Sutton Township** was very much the sort of place from which an ambitious young man (or older man with a family to feed) would have wished to escape, especially when times were hard – which they often were.

Having completed this description of the community at **Sutton. Wood, Chapter Four** will now be used to best describe the housing conditions my Great, Great Grandparents faced around the time of **Edmund's** birth in **January 1832**. In many ways, they were appalling. Most of the sandstone-constructed dwellings consisted of either blind back houses (as in the case of **Harker Street**) or back-to-back houses (as in the case of **Wells Street**). In either case, ventilation would have been inadequate – made even worse by small square sash windows. A poor circulation of air would have produced a greater amount of damp in winter and stiflingly hot conditions in summer. Any perishable food would have quickly deteriorated. In **1850** the average ratio of people per household (*i.e.* average number of people residing in a house within a given area) was **5.7** (as compared to **5.4** in the main Village of **Sutton**). The more expensive houses would at least have contained a cellar; families in cheaper rented accommodation would have had to make do with only one downstairs and one upstairs room. Of the **58** dwellings in **Sutton Mill,** it was found that **20** had **7** or more inhabitants, whilst **32** had **6** or more. The **21** small dwellings of **Harker** and **Wells Street** had over **100** inhabitants who shared **10** privies consisting of nothing more than a tiny shed with open boxes over a pit. Even as late as **1879** a Sanitary Report (quoted in **Wood pp.18-19**) mentioned the *"offensive emanations from the large, uncovered privy middens."* At that time, only four houses possessed proper water closets. Adding to the stench was a large slaughterhouse (sited at the bottom of **Harker Street**) which, it seems, chose to dump some remains into an open midden, **15** feet away from its own door.

Another slaughterhouse (besides the footbridge, just above **Sutton Chapel**) went one better and left it remains in an open field! The sanitary inspector noted that, at the time of his visit, liquid excrement was seen to trickle down the footpath near the slaughterhouse. Frequently blocked stone channels, running alongside the road seemed only to offer a little help in removing the sewerage which discharged into **Glasburn Beck,** (which also received the remains of slaughtered animals alongside the industrial waste of **Bairstow's Mill**). The reservoir beside the Mill was little more than an open cesspit. Hardly surprisingly, wooden clogs were perhaps the most sensible footwear to wear in these conditions. (**Wood pp. 23-24** showed that in both the years **1822** and **1851** there were three *'shoemakers and cloggers.'*) Mortality in the period **1861-1878** was **19** per **1000** and deaths from enteric fever were common. During the time of **Edmund's** birth, (in **1832**) conditions would, if anything, have been even worse. Public Health was only then just beginning to be viewed with grave concern. Admittedly, an **1850** map of **Sutton Mill** (unlike one of **1868**) showed no evidence of a slaughterhouse being present but offensive smells would still have been very unpleasant – especially during the scorching summer months.

Each of the smaller dwellings will have been stone flagged with sparse furnishings, consisting of little more than a dresser, table and chairs and possibly a handloom in the corner. The wall will have supported a row of hooks, needed to hang up heavy overcoats. Beside the single window would have once stood a stone sink known as a *'slop stone'* and opposite to this, a large cast iron cooking range, providing a source of warmth in the winter. If no cellar was available a *'set pot'* (consisting of a jug and bowl) was placed near to it for the weekly wash. Water would have been carried by bucket from a nearby spring. If the household was religious, then bible texts may have adorned the bare white plaster walls. Downstairs will have dovetailed as a kitchen, dining room and wash area. Upstairs was likely to contain one bed and a dresser. The children will have slept on rough sacking, curtained off from their parents. When not working, they would have been encouraged to play outside in the street at all hours and in all weather. The presence of a Sunday School will have acted as a welcome relief from the overcrowding. Disease would spread quickly as would head lice and skin rashes. To survive, one needed to be strong. Most men and women preferred to spend their meagre leisure time outside of the house in either the pub or the Chapel.

The **1841** Census recorded that there were **28** inhabited and **3** uninhabited houses at **Sutton Mill.** (These figures excluded the larger accommodation of **Laith Farm,** which lay on the **north side** of the **Eastburn Road,** just west of

Sutton Mill, and Royds Hill where the Bairstow's lived.) Inside the smaller houses were crowded 168 people, 84 of whom were male and 84 females. On dividing 168 by 28 it was found that there was an average of 6 people per house, (which denoted overcrowding.) In contrast, Ellers had 10 households – plus one uninhabited house. In these 10 houses lived 48 people of whom 25 were male and 23 were female. After dividing 48 by 10, there was found to be a ratio of 4.8 people per house. However, any benefit of less overcrowding was quickly countered by the fact that all the occupations were textile-related, with worsted weaving and spinning being the most common work done. (There was also some wool combing.) The implication here was that house space will have been taken up by weaving equipment. In one way or another, the accommodation at Ellers would have been just as cluttered as that of Sutton Mill – only here a person would be tripping over spinning wheels as well as children!

By retracing the steps taken by the 1841 Census enumerator (from Ellers to Royd Hill) it became possible to discover the likely living place of my Great Grandfather John Smith. Beginning a fair distance to the south of Sutton the enumerator will have called in at the following dwellings, all on the East Side of the old Skipton to Keighley Turn Pike Road:
1.   Longhouse (consisting of 2 households)
2.   Valley Farm (consisting of 1 household – the Cloughs)
3.   High Royd Brow (consisting of 2 households)
4.   Dobby Hall (consisting of 1 household)
5.   Knowle Top (consisting of 4 households)
6.   Briggate (consisting of 1 household of farmers)
7.   Ellers (consisting of 10 households – all in textile-related occupations)
8.   Gott Hill (consisting of 2 households – mainly farmers)
9.   Sutton (consisting of 21 households living East of the Old Turn Pike Road – however, most of the main village was concentrated on the West side)
10.   Mill Lane (consisting of 2 households of farmers at Laith Farm)
11.   Salt Pie (consisting of 1 household of Corn Millers)
12.   Sutton Mill (consisting of 28 households)
13.   Royds Hill (consisting of 2 households, including the Bairstow Family and their servants)

After Sutton, the enumerator will have turned east to go up the Eastburn Road. (An 1840 map of the locality showed that this road ran across to Royds Hill and was then known as Mill Lane). The first row of houses he came to would have been on Tetley Row. A close examination of the 1841 Census

Return for **Sutton Mill** confirmed that a handloom weaver called **John Smith** (and his wife) may have lived at the <u>sixth</u> house from the left on **Tetley Row.** (The <u>fifth</u> house was uninhabited.) This house was almost directly opposite to where the slaughterhouse stood. First-hand observation of this row, (seen on several different visits to **Sutton**) showed that the doorway stood about three steps above **Eastburn Road.** Sadly, this **John Smith** did <u>not</u> turn out to be the **John Smith** who was my Great, Great Grandfather. At the far right of the row was located the premises of **James Murgatroyd,** the village blacksmith. Two doors down from **John Smith** and his wife **Mary** were the **Bassetts** – a family of eight. During tough times (*e.g.* during the **1839-1842** trade recession) many of the inhabitants would have been oppressed with the nagging anxiety of being imminently evicted, with landlords casting their furniture out onto the street. As stated earlier, **Edmund's** place of birth would most likely have been one of the Corn Miller Cottages next to **Bairstow's Mill. John Smith's** occupation as a Corn Miller indicated that he either worked for the **Bairstow** Family – who, after all, were the largest employers in **Sutton** or at the smaller corn mill on the **Crosshills-Glasburn** boundary. If the former was the case, then the balance of probability points to **Edmund** being born amidst the squalor of **Sutton Mill.** Hardly surprisingly, **Sutton Mill** represented an environment from which **John Smith** would have dearly wished to escape. After studying the conditions of his son's birthplace, I could easily understand why **John Smith** had moved to **Cullingworth** by **1836.** (His move coincided with the time when the **Bairstow** Family were beginning to move from Corn to Worsted production.) **Edmund** himself would later display the attitudes of a man brought up during the *'starving 1840s'* when commercial failure often amounted to a death sentence.

During my first visit to the **Sutton** and **Crosshills** area (made on **Monday 22nd November 1999**) I noticed that the (mainly) terraced houses were built of sandstone – now sooty-black with age, but still retaining a very solid appearance. The walls were thick, providing protection against the ice-cold winds that blew up the **Aire Valley.** A second visit to the area, made on **29th December 1999,** this time with my wife and two younger sons, confirmed that **Sutton-in-Craven** was something of a *'smoke trap.'* On what was a clear and frosty winter's day the smoke from one small factory chimney left a sooty blue haze over the town that could be smelt almost as far away as **Crosshills.** Like the spectre of a stranded blue whale, this haze lay trapped at the bottom of the valley. One was left wondering what conditions would have been like when all the mill and house chimneys had belched their contents out into the air. Lung conditions like bronchitis and pleurisy must have been rife. A metal date bar above a passageway confirmed that most of the houses near the **Crosshills Road** had been built in **1862.** Further out (and closer to the Parish Church) lay even more substantial houses, each dating from the late **1870s.**

Steep grassy ridges flanked both settlements. To the **north** lay **Rombald's Moor** and to the **south Shipley Moor.** Personal observations (made during my initial visit) quickly reinforced the impression of bleak *'Wuthering Heights'* country. It was a very typical **Pennine** setting; in winter a damp icy wind will have blown down from the moors, chilling the very bones. However, seeing the sun sink over **Shipley Moor** (towards the end of my second visit) was a very moving experience. As I stood with my family just outside the small **Crosshills** local library, we watched the red glow ebbing out over the ridge, high above **Sutton.** As I looked, I realised that this too was a sight that my distant forbears would also have seen. This common experience somehow brought them closer to me.

Two of the people living in **Sutton** during the early **1830s** was my Great, Great Grandparents **John** and **Ann Smith.** On **Saturday, January 21st, 1832, Ann Smith** gave birth to my Great Grandfather **Edmund.** He was to exert a major influence upon subsequent generations of **Smiths,** lasting well into the twenty-first century. Because of **Edmund,** prospects for the **Smiths** were to be greatly changed for the better. Undeniably, one of the most fundamental influences concerning the **Smith** Family was their original geographical location. During the late eighteenth to early nineteenth century, they had moved around the small settlements of **Cowling, Glusburn, Crosshills, Sutton and Kildwick.** Tomb inscriptions at **Kildwick Parish Church** implied that their roots in this area had gone back a very long way.

In closing, it must be noted that these communities had existed in a world wherein a traditional agricultural society had needed to change so they could successfully industrialise. Here was a pattern in which the slow (and at times almost imperceptible) change of earlier centuries now began, in the eighteenth century, to give way to a period of accelerated change and then of revolutionary economic and technological upheaval. By the time my Great Grandfather **Edmund Smith** was born (in **January 1832**), these changes were well under way. A more exact review of these changes is made in the following section.

Section 6: The Impact of Industrialisation

Concerning Hartley-Smith in Sutton-in-Craven

In **1830** the Industrial Revolution became all too obvious with the building of a new worsted Mill, owned by the **Hartley** family. From speaking to local inhabitants, it was ascertained that at one time the mill had been called **Hartley-Smith mill,** and so a possible (albeit distant) family connection may well have existed, although the **Hartley's** were undoubtedly the prominent shareholders. An **1838** Trade Directory (held in **Keighley Public Library**) listed **Sutton-in-Craven** as having a population of **1,153,** spread over **2,650** acres (compared with a population of **3,240** recorded in the **1991 Census**).

Riley (1996) described how most of the people would have worked at home as weavers or cloth makers. During the eighteenth-century textiles had largely replaced agriculture as the main occupation in **Sutton.** The invention of the *'Spinning Jenny'* (in **1764**) created a new trend toward a greater number of people working alongside one another in larger premises. The latter often consisted of little more than a few cottages knocked together. Nevertheless, by the time **Edmund** was born mass production (for the main part in mills built for the purpose) would have been well underway. Rather surprisingly, given the competitive environment of the time, smaller-scale cottage industries managed to survive by specialising in the production of high-quality cloth. Hence, in the economic sphere, the *'old'* co-existed amicably with the *'new.'* At a lecture given at a meeting of **the Family History Section of the Yorkshire Archaeological Society** on **Wednesday, 13th June 2001,** the local historian **Stephen Caunce** confirmed that, until about **1850,** the old domestic system grew <u>alongside</u> the new factory system. At that time the factories concentrated upon the mass production of a lower quality cloth. It was only after **1850** that power looms could produce the same quality of cloth as the traditional handloom. **Caunce** also remarked that the Woollen Industry was an industry *"that consisted of a lot of little people"* and that its pattern of development was one of steady growth over long years rather than the rapid *'boom and bust'* which characterised the Cotton Industry. Nevertheless, my Great Grandfather's **Edmund's** entrance into this world came at a time when, through intense industrialisation, the Western World was undergoing its most amazing period of economic development since the *'Agricultural Revolution'* **10,000** years previously. In addition, salesmanship was something that would have been instilled in his blood and would later contribute to his own considerable success as a salesman. The aggressive salesmanship of textile representatives from the **North of England** was greatly feared by competitors in places as far afield as **New York** – where these *"pushy people"* were even accused of undermining the **American Constitution!** These *'sales representatives'* knew what it was to go out and seize foreign markets. It was partly their dauntless determination which played a pivotal role in laying the foundations of **Britain's** industrial success throughout the nineteenth century. **Edmund** too portrayed this quality in full measure, and it equipped him to successfully ride-out several severe economic recessions in the later **Victorian** period **(1873-1901).**

One other person to quickly seize upon the opportunities presented by the earlier stages of industrialisation was a certain **John Smith (1718-1793)** who, following his death, was described by the **Kildwick Parish Register** as being *'for many years an eminent worsted manufacturer.'* (Incidentally, **1793** was the year in which **King Louis XVI** of **France** and **Queen Marie Antoinette** were guillotined in **Paris** when the **Jacobean** terror was at its height.) Quoted in **Wood p.34,** this notice meant that **John Smith** must have possessed enough business acumen to have made a success of his trade, despite periods of economic instability.

His work would have required him to travel to **Colne** and **Halifax** to sell his wares in the Cloth Halls there. At **Halifax,** a room could be hired for £2.00 per year or purchased entirely for £30.00. There was no reason to think that dissimilar prices were charged at **Colne.** Whilst working in these Halls **John Smith** would have had to prove himself a very good salesman, needing to strike a good bargain with each customer. He will have made sure that he put across the impression that it was the customer who was getting the bargain! Such a challenge would have demanded a marked degree of *'playacting'* and a strong, fulsome voice to go with it. Somehow, I could easily imagine my own father **Fred** discharging that role with marked enthusiasm. This strong element of effective and successful salesmanship was a characteristic which would become embedded throughout various branches of the **Smith** family. It continues to this very day, especially when I endeavour to sell my services as a Private Tutor in Business, English, History, Religious Studies and various Social Science subjects to enquiring parents and fussy students! Sometimes, in such circumstances, I do feel a *'rush of ancestral blood.'* (As an *'aside'* writing this history has gained me some custom – especially amongst the Indian and Pakistani Communities where being perceived as coming from a *'good'* family helps produce a job offer.) A source of further information about this **John Smith** was his tomb inscription at **Kildwick Parish Church.** This provided the following details: -

John Smith of **Sutton,** upward **50** years a tradesman
August 31ˢᵗ, 1793 75ᵗʰ year
Mary his relict (meaning widow)
December 21ˢᵗ, 1799 83ʳᵈ year

Clearly, there was a man who wanted to be remembered for his business. His epitaph anticipated that of my Great Grandfather **Edmund** who also took pride in his business. **John Smith** was not a direct forbear of **Edmund** but if he was a relative then he would have displayed very typical **Smith** traits. My own instinct (as a family historian) is to believe that there was a loose connection – not least because **Edmund** appears to have manifested the same gift of performing well at business.

Lastly, it's worth noting that this **John Smith** was obviously much better off than his contemporary able-bodied peers. Worst off were the paupers who were paid only **1/-** a day to repair the local roads. During epidemics, it was these same paupers who were sent to clear out the houses of those who had died – the result often being a subsequent reduction of any poor relief needing to be paid out! Once again, the impression emerged that the **Smiths** were an industrious *'middling sort'* of people, spared some of the worst hardships of the times in which they were living.

Other more traditional craft occupations continued and were perhaps even rejuvenated by the arrival of new migrants. The **1822 Baines Directory** listed another **John Smith** as being a stonemason. To possess such an entry indicated that his highly traditional craft must have been doing well. Very small businesses were not usually recorded in this Directory.

A chance encounter with an eighty-four-year-old man (during my first visit to **Sutton**) confirmed that most of the mill working families had intermarried with one another. (This elderly gentleman himself had once worked at a nearby mill.) The fact that **Edmund** married <u>outside</u> the **Sutton** area would impression reinforce the possibility that he enjoyed a status slightly higher than that of the ordinary mill worker. (This point was to be confirmed by later findings.) This gentleman (who spoke with a marked local accent) also stated that there were possibly up to three families of **Smiths** still living in the **Sutton** area. He also disclosed that, during the **1920s,** the **Baptist Chapel** at **Sutton** had been very active, running a well-attended Sunday School and a *'Band of Hope'* Temperance Society. The latter had aimed at encouraging people to give up alcoholic drinks. This Baptist Assembly is still running now, opposite the bridge which spans

Holme (formerly **Glasburn**) **Beck**. It is now housed in a very modern building on the west side of the old **Turnpike Road,** running up to **Crosshills**. Much more will be said about this church and its profound influence upon my family in the second chapter of this history. A later contact with the minister who kindly gave us access to some interesting documentation on **Friday 4th September 2015** would prove most fruitful.

Section 7: Mill Misery

Concerning Bairstow's Mill in Sutton-in-Craven

The first fully recorded worsted manufacturers in **Sutton** were **Joshua Hill** and **Robert Clough** who took up this occupation as early as **1787** (two years before the outbreak of the French Revolution in **July 1789**). However, the family that really brought industrialisation to **Sutton** were the very influential **Bairstow** Family. In **April 1809,** they acquired a Corn Mill in **Sutton.** The whole purchase (which included three *'closes'* of land) had cost **£2,560.** This sum of money showed that the **Bairstow's** were already an extremely wealthy family. (Records confirmed that they had been commercially active for at least the previous decade, having re-opened a Corn Mill in neighbouring **Steeton** on **January 30th, 1798.**) The previous owner of **Sutton Corn Mill** had been a certain **David McCartney.** Apparently, they had taken over a site which had been used for corn milling purposes since **1543.** The limited profitability in that line of business provoked the two brothers **Thomas** and **Matthew Bairstow** to move into worsted manufacturing in **1838.** Like many other manufacturers of the time, they began the changeover by converting the use of the old premises. They replaced corn milling machinery with imported worsted machinery.

Very quickly, the brothers began to construct a large purpose-built worsted factory on the same site as the (now demolished) old Corn Mill. (Stone for both the earlier and later mills had been carted from the four hillside quarries to the **south** and **south-east** of **Sutton**.) Over the **1836-1838** period, substantial rebuilding was to take place on the site and in **December 1838** money had been paid for a temporary dam. Their action demonstrated that a highly enterprising, business-orientated family had not seen much of a future in corn milling. Later cited evidence would show that, by **June 1834,** my Great, Great Grandfather **John Smith** had worked as a Miller in **Cullingworth. In Sutton,** the only way he could have followed this trade on a regular basis was either by working with his father at **Glusburn Corn Mill** or for the **Bairstow Corn Mill,** sited (on what was then called) **Glusburn Beck. Edmund** himself would describe his father's occupation as that of a *'Corn-Miller'* and this description strongly suggested a link with either or both mills at various times. Some nearby tenant farmers (called the **Roes**) also undertook Corn-Milling but were only in operation <u>after</u> the early **1830s,** by which time **John Smith** had moved to **Cullingworth.** The **Roe's** business was only small-scale and would have been unlikely to have provided regular employment – something that **John Smith** needed to survive. Unless he (or family members) had <u>owned</u> an established local business my Great, Great Grandfather **John** would have found Corn Milling to have been a very precarious occupation. No Trade Directories for **Sutton**, **Cullingworth** or **Skipton** showed him ever having owned a large enough enterprise to have gained an entry in their listings.

A review of the archives (at **Bradford Archive Centre**) on **Friday, June 28th, 2002** confirmed that the **Bairstow's** were a substantial family. They held properties and shares in a diverse number of places across the **West Riding of Yorkshire.** They also owned land, cottages and shops. A review of other miscellaneous documents revealed that, in **1831,** the **Bairstow** Family purchased a plot of land near **Silsden** called **New Close** from a **Henry Spencer,** the traditional landowner, for the then considerable sum of **£57 3s 7d.** In this transaction, the **Bairstows** were reflecting the wider trend of the time wherein manufacturing families were taking over from old *'landed'* families who had hitherto been dominant. (Details of the huge archive can be found in **Hudson pp.9-48.** It was fortunate that I needed material only up to the end of **1835.** The whole archive itself carried on into the **1960s.**)

Once I had gained access to the above source the next question was to determine whether the **Smiths** had had any connection with the **Bairstow** Family. I was keen to ascertain whether my family had ever worked for them. Consequently, I had to spend a total of two and a half hours wading through account books, sale ledgers, lists of *'outworkers'* and wage cashbooks. (Outworkers simply did their work at home rather than on the industrial premises and were employed on a short-term *'Commission-only'* basis. Their labour was usually taken on only when a very large order was had to be met.)

Some of the details were written in very faint ink and even in pencil. Also present were badly written rough *'workings out,'* which obscured the important data. Nevertheless, these records were of sufficient detail to allow certain definite conclusions to be drawn. The first showed a business connection between the two families, but only a very limited one. A **John Smith Senior** (his actual full name) was found to have laboured at the new dam in **Sutton**

Mill, constructed from **19/8/1809** until **8/11/1809.** He was paid **6s 6d,** which constituted only a small part of the total (mainly labour) costs of £25 12s 0d. His name had been written against the date **8/11/1809.** A more substantial connection was enjoyed by an **Edmund Smith** of **Sutton** – who featured in the **1834-1843** *'Wage Account Cash Book for Hand Combers'* who were also classed as *'Outworkers.'* (A Hand Comber had to produce the unpleasant job of manually cleaning wool before it was processed in the mill.) It was found that he had been paid: -

£ 5 16s 9d for work done over **1/12/1837-9/2/1838**
£ 7 7s 4dh for work done over **1/12/1838-16/4/1838**
£ 7 15s 6dh for work done over **21/4/1839-7/9/1839**
£ 7 16s 5d for work done over **13/9/1839-29/1/1840**
N.B: h stands for a halfpenny.
However, none of the above **Smiths** was my direct ancestors although they may well have had some relationship with them.

Another interesting transaction took place with the brothers **Joseph** and **Benjamin Smith** who had been wool dealers in **Crosshills.** A *'Purchase/Sales Day Book'* (covering **1830-1835**) had the following entry, dated **October 21st, 1831,** *"J & B Smith Crosshills contra Ce* (or CR). (**Latin** for *'Credit Against') for wool £14 2s 63/4d."* A subsequent entry for **October 29th** showed that they had paid this amount in cash. From this entry, one can deduce that these **Smiths** were prompt payers who liked to keep some cash in hand. A review of the index in this source showed that, despite the large numbers of **Smiths** involved in textiles, only a few had experienced any direct links with the **Bairstow's** Empire. Even the name *"J & B Smith"* came up only once. It appeared that the **Smiths** had wanted to give the **Bairstow** Business Enterprise a wide berth. Presumably, they were keen to preserve their independence, separate from the larger **Bairstow** organisation. Given the working conditions in **Bairstow's Mill** at **Sutton,** they were perhaps wise to have adopted this stance. Overall, the **Smiths** were a very self-sufficient lot, determined to make their own way forward in life. (Incidentally, this independent streak was a trait my own father possessed to a large degree. I have it and so do my sons!) However, later cited evidence would confirm that my Great, Great, Great grandfather **William Smith** did conduct transactions with the **Bairstow** Family. The reality was that they were a family who could hardly be missed. During **1833,** one year after **Edmund's** birth, a Factory Inquiry Commission (quoted in **Wood p. 36**) tabulated weekly factory wages in nearby **Oxenhope Mill** as being: -

2/- for those aged less than **10** years
2/6d for those aged **10-12**
3/6 for those aged **12-14**
4/6 for those aged **14-16**
6/- for those aged **16-18**
7/- for those aged **18-21**
10/- for those males aged **21** or over
7/- for those females aged **21** or over
Working hours were from: -
6.00A.M. −7.00P.M. in summer
6.00A.M. - Dusk in winter.

In **Sutton,** wages and hours will have been at a similar level. At the time of **Edmund's** birth, the most likely future prospect facing many families in the locality would have been working in **Bairstow's** Mill. By a mixture of hard graft and opportunism, a keen worker may have worked his way up to be an overseer, but this was the highest level he could ever reach. By the time of the **1851** Census **Bairstow's** had become the major employer in **Sutton.** This can be seen in a comparison between itself and **Hartley's Mill** (founded in **1830**), made by **Wood p.35.**

Number of Textile Workers	Bairstow's Mill	Hartley's
Men	402	58
Women	12	-
Boys	109	7
Girls	83	-
Totals	<u>606</u>	<u>65</u>

A quick calculation showed that **88.53%** of the **671** textile workers of **Sutton** were employed at the **Bairstow** Mill. The days of small businesses employing a few spinners in their workshop premises were long since over. Even semi-independent handloom weavers (*e.g.* **John Smith** of **Tetley Row**) would have depended mainly upon *'outwork'* from **Bairstow's.** Of the two establishments, **Hartley's** appears to have been marginally more humane in not employing female labour. Nevertheless, as a family, the **Bairstow's** appear to have prospered with the **1861** Census revealing **Thomas** to have been a manufacturer employing **820** persons. The occupational composition of the textile workforce in **1851** (the **Bairstow** and **Hartley Mills** combined) could be broken down into five principal areas, as shown in the following table: -

Occupation	Number	%
Power Loom Weavers	218	32
Hand Loom Weavers	148	23
Combers	95	14
Spinners	111	17
Others	99	14
Total number of textile workers	**671**	**100**

What these figures did <u>not</u> show was the overall trend <u>away from</u> handloom to power-loom weaving. However, when compared to earlier data these figures do lend weight to the supposition that **Edmund's** birth in **1832** came during the middle of a transition from a mainly hand-craft and small business-based textile industry to that a machine power. Single companies enjoyed a near local monopoly in terms of production and employment. A wool merchant of the **1790s** would barely be able to recognise the wool industry of the **1850s.** Far from being tranquil, if impoverished backwater, **Sutton** was a community undergoing dramatic change, (which itself was part of a wider change affecting the whole of **Britain.**) Figures (supplied by **Jay pp.183-4**) revealed that male employment in agriculture dropped from **53%** to **29%** over the period **1760-1840**; whilst those employed in industry rose from **24%** to **47%**. The percentage of the population living in towns and cities soared from **21%** to **48%**. Any failure to adapt to such changes could pitch a family into the nightmare of early **Victorian** destitution. From his youth, **Edmund** would have appreciated the need for *'flexibility'* in the world of business. To do nothing but *'tread water'* was to drown. **Edmund's** own understanding of the world was moulded by the hardships he would have seen and experienced during the **1840s.** To better understand my Great Grandfather, it was first necessary to view him as a product of the *'starving forties.'* His character was very much moulded by the harsh times in which he lived. The price of failure was starvation. As he would have realized, gaining respectability (and the income to go with it) would constitute one very practical way to avoid such a fate. It would not be an exaggeration to portray my Great Grandfather as a man who had been psychologically traumatized by destitution, he saw around him.

Yet the commercial success and prosperity of the **Bairstow** Family offered no defence against the kind of domestic tragedies afflicting poorer members of the local community. A review of heavily eroded tomb epitaphs beside **Kildwick Parish Church** showed that **Thomas Bairstow** and his wife **Elizabeth** lost: -
Elizabeth aged **8** months on **21ˢᵗ August 1846**
Charles aged **19** to **18ᵗʰ?** **February 1861**
Thomas Ingleby aged **18?** On **24ᵗʰ February 1861**
John Samuel infant son **25ᵗʰ February 1861**
Lilla? Aged **11** on **December 29ᵗʰ, 1864**
Agnes aged **16** on **6ᵗʰ March 1867**
Two infants of unknown dates
Thomas Bairstow '*of Royd Hill*' himself expired on **December 2ⁿᵈ, 1867** at the age of **59.** His wife **Elizabeth** followed on **September 30ᵗʰ1878.** She was **63** years old. It's hard not to escape the conclusion that their lives were a case of outward success masking private tragedy. To endure these losses **Thomas** perhaps lost himself in his work. One wonders how his wife will have coped even with a strong supportive family network.

Section 8: Touching Epitaphs

Concerning Smith grave inscriptions at Kildwick Parish Church

Sometimes, burial registers could also be unintentionally revealing about the ways in which life was lost at that time. On **4ᵗʰ March 1775,** the burial register for **1771-1781** entered a **Richard Smith** of **Lothersdale** "*who drowned in the canal!*" (His age wasn't recorded.) The same source also revealed (in an entry dated **9ᵗʰ December 1773**) that a Husbandman by the name of **Francis Stirk** of **Silsden Moor** had lived to be **97.** Similar entries confirmed that it was possible for men and women to live on into a ripe old age. Not everyone died young.

This last point was underlined in the following tomb inscription, lying inside **Saint Andrew's** Churchyard.
"*This stone relives from oblivion the*
Memory of **Thomas Wade** *of* **Silsden Moor** *who*
Lived a life of plainness, uprightness &
Temperance and died **Feb II 1810**
In the **103ʳᵈ** *year of his age*

Also, **Martha** *widow of* **Hugh Hudson** *and daughter*
Of the above **Thomas Wade** *who died* **Mch 2ⁿᵈ 1812 73ʳᵈ** *yr."*

Possible evidence of a genetic predisposition to longevity in the **Smiths** was found on the tomb of a **George Smith** of **Lumb, Cowling,** who'd *"departed this life on the* **6ᵗʰ** *of* **January 1832** *in the* **99ᵗʰ** *year of his life."* His wife (also named **Susanna**) had died on **April 5ᵗʰ1805,** aged **71.** This provides further evidence that the **Smiths** were spared the worst hardships of the time. For them, life had appeared grim rather than desperate.

Especially revealing was the inscriptions that were engraved onto gravestones. Very typically for their time, some of the **Smiths** living in the eighteenth to early nineteenth centuries had a horizontal gravestone. These were lying flat on a pavement leading up toward **Kildwick Parish Church** when I discovered them. They were only found during my second visit to this graveyard, made during a very wet **Monday, February 5ᵗʰ, 2001.** (The first visit had been undertaken on a bright but windy autumn afternoon on **Friday, 29ᵗʰ September 2000.**) The inscription was in old English where the letter *'s'* was shaped like the letter *'f'* without the midline. (Whilst trying to scrape off some moss I slipped and sent a wooden bench keeling over. In my bright blue cagoule and sodden black jeans, I must have looked an amusing sight lying on my back amidst the sleeting rain.) The inscription read as follows: -
"Here lye
The bodies of
Robert *and* **John**
Sons of **William**
Smith *of* **Sutton,**
Who were both
Buried **January 25ᵗʰ1732.**
Robert *in ye* **19ᵗʰ** *year of*
His age and **John** *in*
Ye first year of his age.
Also, the body of
Robert Smith *of*
Sutton *Grandfather*
Of the above-said children.
He died on the **4ᵗʰ** *and*
Was buried on the **7ᵗʰ January 1741** *in the* **90ᵗʰ**
Year of his age.
Also, **William Smith** *son of*

The above **Robert Smith** *and father*
Of Ye above children
departed this life **August 11**th
1742 *in the* **57**th *year of his age."*

There was something very touching about this epitaph. Despite a covering of moss, the inscription was reasonably well preserved although the age given to **John** was something of a guess as it had been chiselled in Latin numerals that were badly eroded. The apparent later insertion of previously omitted letters suggested that the mason had possessed only a limited degree of literacy. From a historical viewpoint, the most interesting feature was the names like **John, Robert** and **William,** which surfaced repeatedly in my own family line during the nineteenth century. These names and the connection with **Sutton** suggested that the people interred here could have been related to my own direct ancestors. Strongly present was a sense of wonder at finding an ancestor who had been born during the English Civil War. His advanced age contrasted with the early death of his two grandsons who appear to have died at the same time. What they'd died from isn't known – but the most probable cause was a highly infectious disease or some form of an accident like a cottage fire. Even in those times (when death was common) their loss must have been a cause of great heartbreak. One curious feature about the tomb was the absence of any female names – were only the names of men judged worthy of remembrance?

A final interesting feature was the proximity of this tomb with that of the successful businessman **John Smith (1718-1793).** This proximity and the shared association with **Sutton** strongly implied a family connection although exactly what this consisted of could not be factually ascertained.

Equally striking details about the early **Smiths** were provided on the following epitaph (engraved on a tombstone adjacent to the path leading to the entrance of **Kildwick Parish Church**).

In memory of
ROBERT SMITH
Late of **Lumb Mill Cowling**
Who departed this life **February 11**th, **1840**
In the **86**th *year of his age.*
Also, **MARTHA** *his wife*
Who died **May 1801**
Aged **40** *years*
"This memorial is erected by one who shared

their parental care and support when
a pupil at the school in connection with this church"
GEORGE SMITH, *their son born at*
Lumb Mill Cowling, April 5ᵗʰ1789
Died at **Manchester, April 1ˢᵗ1865.**

What is fascinating about this epitaph is that it provides further evidence of a deep-rooted family interest in education. This was a very typical **Smith** trait that continues to this day. On a speculative note, was this **Robert Smith** the son of **Robert Smith** the schoolmaster (at **Cowling** in **1751**)? His location at **Lumb Mill** shows the **Smiths** having a connection with the higher, moorland end of **Cowling.**

The Birth Register for **Sutton Baptist Chapel** suggested that *'Laura'* was the middle name of **Robert Smith's** wife **(Martha Laura Smith).** It was perhaps used to distinguish her from other **Martha Smiths** – *'Martha'* being a very common name at the time. (Incidentally, I discovered this tomb on my first visit to **Kildwick** in **September 2000**).

His death at the advanced age of eighty-six lent weight to the view that **Robert Smith** had been a most vigorous man. He had lived even longer than my own father – who had enjoyed the benefits of modern medicine. Moreover, his transfer of loyalties from **Sutton Baptist Chapel** to **Kildwick Parish Church** implied that he had risen in the world because, in his time, people tended to join the **Anglican** Church as they prospered and became more *'respectable.'* Exactly what relation **Robert** bore to my own line of **Smiths** remains a mystery. The family details (given in the **Sutton Baptist Register**) show that he was not a direct ancestor, but a more distant relationship could not be ruled out. Anyway, he was one of the **Smith** of whose personality it was possible to discern something concrete about. His care for others provided an early anticipation of my father's own marked concern for the welfare of other people. In **April 1838,** a **Robert Smith** (aged **4**) was on the Parish Record as having died through *"accidental burning."* Little was discovered about his background except that he'd come from **Cowling** and that his father was a weaver. The name, however, did suggest that he might have been a grandson of the **Robert Smith** interred at **Kildwick.** If this was the case, **Robert** would have heard about this family tragedy when in extreme old age.

Another tomb inscription (also discovered during my first visit), not far from that of **Robert Smith,** provided evidence of a rather macabre sense of humour: *"IN MEMORY OF*

Martha *the wife of* **Benjamin Smith** *of* **Glasburn Hall,** *who died* **January 30th 1817** *in the* **23rd** *year of her age.*

Reflect when thou my grave dost see the next that's made may be for thee."

After that cheerful thought the rest of the inscription read: -
"Also, of **Esther,** *wife of the above named* **Benjamin Smith** *who died on the* **11th June 1827,** *in the* **35th** *year of her age. Also, the aforesaid* **Benjamin Smith** *who died at* **Crosshills October 31st 1834** *in the* **45th** *year of his age. Also,* **James Cowgill** *surveyor* **Bradford** *who died* **August 10th 1878** *aged* **53** *years. Also,* **Elizabeth** *daughter of the above* **[Benjamin Smith]** *and widow of the late* **James Cowgill** *surveyor,* **Bradford** *who died* **May 28th 1887** *aged* **62** *years."*
(During this first visit one elderly lady I met within the graveyard mentioned that an epitaph by a widow for her husband had read *"Rest in peace until I come."* Unfortunately, this headstone no longer existed to confirm her story!)

A great deal was discovered about the above **Benjamin Smith** whilst searching through the marriage register of **Kildwick Parish Church** at The **Northallerton Archive Centre.** I remember a furious thunderstorm raging whilst using microfiche to go through this source on the afternoon of **Friday, June 15th 2001.** He was a *'clogger'* by trade and could sign his name in beautiful script writing. His marriage to **Martha** (formerly **Parkinson,** a spinster of **Cowling**) had taken place on **July 21st, 1814,** whilst his marriage to **Esther** (formerly **Harrison,** a spinster of **Glasburn**) had taken place on **February 22nd, 1824.** Both wives could write neat signatures, as could the witnesses at the two weddings. (These being **Henry Smith** and **John Greenwood** at the first wedding, and **Robert Harrison** and **Jane Smith** at the second.) **Benjamin Smith's** signature also appeared on the marriage certificate of a **John Smith** and an **Anne Wilson** on **24ᵗʰ May 1824.** At **Kildwick,** I had found the gravestone of a man who had known my Great, Great Grandfather *'face-to-face'* in the early nineteenth century! Such discoveries can indeed provoke a sense of amazement. My eldest son is also called **Benjamin** (born on **1ˢᵗ June 1983** in **Leeds**).

Elizabeth, the daughter of **Benjamin Smith's** first wife **Esther,** had been christened on **March 6ᵗʰ, 1824.** Her actual birth date had been **January 24ᵗʰ** of that year. (This **Benjamin Smith** the *'clogger,'* is to be distinguished from a later but possibly distantly related, **Benjamin Smith** who was a wool manufacturer.) This second **Benjamin Smith** (the wool manufacturer) had been baptised at **Kildwick Parish Church on December 25ᵗʰ1804.** The register revealed that he was *"**Benjamin,** third son of **Benjamin Smith** of **Sutton** Yeoman & **Sarah Briscoe** his wife, [born] 21 November."* He'd had an older brother called **Joseph** who had been baptised on **4ᵗʰ July 1803.** The register had stated: *"**Joseph,** second son of **Benjamin Smith** of **Sutton** worsted manufacturer & **Sarah Briscoe** his wife, [born] 30ᵗʰ May."* By**1838** the **Trade Directory** showed that the only **Smiths** worth mentioning in **Sutton** were butchers – but in nearby **Crosshills** was a **Benjamin Smith** and a **Thomas Smith** – both connected to worsted manufacturing. Regarding the former manufacturer, the **1841** Census Return showed: -
Benjamin Smith aged **35,** *"Worsted Manufacturer's Agent"*
Anne Smith aged **35**
Catherine Smith aged **2**
Sarah Anne Smith aged **11**
But the **1841** and **1851** Census Returns showed **Thomas Smith** to have been a single man, born in **1816** whilst **Benjamin Smith,** for his part, disappeared from the area sometime between the two Census Returns. He was to resurface later in an unexpected location. Like the first **Benjamin,** he appears to have been a close associate of my family. On some records, it was not always possible to distinguish between these two men named **Benjamin!**

What was especially apparent from the **1841** Census Return was that the whole area from **Colne** to **Kildwick** was absolutely teeming with **Smiths.** This was in marked contrast to a settlement like **Cullingworth** where other local names like **Craven** were far more predominant. (In **Cullingworth** the **Smiths** only came in ones and twos.) Adding to this complexity was the fact that many of them had identical forenames, with *'John,' 'Mary'* and *'Ann'* being especially common.

On **Friday, 4th September 2014** the Vicar of **Kildwick Church** kindly showed my wife, my second cousin once removed and myself an old burial map of the church. (A photograph shows the vicar, my second cousin and I poring over it.) This very old document confirmed what I'd expected – the tombstones had been removed from their original locations to act as paving stones. Rather like **King Richard III** my ancestors **William** and **Edward Smith** lie buried beneath a car park! The pavement *'headstone'* had been moved upwards to cover a path.

Family tradition (and the **1861** Census) had located my Great grandfather's place of birth to the **Sutton-in Craven** and **Crosshills** district. Although this information narrowed the area of search, a survey of families in **Sutton, Glasburn Township** (which included **Crosshills** village) and **Kildwick** revealed the presence of many **Smiths** in the earlier **1841** Census. Tracing the parents of my Great Grandfather **Edmund Smith** was turning out to be something of a nightmare, especially as the Dissenting Register had revealed that their names were yet another *'John'* and *'Ann Smith!'* Unless great care was taken, it would be all too easy to trace the wrong **John** and **Ann Smith** – and yet <u>even</u> with painstaking care this was precisely what did happen! The correct couple's details were only finally located at **Northallerton Archive Centre** during a stormy, rain swept **Friday** on **June 15th, 2001**. Consequently, many hitherto plausible conclusions had then needed total amendment.

Section 9: Faces They Knew

Concerning village contemporaries of the Smiths

Despite helpful graveyard inscriptions, only a few bare facts are known about the **Smiths** who lived from the late sixteenth to mid-eighteenth century. Hindering any definitive conclusion about some of them was the way the **Kildwick Parish** Burial Register for the years **1720-1743** was missing. Consequently, it wasn't possible to ascertain whether anyone likely to be my ancestor was buried between these dates. The poor handwriting was another problem with these records. However, despite these limitations, it was still possible to use parish documents to gain some insight into the lives of my ancestors by examining those of their contemporaries. Although they may not have known them intimately these were people whose faces, they would have seen in the local village or parish church service. In some cases, their names may also have been known and gossip about them recounted. The following details are taken from **Alec Wood's (1996)** highly informative booklet *'History and Description of the Parish Church of **St Andrew, Kildwick in Craven.'*** His booklet made excellent use of the available Parish Records which are quoted below. Nevertheless, I took the liberty of re-arranging the material **Wood** used in chronological rather than subject order. Doing this should enable readers to trace local and key national events in the lives of my **Smith** forbears. Some of these events would have been a talking point in a remote community where any news would be seized upon. Insertions in square brackets are my own.

'*1581* [burial of] **William Morrison** *son of* **Francis Morrison** *and* **Dorothy** *his wife, a stranger'* [someone outside the locality].

'**John Shackleden** *his wife, his mother and three children all died of the 'peste'* [plague].

'*1587 July 2ⁿᵈ*. **William Scott** *and* **Robert Craven** *buried in one coffin.'*

'*1597 Oct 23ʳᵈ*. **Henry** *the son of no-one, the mother a pauper dying in childbirth.'*

'*1604* **Peter Foster** *and* **Jenny Swayne** *the woman's finger was missing.'*

'*1607 January 15ᵗʰ*. **William Peele** *who perished in the waters having been bruised by the mill wheel when about to break the ice from the revolving wheel.'*

'*1673 To 3 persons for* **150** *crow's heads* **3s 10d, 1s 0d** *was paid for a fox's head, and* **4d** *for a hedgehog.'* [This was payment for small game.]

'*1678* **Francis Rawlings** *was the first* [buried] *in Woollen* [shroud, allowed] *by an act of Parliament.'*

'*1709 pd* [paid] *for clerk's new clothes and making* **4s. 0d.'**

'*1729* **John Wade** *received* **10s 0d,** *per half year for 'looking to the clock'* and **2s 6d,** per half year *for 'whipping dogs out of the church.'* [Popular status symbols at the time, dogs were often brought to church and ended up fighting each other during a service]

'*1746 To Ringers for ringing the* **9ᵗʰ Oct** *being Thanksgiving Day after the* **[Jacobite] Rebellion is 6d.'**

'*1760 Pd, to* **John Beanland's** *bill for candles to illuminate the church on taking of* **Quebec 6s 2d.'** [Note how the parish church acted as a conduit for the major news of the day.]

'1772 Feb 11ᵗʰ [burial of] *George Stanley of Kildwick Dancing Master.'*

'1797 Aug. 16ᵗʰ Mary wife of Hartley Wilkinson, weaver, who died of childbed [fever] *aged 18.'* [One of many deaths of mother and child in childbirth]

'1803 Dec 25ᵗʰ To Churchwardens dinners and liquor on Christmas Day £1 19s 6d.'

'1805 Leather for muffling the bells on hearing of the victory and death of Nelson 1s 0d.'

'1815 paid for a new clerk's clothes and making £4 11s 6d.'

'1815 Oct. 3ʳᵈ The singers be allowed 4s 0d per week but must have a master until such times as the Vicar and churchwardens shall deem them fit to proceed by themselves.' [Evidently, there had been some trouble in the choir] **(Wood pp.18-19)**

On **p.20 Wood** revealed that **Kildwick Saint Andrew** was not immune from the upheavals of the **Tudor** and early **Stuart** period. The following extract demonstrates this point.

"A priest [who must have been an interesting character] *was **Brother Robert Whixley**. He was instituted in **1514** and held the living for fifty-six years. What did he think of the surrender of the monasteries and the religious upheavals during the reigns of **Henry VIII, Edward VI, Mary** and **Elizabeth?** Whatever he thought he remained Vicar until **1571** conforming to the changes introduced by the **Tudor** rules.*

*Mention must be made of the **Rev. Alex Horrocks**, Vicar from **1571-1589,** who after allowing a Puritan Minister, one **John Wilson** of **Skipton**, to preach in **Kildwick** Church, was summoned to appear at **York** for trial. Found guilty they were both imprisoned; **Horrocks** until such time "as he would recant publicly."*

*A curate of note was **John Webster, 1634.** A keen linguist, chemist and teacher, he also served in the **Roundhead Army** as a doctor, later turning to preaching. During a service at **Kildwick**, a boy named **Edmund Robinson** suddenly stood on a bench and began pointing out certain women, denouncing them as witches. The terrified women bribed the boy's father not to inform the Magistrates, but **Webster** in no uncertain manner exposed the fraud – the boy and his father (who made a living in this way) leaving somewhat hastily."*

What side the **Smiths** took in the **English Civil War (1642-1653)** remains unknown. They resided near to the **Puritan** stronghold of **Bradford,** so their sympathies were most likely to have tended in a **Roundhead** direction. Parish records are scanty for that period which suggests a certain degree of disruption. Who knows what my ancestors would have made of such events, but their geographical isolation would have offered them some degree of protection. Maybe – like most of the population – they were just trying to survive. Thankfully, the end of this tumultuous period provided a certain degree of stability and (for some) a measure of prosperity. In this context, it's worth referring to the Will of a **John Emmott** of *'Coweling'* who *was 'a man of substance.'* The old-fashioned English wording made it a difficult document to determine exactly w. Moreover, he had a definite contact with a **John Smith** who owed his estate the not insignificant sum of **£11.00.** All figures are in pounds, shillings and pence.

James Emmott Revill Know Coiling 23rd April 1716

Imprimis His purse & apparrell	5-0-0
Itm Four cows	**15-10-0**
Four little Oxen	15-0-0
Three steers	**7-15-0**
Three young heifers	7-15-0
Three calves	**3-15-0**
One Mare	4-15-0
Two carts, two prs of Wheels, one coupe and Raithes	**1-17-0**
One other cart and wheels	13-0-0
2 old arks	**10-0-0**
2 plows, 1 coulter, 1 share Teams and Traces Yoaks 2 harrows, barkhams, hames and other old hustlement belonging to the same	1-16-0
Shools, forkes and spaides	**8-0-0**
One cheesefatt and other small wright's tools stock in the workhouse	15-0-0
One hack (?) one piece of wood, 2 spinning wheels and tunes	**1-0-0**
Eight sackes one winowing sheet, one saddlerope wantow and other odd hustlements	1-0-0
One colepott, one chafeing dish, one reckon, one frying pan, one baking stone, one pair of Briggs, one pair of tongs	**6-0-0**
Thirteen pewter dishes, two pewter plates and other pewter	1-10-0
7 pans, 4 brass hoddles, 1 candlestick and one morter	**16-6-0**

In potts	3-6-0
One dish board and all the wood vessell	**13-0-0**
1 Longtable, 2 forms, 1 cupboard and 1 long seat	1-1-0
One arke	**7-0-0**
Two glass cases, one bread fleak, shelf board and one watch	5-0-0
17 chairs and Quishings, 1 meat board and stools	**18-0-0**
One bedstead and bedding	1-5-0
Three chests	**1-0-0**
One coffer and old board	1-6-0
One bedstead and bedding	**1-5-0**
One pair of looms, and furniture	6-0-0
One pair of old bedstocks	**2-0-0**
One bedstead and bedding for 2 beds	2-1-0
2 chests	**18-0-0**
3 boards one old arke, 1 form and 3 coffers	9-0-0
In oatmeale	**8-10-0**
Itm in wheat	8-0-0
In beefe and bacon	**2-5-0**
	92-6-6
Debts owing to the Testator by: -	
Stephen Tillitson	
John Tillitson	**21-0-0**
William Laycock	1-0-0
William Parkinson	**6-10-0**
Christopher Hartley	27-0-0
John Smith	**6-0-0**
Robert Shackleton	11-0-0
Henry Moorehouse	**19-5-0**
Robert Watson	13-16-0
Widow Aldersley	**15-0-0**
Richard Brigg	1-2-0
Robert Emott	**4-0-0**
Widow Judgson	10-0-0
Abraham Oxnard	**13-0-0**
William Jackson	6-0-0
Thomas Thompson	**6-0-0**
Daniel Robinson	12-0-0
	1-0-0

The whole sum of this inventory

<u>111- 15-0</u>

<u>204-1-6</u>

John Wilson, Christopher Emmott, George Emmott, Richard Brigg (marks)

Where it was present, wealth was expressed in terms of the ownership of land and property and in the ability to gather rents. The **Smiths** were clearly below the **Emmotts** in terms of status.

The **Cowlings Moonraker's Site** provided further details (retrieved on **Wednesday 9th March 2016**) which I've re-arranged in chronological order. Although the notes contained interesting details, they were very disorderly and extremely difficult to edit: -

"Extract taken from **Wm. Sewell's** *notebook.* **Mr Sewell** *(pupil teacher at a local school). Local historian & teacher d.* **1972** *age* **93.**

*"**14th January 1580 (or 1581)** – **Margareta Hargreaves** drowned in water above mill called* **Ridge Mill.**
Earls of Cumberland *held lands in* **Cowling** *in* **16th** *c. lands sold &* **3** *hamlets,* **Cowling, Ickornshaw & Stott Hill** *which met at Ridge Mill Bridge were divided. Stood on land between where waters meet corn mill. Grindstone found in the beck.*
1622 - Robert Smyth *of 'Ickornshay', yeoman, sold to* **Christopher Smyth** *of the same, tailor, some farm property. In a document relating to the sale, the buyer covenanted to grind all corn at the water mill in* **'Collinge'** *called* **Ridge Mill.**
1622 *- Corn mill destroyed by fire then transferred to* **Lumb Mill.**
David Bracewell *of* **Lower Stonehead (A.D. 1677)** *was appointed to serve as an overseer and master of the poor for one year at a salary of £5 15 shillings. In* **March 1775,** *at the local* **Cowling** *Workhouse. Duties included: To supply vittens (victuals).*
• *To go* **3** *times every week to Workhouse.*
• *To keep all account for work in poor house and for hay getting & shearing.*
Mention of stone for walls taken from **Ridge Mill Plantation** *for walls in connection with repairs to* **Wood House** *in* **1769.** *No mention in records after* **1773.**
The road over 'stonery' to **Wood House** *made in* **1792** *& improved in* **1797.**
Bridle Path through **Dark Wood,** *though we have no evidence of where Dark Wood is.* **Mill Dam** *also mentioned to be in* **Dark Wood."**

Anne Bronte in her autobiographical novel *'Agnes Grey'* also provided helpful information. (It was first published in **1847**.) On **pp.71-72**, it featured a minor character named **Smith** who spoke in what would have been the dialect of my ancestors. He occurred in a scene where the heroine **Agnes Grey** is about to leave home to take up her position as a governess for what would turn out to be an appalling family.

*"I was to depart early, in that the conveyance which took me (a gig, hired from **Mr Smith**, the draper, grocer, and tea-dealer of the village) might return the same day. I rose, washed, dressed, swallowed a hasty breakfast, received the fond embraces of my father, mother, and sister, kissed the cat to the great scandal of **Sally** the maid, shook hands with her, mounted the gig, drew my veil over my face, and then, but not till then, I burst into a flood of tears.*

The gig rolled on – I looked back- my dear mother and sister were still standing at the door, looking after me, and waving their adieux: I returned their salute, and prayed God to bless them from my heart: we descended the hill, and I could see them no more.

*'It's a coldish mornin' for you, **Miss Agnes**,' observed **Smith**; 'and a darksome un too; but we's happen get to yon' spot afore there come much rain to signify.'*

'Yes, I hope so,' replied I, as calmly as I could.

'It's comed a good sup last night too.'

'Yes.'

'But this cold wind ull happen keep it off.'

'Perhaps it will.'

Here ended our colloquy; we crossed the valley and began to ascend the opposite hill."

The amazing feature of this account was the way it dovetailed so neatly with my own research into the early **Smiths. Ann Bronte's** *'Smith'* had possessed a strong business streak, spreading his activities over several different areas – thereby displaying a trait that persistently resurfaced through successive generations of my family. They were an enterprising sort of people. Also (like the real **Smiths** uncovered by my research) her fictional character was certainly not gentry but, nevertheless, his standard of living would have been above the average. He certainly was not a *'common'* labourer or worker. Finally, it is easy to imagine that many of the real **Smiths** were just as taciturn as the one portrayed in **Agnes Grey**. On first reading this extract from **Ann Bronte's** novel (in **April 2002**) I felt as if I was meeting one of my own ancestors. It was a case of literature further illuminating (and certainly adding life too) the huge amount of carefully gathered historical data.

Section 10: The Wider World

Concerning *'The Leeds Intelligencer,' 'The Leeds Mercury'* and Quack remedies for VD

To help convey a flavour of the wider world in which my early ancestors lived extracts will be quoted from *'The Leeds Intelligencer,'* an important regional newspaper of the day. This paper was selected because it covered the whole period from the birth of my Great, Great, Great Grandfather's **William Smith** in **November 1778,** to that of my Great Grandfather **Edmund** in **January 1832.** It is worth mentioning that (from the **1790s** onwards) this publication was **Tory** in its sympathies – in contrast to *'The Leeds Mercury,'* which supported the **Whig Party** (and was much more likely to have been read by **Edmund** himself). It was this political divide which partly explained the different coverage given to the Great Reform Meeting held in **Leeds** on **May 14th, 1832.** The **Leeds Intelligencer** gave a negative coverage, (which highlighted the disorderly aspect of that meeting) whereas **The Leeds Mercury** took great care to give a far more positive impression.

On **Tuesday, November 3rd, 1778,** (the day after **William Smith's** birth) **The Leeds Intelligencer** (price **3d**) contained the following news items: *"The following ships sailed from **Sandy Hook** [off the coast of **America**], under the command of **Lord Howe, August 6th, 1778** – The **Cornwall** of **74** guns, **Eagle Trident, Nonsuch, Raisonable, Somerset St Albans** and **Ardent,** of **64** guns each. **Preston, Centurion, Experiment, Isis** and **Renown** of **50** guns each. **Phoenix** and **Roebuck** with **44** guns each. **Venus** of **36, Richmond, Pearl** and **Apollo** of **32** guns each. **Spitfire** of **20,** besides several armed ships, fire-ships. & c. &c."* Apparently, their mission was to engage the **French** fleet (who were supporting the **Americans**) in the **New York** area. A despatch from **Lord Howe** had preceded this bulletin, which appears to have been extracted from the **London Gazette** and dated **August 17th, 1778.** It seems that, in those days, news about the **American War of Independence** took two to three months to reach Leeds – a vastly far slower speed than we are used to today. Many *'auction'* announcements were also to be found in these newspapers, *i.e.*
"To be SOLD by AUCTION
*By **T. STOOKS,***
*At **BRAMHOPE HALL**, near **OTLEY***
ALL the Valuable Household furniture,
*Belonging to Mrs **VAVASOUR,** consisting of Bed-heads with different Hangings, and Window Hangings,*

Bedding, Plate, Linen, China, Glass & C.
The Sale to begin on Monday the Sixteenth of **Nov.**
Inst. At Ten o' Clock in the Forenoon, and to continue till
All are sold."

This typical announcement has a certain *'market town'* air about it. The list of goods being sold revealed that **Mrs Vavasour** had been a wealthy lady. One wonders whether she'd died or had fallen on troubled times. The following advert was equally revealing: -
*"**VOLTAIRE'S WORK COMPLEAT.***
On Saturday last was published, price only **6d**
Elegantly printed in octavo, and ornamented with a Head
Of the Author, copied from an original bust by the ingenious **Mr Houden** *and engraved by*
Mr Walker,
NUMBER 1. (to be continued weekly) of
A Compleat Edition of the WORKS of the late celebrated **Mr De VOLTAIRE** – *Translated*
From the **French** *by* **WILLIAM CAMPBELL, I.L.D.**
Member of the Royal Academy of Sciences and Belles Lettres
At **Lyons,** **J. JOHNSON M.A** *and OTHERS.*
With Notes, Critical and Explanatory."

This advert was fascinating because it showed that Enlightenment Thinking was spreading – even in a provincial town like **Leeds**. It was <u>not</u> a phenomenon confined to capital cities like **London** or **Paris.** In a very shrewd (yet determined manner) reputable authorities like the **Academy of Sciences** used the **Leeds Intelligencer** as a *'selling point'* to an obviously upper-class genteel audience. The advertisers knew how to appeal to their market. Of interest was the way in which the following public notice provided evidence that the *'pirating'* of **Voltaire's** works was a real problem. This suggested that there was an obviously significant demand for them.
"To distinguish the spurious performances from those
Which really flowed from his pen, as well as to procure
many of his last pieces would have been a task attended
with superior difficulties, had not the present translators
been generously favoured with the assistance of the author's
noble friend the **Marquis de Villette;** *under whose hospitable*
roof he died."

Present was an appeal to traditional **English** snobbery with its love of aristocratic titles. The advertisers clearly knew how to differentiate their product from those of other competitors, who were subtly belittled. They also had a targeted market niche in mind. Their sales promotion was quite brilliant and could rival any *'modern'* advert produced today.

On **Monday, March 13th, 1805,** four days before my Great, Great Grandfather **John Smith's** was born, the **Leeds Intelligencer** (price now **6d**) contained the following news items: -
"CAUTION
The Public are hereby informed that I will not
From the Day of the date hereof, be answerable for
Debt or debts which ***ELIZABETH SARAH REYNOLDSON,***
The Wife of me ***THOMAS REYNOLDSON,***
Leeds, *in the County of* ***York, Taylor,*** *or her son*
WILLIAM PARKER *may contract or have heretofore*
enacted – As Witness my Hand
THOMAS REYNOLDSON,
Rothwell Gaol, March 7th, 1805."

The angry tone of this announcement speaks volumes. What appears to have happened was that **Thomas Reynoldson** had found himself in prison because of debts incurred by a spendthrift wife. She appears to have passed money on to a son of a previous marriage; perhaps she was one of those silly mothers who couldn't say *'no'* to the unreasonable demands of a feckless child. If this was the case, then the result was the enmity of her second husband who was determined to *'wash his hands'* of both his wife <u>and</u> stepson alike; the words were those of a man driven to the last point of utter frustration. An interesting insight had thus been given to some of the domestic conflicts existing at the time.

Another announcement struck a more commercial note and thereby cast some light on the difficult economic conditions of the time: -
"In ***HOPKINS'S BANKRUPTCY***
An Order of Dividend having been lately made
by the commissioners in a commission of bankrupt,
awarded and issued against ***SAMUEL HOPKINS***, *now or*
late of ***Leeds,*** *in the County of* ***York,*** *Merchant, Dealer*
and Chapman.

NOTICE is hereby given

That the fair Dividend will be paid to the Creditors
As have proved their Debts under the said commission, at
the House of **William Ward**, *the* **Bull and Mouth Inn,** *in*
Leeds, *on* **Saturday** *the Thirteenth Day of* **March** *Inst. Between*
the Hours of Ten in the Morning and Five in the
Afternoon – By Order,
CHARLES CARR, *Solicitor.*
Greenfall, March 11ᵗʰ 1805."

The fact that this was one of several *'bankruptcy notices'* appearing on the first page of this paper was indicative that **Leeds** was enduring a period of economic distress. The presence of at least two dissolved partnerships supported this conclusion. However, on the next page was an advert for the Insurance Policies of the **Norwich Union** which had been founded in **1797**. This advert had an eye-catching logo of two hands clasped in a handshake, each sporting two ruff shirtsleeves. Here again, I had the impression that many of our allegedly new *'marketing techniques'* are really not so new after all! Beyond its eye-catching quality, this handshake logo had merit as a marketing tool in portraying an image of trust. (The company in **2018** continues and I have taken out three Accident related insurance policies with it.) The next item of this **1805** publication conveyed some important international news, demonstrating the complexity of both the military and political conflict then raging across Europe.
"THURSDAY'S POST.
LONDON, March 12.
Letters from **Berlin** *speak of very active negotiations*
Between the court and the **Russian** *cabinet –*
The First Court is stated to have received the answer
To her offer of mediation between the former and
That of **France** *and* **Russia** *could only treat in conjunction*
With **Great Britain.** *A defensive alliance is*
also said to be in agitation between **Austria** *and* **Prussia.**
An **English** *squadron of six ships is cruising off*
The coast of **Genoa.**
The poor old Pope is destined to endure new humiliations.
According to report, he is to add to the
Degradation of his [the Pope's] *character by consecrating another*
Usurpation of the **Corsican** *upstart* **[Napoleon]** *at whose heels*
He must lacky till he has erected a new throne in
The Italian Republic."

The **Leeds Intelligencer's** patriotic sentiments are clearly revealed here. Even the Pope was shown a little sympathy because he was an enemy of *"the Corsican upstart,"* **Napoleon Bonaparte.** Great hopes appear to have been placed in an **anti-French** alliance. However, **Napoleon's** stunning victory at the battle of **Austerlitz** on **December 2nd** of **1805** would put an end to them. Mention was also made of various naval manoeuvres in the **Atlantic.** These represented the run-up to the **Battle of Trafalgar,** which **Admiral Nelson** won on **October 21st, 1805.**

On **Thursday, January 19th, 1832,** four days before **Edmund Smiths** birth, the **Leeds Intelligencer** (price now **7d**) contained the following news item: -
*"The anatomy bill, on the motion of **MR WARBURTON,** was read a second time; the only dissentient was **Mr Hunt.** The **Irish** Reform Bill was read a first time, and the second reading fixed for* **Friday** *fortnight."*

The Anatomy Bill was eventually passed and, by loosening the restrictions on human dissection it ended the practice of body snatching, which had been common in **Leeds.** It allowed for *'unclaimed bodies'* from workhouses to be used for dissection purposes. Those unfortunates who were inmates of the workhouse clamoured a great deal against it but to no avail. Most of the parliamentary discussion was taken up with the question of the Great Reform Bill, of which the **Irish Reform Bill** was a part. (There was much, sometimes violent agitation over the whole question of parliamentary reform.) **Leeds** did not escape the economic hardships endemic during this period.
*"SUBSCRIPTIONS FOR PROVIDING CLOTHING and other charitable ASSISTANCE for the POOR of **Leeds** during the ensuing winter. SUBSCRIPTIONS ADVERTISED, £2676. 6d (A long list of subscribers followed with the amounts they had donated, they mainly appear to have come from the wealthier manufacturing and professional classes.) ADDITIONAL CONTRIBUTIONS RECEIVED AT THE DEPOT*
  *Mr **Wm. Holliday,** five Shirts.*
Mr Hunt, Eighteen women's bonnets.
*Messrs. **Saml. Powell** & Son, Six Pair Blankets.*
  JOHN CAWOOD, *Treasurer.*
*The Treasurer will attend at the Depot every Day, next Week, from **11** to **12** o' Clock, for the purpose of receiving Subscriptions."*

This example of middle-class paternalism confirmed that although a commercial centre, **Leeds** was not immune to the socio-economic distresses afflicting the rest of the country. The level of distress was so great that it drove ahead of the agitation for political reform. **Edmund** had been born at a time of great hardship for the mass of the common people. Indicative of this was the frequent outbreak of cholera caused by the dirty drinking water and overcrowded living conditions. A huge cholera epidemic had ravaged **Newcastle-Upon-Tyne** and its outlying settlements, from **11**th to **January 17**th, **1832**. Thirty-six lives had been lost in **Newcastle** proper and another eight in **Gateshead** and one in **North Shields**. At **Newburn** (five miles from **Newcastle**) cholera claimed the life of the Rector the **Rev. Edmondson** on **Sunday, 15**th **January 1832**. *"The following day thirty deaths occurred, and people were falling ill every hour."* This village appears to have been particularly badly hit.

Sadly, there were plenty of quacks willing to exploit the despair of a frequently ill population. Two of them went under the name of **Drs R.** And **L. Jordan** who were concentrating their efforts on something other than cholera: -
"THE VENEREAL DISEASE under its
various appearances and complicated attacks may
be speedily and secretly eradicated from the system by the
use of DR LEWIS'S VEGETABLE PILLS, Price 2s 9d, or
two boxes in one for 4s 6d, which for their salutary effects in
cleansing the Blood from all impurities, whether venereal
or Scorbutic, are of the utmost importance. They are in
the highest estimation for preventing as well as totally
eradicating, every symptom of this destructive malady, and
producing a safe and salutary cure, without
the least confinement, or abstemious regimen; affecting its
purpose independent of those common auxiliaries that
generally, lead to a discovery. So sovereign a remedy should
ever be in possession of such, as either through juvenile
inclinations, or the habits of gallantry, frequent such places
where danger is inevitable, as no change of climate can alter
their power."
[More tedious *'hard sell'* then followed]
"These pills are worthy of a place in the cabinets of masters
and captains of ships; the more so, as they will keep good
in all climates, any length of time, and they have now
borne the tests above 70 years with increasing credit to themselves
and to honour of the author.

*Prepared only by the sole Proprietors, at **23 Park square,***
Leeds. *Private entrance, first door on the left hand, one*
*Door from **St Paul** buildings.*
Drs JORDAN *are to be consulted, as usual, every day*
And on Sundays from Nine to Two o'clock. Patients in the
remotest Parts can be treated successfully on describing
minutely the case and enclosing a remittance for medicine
which can be forwarded to any part of the World. No difficulty
can occur, as the medicines will be securely packed
and carefully protected from observation.
*Address **Drs R.** And **L. JORDAN,** No. **23, Park***
***Square, Leeds,** Money, Letter, paid double Postage."*

These peddlers of false hope appear to have made a profitable income from their quackery as **Park Square** contained office accommodation for wealthier professionals, *i.e.* lawyers. An examination of the site (made on **Friday, 5ᵗʰ July 2002**) revealed that their premises had consisted of a two storey, red brick **Georgian** house, situated above an archway large enough to have accommodated a coach and horses. Although covered over with new brickwork it appears that the side entrance had been set in the wall, underneath this arch. A narrow flight of stairs would have led up to the consulting room. These quacks had chosen an excellent central location for their trade – with the entrance *'tucked discreetly'* away so to have afforded a rapid entrance and exit for their unfortunate clients.

The high degree of literacy displayed in their promotion also betrayed a certain amount of education. Whoever **Dr's R.** and **L. Jordan** were (assuming that was their real names) they knew how to play on the needs of a desperate market. One wonders how much **VD** was spread by customers who perhaps mistakenly thought that they'd been cured by these vegetable pills. Their confidence trick had perhaps cost many lives. Incidentally, a search for their names in relevant **Leeds** Trade Directories proved fruitless. They didn't seem to live on their premises nor were they listed under the headings of *'Druggists'* or *'Physicians.'* This reinforced the impression that they were not proper, bonafide doctors. They had certainly seemed unwilling to advertise their services through these more respectable channels. Sadly, one of **Edmund's** Great Grandson's would also be found by a court of law as guilty of indulging in serious medical quackery, but that is a topic covered far later in this book.

Someone with a more robust attitude to the problems of the day was the following anonymous poet who published these six verses against drink: -

FILL, FILL THE CUP!

Fill the cup, the bowl, the glass
With wine and spirits high;
And we will drink, while round they pass,
To – vice and misery!

Push quickly round the draught again,
And drain the goblet low;
And drink to revelry's swelling strain,
To – Reason's overthrow!

Push round, push round in quickest time
The deepest drop be spent
In one loud round, to – guilt and Crime,
And Crime's just punishment!

Fill, fill again! Fill to the brim
To – Loss of honest fame!
Quaff, deeper quaff! While now we drink –
Our wives and children's shame!

Push round and round, with loudest cheers
Of mirth and revelry!
We drink to women's sighs and tears!
And – children's poverty!

Once more! While power shall yet remain,
Even with its latest breath,
Drink – to ourselves Disease and Pain,
And infamy and death!

The lively beat of this poem suggested that it might have been a satire of an old drinking song. The author may well have participated at some stage in his life in some of the situations described here. His sentiments were identical to those of the **Temperance Movement.** Unlike **Drs R.** and **L. Jordan,** he preferred to challenge rather than to exploit the social problems of his time.

CHAPTER 2: AN ENTERPRISING SORT OF PEOPLE

Section 1: From Richard to Richard

Concerning the first known Smith Ancestor

Nothing else is known about the **Smiths** of the Early Middle Ages. All we possess are the names of the landowners who owned their settlements – the earliest of which was *Gamel* and *Karli,* both dating back to the late **Anglo-Saxon** period (from around **1,000-1066**). These were names that would have been known to my remote ancestors and they suggest a possible **Viking** origin. Whether my ancestors would have seen these men remains questionable as they owned many portions of land across **Yorkshire.** How the pre-recorded **Smiths** survived and maintained their precarious social positions in the face of famine, plague and periodic internal strife isn't known at all. However, the very fact that they did survive would suggest they must have been a hardy lot.

The name *'Smith'* (throughout the **Anglo-Saxon** and **Medieval** periods) pointed to some remote blacksmith fashioning horseshoes and a whole assortment of agricultural implements (and possibly weapons too). These **Smiths** may also have turned to farming whenever trade was slack. Evidence concerning the blacksmith's status is provided by **Patrick Ottaway (2015)** who observed that *"An indication of the vital role of the blacksmith in **Anglo-Saxon England** is to be found in the well-known passage of **Aelfric's Colloquy** in which the pupil speaking for the Smith asserts his primacy amongst the secular crafts. The 'Counsellor' answers: ... You, what do you give us in your smithy but iron sparks, and the noise of hammers beating and bellows blowing? The 'Carpenter' says: Which of you doesn't make use of my craft, when I make houses and various vessels and boats for you all? The 'Blacksmith' answers: Oh carpenter, why do you talk like that when you couldn't pierce even one hole without my craft?'"*

Revealed here is the sense of rivalry which must have existed at the time between village craftsmen. Each will have wished to preserve their standing within their own community. My remote Blacksmith ancestors were of this craftsmen class – above the serfs and ordinary peasantry but below the gentry and their officials. They were a *'middling sort of people,'* proud of their craft and constantly striving to maintain their respectability. Over the centuries, not much was to change.

70

The above represented all I knew about my remote ancestor – that is until **Friday, 4ᵗʰ September 2015** when (in **Skipton** Library) I encountered the man most likely to have been my earliest known forebear. He was another **Richard Smith** and details about him appeared in **Wood p. 7.** These were obtained from the Poll Tax Returns of **1379** (which had to be paid by everyone aged over **16**) with payments ranging from **4d** (*'d'* meaning pennies or pence) to **10** marks depending upon the wealth of the person concerned. Married couples were taxed in pennies as one person. For **Cowling,** details were as follows: -

Collyng	
1. Johannes West & uxor (wife)	iiij.d.
2. Ricardus West & uxor	iiij.d.
3. Willelmus filius Johannis & uxor	iiij.d.
4. Johannes de Totyngton & uxor	iiij.d.
5. Johannes de Paldeyn & uxor	iiij.d.
6. Adam filius Johannis & uxor	iiij.d.
7. Adam del Dobbes & uxor	iiij.d.
8. Willelmus de Merebeke & uxor	iiij.d.
9. Johannes de Tong & uxor	iiij.d.
10. Johannes de Wraton & uxor	iiij.d.
11. Robertus Damson & uxor	iiij.d.
12. Johannes filius Willelmi & uxor	iiij.d.
13. Johannes de Brytwesle & uxor	iiij.d.
14. Ricardus Smyth, *Faber* (Blacksmith) & uxor	**vj.d.**
15. Johannes Dauy & uxor	iiij.d.
16. Johannes Scot & uxor	iiij.d.
17. Robertus Dauy & uxor	iiij.d.
18. Johannes Mason & uxor	iiij.d.
19. Agnes filia Johannis	iiij.d.
20. Willelmus Tillotson	iiij.d.
21. Tillot de Northwood	iiij.d.
22. Seruient (Servent) - Isabella uxor Roberti	iiij.d.
23. Johannes Tillotson	iiij.d.
24. Johannes de Northwood	iiij.d.
25. Robertus del Rode	iiij.d.
Summa-	viij.s. vj.d.

A review of the other poll tax returns of **Glasburn, Sutton** and **Kildwick** revealed no other **Smiths.** This strongly reinforced the view that **Cowling** was the actual home village from which the **Smiths** had originated. As the family expanded, they would migrate down into the more fertile valley below. Insight was also given into the geographical size of my namesake's *'Business'* market. There were no other blacksmiths in the parish, so he would have exercised a local monopoly in an area consisting of **442** known households. These were in the settlements of **Steeton, Farnhill, Sturton**, **Silsden** and **Bradley** (as well as those already mentioned). In all of them, **iiij.d** was by far the most common amount paid, which indicated an area that was poor – even by medieval standards.

When combined with the work provided by passing travellers there would have been enough custom to keep **Ricardus Smyth** busy. He had a very sound *'customer base'* to build upon. The term **'Faber'** not only denoted a blacksmith but also meant *'skilled artisan or forger.'* His craft would have given **Ricardus** extra status in the parish. The higher than typical poll tax amount he paid suggests that he'd managed (in true **Smith** style) to profit from his business. We can even make an intelligent guess about his appearance. As a blacksmith, he will have had a sturdy physique with very muscular arms. To maintain this craft, he would have needed to be in a good state of health. However, he may eventually have suffered from repetitive strain injury and a damaged back caused by the constant lifting of heavy metal objects **Ricardus** will have learned his craft from his father and it perhaps had been in the family since the first settlement in **Saxon** times. A prominent nose may also have been a feature of his – an inherited trait passed down successive generations of **Smiths.**

So, was my namesake a direct ancestor? The balance of evidence would strongly point in that direction. To begin with, there were <u>no other competing family lines in either</u> **Cowling** <u>or in any of the other settlements</u>. Moreover, his status as a blacksmith was just right to position later generations of **Smiths** into the upper peasantry and allow them in future to become respectable yeoman farmers. **Ricardus** was where one would expect a **Smith** to be in the social *'pecking'* order. The name itself would re-surface as late as the mid-twentieth century when I was given the same forename. In addition, the higher than average poll tax return would suggest that he'd made a success of his trade. He appeared to possess that **Smith** business streak that would still be obvious and active several hundred years later.

Finally, for **Ricardus Smyth** <u>not</u> to be a direct ancestor one would have to assume that his line had died out completely and that another line of **Smiths** had later moved into what really was a remote and poor locality. This was in an age when travel was dangerous and usually only undertaken when there was an exceptionally pressing reason to do so. **Colne** and **Skipton** (the nearest market towns) were probably as far as anyone will have travelled. With farms and trades to attend to there was little incentive to go much further afield. Therefore, the theory that **Ricardus Smyth** was <u>not</u> my direct ancestor collapses under the weight of its own difficulties.

What further deductions can be made about my namesake? Sadly, his most formative experience would have been the Black Death (or *'great pestilence'* as it was then known). The remoteness of the area in which he lived would have provided some protection but even then, the death rate will have been in the order of **25%**, with news of its spread causing absolute terror. Whether my likely ancestor was alive at the time remains unknown, but he would certainly have known of survivors. The fact that monasteries like **Fountains Abbey** (which owned the corn mill at **Crosshills**) suffered especially badly may have fuelled religious doubts in **Ricardus Smyth's** mind. He may also have heard rumours (from travellers) of the Hundred Years War raging in **France** and of the Peasants Revolt which took place in **1381.** The latter had taken place because of the poll tax imposed upon workers like himself and his neighbours. (However, his region appears to have been unaffected by it.) The political and sociological horizons of **Ricardus Smyths** world would have been extremely narrow.

Geographically, repeated visits to the site enabled me to make an intelligent guess as to the likely location of **Ricardus Smyths'** premises. A convenient location would have been on the trackway leading to **Colne** where he would have received passing traveller custom. In addition, these premises will have been located near to **Ickornshaw Beck** – a valuable water source. His *'middle'* position (in the *'Return'*) suggests that he lived in the middle of the **Cowling** locality (around the previously mentioned trackway). His products will, in the main, have consisted of horseshoes and agricultural implements. However, he may well have been called upon to produce weapons in times of disturbance. To thrive he will have needed to establish a good reputation in the community; engendering respect from others. As this *'History'* continues to show, a desire for respectability remains an integral part of the psyche of a typical *'Smith.'*

One artefact possibly dates right back to **Ricardus'** time. On **Friday, 4th September 2015** my wife (and a distant female relative) gained access to the interior of **Kildwick Parish Church**. The Vicar kindly showed us the fourteenth-century font where successive generations of **Smiths** will have been baptised (spanning five centuries, **c.1335-c.1835**). Seeing it was a moving experience, augmenting an already very powerful sense of *'connection.'*

Section 2: A Tudor Murder

Concerning a village murder

Violence was never far from the kind of village settlements the **Smith's** inhabited. Lives could really be *'nasty, brutish and short.'* One such case was the murder of **Hugh Blakey** in the **1540s**. Information about this case was obtained from the local historian **Nellie Snell (1927)**. An extract of her work was retrieved from the **Sutton-in-Craven** website on **Friday, 16th March 2018**. It was heavily edited by my wife **June** to improve the quality of its Grammar. This source began by providing some details about **Malsis Hall,** the old manor house of **Sutton.** The family owning it would be directly involved in this case.

The **Copley** family of **Batley** had (at one-time) large possessions (land and property) in that part of the **Aire Valley.** In the fourteenth century a **Copley** was living at **Farnhill Hall,** another at **Glusburn Hall** and yet another, **Robert Copley**, occupied **Malsis Hall** in **Sutton Township.** From about **1341,** some member of the **Copley family** lived at **Malsis Hall** with the name frequently found in local documents of the Middle Ages. (**John** the son of **Adam de Copley** was **Lord of the Manor of Sutton** in **1381** and, given the location, would have been a customer of the blacksmith **Ricardus Smyth.**)

There was a very notable gathering at the ancient **Malsis Hall** on **April 30th, 1484** to witness the signing of a marriage settlement (presumably, accompanied by much pomp and ceremony). Through this, **Lionel Copley** granted to his son **John,** on his marriage to **Agnes,** daughter of **Sir Geoffrey Piggott**, a large part of his land in **Sutton** and other places. The document was signed at **Malsis Hall** with much state. Some of the witnesses to the settlement were the Knights **Sir John Savyle, Sir John Pudsey. Robert Nevile** and **Sir Geoffrey Piggott.** Several decades later in **1541, John Copley,** (evidently than the **Lord of the Manor of Sutton**) in a letter, made the following complaint to **King Henry VIII.**

"To the King our Sovereign Lord - Humbly showeth and complaineth your faithful subject, **John Copley, Esq**. *that your said subject and his ancestors were by the space of* **200** *years and above, lawfully belonged by good and just title of the* **Manor of Malsis,** *and did take the same rents and profits peaceably; one* **Hugh Blakey,** *of* **Malsis**, *yeoman, without any manner of title or grounds, hath of late, with force of arms, in a riotous manner, and against*

*your peace, entered into the manor, and the said **Hugh** hath in forcible and riotous manner, that is to say, with bows, arrows, stones and hot water, keepeth your said subject from the possession of his Manor; and since his unlawful entry hath pulled down, wasted and destroyed divers houses and buildings, hedges and other enclosures, and hath cut down a good part of the woods growing upon the same Manor. And the said **Hugh,** by his further evil disposition, hath many and diver's rights to put his cattle into the pastures and meadows of your said subject, being parcel of his **Manor of Sutton,** where the said cattle destroyed the grass, and when they had done so the said **Hugh** took them out again, early in the morning. And also, the said **Hugh** hath many diver's times destroyed the corn, meadows, and pastures of the tenants of the said **Manor of Sutton** so that they be not able to pay their rents due. And over that, the said **Hugh** since the Feast of Easter last past, hath at several times broken the common pound in **Sutton,** and taken out of the same pound his cattle, being lawfully impounded in the same for hurts and damages done to your said subject. And also, the said **Hugh** of his malicious mind and evil disposition, since Easter last past with an axe did cut to pieces the stocks, made by the inhabitants of **Sutton** for the Punishments of vagabonds and beggars, and did cast great pieces of them into the fire; which aforesaid evil acts will be a perilous example to like offenders unless the said **Hugh** may have condign [a severe but just] punishment. In consideration whereof may it please your highness to direct your gracious writ to the said **Hugh Blakey,** commanding him to appear before your highness and your most honourable council in the Star Chamber."*

Hugh must indeed have been a disturbing member of the community. It would be of interest to hear his point of view and to find out his special grievance against the **Lord of the Manor** and the **Sutton** folk. He seems to have continued troubling the neighbourhood because, two years later, we find that one man, perhaps a relative, could endure him no longer. From the record we find that, on **May 3rd 1543**, *"with force of arms, viz - sticks and knives and other defensive weapons two men, **Richard Garforth** of **Kyldwyke**, husbandman and **Nicholas Johnson**, late of **Sutton under Soun**, mylaer or labourer, of premeditated malice, and by the instigation of the Devil, and voluntarily by the order and procurement of a certain **Thomas Blakey**, late of **Newhall** within the township of **Sutton** under **Soun**, gentleman" assaulted **Hugh Blakey.** This happened between **10** and **11 pm** and on this occasion, we are told that **Hugh** was "then and there in the peace of **God** and of the lord the King". **Richard Garforth** held **Hugh** while **Nicholas Johnson** "with a stick to the value of **3d** which he then and there held in his hands feloniously gave to the said **Hugh Blakey** three mortal wounds ... of which wounds the said **Hugh Blakey** then and there instantly died".*

They left the body in a hut nearby. Evidently, they reported their success to **Thomas Blakey** who seems to have instigated the murder. The record goes on to say that he "*agreed with the same* **Garforth** *and* **Johnson** *and willed and ordered that they, on* **May 4ᵗʰ** *(the next night) about midnight should go to the said shed, and should carry the body of the said* **Hugh**, *then to the water of the* **Ayre** *and should put and precipitate into the depth of the said water, the said body*".

Richard Garforth evidently bought his pardon or turned *'King's Evidence'* for the document ends "*Know ye that we of our special grace and certain knowledge have pardoned the said* **Richard Garforth** *late of* **Kyldwyke** *the murder of the said* **Hugh** *&c, &c... and grant to him our firm peace &c*". **Whitaker**, the **Craven** historian, says that **Cowling**, an adjoining township to **Sutton**, "*in the latter end of the reign of* **Henry VIII** *belonged to* **Thomas Blakey** *who was hanged, and his estate forfeited*". In this and later documents **Johnson** is referred to as "***Nicholas Johnson**, late of **Sutton under Soun**,*" probably he also was hanged.

Malsis was held by the **Copley** family until **1625** when it was sold to **Richard Horsfall**. A member of this family planted the beautiful beech trees, for which **Malsis** has long been noted in the district. However, later in the seventeenth century, The **Spencer** family became the next owners and then in **1865,** the present hall was built by **James Lund.** The carvings over the doors of the old hall have been preserved. They consist of coats of arms and other devices. Most interesting of all is a stone which bears the words "***Avery Copley** built this house*". By **December 2017 Malsis Hall** was being converted into a Care Home after being used as a school.

In **John Copley's** account, **Hugh Blakey** comes across as the village psychopath. The weapons he employed suggest a man with some military experience. He was certainly a man who could not be ignored. Yet to inflict the damage he did he must have been able to draw on some local support. This scenario suggests that **John Copley** (who died later in **1543**) wasn't a well-liked man and that a land dispute lay at the heart of the matter. Evidence for this latter point is provided in a comment made at his Inquisition Post-mortem (that was designed to assess the value of a deceased landowner's estate for taxation purposes). It revealed. *"that he was seized of the following manors "...**Sutton, Malsis, Addingham, Cowling, Oakworth, Sawood** and **Batley**"*. Given his social standing as *'Lord of the Manor,'* **John Copley** may have been instrumental in having **Blakey** and **Garforth** put to death. Indeed, it's possible that the whole thing had been a *'set-up'* by him. Furthermore, it's likely that he possessed sufficient influence to prevent awkward questions being raised. All that can be said with certainty is that there's a lot more to this case than meets the eye. My ancestors could not avoid hearing about it, but thankfully they seem to have the wisdom not to be directly involved. A dose of **Smith** common sense and a keen sense of self-preservation appears to have kept them out of trouble.

Section 3: The Smiths' Step into History

Concerning the Smiths of Cowling and Kildwick Parish

As a family, the **Smiths** only really step into *'recorded history'* in **November 1575** with the following entry (made on **p.1** of the Parish Register of **Saint Andrews, Kildwick** covering the period of **1575-1622**). This recorded the baptism of a certain **John Smith.** Written in **Latin** the entry read, *"Eodem die **Johannes Smith** filius **Willi Smith** et **Gracie** xxoris eiius."* This entry (fourth out of seven entries) for that month revealed nothing about the locality or occupation of these **Smiths.** But it does show that names like *'John'* and *'William'* were in common use by the late sixteenth and early seventeenth centuries. This point was amply confirmed by a review of the Index **(pp. 184-185)** of that source. By this time a population increase had shown a cluster of **Smith** families – so tracing a direct ancestor became much more difficult than in the earlier medieval period.

Of interest is the way the Parish Register revealed that **Johis Smith** had got a **Janet Rycroft,** pregnant through what appears to have been an extra-marital affair. One can only wonder what his wife **Margareta** had thought. With only common forenames to go on it's hard to decide which, if any, of this cluster of **Smiths,** had been my direct ancestors. On a speculative note, I wondered whether the forename *'Johis'* was a mistranscription of *'Johnis.'* However, I found no evidence to prove this. In passing, it's worth noting how other names like *'Overend'* or *'Wilson'* (which re-occur throughout this History) were also present.

The second page of this Register mentions a *'Richard Smith,'* constituting the second out of seven entries for **September 1576.** It reads *"Edvardus Smith filius **Richardi Smithe** et **Eliz:** vxis eius."* At least the forename *'Richard'* is still in use today! The Index confirms that *'Richard'* was a common forename during the period covered by the Register but *'Edward'* far less so. This source also revealed other details about the Late Tudor **Smiths.** Baptisms from the **Register of Kildwick in Craven, Nov 1575-1578/9.** (Retrieved on **Thursday, 21/5/2015**) provided the following list (*'d'* denotes *'daughter* and *'s' 'son.'*

Childs Name		Father's Name	Mother's Name	
RYCROFT,	Johnnes	d. Johis SMITH	Janet RYCROFT	Aug 1578
SMITH,	Alice	d. Thos.	Elizabeth	Sep 1576
SMITH,	Dionisius	s. Wm	Grace	Dec 1577
SMITH,	Edward	s. Richard	Elizabeth	Sep 1576
SMITH,	Helena	d. Robert	Alice	Oct 1576
SMITH,	Hugo	s. Thos	Alice	Aug 1577
SMITH,	John	s. Wm	Grace	Nov 1575
SMITH,	Margareta	d. Johis	Margareta	Aug 1577
SMITH,	Robert	s. Robert	Alice	Jul 1576
SMITH,	Roger	s. Wm	Margaret	Mar 1575/6
SMITH,	Wm	s. Thos	Isabell	Jul 1577
SMITH,	Wm	s. Wm	Margarita	Jul 1578

A **Ricardius Smith** married an **Alicia Peele** on **22nd November 1579**. On **1st July 1588**, either this or another **Ricardius Smith** married an **Anna Whitwham**. This was at a time when the **Spanish Armada** was sheltering from storms in the **Spanish** port of **Corunna**. **August 5th, 1588** saw a battle between the **Spanish** and **English** fleets off **Portland Bill** and on that day a certain **Milo Smith** married an **Agneta Warde**. The remoteness of **Kildwick** would suggest that it would have been weeks before its inhabitants heard anything at all regarding the **Spanish Armada**.

One typical family was that of **Hugonis (c.1560-1621?)** and **Alicae Smith (c.1560-1637?)** who married an on **18/2/1584**. They had at least nine children. They were **Johannes (9/2/1580** – illegitimate, both parental surnames are down as **Smithe**), **Georgius (24/7/1587)**, **Hugo (6/1/1589)**, **Anna (17/9/1592)**, **Agneta (9/5/1594)**, **Gracia (26/12/1594)**, **Aluaredus (12/3/1595** – illegitimate, both parental surnames are down as **Smith) Gracia (28/10/1599** – presumably the earlier **Gracia** had died in infancy) and **Michael (1/8/1602)**. (The dates in brackets recorded their baptism at **Kildwick Saint Andrews**.) **Georgij (1587-1667?)** of *'Collinge'* would go on to marry a **Maria Parkinson** on **7/3/1613**. On **7/1/1620** they baptised their son **Hugh Smith (1619-1699?)** who married **Jennetta Scarborough** on **30/4/1653**. An important community figure, he would help found the first village school and establish a longstanding **Smith** interest in education that continues to this day.

Baptismal records also cast some light on **Geogious**. As an extra detail, it stated *'bap. Colne.LivSut,' i.e.* Baptised in **Colne**, living in **Sutton**. This would fit in neatly with an old family tradition mediated by my cousin **Pamela Smith,** asserting, *'the **Smiths** went to **Colne** and back.'* If this is the case, then it's been an oral tradition that's been preserved for an incredible four centuries. Such preservation can only occur if there were a succession of ancestors sufficiently interested in their origins to have passed it on to their children. It would suggest a strong predisposition to be interested in family history. The *'Georgius'* mentioned here may also be the *'George'* who was a *'senex of* **Cowling'** whose burial occurred on **15th December 1667.** The term *'Senex'* meant old man. If this was the case, he would have been eighty at the time of his death – a marvellous age for that period.

We know barely anything about these early **Smiths.** Before **1700,** the information was too fragmentary to trace a direct line with complete certainty. Some **Smiths** though lived to an advanced age. From the register of **Kildwick** that recorded the date of burials we discover a **Henricus Smith (8/2/1581)** had lived to be **85,** the widow **Jana Smith (6/6/1583)** to be **84,** a **Johis Smith (25/10/1587)** to be **88,** an **Alicia Smithe (29/8/1581)** to be **80,** **Richardus Smithe (16/4/1584)** to be **96** and another **Richardus Smithe (8/3/1590)** of **Steeton** to be an incredible **100!** Their advanced ages contrasted with the many who had died in infancy or as young children. For instance, beneath the above listed **Alicia** was another **Alicia Smithe (7/2/1586)** who was registered as an infant!

Also emerging from Parish Registers were fleeting glimpses of long-forgotten misdeeds. For example, we find that, on **1st November 1630,** a certain **Margaret Emmott** of **Collinge** (an old spelling for **Cowling**) had had her daughter **Anna** baptized at **Kildwick Parish Church.** The father was an **Edward Smith** who may well (given the small population) have been the same **Edward Smith** who had had his son (called **Edwardus** an old form for **Edward**) baptised on **2nd July 1626** when he was married to a woman called **Alice.** (Their marriage possibly took place on **13th February 1608** with **Alice's** maiden name being **Hardie.**) Nor was that all, on **16th April 1666** we find the name *'Edward Smith'* associated with the illegitimate birth of **Hugo,** the son of **Elizabeth Jennings** (also of **Collinge**). An **Elizabetha Jennings** is on record as marrying an **Eduerdus Smyth** on **24th August 1668** whereas the other women and their men vanish. She might be the same **Elizabeth Smith** *"wife of **Edward-Cowling"*** who was buried on **24th October 1676.**

Unless he had tremendous stamina, it's hard to believe that the same **Edward Smith** was involved in both cases that were separated by an interlude of thirty-five years. Was it a case of a son imitating his father? One must remember that, in their forties, a man above the lowest strata of society could still be *'in his prime'* whereas his wife would have been worn out with childbearing. I can recall a portrait dating back to the seventeenth century where a man's younger wife looks old enough to have been his mother. The substantial number of children gathered around them helped to explain this discrepancy in appearance.

Hugo himself appears to have sired at least one illegitimate child. The **Kildwick Parish** Burial Book recorded an **Elizabeth SMITH/PHILIPPS** *"dau. of Hugo & Anna – Cowling" being buried on 9th April 1704."* What appears to be present is a line of **Smiths** characterised by a string of illegitimate births. Whether these were the result of simple romps in the haystack or done to test a woman's childbearing ability remains unknown.

The baptismal register for **Kildwick Parish Church** did confirm that *'Edmund'* was a common **Smith** forename. The earliest entry I found featuring the name **Edmund Smith** was on **13th February 1615.** It recorded the marriage of an **Edmund Smith** to a **Matilda Tempest** who came from a family of wealthy landowners. It took place during the reign of **King James I** just four years after the publication of the **Authorised Bible.** At that time marriage was often a commercial transaction designed to secure property and land. Romance rarely came into it. The other **Edmund Smith's** mentioned in this source included: -

1. **Edmund Smith:** a *'Husbandman of Stott Hill'* who married **Mary Tempest** on **6/1/1757** before having: -
- His daughter **Ann** christened on **18/3/1759**
- His daughter **Sarah** christened on **28/12/1762**
- His son **Robert** christened on **10/2/1765**
- His son **Edmund** christened on **16/8/1767**
- His daughter **Mary** christened on **8/10/1769**
- His daughter **Elizabeth** christened on **22/9/1771**
- His son **William** christened on **2/1/1774** after his father had moved to **Cowling** (Pronounced *'Collinge'* by its residents)
2. **Edmund Smith:** a *'weaver of Cowling'* who married **Jennet Wright** at **Keighley** on **16/11/1761** before having at **Kildwick:** -
- His daughter **Martha,** christened on **20/3/1763,** whilst living at **Green Sike**

- His son **William,** christened on **17/11/1765,** after moving to **Cowling** – sadly **William** was buried at **Kildwick** on **11/1/1766**
- His son **Edward,** (or **Edmund**) christened on **7/6/1767** – sadly he appears to have been the **Edmund** buried at **Kildwick** on **18/9/1768**
- His daughter **Mary** christened on **26/11/1769**
- His son, another **William,** christened on **10/7/1774**
- His son, possibly another **Edmund,** christened on **5/1/1777,** having been born on **17/12/1776** (His parents had followed the conventional practice of naming a new child after a deceased one)
3. **Edmund Smith:** another *'weaver of Cowling'* who married **Jane** at an unknown date before having: -
- His son **John** christened on **17/5/1772**

There was no evidence to link any of these **Edmund Smiths** to my forbear of the same name. From the above list, it's easy to see how frequently re-occurring names could easily confuse any genealogist! It also explained why I was unable (for an extended period) to trace my family line beyond the year **1778.** (In **2018** a **Stott Hill Farm** still existed just off the **Old Lane** above **Cowling.**)

Section 4: An Early Interest in Education

Concerning the foundation of Cowling Charity School

An indenture associated with the clothier **Hugh Smith** (dated **Sunday, 12ᵗʰ February 1665**) revealed an early interest in education. Quoted in **Woods p.69** it directed that part of the rent of **Lower Bawes Edge Farm** should be employed *"for and towards the teaching and instructing in learning of such children within Ickornshaw and Stott Hill only, whose parents were not able to bring them up in learning."* Further details were provided by the **Cowling Moonrakers' Website** that was accessed on **Wednesday, 9ᵗʰ March 2016.**

*"An Indenture dated **12/2/1665** between **Hugh Smith** of **Bawsedge** of the first part and **John Smith,** son of **Michael Smith** of **Fair Place, Abram Brigg** of **Fair Place, Edward Smith** and **William Pighills** of **Stonehead** provided that the income from **Bawsedge Farm** should be devoted to the payment of school wage for necessitous children who could not otherwise afford education (**Stott Hill** and **Ickornshaw**).The lineal descendants of **James Wooler** were forever debarred from all benefits and privileges under this grant. **Hugh Smith** reserved the right to revoke this grant during his lifetime but never exercised it.*

*In **1759** an indenture showing that the land was divided into two portions. One part to be devoted to education as above stated.*

***1795** a further indenture* [dated **21st July**] *showing that the school lands were divided, and part was conveyed to **Robert Watson**.*

*On **May 30ᵗʰ1901** it was taken over by the Charity Commissioners* [Ch. Comm and C.C.] *and a scheme was drawn up with the following persons acting as trustees:*
R.B. Ackroyd (Crosshills) *appointed by Ch. Comm. for life,*
J.N. Lee *appointed by Ch. Comm. for 5 years.*
John Hartley (Cowling Parish Council) *appointed by Ch. Comm. for5 years.*
Thos. Watson (Cowling School Board) *appointed by Ch. Comm. for5 years.*
Ben Snowden *appointed by West Riding C.C. appointed by Ch. Comm. for5 years.*
*The property was sold at auction by **H. Tillotson** at **The Bay Horse** on the **18th February 1902** and realised:*
*Farm Buildings **(Robert Gott)** £430. 0. 0.*
*House in Ickornshaw **(Alfred Hartley)**   £7 .10. 0.*
Total   £437. 10. 0.

*This was invested in **£515. 0. 0** 2.1/2* [the]*% Perpetual Preference Stock of Midland Railway = **£409. 8. 6***
*A further purchase of **£258** of the same stock **£76. 75** was made at a cost of **£198. 0. 4.***
*This provides **£19. 6. 6** from which grants are made at the Governors' discretion."*

From this source and the original document, it was possible to conclude that **Hugh Smith** had possessed a powerful sense of responsibility for his community. As an apparently successful clothier, he was of the *'middling sort'* and his travels to market towns would have broadened his horizons. He would certainly have been able to hear of similar developments elsewhere. Moreover, he lived at a time when attempts to effect widespread political change had ended in failure – a failure highlighted by the restoration of **King Charles II** in **1660.** This meant that any remaining desire for change was best diverted into *'charitable'* local endeavours if trouble with highly suspicious, governing authorities was to be avoided. Support for parliament had been strong in the area and this would have further increased any level of suspicion. In **1662, Puritan** Clergy had been evicted from **Anglican** Churches – which would only have further added to the tension.

So much for the wider context surrounding **Hugh Smith's** benevolent decision. Is it possible to reconstruct these motives for founding this school?

The answer is a cautious *'yes.'* As **Woods p.69** suggested a compensatory mechanism may have been present. **Hugh** could only leave a mark on the indenture which confirms that he was illiterate. He may well have wanted poor children in the village to have what he didn't have – basic literacy. (A similar compensatory mechanism was present in my father who wanted his sons to enjoy the complete Grammar School educational experience he never had.) However, what **Wood** appears to have largely omitted is a possible religious motive. If, as seems very possible, **Hugh** was influenced by **a Protestant, Non-Conformist Christian Tradition** he would have wanted vulnerable children to get into *'godly ways'* by being enabled to read the bible for themselves. A covert missionary motive may well have been present. Also, his decision to establish a charity school may well have been compensation for a failure to achieve wider social change. Parish records of **Kildwick Church** reveal that a **Hugh Smith** was baptized on **7th January 1620** – his parents being a **Georgj** and **Maria Smith** of **Collinge.** His formative experience would have been the **English Civil Wars** and **Cromwellian** Commonwealth, **(1639-1660).** Like his elder brother **Georgius** (baptized **10th August 1617**) he would have seen the failure to effect widespread change. However, both his trade and location would suggest a man more sympathetic to the **Parliamentary** than the **Royalist** cause. Whether he (or other family members) were active combatants, can't be ascertained as militia rolls were scarce and named only officers, **(Family Search: English Military Records).**

One puzzle is the exclusion of **James Wooler** and his lineal descendants. The **1672 Lady Day Assessment** suggests he was a neighbour of **John Smith,** so a quarrel could easily have blown-up between the two men – but why the ban on his lineal descendants? This apparently spiteful measure suggests not so much a quarrel but a long-standing feud! Was his family particularly disreputable? Who knows? But even so, it seems very harsh to deprive generations of **Wooler** children of their only chance of an education. All too evident was an ominous capacity of **Smith** family members to harbour long-standing grudges.

What is apparent is the persistent involvement of the **Smiths** in this charity and its enduring influence. A **John Smith** and **Abraham Brigg** were two of four trustees and only the names of two of the early teachers survive. These were **John Holmes** in **1718** and **Robert Smith** who was recorded in parish records as burying his wife, **Ellen,** on the **5th June 1751.** These noted he was a *'schoolmaster in Cowling.'* The survival of this Charity School suggests it performed a valuable function – although education may well have been confined to boys only. Exactly how many pupils passed through its doors isn't known. Nevertheless, <u>in the mid-seventeenth century was that the link between business and education which is still a feature of the **Smith** family today.</u>

On a more certain note is the long-lasting influence of the above **Hugh Smith's** charity. In **1759 Lower Bawes Edge Farm** was sold but the proceeds went to another (presumably large) farm whose rents could provide further financial support. In **1779** a new school house was set-up, possibly on the East Side of **Ickornshaw**. It lasted until **1848** when it was replaced by a **National School**. However, this didn't mean the end of the **Hugh Smith** Charity. As late as **2nd September 1919** a certain **Edward Smith** was President and, along with his secretary **Ben Snowden,** was responsible for deciding which of **12** applicants should receive £18 **10s** for assisted scholarships at **Glasburn Institute.** As late as **1980 Trustees** were meeting annually to review applications with the aim of providing financial support to **Cowling** students wishing to participate in Further Education **(Wood p.72).** It was certainly some legacy that **Hugh Smith** left behind. Some of its business was subject to discussion at a **Cowling Parish Council** Meeting held on **Monday 5th March 2012** at **Saint Andrews Church, (Mallinson 2012).** The interest my family has in education possesses some very deep roots – remaining strongly present over **350** years after **Hugh Smith's** indenture.

So, was **Hugh Smith** a direct ancestor? I would like to think so, but the evidence is tentative. Parish Records reveal a **Hugh Smith** married a **Jennetta Scarborough** on the **30th April 1653.** By her he had:
Hugh baptized on **14th October 1655** (He was perhaps the **Hugh Smith** who married **Jana Atkinson** on **12th April 1684**)
George baptized on **8th November 1657** (He was perhaps the **George Smith** who married a **Deborah Ellis** on **12th May 1678**)
Edward baptized on **2nd October 1659** (He was perhaps the **Ewardus Smith** who married a **Gracia Bradley** on **31st December 1687**)

Adding to the complication is the presence of a <u>second</u> **Hugh Smith** who shows up in both the **1672** Lady Day List and in Parish records. (Lady Day was the traditional name of *'The Feast of the Annunciation'* in the Church's Liturgical Calendar and occurred variously at the end of **March** and in early **April.**) From this latter source we find that this **Hugh Smith** married an **Ann Smith** of Cowling/Ickornshaw on **16th January 1658** and by her he had: -
Ann baptized on **20th November 1659**
Maria baptized on **17th August 1662**
Margaret baptized on **14th June 1663**

Martha baptized on **29th November 1668**

Exactly which of the **Hugh Smiths** founded the Charity School remains a mystery, but the presence of common **Smith** forenames like *'George'* or *'Edward'* makes the first option more likely. Unlike his namesake, the first **Hugh** had sons to invest in.

Section 5: Becoming Visible

Concerning George Smith of Cowling

The <u>direct line</u> of my family only became visible with the marriage of **Edwardius Smith** and **Margareta Emott** at **Kildwick Parish Church** on **8th October 1700** – the earliest definite date I could trace to an event involving a direct male ancestor. With **Margareta,** it was possible to push back a little further and establish that her baptism had taken place on **30th April 1682** and that also her parents were **Georgius** and **Margareta Emott** of **Cowling.** Unfortunately, there was no trace of a suitable **Edwardius** who was her contemporary. The only other **Edwardius Smiths** on the records were either too old or too young to have been her husband. My guess is that he was born around **1680** and possibly had a slightly older brother named **George.** This absence from local baptismal records was a mystery and no real explanation for it exists other than alienation from the Church. However, an **Edward Smith,** a *'yeoman farmer'* is on record as being buried at **Kildwick** on the **14th September 1753** whilst a **Margaret** *'a relict* [widow] *of Edward Smith'* was buried on **18th May 1757.** Whether they were the same couple as my direct ancestors remained unproven for a long time, but information gathered subsequently confirmed that they had both lived into their seventies which was an extraordinary age for that time – and perhaps a testimony to good living. In terms of social class and location (as well as names), there was a match with my remote ancestors so a long life for both can't be discounted.

Very quickly, children followed the union of **Edwardius Smith** and **Margaret Emott.** There was : -

- **George** baptised **6th July 1701** (my direct ancestor)
- **Maria** baptized **20th December 1702**
- **Robert** baptized **18th February 1704**
- **Margarita** baptized **5th October 1707**
- Another **Margarita** baptized **26th October 1711/2** (the record is not clear, but it suggests that the first **Margarita** had died in childhood).

George may have been named after an uncle of the same name – the uncle concerned having married a **Margarita Brigg** on 7th **November 1699**.

During this whole period, the **Smith's** residence was given as **Cowling**. Baptismal records connected to **George's** own children show that **George** was a yeoman farmer with side-lines in weaving and grocery. If times were prosperous, they could make a profit selling cloth and grocery items, if times were hard they always had the farm to fall back on. Such survival tactics were commonly employed at the time.

An examination of **Kildwick Baptisms** (from **1715-1743**) suggested that **Edward** was one of the youngest (perhaps the youngest son) of **George** and **Mary Smith**. In the following list, the name *'George'* has been underlined wherever it refers to my direct ancestor. An asterisk (*****) has been placed next to those forenames reappearing in the family of **Edward** and **Elizabeth Smith**. (The forename *'Edward'* is constantly used here as it may have been a mistaken transcription of *'Edmund,'* in the original records.)

- **22/11/1726** baptism of **Peter* Smith,** son of **Mary** and **George Smith** *'mercer'* **Cowling**
- **26/12/1728** baptism of **Susanna Smith,** daughter of **Mary** and **George Smith** *'weaver'* **Cowling**
- **21/3/1730** baptism of **William* Smith,** son of **Mary** and **George Smith** *'weaver'* **Cowling**
- **5/5/1733** baptism of **Sarah Smith,** daughter of **Mary** and **George Smith** *'husbandman'* **Cowling**
- **30/6/1734** baptism of **Sarah Smith,** daughter of **Mary** and **George Smith** *'weaver'* **Cowling**
- **29/1/1735** baptism of **Patience Smith,** daughter of **Mary** and **George Smith** *'weaver'* **Glasburn**
- **14/11/1736** baptism of **Jennett Smith,** daughter of **Mary** and <u>**George**</u> **Smith** *'yeoman'* **Cowling**
- **21/8/1737** baptism of **John* Smith,** son of **Mary** and **George Smith** *'weaver'* **Glasburn**
- **27/8/1738** baptism of **Martha Smith,** daughter of **Mary** and **George Smith** *'grocer'* **Cowling**
- **8/4/1739** baptism of **George* Smith,** son of **Mary** and <u>**George**</u> **Smith** *'weaver'* **Cowling** [and likely participator in the land deals of **1788**]

- **3/5/1741** baptism of **Henry* Smith,** son of **Mary** and <u>**George**</u> **Smith** *'weaver'* **Cowling**
- **13/11/1743** baptism of **Edward* Smith,** son of **Mary** and <u>**George**</u> **Smith** *'weaver'* **Cowling** [and likely participator in the land deals of **1788**

The presence of two females named **Sarah** would suggest that the first had died in infancy. At that time, it was common to name a living child after a dead one. It need hardly be added that such a custom could create difficulties for future Family Historians! A *'mercer'* was a dealer in textiles and suggests a family link with that trade going back to the early eighteenth century.

Although the possibility remains that this list might refer to more than one **Mary** and **George Smith** it remains clear that my ancestor **Edward** was the younger member of a large family and this perhaps fuelled in him the ambition to *'get on.'* The *'mixed bag'* of occupations was typical of the region. The bleak **Pennine** area of **Cowling** was not the place to make a steady living by farming alone. To survive, both men and women had to appropriate a variety of skills. The confirmation that **Ed<u>m</u>und** and **Ed<u>w</u>ard Smith** were one and the same person made it possible to push this history back to a far earlier period, tracing my line of ancestors to **1700**. Before this confirmation, there'd simply been a whole cluster of **Smiths** who may (or may not) have been my direct ancestors.

Transcripts of **Kildwick St Andrew's** Parish Records (received from the *'Keighley & District History Society'* on **Thursday, 11th December 2003**) strongly implied that: -
1) My forbears **George** and **Mary Smith** were married on **7th April 1735,** with **Mary's** maiden name having been **Robinson**. This seems to have been after they'd already had six children and had been living together for about a decade.
2) **Mary** appears to have predeceased **George** – her burial having taken place on **26th December 1759** (**George** being recorded as a *'Yeoman'*) whilst her husband's death took place on **2nd September 1764,** when working as *'a weaver of Cowling.'* His death in his sixties would suggest that he'd been a clean living and industrious sort of a man.
3) There were branches of the **Smith** family living at **Cowling** as far back as the late sixteenth and seventeenth centuries, with forenames like *'William,'* *'John,'* *'Edmund'* and *'George'* is commonly used. Sadly, a high infant mortality rate was present throughout this period. Previous analysis in **Section 1** of this **Chapter** would indicate that the **Smiths** of **Cowling** were the direct descendants of the fourteenth-century blacksmith *'Ricardus Smyth.'*

Although only a few bare facts are known about **George** he did display that spirit of enterprise which was to characterise many **Smiths** for generations to come. To *'spread his risk'* and maintain respectability he too had followed a strategy of diversification – as I do today in my profession as a Private Tutor and self-published author, (the latter covering anything from poetry to fiction and theology). Through doing this he will have adequately provided for his family, so keeping them away from the jaws of destitution.

Section 6: Frustrations

Concerning the Smiths of Calderdale

One highly frustrating mystery that took some time to clear up was whether the **Edmund Smith** who was known to have fathered **William Smith** (my Great, Great, Great Grandfather) was indeed the same person as the **Edward Smith** who featured in the relevant records of **Kildwick Parish Church** and **Sutton Baptist Chapel?** Only two options were possible: -
Option 1: **Edmund** and **Edward Smith** were one and the same person.
Option 2: **Edmund** and **Edward Smith** were two different people.
In this context, it's worth mentioning that by **March 1801, Glusburn Township** had a male population of **276.** One can assume that before that period the figure had been lower, probably in the region of **150-250** males during the second half of the eighteenth century.

The following reasons strongly supported **Option 1:** -
1) Matching Characteristics. Both men were: -
- Married to a woman called **Elizabeth**
- Weavers
- Lived mainly in **Glusburn**
- Obvious contemporaries in terms of age
- Mentioned more than once in local records
- Associated with both **George Smith** and my forbear **William Smith**
- Endowed with an enterprising business temperament

2) The Alternation of Names. Both men were never associated together in the same document. Their names would appear sequentially (as was the case when various parish records of **Kildwick Parish** were conflated with the **Dissenting Birth registers** of **Sutton Baptist Chapel.**) For instance, the name **Edmund Smith** would appear when one would have expected **Edward Smith** and vice-versa. This point was seen more clearly when information from both records was collated and summarised, as follows: (Available birth dates are placed in squared brackets and the forenames of direct ancestors are underlined.): -

- **18/10/1768 Ed<u>m</u>und Smith** of **Cowling** *'weaver and bachelor'* married an *'<u>Elizabeth</u> **Pighels** of **Kildwick**, a minor'*
- **21/4/1771** baptism of **Mary Smith** (daughter of <u>Elizabeth</u> and Ed<u>w</u>ard **Smith**) *'wool comber'* **Kildwick**
- **6/3/1774** baptism of **John Smith** (son of <u>Elizabeth</u> and Ed<u>w</u>ard **Smith**) *'weaver'* **Glusburn**
- **20/5/1776, the** baptism of **George Smith** (son of <u>Elizabeth</u> and Ed<u>w</u>ard **Smith**) *'weaver'* **Glusburn**
- **3/1/1779 [2/11/1778]** baptism of <u>**William**</u> **Smith** (son of <u>Elizabeth</u> and Ed<u>m</u>und **Smith**) *'weaver'* **Glusburn**
- **22/7/1781 [21/5/1781]** baptism of **Edmund Smith** (son of <u>Elizabeth</u> and Ed<u>m</u>und **Smith**) *'weaver'* **Glusburn**
- **4/1/1784 [23/5/1783]** baptism of **Henry Smith** (son of <u>Elizabeth</u> and Ed<u>m</u>und **Smith**) *'husbandman'* **Glusburn**
- **22/3/1786 [2/2/1786]** registration of **Betty Smith** (daughter of <u>Elizabeth</u> and Ed<u>w</u>ard **Smith**)
- **14/2/1788** purchase of land at **Glusburn** by **George** and Ed<u>m</u>und **Smith** *'manufacturer'*
- **11/5/1788 [16/3/1788]** registration of **Peter Smith** (son of <u>Elizabeth</u> and Ed<u>w</u>ard **Smith**) *'manufacturer'* **Glasburn**
- **8/4/1791 [7 or 17/3/1791]** registration of **Benjamin Smith** (son of <u>Elizabeth</u> and Ed<u>w</u>ard **Smith**)
- **21/5/1796 [Interred 27/5/1796]** death of <u>Elizabeth</u> **Smith** *'wife of Ed<u>m</u>und of **Glasburn** a <u>**Yeoman**</u> aged **48** years'*
- **20/5/1798 [3/3/1798]** baptism of **Margaret Smith** (daughter of Ed<u>w</u>ard **Smith**) *'Yeoman'* **Glasburn** and **Isabel Harrison** *'2 wife'*
- **13/4/1800 [4/3/1800]** baptism of **Mary Smith** (daughter of Ed<u>w</u>ard **Smith**) *'Yeoman'* **Glasburn** and **Isabel Harrison** *'2 wife'*
- **28/8/1802 [21/8/1802]** registration of **Thomas Smith** (son of **Isabe<u>lla</u>** and Ed<u>w</u>ard **Smith**)
- **8/7/1804 [24/5/1804]** registration of **Samuel Smith** son of **Isabe<u>lla</u>** and Ed<u>w</u>ard **Smith**
- **27/5/1809** death of **Mary Smith**

- **20/7/1811 (Interred 22/7/1811)** death of **Ed<u>w</u>ard Smith** *'of Glasburn a Yeoman aged 67 years'*
- **31/12/1841** death of **Isabe<u>ll</u>a Smith** aged **74**

N.B: Poor handwriting in the original document meant that some of the dates given in this list are approximations. This would also perhaps explain why **Edward Smith's** second wife was variously spelt as *'Isabel'* and *'Isabella.'*

Perhaps the most decisive evidence was the way in which both the names *'Edward'* and *'Edmund'* <u>were associated with the burial records of the same</u> **<u>Glusburn Yeoman.</u>** At the death of **Elizabeth,** he had been known as *'Ed<u>m</u>und'* but at his own death (and on his headstone) the name *'Edward'* was employed. Such evidence provided the decisive clue confirming that *'Ed<u>w</u>ard'* and *'Edmund'* <u>were indeed one and the same person.</u> If they were different it would be necessary to believe in a whole string of implausible coincidences – the most notable being the presence of two men <u>with identical characteristics</u> living in **Cowling** at one and the same time (with only a minor difference in forename). One would also have to believe that, when one man appeared the other vanished and that they both shared the same grave. From direct experience, I'm aware that unusual coincidences <u>can</u> occur in a Family History <u>but not that unusual!</u> This **second** option, of **Edmund** and **Ed<u>w</u>ard Smith** being two different people simply collapses under its own absurdity. There then remained the problem of how this confusion in names originated, especially as most of the relevant records had been written with neatness and clarity.

The most likely explanation was dialect confusion. To a well-bred vicar from outside the region, the two names could have sounded similar. Even in neatly written documents, it was still possible for those using blotchy quill pens to confuse the letters *'m'* and *'w'* and to close the *'u'* so that it formed an *'a.'* If in doubt they would write the phonetic spelling of a name (spelling it as it sounded). A review of **Kildwick** Parish baptism records (from **1678-1714**) quickly demonstrated that the two aforesaid forenames were often confused. <u>It appears to have been a standard mistake.</u>

Despite resolving this mystery, it remained frustratingly difficult to go beyond the birth year of my Great, Great, Great Grandfather **William Smith.** Throughout much of this research, **Monday, 2nd November 1778** remained the <u>earliest</u> date in which it was possible to trace my ancestors. All family links before that time were, for a lengthy period, too conjectural in nature. This meant that I found it very difficult to successfully identify his father. For a lengthy period, I floundered between conflicting options. These were: -

Option 1: **Edmund Smith** (the weaver) who may have been the son of **William** and **Ellen Smith,** christened at **Kildwick** on **7/1/1730.**
Option 2: Less likely, **Edmund Smith** (the weaver) who may have been the son of **Robert** and **Margaret Smith,** christened on **24/4/1730**
Option 3: He could have been the son of a **Robert** and **Elizabeth Smith** christened on **17/4/1735.**
Option 4: He may have been an **Edmund Smith** who married an **Elizabeth Pighels** at **Kildwick** on **Tuesday, 18/10/1768.** However, in this case, a ten-year gap was to follow before they had any children.
Option 5: He was the son of none of these people and was christened somewhere else other than **Kildwick** – assuming he was christened at all!

However, the **Edmund Smith** (in **option 4**) did not appear to be the man who married an **Elizabeth Johnson** on **6/4/1779.** This is because the record of **William's** christening showed **Edmund** as having been married prior to that date. One possibility was that he'd moved into **Kildwick** from another locality *i.e.* **Colne.** However, consultation with the parish records for **Colne** (made on **Thursday 26th January 2001**) failed to find a person with the correct specifications. Attempts to connect him with any of the three **Edmund Smiths** living in nearby **Cowling** also proved unsuccessful, as did the attempt to connect him with an **Edmund Smith** living at **Stott Hill.** (During a walk to **Lund Tower** with my wife on a boiling hot **Saturday, 9th August 2003** the grey stone farm buildings of **Stott Farm** this **Edmund Smith** had lived, were located on a steep hill outside **Cowling.** The surrounding fields were still used for grazing cattle.) For a very long while, barely anything could be discovered about the **Edmund** (or **Edward**) **Smith** who was my direct ancestor. It took an extensive and repeated consultation of the records that had originated from **Kildwick Parish Church (St Andrews)** to resolve this matter and allow me to trace my direct ancestry back to **1700.** As it turned out **option 4** was correct! This occurrence demonstrated all too clearly that in Family History one is often confronted by several equally plausible (or implausible) scenarios. Patience and dogged determination are the key elements needed if any breakthroughs are to be made.

Once these frustrating puzzles had (on **Wednesday 5th, November 2003**) been resolved it was possible to obtain further information about **Edward Smith** and his family. This concerned the discovery of other family events which had taken place <u>prior</u> to the previously confirmed earliest recorded ancestral date (**William Smith's** baptism on **2nd, November 1778**). A copy of **Kildwick Parish** records (received from the **County Records Office** based in **Northallerton** on **Saturday, August 30th, 2003**) showed that, on **November 13th, 1743**, '*Edward son of* **George Smith** *of* **Cowling** *Weaver and* **Mary** *his wife*' was baptised. This was well into the age of **Bonnie Prince Charlie, Frederick the Great** and **John Wesley. King George II** was sitting on the **English** throne and **Louis XV** was ruling over an increasingly discontented **France.** Also, at that time, **France** and **England** were embroiled in the war of the **Austrian** Succession.

Section 7: An Eighteenth-Century Land Deal

Concerning land deals made by the Smiths in Glusburn

A '*Deed of Release*' (discovered at the **West Yorkshire Archive Service Centre** at **Wakefield** on **Monday, July 14th, 2003**) threw far greater light upon the activities of the early **Smiths.** Regrettably, the use of archaic language, dense handwriting and eighteenth-century legal terminology made this a ferociously difficult document to either transcribe or interpret. Indeed, professional help from more than one archivist had to be sought to help make sense of it at all! In outline, it demonstrated that the **Smiths** were purchasing land and property, which they had hitherto held on lease. During the eighteenth century, the law made this a three-way process whereby the lease was '*released*' (terminated) before it could become the freehold property of the purchaser. The following lengthy extract will give a greater idea of the ponderous style in which this document was written, some names and link words like '*concerning*' and '*between*' were penned in red lettering in the original document: -

"***INDENTURES*** *of lease and release date respectively the thirteenth and fourteenth days of* **February** *in the twenty-eighth year of the reign of our Sovereign Lord* **George** *the third by the grace of* **God** *of* **Great Britain, France** *and* **Scotland***, King, Defender of the Faith and so forth and in the year of our* **Lord** *Seventeen Hundred and Eighty-Eight. This release was made between the Reverend* **William Bawdwen** *of* **Stonegap** *in the Parish of* **Kildwick** *and* **George Smith** *of* **Bisko** *within* **Glasburn** *in the Parish of* **Kildwick** *aforesaid yeoman of the two other parts and the lease made between the Revd.* **William Bawdwen** *of the first part, of* **Grace Bawdwen** *of the* **City of York** *of the second part,* **Thomas Chippendale, Stargate** *Gentleman of the third part, the said* **George Smith** *of the fourth part and* **Edmund Smith** *of* **Glusburn** *aforesaid manufacturer of the fifth part and concerning all that fields, or dwelling house, farm and tenancies in situ in* **Glusburn** *aforesaid and generally called or known as* **Glusburn Green,** *write our lease* *out [for the] Turf house and garden to the said belonging and all those several closes and parcels of ground variously called and known as the* **Green, Beanlands, [Wheatlands, Binns, Ryecroft, Lingah] Hopsis** *all of which parcelled out, situated lying and being in* Glusburn *aforesaid in the* Parish of Kildwick *and now in the tenancy or occupation of* **Joshua Clough.**" (Reference **CX**: Page **530** document **719**.)

The remainder of this document stated that, although **William Bawdwen** made this *'release'* a **Matthew Wilson** of **Otley** and **William Philips** of **Silsden** were required to place their signatures as witnesses. A brief note in the margin confirmed that represented here was a transfer of real estate from **William Bawdwen to George** and **Edmund Smith. William Bawden** appears to have been the son of another **William Bawden** whose headstone inside the **Saint Andrew's** Church at **Kildwick** stated, *"Here lieth the body of* **William Bawden** *of* **Stone Gap Esq.** *who departed this life on the* **22nd January** *in the year of our* **Lord 1796** *in the 56th year of his age."* The location of his headstone and designation *'Esq'* confirm that the **Bawden's** were of the gentry class.

Consultation (on **Monday, 14th July 2003**) with a knowledgeable informant experienced in this type of documentation, showed that **Edmund Smith** had been one of five parties involved in the lease. He was now collaborating with a **George Smith** (most likely his brother) to purchase several closes of land, consisting of approximately **32** acres (although some of these could have been later purchases). A first-hand observation made of the area during a visit to **Glusburn** on **Saturday, July 26th, 2003** confirmed that a substantial property had been involved. It had consisted mainly of downward sloping fields, tilting toward **Glusburn Beck** where the Corn Mill was sited. It made ideal pastureland for sheep or cattle. Its purchase suggested that the **Smiths** were ambitious social climbers who were determined to better themselves. They belonged to the yeoman farmer, small business owner and skilled artisan class. Life would have been hard, but most **Smiths** seemed to have earned enough to have provided food on the table. In terms of community involvement, they wouldn't have been leaders like the gentry or clergy but as the *'next rank down'* they would have executed leadership decisions on such matters as how much poor law relief should be distributed and to what families. They would have best been described as *'aspiring'* or *'respectable'* rather than *'prominent.'*

What this crucial document showed was that, in **1788,** (the year **King George III** had experienced his first serious attack of madness) the **Smith** family were *'moving up'* in the world. They were investing in plots of land that was to support them until at least the mid-nineteenth century. On display here was an ability to think and to plan strategically. Also present were social links with the **Cloughs** and **Wilsons** whose names frequently occurred, in association with the **Smiths.** One intriguing question remained; where did **Edmund** and **George** obtain the money for such a substantial purchase? The answer is sadly lost in the swirling mists of time, but the clear implication is that the first **Edmund Smith** had made a success of his business in what appears to have been cloth manufacturing. In the year of **King George's** first mental breakdown, the **Smiths** were actively displaying a notable business acumen.

Reference to earlier *'Deed Purchase Indexes'* (from **c.1760** until **1787**) showed that there'd been virtually no purchasing of real estate in **Glasburn** Township by <u>any</u> party throughout this period. In contrast (during the same period in **Cowling –** only five miles **East** of **Colne**) a considerable amount of purchasing activity had been made by the **Smiths** who lived there. *'Edmund'* was a common forename amongst them. One old family tradition stated that the **Smiths** *'went to Colne and back.'* However, none of the available documentation showed this as ever applying to any of the **Smiths** living in the post-**1778** period. This was the case even though **Colne** was a place for cloth dealing and manufacture. Consequently, any links at this stage would have been purely commercial. Possibly this oral tradition referred to events taking place well before that period. From the scrappy documentation, available and from the fact that my ancestor **William Smith** had married **Susanna Emmot** (a spinster of **Cowling**) in **1799** it was possible to the following order of events.

Around the time of his marriage to **Elizabeth Pighels** in **October 1768, Edmund** (or **Edward**) **Smith** moved from nearby **Cowling** to **Glasburn** and took up a lease. He had prospered sufficiently by **1788** to purchase (along with his older brother **George**) the whole of the land covered by the lease. Despite the discovery of the Land Deed, much remained tantalizingly obscure. But what the Land Deed <u>did</u> confirm was that, by the late eighteenth century, the **Smiths** were obviously bettering themselves. They were keen on self-improvement. In the next century, other **Smiths** would build upon this solid base and continue their climb up the social ladder. They were clearly an opportunistic lot. Should a chance for advancement show itself (as with this land purchase) they would be sure to make the very best of it. Generally, the pattern of settlement followed by the **Smiths** in the late eighteenth century was very typical for the region. For economic reasons, there was a tendency to slowly move down from poorer hillside areas to more fertile lower lying ones. It was the Genealogist **Andrew Todd** who first drew my attention to this trend on **p.104** in the **September 2003** issue of the magazine **The Yorkshire Family Historian.**

Greatly assisting my understanding of my own ancestor's movements were conversations I had with friends inside the **Leeds Asian** community. They informed me that younger sons of highland **Pakistani** families were often encouraged to move into low lying areas to prevent inheritance or land disputes. Usually, this only applied to families living on the edge of highland areas. Those in central highland regions tended to stay put. It was also customary for marginalized younger brothers to *'team up'* to acquire land or to launch a business venture. Although parallels between eighteenth-century **England** and contemporary **Pakistan** should be treated with caution such conversations were invaluable in reconstructing the likely family dynamics operating within the **Smiths** of this period. Members of the **Asian** community had no difficulty in understanding the possible motives of people like **Edward Smith.** Their native communities appeared to be at a similar stage of development.

On a less ambiguous note, we find **Edward Smith** (the weaver) and his wife **Elizabeth** were on record as having the following children christened by the Reverend **John Dehane** at **Kildwick Parish Church**. These were: -

- **William:** my ancestor – born on **2/11/1778** and christened on **3/1/1779**
- **Edmund:** born on **2/5/1781** and christened on **22/7/1781**
- **Henry:** born on **23/11/1783** and christened on **4/1/1784**

1783, was the year **America** finally gained independence from **Great Britain**. At that time, **Edmund** was still living in **Glasburn** but working as a *'Husbandman'* – presumably because weaving had become unprofitable.

Of special interest was how **Edward Smith** tended to rotate between **Anglicanism** and the dissenting **Baptist** movement. This information came as something of a surprise – simply because I too had followed an identical pattern in my own life. It was amazing to see how, despite vastly different socio-economic backgrounds, I had repeated a near-identical pattern of religious affiliation. I found it all too easy to imagine my forbear as a stubborn sort of man who'd easily adopted the role of a critical parishioner.

Extra evidence concerning **Edward Smith** only came to light during a visit made to **Kildwick Parish** graveyard (along with my wife) on **Monday, September 22nd, 2003.** Remarkably, what had been a very wet day brightened up when the bus we were on drove into **Kildwick.** My wife provided invaluable help in transcribing what was often badly eroded *'pavement'* tomb inscriptions. The afternoon sunlight, which cast long shadows, was also a decisive factor in assisting the transcription of the following details. His flat, slab-like tombstone was almost missed because it lay obscured beneath a lot of fallen leaves. It lay a little further up from his son's **William's** tombstone of identical design. A combination of my wife's help and ideal sunlight assisted in the transcription of what was often badly eroded wording. A year or two later and it would have been possible to have retrieved only <u>some</u> of the information.

"Here lieth the body of
Elizabeth *the wife*
Of **Edward Smith,** *of*
Glusburn Hall *who de-*
Parted this life the
21st May 1796 *and*
in the **49th** *year of her age,*
'Hither I gave my spirit up
And trust it in thy hand
My dying flesh shall rest in hope
And rise at thy command.'
Also, **Mary** *daughter of*
The above named, **Edward**
And **Isabella Smith** *who*
Departed this life **May 27th**
1809 *aged* **9** *years.*
Likewise, the above said
Edward Smith *who departed*
This life **July 20th 1811** *in the*
68th *year of his age*
Also, **Ann** *wife of* **Robert Smith**
Who died **October 6th 1840**
The **77th** *year of her age*
Also, of the said **Robert Smith**
Who died **August 15th 1847** *in*
The **78th** *year of his age."*

A transcribed copy of **St Andrew's Kildwick Burial Register** of 1792-1801, (received from the **Keighley & District Family History Society** on **Tuesday, 22nd July 2003**) revealed the date of **Elizabeth Smith's** burial. It contained the following statement: *"27/5/1796 SMITH wife of Edmund of Glusburn a Yeoman aged 49 years."*

As my wife remarked during our visit, the above inscriptions *"appear to confirm that the Smiths were a 'God-fearing' lot."* They also indicated that they'd led sombre lives, characterised by a resigned attitude to suffering. Attempts to discover more about **Elizabeth** initially proved unavailing. A letter from **Northallerton Archive Centre** (received on **Saturday, 27th September 2003)** confirmed her name was <u>not</u> found on the **Kildwick Saint Andrews** parish baptism registers (covering the period from **1745** to **1750**). Her precise date of birth couldn't be ascertained. All that can be asserted is that it had most likely occurred sometime from **October 1747** to **May 1748.** Previously quoted parish records confirmed that she was under the age of **21** when she'd married **Edward** (who as stated before, was confusedly known in some of these records as **Edmund.**)

However, **Edward's** second wife was perhaps the same **Isabella Smith** (of *'independent means'*) recorded as living with a **Mary Smith** (aged **40**) at **Hopsis, Crosshills** during the **1841** Census. The **Kildwick Saint Andrews** Burial Book records interment as occurring on **31st December** of that year. She was **74** at the time of her death. Like many other second wives of the period she had been much younger (by some **24** years) than her husband. The possession of a private income suggests that **Edward** had been a good provider for his family. He seemed to have possessed (in full measure) the *'Smith'* aptitude for business. The fact his son **Robert** chose to be buried alongside him would suggest he'd been a respected figure.

In terms of character, strong similarities did emerge between my Great, Great, Great, Great Grandfather **Edward Smith** and his descendant, **Edmund** who would exercise an enormous influence on the development of my family. Both were shrewd, entrepreneurial figures, keen to rear large families and to provide for them. A mixture of job opportunities and family politics may have explained **Edward's** move to **Kildwick.** The location of his wife's family may also have played a part – even though it was customary for the wife to move to where the husband lived. Both **Edward** and his Great-Grandson **Edmund** knew the value of *'hard graft,'* each having worked their way up from lowly positions in the textile industry. Both had experienced rather erratic connections with dissenting forms of religion, and both had a weakness for women. **Edward** had possibly fathered his first child by **Isabella** (his second wife) out of wedlock. Available evidence would suggest that **Edward** was one of the most entrepreneurial of the **Smiths.** Another two generations were to pass before his like would be seen again – this time in the form of his Great Grandson (and my Great Grandfather) **Edmund Smith.**

CHAPTER 3: MILLS, MARRIAGES AND AMERICA

Section 1: A Corn Milling Background

Concerning the Smiths of Glusburn and some grave inscriptions

On **Friday, July 6ᵗʰ, 2001**, I received copies of the Baptismal Register (for **Kildwick Saint Andrews**) from **Northallerton Archive Centre.** These provided some extra information concerning **William Smith**: *"Baptised: 1779 January 3 William son of Edmund Smith, Weaver of Glusburn & Elizabeth his wife [being born on] November 2ⁿᵈ1778."* This was one of seven christenings, which the Parish Vicar had conducted on **Sunday, January 3ʳᵈ, 1779.** (Unfortunately, the Vicar's surname was too faded to have been recorded, but consultation with **Livett 1932** showed that his name had been **John Dehane.**) During the time of **William Smith's** birth, **George the Third** was on the throne and the **American Colonies** were struggling for independence from **Britain.** This was just at the period when the **British** were consolidating a new Empire in **India** and beginning to experience the Industrial Revolution. Within mainland **Europe** daring novel ideas of political freedom were beginning to take hold in influential, educated circles. They would pave the way for the **French Revolution**, which was to explode with great force in just another ten years. For now, **Louis the Sixteenth** of **France** and his **Austrian** born wife **Marie Antoinette** still seemed secure on their thrones and able to enjoy the delights of the Palace of **Versailles.** Such, in outline, was the state of the world at the time of my Great, Great, Great, Grandfather's birth. During **1803** the threat of a **French** invasion led by **Napoleon** caused a *'Militia Muster Roll'* to be compiled, covering the whole of **Kildwick Parish.** Recorded on this document (kindly provided by the small Community Library at **Crosshills** on **Monday, 5ᵗʰ February 2001**) were the names and trades of the following **Smiths** from **Glasburn Township,** just **North** of **Sutton.**

Henry Spencer Smith – *"Weaver"*
Edward Smith – *"Miller"*
Thomas Smith – *"Mason"*
William Smith – *"Comber"*
William Smith – *"Miller"*
Wilkinson Smith – *"Mason"*
George Smith – *"Weaver"*
Robert Smith – *"Comber"*
Robert Smith – *"Miller"*

What this document showed was how this group of **Smiths** appeared to hold a narrow range of occupations in common – mainly textiles, milling and masonry. They were neither at the very wealthy nor the very poor end of their communities. Given the tendency of militias in those days to include anybody who was even remotely fit, it also seemed apparent that represented here were the most able-bodied **Smiths** at that time. In addition, some of the above **Smiths** might well have been father and son. Statistical extrapolation would suggest a total of **55-70 Smiths** living inside **Glasburn Township** during the early nineteenth century. Clearly, they were very prolific. Of interest was the connection with milling. Throughout this period the same occupation was usually *'passed down'* from father to son and so it seems possible that one of the **Smiths** (listed as a miller) may well have been the parent of **John Smith.** The presence of a **John William** amongst one of **John Smith's** Grandchildren also suggests that, of the three millers listed, **William Smith** was the most likely candidate as my forbear.

A phone call from **Skipton Library** (on **Monday, July 28**[th,] **2003**) revealed that local militiamen were sub-divided into four groups (or classes): -
Class 1: men aged under **30** with no living child
Class 2: married men aged **20-40** with a child under ten
Class 3: married men aged **17-29** with not more than two children aged under ten
Class 4: others not included in the above classes.

The *'miller'* **William Smith** fell into the third class – at that time having one son and one daughter (born in **June 1803**). This extra information confirmed that I had indeed located the correct **William Smith.** His participation in the militia suggested he'd been taught the rudiments of firearm use. However, like many militia members, he may well have spent more time in the tavern than on the local parade ground! The militia as a military force was notoriously undisciplined. They were often the subject of satirical cartoons, lending further weight to the scant regard afforded them by the public.

Also emerging was the limited connection my Great, Great, Great, Grandfather **William Smith** had with the **Bairstow** dynasty – as shown in the following entries (from **p. 341** of *'The Purchase/Sales Book'* **1820-1835**: -
    "1823, March 3rd*'Let **Wm Smith** stable horses for £1 11s 6d – Wm Smith** left the horses 6*[th] ***December."*** (From the Account Book **1801-1839**)
    "11**[th] **June 1835 William Smith Crosshills,

59 11-   1. 1. 25
14

1—1-11 – for 15 Ibs Scotch Wool@ 63/4 per Ib pays £4-
4-10

2

4-5-0"

On **25/6/1835** an entry on **p.343** showed that he had paid off the amount owed of, *£4-4-10* in cash and the remaining *2s 'by discount.'* (Rough workings out preceded this figure.)

*"22nd November 1830 paid **William Smith** for **Comb setting £1-5s-0d**, sundries 8s 3d."* (From **p. 365** e *'The Purchase/Sales Book'* **1830-1835.** This is a slightly more doubtful entry and may well refer to another **William Smith.**)

Unlike most of the other entries, **William Smith** was <u>not</u> a regular customer of the **Bairstow** Enterprise. He appeared only to have had dealings with them when he needed to. The amounts quoted in the *'The Purchase/Sales'* book showed that he did have some spare cash to use. My ancestor was by no means the poorest member of the local community. Like many of his contemporaries, it looks likely that he diversified into various business activities other than agriculture; this included corn milling and textiles. **William Smith** had certainly keen to spread his risk, providing early evidence of that shrewd **Smith** business brain, which had already been manifest throughout successive generations. (It was absolutely fascinating for me to have seen these written financial transactions involving my ancestral family at such a great distance in time.)

The **1841** Census showed two **William Smiths,** both of whom were of the correct age to have been my Great, Great, Great Grandfather. One lived at **Lingah Farm,** just outside **Crosshills,** and worked both as a farmer and a stonemason. The other lived in **Glasburn** itself and was of *'independent means'* – suggesting that he'd made a success in whatever business venture he'd been involved. Preventing any firm identification was the fact that both **Williams Smiths** lived with a **Mary Smith** too! My guess would be the second **William Smith** (as stone masonry was never a business associated with my direct ancestors). Moreover, the fact that he was of *'independent means* would suggest that this **William Smith** had possessed enough financial reserves to help **John**

Smith's family were they ever to fall on challenging times. This is exactly what happened during the mid-**1840s.**

Beyond the above facts, little else could be discovered about **William.** Like many men of a similar background he was shrewd in his business dealings and able to survive by taking on various jobs (other than Corn Milling alone). Also, akin to his first wife **Susanna** (already a spinster from **Cowling**), **William Smith** could also write intelligibly – in stark contrast to his second wife **Martha Brewer** (whom he married on **June 20th, 1822**) who was able only to leave a mark. His respectable occupation as Corn Miller would suggest that he'd enjoyed a living standard slightly above the norm; though this would not have spared him the all too common tragedy at that time of seeing two wives die at a comparatively early age. Also, like many of his contemporaries, he would have flirted with religious dissent. Surviving records (in **June 1805**) showed a connection with **Sutton Baptist Chapel.**

As with his father **Edward** evidence concerning **William Smith** only came to light during the previously described visit made to **Kildwick Parish** graveyard on **Monday, September 22nd, 2003.** With the aid of my wife I was able to transcribe the following details whose accuracy would be carefully checked on subsequent visits: -
"IN MEMORY OF
Susanna *Wife of* **William Smith**
Of **Glusburn** *who died* **April 27th**
1821 *aged* **45** *years*
'Weep not for me my Husband dear
My children weep not [that] *I am here*
For in refrain to **Jesus** *I fly*
If you thus live, you'll happily die'
Also, of **Martha** *wife of the above*
named **William Smith** *who died*
September 21st 1826 *aged* **34**
Also, the aforesaid **William**
Smith *who died* **May 12th 1850** *in the*
72nd *year of his age"*
Susanna's death in **1821** would have come as a terrible blow to her son **John** (my Great, Great Grandfather) who was only aged sixteen at the time. It possibly left him with a fervent desire to perpetuate her memory.

William Smith's own Death Certificate indicated that his demise was due to a stroke. It provided the first evidence of those blood circulatory problems which would dog successive generations of Smiths. (This is something I am all too aware of and take precautions to avoid – through a good diet and regular swimming.)

Registration District <u>Skipton</u>
1850 Death in the <u>sub-district</u> of <u>Kildwick</u> in the <u>County of York</u>
When and where died: Twelfth May 1850 Glusburn
Name and Surname: William Smith
Sex: Male
Age: 71
Occupation: Corn Miller
Causes of Death: Paralysis 6 days Certified
Signature, description, and residence of Informant: X the mark of **Mary Smith** Present at death **Glusburn**
When registered: Twenty-Second May 1850
Signature of Registrar: *John Crossley*

Section 2: A Youthful Marriage

Concerning the marriage of John Smith and Ann Wilson

The **Sutton Baptist Dissenting Register** provided the birth date of my Great, Great Grandfather: *"**John Smith**, the son of **William** and **Susanna** his wife of **Glasburn** in the Parish of **Kildwick** in the county of **York** was born the seventeenth day of **March** in the year of our Lord **1805**. Registered the twenty-third day of **June** of our Lord **1805** by **John Walton** – Protestant Dissenting Minister."* In turn, the **St Andrew's Kildwick Burial Register** of 1802-1812 revealed that my Great, Great Grandfather **John Smith** had had an elder sister **Mary** who'd died on **8th May 1803.** The burial entry confirmed that she'd been the daughter *'of **William & Susanna** of **Glasburn**, a **Weaver**, aged **2** yrs.'* Unfortunately, **Mary** wasn't the only loss suffered by that family. **John** had also had an elder brother whose name had not been recorded. The statement simply read: *"**3/1/1810 SMITH** a son of **William & Susannah** of **Glusburn** a Miller aged **10** years."* Why, unlike most of the other deceased children, his name hadn't been recorded isn't known. He doesn't appear to have been baptised either. Perhaps there'd been a clerical error, or his name was identical to that of his father.

The **North Yorkshire County Council Record Office,** based in **Northallerton,** provided (via a letter dated **Saturday, 10th September 2000**) the following information about the marriage of **William Smith's** son. *"24ᵗʰ May 1824, John Smith of Sutton in this parish, millwright and a minor & Ann Wilson of Sutton in this parish, minor – married after banns and with the consent of parents. Witnesses: Benjamin Smith, Mary McCroben."* Direct observation of this document on **Friday, June 15ᵗʰ, 2001** revealed that, in contrast to the two witnesses who could write very neatly, **John** and **Ann Smith** could leave only a mark. They were illiterate – able only to pen two cross-shaped marks. My desire to get hold of their original signatures had been foiled. Where **John** had met his wife isn't known, but it's possible that they had been co-workers at **Crosshills Corn Mill,** which I visited in **July 2003.** He was only nineteen years old at the time of his marriage.

Consultation with **Pigot's 1834** Trade Directory showed that the only miller of note in **Glasburn** was a certain **Guy Pearson** and he seems to have been the owner of a mill at nearby **Crosshills.** The implication of this finding was that at this period the **Smiths** owned no significant Corn Milling Business. Instead, they appear to have worked for other people. However, **John's** father **William Smith** may have had part ownership of this **Crosshills** mill and this might be the origin of the mill story in *'Family Tradition.'* It was located beside a stream as this tradition said it would be.

Information gathered from *'The Morton Kin Book'* confirmed that **Ann Wilson** came from a large family that lived in **Haworth.** Her parents were **Edmund Wilson** and **Ann Dixon** who'd married on **9ᵗʰ January 1798.** Their children were: -
Elizabeth born on **11ᵗʰ November 1798**
Mary born on **3ʳᵈ June 1801**
Ann born on **22ⁿᵈ March 1803** [my Great, Great Grandmother]
Hannah born on **1ˢᵗ February 1805** [she would emigrate to **America** in **1827**]
Martha born on **7ᵗʰ January 1806**
Harriet born on **10ᵗʰ January 1809**
Henrietta born on **15ᵗʰ October 1811**
John born on **20ᵗʰ January 1814**
Sarah born on **25ᵗʰ January 1815**
Edmund born on **28ᵗʰ January 1817**

Elizabeth would marry a *'Mr. Swire'* and would still be seen actively doing the household washing in **Crosshills** when she was visited by **David Morton** during **27ᵗʰ September 1881.** He noted how the above list of births had been preserved in an *"old record in the handwriting of **Edmund Wilson** in* [the] *Bible at*

Aunt Bettie Swire's."). **David Morton's** account revealed her to be a very sweet and hospitable **Yorkshire** woman who was much loved by family members. She was cared for by her single daughter **Ann Swire.** This venerable old lady would pass away suddenly on **1ˢᵗ August 1885** at the age of eighty-six. In her young days, **Elizabeth** would have found living in a crowded household of girls would have its tensions, especially when times were hard, which they often were in the early nineteenth century. It was a situation that would provoke my great, great grandmother and her sister **Hannah** to move to **Sutton** and then in **Hannah's** case to **America.**

Like most of their contemporaries, **John** and **Ann** had links with their local Parish Church (in this case it was **Saint Andrew's** in **Kildwick Village**). The incumbent for most of this period was a **Rev. John Perring** (who may well have been the archetypal model of one of the three Clergymen featured in **Charlotte Bronte's** novel *'Shirley,'* serialised on **Radio 4** in **July 2002.**) His interest in improving the moral and educational condition of his flock was highlighted by the following inscription on the old schoolhouse, sited just outside an entrance to the parish graveyard: -

"This school was erected
Principally at the expense of
The Revd. **John Perring M.A** *Vicar;*
Aided by a grant from the **National Society**
AD 1839"

This same clergyman baptised the following children of **John** and **Ann Smith.**

When Baptised?	**When Baptised?**
Christened, 4/2/1827	Christened, 6/9/1829
Born, 1/11/1826	Born 29/6/1829
No. 2107	No. 176
Child's Christian Name	**Child's Christian Name**
Samuel Son of	Susanna Wilson Daughter of
Parent's Name	**Parent's Name**
Christian	**Christian**
John	John
Anne	Anne
Surname	**Surname**
Smith	Smith
Abode	**Abode**
Sutton	Sutton
Quality, Trade or profession	**Quality, Trade or profession**

On some documents my Great, Great Grandmother's name would appear simply as **'Ann'** without the *'e,'* whilst **Susanna** sometimes had the letter *'h'* appended to it. Throughout this history, I have used the spelling as it was originally written in a document (even if it contradicted the spelling of other documents). Where possible I have re-constructed the oft-found irregular presentation of a document to give the reader a *'feel'* of what these documents looked like when originally composed.

Warren (1999) pp. 6 & 12 revealed that **John Perring** was a *'pluralist'* Vicar with more than one church under his care. His main *'living'* was at **Kildwick Village,** delegating the services at **Skipton Parish Church** to the care of his curate. In **August 1813,** he called an important meeting of Churchwardens and influential townspeople at **Skipton** to push through the decision to set up a new Parish School there, under the auspices of a special Committee of Management. As its chairman, **John Perring** played a prominent role in persuading wealthy members of the community to make generous donations. In the end, £305 was raised from **82** subscribers with half of the amount coming from six members of the Committee themselves.

The name **Susanna** provided further evidence that **John Smith** was indeed the son born to **William** and **Susanna Smith** in **June 1805.** It was often the case that sons would name a daughter born to them after their own mother. This was particularly the case if the mother had died relatively young and there was a desire to honour her name. **John's** occupation as Corn Miller established another link with **William Smith** and suggested he was following in his father's footsteps and was more likely to have worked at the mill located on the boundary of **Crosshills** and Even in the mid-nineteenth century, there appears to have been a marked lack of literacy in the family. At this stage, he could only leave a mark.

<h3 style="text-align:center">Section 3: A Winter's Birth</h3>

Concerning the birth of my Great Grandfather

Written in a very untidy manner, the entry for my Great Grandfather's birth read as follows: -

*"**Edmund Smith,** son of **John** and **Ann Smith** of **Sutton** in the Parish of **Kildwick** in the county of **York,** was born on the twenty-first of **January** the thousand*

eight hundred and thirty-two. Registered by **David Marsh,** *Dissenting Minister* **April 22, 1832.** (on **Easter Sunday.**)
> *Witnesses* **Robert Clough**
> **John Parkinson.**"

Being registered on the same day as **Edmund** was: *"**John Edward Clough,** son of **Robert** and **Mary Clough.** Was born at **Valley** [Farm] in the township of **Sutton** in the bounds of **York** the twenty-fifth day of **September** one thousand eight hundred and thirty-one. Registered by* **David Marsh,** *Dissenting Minister* **April 22, 1832.**
> *Witnessed* **Geo: Wilson**
> **John Storey.**"

The lengthy gap between birth and registration was not unusual – it seemed common parental practice to ensure the newest child survived the first few weeks of infancy before registering him or her. **Pilling p. 11** revealed that the **Rev. Jonathan David Marsh** was a former student at **Horton Baptist College** in **Bradford.** After accepting an invitation to the pastorate, he *"entered upon his ministry in* **January 1833.** *Considerable numbers were added to the Church during his brief stay, but in* **1836** *he left to take the pastorate of a newly-formed church at* **Ashton-under-Lyme."** At the time of **Edmund's** birth, **Sutton Baptist** was experiencing an interregnum, which was to last from **1826** until **1833.** So, until his own appointment to the pastorate in **1833, David Marsh** was perhaps standing in the place of an absent minister. The Chapel must have had enough respect (or desperation) to have invited him to take up the pastorate. His writing proved to be very poor – one hopes that his sermons were of a better quality!

The Census Returns of **1841** and **1851** revealed that a **Robert Clough** was the owner of **Valley Farm,** on a ridge top above **Sutton.** More will be revealed about his background and the tragedies that struck his family in the next chapter.

John Parkinson was the name of a Sunday School Superintendent at **Sutton Baptist Chapel.** The contacts gained through this position probably explained why his signature as a witness also appeared on the three previous birth registrations. (These covered the period of **1830-1831** – with **Edmund's** being the last. After that period, the newly appointed Reverend **Marsh** took over proceedings.) **Mr Parkinson** was a man who appeared to know everybody who needed to be known. Available records reveal he was received into church membership in **1823.** Born at **Cononley** in **1801,** (when its population numbered **876**) he would have been a near contemporary of my Great, Great

Grandfather **John Smith.** This connection was especially interesting because it showed that **John** and **Ann Smith** had enjoyed contact with someone holding a position of responsibility within this same Chapel. Further information would powerfully suggest that members of my family <u>did</u> enjoy a significant connection with this Chapel. Eventually, **John Parkinson** entered the wool trade to become a worsted manufacturer. In communities like **Sutton** business and church contacts were often closely connected. Furthermore, a man's personal reputation was, to some extent, determined by his skill and honesty in business. (Later cited records showed that a moral failure in this area could lead to exclusion from the Chapel.) *'Respectability'* was the key to *'getting on'* in that sort of community. For his part, **Geo Wilson** appears to have been the brother (or father) of **Ann** as her maiden name had been *'Wilson.'* Together, these people had witnessed the registration of a child who would grow to exercise a profound influence on the future development of the **Smith** family. He would become both a towering and controversial figure who would become a subject of discussion and public lectures well into the twenty-first century.

Section 4: An American Connection

Concerning Family links with America

The origin of my Great, Great Grandmother's family the **Wilsons** only came to light extremely late in this *'Research'* – in **South London** on **Friday, July 13**[th], 2018. It turned out that their place of origin had been the weaving community of **Haworth** – a place later made famous by the **Brontë** sisters. Their story really begins with the birth of **Ann Wilson's** older sister **Hannah** to **Edmund** and **Nancy Wilson** on **Saturday, 25**[th] **February 1804.** At the age of fifteen, **Hannah** joined the **Methodists** and two years later found *'The Prince of Peace'* and became a **Christian** Believer. She seemed to have been a strong-willed young lady, for, despite violent opposition from her parents, she moved to **Sutton Manor** and married a weaver and preacher named **Thomas Sewell Bottomley** on **Monday, 24**[th] **June 1824** – exactly one month after her sister **Anne's** marriage to my Great, Great grandfather **John.** It was in **Sutton** that **Hannah's** first child (also called **John**) was born. Her husband appeared to have entertained radical political views for, in **1827** he and his wife migrated to **America** – landing in **New York** on **Wednesday, 4**[th] **July.** The grounds he gave for leaving **England** were that he wanted to live in a Republic, rather than in *'a land of Lords and Ladies.'* By **1849,** he and **Hannah** had, after some wanderings, settled in **Kentucky** (later to be a major Civil War battleground) and were thoroughly assimilated into **American Society. Thomas** would live to be **89** and become a successful preacher on the **Methodist** circuit – only finally dying on **27th September 1894** in **Hopkinsville, Christian County, Kentucky U.S.A.** (His wife had pre-deceased him at the same place on **3rd July 1882.**) Details on a Family History ancestry site revealed that his birth had occurred on **2nd June 1805**, at **Cononley Woodside** (near the village of **Cononley**) in **Yorkshire, England.** A photograph of **Thomas** in early middle age revealed him to be a lean, ascetic-looking man with a gaunt, pinched face. His eyes were raised upward as if receiving some divine revelation. He looked every inch a fundamentalist preacher of the nineteenth century. In contrast, his wife was a large, **Yorkshire** lady who looked as though she could provide her husband with a dose of sound common sense.

On **5th February 1831,** (when in **Maryland) Thomas** and **Hannah** had a daughter whose full name was **Hannah Wilson Bottomley.** She would live on into her early nineties, not expiring until **28th October 1923** at **Saint Joseph Buchanan, Missouri.** At **Taylor County, Kentucky, Hannah** married a Reverend **David Morton** – a fellow **Kentuckian** who'd been born on **4th June 1833.** A talented preacher with a keen interest in Family History, he rose high in **Methodist** circles and was subject to a **1916** biography by a **Methodist** Bishop (with the splendid name of **Elijah Embree Hoss, 1849-1919).** A photograph of **David** revealed a strong-looking man with a mane of black hair – and an expression which suggested a speciality in *'Hellfire and Damnation Sermons'* – which were popular at that time. In contrast, his wife was a conventional mid-nineteenth century lady in a crinoline type dress, broach and neatly parted hair. She was rather pretty. The following biographical details (taken from *'Texas Archive Resources online'*) provide an outline of his life and career: -

*"**David Morton (1833-1898)** was born in **Russellville, Kentucky,** the third son of* *Marmaduke B. and **Nancy Caldwell Morton.** He studied at **Russellville Male** *Academy, a **Baptist**-related school, later known as **Bethel College.** On **December** *25, 1851, **Morton** had a dramatic conversion experience. A few months later, in the spring* *of 1852, the **Russellville** station quarterly conference of the **Methodist Episcopal** *Church, South (MECS)** granted him a license to preach. In **1853 Morton** was* *admitted on trial to the **Louisville Conference,** and in **1855** he was ordained **Deacon** *and admitted in full connection. **Elder's** ordination followed in **1857.***

*"**Rev. Morton's** ministerial appointments in the **Louisville Conference** of the* *MECS** included: **Mammoth Cave circuit (1853-54); Campbellsville circuit** *(1854-1856); Bardstown station (1857); Owensboro station (1858-1860);** *Agent, Southern Kentucky College at Bowling Green (1860-1861); Elkton**

circuit (1861-1863); Hopkinsville circuit (1863-1864); President, Russellville Female Academy (1864-1868); Agent, Board of Education of the Louisville Conference (1868); Agent, Logan Female Academy (1868-1873); Presiding Elder, Russellville district (1873-1876); Educational Agent, Louisville Conference (1877); Elkton circuit (1878-1879); and Presiding Elder, Louisville district (1879-1882). Morton also served briefly in the Denver Conference of the MECS as Presiding Elder of the Montana district and as Chaplain of the Montana Senate (1876-1877).

David Morton served as a delegate to seven consecutive General Conferences of the MECS beginning in 1870 and as a delegate to the Ecumenical Methodist Conferences of 1881 [in England]and 1891. He was instrumental in the founding of the MECS Board of Church Extension and guided the board as Corresponding Secretary from 1882 until his death in 1898. In 1883 Centenary College, Jackson, Louisiana, conferred upon Rev. Morton an honorary Doctor of Divinity degree. From 1891 to 1898 Morton served as President of the Board of Managers of the Vanderbilt Training School in Elkton, Kentucky.

David Morton married Hannah Wilson Bottomley (1831-1924) on August 8, 1854. Their nine children included Daniel Morton, M.D., who donated the David Morton papers to Southern Methodist University on June 15, 1929."

David Morton turned out to be a crucially important source of information. He seemed to have a passion for family history. Whilst attending the **Ecumenical Methodist Conference** of **1881** (which I've underlined) he would be entertained by my Great Grandparents at **Vernon Road.** And provided a vivid description of both my Great grandparents and their way of life. He liked **Yorkshire** which was a sign of good judgement. I have little doubt that the **Reverend Morton** would have shared the **Gospel** with my forebears if he saw a need. In that period, **Protestant Christianity** was not the useless *'wishy-washy'* pseudo-faith of today. We do know that, during the year of his meeting with **Edmund, David Morton** had preached a sermon entitled, *"A Watch Night Sermon"* based on **John 13:17** which reads, *"For God sent not his Son into the world to condemn the world; but that the world through him might be saved."*

The main relevance of the **Morton's** lay in the vast amount of information they provided in their *'Kin Book'* and with the contacts enjoyed with the **Smiths** over a period of ninety years. In **1913, James** (the eldest son of my Great Grandfather **Edmund**) apparently took members of the **Morton** Family Line for a guided tour (of all the previously described) sites in the **Kildwick** locality. During the First World War the **Morton's** sent food parcels to **James** and on

19th **November 1925, James** received a visit from a **Dr Paul Morton** who was touring **European** Hospitals to research into best medical practice. Some form of contact was maintained in connection with **James'** Granddaughter until they petered in about **1970.** The last known contact was with **David Morton's** Granddaughter, **Mary Morton Hillix (1912-2010)** who had been a teacher and a member of **First Baptist Church** at **Saint Joseph, Buchanan County, Missouri.** Although this link was to fade out it did show that the **Smiths** had long-standing family contacts outside of **Britain**. Whether this present history will renew this **American** connection remains to be seen.

Section 5: Constructing a Genealogy

Concerning the Smith line of Descent

A careful analysis of parish records made in **April 2018,** attempted to construct a genealogy going back before **1700.** This was done by tracing clusters of *'re-occurring forenames'* like *'George'* and *'Edward'* that occurred together across successive generations. As an earlier study showed, **Hugh Smith** the founder of the Charity school had two sons by with those names. (Tellingly, **Hugh** had an elder brother called *'George'* who had been baptised on **10th August 1617.**) However, both the younger **Hugh** and **Edward** appeared to have married several years too late to have been the father of my direct ancestor with the same name. A more hopeful candidate was his elder brother **George** who married in **May 1678** around the right time for my first proven ancestor **Edward Smith** to have been born. Unfortunately, further research showed that although he had two male children around the period of **1680-82,** neither of them was named **Edward.** Reluctantly, I concluded that *'re-occurring forenames'* wasn't by itself a sufficient means of constructing an accurate line of descent. Other evidence would be needed to back it up. This limitation meant I couldn't push much beyond **1700.**

On a more definite note, information (obtained from the **Northallerton Archive Centre** on **Friday, July 6th, 2001**) allowed me to begin drawing a direct line of descent that that eventually led me back to my Great, Great, Great, Great Grandfather **Edward** (or **Edmund**) **Smith** the weaver. Following painstaking studies of relevant information sources, I was able to construct and repeatedly check out the following line of descent: -

1. <u>**Edwardius Smith (c.1681-1753)**</u> who married **Margareta Emott (1682-1757)** on **8/10/1700;** on **6/7/1701** they baptised a son: -

2. <u>**George Smith (1701-1764)**</u> *'A Weaver'* who married **Mary Robinson (c.1701-1759)** on **7/4/1735**; on **13/11/1743** they baptised a son: -
3. <u>**Edward (or Edmund) Smith (1743-1811)**</u> *'A Weaver'* who married **Elizabeth Pighels (1747-1796)** on **18/10/1768** who, on **2/11/1778** gave birth to a son: -
4. <u>**William Smith (1778-1850)**</u> *'A Miller,'* who married **Susanna Emmot (1776-1821)** on **7/2/1799** who, on **17/3/1805** gave birth to a son: -
5. <u>John Smith (1805-1843)</u> *'A Corn Miller,'* who married **Ann Wilson (1803-1844)** on **24/5/1824** who on **21/1/1832** gave birth to a son: -
6. <u>**Edmund Smith (1832-1915)**</u> *'A Commercial Traveller in woollen cloth,'* who married **Rosamond Stamford (1843-1891)** his second wife on **10/12/1867** who, on **23/9/1869** gave birth to a son: -
7. <u>**Fred Heselwood Smith (1869-1939)**</u> *'A Commercial Traveller, selling men's worsted clothing'* who married **Elizabeth Foster (1871-1947)** on **27/6/1899** who on **6/2/1914** gave birth to a son: -
8. <u>**Fred Gordon Smith (1914-1999)**</u> *'A Clothing Representative'* who married **Cynthia Absalom (1923-?)** on **13/12/1941** who, on **3/5/1956** gave birth to a son: -
9. <u>**Richard John Smith (1956-?)**</u> the author of this book, (*'A self-published writer and Private Tutor offering English, Business Studies, Social Science and History'*) who married a tireless proofreader **June Elizabeth Shinn** (birth date **22/12/1956**) on **23/6/1979** in **Newcastle-Upon-Tyne** who, on **14/11/1980** gave birth to a daughter and also to three sons, born in **1/6/1983**, **18/1/1986** and **27/7/1988** respectively. Their middle son became the father of
10. A male, born on **23/7/2009** and a female, born on **2/5/2013** who together will contribute to the future history of the **Smiths.**

One noticeable feature of the first four generations on this list was that most of the **Smiths** were long-lived by the standards of their time. This supported previously cited evidence that they were of hardy stock and had been spared the worst hardships of the historical periods they lived in. Their way of doing this had been to maintain their social and financial respectability through a mixture of shrewd business dealings, strategic marriage alliances, community involvement and self-improvement through education. *'Aspirational'* would be the most appropriate word to describe them.

CHAPTER 4: LOCAL DIFFICULTIES

Section 1: The Kildwick Friendly Society

Concerning the Kildwick Parish Friendly Society

During the late eighteenth and early nineteenth centuries destitution was an ever-present threat. Violently oscillating trade cycles meant that even wealthy manufacturers could end their days in a workhouse. There was no real security during the early industrial period. In response to this situation, *'Friendly Societies'* were set up to provide some form of insurance in the event of sickness or unexpected death. One of these was the **Kildwick Parish Friendly Society,** which had already been established by **1/1/1799**. In exchange for **2/-** paid in by each member per quarter, each would receive **7/-** weekly if unable to work in the case of illness or injury. An entry book recorded the rules of this Society and indicated that drunkenness was a problem **(Wood 1973, p.56).**

KILDWICK PARISH FRIENDLY SOCIETY

January 1ˢᵗ 1799

Rules

1. *Every member to pay* **2/-** *quarterly into the box, besides the allowance for a pint of ale.*
2. *Any members sick or lame or otherwise indisposed so as to render him unfit to work shall receive* **7/-** *weekly.*
3. *When a member shall depart this life, there shall be paid the sum of* **5gns** *(Guineas) out of the box to defray expenses of the funeral*
4. *After payment for* **12** *months to any member, his pay will then be only* **5/-** *per week*
5. *Any member refusing to conform to the rules shall forfeit* **6d** *to the box*
6. *Any member joining the procession in a state of intoxication or behaving disorderly or absent from Divine Service shall forfeit* **1/-** *to the box*
7. *The Master and Stewards to lead the procession, the rest of the members to follow two abreast, each furnished with a sprig of green oak.*

(Presumably, these *'processions'* took place to celebrate the Annual Feast Day – the carrying of a sprig of oak was a custom that perhaps had its origins in an ancient fertility rite.)

To ascertain whether any of my forbears enjoyed a connection with this Society I decided to carefully examine and replicate some of its archives during a visit paid to **Keighley Library** on **Thursday, March 1st, 2001.** As the following extracts, will show, these archives provided some intriguing details concerning the **Smiths** of **Sutton** and other connected families. An insight was also gained into the type of social life enjoyed by the men when they were away from the ladies! (The word *'do'* in the following extract was an old way of saying *'also.'*) Where possible the original layout of the document has been preserved, even if it contains errors and reads badly.

"Annual Day, **October 5th 1826.**

Appointments to Offices for part of the year **1826**
And part of the year **1827.** *As follows viz: -*
James Wilkinson *President*
       Stewards
For **Farnhill, John Wellock**
Do **Cowling, James Snowden**
Do **Thos. Bottomley**
Do **John Riley** *at* **Jackfield, Sutton**
       Committee
Glusburn, Thomas Hopkinson
Connolly, Hugh Watkinson
For **Bradley, Edmund Cockshott**
Sutton, Wm. Dickenson *and* **Henry Spencer**
Steeton, James Lund, Silsden, Henry Pickles, Cowling, John Emmott
 Kildwick, William Davihorn,
Farnhill, Michael Brown *and* **Anthony Spencer Junior**

Committee Room **October 5th 1826**
We the Committee have unanimously agreed that the Committee
Shall in future have two quarts
Of ale on the Annual Feast
Wm. Skinner   **Joseph Dickinson**
    Wm. Heaton   **Wm. Hind**
Wm. Green   **Wm. Wilson**
John Longbottom   **Wm. Stott**
Jonathan Green Wm. Laycock
Richard Brigg."

Based on this resolution it was possible to deduce that those involved in the **Kildwick Parish Friendly Society** liked their ale. This refreshment will have been drunk from pewter tankards – with the participants in this group eating what was likely to have been the very traditional pub fare of roast beef, potatoes and an assortment of vegetables. Conversation at such an event would have revolved around business and village gossip. *"Talking scandal"* may well have proved a popular pastime! An important national event like the recent **Buttershaw** banking crash **(1825-26)** will have been topical. It reputedly ruined half the manufacturers in **Keighley** and almost bankrupted the famous **Scottish** writer **Sir Walter Scott** (even though the **Scottish** banking System was far less badly affected than its **English** counterpart).

The falling price of cotton could also have been a sombre subject of debate. As the ale flowed, some of the conversations at the Annual Dinner must have assumed a bawdier tone. The room in which they met would have been dark, illuminated only by candles and a flickering coal (or log) fire. One interesting name to surface was that of a **William Wilson**, who may have been **John Smith's** father-in-law (or brother-in-law). However, the records showed that **William Wilson's** signature did not appear on any other Friendly Society Records after **October 1826.** This meant that he may never have had any contact with my Great, Great Grandfather **John Smith.**

The first **Smith** to be found in the records of **Kildwick Parish Friendly Society** was a **Robert Smith** of **Sutton,** listed as serving on the Committee at the Annual Feast Day held on **October 4ᵗʰ 1827.** However, the find of most interest was the simultaneous presence at the Annual Day (held on **October 7ᵗʰ, 1830**) of **John Smith** from **Sutton** and **John Parkinson** from **Glasburn,** (sometimes spelt **Glusburn** in old documents). The latter name was important because **John Parkinson** was a witness at my Great Grandfather **Edmund's** birth registration at **Sutton Baptist Chapel** in **April 1832.** At that event, his name had also appeared in association with my Great, Great Grandmother **Ann Smith.** Throughout this period his name was often associated with Great, Great Grandfather **John Smith.** Indeed, **John Parkinson** seemed quite an interesting character in his own right – a most active individual who seemed to have been *'in on'* everything! Such was the extent of his involvement that it was easy to conjecture that *'where there was a Committee there was **John Parkinson!'*** Consequently, his was a name that frequently cropped up in the research for this Family History; it seemed he had to be *'in on'* this enterprise too! As a community leader, he could perhaps truthfully claim, *"everybody knows me."*

To provide some form of context the official committee appointments for this Annual Day will be recorded in full – along with other relevant details. One can assume that to get onto the Committee both **John Smith** and **John Parkinson** will have needed to have been active participants in the Friendly Society for at least a few years. Therefore, it seems reasonable to assume that they will have been present at the same time **William Wilson** was around, four years previously.

"Annual Day **October 7ᵗʰ 1830.**

Appointments to offices for part of the year **1830**
And **1831** *are as follows viz.*
President **Joseph Wilcock**

Stewards
John Clarkson *for* **Silsden**
Samuel Gott *for* **Cowling**
John Dickinson, Sutton
John Heaton, Farnhill

Committee

<u>**John Smith**</u>	*Sutton*
John Shackleton	*Sutton*
Joseph Right	*Silsden*
<u>**John Parkinson**</u>	*Glusburn*
Thomas Walbank	*Glusburn*
Roger Couper	*Connolly*
Roland Harrison	*Cowling*
Frank Restwick	*Farnhill*
John Todd	*Farnhill*
William Hinde	*Steeton."*

Unfortunately, a secretary had recorded all the relevant names so that no original signatures (or marks) were available to compare with those found in other documents. This meant that it wasn't possible to establish for certain whether the **John Smith** (whose name appeared in these documents) was my ancestor or some other **John Smith.** (If he were not it would be necessary to conclude that **John Parkinson** was closely involved with two **John Smiths** from the **Sutton** locality. Given the extent of this man's contacts this was not impossible.)

On the Annual Day of **October 6ᵗʰ, 1831, John Smith** was re-elected to serve on the Committee. **John Parkinson** was one of eleven signatories approving a unanimous (if somewhat obscure) motion *"that in future the stewards shall have the power to stop all deficiencies belonging* [to] *the sick members of this society the first weekly day the fines go to the benefit of the box."* (Among the signatures was one belonging to **Robert Smith** who would later become an influential figure in this Society.) By this juncture, my Great Grandfather **Edmund Smith** was some five and a half months grown inside his mother's womb.

The **Kildwick Parish Friendly Society** Committee minutes also made it possible to trace developments throughout the nine and a half months following **Edmund's** birth.

"Copy of a notice to committeemen

Sir/ A committee meeting is appointed to be held at the
Clubhouse **Farnhill** *at the hour of Seven O Clock*
In the evening on **Saturday** *the 19ᵗʰ instant, when*
Your attendance will be required at the time
And place above mentioned
Sutton, May 16ᵗʰ 1832   *yours* **Wm. Walton**
                                          Clerk."

The reason behind this urgent summons was duly recorded. It showed something of the financial concerns involved in a period of high economic and political uncertainty – where there had been much agitation for parliamentary reform. (**1832** had been the year in which the Great Parliamentary Reform Act was passed.)

"Clubhouse, **May 19ᵗʰ 1832**
The Committee resolves that the **£250** *due*
From the Canal Company to be paid off the
31ˢᵗ day of May *shall be lodged in the*
Savings bank at **Skipton."**

Whilst the Committee bustled about its business, my Great Grandfather would have been suckling from his mother just before being put to bed. Like many wives in the village, she may have been glad that her husband was out for the night. At only five months old, **Edmund** will already have begun to raise his head – looking at those objects and people nearest to him – oblivious of any larger affairs of the world. His exhausted mother may have sung him lullabies to send him to sleep. It was easy to imagine **Edmund** being a rather active if a somewhat delicate baby. **Ann Smith** would not have had the faintest idea that her son was to be the *'lynchpin'* upon which the future destiny of many **Smith**s would rest. She could never have dreamt that the baby she held in her arms would be a source of considerable interest to family members at the beginning of the twenty-first century. And, of course, she could not have foreseen that her own name would be plucked from obscurity and published worldwide on the Internet.

Almost every club has its *'problem member'* and in the case of **Kildwick Parish Friendly Society** that member was **Thomas Greenwood.** Hints of trouble could be seen in the following curt notice: -
"Copy of a notice sent to committeemen
July 12th concerning **Thomas Greenwood**
Sir,
*   The Committee meeting is appointed*
To be held at the Clubhouse **Farnhill** *at the*
Hour of Eight o' Clock in the evening on
Saturday next the **14th Inst.** *when your*
Attendance will be required at the time and
Place above mentioned.

Sutton July 12th   *Yours*
1832   **William Walton**
                              Clerk

Thomas Greenwood would cause more difficulties later on.

Following a period of service lasting two years, **John Smith** was not listed as being appointed for any office on the Annual Day held on **October 4th 1832.** A **James Ramsden** and a **William Heaton** (both of **Sutton**) had taken his place. However, one does find a **William Smith** serving as a steward for **Glasburn** and **Sutton** and an **Edmund Smith** serving as a steward for **Cowling** – the **1841** Census showing the latter as a farmer by occupation. **James Wilkinson** acted as President. **John Smith** may still have been present at this meeting as his one-year term on the Committee had not quite ended. This implied that he was to voluntarily relinquish his responsibilities to this society, possibly because of an impending move. His name was added to the following resolution, which contained some evidence of a financial problem.
"October 4th 1832 clubhouse
We the undersigned committee

Have resolved
Unanimously that in future
*The **3s 6d** pay shall be*
2s 6d Thomas Green
James Laycock   David Snowden
William Dickinson John Holmes
John Smith
John Longbottom
Henry Clapham
William Roe
William Smith."

The other business transacted that day was the direct result of a dispute with the Clubhouse Landlord. As was often the case in such matters the problem revolved around money.

"*Clubhouse **Farnhill October 1832***
The committee, this evening have unanimously resolved
To have the Club Box moved to another House
*In consequence of **Mr Palfryman** saying to*
The committee then sat, that he lost money by
Providing Dinners for the members of the club.
The business was immediately carried over, when
Put to the vote there was not one dissenting voice.
One of the Committee was immediately sent to
***Mr Henry Stirk** at the **Old White Bear** who has agreed*
To take in the Club and provide for them at the
*Same rate now paid to **Mr Palfryman**, the box*
Was accordingly removed this evening,
            October 4th
            1832."

Of special interest was the absence of any dissenting voice. The Committee appears to have given **Mr Palfryman** very short shrift. Perhaps they had been dissatisfied with his services for quite some time. One is left wondering how he felt about the Club's defection to a nearby competitor. However, he managed to survive the defection of the Friendly Society for the **1841** Census showed him remaining in business as an Innkeeper: -

William Palfryman aged **60**, *'Innkeeper'* at **Low Farnhill**
Jane aged **57**
Ann aged **30**
Sarah aged **30**
Richard aged **31** *'Butcher'*
Samuel Parkin aged **35** *'Agricultural Labourer'*
Hugh Watson aged **25** *'Lawyer'*

One can only speculate over what had brought a young lawyer into the locality and why he chose to stay in the same accommodation as an agricultural labourer? **Pigot's Trade Directory** for **1834** confirmed that the name of **Mr Palfryman's** Inn was *'The Ship.'* The entry recording his business details spelt his name *'Palfreeman.'* This was the spelling used in the Parish Monumental Inscriptions for **Kildwick** Parish Church. I examined these at **Skipton** Reference Library on **Thursday, 5/4/2001.** They revealed that **William Palfreeman** had lived to an exceptionally good age for a man in a trade where the temptation to heavy drinking was severe. His inscription stated: -

William Palfreeman of **Farnhill**	**March 30**th, **1860, 86** years
Jane his wife	**June 4**th, **1846, 63**rd year
Harrison infant	
William	**November 22**nd, **1862, 49** years
Jane widow of son **William**	
Thomas son of **William Senior**	**June 15**th, **1875, 54**th year
Alice wife of **Thomas**	**February 4**th, **1899, 74** years

On a separate headstone was inscribed the name: -
Richard Palfreeman of **Bradford** late of **Farnhill, November 24**th,**1863, 43** years

A search of the Marriage Registers for **Kildwick** (at **Northallerton Archive Centre** on **Friday, June 15**th, **2001**) showed **William Palfryman** acting as a witness for quite a sizable number of weddings. The frequent presence of his rather cramped signature implied that he was a popular figure who seemed good to have around on a joyful family occasion where the ale would be flowing freely. He always spelt his surname *'Palfreeman'* phonetically (*i.e.* as it sounded). The signature of his wife **Jane** confirmed that she too was literate. In **1841, Farnhill** was a small township with a total population of **459.** A visit to **Farnhill** (made with my wife on **Sunday, 2**nd **January 2011**) failed to discover the location of **Palfryman's** inn though there were one or two old buildings where it could have been.

The **1834 Pigot's Trade Directory** also revealed the presence of a *'boot and shoemaker'* called **John Parkinson** in **Glasburn.** He may have been the brother of a **Robert Parkinson** in **Crosshills** who, during this period, followed the same trade – although by **1841** he was a grocer.

The Census for **1841** also showed **John Parkinson** to be now living in **Eastburn,** a village just down the lane from **Sutton Mill.** He was living alone except for a **15-year** old maidservant called **Martha Staw!** Ten years later he was married to a **54-year** old lady called **Susanna,** (he himself was then aged **50**). The **1851** Census also revealed him to be a worsted manufacturer who had been born in **Cononley,** (which I briefly visited on my way to **Skipton** on a very wet **Thursday, April 5th, 2001**). Lodging with them was a **Peter Scott** (aged **57**) Minister at **Sutton Baptist Chapel** from **1854** until **1857.** The fact that **John Parkinson** did not appear to have any children perhaps freed him to participate in a wide range of community activities. The **1861** Census revealed that he was no longer living at **Eastburn.**

Significantly, **John Smith** vanished from the scene at a time when I expected him to have done so. Later cited evidence was to confirm that he had left **Sutton** to look for employment opportunities elsewhere. His active involvement in the affairs of the **Kildwick Parish Friendly Society** indicated that, at least until **October 1832,** his life had been free of any traumatic events such as the loss of a wife. Overall, **John Smith** appears to have been a sociable sort of man who enjoyed his ale. However, the same couldn't be said for **Thomas Greenwood** who, as the following extracts show, was to cause yet more problems.

*"The following is a copy of a notice sent to the Committee on the **12th Novr 1834."***

Sir/ A committee meeting is appointed to be held
*At the Clubhouse **Crosshills** at half past seven.*
O Clock in the evening on Saturday next
*The **15th Novr** when your attendance will be required*
At the time & place mentioned.

Sutton Novr 12th   *Yours*
     1834   **Wm. Walton**
                     Clerk

The reason for this urgent request was explained in the following notice.

"The above meeting was convened on account of
Thos Greenwood's *irregular conduct when paying*
On the club who agree to pay the fine
Of **ten shillings & 6d** *specified in the*
17ᵗʰ article, *which fine he promised to pay*
At the Annual Feast Day, next ensuing."

The conduct of this **Thomas Greenwood** must have been very *'irregular'* as the fine of **10/6** almost amounted to the weekly wage of a skilled worker! Something far more serious than turning up drunk at a meeting had been involved. Yet the precise nature of his *'irregular conduct'* can only be guessed at. Whatever it was it must have been rather longstanding and seemed to have involved the misuse of money. Perhaps there had been some arrears in his contributions? At the time of this confrontation, my Great Grandfather **Edmund** had entered the third year of his life and was living away from **Sutton** – now in **Cullingworth** with his parents **John** and **Anne.** By this time, he'd been joined by a younger brother named **Daniel** who had been born on **27ᵗʰ June 1834.** He was to achieve as much as **Edmund** but in a different sphere of activity.

The minutes of **Kildwick Parish Friendly Society** ended in **September 1855.** They consisted of the usual list of names and committee resolutions on mundane administrative matters. Certain key individuals had displayed a long-lasting commitment right up to the end. **Robert Smith** had served as *'Clerk'* from **1839** until **1846** whilst **Benjamin Smith** had acted as *'steward'* for **Sutton** from **7/10/1841** until late **1844.** At the Annual Feast Day (held on **October 4ᵗʰ, 1849)** *"the following persons were appointed to the following offices"* **John Cockshott** was President, **Roland Smith** acted as steward for **Sutton, Robert Smith** (also of **Sutton**) served on the committee, and the ubiquitous **John Parkinson** acted as steward for **Steeton.** Records connected to **Sutton Chapel** show **Roland Smith** to have been a devout **Baptist,** yet despite his evident religious convictions he still felt free to hold a responsible position in a society that met in a public house and consumed generous quantities of ale! Apparently absent during the late **1840s** was any rigid demarcation between Chapel and Public House. Evidence (provided by **Wood**) confirmed that the Temperance Movement did not begin to influence **Sutton Chapel** until the late **1860s.** An earlier generation of Chapel members appeared not to have been troubled by any conflict between their faith and their attendance at the **White Bear Inn.** Their attitude was more akin to that of today rather than the late **Victorian** Era when to be a member of the Chapel was to be identified with teetotalism. The following extract, written in neat script writing, provides confirmation of this point.

"Committee Room **October 5ᵗʰ1854**
In consequence of the members not attending
To put in and nominate officers according to the
Rules of the society the officers now acting
Were obliged to hold office for this year
When it was unanimously agreed
To have the box and society removed to
The **Old White Bear Inn, Crosshills**
When the landlord agreed to furnish
Each member with a dinner on the
Next Annual Feast Day.
The box was removed accordingly.
Robert Smith, *Secretary."*

It seemed that, following several decades of honourable service to its members, the **Kildwick Parish Friendly Society** was now in decline – having been replaced by other forms of insurance provision. Most of its records seem to have petered out in the late **1850s**. Incidentally, the **1841** Census revealed only two **Robert Smiths** living in **Sutton**. One, an agricultural labourer, born in about **1810** (too young to have been an active member in the Society in the **1820s**) and the other a worsted manufacturer, who would have been of the same generation as my Great, Great Grandfather **John Smith**. (This **Robert Smith** had lived at **Low End** on the **North Side** of the **Turnpike Road**.) The high standard of literacy displayed in his role as secretary strongly implied that the **Robert Smith** of the Friendly Society was most probably the worsted manufacturer of the same name.

My Great, Great Grandfather's probable connections with **John Parkinson, Benjamin Smith** and **Robert Smith** have one common feature; these associations were with men engaged in worsted manufacturing. The influence of such connections may have persuaded **John Smith** that working in this growing industrial area would be a good option for his son **Edmund** to follow. Almost of equal significance was the fact that his best friends (or at least close associates) were businessmen. This powerfully suggested that his own commercial reputation as a Millwright (during the **1830s**) must have been a respectable one. In those days, businessmen did not usually associate with those they regarded as being *'disreputable.'* Should they have done so, they would have risked their own personal ruin. Maintaining respectability in the tightly knit communities in which my ancestors lived was hugely valued and something greatly sought after.

Whilst visiting the locality on **Monday, 19th March 2001,** I located *'The Old White Bear Inn, Crosshills.'* An inscription (in a somewhat eroded capstone above the doorway) showed that the building had first been constructed in **1735.** One interesting feature was a flight of stone steps leading from outside to an upper room. This most likely would have been the dining area where the Friendly Society had held their Annual Dinners. The regular clientele would have partaken of their local refreshment downstairs. The Inn was only about twenty-five minutes' walk from **Sutton.** For most of the members, it was perhaps at a far more convenient location than **Mr Palfryman's** Inn *'The Ship'* at **Farnhill.** (Incidentally, the *'White Bear'* Pub at nearby **Eastburn,** is <u>not</u> to be confused with this Public House. In **1834,** this <u>second</u> *'White Bear'* pub was under the proprietorship of a **John Wilkinson.**)

During my 54th birthday celebration (on **Monday, 2nd May 2010**) I managed to visit *'The Old White Bear Inn'* with my wife, middle son, daughter in law and grandchild (who'd been born on **Thursday 23rd July 2009**). Thanks to the kindness of the proprietors we could see the upper room where the Friendly Society had met. It was full of unwanted furniture and other junk but on the whitewashed ceiling, the old beams could be seen, as well as a large stone fireplace. Its structure and décor appear to have remained unchanged since the days of the Friendly Society. They were also kind enough to show us the room once again when my wife and I revisited the premises (along with my second cousin once removed) on **Saturday, 5th September 2015.** (It was still full of the same junk we'd seen previously.) A member of staff divulged that it had, until recently, been used as a small brewery.

A less exciting (but still highly informative document) was the **Kildwick Parish Friendly Society Sick Book,** dating from **1782** until **1853.** It consisted mainly of a list of names and payments. The earliest **Smith** on record was a **Benjamin Smith** who was paid **4/-** for one week's sickness on **July 4th, 1782.** Next on the list was a **John Smith** (not my ancestor) who had received **5/-** for one week's sickness on **February 10th, 1783.** However, perhaps the most interesting entry was that of a **John Smith Senior** of **Sutton** whose sick pay evidently amounted to an old age pension. The length of time he received this form of payment suggested that he had suffered an old age characterised by a great deal of infirmity. He first appeared on the records on **July 7th, 1831,** along with a **John Smith** of **Glasburn.** His payment at that stage was **6/-** per week. By **January**

1832, his weekly payment was **5/-,** by **August 16ᵗʰ** of that year it was down to **3/6,** by **9/9/1833** it had been reduced to **2/6** and to a paltry **1/6** in **April 1838.** It remained at that level until the final payments late in **1838.** My own estimation – based on these records – was that his death had taken place in late **November 1838.** His case showed that the Friendly Society could only meet needs for a rather limited time-period. His last income from this source would barely have paid the rent.

Section 2: The Poor and the Destitute

Concerning poverty in a West Yorkshire Village

One especially fascinating document was the *'Disbursements to the Poor Book'* for **Sutton.** It covered the period from **1785** until **1809,** naming those who were in receipt of poor relief. A review of those listed revealed plenty of **Cravens** and **Wilsons** but <u>not one **Smith!**</u> Even if I had overlooked a few names the fact remained that, in proportion to their numbers the **Smiths** were <u>underrepresented</u> in the *'Poor Book.'* This absence provided <u>decisive</u> evidence that the **Smiths** (in a social sense) was located <u>above</u> the poorest section of the community. They were neither wealthy landowners (like the **Spencers**) nor were they *'up and coming'* industrialists (like the **Bairstows**). Instead, they were more of *'a middling sort of people'* who knew how to be self-sufficient. Their signatures (as witnesses to the fact that the poor relief accounts had been properly examined) provided telling evidence of their *'respectable'* position within their local community.

An examination will now be made of the poor relief distribution for **1805** – the year in which **Admiral Lord Nelson** won his famous sea battle against the **French** and **Spanish** navies at **Trafalgar.**) For ease of clarity, the figures have been placed in table form. Whilst being under the authority of the local overseer, a certain **John Smith** had taken a hand in the administration of this form of welfare. The money will have been released into his care from which he will have distributed it to those most in need.

"Disbursements by **Joseph Craven,** *overseer [& Constable]*
For **John Smith** *at* **[Firtops]** *or* **Spencer's Farm**
1ˢᵗ May 1804 *until* **1ˢᵗ May 1805**

Payments	£	s	d	h/f
Monthly Pay	7	19	4	
Weekly do...	123	13	5	
Funeral Expenses	2	14	6	
Clothing	2	7	10	½
House Rents	16	11	6	
Necessities	18	0	7	½
Overseer Expenses	30	7	7	
Constable	60	8	2	
Mole Catching	4	8	4	
To serving the office	8	[9]	[1]	
Vestry coals –	5	2		
4 Loads **15** and a half				
	275	4	2	½
Due to Old offices **1803**	73	18	1	½
	349	2	4	

N.B: **h/f** = *'Half Pennies and Farthings'*

Following a brief record of collections made to pay for the poor rates, the balance for this period closed with the following statement.

"**June 13ᵗʰ, 1805** –
These accts (accounts) have been examined
& allowed errors accepted
By us **W. Dixon**
Wm. Spencer
John Clough
David McCroben
Robert Clough
John Spencer
Richard Smith
James Lister
Benj. Smith
John Parkinson
Wm. Brigg
Thos. Bottomley."

A particularly fascinating feature about the names I underscored was how the **Smiths** were already enjoying close ties with other families, *i.e.* the **Cloughs, McCrobens** and **Parkinson's** at the beginning of the nineteenth century. This was at a time when my Great, Great Grandfather **John Smith** would have been only a three-month-old baby. Subsequent evidence would show that these ties were also present at the time of my Great Grandfather's birth in **January 1832** and continued well into the second half of the nineteenth century. It seems that these same respectable families had all known one another from the late eighteenth century before industrialisation had really taken hold of **Sutton.** In the main, their chief sources of income had been from farming, milling and weaving.

By **June 1807 Napoleon** was the master of **Europe,** but in **Sutton,** the routine distribution of parish poor relief continued unaffected – although the higher amount spent on weekly relief suggested the presence of economic hardship. This, in part, <u>could</u> have been a symptom of the disruption caused by the troubled political and military situation experienced at the time.

"Disbursements by **Joseph Craven** *overseer [& Constable]*
For **Peter Barritt** *at*
Hill Farms **1ˢᵗ May 1805**
Until 1ˢᵗ May1806

Payments	£	s	d	h/f
Monthly Pay	5	7		
Weekly do...	163	16		
Necessities	14	19	4	
House rents	15	16	9	
Funerals	3	15`	10	
Mole Catching	5	3		
Clothing	6	16	9	
Overseer Expenses	6	12	3	
Constable	51	1	7	
To serving the office	8	8		
Paid to old officer	35	14	11	½
	317	11	5	½
& charging journey to **Huddersfield**		8		
	317	19	5	½

Following a brief record of collections received to pay for the poor rates, the balance for this period closed with this statement: -

"*July 2ⁿᵈ 1807 –*

The above accts examined

And allowed errors accepted

By us -----

Wm. Spencer

John Clough

David McCroben

John Spencer

James Lister---

Joshua Cropley

John Smith

John Spencer, Farmer

John Walton

Hiram Butterfield."

N.B: **John Walton** *was possibly the Pastor at* **Sutton Baptist Church.**

Virtually all the signatures appended to the **1805** and **1807** accounts were neatly written – not one 'mark' was present. This confirmed the high degree of literacy existing amongst this circle of men. Somewhere in or around the township a reasonable amount of basic teaching had been (and hopefully) was still taking place. Not only could these men write their names, but they could also understand monetary accounts. This was a skill that some of my own Business Studies students are struggling to grasp today – even with the benefit of the modern education system!

From **1810** until **1827,** no records of poor relief were available. When they do re-appear as the "***Kildwick** Payments Book for **Sutton** Township*" **John Smith** *was 'overseer.'* He held this post until **April 1833** when **Peter Laycock** replaced him. This **John Smith** wrote in beautiful script style, which was to contrast markedly with the far messier style of his successor. His signature, with its decorative curls around the *'J'* and the *'S,'* and its bold crossing of the *'t'* was identical to that of the **John Smith** whose signature appeared in the **1807** audit. He was clearly too old to have been my Great, Great Grandfather of the same name. (Also, my Great, Great Grandfather was illiterate.) Equally apparent was the fact that this **John Smith** was a man of some standing in the local community. The writing gave the impression of a good administrator who knew his own mind on matters. In addition, the length of his involvement in the depressing area of poor relief indicated a high degree of commitment to his surrounding community. This present history owes much to this **Smith** for the meticulous way in which he kept his documents – extracts of which are now given.

John Smith, Overseer **1827**

Payments	£	s	d	h/f
Disbursts in **April**	100	1	4	
Do in **May**	86	1	5	
Do in **June**	111	4	4	½
Do in **August**	107	15	3	½
Do in **September**	89	6	[0]	½
Do in **October**	50	1	4	½
Do in **November**	53	1	1	
Do in **December**	59	18	2	½
Do in **January**	46	5	[0]	
Do in **February**	174	7	5	½
Do in **March**				
	105	12	9	
	5			
Lost in **Bastardy**	13	8	5	
	106	1	2	
	9			
John Smith	8	8	9	

"Overseer to Town"

A review of these figures appeared to show no seasonal fluctuations. During high summer a plentiful supply of outdoor work should have been available, yet this period showed a <u>higher</u> level of payments than the chilly winter months of **January** and **February** when such employment would have been of limited supply. Why this was the case isn't known. The amount spent on poor relief would have represented a sizeable proportion of the township budget, with only a little left to spare for improvements to the roads and other local facilities. Much of the local labour appears to have been of a casual kind, which could easily be laid-off at the first hint of an economic downturn. Consequently, the amount spent on poor relief could suddenly escalate – as demonstrated in the figures for **December 1831** until **March 1832**.

128

Payments	£	s	d	h/f
December 1831				
Weekly Payments	27	3	2	½
Casual Relief	30	8	8	½
Rents	7	8		
Journeys	8	6		
Totals	65	8	5	

Payments	£	s	d	h/f
January 1832				
Weekly Payments	15	18	4	
Casual Relief	17	5	6	
Rents	6	11		
Journeys		11		
Totals	40	15	10	

Payments	£	s	d	h/f
February 1832				
Weekly Payments	20		6	½
Casual Relief	22	1	3	
Rents	3	10		
Journeys	11			
Totals	45	19	8	½

Payments	£	s	d	h/f
March 1832				
Weekly Payments	47	9		
Casual Relief	100	4	3	
Rents	30	9	6	½
Bills	63	10	3	
Journeys		12	6	
Totals	242	5	6	½

The almost five-fold increase in *'casual relief'* strongly supported the view that, in the above period, there had been a sudden and major *'laying off'* of casual labour.

This problem may have arisen because of the economic and political uncertainty involved with the passing of the great Reform Bill in **June 1832.** However, this event will not have excluded other more localised influences. Whatever these factors may have been, they will have taken place within the context of an agitated national political environment. This could only have discouraged a wider business confidence. The birth of my Great Grandfather **Edmund Smith's** birth (on **Saturday, January 21st, 1832**) occurred amidst some very troubled times. His father, **John** may have needed to look for slightly better-paid work just to feed his family.

Total payments in the fiscal year (covering the period from **1/4/1831** until **31/3/1832**) amounted to **£902 3s 8 1/2d.** Of this amount **£6 11s 1/2d** went *"by balance of bastardy;"* the rest into various forms of poor relief. The last month accounted for over **25%** of the total. As can be seen from the extract below, respectable witnesses had to sign to the fact that the annual totals had been properly worked out: -

> *"Seen and allowed by us this*
> 6th *day of* **April 1832**
>
> **James Laycock**
> **Edmund Smith**

(Was this **Edmund** an Uncle to my Great Grandfather of the same name?)

> **Ferdinand Scarborough**
> **Peter Laycock**
> **Richard Gill**
> **John Teal**
> **Samuel Whitaker**
> **Saml. Gott**
>
> **West Riding**
> **Yorkshire} Passed** *and allowed by us two of his*
> *Majesty's justices of this place for the said*
> *Riding, the same being verified upon the oath*
> *Of* **John Smith,** *this* 7th **April 1832.**
>
> **M. Coulthurst**
> **A. Marsden"**

Obviously, the overseer **John Smith** was a man who could be entrusted with a major responsibility in running community affairs and whose oath could be relied upon by visiting magistrates as well as by the wider community. His position of respectability strongly reinforced the impression that the **Smiths** *were 'a middling sort of people,'* not wealthy, but not exactly poor either.

Over the next fiscal year, total payments were **£895 19s 61/2d,** of which **£3 1s** was spent on *'Bastardy.'* Verifying these accounts on **May 17ᵗʰ1833** was: -

> *James Laycock*
> *John Davy*
> *Edmund Smith*
> *John Parkinson*
> (Whose signature differed from the **John Parkinson** of **1805**)
> *Joseph Brown*
> *Ferdinand Scarborough*
> (An unusually splendid-sounding name)
> *Richard Gill*
> *William Smith*

The two examining magistrates being **Matthew Wilson** *and* **H. H. Bramley.**

By **1836,** the administration had become much more stringent, with the accounts now being examined every quarter rather than once a year. **Peter Laycock** appeared to find it difficult to do his job. On **July 4ᵗʰ, 1836** the witnesses to the figures for the first quarter of the fiscal year, which began on **April 1ˢᵗ** were: -

> *James Laycock*
> *John Smith*
> (Whose signature was <u>not</u> that of **John Smith** the overseer)
> *The mark of* **Richard Gill**
> *Henry Overton*
> *John Binns*

These were the usual number of witnesses one would expect, even though the total payments were **£180 3s 7d** (of which **£3.15** went on the Overseer's salary and **£1 3s 3d** on *'bastardy.'*) However, the following quarter was quite a different story. Virtually everyone wanted to sign as a witness, which powerfully suggested that there had been some form of serious dispute about payments. Respectable members of the community of **Sutton** did not seem to possess much confidence in **Peter Laycock's** ability to properly discharge his role as overseer. However, throughout this period, the **1834** Poor Law Act was putting an end to the old traditional system of *'Parish Relief'* and replacing it with the much-feared workhouse.

"1836

July *Paid*	*26*	*18*	*10*
Aug. *Paid*	*28*	*16*	*1*
Sept. *Paid*	*66*	*7*	
Paid in Bastardy	*3*	*0*	*1*
	125	*2*	*--*

Overseer on Hand

<u>*-5   3   3h (halfpence)*</u>

130   5   3h

Seen and allowed by us
*This **3**ᵈday **Oct 1836***
*For the last **3** months, before*

        Jonas Laycock *Church Warden*
        <u>**John Parkinson**</u>
(His signature was identical to the **John Parkinson** of **1833**)
        James Laycock
        Richard Gill X
        Henry Overton
        Joseph [Becanan]
        John Whitaker
        <u>**Edmund Smith**</u>
        <u>**John** **Smith**</u>
(This **John Smith** was a handloom weaver of **Sutton** whose untidy signature appeared on his own wedding certificate at the time of his marriage to **Mary Overend** on **March 30**ᵗʰ, **1834.**)
<u>**John Smith**</u> (Another handloom weaver of **Sutton** whose tidy signature appeared as a witness to the above wedding)

Richard Green X
John Woollen X
Ths. Laycock
James Gott
Peter Watson
<u>Joseph Smith</u>
William Watson
Roger Shackleton
(Was shown as a *'Slater'* by trade in the **1841** Census)
Wm. Watson Junior
Henry Shuttleworth X
Joshua Wilson
James Hargreaves X
Nicolas Smith X
John Binns X
William Whitaker X
Benjamin Lambert X
John Teal X
Michael Emmott X
Robert Hutchinson X
Isaac Berry
James Emmott X
George Scarborough
William Thompson X
James Whitaker X
<u>John Smith</u>
William Shuttleworth
John Wilson
Peter Walton
James Snowden X
West Riding
Of Yorkshire
Yorkshire} Passed *and allowed by us two*
Of his Majesty's justices of this
Place for the said riding the same being
Duly verified upon the declaration of
Peter Laycock *this* **4**[th] *day of* **Oct 1804**
Matt Wilson
L. Prestow."

None of the three **John Smiths** who had signed this document could have been my Great, Great Grandfather. Nor do any of them appear to have been **John Smith Senior** who was in failing health and dependent upon the relief provided by the **Kildwick Parish Friendly Society.** Although reasonably clear – these signatures did <u>not</u> match the very neat hand of **John Smith** the overseer. Despite blotches caused by what was a very scratchy fountain pen, it was still apparent that the **Smiths** enjoyed a high-level of literacy for the time. The only mark was for a **Nicolas Smith** who appeared to have been an elderly man. He was gone by the time the **1841** Census took place. One typical (and unsurprising) feature was the signature of **John Parkinson** who, of course, had to be *'in on'* this business as he was in every other!

Section 3: Mountains out of Molehills

Concerning Molehills in Sutton Parish

Complementing previously cited documents were the official parish records of **Sutton Township** which contained those same names which had featured in the Friendly Society and in the records of **Sutton Baptist Chapel.** When used in conjunction all three sources offered a very coherent picture of the kind of lifestyle led by the **Smiths** and something of their social position within their local community. Each source also highlighted many of the difficulties facing a community like **Sutton** – as seen in the following extracts taken from the official parish records. (As with the documents from the **Kildwick Parish Friendly Society** I have extracted material which pertains directly to my own (or closely connected) family lines or which offers useful background information about everyday life at **Sutton.** Care was taken to ensure that the material selected was representative of the documentation.)

The endless capacity of small communities like **Sutton** to almost literally *'make mountains out of molehills'* can be seen in the following extract taken from The **Township Accounts Book** (covering the period from **1834** until **early 1839**).
"1836
*An agreement this 9ᵗʰ day of **February 1836***
*Between the inhabitants of **Sutton** and **John***
Shackleton** of **Sutton** that he, the said **John
***Shackleton** engages to take the moles and*
To spread all the molehills in the said
Township for 7 years at 4 pounds per year.
If any complaint be made that he has

Not done his duty, he shall be discharged
From his employ by the consent or
Majority of two-thirds of the occupiers
Present at a meeting convened on
The occasion by giving <u>three</u> months
Notice from the aforesaid meeting.
  *I **John Shackleton** engage and*
Enter into the above agreement as
Witnessed my hand the day and
Year above written.

       X (John Shackleton)

                         *Witness **J. D. Heaton.***"

It appeared that the services of the illiterate **John Shackleton** were <u>not</u> satisfactory because a year later another illiterate worker **George Hudson** had replaced him. He received one-third extra for doing the same work as his predecessor.

*"**1837***
*An agreement made this **5th day***
*Of **May 1837** between the inhabitants of **Sutton** and*
***George Hudson** of **Sutton** that he, the said*
***George Hudson** engages to*
 Take the moles and to spread
All the molehills in the said
*Township for **7** years at*
*£**6. 0s** per year. If any*
Complaint be made that
He has not done his duty, he
Shall be discharged from his
Employ by the consent or
Majority of two-thirds of the
Occupiers present at
A meeting convened on the
Occasion by giving a <u>one</u>-month notice
From the aforesaid meeting
*I **George Hudson** engage and enter*
Into the above agreement
As Witnessed my hand the day and
Year above written.

      X (George Hudson) *Witness **John Jackson.***"

The change (which I underlined) from three to one month's notice indicated that the inhabitants of **Sutton** wanted to speed up the procedure whereby an incompetent mole catcher could be discharged. The existence of such a post showed that industrialization had not yet completely severed this community from its rural roots. Parochial politics were very much on display. In some ways, my ancestors lived in a very small world. Appointing a mole catcher would not have been one of the most exciting of activities – and somewhat frustratingly it failed to provide a long-term solution to the problem. During my visit (made to **Ellers** on **Monday, 19th March 2001**) I could see some surrounding fields were still covered with molehills!

Section 4: A Cluster of Cloughs

Concerning the Cloughs of Sutton-in-Craven

A great deal was discovered about the other families with whom the *'Smiths'* associated. One of the most extensive of these was the **Cloughs.** The Census Returns of **1841** and **1851** revealed that **Robert Clough** (born approximately **1793**) was the owner of a **Valley Farm,** sited atop a ridge above **Sutton.** It lay directly to the **South** of **Salt Pie Farm** and **East** of the **Old Turn Pike Road. Robert** had married a woman called **Mary** – some fourteen years his junior. By **Mary, Robert Clough** had two surviving sons – **Joshua,** born on **8th May 1829** and **John Edward** born on **25th September 1831. John** would have been nearly seven months old when his birth was registered alongside **Edmund's.** The register of **Sutton Chapel Sunday School** showed **John Edward Clough** to have attended there at the age of **14** (from **19/2/1845** until **20/9/1845**). *'John'* and *'Robert'* were very common forenames in the **Clough** family. By **1851 Valley Farm** covered **39** acres, and **John Edward** himself had become an apprenticed shoemaker. Interestingly, a certain **Betty Smith** of **Glasburn** was on record as visiting them. (She was aged **65** and of *'independent means.'*) Following three tragic deaths in **1854, John Edward** inherited the farm. In **1871,** he was recorded as living alone (with a **61**-year-old servant, **Joshua Dewhurst**). The Farm had expanded slightly to contain **40** acres although exactly how it was worked remained unknown. **Wood (p.84)** revealed that **John Edward Clough** had worked as a shoemaker in **Sutton.** He had also married a lady called **Hannah** but died in **1896** without ever having sired any children. During his life, he had become an extremely fervent **Baptist,** which suggested that he was actively engaged in lay preaching. However, his loyalty to the **Baptist** Church did not prevent him from being interred at **Kildwick Cemetery** along with other members of his family.

To the **South East** of **Valley Farm,** just on the **East Side** of the **Old Turnpike Road there** had once stood a farm by the name of **Longhouse.** Yet another **Robert Clough** had lived there during the first half of the Nineteenth Century. He was to play an influential role in the affairs of **Sutton Baptist Church.** (This **Robert** was not to be confused with the **Robert Clough of Valley Farm** itself.)

Astonishingly, the **Cloughs** were probably the only family in **Sutton** who had a reasonably detailed biographical sketch written about them. This was mainly because they were an influential family who had been in **Sutton** since at least the Sixteenth Century. According to **Hodgson (1879) p.65-67,** a <u>third</u> **Robert Clough** had come from a line of *'gentleman farmers'* from **Bent** in **Crosshills.** (In fact, a map marked it lying down **Bent Lane,** West of the **northern** end of **Sutton.**) Another **John Clough,** the father of this third **Robert Clough** had, near the end of the eighteenth century, branched out into spinning and stuff manufacturing. (Records mentioned by **Wood p.84** confirmed that his christening had taken place on **31st May 1752**). He was also reputed to have been the first manufacturer to have set up *"a pot-of-four,"* – a table where four wool combers could work together. His evident intention had been to increase productivity.

In addition, this **John Clough** had owned a warehouse in **Sutton,** used for sorting and storing wool before sending it to combers and weavers. Two of his sons (**Robert** and another **John Clough**) was brought up in the business. By **1822, Robert Clough** was operating as a sole trader in **Sutton**. In that year, he took into partnership his younger brother **John** and purchased the **Grove Mill.** This mill had specialised in cotton spinning ever since its construction in **1797.** By **1826,** the business was prospering but a dispute over its expansion was to lead to the dissolving of the partnership. **Robert Clough** continued in business at *'The Grove'* whilst his younger brother **John** had turned to setting-up his own business in **Ingrow Mill.** In **1831, Robert** made his first expansion of the premises by extending the south side of **Grove Mill.** By the time of my Great Grandfather's birth, **Robert Clough** had obviously had a lot of things on his mind. In **1832,** he decided to enlarge the old wool warehouse (enlarged again in **1862** and eventually replaced in **1872.**) Further expansions to the mill took place in **1836** and **1842. Robert Cough** died in **1848,** his business passing onto his son, yet another **John Clough,** who owned it until his death in **1865.** Like his father, **Robert, John Clough** was a generous supporter of **Methodism.** This was shown in him partly funding the building of several **Methodist Chapels** and schools on the **Keighley Methodist Circuit**.

As can be easily imagined, distinguishing these **Robert** and **John Cloughs** from the ones who owned **Valley Farm** was not easy. Only a careful comparison of dates (made on **Thursday, November 16th, 2000**) prevented me from mistaking one pair for the other. However, it did become clear that both sets of **Cloughs** were closely related. In **Chapter Eleven, Wood** revealed that they shared a common descent from **William Clough** (born in **1676**) who had had seven children by his first wife and six by his second. A weaver and husbandman by trade, it was **William Clough** who had first settled on **Bent Farm**. Like many in his family, he had acted as churchwarden in **Kildwick Parish Church**. Both the **Robert Clough** at **Bent** and the **Robert Clough** at **Valley Farm** (locally known as *'Valley'*) were both to be his Great Grandsons but possibly by different wives. An interesting family connection between this last **Robert Clough** and the **Smiths** also existed. This was borne out by the following inscription on a pavement tombstone located in the grounds of **Kildwick Parish Church** (Discovered during my second visit there on **Monday, February 5th, 2001**.)

"IN MEMBRANCE OF
JAMES
Son of **ROBERT** *and* **MARY CLOUGH**
Of **Valley, Sutton** *who died* **November 25th**
1837 *aged one month.*
Also, of **JOSHUA** *their son who died*
June 14th 1847 *aged* **18** *years.*
Also, the above **ROBERT CLOUGH**
Who died the **19th September 1854**
Aged **62** *years*
Also, the above **MARY CLOUGH**
Who died the **25th September 1854**
Aged **49** *years*
Also, in memory of **BETTY SMITH**
Mother of **MARY CLOUGH**
Who died the **23rd September 1854**
Aged **69** *years.*
Also, of **JOHN EDWARD CLOUGH**
Son of the above
ROBERT *and* **MARY CLOUGH** *who died*
February 19th 1896 *aged* **64** *years.*

Also, of **HANNAH** *widow of the above*
JOHN EDWARD CLOUGH
Who died **March 20ᵗʰ 1906**
Aged **62** *years."*

Incidentally, the death of three **Cloughs** in the space of one week during **September 1854** was suggestive of an infectious disease (like Cholera, which would have arisen from an infected water supply). The inscription itself had been well preserved but it was not quite clear whether **Joshua** had passed away in **1847** or **1846.** This was because the Stonemason had chiselled the top of a figure *'7'* but then completed it with the bottom of a figure *'6!'* However, by adding eighteen years to **Joshua's** birth date of **8/5/1829** it was found that **1847** was the more likely date.

CHAPTER 5: CHAPEL ROOTS

Section 1: A Revival in Christianity

Concerning Local Churches

Volume 1 of **Slater's Directory** for **1855** revealed the presence of several churches in the wider area of **Kildwick.** These were: -
1. Saint Andrews, Kildwick - Rev. T. C. Fawcett, vicar
2. Saint James Church, Silsden - Rev. Richard Heelis, curate
3. Baptist Chapel, Sutton
4. Wesleyan Methodist Chapel, Crosshills – Rev. Paschal Hoskins
5. Wesleyan Methodist Chapel – Cononley, Steeton and Silsden
6. Primitive Methodist Church – Steeton
7. Wesleyan Association – Crosshills.

The Directory also mentioned that *"Sutton is in the Parish of **Kildwick,** stuff and worsted for the **Bradford** market are manufactured there. The only place of worship is the **Baptist Church.** "* The records provided by **Sutton Chapel** were to play a crucial role in highlighting the various activities of some of my forebears and pointing out the social networks within which they moved. Through these activities, I got to know something about them as people and learnt about those things which were of importance to them. I was also able to see how some of their values would last right up to the present day. These included an emphasis on the need to gain a good education which, after <u>six</u> generations, is still a powerful force. Without the survival of these records, the knowledge gained about my ancestors would have proved far less rich. Having been stored since **1975** in the Reference Section of **Keighley Library,** it seemed as if these very documents had been patiently waiting for me to delve into their contents.

In the early **Victorian** era, the Church as an Institution specialised in education, especially in larger population centres. At **Keighley Grammar School,** a **Rev. Thomas Plummer** of **25 Cook Lane** (in the centre of **Keighley**) was on record as being the Headmaster from **C.1830** until **C.1837** – his son **Peter,** acting as that school's *'usher.'* By **1843** the Grammar School was in the hands of the **Rev. Thomas Brayshaw M.A.** and a **Thomas Holgate.** (Unfortunately, the oldest surviving documents of this school were financial records dating back only to **1853.** This prevented any further detailed research.) By placing a high priority upon education **Sutton Chapel** was simply following a very typical trend of the time. In the **Sutton** area, the **Protestant Dissenting Tradition** was very strong – not least because the **Anglican** Parish covered a large geographical area and was difficult to supervise. Nearby **Halifax** was the second largest parish in **England. Charlotte Bronte's** novel *'Shirley'* testified to the fact that the relations between **Anglican** and **Dissenting** Communities were often extremely strained. This could be seen in their unwillingness to agree on the basics of **Christian** belief. There also existed a great deal of rivalry – not least in education.

The fervent **Evangelical Anglican** Minister **William Grimshaw (1708-1763)** often conducted missions in the **Sutton** area during his time as curate of **Haworth Church** (from **1742** until **1763**). In a letter written during the year **1744,** he mentioned that **God** was pleased to visit **Keighley, Silsden, <u>Sutton,</u> Bingley** and other localities (where different branches of my family lived). On **Thursday, October 9th, 1755,** his short-lived diary recorded a busy round of preaching engagements that covered **Otley, Addingham, Silsden, <u>Sutton</u>** and **Newsholme.** Despite travelling about thirty miles he stated that it was a blessed day and that *"he'd much of the Lord's presence in him and with him!"* Precise quotations from those sources will be found in **Cook (1997) p. 81 & 168. William Grimshaw** was a close friend of such well-known eighteenth-century preachers as **George Whitfield (1714-1770)** and the **Wesley** brothers (who founded **Methodism**).

Almost inevitably, the activities of **Grimshaw** would have caused comment at **Kildwick Saint Andrews** – not least because he could easily have been viewed as an intrusive trespasser, meddling in the affairs of a parish that was not his own. Among those well placed to have observed and commented upon **Grimshaw** were those *'respectable'* members in the community who acted as Churchwardens at **Kildwick.** These were **John** and **William Smith** (from early **1747** until early **1748**), **Robert Smith** and **John Gill** (from early **1748** until early **1752** at the latest), **Samuel Smith** and **William Holmes** (from early **1755** until early **1756**) and finally **Joshua Smith** and **Peter Parkinson** (from early **1757** until early **1758**). It was by no means beyond the realm of probability that **Samuel Smith** and **William Holmes** heard **William Grimshaw** preach the Gospel with great fervour at **Sutton** on **Thursday, October 9th, 1755.** What their reaction would have been could only be guessed at, but at **Sutton Grimshaw** did not meet with the violent hostility he'd encountered in places like **Colne.** Here the local incumbent of the local **Anglican** church, the Reverend **George White,** would instigate mob attacks against **Grimshaw** and his lay preachers. In passing, it's worth noting that **George White's** notorious drunken and gambling ways often landed him in the debtor's prison. He was the sort of eighteenth-century **Church of England** Minister satirised in the prints of the painter **William Hogarth.** (After a final spell in a debtor's prison he died in **1751.** It was said that he'd begged **William Grimshaw** to minister to him during his last moments.)

Section 2: A Baptist Background

Concerning the Baptist Church in Sutton-in-Craven

In **1784,** the **Smiths** were in the local *'Dissenting Register of births for* **Kildwick Parish.'** This invaluable document was introduced by **John Walton** in **1785,** the Minister of **Sutton-in-Craven Baptist Chapel** (from **1780** until **1807**). It was to remain in use until its replacement in **1837** by **The National Birth Register.** It had been stored at both **Bradford** and **Leeds Central Libraries.** It showed that **John Walton** was a very methodical man, endowed with a sharp intelligence and a gift for administration. Thanks to this source, possible family connections could now be traced back to the late eighteenth century. Whilst studying it on microfiche, an attempt was made to begin with the earliest entries in **1785,** before moving forward in time until the birth of **Edmund** in **1832.** In **John Walton's** neat script writing, we hear of a **Susan Smith.** Her date of birth provided the earliest entry in the Register. It simply stated, *"***Susan Smith** *the daughter of* **Robert Smith** *and* **Laura** *his wife of* **Lumb Mill** *in* **Cowling** *in the Parish of* **Kildwick** *in the county of* **York** *was born seventeenth of* **August** *in the year of our Lord* **1784.** *Registered the fourteenth of* **May 1786** *by me* **John Walton** *– Protestant Dissenting Minister."* **Susanna** (or **Susan**) was a **Smith** for whom it was possible to gather a little more information. In addition, she appears to have had a sister called **Mary Smith,** born on **14th April 1786** but also registered on the **14th May** of that year.

Evidence of the social problems facing the community at that time came to light in further records belonging to **Sutton Baptist Chapel.** One of these had the rather long-winded title of, *"The book belonging to the Baptized – Church of* **Jesus Christ** *at* **Sutton** *containing: The Church's confession, together with the names of those that have subscribed thereunto, who is a member of the said Church,* **No1, 1780."** The Confession itself displayed marked **Calvinistic** influences – with an emphasis upon the classic **Calvinistic** teachings concerning election and the depraved condition of human nature. Some of it would seem harsh by today's standards. What this confession did show was that the ideological roots of the Church lay in seventeenth-century **Puritanism** as opposed to the more emotional revivalism of the eighteenth century. The evangelical revivals of that period appeared to have largely passed **Sutton** by – although **Methodism** did gain a noticeable foothold in **Crosshills** and other nearby localities.

For an extended period (following its foundation in **1711**) **Sutton Chapel** was a very struggling work, meeting in a converted barn. It seemed to have depended upon visiting preachers and there appeared to be no attempt to keep any records until **1768.** Meetings occurred on a fortnightly or monthly basis. It gave the distinct impression of a work just about *'hanging on'* in the face of severe difficulties. However, some members appear to have maintained an association for of all their lives – whilst others remained a source of considerable trouble to a succession of pastors. It was only possible to establish a coherent narrative of events following the ordination of **John Beatson** as pastor in **1768.** After this *"many were added unto the Church and the chapel was enlarged whilst he was here for about two years. **Mr Beatson** added members, but many were afterwards proved to be unfit to have a name and place in the Church of God. He preached his farewell sermon, **May 27th 1770** – again he preached on **June 20th.**"* The record showed that he went to **Hull** with his wife **Mary.** One may speculate whether he decided to leave the Chapel before problems began to show. If so, it was a case of *'getting out in time.'*

*"When **Mr Beatson** left **Sutton**, it pleased the Lord to send the **Revd William Roe,** who had much work in weeding out some members admitted in **Mr Beatson's** day, but much disturbance taking place and continuing a long time, he thought it his duty to leave the Church. Many died and were dismissed in his day – only three he baptised remain now in the Church. According to the Church Book, the Church consisted of **34** members when **Mr Roe** came to us; he was a pastor for **8** years and supplied sometime before he was ordained. He preached his farewell sermon **August 1st 1779** and removed to **Farsley**. He left the Church with **23** members and was dismissed* (meaning *'moved'* not sacked) ***February 23rd, 1780.** When **Mr Roe** left us the Lord, notwithstanding our manifold offence, was pleased still to be mindful of us and immediately sent unto us the **Rev. John Walton** who preached the first time as a regular supply **August 8th 1779.**"*

On becoming Pastor on **July 11th, 1780** *"he wished to have some regular account kept."* The evident effectiveness of his ministry paved the way for **Sutton Baptist Chapel's Victorian** heyday. Near the beginning of his pastorate, he must have felt confirmed by the rightness of this move when **Mrs Elizabeth Atkinson** was moved to benefit the minister with an annuity of **£15.00** per year with another **£3.00** per year for the poor. This incident showed that **John Walton** could attract loyalty from well-meaning people. Nevertheless, he needed to be very strong-minded because the Church he'd taken over appeared to have represented every pastor's nightmare. It had suffered from a long history of internal dissension and a high proportion of deaths. Confirmation of this lay in the following three lists of names, (the *'exclusions'* having occurred during **Pastor Roe's** tenure).

Deceased
Matthew Green
William Sharp
William Ingham
Mary Ingham
Mary Hudson
Eleanor Smith
Agnes Emmott
Sarah Gill
Ann Clough – died **9/8/1772**
Mary Smith – died **19/4/1780**

Dismissed to other Churches
Rev. John Beatson - to Hull **20/6/1770**
His wife **Mary Beatson**
John Smith
William Roe – to Farsley **23/2/1779**

Excluded
John Greenward Senr. – Shaw House
Edward Duckworth Senior
Margaret Crabtree
Ann Smith
Simon Topham
Rose Topham – restored – excluded
Elizabeth Smith
Richard Gairs
Christopher Mason – added **27/9/1772**
John Tomlinson – added **18/7/1773**
Lydia Duck – added **8/3/1777**
N.B: The last three exclusions consisted of members Pastor **Roe** had initially added to the church.

Further details concerning the administrative disarray facing **Pastor Walton** were provided in a statement following the above list; *"The greatest part of those who now stand as members have no day of the month or year of our Lord when we were joined as members. What circumstances turn up after the coming of* **Mr Walton** *must be looked for* *among our names – excepting* **Mary Smith's** *death.* **David Laycock** *is the first baptised and from thence names begin more regular."*

From the numbers excluded it appeared that **Pastor Roe** had *'purged'* almost one-third of those who had belonged to the Church in **1770.** Moreover, he then subsequently removed three of those whom he himself had made members! Admittedly, some of these individuals (like **Rose Topham** who was also to fall foul of **Pastor Walton**) may well have been *'troublemakers,'* but the high proportion of exclusions and the variety of people involved did raise questions about the quality of **Pastor Roe's** leadership. Either he was a very weak man trying to compensate for this by exerting his authority in a tactless and arbitrary manner, or he was very proud and arrogant, taken up with his own sense of pre-eminence, **(3 John 9).** What may have been on display here was the kind of *'petty popery'* which can still afflict rigid forms of Protestantism. However, in fairness, it must be stated that a place like **Sutton** would have been full of rough characters, many convinced that they could do a far better job of running the Church than the Pastor! Others would have had serious social problems. Gossip too would have been rife. As **Charlotte Bronte** observed in her novel **Shirley,** *"talking scandal"* was a pastime shared by rich and poor alike. There was very little privacy in small settlements like **Sutton.** With hindsight, it was possible to see that faults had probably existed with both **Pastor Roe** <u>and</u> his congregation. Heavily abbreviated extracts from his Chapel Book show that even the wise and effective **John Walton** endured some major difficulties.

In the following list (taken from **The Sutton Chapel Book**) a cross (or **X**) has been inserted against the names of those who could only leave a cross-shaped mark. Such a symbol meant that another person had written their name for them because many of those joining the Church were illiterate. (Overall, illiteracy was found to be higher amongst women than men.) Those words in square brackets denote sections which proved so difficult to read that the original meaning could only be guessed at. Any idiosyncratic spelling given to some names has also been retained. To give a better flavour of how the original source would have read, details of a few names have been quoted in full. (However, reasons of length prevented this being done in every case).

"ROBERT CLOUGH *Junior of* **Longhouse** *– added* **March** *9ᵗʰ* **1769** *– died* **1821**

JOHN GREENWOOD *of Glasburn - added* **June** *1ˢᵗ* **1777** *– died* **3/1821**

JOHN WALTON *- Received from the Church at* **Halifax 20/8/1780,** *ordained Pastor* **24/8/1780**

*X BLAKEY X SMITH X. Excluded **April 19th1781** for professing himself dissatisfied with some of the members, or something else, which we would not discover. But withdrawing from the privileges of the house of God – Church meeting and private meetings and also the Lord's Supper and for saying one thing at one time, and the reverse at another in a contradictory manner."* **Note:** there was one sentence in brackets, which had been crossed out by a thick black line.

*X MARY X GREENWOOD X. Added **24/8/1769.** Excluded for tale bearing and denying the truth - excluded **19/4/1781***

*X ROSE X TOPHAM X. Restored **24/7/1781** but excluded from acting the part of the tale-bearer or mischief maker and for attempting to justify her conduct and character by lies.*

*X DAVID X LAYCOCK X Baptised **30/5/1780** – member **1/6/1780,** excluded **29/5/1783,** restored **4/7/1796,** excluded **2/3/1797** – for persevering in trade after he knew himself unable to pay his just debts. For borrowing money – when he knew himself unable to repay again.*

*JOHN PARKINSON – baptised by **J. Walton** the **20th September** and added to the Church **11th October 1781***

*X JOHN X CRAVEN X of **Sutton Brow** excluded **4th December 1783***

*X ABRAM X HEELAND X – Baptised **6/8/1786,** added (to membership) **3/9/1786** – excluded **8/5/1802** for neglecting to fill his place in the Church.*

*HENRY BANNISTER – Baptised **6/3/1787** – excluded – poor attendance.*

*THOMAS LAYCOCK of **Cononley** – Baptised **19/4/1793** – member **21/4/1793** died **10/9/1854** aged 88 years.*

*MARTHA SNOWDON – Died **October 1795,** interred at **Kildwick (22nd October).***

*SARAH LUND – baptised by **John Walton** and admitted as member **February 7th, 1796** excluded **July 8th1813** for not filling up her place and railing against the Church.*

*ANN LAYCOCK – Baptised **28/8/1796** – excluded **22/6/1797** – non-attendance.*

*ALICE CLOUGH X – Baptised **28/8/1803,** member **18/9/1803,** excluded **8/7/1813,** non-attendance.*

*JOHN HUDSON – (Born **Feb. 7th1713** old stile. In **1804,** he said he had been almost 60 years a member of the Church. Died **September 4th1804** aged 91)*

*MARY PEEL Died **April 3rd1805** aged 85, buried 6th.*

*ELIZABETH WILSON Died **July 16th1807** about 10' o Clock morning, aged 77."*

Having rearranged this list in chronological order (from **1769** through to **1807**) – just after the time when my Great, Great Grandfather **John Smith** was born, some interesting points emerged. The first striking feature was the great age to which some of the people had lived. The only medicinal remedies available at that time would have been herbal in nature. Once people had survived childhood diseases (and childbirth in the case of women) living to an old age appeared to have been a distinct possibility. The above records (taken from *'The Chapel Book'*) implied that **Sutton** was a community in which the basic provisions of life – in terms of food, shelter and clothing – were available to all but the poorest inhabitants. Conditions in **Sutton** would have been better than those found in rural **Ireland** or most of **Europe.**

The second striking point was the absence of drunkenness as a reason for exclusion! In the main, the disciplinary measures taken were for such *'Churchy'* sins as gossip and disputing with the Pastor – rather than for carousing at the nearby Inn. It did seem that **Sutton Chapel** attracted the more respectable elements of the community. Hardcore drunkards would stay away of their own accord. One frequent problem was *'durability'* – new members were sometimes easy to find but difficult to retain, even under the talented leadership of **John Walton.** This was shown by the fact that the most common reason for exclusion was non-attendance. After a week full of toil, people could not be bothered to go to meetings. They were just too exhausted. Perhaps candidates for baptism should have received clearer guidance as to what church membership would entail. At least then there would have been a higher retention rate. Nevertheless, **Sutton Baptist Chapel** took its ministry to the surrounding community very seriously and this was perhaps a factor in fuelling its nineteenth-century growth when membership rose into the mid-hundreds. Of further interest was the fact that those very problems which had confronted **John Walton** still exist today in the modern Twenty-First Century Church. Most Pastors reading this document would quickly recognise a **Blakey Smith** or a **Rose Topham** in their own congregations!

Financially, **Sutton Baptist Chapel** was not immune from the economic pressures caused by the **Napoleonic** wars. A Church memorandum of **1806** (the year in which **Napoleon** was coming to the height of his power following his great victory at **Austerlitz** in **December 1805**) provided confirmation of this. *"Memorandum:* **Thomas Gasforth Esq.** *of* **Steeton** *informs us that he has read a letter from one of the trustees saying that the government has, by Act of Parliament, laid a tax of ten percent upon the interest of bank stocks which took place in* **July 1806** *and reduces the bill which used to be* **£11. 10s. 0d,** *to* **£10. 7s. 0d,** *per half year.*

The stamp duty takes off **£0 3s 0d**

£2 9s 0d} *sum of both*

The bill must be drawn on the **5th** *of* **January** *and on the* **5th** *of* **July** *every year."*

The only other conclusion to be drawn from this document was that the Church had put aside a little money to meet extra expenditure. There was a desire to keep track of its investments.

Following the departure of **Pastor John Walton** (in **1807**) the deacons decided that *"writings belonging to the Church"* should be kept by **Robert Clough** of **Longhouse.** (Situated **South** of **Ellers, Longhouse** was a long grey stone farm building, which is still in use today). That decision was taken on **November 14th, 1808.** The mark of **Alice Clough** was on the minutes of the meeting. It appeared that, in certain instances, women played some part in the decision-making processes at **Sutton Chapel.** Presumably, it was felt that these documents would be more secure in what was possibly a well-guarded farmhouse. A strange set of circumstances less than a decade later would show that this security was not impregnable. **Sutton Chapel** did not obtain another Pastor until **Francis William Dyer** was received in **June 1812** (the month in which **Napoleon** began his disastrous invasion of **Russia**). Students from **Horton Baptist College** had filled the pulpit during the five years *'interregnum.'*

From the early nineteenth century *'The Church Book'* listed people who clearly had associations with my own family. Some of them may well have been closely related to my Great, Great Grandfather **John Smith.** On a more cautious note, it should be stated that following the end of **John Walton's** pastorate in **1807** the quality of writing in this source became somewhat variable – at times bordering on the illiterate. Despite repeated checks, it became impossible to vouch for the complete accuracy of the information provided. Nevertheless, a coherent picture of Church life did emerge.

*"SARAH SMITH+ of Sutton – Baptised by **Mr Edwards** 14/5/1809 added 9/7/1809. Died 18[70]*

*ROWLAND SMITH of Sutton - Baptised 5/6/1809, added 9/7/1809. Died after a short illness but in the faith of [Christ] **May 11th 1857.***

*DAVID McCROBEN of Sutton - Baptised by **Mr McFarland** 5/6/1809 added 9/7/1809 – excluded.*

*X ANN X OVEREND X (Dickinson) Baptised by **Mr Sinkley** 25/6/1809, added 9/7/1809, excluded 8/7/1813. Doubts were entertained respecting her moral conduct, but she wished to withdraw.*

*JOSEPH CRAVEN – of Lower Jack Field – Baptised by **Mr Greenwood** 8th July 1809 and added to the Church **July 9th 1809** – died of apoplexy **April 19th 1814.***

*MARTHA CRAVEN X of Jack Fields – Baptised by **Mr Greenwood** 8th July 1809 and added to the Church **July 9th 1809** – died 1838*

MARGRITT OVEREND *Baptised by* **Mr Edwards 10/5/1810,** *added to the Church* **13/5/1810** *– dead.*

JOHN SMITH *– Baptised by* **Mr Edwards 10/6/1810,** *added* **7/2/1811** *– dead, lived at* **Cranbury Hole**

JOHN SMITH SENIOR *of Sutton – Baptised by* **Mr Wilcocks 29/1/1811,** *added* **7/2/1811** *- dead*

SARAH SMITH *– Baptised by* **Mr Wilcocks,** *added to the Church* **28/4/1811** *– died* **14/2/1818**

JOHN OVEREND *– Baptised by* **Mr Wilcocks,** *added to the Church* **29/12/1811** *– dead*

RICHARD OVEREND *– Baptised by* **Wm. Dyer 3/1/1813** *and added to the Church the same day – excluded for non-attendance*

ELIZABETH SMITH *(now* **WILKINS***) – added* **3/7/1814** *– moved to* **Shipley** *– dead* **25/12/1857**

MARY SMITH *– was baptised on a profession of faith and added to the Church* **July 3rd 1814** *– dead*

WILLIAM CLOUGH *– was baptised on a profession of faith and added to the Church* **July 3rd 1814** *– excluded."*

How much these people would have known about the *'outside world'* was certainly open to question. Those more literate (who hopefully read the newspapers of the day) would have been most interested in the campaigns of **the Duke of Wellington** in **Spain.** One or two survivors of the **Napoleonic** wars may well have returned to their local communities with horrifying tales of the battles they had fought. Any businessman would have fretted about **Napoleon's** attempts to ruin British trade through his Continental-wide blockade. **Napoleon's** banishment to **Elba** in **1814** and his final defeat at **Waterloo** in **June 1815** caused widespread celebration with some mill owners treating their workers to free beer and even a hearty feast. Nevertheless, the impression remained that, for most people in the above list, the campaigns of **Napoleon Bonaparte (1769-1821)** might as well have been in another world. They were too busy struggling to survive to worry about events in far-off Europe. Even the *'better off'* would never have begun to understand the diplomatic complexities of the **Congress of Vienna (1814-1815)** which was to redraw the map of **Europe** for almost a century.

Evidence concerning **John Smith *'Senior'*** emerged with the Baptist Register of **Kildwick Parish Church,** which showed that he was a weaver of **Sutton.** His wife's name was **Mary Smith** and together they produced the following children: -

Benjamin baptised on **21/10/1770**
Mary baptised on **13/2/1774**
Joshua baptised on **26/11/1775**
Jane baptised on **1/3/1781**
Peter baptised on **23/4/1787**
Mary baptised on **21/8/1788**

For the first two baptisms (also known as *'Christenings'*) **John** and **Mary Smith** were living in **Glasburn,** but by the time of **Joshua's** christening they had moved to **Sutton.** The presence of a second **Mary** may indicate that the first **Mary** had died young. It was the common custom in that period to give a new child the name of a deceased one. (This practice can be a source of nightmarish confusion for Family Historians.)

The above details (taken from the **Kildwick Parish Church** Marriage Register) also revealed that **John Smith** and his father **John Smith** *'Senior'* were weavers, both of whom had lived on a farm called **Cranberry Hole** and were each married to a lady called **Mary.** Like many of their contemporaries, they would have combined agricultural work with other work associated with the rising Textile Industry.

In **1811, Sutton Baptist Chapel** decided to expand its premises to celebrate its Centenary. To some extent such a step might have been taken out of sheer necessity as the converted barn in which the congregation met was in a serious state of disrepair. Yet such a move could also be interpreted as a sign of fresh confidence, for the Church Membership was indeed growing. Regrettably, **1811** was one of the worst years to have undertaken such a project. **Charlotte Bronte's** well-researched novel *'Shirley'* (set in precisely that year) showed it to have been a time characterised by terrible economic hardship and severe social disturbances – with even large mill owners finding it difficult *'to make ends meet.'* Moreover, as was often the case with building projects, costs escalated, and the congregation was forced to appeal to **Baptists** as far afield as **Leeds** and **Scarborough** to pay off an outstanding debt of £117.00. (According to the accounts section of *'The Church Book.'* the total cost of the original project had been £180.00 – a vast amount for those days.) The letter appealing for financial assistance possessed that timelessly irritating quality characteristic of all such correspondence. Dated **July 25th 1813,** it began by stating *"Dear Brethren, our circumstances are of such a nature as to lead us to address you through this medium in order to elicit a little of your kind and brotherly assistance."* There then followed a highly verbose and rather defensive account explaining why **Sutton Chapel** needed to raise such a vast amount of money. A sense of embarrassment was very strongly present. Finally, this letter ended with the signatures of **Pastor Dyer, Deacon Thomas Laycock** and **Deacon Robert Clough.** Accompanying the appeal was the following recommendation by the influential **Dr William Steadman** of **Horton Baptist College, Bradford** and **John Fawcett, Pastor** of **Hebden Bridge Chapel.** It stated, *"I am fully satisfied that our brethren at **Sutton** have acted with prudence, and exerted themselves to the utmost of their ability, and do therefore with pleasure warmly recommend their case to the attention of the friends of Christ and his cause.*

> *W. STEADMAN, Bradford*
> *JOHN FAWCETT, Hebden Bridge."*
> (Quoted in **Pilling p. 10**)

Despite this recommendation, the suspicion remains that an absence of coherent financial planning meant that few of the costs had been sufficiently budgeted for. **Sutton Chapel** had not been the first (or the last) Church to have floundered into financial difficulties through an over-ambitious building programme.

Haykin (on **p.21** of the **January-February 2015** of the Baptist publication *'Reformation Today'*) divulged some interesting details about **John Fawcett (1739-1817)** who had ministered at **Rodhill End Baptist Church,** near to **Hebden Bridge.** (Its services were held only every other week.) Converted through the ministry of **George Whitfield (1714-1770)** and influenced by the eccentric **Anglican Evangelical** vicar of **Haworth, William Grimshaw (1708-1763)** he had exercised a long and fruitful ministry, characterised by a passion for revival. According to his son, he kept a portrait of **Whitfield** in his study and *"the very mention of his name inspired the warmest emotions of grateful remembrance."* By **1811, Fawcett** was a highly influential and well-respected *'elder statesman'* figure. An entry in Wikipedia revealed that he was the author of following publications: -

- Poetic Essays, **1767.**
- The Christian's Humble Plea; a poem in answer to Dr Priestly against the Divinity of our Lord Jesus Christ, **1772.**
- Three hymns in the Gospel Magazine, **1777.**
- The Death of Euminio, A Divine Poem, **1779.**
- Another Poem suggested by the decease of a friend, *"The Reign of Death",* **1780**
- Hymns adapted to the circumstances of Public Worship and Private Devotion, Leeds, G. Wright and Son **1782.**

A portrait of him in **1814** revealed **Fawcett** to be a man of large build thick-set features and a rather dour **Yorkshire** looking face. His eyes are watchful and alert. In the background are shelves of books stacked full of what seem to be large theological tomes. He gave the impression of a man who would have bellowed out his sermons. It's highly likely my ancestors would have heard him preach.

Incidentally, **Fawcett's** theological opponent **Dr Joseph Priestly (1733-1804)** was a famous scientist who discovered oxygen and served as a minister at the **Mill Hill Unitarian Chapel** in **Leeds (1767-1773).** Located near the central rail station, the chapel (in **2018**) continues its ministry and is known to provide a venue for events associated with the Lesbian, Gay, Bisexual and Transgender Community. It's also heavily into Interfaith activities. I have visited the building two or three times and was once served a rather tepid cup of tea.

Thankfully, for all concerned, a subsequent record of donations showed that the financial appeal did produce the required funds. **Pastor Dyer** and his deacons were spared the humiliation of a debtor's prison. One donor helping them out was a **Benjamin Smith** who gave the quite generous sums of **10s 6d** – thus showing he was a man with some spare money. Whether he was the **Benjamin Smith** who had acted as a witness at **John Smiths** wedding in **1824** remains unknown.

One literary source (which threw an interesting sidelight into the kind of life enjoyed by the people at **Sutton Chapel**) was the novel *'Shirley'*, first published in **1849.** This invaluable source was written by **Charlotte Brontë** and was set in the period **1811-1812.** However, it may be best to treat it with caution – not least because it represented the views of a middle-class **Anglican** *'looking down her nose'* on working-class **Dissenters**. Nevertheless, **Charlotte Brontë** clearly drew upon what was still living memories of the late **Napoleonic** period. She also knew the area where the early **Smiths** had lived and had an *'acute ear'* for their local dialect. (On reading this novel I gained a very clear idea of how people like my Great, Great Grandparents will have spoken.) Where **Charlotte Brontë** proved most helpful was in her very adept ability to expose religious hypocrisy and to distinguish it from real **Christianity**. This was most evident in her waspish treatment of three awful curates. However, in relation to early nineteenth century **Baptists** (mentioned on **p.10** of *'Shirley'*) the way she vividly described the general level of emotionalism in some of the sermons and the manner a preacher could attract weaver-girls *'in their flowers and ribbons'* struck a contemporary note. Apparently, a dynamic **Baptist** preacher of that period could enjoy a certain amount of *'sex appeal,'* especially when like myself, he was handsome and distinguished in appearance! Whilst reading this novel I was struck by just how little certain aspects of both **Anglican** and **Baptist** Church life had changed over the last two centuries. The types of religious misfits that **Charlotte Brontë** *'lampooned'* so skilfully then are still around today.

During **1813,** pressures (other than financial) were bearing down on **Sutton Chapel.** One of these was the insistent and widespread local demand for a burial ground to be established in the surrounding open land of the newly built premises. Preoccupied with financial survival the leadership responded to this development with a marked degree of irritation – as evidenced by the following brusque announcement: -

> *"Against burying any corpse*
> *In the Baptist Chapel at* **Sutton**

Whereas several persons seem desirous of interring the bodies of deceased relatives in the place in which we assemble for the purpose of divine worship and different individuals have on that account applied to us frequently for our permission so to do. We feel it our duty as members of the Church whose joint property the chapel aforesaid is, to enter on our Church our full determination not to permit any person rich or poor on any account to inter a corpse or corpses in the above-mentioned place of worship.

Several reasons may be assigned for our conduct in this affair, but we think every wise person will be satisfied without requiring any.

This has very unanimously been agreed at our Church meeting **May 19th 1813** *and signed on behalf of the whole by*

> **Robert Clough**
> **Thomas Laycock**} *Deacons*
> **David McCroben**} *Member*
> **Wm. Dyer**} *Pastor."*

The impression created by this document was that of inopportune enquirers being rebuffed in a very abrupt manner. One interesting signature was that of **David McCroben** who appeared to be a highly influential member. The **1822 Baines Trade Directory** revealed that, along with **Benjamin Smith,** he was one of two Cotton Manufacturers present in **Sutton.** This fact added to the view that, socially, his voice carried some weight.

Although possibly justified at the time, the decision taken at this meeting was eventually over-ruled by popular demand. By **1830,** dead members were beginning to be interred around the chapel and by the late **1870s,** it was evident that overcrowding was becoming a problem. I for one am grateful that the first decision was eventually nullified by future events. If **Pastor Dyer** and his deacons had had their way this Family History would have made little progress! Thankfully for me, the burial ground behind **Sutton Chapel** turned out to have been one of the most important sources of information. (If not the most important!) Sheep may have been allowed to graze in the burial ground to keep the grass down.

One problem with the employment of lists as a historical source was their tendency to *'de-personalise'* the people named on them. Lists portray bare facts which often leave the reader speculating about other details, *i.e.* the precise reason for *'exclusion'* or an exact cause of death. Yet behind every name was a real human being with an individual story – someone who had once felt, thought and lived. Only rarely was any extra information available to reveal something more. In the case of **Joseph Craven,** supplementary details were available and the following account, (written in **Pastor Dyer's** neat handwriting) provided a vivid account of his untimely death:

*"Departed this life yesterday **April 19th 1814** our dear brother **Joseph Craven** an honourable and useful member. He died suddenly in a fit of apoplexy as he was returning from **Sutton** to his farm at **Jack Field.** He had conversed with great cheerfulness with his Pastor not much above a quarter of an hour before his death. His funeral sermon was preached by his bereaved Pastor the Sabbath but one after his departure from this vale of tears. The congregation was numerous and affected. A [loving] address from the following words: -*

'Be ye ready, for in such an hour as ye think not the Son of Man cometh.'"

After nearly two centuries one can still feel the emotional intensity contained in those words. Both **Pastor Dyer** and his shocked congregation would have interpreted this unexpected death as a divine *'visitation,'* warning people not to neglect the ways of the Lord. Whilst reflecting upon this point it was easy to imagine that **Joseph Craven** had been a stout, red-faced *'John Bull'* of a figure – someone with a hearty laugh and a warm-hearted concern for others. Even **Pastor Dyer** (who was quite ruthless in excluding people) found him to have been *'an honourable and useful member.'* This minister undoubtedly preached a most moving sermon at **Joseph Craven's** well-attended funeral. Perhaps some of those who heard it would have been awakened to a genuine **Christian** faith.

Following the analysis of previously quoted documentation, it became apparent that the period of **1813-1814** was very much *'a season of trial'* for **Sutton Chapel.** Financially it was in dire straits, with some evidence of poor planning. Also, an unpopular decision had been made concerning the highly sensitive issue of the internment of bodies and a much-loved member had died unexpectedly. Moreover, one long-established member (**Sarah Lund**) had been excluded from the Church in acrimonious circumstances and was busy *"railing"* against it. (She may have felt aggrieved about the decision made about the proposed graveyard.) Her defection suggested that internal relationships within this Assembly were not exactly harmonious. Such afflictions must have compounded the daily trial of living in early nineteenth century Britain – where death, disease, and poverty were all too common. No wonder **Pastor Dyer** referred to this world as being *'a vale of tears.'* The strain he was under must have been considerable. Hardly surprisingly, he left **Sutton Chapel** in **1814** to become Pastor of a Church in another locality. Perhaps the trials he had encountered during his brief pastorate had convinced him that the Lord's blessing was no longer upon his ministry at **Sutton.** He seemed glad to leave and take up the Pastorate of another Chapel at **Baccup** (where that Pastor had recently died). The following interregnum (of four years) at **Sutton Chapel** suggested that **the Baptist Association** had known about its difficulties. If (as seemed likely) this was the case, then **Sutton Chapel** would not have been a prospective Pastor's *'first choice!'* Even when another Pastor was later to be found he became involved in some unusual business concerning the Chapel Book. Moreover, the inferior quality of his handwriting (when compared to that of **John Walton** or **Wm. Dyer**) reinforced the view that the new **Pastor, Joseph Gaunt** was a far less cultivated man than his predecessors. Perhaps the Church trustees who had appointed him felt that a *'rough diamond'* was the best person to deal with the unruly folk of **Sutton.** Should this have been their intention then their decision was later to be borne out by events. During his pastorate, (which lasted from **1818** until **1826**) he added **40** members to the Chapel. This level of success suggested that **Joseph Gaunt** had indeed established a good rapport with the locals of **Sutton.** They would perhaps have recognised and felt more *'at home'* with someone more like themselves. He seemed to have the *'common touch.'*

The following excerpt was one of the most ambiguous findings made during this research. It was obvious that **Joseph Gaunt** and his wife **Ann** had, at one point, been involved in a conflict over **The Chapel Book.** The first paragraph in this said *'Book'* had been crossed out and covered in blotches of black ink in what appeared to have been a deliberate attempt at defacing details. The impossibility of fully reconstructing this paragraph meant that the **Gaunt's** exact connection with the Church in **Bramley** (mentioned in that paragraph) would remain a mystery. Adding to the confusion was the fact that the writing of each was of an extremely poor, semiliterate quality.

*"**Joseph Gaunt** having laboured [among us] in the Lord [moved]... to the Church at* **Bramley** *... He was received as a member on **17/5/1818** [ordained] **3/6/1818**. Also,* **Ann Gaunt** *the wife of **Joseph Gaunt** [received] from the Church at **Bramley** by the Church at **Sutton** at the same time.*

*We do hereby declare that all connection between us as members and the Church at **Sutton** is entirely at an end and as proof of which with our own hands, we have withdrawn our names from the book as witnessed by our hands*

JOSEPH GAUNT
ANN GAUNT

I do most solemnly certify that a book called **The Chapel Book** *which was paid for out of chapel money was frequently brought to our house by **David McCroben** and that I have a distinct recollection of it being left one night and that **Mary McCroben** came for it next morning. I delivered it to her, and other circumstances were connected which I cannot forget.*
ANN GAUNT.*"*

(On the following page was an entry about **Richard Smith** dated **9/4/1820**.)

What were the *'other circumstances'* connected to *'**The Chapel Book**,'* which **Ann Gaunt** *'couldn't forget?'* The answer proved impossible to find but her voice was that of an essentially timid woman obviously caught up in some unsavoury business or congregational power struggle she was later to regret. It was easy to imagine her in a woollen shawl giving a breathless account to scowling Church elders. The exact nature of the problem was not clear, but it apparently involved the disappearance of a Chapel Book that, by rights, was the property of the Church. Why such an event occurred was a mystery, but it involved the **McCrobens** who appeared to have had some role in it. Reading between the lines there seemed to have been a power struggle involving both **Joseph Gaunt** and **David McCroben.** Such struggles were a common feature of early nineteenth century Baptist life. Moreover, the list of exclusions in **Sutton Chapel's** own records showed that ill-discipline was a continual feature.

Yet much remains unknown. Even the date of this incident was uncertain. Its position in the book suggested **1818** but the actual events being recorded suggested that it had occurred around **1826.** The **Gaunts** may have joined the Church in **1818** and then had resigned, only to be recalled to a pastorate lasting until **1826.** Alternatively, they may well have left a blank page in the church book before recording the **1820** entry. This would have been done to leave room for further additions to their record. Unless new evidence comes to light then the full events surrounding this *'cloak and dagger'* business will remain forever unknown. My own instinct was to guess that somehow money had been involved. It was unclear whether the Chapel Book was simply another name for the *'Church Book'* that has proved to be such an invaluable source for this study. If they were the same, then I am truly grateful for this document's survival!

The Birth Register showed that **Joseph Gaunt** had made an early entry on **December 10th, 1818** and his last on **25th December 1826**. His first entry that marked the beginning of <u>his</u> pastorate was made on **29th September 1816** – a fact which raised the possibility that this Register formed an actual part of the Church Book, which had apparently gone missing earlier in **1818**. In his large untidy handwriting, Pastor **Gaunt** had made the following proud entry concerning the birth of his own son (also named **Joseph**). *"**Joseph Gaunt the son of Joseph Gaunt** and **Ann** his wife was born on **Wednesday** Morning (between 6 & 7 o'clock), the 26th of **September 1822** in the Township of **Sutton** & Parish of **Kildwick** in the County of **York**. Registered 29th **September 1822 Joseph Gaunt, Minister."**

Returning to a more factual note, the Church lists did show the existence of another **David McCroben** who was almost the exact contemporary of my Great, Great Grandfather **John Smith**. He was apparently the son of the **David McCroben** who had become a member in **1809** and had subsequently become embroiled in the strange business involving The Chapel Book. **Mary McCroben** (who was either his wife or sister) had acted as a witness at the wedding of **John Smith** the weaver on **May 24th, 1824**. Her neatly written signature provided evidence that she was a literate woman – one who could be entrusted with updating a Chapel Book

After the dramatic episode of The Chapel Book, its list of names continued once again: -
*"**RICHARD SMITH** – added 9/4/1820, having been baptised on 3/4/1820 being Easter Monday - dead*
***MARGARET SMITH** – added 9/4/1820 - having been baptised on 3/4/1820 being Easter Monday died 11/4/1878 aged 78 years at **Kildwick Grange**.*
***WILLIAM SMITH** – Baptised 2/12/1820 and added to the Church 3/12/1820. Excluded **May 1834** - association letter to **Colne June 13th-14th 18[21]** Baptised – twice excluded. Restored to the Church in **September 1848** – dead **October 1857**.*

BETTY SMITH added *2/8/1822* having been baptised several weeks before - dead *23/9/1854*

JOHN PARKINSON – added *3/2/1823*, having been baptised on *1/1/1823* - *2/1848* withdrew, *1/1849* restored – **died 17th December 1875** aged **71 years**

ELLEN SMITH added *21/8/1825*

EMMA PARKINSON – added and baptised *18/7/1829*, withdrew, restored *3/9/1863* – died *25/5/1875* aged **66** years

RICHARD & EDWARD WILSON – added *17/11/1833* – dead *1858* and *1843*. Also, **SARAH WILSON**

JESSE OVEREND – added *12/10/1834*, excluded *7/1841*

ELIZABETH SMITH – added *12/10/1834* – *1845* dismissed to **Hall Green [Chapel] Haworth** [and] received by letter

TITUS WILSON, WILLIAM WILSON (dead *4/6/1876*, aged *63*), **BETSY WILSON** – added *9/11/1834*

ROBERT SMITH – added *5/4/1835*, dead

Being the ordinance day of **June 4th 1837** *the following persons were baptised and received into the Church – having signed the covenant.*

ANN SMITH from **Ellers** – **dead 10/4/1856**

ABIGAIL SMITH from **Sutton** – excluded - **May 1841,** restored in **October 1841** - moved to **Hudson** in **Australia**

ANN MILBURN from **Sutton** – dead *6/1841*

MARY OVEREND from **Ellers** – dead

JOSEPH SMITH from **Glasburn** – added *7/2/1838*, excluded *1853*, restored *1856*

ROWLAND SMITH – added and baptised *3/6/1838*

<u>Added *5/5/1839:* -</u>
ANN WILSON from **Cononley,**
MARY SMITH X from **Cononley**
TITUS SMITH from **Sutton Mill** – added *3/11/1839*

<u>Added *3/5/1840:* -</u> having been baptised the same day
ALICE WATSON – died *6/1846*
HANNAH BERRY – dismissed to **Haworth**
MARY ROE - died *18[58]*
DAVID McROBEN – withdrew, restored *31/1/1867*, died *27/10/1871* – **age 70**
JOSHUA BECK – excluded *1845*
HANNAH RISHWORTH - excluded
JOSHUA SMITH – added *31/5/1840,* excluded *11/1845* – dead *1850*
ROBERT SMITH – added *31/5/1840,* excluded *5/1841* – restored *10/1841*"

What the above-cited names demonstrated was how families like the **Overends, Smiths** and **Wilsons** had formed a particularly close association with the Chapel. Hardly surprisingly, a high proportion of intermarriages took place between these families. **John Smith** the weaver (who wasn't my direct ancestor) had married – first a **Wilson** and then an **Overend.** Another interesting feature was how **William Smith** (not my ancestor) had a definite connection with **Colne.** Evidently, there had once existed quite close links between **Sutton** and the market town of **Colne.**

From about **1840** onwards the Chapel began to provide detailed numbers of its membership. These showed that, within six decades, **Sutton Baptist** had come a long way from being the struggling affair of **1780.** Numeric growth had risen, and this suggested that the Chapel was now performing a highly-respected service in the community. It appeared to have benefited from industrialisation and the population increase of the surrounding area.

The list of new members (from **1841** until **1851**) confirmed the earlier impression of the **Smiths** (and other closely connected families) being strongly represented.
"SUSANNAH SMITH from Sutton Mill – added 11/7/1841, (1852 withdrew,) returned 4/12/1873 as SUSANNAH LAYCOCK
ELLEN SMITH – added 3/8/1845 – Sutton
MAVIS SMITH – added 3/8/1845 – Glasburn dismissed to Easby 7/1/1857
JOHN SMITH – added 21/12/1845 – excluded 1850 – restored January 1852 – excluding 1857
NANCY SMITH – added 2/1846
WILLIAM SMITH – added 8/1846, dismissed to Easby 7/1/1857
MARY SMITH – added 4/4/1847 – now RISHWORTH
SARAH SMITH – added 7/11/1847
RICHARD GREENWOOD
ELIZABETH GREENWOOD - received by letter from Hall Green, Haworth, added 6/10/1849

Added 3/12/1850: -
JANE WILSON (Now EVANS)
SARAH WILSON (Now HALL)
SARAH EVELYN CLOUGH (Now HAUGGAS) – KEIGHLEY PARISH
ELIZABETH WILSON (Now MCNAB) – excluded 1857
MARY SMITH – died 18/7/1874, aged 86
MARGARET WALTON (Now MIDGLEY)

*ELIZABETH HILL (Now **THORNTON**) – died 16/2/1883, aged 46*
MARY TETLEY – died 26/3/1872 aged 65
MARGARET SMITH – added 5/5/1850

Added 7/7/1851
SARAH WILSON
MARY ANN OVEREND
MARGARET WILSON – *added 7/9/1851 (now **WILKINSON**) – moved to America 3/10/1873."*

The above list showed that most of the Chapel's growth during the **1850-1852** period was due largely to an increase in female membership. For some reason, **Sutton Baptist Church** managed to break into female social networks. This success resulted in a situation where ladies would *'gossip the gospel'* and bring their friends or relations to meetings. There they would respond to the **Christian** message and take up Church membership. The relatively low proportion of exclusions suggested that this Assembly managed to successfully meet a variety of female needs. Improved economic conditions may have meant that the womenfolk were less bound by a daily struggle for survival. There was the odd extra penny to spend on Church activities. Not shown in the above selection was the fact that the name *'Walton'* frequently re-occurred on these lists. A telephone conversation with a contact at **Sutton Baptist** did confirm that the **Walton** family had been active members of the Church for three to four generations covering the late eighteenth to early nineteenth centuries. At one stage in this research, it seemed possible that the twice-excluded **John Smith** may well have been my Great, Great Grandfather. However, later findings would nullify this conclusion.

One important source was *"the minutes of the teachers and committee of the **Baptist** Sunday School, **Sutton**, with registers of teachers."* Covering the period from **1837** until **1853** this *'Minute Book'* provided much useful information. However, the presentation was highly variable – poor writing was often marred still further by ink stains, rough calculations and what appeared to be early **Victorian** doodles drawn by a bored *'Minute's Secretary!'* Even worse, the page edges had at some time in the past, become damp and were beginning to crumble away. It was decided that the best way to handle this evidence was to quote some of the more clearly written parts pertaining either to my own family or to families closely connected to the **Smiths**. Portions in square brackets represent my own guess at what keywords meant, whereas portions in curved brackets represent additional information inserted by an unknown party from elsewhere in the book. The following excerpts (from **1837-1840**) were typical of the document and conveyed something of the flavour of Church life: -

> ### "*Sutton Chapel, May 28ᵗʰ 1837*

> *The meeting having opened with singing and prayers,* **Wm. Samuel** *was elected chairman in the absence of* **Wm. Fawcett** *the president.*
> **Judith Wilcock** *was elected a treasurer* (for the next session)
> *The following persons were then appointed as officers for the ensuing year: -*
> **Wm. Fawcett,** *president by virtue of his office as the Minister of the place*
> *Superintendents*
> **John Parkinson** (for the first course)
> **Samuel** (for the second course – a man called **Charles Asquith** replaced him during the annual meeting held on **4/6/1838**)
> **Thomas Wilson** (for the third course)
> (**James Laycock** was serving as a superintendent from **4/6/1838** but had gone by **20/5/1839**)
> *Secretaries*
> **Richard Petty** (resigned in **1839** and was replaced by **John Wilson**)
> **Thomas Berry**
> *Librarians*
> **Richard Wilson**
> **William Wilson** (from **Sutton,** resigned in **1839** and was replaced by **Lawrence Moss**)
> *Treasurer*
> **Thomas Berry**
> *Members of the committee*
> **Matthew Sugden**
> **Duncan Campbell** (**Jesse Overend** replaced him during the annual meeting held on **4/6/1838**)
> **William Wilson** (from **Crosshills**)
> **James Fox** (**Rowland Smith** replaced him during the annual meeting held on **4/6/1838**)

It was ordered that no [pupils] should be separated on the anniversary day.
Those **60** *Circulars be printed for the use of persons who may wish to invite their friends to the Anniversary.*
That **[Martha] Berry** *and* **Mary Ann Clough** *find places for the children and get them tea on the anniversary.*

[Robert] Parkinson, Stephen William, Matthew Sugden and Lawrence Moss were appointed visitors for the next quarter.
(Minutes recorded by) **Richard Petty**"

A distinction appeared to have existed between the Committee Meetings and the actual Teachers' Meetings (the latter of which were held more frequently). The Teachers Minutes tended to be short and to the point – as seen in the following example.
"Teachers Meeting July 2nd 1837
1.   *Ordered that* **Benjamin Smith** *be received as a teacher*
2.   *Ordered that* **Charlotte [Moreley]** *be received as a teacher*
3.   *Ordered that* **Joshua Walton** *be received as a teacher."*

The size of this mainly male dominated Committee showed that the Sunday School was a very large affair, taken seriously by all involved persons. Women tended to be given an auxiliary role and were very much in a position of subordination. There also appeared to be a great concern on formality and order. It was easy to imagine that some of these meetings were tedious in the extreme – hence the doodles in the book. Present at a committee meeting chaired by **John Parkinson** on **30/8/1840** were **David McCroben, Jonas Tetley, Benjamin Smith,** and **William Wilson.**

The above-cited information was particularly illuminating because it showed that, through **John Parkinson,** my Great, Great Grandparents were possibly connected to one person who was actively involved in **Sutton Baptist Chapel.** This strongly implies that they themselves could have enjoyed some contact with this Assembly – albeit a very loose one because they lived further afield. This would lend credibility to the family tradition which stated that *"the **Smiths** were all originally **Baptists.**"*

By the time of the Committee Meeting's **AGM** on **8/6/1840** various personnel changes had taken place *i.e.:* -
The Secretary was now **Wm. Samuel**
The Clerk was **William Wilson**
Assistants were **Robert Parkinson** and **Stephen Wilson**
The Treasurer was **James Laycock**
Superintendent for the first course was **Walter Midgley**
Superintendent for the second course was **Rowland Smith**
Superintendent for the third course was **Thomas Wilson**

The Librarian was **Charles Asquith** – the **1841** Census showed him to be a joiner. At about the same time **Henry Smith** of **Sutton Mill** had been admitted as a teacher.

It was perhaps the long working hours of the time that created the problem of a lack of punctuality. At one Committee Meeting (held on **27/9/1840**) with **John Parkinson** acting as Chairman, **Richard Petty** (acting as Secretary) proposed a motion, seconded by **Matthew Sugden.** This requested *"that the superintendents be requested to ensure the teachers in their respective courses to be more punctual to the time of opening the school. Present, Males 13, Females 9."* The minutes also showed that, by **6/1/1841, Titus Smith** (who had become a member on **3/11/1839**) was serving on the Sunday School Committee. The **1841** Census showed him to be a Worsted Weaver, living in **Sutton Mill.** It also confirmed that he had been born in **1780,** the year **John Walton** had become Pastor. He would have been in his late fifties when he became a member. This **Titus Smith** had also ensured that the births of his two daughters **(Hannah** and **Charlotte)** had been registered at the Chapel in **1811** and **1814.** By drawing together information from a variety of sources it became possible to supply biographical details about individual people. These sources also confirmed that different branches of the **Smith** family had formed a major and enduring presence at **Sutton Chapel.** Their spiritual roots had indeed been Baptist.

Section 3: Sutton Sunday School

Concerning a Baptist Church's contribution to education

Provided by the *'Teacher's Minutes'* was helpful statistical and financial information concerning the actual running of the Sunday School. The following Table (compiled by the teachers themselves) shows the number of Sunday School Scholars – thus confirming that the Church had undertaken a very major educational work at a time of much socio-economic hardship. The sheer scale of its efforts could only be commended. Clearly, Sunday School work at the Chapel enjoyed massive support from within the surrounding locality. The education facilities it provided were obviously highly regarded.

	On the books May 21st, 1837		Admitted during the year		Totals	
	Male	Female	Male	Female	Male	Female
Scholars	74	79	51	44	125	123
Teachers						
1st course	12	12	4	4	16	16
2nd course	12	12	1	4	13	16
3rd course	10	11	3	3	13	14
Totals	34	35	8	11	42	46

	Dismissed during the year		On the books, June 2nd 1838	
	Male	Female	Male	Female
Scholars	2	9	123	114
Teachers				
1st course	3	4	13	12
2nd course	1	3	12	13
3rd course	2	2	11	12
Totals	6	9	36	37

Beyond legibility, one difficulty with these figures was the absence of any consistent system of presentation. This point was confirmed when an attempt was made to compare these figures with those of subsequent academic years.

	Number of Scholars	Number of Teachers
Number of Scholars on the Books, May 6th, 1838	237	73
Admitted during the year	27	22
Dismissed	32	9
Number of Scholars on the Books, May 5th, 1839	232	84

	Number of Scholars	Number of Teachers
Number of Scholars on the Books, May 6th, 1839	229	86
Admitted during the year	20	13
Dismissed	90	9
Number of Scholars on the Books, May 5th, 1840	229	99

The financial returns revealed much in the way of interesting information. They showed exactly where the income from this work was coming from and where it was going. Also displayed was a certain degree of generosity when rewarding scholars.

Receipts	£.	S.	D.
Balance from last year			6
Collection 18/6/1837	16	2	1
Two books sold to Richard Petty		1	6
By balance due to treasurer	1		3h
Total	16	5	4h

Expenditure	£	S.	D.
By expenses last anniversary	3	15	0
By Whit Monday		19	10
By Rent	5		
By attending Night School		17	8h
By propitiation of attending			

	£.	S.	D.
alterations in Chapel	4	8	6
By rewards		14	9
By Books and copies		9	7
Total Balance by 4/6/1838 Committee Meeting	16	5	4h

The Minutes showed that *"after the business had been transacted by* **Mr Matthew Sugden** *and* **Wm. Fawcett** *addressed the meeting and the whole was concluded with singing and a prayer."*

Receipts	£.	S.	D.
Collection 18/6/1837	21	6	3h
T.W. for Books		9	
Total	21	15	3h

Expenditure	£.	S.	D.
By Rent	5		
Coals	2		
Sweeping		10	
By expenses last anniversary	2	16	6
Books	2	14	6
Sundries		13	10h
Whit Monday Balance	1	12	9
Total Balance by 20/5/1839 Committee Meeting	21	15	3h

From this date, it became immediately apparent that the Sunday School was largely dependent upon individual giving. There were neither grants nor any other sources of income from outside the area. The general level of giving was indicative of a solid core of commitment. Those at the Chapel were determined that this work should succeed in bestowing a basic level of education. Lending further support to this view was the substantial number of obviously very busy people willing to give what little spare time they had to volunteer as teachers. In operation at a Community level were the principles of *'self-help'* taught by the well-known **Leeds-based** author **Samuel Smiles.** A succession of zealous Pastors also took an interest in establishing activities for young men, with Night Classes being conducted for *'their mental advancement,'* (**Pilling et al P.11).**

Sometimes material outside of the archives of **Sutton Baptist Chapel** would give more insight into some of its active participants. Both the **1841** Census and modern sources like **Whittaker** and **Wood (1992)** revealed that **Richard Petty** had been a Schoolmaster, living at **North Street, Crosshills**. His school was founded in **1775** and was to last until **1857** – by which time it was known as *'The Richard Petty School.'* Apparently, the schoolroom consisted of one large room, **30** feet in length and **18** feet wide. It had five writing desks and a *'master's desk'* in front of the fireplace. Its pupils consisted of **17** boys, a few of them boarders. One senses that **Richard Petty** would have put to most effective use the two books he'd purchased from the Sunday School.

A review of the monumental inscriptions for **Kildwick Church** revealed: -
Richard Petty of Crosshills June 21st, 1861, 60 years
Margaret his widow **January 18th, 1884 - 84th** year
Martha infant
For Remembrance
Charles eldest, died **Sutton 1896**
Joshua second son died **Preston 1894**
Richard third son died **Brisbane 1899**
Francis William fourth son died **January 2nd 1918 - 80th** year
An interesting feature of this epitaph was the way in which a man who had once been very involved in the **Baptist** Church could have chosen to be buried in the local **Anglican** graveyard. Nor was his behaviour unusual, for other families (*i.e.* the **Cloughs** and some branches of the **Smiths**) followed this very same pattern; high involvement in the **Baptist** Church followed by burial in the **Anglican** Cemetery. It seemed as if the **Church of England** was still being used for *'dispatching'* purposes – though not for *'hatching'* or *'matching,'* (christenings and weddings).

Throughout the **1840s** and early **1850s,** the whole of the Sunday School prospered. On **8/6/1840** the balance stood at £**24. 14s 6h** – during a time when a severe economic recession was provoking large-scale Chartist agitation! In the more prosperous **1850s,** the balance grew even higher at £**35.00** for **26/6/1852** and £**36 12s 9d** for **19/6/1853.** In those days – education (along with religion) provided hope for people who were bearing the full brunt of industrialisation. It also provided a way for overworked parents to get their children away from overcrowded living conditions – especially on Sunday afternoons when their parents would value some real peace and quiet.

Nevertheless, even though Sunday School work met an evident need and grew in terms of financial prosperity this did not automatically mean it was free from problems. On **9/8/1849** *"A teachers' meeting was held this day at [this Church]. It was resolved that a monthly teachers' prayer meeting be held on the last Sabbath of every month to commence at 5 'o' clock for the purpose of the instructions given and labours exercised in the Sabbath School. **Rowland Smith Junior.**"* The information here was especially fascinating because it provided a glimpse into the spiritual life operating behind the Sunday School work. It showed that it existed on a dynamic of prayer. One could easily imagine any prayer meeting led by a **Smith** would be somewhat verbose and long-winded in nature. Even in those times, the **Smiths** appeared to have been a family who liked the sound of their own voices! (Significantly, **1849** was the year after **Karl Marx** and **Frederick Engels** had published their *'Communist Manifesto.'* Their diatribes against political opponents showed that sectarian feuding was not something confined to the **Christian** Church alone.) A likely reason behind this recourse to prayer could be found in the details of the teachers meeting held on **11/11/1849.** It was during this meeting that both **John Smith** and **Samuel Smith** proposed a motion *"that absent teachers should have their names read out at successive teachers' meetings."* One victim of this exercise of group pressure was certain **Mary Smith.**

By **1/4/1850 Samuel** (who was a farmer) had become Treasurer on the Sunday School Committee whilst **Rowland Smith** was Librarian. Also, remaining on the Committee (but not serving in any office) was **Jonas Tetley** who had been a next-door neighbour to **John Smith** (the weaver) at the time of the **1841** Census. The persistence of these names over a decade was indicative of a strong degree of commitment to this work. Perhaps the longest track record was that of **John Parkinson** who was still chairing committees until the year of his death in **1875** – but by that time it was for the **Glasburn Mission,** a work which had been established by **Sutton Baptist Church.** For a certain type of personality,

Committees can be a highly addictive activity. **John Parkinson** appeared to have been a natural born Chairperson.

Other written records concerning the Sunday School (from **February 1845** until **March 1846**) were in the **Local History Reference Section** of **Keighley Library.** These included the *'Scholars Register'* for that time period and the *'Sunday School Minutes Book.'* With **287** admissions in the **5** to **15**-year age range, it was a thriving work, overseen by a large (but variable) number of teachers. The two main subjects it offered were maths and reading. Clearly, the Church was making a brave attempt at providing what seemed to be the only large-scale educational service in the area. Despite the classes being very popular throughout the district, my Great Grandfather's name **(Edmund)** did not appear in the list of pupils. Neither did his name appear in the **1841** or **1851** Census Returns for **Sutton** or **Crosshills** – although these were very settled communities with insignificant rates of migration – even during periods of economic difficulty. (The latter included the **1839-1841** textile recession which brought considerable hardship to the mill workers of **Manchester**.) For reasons that will become clearer later, **Edmund** retained a strong attachment to his place of birth. He must have had some other links beyond being born there.

However, this Register did show that a sizable proportion of **Smiths** in **Sutton** were **Baptists**. Like many of their contemporaries, the **Smiths** were greatly concerned with religion, education, and social development – they lived in the age of *'self-help.'* Despite many positive services offered by the Sunday School, a combination of low attendance and high turnover rates would have made it difficult for children to pick up any more than a basic knowledge regarding literacy and numerical skills. Even the Sunday School's Minutes Book was at times badly written and blemished. It contained rough workings out of financial transactions, blotchy ink stains and what appeared to be early **Victorian** *'doodles'* – no doubt made during the more tedious sections of a Committee meeting.

Found within the *'Scholar's Register'* was an example of the kind of work that teachers of this period inflicted upon their charges. Printed on a crumpled piece of paper were some Arithmetic and English exercises. The latter included two fragments of a rather charming story called *'The Animals that Ran Away.'* A start will be made with some of the Arithmetic where forty-one questions were asked. As can be seen from the following extracts, the exercises got harder as they went along. Question numbers were placed in brackets

(1) **97351 X 2**
(5) **54917 X 4**

(9) 45897 X 6
(13) 60839 X 8
(17) 26948 X 10
(21) 89657 X 12
(25) 239765 X 2, 3, 4.
(28) 3974268 X 7, 8.
(31) 893746 X 16, 17, 18.
(35) 962503 X 19, 21, 34
(39) If Tom has 40 apples, Jane 101, Kate 7562, and if Bill takes 9 from each, how many remain?
(40) If every inn in England has 6 horses in its stables and if there are 517 inns, how many horses are there in all? [Work this first as an addition, and then as a multiplication sum.]
(41) In a desk, there were 6 drawers, each drawer was divided into 8 compartments and in each compartment, were 87 pounds. How many pounds did the desk contain?

Not very nice work for a child to do at any time of the day! However, it was largely through the English exercises (like the one below) that an attempt was made to nurture the right moral values into a child.
Up be watchful! Day is dawning!
Softly steals the gleams of morning,
Thank thy God who guards the night
And who brings the morning light.
[Write from dictation the last four lines of the last verse]"

Only the last two verses of the following twelve verse moralistic poem survived.
11.
If he had thought how tender hearts
Love every living thing,
And would not hurt the lowest beast
And bird upon the wing;

12
And how the good and kind can feel
E'en for a bird distressed,
I think he would have left the eggs,
In Robin's pretty nest.

[Write from dictation the ninth verse.]

The story *'The Animals that Ran Away'* was written for the same edifying purpose. Only the pupils were expected to *'spell and write'* words like *'animals, consider, ploughing, quality, appearance, company, resolved.'* It would have been worth quoting if only a full copy of it was available. The degree to which children in places like **Sutton** absorbed its moral message probably varied from case to case. Then, as now, their home background would have been the decisive factor. Overall, the impression generated was one of an unbridgeable gulf between the world of the Upper Middle-Class **Victorian** moralist (who would have designed this sort of literature) and rough working-class children in **Sutton.** The latter could only look forward to a life of hard manual work, alleviated by alcohol. Even today, the gulf between educational experts and the pupils (who often act as the unfortunate *'guinea pigs'* for their theories) remains a perennial problem in education. Pity the teachers caught between the two parties!

Three years after the passing of the **1870 Foster Education Act** what had become the **Baptist Day School** now became **The Baptist Sunday School.** This new *'Board School'* met in the former premises of the **Baptist** Day School and remained there until **1896** when purpose-built buildings became available, **(Wood p.65).** By that later period, there co-existed within **Sutton** a very typical denominational rivalry with the Parish Church of **Saint Thomas,** (consecrated on **21/12/1869**). In the village, a three-way split existed between *'Church'* people, *'Chapel'* people and godless *'roughs.'* This type of division was very common in the **Victorian** era.

Despite its well-documented problems, it was still possible to feed a marked degree of respect for the Sunday School work of **Sutton Baptist Chapel.** Whatever its shortcomings, it at least attempted to offer a positive service in an area of severe socio-economic hardship. Most of those who played their part in this educational activity really did have the best interests of the children at heart. Given the horrendous conditions of the time, their efforts were truly heroic. They accepted the value of combining strong **Christian** belief with an emphasis on education and a determination to serve their local community. In their own quiet way, the **'Sutton Chapels'** of this world did far better than the revolutionary ideology of **Karl Marx (1818-1883)** with its secret police torture chambers, *'Gulags'* and mass execution pits. Perhaps the time has now come to appreciate the achievements of such places. They stand as a rebuke to the militant atheism so popular during the first decade of the twenty-first century. Far from being the *'root of all evil,'* religion in places like **Sutton** was the foundational basis of that which was solidly good.

Although rather idealised, the following paraphrased notices concerning two Pastors, **(Pilling pp. 13-14)** convey something of the flavour of life at **Sutton-in-Craven Baptist Chapel** during the **Victorian** period: -

*"The Rev. **William Elisha Archer** became Pastor of the Church on **May 12th 1861** and retained the office for nearly a quarter of a century. **Mr John Walton,** (a descendant of Pastor **John Walton**) the Church Secretary mentioned earlier, thus described **Mr Archer's** characteristics: 'He was a great thinker and the way he prepared and wrote his sermons showed him to be a man of method. He made it a point to be in the pulpit always five minutes before the service began. As a preacher, he appealed to the heart and conscience. His language was always choice, and his sermons were all based on the foundation truths of the gospel. During his long ministry, he baptised and received into fellowship **334** members... The Chapel was taken down and rebuilt in an enlarged and improved style. **Mr Archer's** ministry closed on **23rd September 1883**. In his retirement, he resided first at **Harrogate** and then at **Leeds,** near which he died at an advanced age.*

*The Rev. **John Aldis Junior** was his successor and commenced his ministry on **23rd January 1884**. During his seven years' pastorate, the present large and beautiful school premises were erected, and certain structural alterations effected in the Chapel at the cost of £5,770...*

*The good work done by **Mr Aldis** during his ministry cannot be tabulated, though in manifest results his ministry was richly blessed, for he baptised **117** new members. After further periods of ministry at **Batley** and **Little Leigh** near **Northwich,** he died at the latter place after a very short illness on **27th November 1900,** deeply lamented by a sorrowing people. His remains rest in the **Sutton Baptist** burial ground, near the scenes of his former gracious ministry."*

Amidst driving rain (on **Monday, February 5t, h 2001**) I came across **Pastor Aldis'** headstone. Its inscription confirmed that he was a man who had experienced both personal tragedy and the heartfelt respect of his congregation.

'In loving memory of
Lizzie Aldis
Who fell asleep
April 30th 1886 *aged **19** years.*
*Also, of **John Aldis***
Father of the above
*Born **July 30th 1837,** died **November 27th 1900.***
A faithful minister and Pastor at
Sutton Chapel *for **7** years **1884-1891***

'So, he giveth his beloved sleep.'
Also, of **Elizabeth**
Widow of the aforesaid
Born **June 25ᵗʰ1840**, *died* **May 10ᵗʰ1919.**
'Even to your old age, I am He.'

During their ministries, both **Pastor Archer** and **Pastor Aldis** would have met my Great Grandfather, though sadly in rather tragic circumstances. Following many years of absence from **Sutton, Edmund** would have spoken with them face-to-face and from them, he would have heard the Gospel message. How he responded to it is not known.

Part 1 has shown that the **Smiths** strove for respectability through a variety of means. Clearly, **Baptist** Chapels like those at **Sutton** were viewed as important vehicles whereby this quality could be gained. By providing a rudimentary education and opportunities for *'networking'* they were often also the means whereby individuals could *'better'* themselves. That sought-after *'respectability'* would also be gained through the services (at a price) of self-help groups like **'The Kildwick Friendly Society.'** It provided some degree of protection against ill-health and poverty. It helped the more highly regarded members of society to avoid the risk of destitution. The main threats posed to respectability was the unpredictable trade cycle which could hurl wealthy mill owners into the workhouse. Another threat was *'demon drink'* which could be the ruin of many a family. All these were threats my ancestors would have encountered during the time periods in which they lived. Generally, they appear to have overcome them.

CHAPTER 6: CULLINGWORTH CONUNDRUMS

Section 1: An Astonishing Discovery

Concerning John and Anne Smith's move to Cullingworth

So <u>where</u> did the **Smiths** go after they left **Sutton** in late **1832** to early **1834?** The answer was not at all easy to find. At first, **Colne** seemed the most likely destination because family tradition had pointed to a strong association with this locality, and indeed the records of **Sutton Chapel** showed a **William Smith** having spent some time in **Colne.** However, just as this Family History was nearing its completion, what seemed to have been a clearly proven connection with this market town itself was deftly overturned by fresh evidence from such sources as the **Baptismal Registers for Kildwick** and the **1841** Census. My extensive research into this market town had very nearly convinced me of some plausible (but what would prove to be very misleading) conclusions. What I thought to have been viable conclusions were now wholly disproved. This caused me to be warier of wholeheartedly trusting in <u>any</u> historical sources. I needed more in the way of <u>corroborative evidence</u> before I could even be remotely certain of anything.

The first clue to the **Smiths'** reallocation was provided by an entry in **Kildwick Parish Church's Baptismal Register,** found at **Northallerton Archive Centre** during a stormy **Friday, June 15th, 2001.** One particularly astonishing discovery surrounded **Edmund's** birth – having been registered at a Dissenting Chapel in **Sutton** on **April 22nd, 1832** he was then christened (along with his younger brother **Daniel**) in the **Anglican** Church of **Kildwick Saint Andrews.** This led to a drastic reinterpretation of this Family History. My eyes nearly *'popped out of my head'* when the following details appeared on the micro-fiche – not least because I was trying to trace the details of quite another **John** and **Anne Smith,** of whom for the previous nine months I had been fully convinced were my true Great, Great Grandparents! When this discovery was made, there was a loud clap of thunder that perfectly reflected my mood at the time!

When Baptised?	When Baptised?
Christened, 3rd August 1835 Born, 21st January 1832 No. 1133	Christened, 3rd August 1835 Born, 27th June 1834 No. 1134
Child's Christian Name Edmund Son of	**Child's Christian Name** Daniel Son of
Parents' Christian Name John Anne	**Parents' Christian Name** John Anne
Parents' Surname Smith	**Parents' Surname** Smith
Abode Cullingworth	**Abode** Cullingworth
Quality, Trade, or Profession Miller	**Quality, Trade, or Profession** Miller

The officiating minister was the **Reverend John Perring** who would now have been approaching his seventieth year at the time of this christening ceremony. Some unusual features were wrapped up with this document. Firstly, although it included **Sutton, Kildwick Parish** did <u>not</u> cover **Cullingworth,** which belonged to the neighbouring Parish of **Bingley.** Normally vicars were very firm about infants being christened in their own Parish; this was because they did not want to risk any appearance of rivalry with a neighbouring clergyman. The only conceivable reason as to why **John Perring** would have allowed the christening of **Edmund** and **Daniel** to have taken place in his Parish was because **John** and **Ann Smith** <u>already possessed strong family links within it.</u> This implied that their move from **Sutton** had taken place in the past year or two. However, my forebears do not appear to have put deep roots into their new abode at **Cullingworth** – having left it by the time of the **1841** Census. Secondly, in an age marked by strong **Anglican** and **Dissenting** hostility, they displayed mixed denominational loyalties. Through registering **Edmund's** birth at **Sutton Chapel, Anne** had provided decisive evidence of **Baptist** sympathies among my direct ancestors. However, christening him later in an **Anglican** Church appeared to indicate that these sympathies were not yet firmly fixed. A final surprise was the discovery that **Edmund** had a younger brother named **Daniel!**

Supplementing the above source of information was the following Birth Certificate, received by post on **Saturday, July 14ᵗʰ 2001.** It referred to the birth of **Edmund's** younger sister **Ann** in the *"district of **Bingley** in the County of **York**, Registration district **Bradford**."*

1. **When and where born:** Twenty Fourth of **December 1838** at Cullingworth
2. **Name if Any:** Ann
3. **Sex:** Girl
4. **Name and Surname of Father:** John Smith
5. **Name and Surname of Mother:** Ann Smith, formerly Wilson
6. **Occupation of Father:** Corn Miller
7. **Signature, description and residence of informant:** The Mark of **'X'** **Anne Smith,** mother, **Cullingworth**
8. **When registered:** Seventeenth January 1839
9. **Signature of registrar:** Edward Sutcliffe

This document showed that, even by her mid-thirties, my Great, Great Grandmother had still not learnt to write. Very probably, the pressures of motherhood had prevented her from ever having enough time to learn this increasingly important skill. Unlike her older siblings, **Ann** was <u>never</u> christened into the **Anglican** Church. **Edmund** and **Daniel** were the last **Smith** children to have undergone this rite at **Kildwick Parish Church.** Their move to **Cullingworth** had broken a long-standing connection that had lasted centuries.

Section 2: A Hamlet near Bingley

Concerning the settlement of Cullingworth near Bingley

On **p.45** of the first part of **Pigot and Co.'s 1834 National Commercial Directory, Cullingworth** was described as *"a hamlet in the parish of **Bingley** in the upper division of **Skyrack Wapentake, West Riding;** about 3 miles **W. (West)** from **Bingley,** the like distance **S. E. (South East)** from **Keighley,** 7 from **Bradford,** and 8 from **Halifax.** The inhabitants of the hamlet, for the most part, are employed in the manufacturing establishments, the principal of which is that belonging to **Messrs. George Townsend and Brothers,** worsted spinners and yarn manufacturers. There are two places of worship, one for **Methodists,** one for **Baptists,** and a license has been granted to convert the **Odd Fellows Hall** to the service of the established Church. A Sunday School is in the village. Population returned with the parish of **Bingley."* During a telephone conversation with the **Bradford Archive** (made on **Tuesday, 19th June 2001**) I learnt that the **Parish Church of Saint John** was not opened until **1849** and that its burial records dated from **1853**. In the **1830s** the **Baptist** and **Wesleyan** Chapels were alone in meeting the spiritual needs of the community. A reference to a map of **1850** revealed that **Mannwell Beck** ran through **Cullingworth**. Presumably, any Corn Mill would have been located next to this stream, harnessing its waterpower to drive the machinery.

Direct observation (made during a visit on **Thursday, July 19th, 2001**) confirmed that **Cullingworth** was a triangular shaped village lying on a steep valley side. A few mill cottages dotted the valley bottom near to a crossing point called **Cow House Bridge,** underneath which flowed the shallow **Eller Carr Beck**. A **Wesleyan Chapel** had been constructed in **1824** but was now a private residence. This watercourse was only a couple of minutes' walk from the **Baptist** Chapel. **Cullingworth** lay beneath some very bleak moorland, which was upon large rubbish tip whose pungent stench hung in the air. Many birds hovered above it, looking for easy pickings.

A visit to the **Bradford Archive Centre** (made on **Thursday, 21st, June 2001**) revealed more details about **Cullingworth**. According to **Cudworth (1876) p. 251,** *"A corn mill and a worsted mill were built in **Cullingworth** by **Mr John Briggs** about forty years ago; the former being worked some years by **Benjamin,** son of **Edward Craven**, the latter by **John Anderton** before his removal to **Bent's Mill**. These premises have been enlarged by **Messrs. Townsend** and adapted to their business. A weaving mill was also built by **Mr Wilkinson** of **Harden** at **Cowhouse Bridge** for **Mr William Harrop** and was worked by him for some years. This is known as **Woodfield Mill,** and is also the property of **Messrs Townend.**"* One useful point of information were the details concerning a new Corn Mill being built in about **1835,** the approximate time of **John Smith's** arrival at **Cullingworth**. The convergence of these two facts did suggest that my Great, Great Grandfather had arrived in **Cullingworth** to take up a position in this new mill. One mystery was the failure of his employers to hire a local man – but perhaps **John Smith** was good at his job and had been recommended for the position by someone in **Sutton**. **Part 1** of the **1841 Pigot Trade Directory** showed that the only Corn Miller of note in **Cullingworth** was a **Benjamin Craven,** so it seemed that he was the employer for whom my Great, Great Grandfather had worked. The only other accessible Corn Millers were **Abraham Hardy** and **James Pearson,** both of whom were based in nearby **Thornton**. However, **Benjamin Craven** remained the most likely candidate to have employed **John Smith.** Moreover, the close association he had with **Benjamin Craven** and **John Briggs** at the local Baptist

Church would suggest that **John Smith** worked in that location. Employment there could have represented a small step-up in the world.

Further details concerning Corn Mills in this locality were provided (on **Monday 13th July 2015**) in an e-mail from **Diana Tottle** of the **Cullingworth Family History Group.**

"There seem to have been several Corn Mills in and around the village circa **1830,** *though there is now no longer any visible evidence.*

Corn Mill on Mill Street.
"It is thought there was a steam corn mill with a drying kiln and engine house worked by **Benjamin Craven,** *son of* **Edward Craven** *of* **Eller Carr Mill.** *The mill provided grain for* **John Briggs** *who was then described as a Corn Dealer"*
This information from **A. Holmes***, who also mentions the reference in* **William Cudworth's** *book,* **"Round and About Bradford"**

Corn Mill at Cow House Fold.
"There may have been a corn mill at **Cow House Fold** *(just northeast of the village)* **c.1830***"*
This reference from **Cullingworth Conservation Area Assessment 2003** *See:* www.bradford.gov.uk

Corn Mill at Hewenden
Hewenden *is a small valley very near* **Cullingworth** *and there were at one time several mills on the length of its small waterway.*
An article by **Astrid Hansen** *"Mills of the* **Hewenden Valley** *– part 1" is online at* www.mycommunityhub.co.uk

In most cases, we think the miller would have lived in a cottage attached to, or very near the mill. Maybe the **1841** *Census may help?*

Bradford Local Studies Library *have several maps covering the area and there is a Tithe map covering the* **Cullingworth** *Area on the 'Tracks in Time' web site,* **Bradford area.***"*

A review of some early maps of **Cullingworth** (held by the Family and Local History Section of **Leeds City Library)** suggested that the Corn Mill could once have stood on **Eller Carr Beck,** to the left of **Cowhouse Bridge** and not too far distant from **Woodfield Mill.** The latter is now a long, newly cleaned sandstone building, located on the right-hand side of this crossing point. It has been converted into private accommodation; a stone inscription on the rear of this building reads, *"Woodfield Mill, Converted 1999."* Some old mill cottages are still standing next to the road adjoining this building. It was probably inside one of these cottages that **John Smith** lived with his family. As will be seen presently both his wife and **Ann** and himself had a very significant association with the **Cowhouse Site**.

Section 3: An Ancestor Baptised

Concerning Baptist Revivalism in 1830s Yorkshire

Cudworth p. 253 provided some useful details concerning **Cullingworth Baptist Chapel,** whose records were thankfully found in **Bradford Archive Centre.** *"About **1835** the **Rev. M. Saunders** of Haworth, being invited by **Baptist** families in and near **Cullingworth,** held services in the village, and engaged in the **Odd Fellows Hall** for public worship. This effort resulted in the formation of a **Baptist** Church and a Sunday School, and the erection of a Chapel in **1837**. The latter is an unpretending but convenient building and was erected from a design by **Mr Nichols** of **Hewenden**. The founders of the **Baptist** Church were **Messrs. W. S.** and **R. S. Nicholas, Thomas Green, John Robinson, Robert Hartley, Jonas Sugden, Sarah Taylor, Isaac Constantine, Abraham Moulding** and **Ellen Gregson**. The Rev. **J. Harvey** was the first pastor and was highly respected by all in the village."* Sadly, this last point was not strictly accurate. Incidentally, **The Odd Fellows** were a Friendly Society founded at **Manchester** in **1810.** Many of its rituals had (and still <u>do</u> have) affinities to those of the **Freemasons**, although **pp. 26-27** of the *'Spring 2001'* issue of their **Odd Fellow** magazine portrayed a slightly touchy sensitivity on this point.

A more detailed account of the Chapel's origins was provided in *'The Minutes Book,'* covering the period from **15th June 1836** until **30th June 1847,** (with a two-year gap from **14th July 1840** until **4th July 1842** and another gap from **14th June 1843** until **1847**). Despite its somewhat ponderous use of religious language, this *'Minutes Book'* was an invaluable source in reflecting something of the religious fervour common in the early nineteenth century. The following extract begins with an account (date unknown) of the missionary activity which had preceded the foundation of this same Chapel. This missionary work had been based around **The Odd Fellows Hall**, known also as **The Lodge.** It seemed that the establishment of a new chapel at **Cullingworth** began amidst some very high, (perhaps unrealistically high) hopes: -

"The establishment of a Church of **Christ** *is a blessing of the highest order, the means of* **Christian** *fellowship which is one of the greatest privileges. A reason for devout thanksgiving – when it is considered that a church formed on the model contained in the New Testament, is an image of that blessed abode, where the followers of the Lamb shall behold his glory and sing his praises and stand in immediate connection with our welfare in an eternal world. It must evidently appear interesting and instructive to trace its rise and progress. Trusting that [as] the Church of God we have had the happiness to see formed at* **Cullingworth,** *shall continue till the time of general assembly of the firstborn, whose names are written in heaven. We briefly record the manner of its commencement for the use of those who may arise after us to dwell in the house of the* **Lord**, *to behold His beauty and to inquire in His temple.'*

As early as the year **1820,** *or even before that period, thoughts of establishing the preaching of the Gospel at* **Cullingworth** *had occupied the minds of leading members of the* **Baptist** *Denomination in the adjacent towns; and though they did not accomplish their pious design, yet it seems to have had the good effect of stirring up the* **Wesleyan** *brethren to increased exertions. Since that time the subject was occasionally referred to, and though no decisive steps were taken there were a few persons living in the neighbourhood who continued attached to the* **Baptist** *cause and waited till the opportunity should arrive of seeing their desire realised.*

The prosperity and increasing population of the village awakened fresh attention and during the summer of **1835,** *the* **Revd M. Saunders** *of* **Haworth** *consulted with the* **Revd D. Taylor** *of* **Bingley** *on the measures which ought to be taken, being encouraged by a liberal promise of support from* **Mr John Briggs of Cullingworth.** (After the word, **'Briggs,'** another hand inserted the telling words, *'but never paid.'*) *The want of a suitable room has hitherto prevented a commencement from being made. Towards the close of the year, this difficulty was removed. A commodious room was erected by* **The Society of Odd Fellows,** *who signified their intention to let it for the use of a religious body.* **M. Saunders** *immediately treated with them and agreed on a moderate rent for the occupation of the room on the Sabbath, and one evening in the week.*

On **Tuesday,** *the* **16**th **February 1836** *the Room called* **'The Lodge'** *was opened for Divine worship and sermons were preached on the occasion by the* **Rev P. Scott** *of* **Shipley,** *and the* **Revd Blair** *of* **Wilsden***; and on the following Sabbath by the* **Revd J. Ackworth [M.A]** *&* **D. Taylor** *of* **Bingley.** *The attendance was highly encouraging, and a good spirit evidently prevailed.*

On the **24**th *of* **February 1836,** *a meeting was convened when sixteen friends (including the* **Revd M. Saunders**) *were appointed as a Provisional Committee – with a Treasurer and Secretary for one year and a plan of supplies for three months was presented by* **M.**

Saunders. It was agreed that a quarterly collection should be made, beside which a private subscription was opened for the purpose of defraying the incidental expenses connected with carrying on the work of God.

*At a meeting held on the **18**th of **March**, it was resolved to establish a Sunday School. A considerable number of persons engaged themselves in this good work as teachers. Superintendents were appointed toward the close of the month with about **50** Scholars, the numbers have subsequently increased to upwards of **100**.*

*On the approach of the annual vacation at **Horton Academy**, it was thought advisable to invite one of the students to supply at **Cullingworth** during that time and it was hoped the opportunity he would have of visiting the people at their homes would greatly tend to promote the cause of religion and to encourage those who were anxious for the blessings of salvation. **Mr Harvey** had won the affections of the friends was chosen to this duty was brought to labour among them in the first week of **May.** At this period, the congregation averaged about **200** persons, many of whom were, previously to the opening of the **Lodge,** living in the neglect of the ordinances of religion without **God** and without hope in the world. A great effectual door was opened for the preaching of the **Gospel** at **Cullingworth** – the good hand of the **Lord** was evidently with his servant – the attendance increased, the faithful were stirred up to greater diligence, backsliders were reclaimed, and sinners converted. A spirit of supplication was prayed out, prayer meetings were established from house to house, as also the Sabbath morning & evening and experience meetings were held with many benefits. This sacred flame of holy piety kindled by the grace of God at **Haworth** was felt at the beginning of the year. Large additions were made to the Church and under the fostering care and zeal of the **Revd. M. Saunders** and others the influence extended to neighbouring villages – may it never expire but spread more and more until it is lost in the full blaze of an eternal day.*

*The opportunity was embraced of forming a **Christian** Church, the materials were prepared by the **Lord**, living stones fit to be built together in **Christ**, and thus the way was opened to the full privileges of the gospel dispensation. **Wednesday, 15**th **June [1836]** was appointed for the solemn service of erecting this spiritual temple to God. The Revds. **B. Godwin, M. Saunders [O] Foster, [W. Jordan]** and other Ministers attended to conduct the interesting proceedings of that day. Seven persons (out of the twelve baptised) made a public profession of their faith in **Christ** by baptism in the stream at **Cowhouse Bridge**. In the afternoon, **B. Godwin** discoursed in a very instructive manner on the nature and character of a **Christian** Church; after which, addressing himself to the candidates for communion. He desired them to give to each other the right hand of fellowship; on their having done so he acknowledged and pronounced them a Church of **Christ,** and in an affectionate manner shook hands with them all. Twenty-five persons were thus united in the **Lord. 14** [Brothers] and **8** sisters - **3** of whom were received by dispersion from **Hall Green, Haworth,** 2 from*

West Lane, Haworth, 12 by baptism, (it appears that five of those baptised, including John Smith, had already professed their faith before this ceremony) and 5 who had previously been in connexion with other Churches, from whose Communion they had withdrawn from various causes.

The members then chose three persons from among themselves, by ballot, to serve the office of Deacon, John Robinson, Wm, S. Nichols, and Richard S. Nichols; whom [the Revd] Saunders, in a fervent prayer, commended to the care, guidance and counsel of the Great God and Head of the Church.

Mr Jordan next offered some admonition on the words of Scripture "Be vigilant." The Lord's Supper was then celebrated. The hearts of the brethren were greatly encouraged by this means of grace and by the presence of about 100 followers of the Redeemer from neighbouring Churches, who sat down with them, in obedience to the gracious commandment of the Lord, "Do this in remembrance of me."

The people being again assembled in the evening; Mr Foster gave the charge to the Deacons, setting before them, affectionately and faithfully, the duties God has called them to perform and Mr Godwin concluded by an exhortation, founded on the words: "Well done thou good and faithful servant, thou that hast been faithful over a few things, I will make thee ruler over many things."

Thus far were the servants of God directed by his good providence, "This is the Lord's doing, it is marvellous in our eyes;" and his merciful hand is still with them so that they prosper; their numbers increase, and their union is cemented.

Mr Harvey, having gained the esteem and the love of both the church and congregation has been unanimously invited to accept the Pastoral charge and arrangements are making for building a Chapel. May the Lord be pleased to make the handful of servants to flourish and may 'the little one become a thousand!' O, Lord! Grant that this hill of thy Zion, which thou dost establish, may even be as the Churches of Smyrna and Philadelphia, which thou didst approve. May it be rich towards thee in humility, in love, in faith! And let the beauty of the Lord our God be upon us and establish through the work of our hands upon us, yea the work of our hands establish thou it!"

This fascinating description showed that **Cullingworth Chapel** was formed amidst an atmosphere of **Protestant Revivalism** where anything seemed possible. One problem with such a vibrant and expectant atmosphere was the fostering of unrealistic expectations which, if unfulfilled, could possibly lead to a trail of acrimony and disillusionment. Such was to be the case at **Cullingworth**

Chapel. Demonstrated was the point that a sound **Christian** work cannot be sustained by emotionalism. Other qualities, like common-sense realism, are also required. The mistake made at **Cullingworth** was to allow powerful religious sentiment to cloud judgement. It is one enthusiastic **Christians** can easily make.

Of more direct relevance to this Family History was the possibility that a **John Smith** was one of those who was baptised on **June 15th, 1836** at **Cowhouse Bridge.** (Baptisms appear to have been carried out in three relays, with different ministers baptising at various times of the day, each group ranging in size from two to five people. Later evidence confirmed that this **John Smith** was indeed my forbear and it was an amazing experience to read a detailed account of his formal initiation into **Christianity,** now preserved for future generations of **Smiths.**

John Smith appeared to have shown an interest in church business before his baptism and had obviously given serious thought to this public commitment to his faith. He had attended the Opening Meeting held at the **Odd Fellows Hall** (*'The Lodge'*) on **24th February 1836,** the account of which made for informative reading. To facilitate reference, I underlined the name of my ancestor. I also placed the names of the committee members in list format whilst inserting any other known extra details about them in square brackets.

"The Minutes Book of Management for conducting Divine Service in the **New Lodge,** ***Cullingworth,*** *which was opened for the purpose on Tuesday,* **February 16th** *in connection with the* **Baptist** *Denomination.*

The Lodge, Cullingworth, February 24th 1836

A meeting of a few friends of the cause having been convened, prayer was offered for Divine direction and **Revd Saunders** *of* **Haworth** *being called to the chair instructed the business of the meeting by stating the object to obtain for which they had been assembled.*

The following friends were appointed to a Provisional Committee for the ensuing year with the power to add to their number:

John Brigg: [The builder of the then new local Corn and Textile Mills. On some documents, his surname was sometimes spelt, *'Briggs.'* He appeared to have been an influential figure in the community.]

Wm Ellison
A. Moulding
Thomas Sutcliffe
John Smith [a Corn Miller who was my Great, Great Grandfather]
Jonas Sudgen [formally received from **West Lane, Haworth** on **15/6/1836**]
John Robinson *[formally added to the Church on 15/6/1836]*
John Greenwood
Thomas Craven
Edward Craven
Ben Craven [Manager at the Corn Mill built by **John Brigg** and son of
Edward Craven]
John Craven *[formally received from* **Hall Green, Haworth** *on* **15/6/1836**. *He later moved to* **Bradford**]
Wm Nichols
R. Nichols
Saint Bland and
Revd M. Saunders *[from* **Hall Green, Haworth** – *he had hitherto been conducting 'cottage meetings,' having been invited to the locality by some of the* **Baptist** *families living within* **Cullingworth**].

Resolved

Resolved 1st that **Wm. John Brigg** *be Treasurer for the coming year*
Resolved 2nd that **W. Tho. Sutcliffe** *be Secretary for the following year*
Resolved 3rd that five persons constitute a quorum for the transaction of business
Resolved 4th that the committee meets once a month & oftener if need be
Resolved 5th that the plan for supplies submitted by **M. Saunders** *be accepted*
Resolved 6th that [voluntary] collection shall be made towards repaying all expenses
Resolved 7th that some of the [forms] be let [off] at 6d and a quarter for each sitting

Adjourned"

John Smith had also attended at least two other meetings – one on **18th March 1836** [called by the Committee of Management] and a special meeting on **7th April 1837**. He was at the Open Meeting held on **28th April 1836** when the Church had resolved unanimously to allow only those baptised by full immersion to participate in Communion. He did not, however, appear to have attended a Committee of Management meeting, held on **5th March 1836**.

The writing for the meeting held on **18ᵗʰ March 1836** was very poor and the help of an archivist was required to interpret some of the words, [at **Bradford Archive Centre** on **Monday, 8ᵗʰ July 2002**]. With her invaluable assistance, most of the details could then be recorded.

> *"Lodge, March 18ᵗʰ1836*
> *Present* **Rev. M. Saunders, J. Brigg, J. Sutcliffe R. S. Nichols, J. Sudgen, B. Craven,**
> **J. Smith J. Craven W. Ellison, J. Robinson**
>
> ### The minutes of the former meeting were read and confirmed.
>
> *Two delegates being present leave was asked to establish a Sunday School and assurance given that any additional cleaning be defrayed, and the paintings screened to preserve them from injury.* [Underlining in the original.]
> *Also*
> *That permission be granted to affix*
> *Back to six forms for the accommodation*
> *Of aged and weak persons.*
> *Also* [the following resolution was indecipherable.]
>
> *To adopt as an experiment for one quarter the principle of support recommended in minute **8**.*
> [This financial support was to be gained through the issue of quarterly collections.]
>
> *A list of teachers for the Sunday School was*
> *Opened and other necessary preparations proposed."*

Provided here was the firm evidence of an ancestor supporting a new educational project. Ironically, this discovery was made whilst I was engaged in a not too dissimilar enterprise in the **Manchester** area! Sunday Schools were regarded with immense importance because they represented the only means whereby children could learn to read and write. It was fascinating to discover further evidence of a keen **Smith** interest in education. In **1836, John Smith** had not yet learnt to sign his own name, yet already present was a noticeable desire for self-betterment. Such a desire appears to have been kindled by his affiliation with the **Baptist** Church.

At the second *'open'* meeting (also at the Lodge) **John** was known to have attended the Church, *"resolved unanimously that, as it is the opinion of the* **New Testament** *(which is the* **Christian** *rule of faith and practice) that we have no authority over* **Christ** *and his* **Apostles** *to admit unbaptised persons to the* **Lord's** *Supper that we acknowledge no baptism as valid save that of immersion of believers on a profession of their faith in the* **Lord Jesus Christ** *of their repentance towards* **God,** *that the admission of unbaptised persons into the church would break down the barriers that separates it from the world and would sanction the neglect of any or all the ordinances of the* **Christian** *religion and would inevitably lead to dissatisfaction, contention and disorganisation that may better keep the unity of the spirit in the bond of peace and hand down to posterity an example worthy of this imitation. We agree to admit no non-baptised person to the* **Lord's** *Supper – or into Communion as a Church."*

Clearly, these were the words of a group keen to establish its corporate identity in the face of competition from the nearby **Wesleyan Church.** They were also the words of a group struggling for internal cohesion. However, later events would show that it had been totally naive of them to expect such rules to have saved them from *'dissatisfaction, contention and disorganisation.'* Later events would show these aplenty! I'm afraid that the example **Cullingworth Chapel** gave to posterity was one most other congregations would do well to avoid!

From these (and other *'Meeting'* transcripts) emerged a clear impression of a **Christian** group determined to build its work upon sound foundations, even though it could be argued that to have sixteen on a Management Committee was rather too large a number. Throughout the proceedings, the moving force appears to have been **Revd M. Saunders** who was perhaps instrumental in devising the following Bible-Based *'Covenant of Faith.'* Here again the Chapel was trying to do things *'by the book'* – in this case, *'the good Book!'* All underlining and **'X'** shaped marks were present in the original document but seem to have been inserted later. Someone had struck out some words, which I subsequently replaced within boldly pointed brackets, {}. The same person also appears to have been responsible for the underlining.

Section 4: A Solemn Covenant

Concerning the formation of the Baptist Church at Cullingworth

The Solemn Covenant of Church Communion

"*We, a small handful of the unworthy dust of* **Zion,** *usually assembling for the worship of God at the* **Baptist** *Chapel* **Cullingworth,** *and conformity to the example of* **Jesus Christ** *and his faithful followers, recorded in the* **New Testament,** *immersed in water in the name of the* **Father,** *and of the* **Son,** *and of the* **Holy Ghost,** *having first given our own selves to the* **Lord** *are now met together with one accord to give up ourselves one to another, by mutual consent and Solemn Covenant according to the will of* **God,** *with deep humiliation for our own past sins, and earnest prayer to God for pardoning mercy, and assisting, persevering and preserving Grace, we say with our hearts we are the* **Lord's** *and subscribe unto him with our hands, in manner following ------ namely,*

1stly *We this day approach* **Jehovah, Father, Son** *and* **Holy Spirit,** *the One, only true and living* **God,** *for our* **New Covenant God,** *and all-sufficient provision, and give up ourselves to Him alone for his peculiar people in a perpetual Covenant never to be forgotten.*

2ndly *We receive and submit to the* **Lord Jesus Christ,** *as our alone Saviour, Prophet, Priest, and King; in whom alone we trust for Wisdom and Righteousness, Sanctification and Redemption.*

3rdly *We devote and consecrate ourselves as living temples to the* **Holy Ghost,** *our Sanctifier, Guide and Comforter, whose gracious operations and heavenly conduct we desire daily more and more to enjoy, experience and follow.*

4thly *we take the Holy Scriptures of the Old and New Testament as* <u>the only ground and rule of our Faith and Practice</u> *desiring, through the help of his Grace, therein promised to be in all things conformable to the Holy Will of* **God,** *therein revealed.*

5thly *According to the tenor of which divine Oracles, and depending for the performance only on the Divine help and assistance therein promised – as deeply sensible that* <u>we are not sufficient</u> *of ourselves,* <u>but that all our sufficiency, both to will and to do that which is good, is of</u> **God,** *whose grace alone is sufficient to enable us to do the following things through* **God** *strengthening us – in a single dependence on whom, and as in duty bound, we now covenant with God, each for ourselves and jointly together*

1stly *to worship* **God** *in spirit and in truth, to observe his commandments and keep his ordinances, as he hath delivered them to us.*

2ndly *To subject to that divine order and discipline which* **Jesus Christ** *our only King and Lawgiver hath appointed in his Church; X* <u>and not to forsake the assembling of ourselves together for the public worship of</u> **God** *in its appointed seasons; but to continue steadfastly in our relation to one another, and to fill up* <u>our</u>

own places duly in the House of God, and cheerfully maintain his worship therein, to the best of our capacity, until death or evident calls in divine Providence shall separate us one from another. X

3rdly *to love one another with pure hearts fervently, and endeavour to keep the unity of the Spirit in the bond of peace for the honour of our God and our mutual good unto edification*

4thly *We will also make it our care, through the aforesaid help, to walk before the* **Lord** *in our own houses, with upright hearts, and to keep up the worship of* **God** *therein by daily prayers and praise to God, and by diligent reading of the Holy Scriptures, that the Word of God may dwell richly in us.*

5thly *and {as we have given our children to the* **Lord***, by a solemn dedication} we will endeavour through divine help, to teach {them} our children the way of the* **Lord***, and command them to keep it, setting before them a holy example, worthy of imitation, and continuing in prayer to* **God** *for their conversion and salvation.*

6thly We will also endeavour by the grace of God *to keep ourselves pure from the sins and vices of the times and places wherein we live, and so be holy in all manner of conversation, that none may have occasion given by our own unholy lives to speak evil of* **God's** *holy ways.*

7thly *and all this under an abiding sense that we must shortly give up our account to Him that is ready to judge the quick and the dead, unto which Solemn Covenant we set our hands in the presence of the all-seeing Heart."*

One fascinating feature was the way in which someone had underlined all those areas where the Church seemed to be visibly failing by the time of **Pastor Joseph Green's** arrival in **1842**. This made it most likely that it was **Joseph** who had made those underlines and to have deleted the document at the places denoted by the pointed brackets, {}. He seemed to have been a rigorous and thorough man, assessing his congregation's behaviour against the standards to which they should have been adhering.

The following financial information was found in the *"Accounts of the **Baptist** Church at **Cullingworth"** for the year **1836,** compiled by **John Briggs** and **Thomas Sutcliffe.** (The symbol *'h'* stands for a halfpenny.)

The Treasurer and Secretary John Brigg

Date	Collection	Amount		
1836	Total Collected;	£	s	d
Feb 16	At the Opening Services	16	7	
	1st Quarterly Collection	2	17	1h
	1st Quarterly Subscription			
	W. Ellison	10		
	J. Briggs		1	5
	A. Moulding		2	6
	B. Craven		10	
	Thos. Sutcliffe		2	
	Jonas Sugden		2	
	John Robinson		2	
	Jn. Greenwood		10	
	Jn. Craven		5	
	Jn. Smith		2	
	A. [Heeland] (Donation)		2	6
July 31	2nd Quarterly Collection	3	13	6
Nov. 15	3rd Quarterly Collection	3	17	9
	Cash for Bible from the Odd Fellows	1	1	
	Subscription of **Sutcliffe & Hudson**			
	for table and music stand	1	1	
		32	6	10h
1837				
Feb 16	Total balance on hand	9	8	9h

Committee of Management for the Lodge – Secretary, Thomas Sutcliffe

Date	Expenditure	Amount		
1836		£	s	d
Feb 16	By acct 2/ By printing 8/		10	
Mar 18	By cash for Bible	1	1	
May 10	By Rent	2	10	9
21	By covers for front desks in Lodge		10	
27	By sundry fittings to Jn Smith as paid		7	10
,,	By supplies for Horton College to April 24		3	12

„	By 4 [forms] & back nails to old ones		2	4
„	By table & music stand	1	0	6
June 24	By Mr Harvey for Easter Supply	5		
Nov 9	By Rent for Lodge Room	5	9	
Dec 4	By Jn Smith's a/c		10	h
	By candles		3	h
	Balance	9	8	9
		32	6	10h

The Account Book showed **John Smith** pledging the very small sum of **2s** for the quarter covering **February 16th** until **May 22nd, 1836** (compared to the **10s** pledge of his possible employer **B. Craven**.) Significantly, in **7** of the **11** recorded cases, the amount pledged to the chapel lay in the **2s** to the **2/6d** range. These small figures suggested that most of the active participants in this new Chapel were people of only limited financial means. Hardly surprisingly, mention was made in the records of it being a poor church. Certainly, it was unlikely to have afforded to pay for <u>both</u> a new Pastor <u>and</u> the costs of a new £900 building at the same time. (Not to mention the costs of running a new Sunday School.) Even if the congregation have given **£25.00** per year to cover the costs of the new building, it would still have taken **45** years to have been fully repaid! These figures showed that the fellowship would either very quickly run into a major *'cash flow'* crisis or be forced to resort to dubious methods of fundraising. It seemed **Cullingworth Chapel** had tried to expand too quickly in too short a time. They would later come to regret their over-ambitious plans. As a **Christian** believer, I can't help but wonder why the leadership didn't pray and ask for divine wisdom before embarking upon the various projects that got them into such financial straits, **(James 1:5)**.

It was interesting to note the **7s 10d** being paid into **John Smith's** account on **May 27th, 1837** for *'sundry fittings.'* By **December 4th** of that year, another **10s and half-a-pence** was paid in. Apparently, **John Smith** was playing an active part in furnishing the new Chapel even though he was not on the *'Building Committee.'* (Neither he nor **Ann** had served on the Sunday School committee either. Sadly, *'The Sunday School Minutes Book'* did not contain the names of those children who attended its classes during this period) The implication of these figures was that he had supplemented his income as a Corn Miller by doing odd jobs – a practice very typical of the time. In general, the picture emerged that **John Smith** was a very useful Chapel member who could be relied upon to repair or make new fixtures. He also served on the occasional committee but was not required to discharge those tasks which involved strong numeric or literacy skills. In addition, he was willing to make a financial contribution – despite having limited means. He seemed very much to be a *'loyal stalwart,'* willing to put in a helping hand, although not eloquent enough to have been considered for preaching or for some higher form of *'Church Office.'*

A quick review of the available records did show **John Smith** as having served on the provisional Chapel Management Committee. This body had lasted from **Tuesday, February 16**th until **December 1836** when the new six-member *'Building Committee'* had superseded it. **John** did not serve on this later committee but attended open meetings conducted under its auspices. The members of this later Building Committee appeared to be influential figures in the community. Their names were **Edward Craven** (whose son **Benjamin** acted as Manager at the new Corn Mill), **W.S. Nichols** (Textiles Manufacturer), **William Craven** (Builder and Constructor), **William Ellison, John Briggs** (Shopkeeper and Grocer) and **John Greenwood.** With their previous track record of success, it did not appear that much could go wrong. Consequently (after full consultation with the members) it was decided, at a meeting held on **6**th **June 1836,** to erect a new Chapel. The surviving records of **Cullingworth Baptist Chapel** showed an **Ann** as well as a **John Smith.** Her name cropped up in the following minutes for the year **1836:**

"Minutes of Church Meeting held **July 22**nd *the baptising having been postponed for a week.*

The following persons came before the Church, **John Berry, Wm. Wilkinson, Wm. Lund, Elizabeth Shoesmith. Priscilla Waddington, Hannah Townsley, Ann Smith,** *Jane Taylor, Martha Craven, Ann Sutcliffe, Mary Huntley and* **Joseph Sutcliffe**

*Resolved 6*th *to accept them in full communion in their having been baptised*

*Resolved 7*th *The committee having made this request – it was to purchase* **1500** *yards of land more or less belonging to* **W. Waddington** *sited opposite to the gate of* **Messrs Townend** *and contiguous to the road*

*Resolved 8*th *To invite* **W. J. Harvey** *to become Pastor of the Church at* **Cullingworth** *on the termination of his studies at* **Horton** *– adjourned."*

Ominously, there was no written record of anyone asking whether this pioneer work could afford to purchase both new land and hire a new Minister. Nor did anyone question whether it was wise to plunge an obviously inexperienced Minister into a situation where a great deal of mature judgement would be required. With hindsight, it was possible to see that, for all its concern with outward forms, the decision-making skills of this provisional Management Committee left a lot to be desired. They were rushing in to build a new work far too quickly. The members of this Chapel had much zeal but too little wisdom to give it a sense of balance. One can only wonder what had happened to their native shrewdness. Perhaps there was a misguided desire to imitate the successful **Haworth Congregation.** If so, there was a failure to realize an approach that was right for **Haworth** may not be right for **Cullingworth** – a smaller, less stable community with far fewer resources.

In the membership lists, **John** and **Ann Smith** occupied thirteenth and thirtieth positions respectively. Details were also included about **Simon Mead** because of the interesting location of his death, which showed that even a remote **Yorkshire** villager could have contacts with a very different part of the world.

Name 13. John Smith X
When Recorded: June 15th, 1836
How Recorded: By Baptism at Cowhouse Bridge
By whom Baptised: Reverend M. Saunders - from Hall Green Baptist Church in Haworth
Dismissed: Removed to Skipton
Separated: December 21st, 1842

Name 16. Simon Mead X
When Recorded: June 15th, 1836
How Recorded: By Baptism at Cowhouse Bridge
By whom Baptised: Reverend M. Saunders
Dismissed:
Separated:

Name 30. Ann Smith X
When Recorded: July 24th, 1836
How Recorded: By Baptism at Cowhouse Bridge
By whom Baptised: Reverend James Ackworth, M.A. – President of Horton Baptist College, Bradford
Dismissed: Removed to Skipton
Separated: December 21st, 1842

NB: Simon Mead died on **July 17th, 1837 in Chicago, Illinois,** *"on his way to settle with his brother."*

192

The *'separation date'* could be recorded some considerable time after an actual removal to another location. All three names had X shaped marks beside them in the original lists (as distinct from a neater, later copy which I had reproduced at **Bradford Archive Centre** for statistical tabulation purposes) suggesting that all three new members were illiterate. **Ann Smith** was one of twelve people baptised on **July 24th, 1836,** only four of whom were men.

The names of **John** and **Ann Smith** also appeared as signatories in a rather grovelling letter sent to **Joseph Harvey,** begging him to be Pastor. Dated **July 24th, 1836,** it showed them both as established Chapel Members with whom were they formalising an important request.

> *"Copy of invitation to* **Joseph Hartley** *by the* **Baptist** *Church at* **Cullingworth** *requesting him to accept the* <u>*Pastoral charge over them*</u>.
>
> *The Church of* **Jesus Christ** *meeting in* **The Lodge, Cullingworth,** *to their esteemed and beloved brother* **Joseph Hartley.**
>
> *We fervently thank our* **Heavenly Father,** *the great shepherd of the Flock, who in his gracious Providence, directed you to labour amongst us during the recent vacation, and who honoured you in the manifestation of his grace to the awakening of careless sinners and the great edification of them who feared God. The* **Holy Spirit** *hath hereby stirred up in us such a love to your person and such an esteem for those gifts of sympathy and communication with which he hath especially blessed you, that our hearts our enlarged toward you.*
>
> *Amidst the greatness of the* **Lord's** *work, we see our insufficiency and weakness. We see the wisdom of the head of the Church in appointing the Pastoral Office, and we humbly but earnestly pray that our wants may be supplied, and the Church built up a glorious temple to the praise of* **God,** *by His appointed means – that we may be blessed in the labours of one whom the spirit of the* **Lord God** *hath anointed to preach good tidings to the meek, to bind up the broken hearted, to proclaim liberty to the captives and the opening of the prison to them that are bound.*
>
> *We are highly favoured in the ministry of those who so acceptably distribute amongst us the bread of life on the* **Lord's** *day, yet we feel the want of one who may discharge the equally important duties of the Pastoral Office during the week, by spiritual intercourse and the maintenance of prayer meetings, preaching and social religious instruction; that enquiring souls may be brought in, the wicked awakened, the borders of Zion be enlarged, and her inhabitants directed and stimulated by such superintendence to diligent labour in the Lord's vineyard.*
>
> *To you beloved Brother, we look on him whom Providence has designed to fulfil these duties among us, our affections unite in you as those of one heart and our prayers and endeavours shall be constantly directed to promote your comfort and prosperity, should you be stationed over us.*

We do therefore most affectionately and unanimously invite you to take oversight of us on the expiration of your term of studies.

May the wise and gracious Spirit guide your decision.

To him, in whom we are and whom we serve, we humbly commend you. Brother pray for us

July 24ᵗʰ, 1836 *(Signed by)*

Wm, S. Nichols, and **Richard S. Nichols** *&* **John Robinson** – *Deacons*
T Shoesmith, W. Wilkinson, Joseph Sutcliffe, Abrm Moulding
Jonas Sudgen, Isaac Constantine, W. Ellison, Jn Smith, Wm Lund,
Simon Mead, Robt Hartley, Cornelius Taylor, Geo: Hethrington,
Thos Ellison, John Berry,
Sarah Taylor, Ellen Gregson,
Ruth Sutcliffe, Rebecca Waddington, Nancy Sandham,
Marianne Craven, Emma Craven, Martha Craven,
Ann Smith, Hannah Townsley, Priscilla Waddington,
Elizabeth Shoesmith, Anne Sutcliffe, James Taylor, Mary Utley,
Grace Tilotson -- *Members."*

Including the three Deacons, there were eighteen males and fourteen female members – hardly large enough a number to sustain both a major building project and a full-time minister. Ominously, there seemed to be an unwillingness to choose between hard alternatives.

Section 5: A Failure in Ministry

Concerning the problems of a nineteenth-century Baptist minister

Through this correspondence, a great deal of emotional pressure and flattery was being exerted on the Chapel's prospective Minister. Hardly surprisingly, he was rather wary in his response, laying down strict conditions before he would accept the post. One of these was a demand for four weeks leave. From the onset, it was obvious that desperation for strong leadership made **Cullingworth Chapel** far keener to have **Joseph Harvey** than **Joseph Harvey** was to have them! Evidence from his correspondence revealed that he already entertained strong doubts about the Chapel's financial viability. This apparently young and rather insecure man perhaps wondered how the Church could feed him! He may also have felt that its members were rather unrealistic in their expectations of what he could do. A sense of unease was already present in his very first reply.

*"To the Church of **Jesus Christ** meeting in the **Lodge, Cullingworth***
Beloved Brethren,
Having received from you an invitation to become your Pastor, and sensible that this involves
important consequences; I cannot presume to answer your request until I have had time for
*serious consideration and prayer that this may be afforded, I beg your indulgence for **2** months,*
when you shall, (God willing) hear from me again.
Wishing your continued and increased prosperity and requesting an interest in your prayers.
*I remain dear Brethren, your brother in Christ **J. Harvey***
 Horton Academy, July 30th, 1836"

At this point, the Chapel perhaps should have taken the hint and either looked for another Pastor or better still, done without one until their financial situation had improved. By the end of **September 1836,** it was obvious that Pastor **Harvey** was playing *'hard to get.'* He appeared to be going out of his way to lay down stringent conditions, possibly in the hope that the congregation of **Cullingworth** would withdraw their offer – without him having to suffer the embarrassment of refusing it! Yet even at this stage, no one in the chapel appeared to have entertained any other notion other than the original request that Pastor **Harvey** lead them. This lack of discernment was evident in the minutes for **September 25th, 1836.**

*"Lords' day **Sept 25th** the members of the Church were requested to stay after the service to consider propositions made by **Mr Harvey** previous to his accepting the invitation of the Church*
*Copy of **J. Harvey's** proposals to the **Church of Christ** at **Cullingworth:** -*
***1st** that he should only preach two sermons on the **Lord's Day** to the same people*
***2nd** that he should have one month every year at his disposal, and that the Church should find supplies (meaning supply preachers) during that time*
***3rd** that he wished to be exempt from begging for the Chapel*
***4th** that he desires to know what they can do towards his support*
*If these proposals meet with the appropriation of the Church, he will accept their invitation for 6 months with the prospect of settling if the providence seems favourable, **September24th 1836."***
*The Church's reply. **Cullingworth Sept 25th, 1836***
Dear Sir,
Your three first propositions have met the appropriation of the Church and touching the fourth the following resolution has been come to – that the Church will do all in its power to make you comfortable and will give you a more decisive answer when the Chapel is built

*To the **Revd J. Harvey***
*(Signed by) **John Robinson, Deacon"*** [who could write in a very clearly]

Such an evasive reply on the matter of his support would hardly reassure an already doubtful **Pastor Harvey** that **Cullingworth Chapel** was in any position to ever successfully provide for him. Any doubts he would have had about accepting their offer could only have been reinforced. Moreover, he could easily have drawn the conclusion that this congregation wanted a pastor *'on the cheap'* – very possibly it did!

Another early indication of trouble was this letter received from **Isaac Constantine** thanking his fellow members for readmitting him to the Church following a period of estrangement. It was written in beautiful script writing.

"Sykes Dec. 3rd1836

Dear Brothers and Sisters in ***Christ,***

*The note of Brother **E. Wadsworth** informing me that by the unanimous consent of your church my unworthy name had been restored to the church book by some misadventure only reached me on **Monday** night. I beg now to express my sorrow that I ever requested it to be withdrawn and think I did wrong, pray for me that I may be forgiven. I take this opportunity for thanking you for this mark of your **Christian** confidence and hope. Let my life be long or short I shall not be unmindful of my obligations to my fellow members. Had I known in time I believe that notwithstanding my severe indisposition I should have been with you at the **Lord's Table** on **Sunday** last. May the **Lord** accept the will for the deed and now my dear **Christian** friends I beg an especial interest in your prayers, and I will not forget you in mine.*

*On a review of my former connection with you, although never quite destitute of the eventual qualification to the true **Christian**, yet I find a sad and mournful deficiency existed in my own case. Brotherly love is not only necessary to the prosperity of the church but also to individual progress in the divine life. Love covers a multitude of sins and enables us to bear each other's burdens and so fulfil the law of **Christ**. It is that prominent mark which separated the world from the church and is the brightest evidence of our having experienced that divine change so essential to salvation.*

*The love of **Christ** shed abroad in our hearts has also a counteracting influence over all our principles, disputations and actions and in dealing with our erring Brothers or Sisters with what tender and anxious solicitude should we endeavour to reform and restore such as one to his or her proper state of mind and were we on all occasions to pursue such a train of actions in dependence on divine influence and grace then I think much good would be the result. May the head of the Church preside over us and direct my brothers and sisters of the **Cullingworth***

Baptists in the prayer of your unworthy Brother in **Christian** *Love,* **Isaac Constantine.**"

After reading this letter one was left wondering *'What happened here?'* It appeared that the most interesting things were those left unsaid. Obviously, there had been some disputation in which **Isaac Constantine** had perceived a lack of charity. No details were given over what had caused the rift and none were found in other records such as *'The Minute Book.'* This would suggest that the matter had not been all that serious; the fact that a restoration to membership was possibly reinforced that conclusion. Overall, **Isaac Constantine** seemed to be genuinely grateful for a hard-won reconciliation. He appears to have suffered from depression, yet the suspicion emerged that his letter was a little too fulsome to be wholly genuine. The writer was not above a little self-serving grovelling! Also present was a tendency to skirt around issues. In terms of style, the letter was certainly something that could easily have come from a **Charles Dickens** novel. This would suggest that **Isaac Constantine** was a well-educated man. His home address of *'Sykes'* appears to have been that of an outlying farm – a conclusion reinforced by the fact that it wasn't found during a search of the **1841** Census Return for **Cullingworth** and its immediate vicinity. This search had taken place on **Monday, 8th July 2002,** the day I first transcribed the above letter at the **Bradford Archive Centre.**

Another mystery was the identity of **E. Wadsworth** – a name which did not surface on any of the membership rolls of the chapel. However, the Sunday School Teachers Minutes Book revealed that he was a Sunday School Teacher who had been asked by the relevant Committee to help set it up on **10th July 1837.** Neither his name nor that of **Isaac Constantine** featured in any Trade Directory for the **Cullingworth** locality. This would suggest that in terms of wealth they did not number among the top one-fifth of the population.

Overall, **Isaac Constantine's** letter was interesting because it had been written by a man who would have both seen and conversed (if only on a formal basis) with my Great, Great Grandfather, **John Smith.** Another interesting feature was the way it covered the affairs of a group to which my ancestor had belonged. It also provided evidence that tensions had been present from the very beginning. These were to grow ever more acute as time passed. On **11th April 1837** *'The Minute Book'* revealed that *"Discreditable reports being in circulation respecting* **Bro. Hartley** *of having for some time being also not in attendance of the worship of* **God,** *Brother* **Robinson** *and* **Wilkinson** *were deputised to converse with him."* He was eventually excluded on the **3rd August 1838. Isaac Constantine** was to have another *'run in'* with the church sometime later.

Details, (kindly provided by **Julie Skellern** of **New Zealand** in late **December 2003**) made it possible to construct the following simple *'Fact File'* concerning **Isaac Constantine** (one of **Julie's** ancestors.) They formed a useful context to the letter just quoted. His service with the **British Army** in the **Spanish Peninsular** suggested that he had been a brave man.

"Name: Isaac CONSTANTINE 3rd

Birth: *ca 1787 Haworth*
Baptism: *31 Jul 1787 St Michael & All Angels, Haworth*
Residence: *1851 Sun Street, KEIGHLEY,*
Residence: *1841 Hope Street, KEIGHLEY*
Residence: *1830 Rycroft (Hamlet near Harden) Bingley Parish,*
Residence: *1817 Rycroft (Hamlet near Harden) Bingley Parish,*
Death: *1857 Keighley*
Occupation: *Wool comber (1817), Peninsular Wars – British Army, Weaver (1830), Teacher of Leading & Lodging House Occ. (1851)*
Father: *Benjamin CONSTANTINE (ca1765-)*
Mother: *Margaret WILSON*

Spouses

1) Alice HOLMES
Death: *before 1830*
Marriage: *11 Mar 1811 Haworth*
Children: -
Benjamin (1811-1846)
Nanny (ca1815-1882)
Thomas (ca1817-?)
John (ca1821-?)
Holmes (ca1826-?)

2) Hannah PRESTON
Birth: *ca 1801*
Residence: *1830 Rycroft*
Death: *Mar 1851 Sun Street, KEIGHLEY,*
Burial: *30 Mar 1851 Keighley,*

198

Father: *PRESTON*
Marriage: *27 Dec 1830 Bingley*

Notes for Isaac CONSTANTINE 3rd
Thomas is baptised to **Isaac & Alice** *in* **Bingley**, *but* **Benjamin** *is baptised just to* **Isaac** *in* **Haworth!** *Other baptisms for his children (and there may be more) have not been found.*

Joseph *(the bath proprietor) refers to his Uncle* **Isaac** *being at* **Cullingworth**.... *in the* **1830s** *to* **1846** *and the tiny village of* **Rycroft** *(some* **28** *households) is just up the road from there - both fall in the Parish of* **Bingley.**

Last Modified: *27 Dec 2003* **Created:** *4 Jan 2004*

Source: Julie M. Skellern
NEW ZEALAND 1750
email: jools@maxnet.co.nz"

Matters rested whilst the Chapel building was being constructed in **1837** – the year Queen **Victoria** came to the throne. The **Revd J. Harvey** came only to preach and help with baptisms. (He baptised one man and three women at **Cowhouse Bridge** on **July 30th, 1837**. During **January 7th, 1838** he baptised another one man and three women in the new Chapel.) Only at *"a Church Meeting held in the vestry* **February 2nd1838"** was the question of his pastorate reviewed. It seems that during this interlude, **J. Harvey** had been unsuccessful in his plans to find another Church to take his services. Looming into view was a dangerous situation in which a desperate congregation was looking for the services of a Pastor who himself was, because of financial pressures, increasingly desperate to find any position – no matter how unsuitable. In terms of ministerial material, **Cullingworth** was in danger of taking on board a *'reject'* by other Assemblies. An unhappy situation was in the making. Undertones of this can be found in the following extract from the minutes of the meeting, which commenced at *"***Friday** *evening* **8 o'clock February 2nd, 1838."**
Brother Harvey *having signified his determination (after many difficulties and much prayer, and contrary to all his former plans) to accept the cordial invitation of the Church (agreed unanimously by the congregation) to its Pastoral Superintendence he requested to know what support could be provided for him, and also stated his conscientious objections to the usual mode of Ordination and Recognition. It was therefore resolved that under present burdens of the Church and its limited resources, that sum cannot be guaranteed which the Church would desire to give and to which* **Bro. Harvey's** *services entitle him and that sixty-five pounds per*

annum with the use of the house be proposed, allowing one month's absence in the year as before stipulated, the church during that time to provide supplies. **Bro. Harvey** *also had reserved to himself the option to avail himself of such assistance as he may be able to procure for one of three services of the* **Lord's** *day and conceding to the Church the remainder of the stipulations agreed according to the minutes* **Sept 25th 1836."**

The ominous words here were, *"agreed unanimously by the congregation."* This provided decisive evidence that not <u>one</u> person was willing to publicly challenge the wisdom of appointing, at a time of severe financial difficulty, a Minister who seemed to raise one obstacle after another concerning the taking up of his position. No one asked the obvious question as to whether he was only considering the appointment because he had no better Church to go to. Nor did anyone query whether it was appropriate to appoint a Pastor when the Church obviously could not afford one. The impression conveyed in these documents was of a Chapel whose decision-making processes were seriously flawed. There was an over-eagerness to gain the *'respectability'* of having a properly accredited Minister – just like any other church. Although the motions of consulting the members were gone through, there was the possibility that Church meetings were commandeered by a few domineering personalities bent on having their own way. Later events would show that just such personalities did exist. Regrettably, nothing emerged to confirm that **John** and **Ann Smith** ever opposed such a dangerous status quo. They were perhaps too young in the faith to have done so.

On **Sunday, 23rd February 1838, Pastor Harvey** was received into the ministry at **Cullingworth Chapel,** amidst what appears to have been a rather grand ordination tea. At a meeting conducted under his auspices, it was *"resolved that the first subject for consideration be the Sufficiency of the Word of God as contained in the Old and New Testaments, for direction in faith and practice.*
Resolved that **Mr Giles** *of* **Leeds** *be requested to present the sermon on the Anniversary of the Chapel.*
Resolved that **W.S Nichols** *be allowed the use of the schoolroom except on the Lord's Day for the purposes of tuition on such matters as may be arranged at the next meeting."*
William Nichols was dismissed to **Bradford Church** on **July 1st, 1840,** although later evidence shows that he was still in the **Cullingworth** locality during the middle of that month.

To the embarrassment of everyone concerned, the **Revd. J. Harvey** turned out to be a one-month wonder. All the efforts taken to cajole him into accepting the ministry at **Cullingworth Chapel** had been a sheer waste of time. Undeniable proof of this point was found in records dated **March 23rd, 1838.**

"At a special meeting of the Church conveyed by notice to the members personally, **March 23rd Friday** *at* **8** *in the vestry. After the devotional exercises the following communication from* **Bro. Harvey** *was submitted to the Deacons.*
Copy
To the Baptised Church of **Jesus Christ** *meeting in* **Cullingworth Yorkshire:** -

My beloved brethren! Grace, mercy, and peace be multiplied unto you.

Since my first knowledge of you, I have every reason to bless **God** *on your behalf, because of the great things he has done for you. I feel thankful to the* **Father of all mercies** *for any token of his favour bestowed upon us and for peace and comfort attendant on acquaintance. Notwithstanding all that has been enjoyed and done, I am under the necessity of resigning my pastoral charge over you. And of separating myself* <u>altogether</u> *from the communion of the* **Particular Baptists.** *I dare no longer continue in association with a body of professing* **Christians,** *which prostitute the worship of* **Jehovah;** *by allowing the ungodly to unite therein and make the world its ally, in maintaining the cause of God by seeking contributions from it.*

(Was this a reference to seeking contributions from the **Odd Fellows** whose rituals **J. Harvey** may well have disliked for religious reasons? The accounts quoted previously did show at least one sum of £1 1s having been raised from that quarter to purchase a Bible. Another *'worldly'* donor may well have been the business of **Sutcliffe & Hudson** who likewise had provided £1 1s.)

My views have not been hastily formed, for they are the result of much prayer, meditation, and searching the scriptures. The sacrifice I now make is on <u>my own part</u> *a very great one. I have much feeling and many interests to relinquish. Yet if the sacrifice were tenfold greater, such is the force of truth on my conscience that I must make it. What am I, that I should withstand* **God?** *This I dare not do on any consideration; for I am fully persuaded in my own mind, that I am now doing my duty by handing in my resignation, and at once coming out from a communion, which I believe to be in practice erroneous. Such is the plain direction given in the word of* **God,** *which is not to separate a society but to come out from those who maintain a fellowship with the world, which the scriptures forbid.* **Viz 2 Cor: 6:14-18 & Rev 18.4.**

In leaving your communion and neighbourhood, I can assure you that I shall retain the warmest affection for you all, and a grateful remembrance of the repeated kindness' you have showed me on various occasions. I take this opportunity of returning my sincere thanks for your forbearance with me amidst the numerous imperfections, which have blended with the performance of my pastoral duties. Believe me, you shall not be forgotten at the throne of grace. My prayers to God for you shall be that the **Lord** *may lead you with all truth and preserve you until that day when we shall meet at the bar of our judge & that we may be found of him in peace. Until that period, cleave close to* **Christ** *with full purpose of heart. Be much in [prayer] with your Father and friend. Be diligent Bible students and the* **God** *of peace shall bless you, with the knowledge of his will, and with hearts to do and submit to the same.* (All underlining was present in the original document.)

Let me remind you that we part in peace, that I have no personal nor private animosities; that I do not blame you for not seeing as I see, and that I only ask in [grace] to be remembered by you when you are enjoying meetings with God, unto whom I now commit you, and shall ever remain, your brother in Christ.
Signed **J. Harvey**

The Church, after discussion, in consequence resolved that the faithful & zealous devotion of our beloved pastor to the welfare of sinners and the interests of this church – the unconscious affection of the church and congregation of him – and the blessing of God manifest on his labours – cause his present communication to be received with the deepest regret."

Somehow it was very easy to imagine the stunned expressions on the faces of all the listeners as that letter was read. Among the dismayed gathering were two people who were direct forebears. However, **J. Harvey's** severance from the Chapel was not as decisive as his letter made out. He was still performing baptisms until **July 8th, 1838** – possibly while he was working his period of notice. Nor did he leave the neighbourhood for he was still ministering in the **Bingley** locality toward the end of **1839**. Only then did this somewhat curiously weak man vanish from the scene.

Although an abundance of other evidence confirmed that his criticisms of the congregation were valid, one would have been more impressed by his letter if he had displayed real humility by openly admitting that he had been wrong to have ever taken up the offer of a Pastorate at **Cullingworth Chapel. Joseph Harvey's** mistake had been to accept a position for which he had had no real calling. Beneath the pious wording of his correspondence there lay the distinct impression that he was heartily glad to be rid of this assembly. It seems he had never really wanted to be so closely involved with it in the first place. Overall, it was a case of a minister having been unable to identify with his congregation or to have *'fitted in'* with their requirements. Having said that, some of the congregation's requirements do appear to have been unreasonable; it was evident that their *'ideal minister'* would be someone good at writing begging letters. Yet in fairness to **Cullingworth Chapel, Pastor Harvey** did receive a gift of eight pounds for the services he had rendered. Such an act possibly spoke of a guilty conscience for having pressed the position upon him in the first place.

Thus, **Cudworth's** statement about **Pastor J. Harvey** was not confirmed by historical sources emanating from within **Cullingworth Chapel** itself. (See Bibliography for precise details of these sources.) I found the copy of **J. Harvey's** letter to have been rather peevish in tone. His letter formed the basis of his excuse to leave. In addition, he should have had the common sense to have ascertained what the fundraising methods were before accepting the post. As so often in church life a failure to ask the right questions at the right time had led to an unnecessary dispute.

An entry in the Minute Book for **1st June 1838** noted that the Chapel was without a Pastor, (the term was used interchangeably with *'minister'*) but had received seventeen new members by baptism and one by letter of recommendation, thus bringing the total membership to **69**. The outstanding debt on the new building was **£650.00**. (This was a huge amount for those days!)

At a district meeting held on **December 4th 1838,** *the* **Bradford District Committee** *recommended that* **Bingley** *and* **Cullingworth** *Chapel pool funds so that they could share the same minister. Two days later at "a Special Church Meeting after the afternoon service and in the schoolroom … it was proposed that* **J. Harvey** *be requested to become the Pastor of the two Churches – the members of* **Bingley** *being agreeable."* (The records showed that deputies from **Bingley** were present at this meeting in **Cullingworth**.) However, at the Church meeting of **January 11th** in the following year, *"it was reported to the Church that the resolution of the last meeting has been communicated to* **J. Harvey** *personally and that the following was his reply:*
"After most serious deliberation and prayer, I am constrained to reply in the negative to the invitation I have received from the Churches at **Cullingworth** *and* **Bingley.**"

Here were the words of a man who had made up his mind. No ambiguity was shown this time around. He was ever so politely telling the two assemblies to *'get lost.'* He must have felt a profound sense of mistrust toward their leaders for him to have adopted this stance. The overall impression conveyed by his correspondence was of a rather evasive, weak man wanting to use any excuse to leave a situation in which he'd never really wanted to fit. His correspondence seemed always to be characterised by a rather sad lack of personal honesty.

Section 6: Chapel Troubles

Concerning divisions within a nineteenth-century Baptist church

In **May 1839,** the Chapel was still looking for a new Minister (they did not receive one until **July 1842.**) By this time the Assembly still listed **69** members. In the previous year, four members had been added by baptism, and four had been lost, (**3** by exclusion and **1** by moving to another Chapel). These figures were interesting because they revealed that **J. Harvey's** resignation had not generated a significant loss of membership. Such data confirmed that any support he had enjoyed within the Church had been of a very limited nature. He had <u>not</u> been a charismatic leader who could draw on large numbers of people for support.

Sadly, as the months passed, **Cullingworth Chapel** fell into complete disarray, as is shown by the following extracts from *'The Minute Book'* that probably recorded only snippets of what was going on: -

*1/11/1839: "that bro. [Ellison] be appointed to visit **Sister Sandham** over the complaint of **Sister S. Taylor**."*

*29/11/1839: "that the resignation of bro. **Sandham** of his post of Deacon be accepted and that he be continued as member of this Church."*

*10/1/1840: "Resolved that **Isaac Constantine** be excluded for continued neglect of the worship of God among us.*

*The withdrawal of **Elizabeth Holmes** and **Ann Sutcliffe** was received.*

Second that members absent from the Lord's Supper for three months without sufficient reason be thereby excluded."

8/5/1840: "It is painful to report to you the state of Church during the past year. We are yet without a pastor – and have suffered so much from the want of that vigilance, reproof, encouragement and co-operation, which a judicious and active leader would have afforded to us." (This was part of a *'begging letter'* sent by the Deacons to the **Baptist Association** concerning the Chapel debts.)

One person who, in the end, was reconciled with the Chapel was **Isaac Constantine.** He was restored on **28**th **November 1856** then died in **March** of the following year. The cause of death was attributed to old age. Somehow one feels that **Isaac Constantine** was as much sinned against as sinning. It must be recalled that he was a man whose previously quoted letter had manifested a profound distaste for any form of conflict and by **1840** there were conflicts aplenty. Given the acrimony that was present **Isaac Constantine** may well have been right have kept away from it all! In addition, it must also be remarked that it had taken **Isaac** almost seventeen years to have plucked up enough courage to have returned. This does not speak of a man with fond memories. Perhaps, in the end, he was *'hedging his bets'* for the afterlife! Apart from my Great, Great Grandparents themselves, **Isaac Constantine** was the only layperson connected to the Chapel whom I felt I'd got to know as an individual in a positive way. The discovery of his letter had represented a major finding.

By **14th July 1840** membership was down to **60,** with **14** being non-resident – the latter apparently including **John** and **Ann Smith.** This decline may have been instrumental in persuading **John** and **Ann Smith** to sever all contact with this Assembly. At the very least it would have left a very charged atmosphere and it was symptomatic of an assembly having turned inward on itself. The situation had involved a *'Brother **Benjamin Sandham'*** who'd been baptised on **September 4th, 1836** before being elected to the office of Deacon on **16th February 1838.** He appears to have got into trouble over a pecuniary matter.

> *"At the Church Meeting on **July 14th 1840**, present **30** members **W. S. Nichols** presiding, **Bro. Green** detailed the proceedings of the Deacons in reference to the reports against **Bro. Sandham** that stating that dissatisfaction had been expressed with his conduct therein*
>
> *Resolved (two Resolutions) that the Church approves the conduct of the Deacons in **Bro. Sandham's** case*
>
> *Also, resolved that the Deacons be requested not to call in other members to advise them, or act in conjunction with them in matters belonging to their office was withdrawn on the Deacons expressing their determination not to do so except in cases of extreme emergency.*
>
> *Resolved that the evidence against **Bro. Sandham** received by the Deacons & others at their meeting for that purpose be read to the Church.*
>
> *That evidence having been read and all other charges brought forward which any member thought proper against **Bro. Sandham** was allowed to question the witnesses present respecting their evidence, and to offer explanation and defence of his conduct.*
>
> *On the proposal that the Church do express its opinion by ballot whether **Bro. Sandham's** conduct on the evidence and defence produced had been consistent as a member of the Church.*
>
> *Resolved (By a majority of **16** to **12**) that the conduct of **Bro. Sandham** had been consistent. Adjourned"*

Bro. Sandham had won only a hollow victory – the membership list showed that he had chosen to withdraw from the Church on that very same day. In passing, I wondered whether this unpleasant affair had provoked my forebears to leave this assembly. Was it the *'final straw'* for them? They would certainly have realized that the **Cullingworth Chapel** had become rather toxic.

After this entry, *'The Minutes Book'* fell silent for almost two years. The failure to keep up with it was another sign of disruption at **Cullingworth Chapel.** When entries were again resumed, they began with the following uncomplimentary description of its condition, written by **Joseph Green,** five days after he took up the Pastorate on **July 4th, 1842.** Not from him the diplomatic equivocations of his predecessor – **Joseph Green** were of an altogether more decisive nature. Unlike the more hesitant **J. Harvey,** he was certainly not a man to mince words with anyone. Indeed, **Pastor Green** appears to have been something of an autocrat, one who did not suffer fools – least of all religious fools – gladly. Such traits were going to be needed, for by the time of his arrival the Assembly was in total disarray. The extent of this was highlighted by **Pastor Green's** first entry in *The Minutes Book.'*

> *"The following was penned by* **Joseph Green,** *their Pastor.*
>
> *From the time of the last minutes being entered the church entered upon a sad course of contention, confusion and decline. It is needless and impossible to enter into detail respecting its downward progress. Suffice it to say the pulpit was supplied by students from* **Horton** *and lay brethren in the neighbouring Churches, the congregation continued to decline until the writer of this account first visited the place, the congregation had dwindled down to* **60** *persons. I came here first on the* **2nd Sabbath** *in* **January 1842** *and supplied the pulpit for* **1** *month during which time the congregation doubled its members. Feeling concerned for the state of things I gave up my pastoral charge at* **Soham, Cambridgeshire,** *and in* **July** *following came to reside here for* **1** *year in order to try the station to see if it was possible to raise it from its awful state. An examination of its state had convinced me that I had undertaken a task of no ordinary difficulty.*
>
> *The Sabbath school was under the direction and control of* **Socialists, Deists** *and* **Chartists,** *who had introduced several volumes of novels of a very questionable character amongst the books. No words can describe the awful condition of the Church. All discipline was at an end, the prayer and experience meetings existed only in name, while very few came to the Lord's Table. And how could it be otherwise with a raw inexperienced people, utterly ignorant of the nature and design of Church order and divided in their views of divine truth. I think I have never met such a motley mixture of* **Arminians, Calvinists,** *and* **Hypers** *in my life.* (Very briefly, **Arminians** emphasised the role human freewill played in choosing the moment one could come to faith in Christ, **Calvinists** highlighted the role of Divine Sovereignty in the creation of this faith, whilst **Hypers** were extreme **Calvinists** who bordered on fatalism in their attitude to Divine election. All three factions still exist today, each within different branches of Protestant Christianity.)

Finding such to be the state of things I requested the members to meet me in the vestry and after stating to them my view of their condition and informing them that I would have nothing to do with their past quarrels and dissensions I proposed that I should dissolve their Church-state and begin afresh. To this everyone heartily consented. [They probably did not have much choice!] *The following resolution was then proposed and agreed to.*

*Resolved that as there has been so much amongst us which has been unchristian and ungracious we agree to bury all our differences and begin afresh and in token thereof to sign the church covenant [and] after the Deacon had engaged in prayer the whole number present **20** signed the covenant. It was resolved: -*

1. *That if any member shall again introduce our former difficulties he has to be instantly expelled from the Church*
2. *That none of the former members shall be allowed to sit down with us at the Lord's table until they have signed the covenant and consented to bury former differences*
3. *That the Pastor and Deacon be requested to visit and affectionately invite our brethren who are absent to unite with us on the foregoing conditions*
4. *That those members who are living in other places at a distance be urged to obtain their dismissals to the churches where they reside.*
5. *That those who shall not have complied with our invitation to unite again with us or obtain their dismissal from us by Christmas shall then be separated from the Church. These things being attended to **Wm. Wilkinson** (who sometime withdrew from the Church) was restored. These resolutions were agreed to **July 9th 1842** and that the meeting was adjourned to **July 16th**.*

July 16th *several friends signed the covenant making the number in communion now **34**. Leaving **29** who have not yet done it.*

*Agreed to hold the Prayer meetings in the vestry on Monday evenings and an experience meeting on Wednesday evenings. Except once a month when there shall be a Church meeting, which is appointed to be held on the **2nd** Wednesday, Also the Lord's supper, which is to be administered on the **1st** Sabbath of the month.*

*Resolved that the seat-rents be made on the **2nd** and **3rd** **Sabbaths** in **January, April, July** and **October**.*

*Agreed that for the future the gravedigger shall have **3d** for digging a grave and the minister **1s 6d** for his fee. Application for graves to be made to the Pastor and Deacon.*

*Agreed to have a public collection every quarter for incidental expenses to be made in **Sept, December, March** and **June**.*

August 17th **Martha Parker, [Olivia] Hanson** *and* **Thomas Heay** *appeared before the Church, related their experience and accepted baptism and church fellowship. They were baptised **August 20th**.*

> *October 19th Hannah Binns, Mary Ann Craven and Thomas Dinnean (who had been a Papist) were received as proper persons for membership. Baptised October 30th.*
>
> *November 16th Mary Wright and James Briggs were accepted for membership. Baptised Nov 27th. Messengers having previously been sent out to Hannah Ackroyd they reported their message to the Church when the Church solemnly separated her from its communion for her conduct. Messengers were also appointed to visit John and Mary Berry to admonish up their place in the Church."*

The removal of **John** and **Ann Smith** from the fellowship was handled in Pastor **Green's** usual brusque manner. *"Dec 21st Berry's case postponed.*

> *Separated for not filling up their places, John and Dinah Robinson, John and Ann Smith, John and Mary Holmes, Ellen Gregson, Thos. Constantine, Joseph Tatham and Elizabeth Greenwood.*
>
> *Dismissed Joseph Sutcliffe to Bradford, 2nd Church."*

Despite some practical contributions to the life of **Cullingworth Chapel** neither **John** nor **Ann Smith** was prepared to remain there. Perhaps by the middle of **1840,** it had already dawned on **John** that the Assembly was in such a bad way that the best course of action was to take himself and his family out of it. (Anyone involved in a similar Church situation today could well sympathise with his decision.) Paradoxically, the evidence cited later in this history would show that **John's Baptist** roots had not been entirely severed. My Great Grandfather **Edmund** was to return to those roots in a very surprising manner. Some light of faith had, after all, been kept burning.

As something of an aside **John Robinson** (who had been the Deacon so anxious to obtain the services of **J. Harvey**) was himself actively excluded. By this time, he may have become a thoroughly discredited figure. However, his neat handwriting was to be greatly missed – the records becoming somewhat untidy following his exit.

Ironically, **Joseph Green's** pastorate was not to last long either. Within eleven months of his taking up the call to be their minister (on **July 4th, 1842**) he had left. An entry laconically stated, *"Dismissed our Pastor Green, his wife and his servant to Golcar 12th June 1843."* (**Golcar** was a Township near **Huddersfield.** In **1841,** it covered an area of **1560** Acres and had **3598** inhabitants.) There was one last entry in the minutes about a minor administrative matter on **June 14th, 1843** and then they fell silent again until **1847.** The Chapel still did not seem able to put its affairs into any kind of order. Its members were always looking for a strong leader to sort out their problems for them.

Following a painstaking search through relevant documents, I can only conclude that my possible Great, Great Grandparents had been wise to have left **Cullingworth Chapel** when they did. Bearing testimony to a marked sense of alienation was the fact that, despite being given over five-months grace, they had never replied to the request to obtain a dismissal to the Church at the place where they now resided. By this lack of action, **John** and **Ann Smith** showed that they wanted to place the many troubles associated with that fellowship firmly behind them. Another irony was that they probably came out of this story in at least a little better light than the Assembly from which they had been dismissed. Approximately **175** years after being first made, their decision to have left **Cullingworth** Chapel had, (through this history) been vindicated.

Despite his short stay, **Joseph Green's** drastic measures did possibly contribute to this Assembly's survival. By **1870 Cullingworth Chapel** could successfully enlarge its premises and install an elaborate entrance, complete with sandstone pillars. It still had enough resources to renovate its premises again in **1909.** However, during a visit to **Cullingworth** (made on **Thursday, July 19th, 2001**) a contact I met there divulged that the Chapel had closed about *"twenty-two years previously when only about five **Baptists** were left."* (Apparently, they were elderly women who used to hold whist drives.) The membership book showed that the last names had been entered in **1980.** All but three of the twenty-two names were women. Following its closure, this grey sandstone building had become a private residence which, up to the present time, has had up to two different owners. A thorough building survey revealed that there'd been minor structural flaws in its original construction, with a slight misalignment in the walls causing problems to the roof and brickwork. The overall impression was of a building having been thrown up in a hurry. **John Briggs,** (who'd been responsible for the construction) did not seem to have had his heart in the job, presumably because there'd been no major financial gain to be made from it. During my visit, it was undergoing a major renovation. A round stone near the roof bore the inscription *"Baptist Chapel 1837."* There were still tombstones in the grounds.

An interesting notice in 'The Minutes Book' pointed to at least one reason why this Assembly had run into problems. *"After contending with many difficulties over the erection of our new Chapel (occasioned by the depression of trade) we had the pleasure of opening it for divine Worship on **October 11th [1837].** We have built our walls in* *troublesome times"* (name indecipherable). This showed that its prosperity had depended heavily upon the economic condition of a community already operating on the margins of existence. Possibly it was this trade depression which had prevented **John Briggs** from honouring a generous financial pledge. Pastor **John Whittaker** had been forced to resign because of the impracticability of supporting a family of three children on a wage of **15s** a week (which the chapel members themselves were barely able to afford). In his long and badly written resignation letter **(3ʳᵈ February 1847),** he'd made it very clear that it was only the lack of money which had provoked his resignation. He had no personal animosities and he had in fact left the Chapel in a more unified state than he had found it. Also mentioned was his background as a mill worker and his resentment at not having obtained financial support from the **Itinerant Society** because he had lacked a College-based Theological Education. Maybe because of his working-class background he'd lacked the financial (and quality time) resources needed to study at theological college. Nevertheless, he appears to have been genuinely liked by the members of the Chapel and would have remained Pastor if economic conditions had been more favourable.

Laying aside any personality clashes and misjudgements by the leadership, there remained a very real and long-term problem. This consisted of the Church's often inadequate and precarious financial position. During good times, a Minister could just about be afforded, but in the all too frequent tough times, this was not the case. Moreover, its membership (totalling about seventy not generally, wealthy people) would have been the maximum it would most likely have generated within the village. (Membership rarely went above that figure.) Consequently, the Congregation was always on the borderline of being able to support a minister. These points were brought out by the Deacons who, at the end of *'The Minutes Book'* wrote;

"A Short History of the **Baptist** *Church at* **Cullingworth 1837–1911:"**

"The Commercial condition of this village does not encourage the belief in its increase in population and trade expansion in the immediate future. Seeing that it has remained comparatively unproductive since **1837** *to the time of the writing of this article worsted spinning being the only trace of industry. In consequence, large families are regularly leaving the district for large towns in order to find more lucrative and varied employment and for growing up sons and daughters. Obviously, the Churches find this to be a constant reducing tendency and regular disappointment. This accounts to a great extent for our inability to support a pastor continuously unaided. Six Pastors since* **1837,** *namely* **Rev. J. Harvey 1837, J. Green 1842, Whittaker 1847, Spencer 1863, Berry 1876, Smith 1879** *and* **Davis 1892.**

These pastorates were mainly for short-term service. In the interval, the pulpit has been creditably supplied by students from **Rawdon College** *and by Preachers."* (In **1911** the Chapel had **70** members, **120** attendees at the Sunday service and **140** Sunday School Scholars. Characteristically, it was in debt to the tune of £**350** – incurred because of building operations.)

Although a persistent problem of limited financial resources had been present, it was worsened by the misjudgements caused by *'conventional chapel thinking.'* In this instance, a congregation requiring a chapel building hurriedly created one even when it would have been in everyone's interests <u>not</u> to have done so. The driving force was this almost palpable sense of wishing to be *'respectable.'* This had obviously been the case at **Cullingworth** – a community desperately vulnerable to any *'downturn'* in trade (which happened frequently). This *'chapel thinking'* also caused this church assembly to hanker after a Pastor even when it couldn't afford one. No one had ever raised the common-sense point that the persistent lack of resources to pay for a Pastor was a sign that the good **Lord** didn't want them to have one! For **Cullingworth,** a rule by elders would have been a far more feasible (and biblical) option. Sadly, this alternative was never considered. One suspects that if it <u>had</u> ever been suggested then it would have been given very short shrift. When it came to Church Government **Cullingworth Chapel's** rule of faith owed more to **Baptist** Tradition than to the New Testament. Consequently, a ridiculous amount of time was wasted on *'Minister chasing.'* For all his many good points, **Pastor Saunders** appears to have been the originator of this problem, for it was he who had first moulded this Assembly along conventional **Baptist** lines. Care should have been taken to follow the Apostle **Paul's** example in **Titus 1:5,** where priority was given to placing Churches (people rather than buildings) under a proper Eldership. **Cullingworth Chapel** would have fared better if they'd done this, rather than having concentrated solely upon the building and Pastor. Given its ceaseless difficulties, I came to wonder whether **Cullingworth Chapel** was a product of human enthusiasm rather than an authentic work of God. Highly applicable were the following words from **Psalm 127:1-2,** *"Except the Lord build the house, they labour in vain that build it: except the Lord keep the city, the watchman wakes but in vain. It is vain for you to rise up early, to sit up late, to eat the bread of sorrows: for so he giveth his beloved sleep."* Was **Cullingworth Chapel** a case of *'being wrong because it was never fully right in the first place?'*

Leaving aside this speculative point, it's clear that mixed spiritual influences constituted another fundamental problem blighting this Assembly. Evidence for this was provided in **Joseph Green's** account. One particularly unsettling influence was that of the **Odd Fellows Friendly Society,** which had some form of connection with **Cullingworth Chapel** from its very beginning. It's difficult to see how its rituals could be reconciled with the beliefs and practices of a bible-centred form of **Protestantism.** Testifying to the size and importance of this 'Order' was the following tomb inscription found in the graveyard of **Saint Mark's Church, Woodhouse, Leeds.** (This largely derelict Church was formally closed on **Sunday; July 15th, 2001.** I had attended its final service, held under the auspices of the **Headingley Deanery.** Its decaying interior had reeked of damp rot and some of the once beautiful windows had been smashed by vandals.) The inscription was discovered whilst going for a walk with my wife during **Boxing Day 2001.** It was finally transcribed on **Monday, May 13th, 2002** and showed that like **Cullingworth Baptist Chapel,** mixed spiritual influences had been present almost from the moment of this Church's foundation in **1826.**

In memory of
WILLIAM ALEXANDER
who died Dec. 13th, 1862
age 58 years.

This monument was erected
By the members of the Leeds district,
Of the Independent Order of
Odd Fellows, M. U.
In recognition of his zeal & integrity
Displayed by him in carrying out
The objects of the order

He was initiated in the year 1831, and
Immediately took an active part in the
Management of this lodge.
In 1836 he was elected
Grand Master of the district
And in 1840 corresponding Secretary,
Which office he held up to the
time of his death

He attended 21 A.M.CS and in 1858 was
Elected grand master of the order,
Numbering at that time
Upwards of 400,000 members.

He fulfilled the duties of his various
Offices, with honour to himself and
To the advantage of those by whom
He was appointed."

On the plinth were added the words: -
"REQUISRAT IN PARR"
(**Latin** for *Rest in Peace.*)

The second inscription showed that this man was not immune to the domestic tragedies which could blight even the most respectable of **Victorian** Households.

"In memory of
Anthony Adamson Alexander
Son of the said
William Alexander
Who died 1ˢᵗ May 1835
Age 6 years.

Also, Ann Alexander
Daughter of the above who died,
January 6ᵗʰ· 1865,
Age 29 years

Also, of Elizabeth
Wife of the aforesaid
William Alexander
Born April 6ᵗʰ· 1803
Died October 25ᵗʰ· 1887"

In an alcove at the top of his inscription was a sculptured portrait of **William Alexander.** It showed a man with a domed forehead, long bushy sideboards forming into a beard (but no moustache) and a slightly bulbous nose. He was wearing a necktie. The expression on his face appeared to be as smug as the inscription beneath it.

Section 7: A Man Called Moses

Concerning the missions of Hall Green Baptist Chapel, Haworth

A surprisingly large amount of information has been discovered concerning the man who initiated **John** and **Ann Smith** into the **Baptist** faith. His name was the **Reverend Moses Saunders,** Minister at **Hall Green Strict Baptist Church** from the time this said building was first constructed (in **1825**) until his replacement by **Thomas Hanson** in **1847,** (who came from nearby **Golcar Chapel.**) Details concerning the history of **Hall Green** were provided by a **Marjorie H. Day** – herself a long-time member of the Chapel until shortly before her death (at the age of **84** on **9th August 1996**). She'd made the final corrections to her booklet only a week before her death. Despite a paucity of original records, the following extracts from her lucidly written history confirm that she'd managed to obtain a significant amount of information concerning the man who'd been an *'Apostle'* to the **Smiths.** I have placed **Day's** quotations in the order in which she gave them. In her <u>first</u> section, entitled *"Beginnings,"* she stated: -

*"Our own story really starts in **1824,** but many years prior to this – in **1781** – half a dozen non-conformists – dissenters as they were known at first – started holding services in **Leach's Barn,** just by the entrance to the **Goit** at the bottom of **Brow Road** in **Haworth.** Evidently, there was a growing worshipping community there for **40** years, and as numbers increased and they were outgrowing the barn; they decided to build a Chapel. Acquiring some land of **Edward Ferrand** of **St Ives, Bingley, Lord** of the Manor of **Haworth,** in **1824** they built our present Chapel on the village green opposite the **Old Hall.** Descendants of one **John Moore,** who helped physically in the Chapel building, are in membership to this day, to the sixth generation. The Chapel cost £1,700 to build and the schoolroom upwards of £200. One of the signatories of our trust deed was the **Rev. Patrick Bronte** of **Haworth** Church"* (**Day p.1.** This indicates exceptionally good relations between the **Anglican** and **Non-Conformists** in the area – as **Patrick Bronte** was, in effect, giving his blessing to the competition; this act displayed a certain broad-minded attitude on his part. Eighteen men acted as the first trustees.)

*"It is unfortunate that many of the Chapel records and minutes of church meetings have been lost. We have no details of the opening in **1825** of the Chapel, but we have an anniversary hymn sheet of **1826,** the date **23rd April.** The preacher was the **Rev. Godwin,** classical tutor of the **Baptist Academy, Bradford.** On the hymn sheet was printed an appeal from the Sunday School Committee to the inhabitants of **Haworth** and its vicinity. They gave a brief statement of school activities and needs and we're confident of the "support of the*

friends of **Christ** *in helping to rescue many of the rising generation from the paths of vice and wretchedness, and of training them up for virtue, happiness and immortal life."*

15 years after its opening it was found necessary to enlarge the Chapel and additions were made to the organ gallery and vestries. In **1841** *an organ was installed, built by* **Nicholson** *of* **Rochdale**.*"* (**Day pp.1-2**)

"The Sunday School was also very well attended, there being **281** *scholars and* **107** *teachers on the register at one period. People attended the school and Chapel from far and near, and for most folk, the only means of getting to the services was on foot. One family walked every Sunday from* **Hewenden,** *which is halfway to* **Bradford**. *Others walked from* **Oakworth, Ingrow, Stanbury, Queensbury** *and from distant farms on the moors surrounding* **Haworth**. *No wonder there are entries in the school book like: "***John Pickles***, no clothes to come in;* **Widdop** *brothers, no boots."*

Each year, when they elected the various officials to run the school, men and women were appointed to visit all the absentee scholars and teachers and report back. In **March 1844**, ten people did this job, dividing **Haworth** and **Oxenhope** into five areas, each area covered by two visitors. On **March 20th,** they brought their reports to a committee meeting. **James Winterbottom** and **Abel Wadsworth** had visited **17** people and found a number sick, some had left, some *"lie too long in the mornings,"* one or two *"will come again when the weather is better."* One boy must have given some trouble in the school – *"he left for the Methodists – good rid."* Of another crafty boy, *"his father does not know but he comes."* **James Feather** and **John Ratcliffe** visited **12** people and brought back similar reports. *"Mrs* **Tidwell's** *lass, no hat, but will come again." "Widow* **Kay's** *lass, sick." "***John Redman*** *very wild and has jobs to do for his grandfather but will do better."* *"***Thomas Wilkinson's*** *lass too cold to come but will come again."*

In the beginning, they drew up a set of rules for the running of the school. These are written out in beautiful penmanship in The Minute Book, dated **1825**. The Old English long **'s'** (which is like an **'f'** without the crossbar is used:
'That the business of this institution be managed by a treasurer, superintendents, secretary and committee to consist of nine persons, with the power to add to their number, three of whom will be competent to act.'

The committee numbered **20** and even later, and sub-committees were formed from time to time to look after special projects. For almost **100** years there were four superintendents, and the secretary had an assistant. Morning school opened at **8.30** in the summer months, at **9 o'clock** in the winter months. Afternoon school was at **1 o' clock.** After both sessions, there was a Chapel, and everybody had to go. *"The committee and teachers are to meet the last Monday evening in every month to transact the business of the institution."*

Teachers had to be proposed, and thereafter to appear and be received at a committee meeting. Rules of behaviour both for teachers and scholars were strict. Punctuality, order and decorum were resolutely expected and observed. *"The superintendents and teachers are requested to embrace every opportunity to communicate religious instruction to the children under their care."* *This may sound to us a strange injunction in a* **Sunday School** *until we remember that in those days there was no compulsory education, so it was essential first to teach the children to read."* (**Day pp.2-3**)

"In **1825** *the treasurer was instructed to order certain quantities of spelling books of various grades, pasteboard and alphabet sheets. Testaments at one shilling from the Bible Society at* **Haworth,** *and several dozens of* **Watts'** *Divine Songs for Children; the children were allowed to have Bibles, Testaments and Hymn Books by paying for them at 1d per week.*

Scholars were given 'tasks' to be learnt during the week and repeated the following Sunday morning, those most proficient to repeat the tasks publicly to the Superintendent were rewarded according to merit." (**Day p.3.** These rewards consisted of medals based on proficiency or regular attendance. Book prizes were also awarded at **Christmas**.)

In her <u>second</u> Section, entitled *"Early Days in Sunday School."* **Day** stated: -
"By the early summer of **1826,** *it would seem that the* **Hall Green School** *was proving popular if the quantities of books ordered are anything to go by. Bibles, Testaments, spelling books and record books were frequently sent for. During the summer eight more teachers were engaged, and still another order for books of all kinds was made, including* **100** *copies of* **Watts' First Catechism. Robert Hartley** *was appointed to examine the boys and* **Martha Greenwood** *the girls in their catechisms.*

Rules of behaviour continued very strictly, indeed had to be with **180** *children, later increasing to* **280,** *being taught at the same time in the open schoolroom. The scholars were to walk in an orderly manner up into the Chapel after Sunday School, led by their teachers, and "each scholar is to put his hat under the form on which he sits." Twelve teachers sat in their turn with the scholars in Chapel, to ensure good behaviour. In* **March 1834,** *it was resolved to appoint four persons as over-lookers in the school, and that rods be provided for them! The rods were to help maintain order among the children. Later on, the 'stick carriers' were also deputed to sit, in their turns, with the children in Chapel. For persistent unruliness and excessively bad* *behaviour, the punishment was exclusion from Sunday School until an apology had been received by the Superintendent.*

In the earliest days, **Hall Green School** *was a member of the* **Sunday School Union** *in* **Leeds,** *and our delegate was the* **Rev. Moses Saunders,** *our Pastor. Questionnaires were sent out by the Union. In* **1826,** *after giving details about the number of children and officials, we replied, in answer to the questions: "Do all the children regularly attend preaching in the Chapel? If not, why not?" "They all attend regularly." "Have you a select class?" "There is no select class at present."* (**Day p.4.** A *'Select Class'* was for adults. Men and Women met in different classes. They were first formed at **Hall Green** in **October 1853** and lasted until the Interwar period.)

"In **1826** *the Union wanted to know: "Have any beneficial effects been observed in the children, parents or neighbourhood, from the labours of the teachers?" Answer: "We think good has been done."* (It is interesting to note that this answer had been penned by the man who was to bring my Great, Great Grandparents into the **Christian Faith.**)

"Reward books and stationary were bought of the Union." (Parcels from the Union were conveyed to the **Bradford** warehouse of the Secretary **William Greenwood Junior** of **Oxenhope** who then brought them to the Chapel. The **Greenwoods** were worsted manufacturers who owned two mills in the local area. A **John Greenwood** was treasurer, but in **1834** he died *"much lamented"* and **James Greenwood** was appointed his successor.)

"For the most part, however, **Hall Greeners** *have been humble, hard-working folk, the majority working in mills, but with a sprinkling of shop-keepers, a farrier or two and a few teachers,"* (**Day pp.4-5**)

"In **January 1828,** *the School Committee met to discuss the formation of a Union of the various schools in the neighbourhood and decided to request the* **Reverend Patrick Bronte** *to call a meeting for that purpose, each school in the area to send two delegates.*

We have no record of the meeting **Parson Bronte** *was asked to call, but we know that a* **Sunday School Union** *was formed at* **Keighley** *in* **1853,** *and we joined it, indeed we helped in the expenses of its formation.*

By the year **1834,** *as more and more people had learned to read, there was a continuing thirst for knowledge and for reading material, and a library was established. From time to time, monies were allocated out of school funds to buy more books and a system of rewarding the* *children of the library was started. By* **1840,** *it appears that the users of the library had read everything, and* **Mr Saunders** *was asked to examine and compare the* **Cullingworth** *Baptist library books with those of* **Hall Green** *and to take a valuation of each, "If found to be somewhat alike, a complete exchange is to be made."*

In **September 1848,** *it was necessary to appoint five librarians, as the library was now open on Wednesday evenings. At this time, too, there was a resolution that a night school should be started for teachers and scholars at their own expense."* **(Day p. 5)**

In her <u>third</u> Section, entitled *"Red Letter Days"* **Day** recounted: -
"For the **1827** *occasion* (the second anniversary), *we read from the minutes: "That* **Rev. M. Saunders** *and* **John Earnshaw** *are to give the necessary instructions to the children in singing." Their performance must have been a success because it was resolved "that* **John Earnshaw** *receives the thanks of the Committee for his assistance in teaching the children singing and that he receive fifteen shillings as a small remuneration for his services." Also "that* **Archibald Leighton** *receives* **3s, George Bland 2s** *and* **Robert Hartley 5s** *for erecting the platform with thanks for their services."*

John Earnshaw *continued to be a singing teacher for many years, assisted later by* **Thomas Murgatroyd.** *They were each paid a "consideration for their trouble."* **Archibald Leighton** *continued to erect and dismantle the platform, with or without helpers and then given a little monetary appreciation. It seems odd to us in these days that people who did jobs for the Chapel and school should be paid, but wages were very low, and most of the people who come into this story lived very frugally at best. There was, of course, no 'sick pay' or unemployment benefit for* **80** *years after this time, and when these misfortunes came people suffered desperate privation. So, it was thought good evidently, to give out a little 'encouragement money' too willing helpers.*

In the **1840s** *the anniversary was moved from* **April** *into* **May.** *Ministers were invited from the nearer towns in* **Yorkshire** *and* **Lancashire** *and even from* **Liverpool.**

From the earliest times, tea was provided for the anniversary singers – a practice which has gone on until recent times." **(Day p. 6)**

"Work was very hard, hours long. No such things as tea breaks; they came in during the Second World War. Mill owners were in some cases Fatherly figures, who nevertheless inspired awe, and of course – like Fathers – were strict in **Victorian England.** *They employed Mill Managers who, with their seemingly great power, were often domineering. The overlookers and lesser bosses, with some authority over ill-paid weavers and spinners, were often overbearing, sometimes cruel. Operatives were afraid of losing their jobs and for the most part, did not answer back.*

Employees of that day had no protection against harsh treatment. Employers could indulge their whims and there was no redress. As yet, there were no funds to draw on to keep the 'wolf from the door,' except what a man had himself 'put by' against the evil day.

So, life was a struggle, but it was not all grim. There were occasions of joy, laughter and fun. Ordinary people got their pleasure from simple things. Most families were connected with a place of worship, around which their social, as well as religious life, revolved. **Whitsuntide** *was one of the highlights of the Sunday School year, and all places of worship had processions, teas and games. Indeed, in some of the* **Lancashire** *towns and cities today, beautifully dressed processions are still a spectacular feature of* **Whitsuntide.**

The **Whitsun** *treat was established in the very beginning.*

The children were "each to have a cake and beer given them," but not before they had listened to a few addresses and done a very long walk "in the best order possible." Doubtless, the 'band of music' marching along at the front of the procession helped to keep them going in good order. In **1843,** *for some reason, it was decided to "dispense with the band, nevertheless thanking the* **Tansy End Band** *for their kind offer." But in* **1851** *the band was again engaged. As well as the children's treat, there was also a public tea laid on, and for this, you bought a ticket costing* **4d** *to* **Hall Greeners, 6d** *to those not connected with the Chapel. About* **150** *adults sat down for tea,"* which mainly consisted of homemade bread, currant buns, cakes and tarts. **(Day p. 8-9)**

"For the **1835** *treat, it was decided "that the* **Rev. M. Saunders** *engage to prepare lemon ale for drink for the children." But before many years had gone by the selection of drinks was out, and it was tea all round, adults and children.*

There must have been some disorderly 'gate-crashing' at the **1846** *celebrations, with our own scholars missing their school buns altogether, so in future, the children must wait for their names to be called before being given their 'cake' and the door would be policed to prevent children not entitled from entering. After all this festivity, there came the annual meeting, when a fresh committee and officers were elected each year."* **(Day p.9)**

In her <u>fourth</u> Section, entitled *"Early Pastors,"* **Day** revealed that: -
"We have a somewhat blurred picture of the early Pastors of **Hall Green.** *The* **Reverend Moses Saunders** *was the first. (We called our Pastors 'Reverend' in those days. He was Minister from* **1825** *until* **1847** *when he moved away from* **Haworth.** *It seems he kept himself very busy in the work of the Sunday School as well as the Chapel.* **Mr Saunders** *had a keen interest in missionary endeavour and in his day, there was a regular missionary*

prayer meeting. **Mrs Martha Saunders** *too was busy with schoolwork, teaching and "examining the girls in their catechisms." It is apparent that* **Mr Saunders** *did a good deal of visiting and was usually in one of the teams deputed to seek out absentee scholars and teachers. The committee got very concerned from time to time about absenteeism. In this day, we would say that there was plenty of excuses, indeed good reason for it, in view of the hard life people had and their need for a bit of extra rest at the weekends."* (**Day p.9-10**)

Day's chief value as an information source was in how she complimented the details she'd already gained from other sources connected to **Sutton** and **Cullingworth Chapels**. She conveyed something of the lives led by early nineteenth century **Baptists**. It was possible to learn a little of what **Moses Saunders** was like as a real human being as distinct from just a name on a list. Although naturally biased in its favour, **Day** gave the convincing impression that, during **Reverend Saunders'** ministry, **Hall Green** was a thriving and robust Assembly. However, it was perhaps the success of this *'work'* at **Haworth** which persuaded **Moses Saunders** that something similar could be repeated at **Cullingworth**. If this was the case then he had fallen into the common missionary trap of assuming that one approach, which had worked successfully in one place, would also work successfully in another. Regrettably, this would not be the case – as previously described events showed.

One source failing to provide any data was the **1841** Census. An extensive search (undertaken on **Wednesday, June 12th, 2002**) showed nothing. Yet **p.329** of the **1837** and **p.441** of the **1847 White's Trade Directory** contained the following entry *"Saunders, Rev. Moses (Baptist)."* He was recorded as living in **Stanbury** and **Haworth,** which were precisely the areas I had looked at two or three times already. The only likely explanation for this absence from the Census Return was to presume he'd been away from the area on some sort of itinerant work. The **1847** Directory did reveal a Baptist Minister called **John Winterbottom** (the **1841** Census had recorded him as aged **45,** married with two boys and two girls), but he was the Pastor of a Chapel at a different end of **Haworth.** There was no obvious direct connection with **Moses Saunders.** For **Brontë** lovers, the **1841** Census did reveal: -
Patrick Brontë aged **61,** *'Clergyman'* born in **Ireland**
(Listed as *"Brontë Patrick A. B. Incumbent"* in the above-cited Directories)
Elizabeth Beaumont aged **60,** *'Independent'* born in **Cornwall**
Emily Jane Brontë aged **20,** born in **Yorkshire**
Ann Brontë aged **19,** *'Governess,'* born in **Yorkshire**
Martha Brown aged 15, *'Female Servant,'* born in **Yorkshire**

The **1847 White's Directory** revealed that the proprietor of the **Black Bull Inn** was an **Abraham Wilkinson**. It was in this establishment that **Patrick Brontë's** son **Branwell** spent the last two to three years of his life drinking himself to death. (His demise in **September 1848** came about largely because of pulmonary tuberculosis and alcoholism). In contrast to his sisters and father, his had been a wasted life; he'd shown no resilience in the face of failure. I suspect my ancestors would have viewed him as something of a *'wastrel.'*

From information provided by the **1822 GENUKI Bradford Website,** it was found that **Haworth** was in the parish of **Bradford, Morley**-division of **Agsbrigg** and **Morley**. This was within the larger Liberty of **Pontefract**. It was **4** miles **S.** of **Keighley, 7** from **Bradford, 8** from **Halifax, 9** and a half a mile from **Colne** in **Lancashire**. It had no market fairs, On **July 22** there was a market for *'pedlary ware'* and on **October 14** there was a market for horned cattle. The population numbered **4,668**. Present was a Chapel of Ease dedicated to **St Michael** which had the Vicar of **Bradford** as its patron. The population appears to have been much too high for **Haworth Village** and may either be a misprint or (as seems more likely) included outlying areas. What this extract did not show was that, in **February 1820, Patrick Brontë** had arrived in **Haworth** to take charge of **Saint Michael's** with his ailing wife and six young children. His wife subsequently died in **September 1821** – possibly of cancer and was only **38** years old. This marked the beginning of domestic sorrows, which would mould the literary genius of the three daughters who survived into adulthood.

In conjunction with records from **Cullingworth Baptist Chapel,** these other sources of information provided an illuminating insight into the character and gifts possessed by **Moses Saunders**. He was the sort of man who knew his Scriptures, an activist who possessed many positive qualities and not a few weaknesses too. If a project was sound, he would zealously propel it along until a great deal had been accomplished. Conversely, if (as appeared to be the case at **Cullingworth**) a project was <u>not</u> soundly based then he would keep it going long after it should have stopped. More thoughtful people would have asked, *"Is it worthwhile persisting in this work, given the endless financial and personal problems being encountered?"* **Pastor Saunders** may well have replied, *"But didn't the Apostles endure many problems with the Congregations they established?"* This will certainly have been a fair point, but he would also have been aware that any **Christian** endeavour needed to bear *'good fruit.'* It firstly needed time and attention to see if it would work out. However, if it proved to be persistently bad then the best course of action was to apply the advice contained in **Luke 13:6-9** and *'cut it down.'* In the case of **Cullingworth Chapel,** the fruits were so bad that, by **1842,** a completely new beginning needed to be made. This would suggest that either a Chapel should never have been founded there in the first place or alternatively it was a work *'born before its time.'* In either case, there had been a failure of discernment. Perhaps against his better judgement, the **Reverend Saunders** had allowed himself to be carried away by the popular enthusiasm of the **Baptists** at **Cullingworth.** They may well have broken away and joined some other denomination if he hadn't supported their endeavours to find a *'proper'* Chapel. Perhaps he'd also felt it better to stay on the scene rather than leave immature believers to become subverted by some other group like the Chartists. **Cullingworth** was a *'baby'* he just could not abandon. His motives had been clearly honourable, but sadly his name was to become associated with a work which simply did not prosper, and which appears to have exercised a distressing influence upon my Great, Great Grandparents. Nevertheless, **Pastor Saunders** must take credit for introducing the **Smiths** to a more-or-less biblical form of Christianity. In that capacity, he was truly their spiritual mentor.

Pastor Saunders had a gift for leadership and a willingness to engage in humble tasks, *i.e.* preparing lemon ale for the children. His commitments at **Haworth** were such that he could give only a very limited amount of time to the affairs at **Cullingworth.** Perhaps he was too busy! Moreover, at **Hall Green,** the fruit of his ministry was (and still is) good. An attendance (by my wife and myself) at two services on **Easter Sunday, March 31st, 2002** revealed that **Hall Green** still possessed a very lively congregation, robustly loyal to those same Gospel teachings which **Moses Saunders** himself had faithfully propagated all those years ago; indeed, he would have recognised everything except the modern style clothing and some unfamiliar words in the spoken **English** language. He would also perhaps have found the sermons a little too short and observed that those attending looked surprisingly well fed when compared to the people of his own time. What the **Reverend Saunders** could never have guessed was that one day, a descendant of two people he had himself evangelised would be attending this very same Chapel to obtain information about him! Should this knowledge somehow have ever reached his ears, then he would undoubtedly have attributed this development to divine favour.

Perhaps the biggest vindication of **Moses Saunders'** ministry has been how **Hall Green Baptist Church** is still a thriving concern – with up to one hundred people attending the morning service. On **Saturday 18th July 2015,** my wife and I visited the bookshop and coffee area in the pleasantly furnished basement of the church. Conversation with an eighty-eight-year-old gentleman (whose own family had been in the Church serving as Deacons and Sunday School Teachers) revealed the following details: -

It had been **Pastor Saunders** who had relocated the Church from a converted barn (in around **1824**) to the present site. The Sunday School used to meet on the premises (now in the basement café area where we were sat around a table, enjoying tea and biscuits.) There may have been as many as two hundred children crowded into it, each one endeavouring to learn **Maths** and **English.** As supplementary subjects, the Boys would learn **carpentry** and the Girls needlework (occasionally inspected by **Charlotte Brontë** who would peer through her glasses). Looking around the same area now I feel that Health and Safety Officers would throw a fit! So many children thrown into a small space!

All the details to do with **Cullingworth Chapel** showed that **John** and **Ann Smith** were somehow closely related, but it would take a long time to firmly establish that they were really my Great, Great Grandparents. Adding to the confusion was the **1841** Census for **Bascroft**, **Cullingworth** which recorded quite a different **John** and **Ann Smith!** The latter couple's children had been born around the same time as **Edmund** and **Daniel.** Confusion was heightened by the way they'd lived next door to three wool combers, also named **Smith,** (**William** aged **20**, **James** aged **18** and **John** aged **14**). Regarding **John** and **Ann,** his Census showed a household containing: -
John Smith aged **45**, Wool Comber
Ann Smith aged **50**
Benjamin Smith aged **20** Wool Comber
Francis Smith aged **16** Wool Comber
[Laura] Smith aged **11** Worsted Mill Worker
George Smith aged **8** Worsted Mill Worker

These people possessed <u>none</u> of the right occupational or personal characteristics to have been **Edmund's** parents. So, the problem arose over exactly which **John** and **Ann Smith** the records of **Cullingworth Baptist** Chapel were referring to? Present was a serious conundrum needing further research to unravel it. My next step would be to examine the **1841** Census Return for **Skipton** to ascertain whether the **John** and **Anne Smith** located there had characteristics matching those of my ancestors. I also needed to throw further light on the family tradition claiming, *'the early **Smiths** were **Baptists** or Congregationalists.'*

CHAPTER 7: MAYHEM IN SKIPTON

Section 1: A Large Market Town

Concerning the market town of Skipton

After discovering the facts (mentioned in the previous chapter) concerning **John** and **Ann Smith,** the next logical step was to check the identity of the **John** and **Ann Smith** who had moved to **Skipton.** Only then would it be possible to ascertain whether they had characteristics matching those of my Great, Great Grandparents. As **Skipton** was a large market town with an old **Norman** Castle at its centre, it was decided to begin with the district nearest the mill bridge, as this was the locality most likely to have possessed a Corn Mill. Consequently, much of the afternoon of **Friday 22nd June 2001** was spent in **Leeds Central Library** running through reels of microfiche looking at the **1841** and **1851** Census Returns for **Skipton.** Only after examining five districts did the decisive piece of evidence slide into view. The time and trouble had been worthwhile – the characteristics <u>did</u> match – indeed they matched perfectly. After over nine months pursuing the wrong **John** and **Ann Smith,** I had at last found the right ones – my own true family roots had been uncovered! The information was revealed in the following Census information for **Skipton-in-Craven: -**

<u>1841 Census Return for Greenside</u>
(A yard adjoining the south side of New Market Street, below number 38)
John Smith aged **36** *"Miller"*
Ann Smith aged **38**
Samuel Smith aged **14**
Susanna Smith aged **12**
Edmund Smith aged **9**
Daniel Smith aged **7**
Ann Smith aged **2**

<u>1851 Census Return</u>
(For the twenty-third house along the north side of New Market Street)
Samuel Smith aged **24** *"Corn Miller"* **Keighley**
Ann Smith (wife) aged **27 Skipton**
William Smith (son) aged **3 Skipton**
Daniel Smith (brother) aged **16** *"Pupil-Teacher"* **Bingley**
Hannah Smith (sister) aged **9** *"at home"* **Skipton**

John Smith (brother) aged **7** *"Scholar"* **Skipton**
Martha Emmott (sister-in-law) aged **22 Skipton**
Mary Emmott (niece) aged **9** months

Notes accessed from **Skipton Reference Library** provided the bracketed information beneath the underlined title row – they were <u>not</u> on the original Census Returns. Reference to an **1852** map of **Skipton** suggested that when living in one of the five dwellings at **Greenside** (near the shallow **Eller Beck**) the **Smiths** may have inhabited a corner house just behind some outdoor privies. The next house up from there was no **36/38 New Market Street,** where a family of Cotton Spinners called the **Vines** had lived (possibly along with another family). The smell from the privies in the summer must have been dreadful. The **1851** Census appeared to show a marked decline in living conditions in **Greenside** because fourteen families were now crowded into one block, whereas a decade previously it had held only five. The occupations followed by members of these households also appeared to be of a lower socio-economic status. An old newspaper cutting in **Skipton Museum** showed that these slum conditions had continued until **Greenside's** demolition in **1958** – the wry comment being made that *"a more unsuitable name for those squalid houses could hardly have been devised."*

Various Trade Directories showed the only significant corn mill being sited at **Mill Bridge**, near the **High Street** – about ten minutes brisk walk from **Greenside**. Known as **High Corn Mill,** it had been used for corn milling purposes since at least **1310** when tenants of the castle had paid for its use. The actual mill building still stands. (**John Smith** himself will have known of it and it will be described further on in this chapter.) During the **1840s** a **Thomas** and then a **John King** (both listed as *'Corn Merchant'*) had owned it. Whether they were father and son, or brothers was not clear.

Direct observation of both photographic and on the ground evidence (during a second visit made to **Skipton** on a sultry **Wednesday, June 27th, 2001**) confirmed that the move from the crowded conditions at **Greenside** to the more substantial property at **23 New Market Street** represented *'a step up in the world.'* It was evident that the **Smiths** had prospered. This dwelling had originally been an armoury in the seventeenth century, but the first private owners had already moved in by the **1690s**. In **1811** a landlord called **John Preston** had purchased the property. During the **1850s,** he (or his legal representatives) were still renting it out to respectable tradesmen. Notes provided by **Skipton Reference Library** showed that **Samuel Smith** lived at

No. 23 until **1858.** The tenants after him were **Peter** and **William Smith,** (a handyman). Whether they were related to **Samuel** is unknown.

The **1851** Census implied that **Edmund's** family was, at that time, devastated by the loss of both parents **John** and **Ann Smith.** When **Edmund** was still in his teens they appear to have died at an early age, leaving **Samuel** to shoulder the burden as *'family head.'* Throughout this period of mourning, and with burial costs to pay there must have been immense financial pressure and **Edmund** would have had no alternative but to have taken up a trade as soon as he was able. This would account for his absence from **Samuel Smith's** crowded household, as recorded in the **1851** Census.

About three doors down, on the other side of the road, was a **Benjamin Smith** whom the **1841** Census had recorded as being a *"Worsted Manufacturer's Agent,"* living in **Crosshills.** The **1851** Census revealed the following details about himself and his family.

Benjamin Smith aged **46** *"Wool Dealer"* **Sutton**
Anne Smith aged **46** (wife) **Kettlewell**
Catherine Smith aged **12** (daughter) **Glasburn**
Sarah Anne Smith aged **11** (daughter) **Glasburn**
Emma Robinson aged **25** (sister-in-law) *"Commercial Traveller's wife"* **Cambridge, Ely**
Elizabeth Smith aged **39** (unmarried sister) **Sutton**

Records from the **Kildwick Parish Friendly Society** suggested that his move to **Skipton** had taken place in **1844.** It seemed apparent that **Benjamin** was a family relation of **Edmund,** that he was in the wool trade and that he employed at least one Commercial Traveller – the same occupation **Edmund** was to follow. Possibly **Benjamin Smith's** move to **Skipton** had been prompted by a desire to help **Edmund's** family during a time of crisis – the nature of which will be explored in subsequent sections. By **1845,** three traumatic events had occurred that was to permanently shape **Edmund's** character.

Section 2: A Disruptive Process

Concerning the effects of industrialisation around Skipton

Despite its market town appearance, **Skipton** could not avoid the disrupting processes of industrialisation. Like other settlements associated with my forebears, a dramatic increase in population was to take place from **1801** until

1851. With the aid of information provided by both **Skipton Museum** and the **Museum of Science and Technology** at **Manchester** a simple chronological outline will show the main developments of **Skipton's** partial industrialisation: -

1785: High Mill becomes the first major Cotton Mill in **Skipton.** Located some way behind the castle (<u>not</u> to be confused with the previously mentioned **High Corn Mill** dating from the Middle Ages and which occupied a more central location).

1822: The Baines Trade Directory lists five Cotton Manufacturers including:

- **William Beesley, Spencer Street**
- **Isaac Dewhurst, New Market Street**
- **William Sidgwick, Mill Place**
- **John Tillotson, Belmont**
- **Storey Wilkinson, New Market Street**

1828: John Dewhurst founds **Belle Vue Mill**

1829: Power looms are introduced to **Skipton** by the firm of **Dewhurst**

1831: Dewhurst's first mill is rebuilt following a fire. It changes from worsted to cotton manufacturing

1835: Baines *'History of Cotton Manufacture'* records the presence of six mills in **Skipton,** employing a total of **605** people.

1840: Sidgwicks begin to operate **Low Mill** to weave and weft more cloth

1842: A serious economic downturn provokes mill owners in **Manchester** to cut the wages of their operatives. This provokes strike action and disturbances which spread further afield to parts of **Lancashire** and then onwards to **Skipton.** In that year, *'The Chartist Movement'* reached its the peak, campaigning for the implementation of the following **Six Points** of *'The Peoples Charter.'* Published in **1838,** it made the following demands: -

1) *A vote for every man twenty-one years of age, of sound mind and not undergoing punishment for crime.*

2) *The Secret Ballot – to protect the elector in the exercise of his vote.*

3) *No Property Qualification for Members of Parliament – thus enabling the constituencies to return the man of their choice, be he rich or poor.*

4) *Payment of Members – thus enabling an honest tradesman, working man, or another person, to serve a constituency when taken from his business to attend the interests of the country.*

5) *Equal Constituencies – securing the same amount of representation for the same number of electors, instead of allowing small constituencies to swamp the votes of large ones.*

6) *Annual Parliaments – thus presenting the most effectual check to bribery and intimidation, since though a constituency might be bought once in seven years (even with the*

ballot), no purse could buy a constituency (under a system of universal suffrage) in each ensuing twelvemonth; and since members, when elected for a year only, would not be able to defy and betray their constituencies as they do now."

The **Chartist Movement** originated from a sense of disillusionment with the perceived inadequacies of the **1832** Parliamentary Reform Act whose failure to enfranchise the working classes was deeply resented – as was the much-hated Poor Law Act of **1834.** Its formal foundation can be dated to **January 1837** when the People's Charter was drawn up – although this charter drew upon already known radical political ideas, present since the **1790s.** During *'bad'* years (*i.e.* **1839, 1842** and **1848**) **The Chartist Movement** tended to draw mass support from those whose grievances were more decidedly economic in nature. This often led to any disturbance being labelled as **Chartist.** In fact, **Chartism** was part of a **European** wide discontent which exploded in **1848.** Across the continent, a whole series of revolutions broke out. These were only suppressed with great difficulty. (In **France,** the government was toppled.)

Israel Roberts (1827-1881) on **pp.13-14** of his moving autobiography attributed *'The Plug Riots,'* (which also affected **Leeds**) to Chartist agitation. Over the course of the next several decades, the first five demands of the **Chartist Movement** were eventually to be met. As to the sixth point, **Chartist** leaders themselves quietly abandoned it due mainly to reasons of practicality. In the short term, however, the **Chartist Movement** was a failure, often beset by scandal and leadership infighting. With improved trading conditions in the **1850s,** support for the **Chartist** cause ebbed and by **1855** the Movement had effectively ceased to exist. Nevertheless, the agitation sometimes associated with the **Chartist Movement** did produce its casualties. During my last archive visit to **Colne** (made on **Thursday, July 26th, 2001**) I came across the following moving inscription, located inside the municipal cemetery.

"Here Lieth all that is mortal of
Martha, *wife of* **John Halsted**
Of **Colne***, who departed this*
Life the **18th** *day of* **December,**
***1829** Age **60** years.*
Also, of **JOSEPH** *their Son, who was*
Barbarously murdered in the **44th** *year*
Of his age, while engaged in his duty as
A <u>special constable</u>*, during the* <u>Riot,</u>
Which took place in the Town, on the
Evening of the **10th August 1840,** *leaving*

Four orphan Children to lament
Their loss
Also, the above **JOHN**
HALSTED *who died* **April 5ᵗʰ 1848"**

Like most tomb inscriptions, the words were in block lettering. However, those I have underlined had been placed in Italics as if the designer of this inscription wanted to make a point for future generations to ponder upon. After recording this inscription, I was left wondering about the fates of the four orphans who had been left behind.

On **Friday, 11ᵗʰ July 2003** I received the following Death Certificate from the **Burnley Registrar Office;** it threw light upon the violent way in which **Joseph Halstead** had met his death.

Registration District <u>Colne</u>
1840 Death in the <u>sub-district</u> of <u>Colne</u> in <u>Lancaster</u>
1. When and where died? 1840 August Tenth, Colne
2. Name and Surname: Joseph Halsted
3. Sex: Male
4. Age: Forty-Three Years
4. Occupation: Cotton Spinner and Cotton Manufacturer
5. Cause of death: A blow from an iron rail, wilful murder
6. Signature, description and residence of informant: R. Hargreaves, Coroner, Blackburn
8. When registered: Fourteenth August 1840
9. Signature of registrar: John Conyers

With incidents like these, it's easy to see how the **Chartist**s discredited what, in many ways, was a just cause. The above information helped confirm the presence of a very violent element within early **Victorian** society. Not long after this sad incident, my Great, Great Grandparents would too find themselves caught up in this kind of violence.

Section 3: The High Street

Concerning the inhabitants of Skipton High Street, circa 1840

Although able to provide useful statistical information concerning population growth, Census Returns were unable to convey a feeling of what daily life was like in **Skipton.** What were the sights and sounds to be seen and heard there? From a review of *'occupations'* alone it could be readily deduced that the wealthier and more respectable families lived in those houses facing the main street, whilst the poorer families *'made do'* as best they could in such crowded and tumbledown places as **Greenside.** To move from a yard cottage to the main street house was surely regarded as a sign of rising prosperity. Fortuitously, a print (circa **1840**) had been made by the local-born artist **Richard Waller (1811-82),** entitled *"A view of **Skipton-in-Craven.**"* (Earlier prints of **1830** showed sheep being driven up the **High Street** in the general direction of **Holy Trinity Church.**) Copies of this print can be found in **Rowley (1969)** and **Hatfield (1991)** – the latter source giving a very helpful commentary on the specific names and occupations of the people in the print. This, along with a picture of **High Corn Mill** in **Walter (1991) p.44** provided a basis for the following historical reconstruction:

*'As my Great, Great Grandfather **John** hurried his way up the heavily rutted **High Street** to his place of work at the Corn Mill he passed a mixed assortment of buildings. Some stood a grand three stories high, whilst others (of a meaner cottage-like appearance) could muster only two. At the very top end of the street was a tollbooth with a 'birdcage' belfry. To the left of this (and breaking into the horizon) was the imposing medieval tower of **Holy Trinity Church.***

*In the foreground, **John Smith** observed a party of half a dozen men working around a covered wagon in the road. They were busy loading up wooden crates. A plump man in a country smock received a tankard of ale from a small boy in a peaked cap. The men had long sideboards and were stripped down to their shirtsleeves. None of them appeared to be suffering from any form of hunger. Standing patiently beside the cart and looking away from one another were two horses – one dark and the other white. Further behind the wagon, two carts stood at right angles to one another. Around these were five other labourers – this time wearing smocks and country caps. It was clear that the commerce of **Skipton** was heavily dependent upon a rural clientele.*

***John** carried on walking and further to his left stood a grey horse tethered to a pavement post. High-up – and poised steadily on a ladder, (repairing brickwork to his shop) was **Sammy Lister.** A man stood below him on the ground, his back turned to **John.** Two other men stood nearby, each wearing cloth caps and waistcoats, facing the stout red-faced Cobbler and ex Chartist **Jack Hudson.** A workman near to **Jack** was kneeling – evidently trying to pick something up.*

Continuing along the left side of the street was a taller building (which belonged to the stonemason **Joshua Crossley**). On the adjoining **(Sheepscar Street)** side of this building was the beer house, known locally as **Hell's Kitchen**. Further down **John** could glimpse steam rising from the flagstone pavement and he guessed that the Cooper, **Tubber Scott** was at work. His habit of working out on the street had led to a public outcry eventually resulting in court action in **1831.** Nevertheless, with true **Yorkshire** stubbornness **Tubber** had carried on regardless and consequently, he was not a well-liked man. He gave no thought to the needs of others. Still further up was the saddler's shop run by **Frank Wade.** Dividing the **High Street** into two was the toll booth with inside stairs leading up to the courthouse where inquests were held. Sharing the ground floor of the tollbooth were the premises of **John Cork** the barber and **George Hird** the umbrella mender. Cells were in the basement of the toll booth conveniently near the **Fountain Inn**. Hardly surprisingly, the cells were the next port of call for some of its clientele! Near the top of the street at the left side were the premises of another saddler (named **Richard Proctor**) and the well-known ironmongers **Manby's,** which first began trading in **1817**.

The first building on the right-hand side of the **High Street** belonged to a shoemaker, a cousin of **Edwin Calvert**, (himself buried immediately outside **Christ Church**). Standing in front of the doorway and ringing a bell was the parish beadle **Andrew Parker.** His blue robes and old-fashioned tri-corn hat added to the dignity of this upright silver-haired figure. It was easy to imagine him ringing the bell very loudly to attract attention to an important notice. He looked the sort of man who would have been very proud of his office. A little further down, wearing a white apron and cap and standing outside the doorway was **Jinny Wharton,** wife of the landlord of the **Wheatsheaf Inn.** The next two shops belonged to **John Briggs** the clockmaker and **Mary Buck** a linen-draper. Waiting outside the drapers was the open carriage and horse of **Miss Currer** of **Eston Hall.** Her servant stood alongside the brown horse, waiting for his mistress to finish her shopping. He probably longed for a tipple at the **Hole in the Wall Inn,** near the drapers. A two-storey building belonged to **William Young,** the draper and silk merchant. His immediate neighbour was **Hannah Thompson** who owned the hatter's shop. Next door but one was the imposing financial building of the **Craven Bank,** facing **the Market Cross.** Continuing in an unbroken line were more shops including **John Hurtley** the chandlers and the wine and spirits shop of **Birtwhistle** and **Mitchell.**

Just before reaching **Holy Trinity, John Smith** turned left and walked down toward the **Springs Canal.** This waterway would often be crowded with barges and other forms of canal transport. He would have seen the three stories of the **High Corn Mill** standing to the left of the canal, separated from it only by a narrow dirt path. A wooden hut-like structure jutted out from the top of the mill wall, above the canal towpath. This allowed for the lifting of goods directly to and from the waiting barges below. Running near this grey and impressive building *was a fast-flowing stream, which powered the large slowly spinning waterwheel, itself reaching as high as the second storey. Finally, **John** entered this same building (at the canal side) to begin yet another day of arduous work.'*

My own second visit was made to **Skipton** on **Wednesday, June 27th, 2001**. The mill building itself was still in active use for commercial purposes. It looked very impressive and, although, in a decayed condition, the waterwheel was still in place. Who knows whether **John** may well, at times, have been on hand to repair it whenever the need had arisen? However, the present water wheel is the second (and smaller of the two) known to have run this mill. Exactly when the first went out of use (to be subsequently replaced by this smaller wheel) is not known. My wife and I took photographs of this site during the third visit to **Skipton** made on **Saturday, July 14th, 2001.**

Section 4: A Chartist Riot

Concerning the *'Chartist Plug Riots'* in Skipton

When the **Smiths** were first settling down in **Skipton** (during the early **1840s**) many textile weavers (including the two **John Smiths** of **Sutton**) were now, being faced with starvation. **Wood p.36** showed that, during **1820,** a handloom weaver could earn **6/-** for a **30**-yard piece of cloth, representing a week's work. In **1840** the figure was down to the starvation rate of **2/-**. Nor could the manufacturers afford to pay any more as they were only making **1d** for every piece of cloth sold. Even if a weaver had worked a flat out **90-hour** week he would, at the most, have earned only **3/-** half of which will have gone on the rent for a cheap back-to-back house, with very little left over for necessities. Larger families were often faced with starvation or the dreaded workhouse at **Keighley.**

According to **Israel Roberts p.20,** wheat, bread and bacon in this period were rarely indulged-in luxuries. The diet of the poor consisted, in the main, of porridge, oatmeal cake with potatoes and cornbread, the latter as often as hard as stone! Gin and water were drunk from black earthenware pots because glasses were too expensive to buy. The quality of food was often very poor. **Roberts p.22** mentioned his mother recalling the time when flour was of such inferior quality that, when baked, it would run thin and drain down the outside facing of the stove. This was even though it cost sixpence per pound in weight. The adulteration of flour with dust and other (sometimes dangerous) additives was a very common practice – and one in which The **High Corn Mill** itself may well have indulged. One thing which is clear from **Robert's** account is that my **Edmund** grew-up during a time of unspeakable hardship. Starvation would become a real possibility if his parents suffered any mishap. From his early years, he would see what destitution did to people. With good reason, the period he grew up in was known as the *'hungry'* or *'starving'* forties. To come through it and make something good of his life testifies to an incredible resilience.

In view of these near-starvation conditions, it was hardly surprising that serious disturbances broke out. In **Leeds** itself, the Riot Act was read and the Mounted Hussars (under the command of **Prince George,** the Duke of **Cambridge**) had been used to disperse a hostile crowd. (Earlier on this crowd had been extorting money (up to several pounds) from some mill owners by threatening to let off the water from the steam boilers.) According to **Roberts, p.14** one agitator in **Yeadon,** near **Leeds,** had boasted, *"We shall have levelling someday and when we have I shall have Esholt Hall."* Individual acts of sabotage also took place, *i.e.* in **Sutton** where one manufacturer called **John Preston** was to receive compensation of £**72-17-0** for the expenses incurred due to the smashing of his power looms. By **August 1842 Britain** was teetering on the edge of an all-out *'Class war!'*

In an angry reaction to their distress, weavers (some of whom had been wandering up and down the region looking for work) produced the following rhyme: -
"What do we want? Our daily bread,
Fair reward for labour done,
All our wants are merged into one.
When the fierce fiend hunger grips us,
Evil fancies clog our brains
Vengeance settles on our hearts
And frenzy gallops through our veins!"

Possibly this (or a similar rhyme) would have been chanted by a **3,000**-strong mob as they left **Colne** in **Lancashire** for **Skipton** with the intention of bringing the **Dewhurst** and **Sidgwick** Textile Mills to a standstill. It must have been a frightening (or perhaps an exhilarating) spectacle for a ten-year-old boy, seeing them in **Skipton** on a sweltering hot summer's day, armed with wooden clubs and loudly threatening insurrection. In **Edmund's** own heart the sight of these desperate men would have reinforced his conviction that poverty was a curse to be escaped by whatever means possible. He would have seen for himself how hunger could make animals of even the mildest of people. **August 16th, 1842** was perhaps a day he would remember for the rest of his life. It was the first if three traumatic events at a formative stage of his life. Meanwhile, **Edmund's** father **John** would most likely have been helping to guard the **High Corn Mill** against any risk of looting. **Edmund** would have spent at least part of the day at home with his mother **Ann** who will have been in great fear for the safety of her husband. She would also have been terrified of receiving unwanted attention from any intruders. **Chartist** mobs were known to break into people's houses and steal things.

When combined with modern sociological analysis of crowd behaviour, local historians like **Rowley (1983)** made it possible to reconstruct the precise events surrounding this riotous episode in the lives of my ancestors. Facilitating my understanding, was my own observation of the **Leeds, Hyde Park** riot on **Monday, 10ᵗʰ July 1995**. Whilst gazing at **The Newlands Pub** being burnt down, I gained much insight into how well-organized mobs worked. (Admittedly, being a bystander on the street was a rather daunting experience.)

The first thing to state about the **Chartist** Riot in **Skipton** was that this crowd was not just a spontaneous mob, but rather a well-planned protest march – one designed to intimidate and to bring to public attention the grievances of those suffering severe hardship – in his instance, following the Trade Depression of **1842.** It was also used as an occasion to extort money and demand much-needed food and provisions. A white band tied around the upper arm would distinguish the main leaders from their followers. Their chief spokesman was a **William Smith** who seemed able to display that *'gift of the gab'* common to so many **Smiths.** Awaiting him in **Skipton** were the magistrates **Matthew Wilson Senior, Matthew Wilson Junior** (later **Sir Matthew**), **Cooper Preston, James Braithwaite Garforth, Hastings Ingham** and **Thomas Birkbeck.** Forewarned of trouble the aforesaid magistrates had *'sworn in'* numerous *'special constables'* to assist old **Thomas Laycock,** the Parish Constable for **Skipton.**

Like all mobs, there was a precipitating factor, and in this case, it had been a visit paid to **Colne** by the distressed textile operatives of **Burnley.** They, in their turn, may well have been stirred by the example of the operatives in **Manchester** who had decided to go on strike in protest at a cut in their wages. Once in **Colne,** the agitators had persuaded their equally distressed compatriots to march on to **Skipton** with a view to bringing the mills to a standstill. They hoped to achieve this by pulling out the water plugs from the wagon-boilers which were needed to power the factory machinery. (Hence these disturbances were later to become known as the *'Plug Drawing'* or *'Plug Riots.'*) Once this objective had been accomplished then the hope was to win over the **Skipton** workers, take nearby **Addingham** and raise the whole region in revolt. **Skipton** was a hugely strategic location – one able to provide a very useful route from **Lancashire** into **Yorkshire**. As the local magistrates knew only too well, its loss to the rioters would cause very severe problems for the governing authorities. Consequently, they were determined to try and contain the disturbances at **Skipton.** Much would depend upon the feelings of the local population. If they strongly sympathised with the protest marchers, then the town would be lost. However, one factor operating in the magistrates' favour was that **Skipton** was a very conservative market town with many *'respectable'* trades-people. They would deeply resent any disruption created by an outside incursion – especially by a threatening mob that had come over from **Lancashire** of all places!

Once in **Colne,** the next stage of convergence would begin with a general assemblage of people prepared to march forward to **Skipton.** Contemporary accounts were to describe this as a terrifying sight, with men marching four abreast, each holding a club to intimidate and bring security against possible attack. Behind the men came the women and children. As the march continued along the **Broughton Road,** sympathisers (or those looking for trouble) would join it. On their way to **Skipton** acts of intimidation took place. At **Barnoldswick** and **Easby** they took the shuttles from the handloom weavers who were almost as poor as they were, and so immobilised their looms. This act could hardly have won them much sympathy. At **Aireville Grange** they demanded milk from a mother with a five-year-old boy. One party visited **Gargrave** and stopped the mills there before re-joining the main party. Such acts probably alienated would-be supporters who saw their own livelihoods being endangered. Meanwhile, the inhabitants of **Skipton** could only wait with mounting fear over what was likely to come. Their reaction was understandable, given the fact that, as a market town with just under **5,000** inhabitants, it was now being faced with an invasion from a hungry and potentially violent **3000** strong mob! Businesses ceased trading, shops closed early doors securely fastened and the windows of the wealthier people were shuttered up. Such acts hardly testified to a keen sense of local sympathy for the protestors. Trouble was expected. Yet it was at **Skipton** that this threat would have to be contained. The scene was set for the next phase of crowd behaviour – confrontation!

To ascertain the mob's intentions, the two magistrates **Ingham** and **Birbeck** parlayed with **William Smith** who openly declared that their intention was to stop the mills and *'turn out'* the operatives. (The fact that they had to be *'turned out'* demonstrated a lack of local support – from workers who would have been expected to have sympathised with the protestors' aims.) **Ingham** stressed that the people of **Skipton** were *'much alarmed'* and he asked the **Lancastrians** not to resort to violence or enter any shops or houses. **Smith's** response was to assure the magistrates that no intention existed to injure life or property. It seemed as if both parties wanted to reduce the risk of violence. Whilst the mob marched into the town **Ingham** rode furiously to **Colne** to call out the military garrison based there. (Why had it not been rallied earlier to halt the trouble?) During his absence, **300-400** rioters visited first **Dewhurst's Mill,** and then **Sidgwick's** newly opened **Low Mill,** before moving on to **Sidgwick's High Mill.** At each place, they stopped production by drawing water from the machines. In response, the magistrates appointed respectable persons (including **William Paget** – Clerk to the Solicitor **Thomas Brown**) to be present at certain sites, to act as witnesses. At **High Mill,** the mob was at first driven back but then returned to *'pull out the plug'* and turn out the workers. Following this success, the crowd demanded money and warned that further mischief would take place if the mill re-opened without the *'plug-drawers'* consent. **Smith** ordered the mill to be kept idle until delegates at **Manchester** had determined the rate of wages. **Christopher Sidgewick** (who had retired in **1833**) promised to pay a sovereign to the mob as a token of submission. He then asked who their leader was, and **William Smith** stepped forward. In what appeared to be an attempt to defuse a tense situation **Smith** ordered the crowd to disperse and within the next fifteen minutes this is what they did. **Christopher Sidgewick** then paid his sovereign to **William** to bribe the crowd to move away. Both parties appeared anxious to maintain some control of the situation.

On the outskirts of **Skipton,** with the leaders busily attempting to immobilise the outlying mills, discipline amongst the rest of the protestors in the centre of **Skipton** began to break down. Crowds took to wandering around the town, breaking into shops and houses, stealing property, seizing food and demanding money. In some cases, householders had food already provided in advance – knowing full well that this would be one of the most common demands. Whether **John** and **Ann Smith** were ever subjected to the mob's attention remains a matter of speculation. (Nothing in family tradition indicates they were – perhaps **Greenside** was too poor a locality to be worth their while.) There were richer pickings to be had on the **High Street.** Such scenes of disorder meant that most of the pre-conditions for a major riot had slotted into place. The final pre-condition galloped in with the **11th Hussars,** accompanied by the **61st Regiment of Foot.** It had taken them three hours marching in sweltering heat to arrive from **Colne. Captain Jones** was their commander.

Backed by military authority the magistrates now felt they could begin to take firmer measures. (They must also by this stage have been confident of local support.) **Matthew Wilson** read (possibly twice) a copy of the **1716 Riot Act** from the Town Hall steps but was ignored. **Hastings Ingham,** (who appeared to have displayed a great presence of mind throughout the day) rode around the town reading the very same Riot Act, but he too was ignored. He will have shouted out the following words: *"Our Sovereign Lady the Queen chargeth and commandeth all persons being assembled immediately to disperse themselves, and peaceably to depart to their habitations and to their lawful business, upon pains contained in an Act made in the first year of* **King George** *for preventing tumultuous and riotous assemblies. God Save the Queen,"* (Quoted in **Rowley p.68**)

A ruse was then resorted to; the well-respected, elderly timber merchant **John Settle** offered the rioters one of his fields with the added provision of beer and refreshments. In the exposed location of **Anna Fields,** the crowd could be more easily dispersed and the possibility of a nasty street battle in **Skipton** avoided. Somewhat naively the crowd complied, only to find themselves followed by the magistrates who kept on reading the Riot Act. One of the magistrates, **Cooper Preston** of **Flasby Hall** seems to have panicked, repeatedly calling upon the troops to fire onto the protestors. He was met with a firm rebuke from **Captain Jones** who reminded his somewhat fearful men that he was their commander and that they must obey him alone. After regaining control this military man then ordered his troops to fix bayonets and charge the still restless mob that had assembled in **Anna Fields.** In response one of the mob leaders **William Spencer** shouted at the mob to remain firm and stand still. However, this was not to be and as the mob fled up the nearby lane he (along with **John Spencer** and **James Dakin**) led the rioters in stone throwing. During the melee, one of the magistrates **James Braithwaite Garfoth JP** was cut off from the troops. Apparently, to signal his presence he waved his stick in the air. This was interpreted as an aggressive gesture and in response one of the rioters struck him full in the face with a club, smashing his spectacles, blinding one eye and knocking out several teeth. After some more stone throwing the mob dispersed. They left behind one dead soldier.

Six leaders were arrested and conveyed to the **Devonshire Hotel** in **Skipton** where, after a preliminary examination by the magistrates, they spent an uncomfortable night under guard. (This was the **Hotel** on the **south side** of **New Market Street;** about five minutes' walk away from **John** and **Anne Smith's** home.) Next day they were conveyed by coach to **York Summer Assize Court,** under the supervision of **Hastings Ingham** and **Captain**

Jones. At their trial, it was apparent that the judge had already made up his mind concerning the verdict. Sentenced on **September 5ᵗʰ, 1842,** the names of the six arrested leaders were: -
William Smith aged **46** – received **12** months imprisonment with hard labour.
William Spencer aged **47** – received **6** months imprisonment with hard labour.
John Spencer aged **50** – received **6** months imprisonment with hard labour.
John Harland aged **38** – discharged for lack of evidence.
Edward Hey, aged **32** – discharged for lack of evidence.
James Dakin aged **27** – received **6** months imprisonment with hard labour.

William Spencer's plea for leniency on the grounds he had a wife and eight children to provide for went unheeded as did the argument of **William Smith's** Defence Council that he had led a starving mob in a very creditable manner. The mayhem in **Skipton** had ended with the clanging of prison cell doors.

Beyond causing some temporary disruption, the protestors had failed to achieve what had possibly been over-ambitious goals. This failure could be attributed mainly to poor discipline, and to the calm (yet determined presence) of mind of some of their opponents such as **Hastings Ingham**. However, perhaps the chief cause was the unwillingness of most of **Skipton's** population to join them. Far from conveying the impression of being a victimised people with a just cause, the behaviour of the demonstrators had simply confirmed the prejudice that they were *'outside'* troublemakers – whose behaviour was a threat to the decent law-abiding citizens of **Skipton.** The fact that they had come into **Yorkshire** from **Lancashire** had served only to discredit their cause even further. (Rivalry had existed between these two counties from time immemorial.) In the end, what at the time was known as *'the turn out riots'* failed because there had been no real attempt to win over the people of **Skipton;** all the magistrates did was exploit this omission. Even so, it had been a very nasty business and was to live on in local memory.

Precisely how my ancestors reacted to the *'Plug Riots'* remains lost in history, though undeniably it would have formed a major source of discussion as did the **Hyde Park** riots I lived through. It seems likely that, as a boy of ten, **Edmund** would have retained deep impressions of these highly charged and dramatic events for the rest of his life. The fact that he (and other members of his family) took the *'High Road'* to **mid-Victorian** respectability suggested a marked lack of sympathy with both the actions and underlying attitudes of the rioters. Also, the evidence that **John** and **Ann Smith** had moved away from **Cullingworth Chapel** at precisely the time its Sabbath School had been taken over by

Chartists surely denoted their lack of commitment to radical political causes. **John Smith** did not stay behind and lead the workers of **Cullingworth** in action against their employers.

In general, the **Smiths** of this period appeared to have been more concerned with the making of money than with *'putting the world to rights.'* Respectability – not revolution – was their goal. They saw that the road to social, (as well as individual) betterment lay through arduous work and good business sense rather than through political agitation. Perhaps in the long term, events were to prove them right.

Section 5: A Tragic Accident

Concerning a fatal accident in Skipton Corn Mill

Providing firm evidence of my Great, Great Grandparents' presence at **Skipton** during this disturbing period of *'The Plug Riots'* were the following details concerning the births of their children **Hannah** and **John:** -
1. **When and where born:** October Third, 1841 Skipton
2. **Name if Any:** Hannah
3. **Sex:** Female
4. **Name and Surname of Father:** John Smith
5. **Name and Surname of Mother:** Ann Smith, formerly Wilson
6. **Occupation of Father:** Miller
7. **Signature, description and residence of informant:** John Smith, Father, Skipton
8. **When registered:** October Twentieth, 1841
9. **Signature of registrar:** E. Tindal

1. **When and where born:** July Twenty Seventh 1843 Skipton
2. **Name if Any:** John
3. **Sex:** Male
4. **Name and Surname of Father:** John Smith
5. **Name and Surname of Mother:** Ann Smith, formerly Wilson
6. **Occupation of Father:** Miller
7. **Signature, description and residence of informant:** John Smith, Father, Skipton
8. **When registered:** August Twenty Third 1843
9. **Signature of registrar:** E. Tindal

Sometime between **June 1836** and **October 1841,** my Great, Great Grandfather had learnt to sign his own name. This showed a determination to overcome his earlier problem of illiteracy. Unfortunately, copies of his signature were not available from the local register office at **Harrogate.** (This same office was also unable to find details of the marriage of **Samuel Smith,** even though several Parish Registers were looked at, including those of **Kildwick.**)

A far more persistent threat to the health of **Skipton's** population was the one posed by filthy living conditions. These were worsened by a five-fold increase in the number of inhabitants; from **2,305** in **1801** to **11,986** in **1901.** The unwillingness of *'The Castle Estate'* to sell off any of its land for building purposes until the **1850s** heightened an already severe problem of overcrowding. A Public Health Act Report of **March 26th1857,** (cited in **Warren (1999) pp.3-5**) revealed that, after considering the **137** infant deaths in this period, the average life expectancy for the good economic years of **1852-1856** was a meagre **35.7** years. Unfiltered drinking water was conveyed in wooden pipes from two reservoirs on the border of **Rombald's Moor.** The **22** *'water closets'* (toilets) in the town leaked excrement through their walls and out onto the road or into the local beck. Many families shared the same privies or were thankful to have **Holy Trinity** churchyard in which to relieve their natural wants! About **20%** of the houses were *'back to back'* and consequently suffered from extremely poor ventilation. One family of ten, with children in the **5-21** age range, lived in only one room unfit for human inhabitation. Another of nine lived in similar circumstances (in this case the children were in the **1-18** age range). The only surprising feature was that there had been so little typhus. One recent sign of progress had been the introduction of gas lighting supplied by a private company. In response to the **1857** Public Health Report, a Local Board of Health was established in **1858** in **Skipton.** Sadly, its arrival came too late for **John** and **Ann Smith** who had already died. Attempts to find their names in any **Skipton** Graveyard Register or in the **Sutton Chapel Burial Book** proved unavailing. However, after much effort, their death certificates were eventually traced and received on **Friday, 21st September 2001.** These documents revealed that tragedy had occurred in **Edmund's** early life; at the age of eleven, he had been left fatherless. The death of his father formed the second major trauma of his life and must have created a gnawing sense of insecurity. One day he off to work, the next day he was dead.

Registration District Skipton

1843 Death in the **sub-district** of **Skipton** in the **County of York**

1. When and where died? November 14th, 1843

2. Name and Surname: John Smith, Skipton
3. Sex: Male
4. Age: 38 Years
5. Occupation: Corn Miller
6. Cause of death: Accidentally Killed
7. Signature, description and residence of informant: Thomas Brown of Skipton, Coroner for Yorkshire
8. When registered: November 18th, 1843
9. Signature of registrar: E. Tindal, Registrar

Significantly, family tradition mentioned *'a terrible mill accident'* through which *'a relative'* of **Edmund** was reputed to have lost an arm through falling into some machinery. Tradition also added that the family had moved to **Leeds** *'sometime after this accident.'* This oral tradition had apparently originated from **Edmund** before being relayed to my Grandfather who, in his turn, had relayed it to two of his children. They had then passed it on to a certain cousin of mine. It appears likely that it contained a garbled version of **John Smith's** death. As a trained Millwright, he would have dealt with machinery daily. However, mill accidents were an all-too-frequent occurrence. An e-mail (received on **Saturday, 29th June 2002**) from the newly established Mill Archive) threw some light upon the possible cause of **John Smith's** death. *"It is all too easy to become too familiar with the machinery and to forget the incredible momentum the gears and shafts possess. If you get caught there is no chance of the mill stopping quickly (assuming, there is someone to help). This was in the days long before safety screens were installed. In the professional journal 'The Miller,' even in the **1890's**, the deaths of a number of people each year were reported."*

The balance of evidence strongly suggests that it really was <u>this</u> **John Smith**, (**Edmund's** own father) who had been the relation to have lost his arm in a machine accident – and had died tragically as a result. The timing was right – as was the occupation. Family tradition suggested that the accident had been *'a terrible one'* and that sometime after it the family had moved to **Leeds**. It's very likely that my Great Grandfather **Edmund** will have acquired a lifelong aversion to machinery.

Clearly, my Great, Great Grandfather's death had been a terrible one. It would have left his family in a profound state of shock. In addition, it will have made a striking impression upon **Edmund** who, at the time of his father's death, was at a very formative age. However, things were to worsen for, at the age of twelve, he was to be left a complete orphan during one of the harshest decades of the industrial revolution. From nearly his earliest years, **Edmund** will have been convinced of have seen the need for financial self-sufficiency. This resolute attitude will have made him outwardly enterprising but inwardly closed and less approachable as a human being.

Unfortunately, around the time of **John Smith's** death, **Skipton** had no newspaper and any contacts made with various archive offices only confirmed that the Coroner's report would have long since been destroyed. (This was because the report belonged to the Coroner rather than to any governing authority.) Consequently, the exact cause and location of my Great, Great Grandfather's death remain unknown. However, **John's** death seemed to have precipitated the rapid decline of his wife **Ann Smith,** as validated by evidence provided in her own Death Certificate.

Registration District <u>Skipton</u>

<u>1844</u> **Death in the** <u>**sub-district**</u> **of** <u>Skipton</u> **in the** <u>County of York</u>

1. When and where died? October 7th, 1844

2. Name and Surname: Ann Smith, Skipton

3. Sex: Female

4. Age: 41 Years

5. Occupation: Widow of John Smith, Miller

6. Cause of death: Consumption

7. Signature, description and residence of informant: Wm. Smith present at the Death, Skipton

8. When registered: October 9th, 1844

9. Signature of registrar: E. Tindal, Registrar

It was easy to see **Ann** had been worn out by eight known pregnancies – these being **Samuel** (born on, **1st November 1826** at **1.00 pm**), **Susannah Wilson** (born **29th June 1828**), **Edmund** (my Great Grandfather born **21st January 1832**), **Daniel** (born **27th June 1834**) **Ben** (Born **15th April 1836**, who appeared to have died in infancy), **Ann** (born **24th December 1838**), **Hannah** (born **3rd October 1841**) and **John** (born **27th July 1843**).

To have seen **Ann** repeatedly cough-up blood and endure what was then known as *'a decline'* must have been highly distressing for all family members. For **Edmund,** it would have his third traumatic experience in the space of just over two years. The **William Smith** who had acted as the informant may well have been **Ann's** father-in-law. If this were so, then his presence showed that members of **John Smith's** family had been rallying around his orphaned children – possibly to save them from the Workhouse. **John's** eldest son **Samuel** will have shouldered a particularly heavy burden in becoming the new *'head of the family'* whilst still in his teenage years. The fact that he and his brothers came to hold respectable positions in **Victorian** society showed that the **Smiths** had not been destroyed by this double bereavement. They avoided sinking into either destitution or alcohol abuse. The fact that **Samuel** and his brothers survived what appears to have been the worst crisis recorded in this family history showed that their lives (and those of the relatives who came to help them) were based upon sound moral values – standing them in good stead throughout these most difficult of years.

The precise burial place of my Great, Great Grandparents has remained unknown. A previous review of the Burial book for **Sutton Baptist Chapel** eliminated that location; whilst information provided by the **Northallerton Archive Centre** confirmed that they were <u>not</u> interred at **Holy Trinity, Skipton** nor at **Kildwick, Saint Andrews**. This left only the nearby **Congregational Church,** which had been opened in **1839** (the large **Raikes Road Cemetery** would not be open until **1846**). The fact that this Chapel had links with the **British School** attended by **Daniel** increased the likelihood that it was here that **John** and **Ann Smith** were buried. Moreover, it would only have taken several minutes to have carried their coffins from their home at **Greenside** (just off **Market Street**). Unfortunately, their names were not in the Monument Lists held by **Skipton Library.** This would suggest that they were either too poor to have afforded a headstone – or as was very possible – the headstone itself had worn away when the remaining inscriptions had been listed a century and a half later. Repeated attempts to locate their burial site simply proved unsuccessful. Complicating this research was the fact that the Burial Book for this Congregational Chapel was itself impossible to trace. However, following the above process of elimination, the **Congregational Cemetery** does seem to have been their most likely resting place.

Throughout this traumatic period, **Edmund** would have lived in a household mourning the loss of their father and then their mother – the main breadwinner and housekeeper respectively. From the early age of eleven, he will have been familiar with the presence of death. This may perhaps explain why he would later acquire such a dour nature and the reputation for being domineering.' The atmosphere in the home at that time would have been thick with gloom and worry about the future. The most immediate priority will have been to look for work to help rescue the family from penury. Any education he may have enjoyed up to this point will have been cut short. This may well have created an inner feeling that he somehow *'missed out'* on life. He would have been only too aware that he lived in a world which showed only a little compassion for widows and orphans. He may also have wanted a job which <u>did not</u> place him close to any machinery.

CHAPTER 8: A DEDICATED SCHOOL TEACHER

Section 1: Four Brothers

Concerning four strong men

On **Wednesday, 4ᵗʰ July 2018** (as fresh revelations about **Edmund** began to pour in) I received an email photo attachment which portrayed his three brothers and himself. Each was crammed (rather uncomfortably I thought) into a small photographic studio run by a **Charles Henry Braithwaite** based at **7.5A Briggate Leeds.** Further details about this photographer can be found at https://sites.google.com/site/leedsandbradfordstudios/home/charles-henry-braithwaite This website revealed that, in **1857, Braithwaite** had "*opened his own studio at* **Reinhardt's Yard** *between* **Reinhardt's Druggist** *and* **Megson Stationers** *near the top of* **Briggate, Leeds**. *He launched his portrait business with some success when he was commissioned to take a portrait of* **Lord Brougham** *at the residence of* **James Kitson, Little Woodhouse**. **The Leeds Mercury** *reported (on* **7th Nov 1857**) *that 'notwithstanding the dullness of humidity of the atmosphere* **Mr Braithwaite** *was successful in obtaining an admirable likeness with which his Lordship expressed himself very much pleased.'*" By **1881** he had risen sufficiently high in his profession to have taken a photograph of Prime Minister **William Gladstone.** (To appreciate the high standard of his work all one need do is Google the words '*C. H. Braithwaite, Photographer, Briggate Leeds.'*) It appears the **Smith** brothers had gone to the best photographer in town.

All '*suited and booted*' their style of jackets and approximate ages would suggest that the photograph had been taken in the mid to late **1860s.** What the special occasion was which had led these very busy men to congregate for this photoshoot in **Leeds** remains unknown. However, it may well have been around the time of **Edmund's** marriage to **Rosamond** – in **December 1867.** Their heavy clothing did suggest a period in winter. I can't think of any other event being big enough to have warranted this special '*all brothers together*' photo. All four **Smiths** are formally attired with their shoes shining and all sporting beards and the long **Smith** nose. The photograph '*captures*' them at an interesting time in each of their lives – when they're knowingly moving away from their rural roots to live as respectable members of the urban middle classes. The one nearest to those roots would be the bespectacled **Samuel** (standing on the left) with his luxuriant curly hair giving him the appearance of a benevolent Santa Claus. He seems to have a large labourer's hand. Of the brothers, he's the most relaxed, emanating a calm patriarchal authority. On **7ᵗʰ**

July 1851 he had married a certain **Anne Smithers** and together they raised a family continue with corn milling. He left **Skipton** and (following a period in **Huddersfield** in about **1858**) he came to **Holbeck, Beeston** which is now part of **South Leeds**. The **1881** Census revealed that he was living at **8 Globe Road** in **Holbeck** and was a *'Master Corn Miller'* with eight men and a boy working for him. He seemed to have been prospering. However, an entry in the diary of his nephew **James** confirmed that he *"died, after **over 7** months in bed.* This was on the evening of **30th June-1st July 1886.** A previous problem with dropsy dating back to the previous **February** and a very evident problem with his weight suggested he'd suffered a massive stroke which a common problem in the family. However, a probate document dated **13th July 1887** revealed that his death had occurred on **1st July 1886** at **3 Cambrian Terrace, Holbeck Beeston.** His personal estate amounted to **£3,439.5.3** that confirmed he'd made a success of his trade. The executors of his will were two of his sons, **Edmund Smith** who was a *'Corn Factor'* living at **119 Woodhouse Lane** and **John Smith** of **Sweet Street, Holbeck** who was a *'corn miller.'*

During his visit to **Yorkshire** in **1881, David Morton** described **Samuel** then aged **56** and weighing **200** Pounds as being *"a rough **Yorkshireman,** self-made, self-reliant, blunt and brave, a high-toned generous and kind fellow who has friends and enemies – warm-hearted, witty, waggish – would be a character anywhere."* Duly noted were his *"fine mill and neat, substantial residence"* which would be worth **$20,000** in **Louisville**. His wife was praised for being *"a devoutly pious* **[Methodist?]** *class-leader. Her highest pleasure in service, **God** and the Church – as near a Saint if common report of her maybe relied on. She is a cripple but manages to get to Church and do Church Work. Is well-read and sensible, adored by her husband and* [six living] *children."* Of all the brothers **'Sam'** as he was known was the one who stayed closest to his rural roots. Interestingly a review of census Information undertaken on **Wednesday, 8th August 2018** in **Leeds Central Library** confirmed that he'd moved to **Leeds** in around **1860,** roughly the same time as his younger brother **Edmund.** Whether the two near-simultaneous moves were connected couldn't be proven. For both, of these brothers **Leeds** was a place of opportunity.

Positioned behind both himself and **Edmund** stands **John** – the youngest brother and the smartest-looking. He was also known as **'Ben'** by family members. His black beard is well trimmed with his prominent forehead edged by a line of receding curly hair. He's pushing himself forward as if wanting to be noticed, but a look of uncertainty crosses his face. **John** appears to be finding life a struggle and seemed to lack that inner strength of character – which was more noticeable in the faces of his brothers. Like his brother **Edmund, John** would be a Commercial Traveller in the drapery line. However, he would be based in **Rochdale, Lancashire.** He too would marry and have children. His death came on **Thursday, 14th October 1909** at **Cleveleys** (located four miles **North of Blackpool**). A **Manchester** Probate Document of **1st November** confirmed that he managed to leave **£439.13.2** to his wife (also called **Anne**). In **2018,** this would be the equivalent of **£50,824.55.**

Seated beside **Samuel** (legs crossed, and arms folded) is my Great Grandfather **Edmund,** his eyes boring straight into the camera. He has a look of defiant belligerence about him as if he's wondering, *'How much is this tomfoolery going to cost me?'* He doesn't seem to want to be there. On display is a resplendent beard, domed forehead and receding crown of curly hair, which, in his case, appears to be either fair or grey. He bore some resemblance to **John.** In this instance (and in contrast to **Samuel** his elder brother) **Edmund's** face is that of a Santa Claus from a horror movie! His bulky frame only adds to his formidable appearance, bedecked as he is with a pocket watch resting against his paunch. Rather surprisingly his trousers are slightly rumpled. The impression gained is of a large *'mountain of a man'* who may well have been quite terrifying to have had as a parent! Here was a man <u>never</u> to be trifled with and with whom an argument was <u>never</u> to be lightly undertaken! I suspect that, for **Edmund,** anger management could well have been an issue.

Little of this was hinted at in **David Morton's** description of him. "*Edmund owns two elegant residences adjoining in a fashionable part of **Leeds**. In one of which he lives, renting the other. His house is splendidly furnished and the two are worth **$12,000**. He is a Commercial traveller representing a large dry goods house in **Glasgow Scotland** with a branch house in **Leeds** in charge of his son. He lives extravagantly and I suspect fully up to his income.*" **David Morton** was the only source suggesting that my Great Grandfather had connections with a Church – albeit for reasons of social respectability. "*Edmund Smith is a steward in the fashionable **North Church** of **Leeds** – a man of much more polish than his brother, a pleasant plausible fellow who gets good wages and spends them and likes to have his friends around them. His wife* [my Great Grandmother **Rosamond**] *is about five feet high and weighs a full two hundred. Is gay, dressy and stylish, was with us very cordial and pleasant, but **Sam** shrugged his shoulders every time he spoke of her. She is his second wife. **Edmund's** two wives have had **16** children, **11** I believe of whom are living. We saw most of them at home.*" The reasons for **Samuel's** dislike of **Rosamond** remained unknown. A photograph taken of my Great grandmother in **June 1882,** confirmed the accuracy of **David Morton's** description. However, I was unable to identify the *'fashionable'* Church **Edmund** served as a steward as **North Leeds** was home to a number such places.

Seated at the front (in what again appears to be an uncomfortable pose) and with his arms folded is **Daniel** the second youngest brother. He appears to be sitting on an undersized chair, his legs bent to the left at an awkward angle, trying valiantly not to topple. A gold watch chain can be seen beneath his folded hands. His beard is slightly forked and his forehead less prominent but still bedecked by a fringe of curly hair. **Daniel's** face is especially interesting – his eyes telling of someone who's seen a lot of suffering, but one who knows his duty and is determined to see things through. **Daniel** possessed that type of sturdy inner calibre needed to make a very dedicated school teacher. Of the four brothers, it's **Edmund** and **Daniel** who portray the strongest personalities. When my mother gazed at the photograph (from her Nursing Home bed on **Saturday 7th July 2018**) she chirped, *"they're all good looking."* Somehow, I think that certain **Victorian** ladies (desiring economic security and respectability) would have agreed. Incidentally, the fact that my mother was still living to see these latest revelations was an event worth recording in itself. In her extreme old age, she was seeing the near completion of this *'Family History'* (which also contained the account of her own life within its pages). This chapter will focus on **Daniel,** because unlike his brothers he and his wife **Elizabeth** had no children who could perpetuate their name. I also found him to be a very interesting person who shared my passion for education.

Section 2: A Skipton Education

Concerning the British School at Skipton and Samuel Farey

One fascinating detail in the **1851** Census Return was **Daniel Smith's** connection with education as a *"Pupil-Teacher."* Now – approximately one hundred and sixty-five years further on – this link with the teaching profession is still very much alive in the **Smith** family. Since **October 1990,** I have taught a wide range of subjects to mainly adult students on a private basis. These subjects have included **Economics, History, Politics, Psychology, Sociology, Theology,** and **Business Studies.** It appears that my role in the family saga has been to combine the business side – as represented by **Edmund** – with the education side – as represented by **Daniel.** Unbeknown to me, I have spent much of my life building upon the heritage first laid down by these two men (as well as other ancestors too.)

Warren (1999) p. 15-17 stated that the Pupil-Teacher system had been established by **Sir James Kay Shuttleworth,** (Committee Secretary of the

Council of Education, formed in **1839**). It was this august body that began the School Inspection System in **1846.** Part of its mode of operation allowed for the payment of government grants. However, receiving these was conditional upon the meeting of certain criteria set down by the School Inspectors. The Pupil-Teacher system represented a major reform, in the sense that cheap and untrained *'Monitors'* were replaced by fully apprenticed Pupil-Teachers, (minimum age **13**). Pupil-Teachers were eligible to sit for qualifying examinations called **Queen's Scholarships** held at a Training College – and all paid out of government expense. Two key concepts underpinned this measure; firstly, that this apprenticeship system could, using the Pupil-Teacher model, be successfully introduced into the area of education – and secondly, that this represented the best method of teaching classes of up to **60** pupils. During the same time that the Master taught varying age ranges and different subjects at set times of the day, the Pupil-Teacher would instruct smaller groups in the very same hall. Superficially, this was a very poor way to teach, as the master's voice would have been in the background, but it was the method used at the time. The three main occupations of; oral instruction, reading aloud and silent occupation largely dominated the lessons. Rote learning still prevailed although there was beginning to be some attempt to break with the idea that the Master was merely a *'Drill Sergeant'* of young children. Scripture study and learning a Church Catechism by heart ranked in importance alongside the *'three **Rs** '* of reading, writing, and arithmetic. Indeed, it could be argued that Religion could be included as a fourth **'R'** because the **Victorians** valued it so highly. By today's standards the education children received throughout this period was terribly narrow, but nevertheless, it did help instil moral values and lead to an improvement in memorising skills. In a period of scarce educational resources, boys were given greater priority over girls, who were sometimes placed in the charge of lowly, untrained female assistants. Schoolmasters themselves were often to be feared, with the swish of a cane a frequently heard sound in many a **Victorian** School. However, some Schoolmasters became well respected and almost revered by their class pupils. A faded old **Victorian** photograph of the **British School** (on display at **Skipton Museum**) showed the Master, **Samuel Farey,** to have been a plump grey-haired man, with *'large mutton chop'* side whiskers (fashionable in the **1840s**) and an extremely serious expression. He was certainly a figure to be respected. Later evidence would confirm that he was not a brute in the mould of **Mr Squeers** – the fictitious schoolmaster of **Dotheboy's Hall** in the **Charles Dickens** novel **Nicholas Nickleby.** In his approach to both staff and pupils, he would be *'firm but fair.'* There did appear to be a very strong caring side to his character.

The nonconformist links of **Daniel** and my Great Grandfather **Edmund** suggested they would have attended this **British School** rather than the **Anglican**-based Parish School. Constructed in **1844,** the **British School** adjoined the **Zion Independent Congregational Chapel,** which itself was a large imposing building of Neo-Gothic design, sited on **Market Street.** Built in **1839,** this chapel had a bird-cage shaped bell tower, which protruded upward from the centre of its long-slanted roof. Perched on the very top stood a cockerel weather vane. In contrast to this towering chapel building, direct observation (made with my wife on **Saturday, July 15th, 2001**) showed that the **British School** itself was a much lower and longer barn-like building. It seemed to cast a perpetual shadow over the small schoolyard and its two outside privies. (The building itself had long since closed as a school – indeed it was now being used for business purposes.) Access to the interior of this building was gained on **Friday, 4th September 2015.** This was achieved with the help of our second cousin (once removed) who introduced us to the business proprietor (a paper supplier) by stating, *"Hello, we're three weirdo family historians. Would you mind if we looked at your premises?"* Somehow, the line got us in, and I quickly ascertained that, despite a lowering of the ceiling to accommodate upstairs offices, much had remained intact from **Samuel Farey's** time. There were still the air vents in the walls – positioned to allow *'clean'* air into the hall. Also, the rectangular double windows were very firmly in their original positions. Each window contained 24 square shaped panels, divided by an extra thick frame into two main sets of twelve. Each double window contained a total of 48 panes. It was an incredibly moving experience to be standing inside a building once so closely associated with my family and an early **Victorian** schoolmaster who knew them.

The **1852** map for **Skipton** confirmed that the school's location was on the **South** side of **Otley Street,** adjacent to what is now **Saint Andrew's Church** (built in **1914**) and just behind the graveyard on the **north** side of **New Market Street. Daniel** and his elder brother **Edmund** could easily have walked to this school within several minutes. Perhaps both lads knew what it was like to have been caned by *'old mutton chops.'* His photograph had revealed a rather formidable figure – one likely to inspire terror in small boys. Yet also present on his face was a deeply caring expression. He appeared to be one of those masters who would have inspired respect as well as fear. Like most schoolmasters of the time, he would have been a very methodical man.

Part 2 of the **1848 Slater's Trade Directory** showed **Samuel Farey** to have been Master of the **British School,** with **Ann Robinson** as Mistress – both residing in **New Market Street.** A thesis by **J. Foster (1974)** held by the

Brotherton Library of **Leeds University,** revealed some interesting details about this man. According to **Chapter Six, Section (a), Samuel Farey** had been in charge from its very foundation in **1844** (when the School had been established under the patronage of the wealthy mill owner **John Dewhurst** who himself had ceremoniously opened the New School Room at a personal cost of £**350**). He would remain as Master until **1866.** He was the first teacher in **Skipton** to have obtained a Government Certificate, gained at an examination held in **Manchester** during the spring of **1849.** An Annual Report of **1850** had praised him for his industry, devotion to work, intelligence and spirit in creating a useful, improving school. He seemed to have been a positive role model for anyone wishing to enter the teaching profession. His annual salary had been £**60.00** – which simply didn't compare to that of the School Mistress **Miss Robinson** who was paid a meagre £**15.00,** despite being praised by the Management Committee for her diligence. By **1855,** the success of the school had attracted extra government grants and each annual wage had risen to £**143.00** and £**36.00** respectively. In the following year, **Miss Robinson** was to resign citing ill health as a reason. Although nominally Inter-Denominational, the school had been closely connected to the **Congregational Chapel** next door. In **April 1854, Samuel Farey** had persuaded his Pupil-Teachers to attend this Chapel, supposedly for congregational singing. When a new Infant's Mistress, **Elizabeth Smith** was appointed in **1857** – one condition of her acceptance was that she would attend the **Congregational Chapel.** Church members largely supported the School's Management Committee whilst the Pastor of the **Congregational Chapel** acted as its Secretary – his deacons filling other positions. The **Dewhurst** family (who were also influential Congregationalists) traditionally provided the position of Chairman and Treasurer. In effect, the School Committee was a *'closed shop,'* run by the same narrow circle of people. Over the period of **1844-1859** more than half the Pupil Teachers appointed were **Congregationalists.** An extremely vague tradition in my family mentions that some of the early **Smiths** had been *"Baptists or Congregationalists."* The evidence gathered to date in this *'History'* would suggest they had been both. They had followed different denominational allegiances over different time periods.

Pupil-Teachers were usually *'hand-picked'* from those considered to be intelligent and have a good, preferably religious-moral character. (In his conclusion to **Chapter six, Foster** showed that their social background was mainly lower middle class or respectable working class – with a high proportion of small businessmen *e.g.* Coal Merchants, Drapers, Innkeepers, Joiners and Grocers. The lower working classes were largely bypassed.) Another consideration was whether the Pupil-Teacher had the ability to encourage others to learn and to pass the government tests, which provided *'objective criteria'* as to whether the school was succeeding. The fact that **Daniel** evidently fitted this model provided a very good testimony to his character and indicated that he'd received sound parenting. In those days, a boy's family background was significant when being considered for such a position. The son of the town drunkard or irreligious sceptic would <u>never</u> have been chosen.

Upon entering the schoolroom **Daniel** would have found a rather cavernous, church-like interior, with long benches, each seating up to six pupils apiece. The walls will have been festooned with pictures, maps and scripture texts – all adding a note of colour to the otherwise drab and austere surroundings. The Master himself will have sat down on a large throne of a chair, positioned behind a heavy wooden desk, elevated on a slightly raised platform. Equipment will have been sparse, consisting mainly of slate tablets and chalks. Only when a pupil's work had been substantially corrected would it be placed into a copybook. As the examples from **Sutton Baptist Church** showed, the reading material was often moralistic in tone, pointing out the dire of any bad behaviour. What was regarded as higher forms of culture would be mediated through the rote learning of poetry and the sitting of English comprehension tests – that was all based on edifying pieces of literature. Mathematical problems were geared to preparing children (boys especially) for the world of trade. Needlework was a skill taught only to the girls.

Throughout his apprenticeship, **Daniel** will have had to deliver *"model lessons,"* with his teaching critically observed by either **Samuel Farey** or a Government Inspector. In return, he will have received *'before'* or *'after school'* personal tuition. He will also have benefited from the school's Management Committee's decision of **1848** to lend money to such Pupil Teachers as **Daniel** to pay for the books he will have needed to use. As Pupil-Teachers usually commenced their work around the age of **13** or **14** this will have been the most likely age that **Daniel** began his own teaching apprenticeship. As his days will have been taken up with teaching activities, so any studying will have taken place in the evening by candlelight. This wouldn't have done much for his eyes. If certified, my Great Grand Uncle may have expected to receive £**10.00** wages in his first year and £**20.00** in his second. The government could augment this modest salary by £**20**-£**30.00** per year depending upon his class of *'Teaching Certificate'* and the length of his College Course. By the **1860s** a trend had begun toward teaching in individual classes rather than in large open halls. This led to a desire for improved classroom accommodation with partitioned-off areas. All too often

Pupil-Teachers acted as unofficial Caretakers and Servants. In **1854** four Pupil-Teachers at the **British School** in **Skipton** complained in a written letter (to unknown government authority) that they had been forced to undertake such menial tasks as lighting fires and sweeping floors. (Their names were **M. Ackernley, Barnes, Calvert** and **T. Holmes.**) A somewhat embarrassed Management Committee firstly *'admonished'* these boys before relieving them of their weekly task of cleaning the stove! In the last year of their apprenticeship, they were relieved of all menial tasks to have the time to prepare for the **Queen's Scholarship,** which would give them entrance to College and a formal teaching qualification. In **1856** classrooms were made available from **6 a.m.** until **9 p.m.** for private study. Despite such concessions, a degree of ambiguity still surrounded the status of the Pupil-Teacher because, in practice, many were neither quite a pupil nor quite a teacher! The retention rate was poor, in that, following the completion of their training, many dropped out of education altogether and became Clerks instead. They had used their position as a stepping-stone to something better. In **Skipton,** the easy availability of alternative work ensured that the retention rate was poorer than in other localities. Out of the **38** Pupil Teachers identified by **Foster** (covering the period from **1846-1870**), a total of **14** failed to finish their apprenticeship – a failure rate of nearly **40%. Daniel** must have liked teaching enough to have completed it. Whether it was **Christian** idealism that motivated him cannot be proven, but it seems likely given his faith background. The early death of his parents would have prompted him to think about his own mortality.

Sometimes there were personnel misdemeanours too. In **1857, Ackernley** and **Holmes** caused a minor scandal by appearing in a theatrical exhibition held in the large room of the **Devonshire Hotel** on **Market Street.** An exasperated Management Committee warned them not to repeat this type of conduct and urged their parents to prevent any risk of it ever happening again. One monitor, **Frederick Manby,** was obliged to leave the **British School** at **Skipton** in **1849** because he had lacked the capacity to accomplish his tasks. The date of his forced departure confirms that he will have been personally known to **Daniel.** In addition, the Pupil Teacher **Thomas Peacock** was dismissed from the **British School in 1860** for repeated acts of theft!

Due to the factors mentioned above, the government concluded they were getting only a poor return for their initial expenditure. In **1861** direct payments to teachers ceased and a new *'Payment by Results'* scheme was introduced. Grants were paid to schools on condition they obtained certain results in the areas of attendance and attainment. Nevertheless, despite its problems the Pupil-Teacher

Scheme had been a courageous attempt to respond to the pitiful lack of public education in the early **Victorian** era. Through it, **Daniel** had provided further evidence of what would later become a family passion for education. His brother **Edmund** was also to place immense value upon education. Perhaps both boys had been ashamed of their parents' inability to have *'mastered their letters.'* Both alike appeared to have shared a passion to *'get on in the world'* although **Daniel's** teaching profession (and the locations in which he exercised it) suggested that he was the more idealistic of the two brothers. He had a real concern for the poorer, more vulnerable sections of **Victorian** Society. On a personal note, I would eagerly have eavesdropped on some of the conversations between these two brothers concerning the great social issues of their time.

Section 3: Hardship in Stalybridge

Concerning Daniel Smith and the Cotton Famine at Stalybridge

Daniel Smith was one of three Pupil-Teachers from **The British School** who was to make teaching his vocation. The other two were **John Grayston** (who became Second Master of the **British School** at **Halifax**) and **William Porrit** (who became Head of the **Smyth Academy** at **Wakefield**). The actual Teacher Training College (which **Daniel** at one time must have attended) stubbornly refused to be discovered. Perhaps that's where he'd met his future wife a school teacher named **Elizabeth Douglas Smith**. On **Thursday, 3rd November 1859,** they were married by the *'minister'* **Henry Kendall** at an *'Independent Chapel'* in **Darlington, County Durham.** (**Elizabeth's** father **George**, a *'Gardener,'* was one of the witnesses. A **Jane Smith,** was the other.) Their marriage certificate confirmed she had been living at **Belle Place Darlington** whilst **Daniel** was a *'Teacher at School'* at *'Stalybridge near Ashton Under Lyne.'* (Husband and wife teaching teams were not uncommon during this period.) By **1860** my Great Grand Uncle had become the Master of **The British School** at **13-15 Kay Street,** in the borough of **Stalybridge,** near **Manchester.** He had succeeded **Frederick Hutchins,** the previous Master. (**Tameside Local Studies & Archives Unit** at **Stalybridge** kindly provided these details.) This establishment had the capacity to teach **400** boys and girls.

In **1874, Daniel** and **Elizabeth** were living at **18 New Spring Bank Street** in the Township of **Duckinfield,** also part of the borough of **Stalybridge.** (An old photograph of unknown date showed terraced houses situated on a steeply sloping street. They possessed a small front yard and belonged to those who were *'aspiring upward'* in terms of social class.) By **1878, Daniel** had been replaced by a **Henry Tinker** who lived in **Stamford Street.** The name **Daniel Smith** did not appear in the Index for the **1881** Census. His place of abode for the **1861** and **1871** Census Returns could also not be traced. A visit to **Stalybridge** (made on **Tuesday, October 16ᵗʰ, 2001**) confirmed that the whole area around the old **British School** had been demolished in about **1966** to make way for a trim new housing estate. In many cases, even the old street names had gone, so pinpointing the school's former location was not an easy task. Despite some improvements **Stalybridge** still seemed to embody the saying, *'it's grim up North.'* A cloud of depression seemed to hang over this community. The economic life had been sucked out of it. **Stalybridge** was the least favourite place I visited while researching this history.

A final visit made to a rain-sodden **Stalybridge** on **Monday, July 1ˢᵗ, 2002** uncovered only a few extra items of information concerning **Daniel Smith** himself. With the help of a Trade Directory (provided by the **Local History Section** of **Stalybridge Library**) it was found that, in **1864,** his address was given as **Eastwood View,** located on **Chapel Walk** (shown on a local map of the area). In **1874** his address was **Hough** (pronounced *'Huff')* **Hill.** Reference to another map revealed that **New Spring Bank Street** lay at the bottom of this hill. However, a careful search of the relevant areas in the **1871** Census showed that he had not yet moved to this address. **Daniel Smith** remained untraceable. Thankfully, greater progress was made with the **1861** Census where **Daniel** (and one of his own Pupil Teachers) were traced despite the awful handwriting of the Census Enumerator!

1861 Census Return
(Chapel Walk, just outside the boundary of Stalybridge)
Daniel Smith aged **26** *"British School Teacher"*
Cullingworth, Yorkshire
Elizabeth Smith (wife) aged **24 Scotland**
John Smith (brother or brother in law) aged **18** *"Gentleman's Domestic"*
Mansfield, Yorkshire
1861 Census Return:
(35 Leach Street, Duckinfield, Stalybridge)
Elizabeth Wood aged **51** *"widow"* **[Cumbria]**
Joshua Wood (son) aged **21** *"Cotton Spinner"*
Doncaster, Yorkshire
Ralph Wood (son) aged **19** *"Pupil Teacher at the British School"*
Doncaster, Yorkshire

It appears that **Daniel** had recently married near the beginning of his teaching career at **Stalybridge**. However, despite repeated searches, no trace could be found of his marriage certificate which would suggest that he'd married in **Scotland**. His brother (or brother-in-law) **John** was keen to emphasise that he was a *"Gentleman's Domestic"* rather than a mere servant. Was this an early manifestation of the old **Smith** vice of snobbery? One can only wonder! By the time of the **1871** Census **Daniel** had moved away from this address.

What could be firmly established was that **Daniel** appears to have made a success of running a school – many of whose pupils will have come from working-class families, most employed in the surrounding nineteen cotton mills (According to **Haynes p.8** various mills employed a total of **10,400** people in **1861.**The total population of the Borough at that time was **24,921**). **The Craven Weekly Pioneer** dated **Saturday, March 25th, 1865** had the following news insert: *"A SUCCESSFUL TEACHER – Mr D. Smith, formerly a pupil teacher in the Skipton British School, now master of the Stalybridge British School, received this year from E. H. Brodie, Esq. Her Majesty's Inspector of Schools the following entry in his certificate: - "This is a very well managed School, excellently taught, and in good order." It was found that 97 and one-third per cent had passed in reading, writing and arithmetic. The number presented for examination was 275, all of whom passed in writing and dictation; 269 in reading, and 258 in arithmetic."* (Information kindly provided by **Skipton Library** on **Thursday, October 18th, 2001.**) These excellent results reflected well on the vigorous work of **Daniel Smith** and his fellow teachers.

Daniel must have had enormous dedication to have produced the above results. His achievement was all the more remarkable because his school was located in what, in many ways, was a socially blighted mill town. In **1863 Stalybridge** had suffered badly from disturbances caused by mill workers being thrown out of work because of the *'Cotton Famine'* that had arisen from the disruption in trade caused by the **American Civil War. Haynes pp.8-9** noted that only three mills were working full time and eight had stopped. The result was that over **50%** of operatives were unemployed and **40%** were working on *'short time.'* By **1871**, the number of mill workers was **7,785** out of a total Borough population of just over **21,000** – the reduced figures being mainly due to emigration. Like many local teachers, **Daniel** may have been obliged to teach literacy skills to resentful, unemployed workers who will have been forced to attend classes to gain entitlement to relief. In **1870,** he would have been legally bound to implement the changes brought about by the Education Act of that year, which made school attendance compulsory. Contemporary photographs showed that the local School Board was one of those awful bodies dominated by pompous looking ex-army officers, opinionated mill owners and feline looking clerics. **Daniel Smith** may well have not enjoyed an easy time in **Stalybridge.** Yet here was someone deserving much respect in his singular dedication as a teacher. In **1871,** he was still at **Stalybridge** (near **Manchester**). The Census Return for that year showed him to be living at **Lawton Head**, just outside the boundary of **Stalybridge,** near **Manchester**. His household consisted of: -

Daniel Smith aged **36** *"British School Teacher"*
Cullingworth, Yorkshire
Elizabeth D. Smith (wife) aged **34 Scotland**
Thomas D. Smith visitor aged **21** *"Architectural Draughtsman"* **Darlington, Durham**

By **1881 Daniel** had moved – not to an easier location but to a more difficult one – **Salford** near **Manchester.** This was an especially surprising development because having done private tuition there myself (in late **2001**) I could see that **Salford** (with its rows of barrack-like terraced houses and stray wandering dogs) would have been a challenge for any teacher. The fact that **Daniel** chose to work in such a location says volumes about his dedication as a teacher. It seems to imply that he viewed his teaching as a vocation rather than a *'free meal ticket'* to the middle classes. **Daniel** appears to have had a very robust social conscience – possibly deriving from strong **Christian** beliefs and his own hard background. No one at that time would normally have chosen to teach in **Salford** unless they'd been very dedicated or felt a very strong sense of calling.

Section 4: Telling Links

Concerning Daniel Smith and the Farey Family of Skipton

The **1881** Census Return is of special interest because it shows the personal associations **Daniel** enjoyed: -
1881 Census Return
(13 Thurlow Street, Salford near **Manchester)**
Daniel Smith aged **46** *"School Teacher, British"*
Cullingworth, Yorkshire
Elizabeth D. Smith (wife) aged **44 Scotland**
Jane Gibbs Farey aged **26** (Visitor) **Yorkshire, Skipton**
Sydney Farey Gunnel aged **6 Yorkshire, Wyke**
More than **Edmund, Daniel** appeared to have kept close to his roots. Especially significant was the close and prolonged contact with the **Farey** family. Clearly, **Daniel** had respected his old schoolmaster enough to have stayed in contact with his family over a sustained period. This lends weight to

the view that **Samuel Farey** had been an outstanding teacher. This close relationship with the **Fareys** of **Skipton** was confirmed by the Census Return for **1891** which shows the **Fareys** and **Smiths** under one roof, evidently for a larger social occasion – whatever that may have been at the time.

<u>**1891 Census Return**</u>

(28 Belleview Terrace, Skipton)

Henry Stanley Farey aged **68** *'Coloured Goods Manufacturer'*
Northamptonshire, Rattany
Annie McKay aged **70** *'wife'* **Scotland**
Jane Gibbs aged **36** *'Daughter'* **Yorkshire, Skipton**
Ada Annie aged **32** *'Daughter'* **Yorkshire, Skipton**
William R G Farey aged **30** *'Coloured Goods Manufacturer'*
Yorkshire, Skipton
Daniel Smith visitor, aged **56** *"A Schoolmaster"* **Yorkshire, Cullingworth**
Elizabeth Douglas Smith visitor, aged **54 Scotland**
Annie Northrop aged **28** visitor, *'Teacher in Mathematics and Grammar'*
Lanarkshire, Scotland
Henry Stanley Farey visitor, aged **31** *'Leather Traveller'*
Yorkshire, Skipton
Alice Dewey aged **23** *'General Servant and Domestic'*
Lincolnshire, Gainsborough

The final Census entry for **Daniel** in **1901** shows him as being retired and living in **Hyde, Stockport**. The precise entry is as follows.

<u>**1901 Census Return**</u>

(Low Bank – Parish of **Compstall St Paul, Hyde, Stockport)**
Daniel Smith aged **66** *'Retired Elementary Schoolmaster – living on own means'*
Elizabeth D. Smith aged **64**

One clear impression from the review of **Daniel's** life was that he and **Edmund** were as different as *'chalk and cheese.'* Where **Daniel** was the social conscience of the **Smith** family, working amongst the poor and deprived children of grim **Lancashire** mill towns; **Edmund** was the business brain, keen to get ahead and make some sort of name for himself. **Daniel's** reaction to early hardships was to empathise with the poor whereas **Edmund's** was to escape poverty through a mixture of demanding work and advantageous marriages. In retrospect, it's difficult to see how the brothers would have got on – yet in the end, **Edmund** provided the family line in which **Daniel's** story could be told. **Daniel's** childless state did not mean that he would be forgotten. Personally, I've been astonished at how my own geographical paths have often crossed with those of **Daniel Smith's** – especially when, with the help of a certain **Pakistani** agent and a former student of mine, I undertook private tuition in the **Manchester** area from **September 2001** until **April 2007**. I remember being driven around **Salford** and **Stockport** by him. my He persistently took a great interest in the developments of my Family History. I would often recount the latest discoveries as he chauffeured me back to **Leeds** along the **M62** Motorway late at night, classical music (via **Classic FM Radio**) quietly playing in the background. He once remarked that I had *"an undeserved gift for attracting chauffeurs who gave free lifts."* His view was that I was *"meant to write this history."* Sometimes, he would amuse me with his hilarious impersonations of the then **Archbishop of Canterbury, Rowan Williams.** They were hilarious.

I had begun discovering the details concerning my Great Grand Uncle's teaching career in **Stalybridge**, just as I was beginning some teaching in the **Manchester** area! (My first teaching engagement there had taken place on **Monday, September 3rd, 2001.**) I had first discovered the teaching connection whilst looking through a copy of **Foster's (1974)** Thesis at the **Family History Section** of the **Yorkshire Archaeological Society** (on **Tuesday** afternoon, **September 25th, 2001** with a **Reformed Jewish** girl). Unbeknown to myself, I had already (to some extent) been retracing **Daniel's** very own footsteps! It was inspiring to find that I was renewing an old family connection by doing something in which I felt thoroughly at home. Equally, it was personally exhilarating to work as a Private Tutor in the vicinity where **Daniel Smith** himself had once taught.

Daniel Smith died on **4th February 1906** at **Low Bank, Romily, Cheshire.** Given his occupation and relatively young age, it was dismaying to find that the cause of his death was given as *"Senile decay and heart failure."* His brother **John** (of **4 Roach Place, Rochdale**) was in attendance. This was a sad end to a useful and well-spent life. Overall, **Daniel** came across as the most sympathetic of the four **Smith** brothers. Surprisingly, his effects amounted to a sizeable **£4,919.14.8.** A **London** based Probate Document revealed that his younger brother **John Smith** (documented as a *'Commercial Traveller'*) and a certain **Robert Innes** were *'Administrators.'* An entry (made by his nephew **James** in a photograph album) revealed that **Daniel** had left **£4,000** to a *'School Company'* (worth **£472,374.99** in **2018**). **Daniel's** devotion to education had remained intact until the end, but how he'd gained such this amount of money working as a humble School Master? A clue was provided by a badly written entry in **James'** photograph album. It implied his uncle was an owner of five schools. This, therefore, could have been the source of his income. If so, he wouldn't be the last **Smith** to employ their business skills in the service of education.

CHAPTER 9: BURNLEY APPRENTICESHIP

Section 1: A Start in Retail

Concerning *'The Swann Inn'* Burnley

A review of **Ancestry.com** on **17th** May **2007** finally cleared away any mystery concerning **Edmund's** whereabouts during the **1851** Census. From the Census Record, it could be seen that he was living in a very crowded household with a strong female influence. Relevant findings are presented below.

<u>1851 Census Return:</u> **For 36 St James Street, Burnley, Lancashire**
Joseph Lee aged 31, Head *"Linen & Woollen Draper"* **Yorks, Grassington**
Elizabeth aged **30,** Wife **Long Preston**
John aged 8, Son **Skipton**
Mary aged **4,** Daughter **Skipton**
Ann Pulman aged **26,** Sister-in-Law *"Proprietor of Land & Houses"* **Long Preston**
Mary Pulman aged **17,** Sister-in-Law *"Proprietor of Land & Houses"* **Long Preston**
<u>Edmund Smith</u> aged **19,** Lodger *"Draper's Apprentice"* **Sutton**
William Thompson aged **17,** Lodger *"Draper's Apprentice"* **Calton**
William Stowell aged **16,** Lodger *"Draper's Apprentice"* **Lancs, Marsden**

Of note was **Joseph Lee's** connection with **Skipton,** which seemed to have lasted until the birth of his daughter **(Mary)** in **1847.** This would suggest that he already had prior knowledge of **Edmund** before moving to **Burnley** and evidently thought that he was prospective apprentice material. **Edmund** may have initially come to **Joseph's** attention through the latter's contacts with **Williams Smith's** family. **Edmund** would most likely have begun his apprenticeship around the age of fifteen or sixteen (around **1847-8**) and finished it when aged twenty-one in **1853.** We do know that by **1857 Edmund** was well out of the **Burnley** area.

My own two visits to **Burnley** (made on **Thursday 30/8/2007** and **Monday 8/9/2008** respectively) confirmed that it would have been a grim environment for a young man from **Skipton.** Whilst visiting, I was struck by **Burnley's** oppressive atmosphere which almost rivalled that of **Stalybridge.** One thing which **Edmund's** work as an apprentice would have impressed upon him was the vast gulf existing between the rich and poor. Forming within him would have been a determination to be on the *'rich'* side of the class barrier. A description of the type of environment **Edmund** would have worked in was provided by **Stratmann (2004) pp.6-7.**

"The stock of a traditional draper was then divided into two areas, each with its own buyer. There were heavy goods: rolls of plain and print fabrics, silks and velvets, wool and linen, table cloths, sheeting and towelling. There was little in the way of made-up garments; the exceptions were plain capes of merino wool, and at the luxury end of the market, colourful woven shawls. A woman who wanted new clothes either made her own or had them made for her. The fancy department stocked the smaller items which were carefully tucked away in boxes or drawers. There were all kinds of edgings and borders, the most expensive of which were fine lace, as well as sewing thread, handkerchiefs, neckerchiefs, gloves, crisp wide ribbons to trim bonnets, narrow ribbons to tie shoes."

The overall impression conveyed by this description was that of **Edmund** having to work in a very crowded environment – where impatient customers were capable of inopportunely awakening the apprentices by banging on the door in the early hours of the morning!

Evidence for the appalling level of deprivation existing in **Burnley** during **Edmund's** stay was provided by the news stories of *'The Burnley Advertiser'* (located with the kind help of the staff of **Burnley Library).** These stories have haunting echoes for today. It was not unknown for women to be attacked and robbed, or for beaten wives to be left for dead in the street with no one willing to intervene. Earlier in the nineteenth century, it had, like **Colne** and **Skipton,** suffered from an entire range of economic and political disturbances associated with the Industrial Revolution – not to mention the dreadful housing conditions and outbreaks of disease. However, by the time **Edmund** arrived conditions were beginning to improve with shopkeepers enjoying a more comfortable living, viewing themselves as deserving members of the more *'respectable'* classes. However, for the working classes *'prosperity'* simply meant having enough to get by on and the ability and means to avoid complete destitution. Real prosperity would have been confined to the old landowning – and now the newer professional-manufacturing classes. The latter's womenfolk will have wished to purchase those very same Fancy Goods on offer at **Joseph Lee's** shop. At a very formative stage in his life, **Edmund** will have learnt how best to ingratiate himself with such people. This would greatly benefit him.

Emphasising the grimness of **Burnley** was a painting drawn in **1854** by an unknown artist. Depicted was a view of the town as viewed from **Spring Hill.**

(It is featured on the cover of **Hall's Short History of Burnley,** published in **2002.**) It showed **34** factory chimneys, some billowing thick black smoke out into the air. (This was possibly an underestimation as the picture was cracked and faded in places.) There was a sharp pictorial division between the town and the countryside – the latter showing a field of six black sheep (possibly blackened due to grimy soot deposits from the chimneys). The field lay above a sloping road, itself flanked by grim terraced houses and larger industrial premises. A few people stood about, wearing the top hats and bonnets of the more prosperous classes. The **Burnley Saint Peter's Heritage** website accurately stated that in this drawing *"South Parade and Market Street (now Manchester Road) lead into the centre of the town. Numerous mill chimneys indicate how important the cotton industry had become, but sheep still graze near the town centre. On the left can be seen the railway viaduct opened in 1848 when the railway reached Burnley. On the right are the railway goods yard and the roof of Thorneybank Station."*

This illustration underlined the fact that, from the late **1840's,** there was money to be made in **Burnley.** It really was a case of *'where there's muck there's brass.'* As **Hall p. 19** remarked, *"After about 1845 the cotton trade expanded. This led to a rise in wages and a general improvement in workers' conditions. Burnley was entering its period of greatest prosperity."*

However, my <u>second</u> visit made to **Burnley** (on **Monday, 8th September 2008**) raised questions about this very same **1850** picture. By following the curves of the road, it was possible to find the artist's original vantage point. It simply wasn't possible for the artist to have seen <u>all</u> the features which he eventually portrayed in his pictures. For example, the **Manchester Road** veered off at too steep an angle to be seen. In addition, the artist appears to have got the scale wrong. The rail viaduct appears far larger than it was. The one thing he did get right was the direction followed by the **Manchester Road.** Overall, the picture represented more of an impressionistic cartoon rather than an accurate representation of a known location. The lesson learnt from this was the need to make allowances for artistic license in the depiction of places. In terms of accuracy, the previously described picture of **Skipton** seemed far better, its features fitting those depicted.

An **1848** map confirmed that **St James Street** was the *'commercial heart'* of **Burnley.** It ran in a slight bow-shaped curve, either side of the **Market Square.** Adjoining the square (at **44 Saint James Street**) was a Public House which had been converted from earlier farm premises. It still stood as licensed premises during my <u>first</u> visit – and was known as the **Swan Inn.** It had gone under this same name throughout **Edmund's** stay. However, the original shop (on **36 St James Street**) had long since gone, being replaced by an educational stationer. I couldn't help but be struck by the irony that, yet another site associated with **Edmund** was being used for educational purposes. A picture of **Burnley Town Centre** in **1854** confirmed that **Joseph Lee** had chosen a major prime-site location for his business – only two or three doors away from the town square. The picture showed a few respectable middle-class people milling about its central gaslight with one or two horses leading light two-wheeled carriages. One lady in a crinoline was heading toward **36 St James Street** whilst taking a sideways glance at *'The Swan Inn.'* She was the type of lady with whom **Edmund** would have had to do business. Such customers could be very demanding. Their very presence may have created the impression in **Edmund's** own mind that one way to climb the social ladder would be to marry just such a lady – preferably one with money! Reinforcing this impression will have been the presence of the **Pulman** sisters. It's more than likely that, living with an ambitious apprentice and two single women of private means in a very limited space may well have created some serious, emotional entanglements. The representation of the market square in the picture was undoubtedly idealised (for instance, no horse droppings were shown) but it did show the type of clientele who may have called into the Draper's shop in **St James' Street.** A round blue metal plaque on *'The Swan Inn'* revealed the following details:

"BURNLEY HERITAGE SITE

THE SWAN INN

Originally a farmhouse, this building was converted into an Inn towards the end of the eighteenth century. Here, the town committee (a forerunner of the council) met during the years **1816-1844.** *Below the Inn can be seen part of the lock-up jail opened by the town committee in* **1819,** *Sponsored by* **Daniel Thwaites Brewery"**

A peep through the window of this establishment during my <u>second</u> visit on **Monday, 8/9/2018** confirmed that the meeting room had remained largely unchanged from the nineteenth century. The old coal fireplace was still in place as was the chestnut coloured oak furniture. An early nineteenth century *'feel about the place'* had been preserved. A glance at the jail in the rear suggested that it could hold several people. It seemed likely that many a client of **Burnley's** drinking establishments would have endured a sobering and uncomfortable night on its cold stone floors.

Section 2: It's Bad in Burnley

Concerning the grim conditions in nineteenth-century Burnley

In **Burnley, Edmund** would have quickly become all too aware of the dire consequences of *'not getting on.'* Outside the commercial heart of **Burnley,** there was complete squalor. A ballad (written in **1850**) described the **Wapping** slum district of **Burnley, (Townend 1999, p.58): -**

"The refuge of the desolate
The stronghold of the bad
And home to many great events
The child without a dad"

Census Returns for **1851** revealed a population of **20,828** as compared to **14,228** in **1841** and **10,026** in **1831**. In the space of two economically unstable decades, the population had almost doubled, with migrants coming from as far afield as **Cornwall** and **Ireland.** During **Edmund's** time, there were about **9,000** handloom weavers belonging to the various firms engaged in spinning. Such a population would have mainly been young, especially amongst the working classes. Relatively few old people would have been seen. During warm summer evenings or on **Sundays** the cobbled streets will have been crowded with ragged and barefooted young children. In such localities, life was often lived out on the streets. Such demographic pressures led to a re-organization of the town's local governance under a *'Local Government'* Act of **1846.** It was passed *"for the better paving, lighting, cleansing, regulating and improving the town and for better supplying the inhabitants with gas and water,"* (quoted in **Hall 1977, p.23**). Any regulations were to be implemented by a body of sixty commissioners, elected by the ratepayers. However, in **1853** the high rate of one shilling per pound (paid to implement this Act) came under sharp criticism from ratepayers. In **1854** a further *'Improvement Act'* allowed the Commission to take over the local Gas Company. During the same year land for a **Burnley** public cemetery was purchased and opened in **1856**.

Although well-meaning such measures did little to alleviate the grave social problems afflicting **Burnley.** In **1841**, two youths were sentenced to death after compelling an old and crippled man to climb the steps of his cellar only to have thrown him back with such violence that he'd died. **Bennett (1948 Part III p.251)** revealed that during the trial, one of them had said: *"It was all a game."* Such a headline could have been seen in today's newspapers. In **1848** and **1852 Edmund** may well have seen two men confined to the stocks for disorderly behaviour, **(Bennett p.253).** If so, this will have made him even more determined to keep to the *'straight and narrow.'* The memories of youth are vivid and such incidents would have left an abiding impression. It's hard not to conclude that he chose to lead a life of prim respectability in response to the degradation he'd seen in **Burnley.** To **Edmund's** way of thinking, being working class meant poverty, drunkenness and misery whilst being middle class meant prosperity, sobriety and comfort. Reinforced would have been any hard lessons he'd learned from **Skipton.** It seems that **Joseph Lee's** shop had been a something of a refuge for besieged respectability.

Contributing to the problem of lawlessness was the *'binge drinking'* culture which pervaded the town – especially amongst the **Irish** population. **Bennett (Part III p.256)** mentioned that **26** hotels, **43** taverns, **42** beer houses and **75** Off-Licenses were recorded in the **1851** Census. (This was not to mention the many illegal distilleries which were also known to exist.) Innocuous names like, *'the Spotted Dog,' 'The Bird in Hand,' 'The Hand and Shuttle' 'The Druid's Arms'* and *'The Rose and Shamrock'* (for the **Irish**) often concealed an ugly reality of angry brawls, battered wives, starving children and cockfighting. At *'The Poets' Corner'* in **Curzon Street,** lay a large pit in which betting onlookers could see a dog kill **100** rats in eight and a quarter minutes. A less brutal attraction was that provided by *'The Half Moon'* which employed Music Hall Artists to attract customers, **(Bennett 1985, Part IV p.15).**

Alcohol was undoubtedly responsible for many acts of calculated and mindless brutality. A wooden seat (near to the **Manchester Road** railway station) had to be removed because it became a centre for unruly conduct. Gangs of ten to twelve drunkards would attack passers-by (including women) with knives and poles. Garrotting was another common offence and even the Police had to patrol in pairs. Gangs of up to **200** hooligans would hinder them from making an arrest. People were not even free from being burgled and assaulted in their own homes. Hooliganism was such a problem that in certain places local landlords threatened to close the roads. *"Evidence of the low standard of morality is seen in a record of **1861** which shows that in that year in **Burnley** there were **51** husbands and **147** wives then living who had been married at the age of **15** or under,"* **(Bennett IV p.17).** This data provided sober evidence of a horrendous level of sexual abuse.

Annually, **500** cases of drunkenness would be brought before the magistrates and that was <u>after</u> the police had been instructed to only make arrests if the act of drunkenness was associated with another crime, *i.e.* leaving a cart and horse to wander unsupervised about the street. Indeed, *"ordinary drunkenness was generally regarded as a regular part of the life of some sections of the community,"* **(Bennett**

Part IV p.16). In reaction to such excesses the *'Total Abstinence Society'* was founded in **1846** – thereby showing that **The Temperance Movement** was a growing influence. Providing further assistance were the flourishing Sunday Schools and the influence of powerful denominations like the **United Methodist Free Church.**

As an apprentice, my Great Grandfather's drinking habits would have been controlled by his Master who would <u>not</u> have wanted those under him to be a source of embarrassment. There were often harsh penalty clauses included in any apprentice agreement to prevent the *'demon drink'* from being a problem. The balance of probability would suggest that my Great Grandfather had been a highly self-disciplined young man by the standards of his day. Yet **Edmund** will have needed to have been very quick-witted and *'streetwise'* to have survived unhurt in such an environment. Admittedly, the very long hours he worked in the shop would have kept him away from the worst spots for much of the time. However, when out in the streets, he will have needed to keep his wits about him, watching out for any trouble or imminent danger. To escape such pressures, he may well have taken solitary strolls along the canal towpath – this was overshadowed by a huge multi-floored warehouse looming above it. During the summer months, children were known to bathe in the canal's filthy water.

Yet there were worse things than the high crime rate. There was a brief cholera epidemic in **1852,** mainly confined to the impoverished **Irish** Community of the **Finsleygate** slum. For the first half of that year, **546** deaths were recorded – of which **96** were due to infectious disease; **30** to Smallpox, **23** to Typhus, **23** to Measles and **20** to Scarlett Fever. The mortality rate was **30** per **1,000.**

In **August 1852,** the weavers held a meeting in **Burnley Market Square** to campaign for a **10%** increase in their wages. Initially, the master's appeared to agree but on **October 28th** they declared a *'lockout'* and **56** mills closed in **Burnley** and the surrounding locality. In **Burnley** alone, **12,000** operatives were left unemployed with **509,000** spindles and **17,000** looms lying idle. A mass meeting held the next day resulted in deploring disorders in **Wigan.** At another marketplace meeting (held on **2nd November 1852**) a speaker from **Stockport** urged the workers to *"stand firm."* **Edmund** may well have heard this speech because it was made just outside the shop door. There was quite literally *'trouble on his own doorstep!'* He would have heard the noisy clamour and seen the hordes of ragged, desperate men gathered there. Memories of the **Chartist** riot ten years earlier in **Skipton** may well have come flooding back into his mind. Any determination on his part to avoid poverty and eventually <u>not</u> work for a master will have been strongly reinforced. When the strike began to cause hardship, the clergy opened **Sandygate School** to teach writing, reading, history and geography to the unemployed. A relief committee managed to raise just over £112, using it to distribute food to about **2,000** families.

On **19th December 1852,** the mill owners met in the **Bull Inn** next to the Drapery Shop. The spinners gained a **10%** wage increase whilst the weavers gained nothing and were put on a four-day week. This *'divide and conquer'* strategy appears to have worked because the strike ended. In **May 1854,** the weavers formed an **Emigration Society** to aid movement abroad. In **July** of that year, the **Chartist Movement** had its final upsurge at nearby **Deeplay.** Thousands attended a meeting where there was a plea for some form of land distribution and a protest about wage reduction. However, despite this high attendance nothing was accomplished. Internal divisions, effective government action and improved economic conditions meant that the spirit had gone out of Chartism. It now seemed to barely exercise any influence at all.

During my very productive visits to **Burnley,** I expected to find a great deal of detail about the milieu wherein **Edmund** had lived-out his formative years. I wasn't unduly surprised to discover that **Burnley** offered a landscape dotted with Chapels – including the nearby Congregational Chapel in **Bethsaida Street.** As in **Skipton, Cullingworth** and **Sutton,** the Churches did invaluable work in providing Sunday Schools, household visits and charitable relief. As **Bennett III p.322** justly observed, *"Religious bodies were the most powerful force in the struggle against evil and did more than anything else to raise the moral tone of the people. The enthusiasm of members of Churches and Chapels merits the highest praise and admiration and a large number of places of worship is a testimony to their keenness. From the minute books of wardens, stewards, and secretaries one may recite the great amount of self-sacrifice that was entailed in regularly praying at open-air meetings and in cottages and in voluntary work of sick visiting and in the self-imposed task of Sunday School Teaching... pulpit oratory inspired with religious fervour and social agitation and led* **Burnley** *people to accept a more compassionate view of life."* Once again it was a case of religious faith acting as a means of social improvement. It gave hope to the lives of the working people.

However, I was a little more surprised at the speed at which the **Victorian** Information and Communication revolution was affecting **Burnley.** In **1847** the **East Lancashire Railway Company** extended the **Colne** to **Burnley** line, opening **Bank Top Station** in **September 1848.** The very next year, the line was extended to **Manchester** and in **1850 Bank Top Station** took **83,000** bookings (rising to **226,000** in **1866).** By the end of **1850 Thorneybank Station** had also been opened. A sign that **Burnley** was making a final break with its pre-industrial past came when **Richard Rothwell** (the last of the **Burnley** stagecoach drivers) closed his business and sold all his coaches and wagons, along with most of his horses. It seems that **Edmund** would have arrived in **Burnley** by coach or cart only to leave it by train. One other sign of greater communication was the removal of the Post Office from **Fleet Street** to larger premises in **Saint James's Row**. In 1853 the first telegraph link was established in the new Post Office – connecting it to **Bank Top Station**. The initial charge was **1s** for **20** words to **Manchester** and **5s** for **20** words to **London**. (However, the price was soon reduced to **2s 6d**). The effect of this *'Victorian Internet'* was to enable Businesses to know what was happening in their respective markets. **Burnley** was an early adopter of this new form of communication as the **Telegraph** had only been invented in **1843**. Clearly, my great-grandfather would have been aware of changes happening at a dizzying pace and will have needed to adapt quickly to survive economically. One unexpected result of my visits to **Burnley** was the discovery of just how much **Edmund** had benefitted from these preliminary stages of **Globalisation**. When he arrived in the community it was still in the age of the stagecoach but when he left, it was in the age of steam.

Perhaps the most surprising feature of my visit was the amount of detail available about **Edmund's** working environment. It was located on a street in which commercial respectability co-existed with private and industrial squalor. **The Old Bull Inn** next door will have been very rowdy at night and only sheer exhaustion will have guaranteed a good night's sleep. **Bennett, Part IV p.5** reveals that, in **1850, St James Street** *"was then a narrow and irregular street, lined with buildings of every type including mills, warehouses, stables, slaughterhouses, pig sties, shops, wooden huts and dwelling homes. At six points buildings projected so far into the street that carts couldn't pass either side of one another."*

Section 3: Hard Graft

Concerning the life of a Victorian Draper's Apprentice

Life as a Draper's Apprentice was very hard, as seen in the following quote from **Stratmann p.7**. *"The life of a draper's apprentice was one of unremitting effort. As the lowliest member of staff* [he] *would have risen at about 7 a.m., and helped take up the shutters, then cleaned and polished the exterior of the shop. He might also have had to do heavy portering work, carrying and arranging huge rolls of fabric, as well as attending to the wants of customers. The hours were long, and even if the shop were shut at 10 p.m. there was* *tidying and cleaning to do afterwards which would have kept him busy beyond midnight. Whilst the young men's assistants would have had a room of their own to sleep in, apprentices were often accommodated on truckle beds beneath the counter."*

In **Burnley,** an improvement in working hours took place only in **1854** – too late for **Edmund** to have benefited from it. This point was recorded on **p1** of **The Burnley Advertiser, 1ˢᵗ October 1854.**

"EARLY CLOSING – The Drapers have issued an announcement stating that their respective places of business will be closed at 7.00 p.m on the evenings of Tuesday, Wednesday, Thursday, and Friday. We always hail announcements of this description with pleasure and we trust that the Grocers and Tea-dealers will be next to take up the movement. Nothing can be said in favour of late shopping, either of the tradesman or the customer, and we trust that immediate steps will be taken to secure the closing of all our shops at a reasonable hour. The assistants and apprentices thus relieved from late attendance at the counter will do well to become members of the local institutions devoted to the improvement of the mind. They will show themselves worthy of the boon and prove to their employers that they do not seek additional time for the purposes of misspending it."

Even the more benevolent owners expected *'hard graft'* from their apprentices. However, the environment could be made all the grimmer if the owner was a petty tyrant. This was emphasised by a **Victorian** observer (writing in the **1870s** – when conditions had improved since **Edmund's** days in **Burnley**). The source was **Hawley (1878, pp.15-16)** quoted in **Stratmann pp.7-8.** A draper's shop could endure *"perpetual martial law. Everyone, from the highest rank to the lowest, had to obey blindly the commands which may be given. Soiled goods, inferior goods, all must be sold in the way which is prescribed. No scruples of conscience are allowed, the merest observation receives a summary dismissal. One is painfully impressed by the frightened looks which announce the sudden appearance of the Caesar of the establishment. No regiment in parade receives a stern colonel with greater fear, whilst the eyes of the scared servants follow nervously the steps of their master. This all-important personage, well impressed with his own dignity, paces majestically up and down (no doubt as he thinks), to the intense admiration of his feminine visitors. If for business reasons you have to inquire about the character of that man, do not seek any enlightenment from any of the suffering beings who live in these places; their mouths are sealed...Though companions in misery, the inmates do not even trust one another...But... let the servant leave the master; it is then you will receive the information you want, for who knows a master better than his servant?"* **(Hawley C. (1878) The Drapery Trade Before the Public, John Haywood, Manchester).** Adding to any discomfort was the fact that (in early **1852) Joseph Lee's** premises were undergoing substantial refurbishment. Detailed evidence for this was provided in the following press release, taken from **Issue 1, p.2** of *'The Burnley Advertiser'* in **March 1852.**

BRITANNIA HOUSE.

GENERAL DRAPERY ESTABLISHMENT.

JOSEPH LEE,

Begs to inform the public that extensive alterations to the old-established premises

36, ST JAMES' STREET, BURNLEY,

(Next door to the Bull Hotel) being completed, the Shop is now re-opened for Business   J. L. begs to state that in addition to his previous stock, he has now on Sale the remainder of the

VALUABLE STOCK-IN-TRADE,

Purchased from the Assignees of Mr John Watson, of Skipton, Bankrupt, amounting at Stock Book Price to £1772 11s 3d. Consisting of Rich, Novel, and costly Silks, Shawls, Merrinoes, Cobourgs, Alpacas, barrages and Delaines, Pure, Genuine and Warranted Damasks, Table Linens and Sheetings, Hosiery, Gloves, British and Foreign Lace, Bonnets, Ribbons, and a General plain and Fancy Stock. The above being well selected and bought at a large discount, will be offered at prices which must command an immediate Sale. The remainder of the Winter Stock at extremely low prices. J. L. wishes to call particular attention to his West of England and Yorkshire broad and narrow Cloths, Fancy Trouserings, Doeskins, Vestings, & Co. Observe the address 36, St James St., Burnley.

To obtain such detailed knowledge of the conditions in **Edmund's** workplace was a most astonishing find. **Joseph Lee** certainly knew how to advertise and to profit from the misfortune of others. He knew exactly what sort of business he was in. These were formidable business skills to pass onto my Great Grandfather. Such skills were needed because a review of **Slaters 1848 Journal** revealed the presence of **15** *'Linen and Woollen Drapers'* **10** of whom were on **St James' Street** – but none at no. **36.** (In passing it's worth mentioning that Trade Journals usually referred to the situation described two or three years previously). In **1854 Joseph Lee** appears on **p.434** of the *'History,*

Topography and Directory of Mid-Lancashire,' still under the heading of *'Linen and Woollen Drapers.'* The entry read *'Lee Joseph 36 James Street.'* He was one of **23** entries with other drapers being at **20, 39, 43, 47, 73** and **91 Saint James Street**. There does appear to have been a real Darwinian struggle to survive in what was an extremely competitive market. Only the exceptionally entrepreneurial could prosper. An **1865** entry (from the same source) confirms that a Drapery Business had survived at **no. 36** – but it was run by a **Francis Horsman. Joseph Lee** had vanished from the scene.

By that period **(1865) Edmund** had long-since gone. Tellingly, when next heard of, he's many miles away – in **Pannal** near **Harrogate.** The impression conveyed by such a move was that he seemed relieved to have left **Burnley** behind him. Also, when he went into the Drapery business on his own account it was as a *'traveller'* and <u>not</u> as a *'shopkeeper.'* Perhaps he'd come to view the premises at **36 St James Street** as something of a prison. Certainly, family tradition pays ample testimony to **Edmund** having possessed a domineering, harsh streak (which can develop in a person brought-up in conditions of great hardship). Whatever else his apprenticeship had taught him it was that poverty was a degrading condition which had to be avoided through a mixture of hard graft, commercial opportunism and marriage to a young lady with her own capital. **Edmund's** first attempt to gain capital through an advantageous marriage may have failed in **Burnley,** (assuming such an attempt had been made in the first place). A further attempt would succeed, but with lasting consequences that would still be a talking point amongst the **Smiths** up to five generations later. His hankering for respectability was of a very proactive kind. and was perhaps the central motivating force in his life. He really wanted to *'be someone'* and perhaps to be remembered long after his demise. If that really was the case, then he certainly succeeded.

CHAPTER 10: RURAL INFLUENCES

Section 1: The Village

Concerning the village of Burton Pidsea in East Yorkshire

Burton Pidsea lies twenty miles **South West** of **Bridlington** and ten miles **North East** of **Hull.** A first visit there (made with my youngest son – then aged eleven years) on the afternoon of **Thursday, April 20th, 2000** confirmed that the area was still largely agricultural in nature. Successive generations of **Smiths** were known to have visited **Bridlington** for their summer holidays so there just might have been some longstanding connection with the region – even though **Bridlington** itself was **20** miles away to the **Northeast. Helen Hastings** (**Edmund's** first wife) and **Rosamund Stamford** (his second wife and **Helen's** niece) both lived at **Burton Pidsea.** Family tradition has it that **Helen's** family had been *'well off'* enough to have provided a generous dowry on her marriage to **Edmund.** Making use of this money will have enabled **Edmund** to enter the *'respectable'* middle classes – something of huge importance to him. For his part, he would have acted as the capable businessman and protector to a woman threatened with being alone in a society where women had precious few rights. Evidence (seen later) implies that the marriage took place largely for economic rather than romantic reasons. **Edmund** may have already demonstrated his own business acumen to **Helen's** family – thereby showing he was a man who would put her money to effective use. His skills, both in business and in the use of money, were two qualities that my Great Grandfather regularly displayed. He most certainly was not an improvident rake – indeed by any reckoning he was incredibly self-disciplined.

Further information (via the *'Internet'*) provided more details about **Burton Pidsea.** These are arranged in chronological order.
1823: The most common occupation is farming – one of twelve of the farmers in the area being a certain **Richard Hastings.** Other trades are those of a typical village – as seen in the occupation of a **John Stamford** who is one of two wheelwrights in the area.
1847: The wheelwright **John Stamford** owns land in **Burton Pidsea** and in the nearby locality of **Elsternwick.** An **1857** Trade Journal reveals that **'*The Wesleyans'*** erect a chapel whilst the **Primitive Methodists** still meet in a cottage.

1851: The **Census** recognizes this community as consisting of **1,980** acres. Its chief speciality lies in arable farming where such crops as wheat and barley are produced in abundance.

1892: With a slightly declining population **Burton Pidsea** (fluctuating around the **350** mark) resides in an area of **2,302** acres and is situated on fertile but flood-prone clay soil. However: -

- The **Hastings** family have either *'died away'* or married into other families.
- The **Stamford's** are a noticeable presence with **Edward Stamford** having risen to become a yeoman farmer. (The **Stamford** Family later become rather important landowners in the region, showing that a degree of upward social mobility is possible.)
- Near the heart of the village lies **St Peter and St Paul's Church**, with its imposing large tower.

It was apparent that the **Hasting** and **Stamford** families were closely through marital connections. Marriage would also be the median whereby they would enjoy a close relationship with my Great Grandfather, **Edmund.**

Reinforcing the above information was data taken from various Census Returns for **Burton Pidsea.** In contrast to **Sutton,** this area (as already stated) was primarily agricultural with only a sprinkling of village trades. A certain **Thomas Hastings** (aged **52**) was there for the **1841 Census**, along with his wife **Elizabeth** (aged **51**) and another lady – possibly a sister-in-law **Charlotte Pinter** (aged **49**). He was on record as being of *'independent'* means. This fact strongly implied that there was some money in the family. He was a next-door neighbour to **James Hastings** who was presumably his brother. Further details from the Census Returns are recorded below: -

1841 Census Return.
(Burton Pidsea had 82 inhabited and 3 uninhabited houses)
James Hastings aged **55** *"farmer"* **Burton Pidsea**
Mary Anne aged **19** – (later married to **John Stamford.** She was to be the mother of **Rosamond, Edmund's** second wife).
Helen aged **16**
(Later to be **Edmund's** first wife)
William [Trains] Aged **20** *"servant."*

1851 Census Return
(Burton Pidsea – including Roos Gate; the village had 87 inhabited and 9 uninhabited houses)
James Hastings aged **68** *"farmer – owning 66 acres, employing one man."*
Ann Hastings aged **59**
Robert Willington aged **22** *"agricultural labourer"*
Hannah Richardson aged **14** *"House servant"*

1861 Census Return
(Burton Pidsea – including Roos Gate; the village had 84 inhabited and 7 uninhabited houses)
James Hastings aged **78** *"retired farmer"*
Rosamond A. Stamford aged **17** grand-daughter
(Later to be **Edmund's** second wife)
Sarah Collinson aged **17** *"Servant,"* born in **Hull**

One strange feature of the **1851** Census was the absence of any children in the **Hastings** household. **Mary Anne** was by then married to **John Stamford**, whilst **Thomas** (who, in the normal course of events would have been expected to have taken over the running of the farm) was living with his younger two sisters **Helen** and **Elizabeth in Hull.** He was running a Drapery business. Like **Edmund, Thomas Hastings** had perhaps wanted to break away from his home background. The fact that two of his sisters had joined him was possibly indicative of a major family rift. At the very least it betrayed a hankering for an alternative way of life. The farm would have been commercially viable, so poverty did not appear to have been a major factor in provoking their move to **Hull.** The mass exodus of all his children from an apparently prosperous farm made me wonder whether he'd been abusive. They certainly, didn't want to stay around him.

The above-cited Census Returns also make it clear that the **Hastings** family tended to be very long-lived. A certain **Elizabeth Hastings,** aged a phenomenal **95**, was recorded in the **1841 Census.** Her connection to other members of the **Hastings** family is not known – although she lived with a certain **Richard Hastings** (a shoemaker aged **55**) and a **Hannah Hastings** who was aged **40.** By **1851, Richard** and **Hannah Hastings** were still alive and (despite being aged **69**) **Richard** had gone in a new and enterprising direction regarding his work. The Census for that year provided the following details about this family: -

Richard aged **69** – cordwainer, master of two men
Hannah aged **49**
George Brown aged **6** – scholar
George [England] Aged **28** – cordwainer and journeyman
Thomas Clarke aged **17** – apprentice cordwainer
Robert Brown aged **14** – apprentice cordwainer
William [Dring] Aged **21** – lodger

Edmund was to bestow the *'Hastings'* names on some of his own children, *e.g. 'James' 'Ann'* and *'Hastings.'* This powerfully suggested a somewhat close connection; **Edmund** may have felt a sense of gratitude to the **Hastings** family for having given him a *'leg up'* in the world. He also subsequently named his family home *"Hastings Place."* Sadly, his gratitude to **Helen,** his first wife, appeared to have been rather less noticeable. Worthy of note was how my Great Grandfather had successfully ingratiated himself into a normally closed rural-based family. The latter, in times past, will normally have married from within their own community. Once again, **Edmund** was defying a conventional social norm – even if he had to *'make do'* with **Helen** who was some years his senior. It's difficult to imagine either **Helen** or **Rosamond's** respective fathers giving their approval unless **Edmund** had something of an exceptional quality about him. To his future-in-laws, he must have appeared as a man with rising prospects. This reinforces the view that my Great Grandfather was not left in a poverty-stricken situation following the death of his parents. Someone somewhere seems to have given him a basic education and an opportunity to begin life as a Commercial Traveller. This is not to deny that his early life was not without its psychologically damaging hardships – but they do not seem to have been on such a scale as to have curtailed his prospects for social advancement. Two samples of his neat copperplate handwriting confirm that he had received what was, by the standards of the day, a reasonably good education, possibly at **Skipton's British School.** His work in business will have demanded a basic competence in the three *'Rs'* of *'reading, writing and arithmetic.'* The obsessive desire to give his own children a good education supports the view that, during his boyhood, **Edmund** had met an exceptionally inspiring teacher, although whether this was **Samuel Farey** cannot be proven. The value of education had meant a great deal to him. He may well have directly witnessed the problems that illiteracy had caused his parents in a period when the skills of reading and writing were becoming ever more necessary for daily living.

In contrast to **Sutton, Burton Pidsea** appears to have suffered from an outflow of population, with many of the younger people migrating to **Hull.**

Amongst those who moved out were the local weavers – unable to compete with the mass-produced cloth then beginning to flow into the village. Evidence for this emerged in the high proportion of empty houses. There also existed a relatively high percentage of elderly people. Presented here were two very different socio-economic effects of the Industrial Revolution. In **Sutton's** case, Industrialisation had galvanised the life of the community, reinforcing such traditional structures as the **Baptist** Church – which only entered its heyday some one hundred and fifty years after its foundation. Also revitalised were the handloom weavers who were free to specialise in highly profitable luxury cloth. With **Burton Pidsea** the effect was very different. Although it survived, traditional village life was weakened, with the more vigorous younger members moving out to nearby **Hull.** Hence the Industrial Revolution had the effect of either strengthening or weakening the life of these local communities. (A footnote in **Jay p.182** suggested that the term *'Industrial Revolution'* was first used in **1837** by a French Revolutionary called **Louis-Auguste Blanqui** but was popularised by the economic historian **Arnold Toynbee (1852-1883)** in a series of lectures delivered at **Oxford University** in 1880-81.

Section 2: Field Enclosures and Disorderly Inns

Concerning a disorderly Inn

Inhabited from the very earliest of times, the modern history of **Burton Pidsea** really began with **The Enclosure Bill** of 1762. An abbreviated account will now be given, taken from the local historian **G. T. Asquith (1953)**:

*"It is quite likely that many people in **Burton Pidsea** knew little or nothing of this plan to fence – in the big fields where they and their forefathers had grazed cattle for centuries. The landowners who went to parliament had no need to tell anybody.*

In our village, some of the richer landowners did not agree and there was quite a storm, but in the end, the fields were enclosed.

After the enclosure of the lands, some of the poorer people were very badly off. They had nowhere to graze their cows, nowhere to keep their pigs and geese; they lost the wood they could gather from the North field, they had no butter, eggs or meat to sell to help eke out their small earnings. Many of these poorer people left the village to work in the towns, and others became day workers on the new big farms.

These big farms must have prospered because, in the early years of the nineteenth century, many of the larger houses in **Burton Pidsea** *were completely re-built and enlarged. One landowner boasted that he could ride from* **Burton Pidsea** *to the sea on his own land."* **(Asquith p.13)**

Among the beneficiaries of the *'Enclosure Movement'* were the **Stamford** and **Hastings** families. One member of the **Stamford** family started up a local foundry whilst his son invented the **Stamford Plough,** specially designed to dig deep into the heavy clay soil surrounding the village. **Asquith's** account also emphasised the remoteness of this community.

"Travelling from **Burton Pidsea** *was not very easy. Until the new road to* **Daisy Hill** *was made, the road to* **Hull** *was a very winding affair. It left* **Burton** *by* **Greens Lane,** *then wound round by* **Burstwick** *to* **Hedon,** *from* **Hedon** *the road turned north to* **Preston** *and* **Bilton,** *entering* **Hull** *by* **Holderness Road,** *which went through open country almost up to* **North Bridge.** *In* **1820,** *it took* **David Tavender** *or* **Peter Drew,** *the village carriers, five hours to reach* **Hull** *with their horse-drawn wagons."*

From **Hull,** *there were stagecoaches to all parts of the country, but we should consider them very slow, uncomfortable and dangerous. In* **1840** *there was a significant improvement for on* **July 2nd** *a railway was opened from* **Hull** *to* **Selby.** *Fourteen years later a railway came nearer to* **Burton Pidsea** *for a line was opened from a station in* **Hedon Road** *to* **Withernsea.** *People were quite pleased to walk three and a half miles to the nearest station. Later a railway was planned to run from* **Hedon,** *near to* **Burton Pidsea** *and* **Humbleton** *to* **Aldbrough,** *but this line was never completed."* **(Asquith P.14)**

Details of relevant **Stamford** family connections can be found in the following outline – the information having been kindly provided by **Peter Stamford** of **Canada** and **Barbara Stamford-Plows**: -

1. Robert Stamford (Dates unknown) on an unknown date married his second wife, **Elizabeth Hall**

2. John Stamford (1733-1818) who, on **16/5/1760** married **Hannah Beck (1735-1821)**

3. John Stamford (1761-1840) A Carpenter and Licensee of *"The Nancy"* Public House who, on **1/12/1788** married **Ann Curtis (1765-1818)**

4. William Stamford (1789-1850) A Carpenter who, on **6/4/1814,** married **Elizabeth Benton**

5. John Hesslewood Stamford (1821-1878) A Carpenter and Wheelwright who, on **12/10/1842** married **Mary Ann Hastings (1821-1875)** the daughter of farmer **James (1784-c.1875)** and **Ann Hastings** and elder sister of **Helen**

Hastings (1824-1866) – first wife of my Great Grandfather **Edmund Smith (1832-1915)**. **Helen** married **Edmund** in **Hull** on **10/12/1857**
6. **Rosamond Stamford (1843-1891) Edmund's** second wife and my Great Grandmother. She married **Edmund** in **Leeds** on **17/12/1867**

One way to escape any feeling of isolation in a remote community like **Burton Pidsea** was through drink. Transcribed below is a letter (dated **16th September 1808**) complaining about the management of a public house called *'The Cross-Keys Inn.'* The manager in question was a certain **John Stamford (1763– 1840)**. A genealogy (kindly provided by a member of the **Stamford** family) confirmed that he was the Great Grandfather of my Great Grandmother, **Rosamond.**

"We the 'propriation' and inhabitants of **Burton Pidsea** *thinks it necessary that our public houses should be reduced and as* **John Stamford** *has 'keeped' very bad rules for on* **Sunday 28th August** *last a party of tipplers resorted and met 'thire' (there) and got intoxicated in liquor and didn't stop tippling until morning and disturbed the neighbours of their rest on Sunday 4th* **September** *last and several other Sundry times too tedious here to mention has disturbed the same and so for that reason and several others we ourselves humbly desire and it is our request that his 'Majesties' Justices of the peace will keep him from the licence.*

'Sind' at **Burton Pidsea Sep16 - 1808**

William Clapham
[Church warden]
[Overseer of the Poor]
Joseph Sool
[Constable]

Inhabitants
David Mair
Joseph Tavender
Peter Drew
?   Salmon
John   ?'

Clearly, this **John Stamford** did <u>not</u> belong to the more respectable section of the community! He subsequently lost his license. It is worthwhile noting that there are no longer any **Claphams, Sools, Mairs, Tavenders, Drews** or **Salmons** living in the village. Only the **Stamford's** remain. The **Cross-Keys Inn** is now a couple of red brick cottages, south of the Churchyard. There still exists traces of an old doorway through which the said drunken tipplers will have staggered to then brazenly disturb the respectable inhabitants of **Church Street!**

A memorial inside the Church read *"In memory of **Leonard Clapham** son of **William Clapham** who departed this life **April 4ᵗʰ 1839** aged **41** years."* The size of this and other **Clapham** memorials confirmed the impression that they were one of the wealthier and more prestigious families in the village. Such evidence showed that **John Stamford** had managed to alienate some influential people. A curt inscription that just gave his name on the grave implied that even members of his own family appeared not to have thought too highly of him. He seemed to have been a *'hard living'* man.

One source of local pride was the breeding of prize horses. One such racing horse went by the name of **Nancy** and was featured in **Asquith.** This horse was of special interest because it featured in a piece of village news that my Great Grandmother **Rosamond Stamford** would have heard about as a young child: *"There was great excitement in the village in **1851** for a locally bred horse, the **Nancy,** won many races and from the money which was won **Mr Baxter** built **Nancy Row. Mr Baxter** had some strange ideas and refused to allow the houses in **Nancy Row** to have any front doors. Another building named after this famous horse was **The Nancy Inn. Cadger Row,** again without front doors, was named after a dog,"* **(Asquith P.15).**

The **Nancy Inn** is still in existence and has a colourful pub sign showing the horse with its owner **Mr Baxter** (who looked like a stocky, weather-beaten country type) and jockey. It was first constructed in **1832.**

Section 3: Rise of the Stamfords

Concerning the Stamford and Hastings families in East Yorkshire

The Census Returns for **Burton Pidsea** made it possible to trace the rise of the **Stamford** family and see its ever-closer links with the **Hastings.** Living next door to **William Stamford (1789-1850)** was his son **Cornelius Stamford** (a *"wheelwright"* aged **25**) and his wife **Ann** aged **27.** (She died on **July 20ᵗʰ, 1845** aged **31** years. Her highly moving epitaph read *"Faithful and industrious wife, loving and beloved through life, patient and serenely sighed, meekly moved her head and died."*) This **Cornelius Benton Stamford (1816-1888)** was the elder brother of my Great, Great Grandfather, another **John Stamford (1821-1878),** who was living away from **Burton Pidsea** during the **1841** Census.

278

1841 Census Return
(This showed that the village had 364 inhabitants, of whom 174 were male and 190 female)
William Stamford aged **50** *"wheelwright"* **Burton Pidsea**
Ann Stamford aged **15**
Hannah Stamford aged **15**

1851 Census Return
(*'In the Back Lane'* close to the Corn Mill near where the Stamford family lived; This *'Return'* also showed that the village had 394 inhabitants – of whom 209 were male and 185 female)
John Stamford aged **30** *"millwright employing 6 men"* **Burton Pidsea**
Mary Ann Stamford aged **30**, born in **Hull,** the daughter of **James Hastings**
Rosamond aged **7** *"scholar"* **Burton Pidsea** (Later to become **Edmund's** second wife)
William Stamford aged **4**
John Stamford aged **3**
Anne Stamford aged **1**
Ann Hodge aged **13** *"House servant"*
Francis [Stockton] aged **20** *"Millwright apprentice"* **Lincolns Buff**
William Hudson aged **18** *"Millwright apprentice"* the nearby village of **Keyingham**

1861 Census Return
(This showed that the village had 408 inhabitants of whom 213 were male and 195 female)
John Stamford aged **40** *"farmer, wheelwright owning 72 acres and employing 2 men"*
Mary Ann Stamford aged **40**
John Stamford aged **13**
Anne Stamford aged **11**
James Stamford aged **9**
Edward Stamford aged **7**
Mary Stamford aged **5**
Helen Stamford aged **3**
Elizabeth Stamford aged **21** *"farmer's widow"*
Charles Carter aged **25** *"wheelwright,"* **Burton Pidsea**

John Stamford married **Mary Ann Hastings** on **12th** October 1842 at **All Saints Church, Sculcoates. Mary Ann Hastings** was then living away from her father at **Sykes Street** in **Sculcoates.** (This again illustrates an unwillingness of any of **James'** children to remain on the family farm with him.)

Like **Edmund, John Stamford** was an entrepreneurial figure. After trying his hand as a millwright, he then settled for being a farmer and, as such, progressed and expanded slowly as the years went by. Admittedly, he was a beneficiary of the **mid-Victorian** agricultural boom, but he certainly seems to have taken advantage of any available opportunities. Such enterprise suggests that **Edmund** would not have fooled **John Stamford** if he had been a mere confidence trickster. He must have possessed some very solid qualities to have given **John** a favourable impression. To his own credit, **John Stamford** was charitable enough to have taken in old **James Hastings** under his roof. This act of kindness suggested that the relationship between the two men must have been tolerable – although it would have fallen to his wife to have cared for her elderly father. We also have the interesting spectacle of both **John Stamford** and **Edmund** naming their respective sons after **James Hastings.** These actions indicated that **Edmund** at least had a respect for **James Hastings.** Whether any direct business connection had existed between my Great Grandfather and **John Stamford** is not known – but seems unlikely given their different trades.

1871 Census Return
(At 27 Church Lane, this showed that the village had 373 inhabitants of whom 185 were male and 188 female)
John Stamford aged 50 *"Farmer, owning 74 acres and employing 2."*
Mary Ann Stamford aged **50**
John Stamford aged 23 *"Farmer's son"*
James Stamford aged 2
James Hastings aged 89 *"retired farmer"*
Susan Longman aged 13 *"servant,"* born in the nearby village of **Ryehill**

1881 Census Return
(At 79 Church Street, this showed that the village had 352 inhabitants of whom 172 were male and 180 female)
James Stamford aged 28 *"Wheelwright Master"*
Helen Stamford aged **23,** sister *"Housekeeper."*
Sarah Fairbank aged 20 *"General Servant"* born in **Hull.**
Samuel Calley aged 29 *"Blacksmith"* born in **Beverley**

1891 Census Return.
(This showed that the village had 342 inhabitants of whom 165 were male and 177 female)
Edward Stamford aged **37** *"House and Iron Foundry owner"*
[Annie] Stamford aged **27**
Edward Stamford aged **7 months**
Edward J. Hodgson aged **16** *"Ironmonger's apprentice"* born in **Hull**
[Lillie] Grantham aged **19** *"General servant and domestic"* born in **Aldbrough**

Sometimes these Census Returns would shed an interesting light upon some of the problems of rural life. The **1871** Census had recorded a certain **Thomas Swift** – an **Irish** agricultural labourer who lived in barns. Such abodes suggest he had been an alcoholic. The population growth enjoyed by **Burton Pidsea** from **1841** until **1861** indicated that the village had benefited from the **mid-Victorian** agricultural boom, which ended in the early **1870s.** By the late half of the nineteenth-century migration to nearby **Hull** would have once more become an attractive prospect. This point was implied in the population decline, as evidenced in the **1871, 1881** and **1891** Census Returns.

Another excellent source of information was the Parish Register of **St Peter & St Paul's Church, Burton Pidsea,** stored at the **East Ridings Record Office** at **Beverley**. My youngest son and I looked at this material on the morning of **Thursday, April 20th, 2000**. We subsequently drew up a Table. Sadly, the original material (showing the officiating clergy for the baptismal register) had been illegible due to severe damage. (A plaque in the Parish Church revealed that the incumbent from **February 1717** until about **1763** had been the Reverend **John Pearson**. From **31/10/1763** to about **1788** it was the Reverend **Thomas Bowness. Jonathan Dixon** succeeded him on **20/5/1788**. Sometime in **1832 Joshua Smyth** had replaced the Reverend **Dixon**. A Trade Directory confirmed that, by **1840,** the incumbent at **St Peter & St Paul's** was a **Rev. Joshua Smyth.**) The names of those clergymen recorded in the register underneath his were, thankfully better preserved.

In addition, the column entitled *'By whom the Ceremony was performed'* was omitted due to the barely legible signatures of those curates who had performed the Ceremony. The names *'Isaac Dixon, L. Raine'* and *'Joseph Lightfoot'* could only just be made out. A Trade Directory for **1820** gave a figure of **378** for the population of **Burton Pidsea**. A Trade Directory for **1840** estimated the vicarage to have a very high value of £**4,200**. *"The Deans and Chapters of York"* were the *"Patrons and Appropriators of this Church."*

When Baptised? 1783, Oct 31st
Child/Children's Name: Thomas
Parents' Name (Christian): Richard
Surname: Hastings
Abode: Oustwick
Quality, Trade or Profession: Farmer

When Baptised? 1784, Mar 30th (Seems to have been born on the 20th)
Child/Children's Name: James (later, the father of Helen Hastings)
Parents' Name (Christian): James
Surname: Hastings
Abode: Burton Pidsea
Quality, Trade or Profession: Farmer

When Baptised? 1789, September 20th
Child/Children's Name: William (Later Grandfather of Rosamond Stamford)
Parents' Name (Christian): James
Surname: Stamford
Abode: Burton Pidsea
Quality, Trade or Profession: Carpenter

When Baptised? 1821, Feb. 22nd Reference No.120
Child/Children's Name: John Hesslewood Stamford, (later father of Rosamond, Edmund's second wife)
Parents' Name (Christian): William & Elizabeth
Surname: Stamford
Abode: Burton Pidsea
Quality, Trade or Profession: Wheelwright

When Baptised? 1822, Oct 25th No.145
Child/Children's Name: Ann Elizabeth, daughter of
Parents' Names (Christian): William & Elizabeth
Surname: Stamford
Abode: Burton Pidsea
Quality, Trade or Profession: Wheelwright

When Baptised? 1823, Born May 16th Bap. May 26th No.154
Child/Children's Name: Thomas Hastings,
(Elder brother of Helen Hastings)
Parents' Names (Christian): James & Ann
Surname: Hastings
Abode: Burton Pidsea
Quality, Trade or Profession: Farmer

When Baptised? 1824, October 24th No.174
Child/Children's Name: Helen (later Edmund's first wife), daughter of
Parents' Names (Christian): James & Ann
Surname: Hastings
Abode: Burton Pidsea
Quality, Trade or Profession: Farmer

When Baptised? 1824 October 26th No.175
Child/Children's Name: Hannah Maria, daughter of
(Was baptised by the same illegible curate as Helen)
Parents' Names (Christian): William & Elizabeth
Surname: Stamford
Abode: Burton Pidsea
Quality, Trade or Profession: Wheelwright

When Baptised? 1828, April Born April Born 2nd, Bap. 9th No.225
Child/Children's Name: Elizabeth (younger sister of Helen Hastings), daughter of
Parents' Names (Christian): James & Ann
Surname: Hastings
Abode: Burton Pidsea
Quality, Trade or Profession: Farmer

From the details provided it was clear that the spiritual life of both the **Hastings** and **Stamford** families centred upon the local **Anglican** Church. This supports the view that they belonged to the more *'respectable end'* of village life, as the Dissenters tended to attract those who were not so well off. Unlike many of the **Smiths** in **Sutton**, both the **Hastings** and **Stamfords** were not dissenters. **Helen Hastings** was baptised only two days before a **Stamford** child. This implied the possibility of a close link between the two families.

Section 4: Helpful Sources

Concerning the Hastings and Stamford's of Burton Pidsea and Hull

Equally helpful was the *'Monument Book'* for this **St Peters and Pauls Church, Burton Pidsea,** (Referred to in our first visit to **Hull** on **Wednesday, April 19th, 2000.**) This source not only threw fresh light upon the lifespans of key individuals like **John Stamford** but also made possible the tracing of relevant family roots well back into the eighteenth century. Especially highlighted were the close marital links between the **Hastings** and **Stamford** families. Relevant excerpts concerning the <u>probable</u> Grandparents of **Helen** are given below. (Sadly, her parents **James** and **Ann** appear to have been interred elsewhere.) I will first quote from the register entry and then record the relevant monumental inscription which was often transcribed in foul weather.

<u>Parish Register:</u>
1822, Aug. 11th Richard Hastings, Burton Pidsea 63
1785, Feb 3rd. Sarah, wife of Richard Hastings, shoemaker

Sacred to the memory of
RICHARD HASTINGS
Who departed this life
August 9th, 1822 *aged 63 years*

Also
SARAH *his wife who departed this life* **February 1st, 1785**
Aged 29 years
'Afflictions sore long time I bore
Physicians were in vain
Till God did please to (give) me ease
And freed me from my pain.'

It is worthwhile noting the low view taken of eighteenth-century medicine (as depicted in the verse) in what seems to have been a case of prolonged illness. For this poor lady, death came as a release. Yet she managed to give her husband two children who were baptized on the same day. Sadly, she only saw them for less than eighteen months.

Parish Register:
1838 Mar. 21 Mary Hastings, Burton Pidsea, 56
In memory of **Mary,** *wife of*
RICHARD HASTINGS *who died* **March 18th, 1838**
Aged 56 years.
'From night on earth to Heaven's unbroken day…' (Remainder of verse eroded)
Her Death Certificate revealed that the cause of death was *'Apoplexy,'* while the person in attendance at the death was **'David Clappison, Apprentice, Burton Pidsea.'** No Doctor certified the cause of death,

These inscriptions confirm that **Richard Hastings** had progressed from being a humble shoemaker to becoming a prosperous landowner. Presumably, his progress had come about largely through advantageous marital alliances. The **Stamfords** also enjoyed a certain degree of upward social mobility. Interred in the parish graveyard were the people who may have been schoolteachers. They were *"***Thomas Ford** *who died* **August 21st, 1840** *aged 64 years"* and *"***Mary** *wife of the above who died* **March 27th, 1847** *aged 66 years."* On **October 15th, 1817** they lost an infant son called **Henry John.** He was recorded as being the son of *'the schoolmaster.'* A review of old maps showed no separate school building for that time, so presumably, they'd followed the typical practice of their time and held classes in their own home. **Volume 2** of **The Baines Directory** showed that (in **1822**) **Thomas Ford** had worked as *'a grocer <u>and</u> a schoolmaster.'* Eighteen years later he was still a schoolmaster but now combining this with being a farmer. Apparently in those days, one could not earn a sufficient living in school teaching alone.

I was unable to find any inscription for **James Hastings** (my Great Grandfather's father-in-law) during two visits made to **Burton Pidsea.** In a private e. mail on **Monday, 16th July 2018** a contact disclosed, *"even in* **1980,** *when we talked to the vicar she looked through the record and it's not there and was compiled of readable stones in* **1980.***"* So, the grave was lost. However, a note taken by my Great Grandfather's eldest son (also called **James**) retrieved matters. It divulged:
"From gravestone in Churchyard **St Peter, Burton Pidsea Holderness**
Anne *wife of* **James Hastings**
Died **12 July 1861**
Those who sleep in **Jesus** *will* **God** *bring with them*
James Hastings
Died **10th July 1872**
Aged **90** *years*

*Taken on Saturday **20th July 1935**"*

Inscriptions relating to the parents, grandparents and great-grandparents of **Rosamond Stamford** read as follows:

<u>Parish Register:</u>
1818 Dec. 5th Ann wife of John Stamford, Burton Pidsea, 53
1815 Aug. 4th Hannah dtr of John Stamford, Burton Pidsea, 10
Sacred to the memory of
***ANN** the wife of*
JOHN STAMFORD
Of BURTON PIDSEA
*Who departed this life **December 2^{nd?}***
***1818** Aged **53** years.*
"Here lies a tender partner dear,
Since she is gone I greatly fear
That such a one is hard to find
To comfort those who are left behind."

*Also, **HANNAH** their daughter,*
*Who died the **2nd of August 1815***
*Aged **10** years*

<u>Parish Register:</u> Nov. 14 John Stamford, Burton Pidsea, 79
Sacred to the memory of
JOHN STAMFORD
*Who died **November 10^{th,} 1840***
*Aged **80** years.*

The discrepancies existing between different records suggested that his birthday could have been anywhere between the late **1760** and early **1763** period. It is interesting to note the lack of any flowery epitaph. The curt tone of his inscription may possibly suggest that his family had not been overly sorry to have seen him dead and buried. His Death Certificate showed that the cause of death was *'Decay of Nature,'* which suggested the senility that can be associated with old age. The person in attendance at his death was ***'John Stamford, nephew.'*** The cause of death was certified by the registrar ***'William Little.'*** He recorded **John Stamford** as having been a *'Joiner.'*

Parish Register: Feb. 8 William Stamford, Burton Pidsea, 60
Sacred to the memory of
WILLIAM STAMFORD
who departed this life
February 5th, 1850
Aged 60 years
'Though lost to sight
still to memory dear.'

The Death Certificate revealed that the cause of death was *'Apoplexy,* **4 days,'** while the person in attendance at his death was a **'Francis Acey'** who was illiterate and left only his mark. No Doctor certified the cause of death. The location of his death at **'Cross Mere Hill'** in the **'Parish of Aldborough'** suggests that he may have collapsed outdoors whilst engaged on some farm work. The probability that the person in attendance seemed to have been a farm labourer further reinforced the possibility of an outdoor collapse. The term *'Apoplexy'* denoted a collapse or fit (which may have been due to conditions ranging from epilepsy to a heart attack or a stroke). Nineteenth-century medicine could be rather vague over the precise cause of a person's demise.

Parish Register:
June 4th Mary Ann Stamford, Burton Pidsea 54.
In affectionate remembrance of
MARY ANN STAMFORD
The beloved wife of
JOHN STAMFORD
Who died **June 2nd, 1875**
Aged 54 years.

The Death Certificate noted that she was the **'wife of John Hesselwood Stamford, a farmer.'** The cause of death was *'Dropsy, 1 month.'* The person in attendance at his death was **'John Benton Stamford,** *son,* **Burton Pidsea.'** The cause of death had been certified by **'Dr T. R. Johnson – LA, S. & MRCS.'**

Parish Register: Nov 30 John Stamford, Burton Pidsea 58
In affectionate remembrance of
JOHN STAMFORD
Who died **Novbr 27th 1878**
Aged 58 years.

His Death Certificate stated that the cause of death was *'Haematemesis, Ascites, 1 month,'* while the person in attendance at the time of death was *'H. Stamford, daughter.'* The cause of death had been certified by *'Dr T. R. Johnson – LA, S & MRCS.'* *"Haematemesis, Ascites,"* means a vomiting of blood and a bloated (fluid-filled) abdomen respectively. Both symptoms could be attributed to a variety of causes including heart failure, kidney or liver disease.

Also interred was a **Hastings Stamford** who died on **September 27th,1888** aged **2** years and **7** months. Being *'the darling son of Edward and Ann Stamford,"* he appears to have been **Rosamond's** nephew. His name testified to the long and enduring connections with the **Hastings** family. **Rosamond's** Grandmother, **Elizabeth Stamford** presented something of a mystery in relation to her resting place. Unexpectedly, there is no record of her being buried at **Burton Pidsea.** For some unexplained reason, she was not interred alongside her husband **William.** Either parish records are incomplete at this point or one can only conclude that she had died some distance from the village, her body not having been returned to **Burton Pidsea** for burial.

My Great Grandmother's birth had been recorded in the *"Sub-district of Patrington in the County of York."* Other details are in *'Table'* form as follows: -

1. When and where born: November Sixth, 1843, Burton Pidsea
2. Name if Any: Rosamond
3. Sex: Girl
4. Name and Surname of Father: John Hesslewood Stamford
5. Name and Surname of Mother: Mary Ann Stamford formerly Hastings
6. Occupation of Father: Joiner
7. Signature, description and residence of informant: Mary Ann Stamford, Burton Pidsea
8. When registered: November Twenty-First, 1843
9. Signature of registrar: William Little

A point of interest concerned the origins of **John Stamford's** middle name *'Hesslewood.'* A quick review of relevant maps confirmed that the name *"Hessle"* was common-place and found in both **East** and **West Yorkshire.** There was, for instance, a *'Hessle Road'* near **Hull.** However, why the **Stamfords** adopted it remained a mystery. One likely explanation was the proximity of a *'Hesslewood'* (a real wooded area) to **John's** own place of birth or near that of one of his ancestors. *'Hessle'* itself was probably a local pronunciation for the word *'Hazel.'*

An e-mail received on **Saturday, 15ᵗʰ September 2001** gave fresh insight into the possible origins of *'Hesslewood.'* According to this source (which appears to have been thoroughly researched) **John Stamford's** mother had been born as **Elizabeth Benton** at **Winterton** in **Lincolnshire** on 7ᵗʰ **October 1786.** Her father's name had been **Cornelius** and on **15ᵗʰ June 1784,** he had married **Elizabeth Atkinson** who was the daughter of **Edward Atkinson** and **Elizabeth Heaslewood.** She had been baptised at **Winterton** on **November 26ᵗʰ, 1758,** (her parents having married in the same location on **May 18ᵗʰ, 1756.**) Thus, the name **Hesslewood** originated in **John Stamford's** maternal Great Grandmother! If this was the case, the name **Hesslewood** has been passed down the **Stamford** and **Smith** lines over the course of two centuries – not ceasing being used until my late **Auntie Madge's** death in the **1980s.** Such a long transmission surely bears witness to the enduring nature of family tradition. It also highlighted **Elizabeth Benton's** determination to preserve old ancestral names in her family. Many of her children (including **John Stamford's** elder brother **Cornelius**) had been named after earlier forbears.

Some fresh light was shone on the community of **Burton Pidsea** during a visit made by my youngest son and myself on a very wet **Thursday, April 20ᵗʰ, 2000.** We quickly noticed how different the countryside was to that of **Sutton-in-Craven.** In this area, the land was almost completely flat, the thick clay soil made the fields prone to flooding and arable rather than sheep farming was far more prominent. Much of **Burton Pidsea** had now become a *'dormitory suburb'* of **Hull.** The old **Wesleyan Chapel** (erected in **1847** to accommodate **150** persons) had long since gone. A bungalow now stood on its former site, just west of the garage on the main road. Nevertheless, some of the original premises still stood – alongside modern-day red brick bungalows and semi-detached houses. These dwellings showed a little of what it must have been like to have lived in the days of **Helen** and **Rosamond.** Situated in the back lane were rather grandiose grey stone Manor Houses (once owned by the wealthier families of the time). A twelve-foot tall grey stonewall (dating from **1843**) guarded the privacy of what once were very large grounds. In contrast, the Millwright's house (situated next to the old Corn Mill) looked to have been the dwelling of a respectable and prosperous craftsman but could never have been construed as a Manor House. It was a red brick dwelling surrounded by lovely gardens – where **Rosamond** may have played as a child. It seemed to have portrayed the promise of wealth rather than its actual reality.

At the heart of this near-rectangular shaped settlement could be found the old village Church of **St Peter & St Pauls,** sited at the other end of the village, some ten minutes' walk away from the old **Stamford** dwelling. According to **Miles and Richardson (1911) p. 138** this medieval Gothic Church *"is an old cobblestone building in the later English style; it has a chancel, nave, vestry, brick porch and embattled tower at the West End, with three bells."* First-hand observation (made during our visit) confirmed this description. Inside, the Church furnishings were very simple; there was none of the **Anglo-Catholic** clutter of **St Mary's, Lowgate** in central **Hull.** The walls were whitewashed, and there were only a few monuments on them. At the back stood a sandstone font – like the one where **Helen** was once christened as a baby. Above the door were two-pointed wooden plaques containing **The Ten Commandments** and **The Apostles' Creed.** Poor weather conditions forced my youngest son and myself to stay inside the building for quite some time. Neither of us was disgruntled at this apparent inconvenience, as the atmosphere was very peaceful. We were in the place where our forebears had prayed and participated in the rites of the **Anglican** Church. Between cloudbursts of cold sleeting rain, we dashed into the Cemetery and recorded as many details from the graves as we could. Many of the graves had already been removed, but I did note the headstone of **William Stamford** (he'd lived from **1789** until **1850).** The monument was simply a six-foot high slab of pointed sandstone; it was very typical of many others in the cemetery. Once these tasks had been completed we rushed to the nearby Village Post Office. It was here that I engaged in conversation with one or two customers and found that the **Stamford's** were still farm owners in the area. In contrast, the **Hastings** family seems to have died out a long time ago. From this information, I could contact two surviving members of the **Stamford** family and obtain other relevant details, now included in this research. This visit had proved invaluable in providing additional information concerning the background to **Edmund's** two wives. However, it was only later established that the farm of **James Hastings** had been called *'Buzzard's nest.'* It still stands on the main road, less than half a mile to the East of the village. Apparently, there is an iron bar above the entrance to the building with the letter *'H'* inscribed upon it. The **Stamfords** had owned the land surrounding this building until they sold it off during the **1960s.** This piece of information lends weight to the view that the land once owned by **James Hastings** had passed down into the hands of the **Stamford** family following his death. Ordnance Survey Maps of varying dates confirmed it as a sizeable property with a large courtyard. In its day, it had perhaps been a prosperous establishment. However, first-hand observation (made during a second visit to **Burton Pidsea** on **Saturday, April 14th, 2001**) seemed to show that many of the original buildings had been demolished. The remaining red brick building looked somewhat bleak standing behind a windbreak of trees in a mildly undulating field.

Section 5: A Draper's Shop in Hull

Concerning Thomas Hastings in Hull

Akin to **Edmund** himself, **Helen** was to leave behind her what seemed to have been an extremely restrictive background. Evidence lending weight to this theory was found in **Leeds Central Library** on **Friday 11ᵗʰ February 2000** in the form of an **1857** Trade Directory. It gave details concerning a Retail Outlet in the centre of **Hull**. The relevant entry stated; *"**Hastings & Heron, linen & woollen drapers & hosiers, 52 Lowgate.**"* The **Lowgate** district was situated above the port area in the centre of **Hull**, an ideal location for any shop. The **1851 Census** held on **Sunday, 30ᵗʰ March** revealed the following inhabitants were dwelling at **52 Lowgate**: -

Thomas Hastings aged **27**, from **Burton Pidsea**, *"Linen woollen draper"*
Helen Hastings aged **26**, sister from **Burton Pidsea**, *"Housekeeper"*
Elizabeth Hastings aged **23**, sister from **Burton Pidsea**, *"Housekeeper"*
Samuel Heron aged **24**, from **Gaston** *"Linen and woollen apprentice"*
David Tindal aged **21**, from **Linton** *"Linen and woollen apprentice"*
Thomas Hindley aged **16** from [**Histerton**] *"Linen and woollen apprentice"*
James Hastings aged **13** from **York Homerton** *"Linen and woollen apprentice"*
Helen Ellerker aged **25** from **Beverley** *"House servant"*

Like the similar establishment in **Burnley**, this crowded household would have had its tensions. One can only wonder why **Helen** failed to marry the promising **Samuel Heron** who would later be taken into partnership. That would have been the expected course of development. Yet for some reason, this didn't happen. Sometimes, the non-events of history can be as telling as actual events.

Standing on the opposite side (at **no. 30 Lowgate**) was **St Mary's Church** where the **Rev. John Scott M.A.** was rector. Trade Directories revealed that he also served as a lecturer in the nearby **Holy Trinity Church**. A memorial plaque in **St Mary's** gave a few extra details concerning himself and his wife – those were recorded during a second visit made to the Church on **Friday, 18ᵗʰ August 2000**. (The first visit having been made a few months previously on **Wednesday, April 19ᵗʰ**).

"TO THE GLORY OF GOD

*In pious and thankful remembrance of **Amelia Scott**, wife of the **Reverend John Scott** M.A, vicar of this church of **Saint Mary Kingston-Upon-Hull 1834-1865**. The window in the tower was given by her children. She died **April 19ᵗʰ1895** aged 86."*

Although these words were probably sincere, they do reflect the somewhat sentimental piety of the time. With his business-orientated mind, **Edmund** would probably have had little time for such displays of religiosity.

The above information gave the definite impression that **52 Lowgate** was a small but thriving business, employing four apprentices. One of these apprentices (**Samuel Heron**), was sufficiently capable to have been taken into partnership by **1855.** (By **1861,** he was running his own drapery business at **12 Lowgate,** whereas **Thomas Hastings'** business had disappeared.) The presence of a *'house servant'* (who would have been paid £15 to £20.00 per year in wages) also denoted a modest degree of prosperity. She would have been employed to undertake the heavy menial jobs that were perhaps beneath the dignity of **Helen** and **Elizabeth.** However, there would have been enough household chores to have easily kept all three women busy. Furthermore, **Thomas Hastings** would (at least in part) have had to pay for the upkeep of his sisters, the wages of four apprentices and the rent (or lease) of an expensive City Centre Premise. To cover these costs (without incurring debt) suggested a substantial annual income that was at least in the £300 to £400 range. The taking on of **Samuel Heron** into partnership also implied that – from **1851** until **1857** – the business was enjoying a healthy degree of growth. Considering such evidence, it was possible to see why marriage into the **Hastings** family would have formed an attractive prospect for **Edmund.** With his shrewd business sense, he will have seen the opportunity of receiving a generous dowry plus future custom from a thriving business. In short, the **Hastings** represented a means of gaining a firm position inside the respectable **Victorian** middle classes. Both my younger son and I were convinced that the grand buildings, situated so elegantly in the centre of **Hull,** would have persuaded **Edmund** that there was more than ample opportunity to make money in that city.

In contrast to the men, the two **Hastings** sisters (classified, as *'Housekeepers'* in the **1851** Census) seem to have stayed in the background but nevertheless played important practical roles. Being a housekeeper in **mid-Victorian** times was easily a full-time occupation, involving much cooking and cleaning. Presumably, they were also in charge of the daily shopping. This may well have involved a careful checking of food purchases – ensuring that they'd not been adulterated in any way. They had perhaps moved to **Hull** to have enhanced their marriage prospects. Overcrowding at **No. 52 Lowgate** may well have been a problem which might have generated severe family tensions. Evidence for this point was confirmed by an old illustration of **51 Lowgate** which stood on the corner of **Bowl Alley Lane.** This clearly showed the house consisting of two main stories with attic accommodation above them. Most of the ground floor would have been taken up with the shop. It was perhaps in the shop that the apprentices slept. Behind the shop was the kitchen where **Helen** and her sister will have done all the cooking. Above the shop lay the storage areas and the master bedroom where **Thomas** slept and perhaps kept his account books. In the attic, **Helen** will have shared a bedroom with her younger sister **Elizabeth,** whilst any maids would have been confined to smaller attic accommodation. A review of a large-scale street map of **1853** (viewed at the Archive Centre in **Hull** on **Thursday, April 20th, 2000**) confirmed that the interior of the building possessed a reverse *'L'* shape in which the horizontal part of the *'L'* would have been on **Lowgate.** This plan also showed that (in contrast to **no. 53**) the premises of **Thomas Hastings** did <u>not</u> possess a bowed window protruding outward into the street. The window, in this case, would have been a six-foot-high large oblong shape and a width of ten to twelve feet. It would have provided an excellent viewing window for all the goods on offer. The plan also showed a few small outhouses at the back. Some of these may have acted as storage areas for a large amount of stock. The remainder may possibly have been outside toilets. A conversation with the chief archivist confirmed that the house was **Georgian** in style, with the inside consisting of a *'rabbit warren of rooms.'* Its location in a city centre **High Street** made it an ideal place to conduct a business of this type. By the end of the nineteenth century the old shop had gone; replaced in **1899** by a newly built grand office building, designed by the then well-known architect **Broderick.** Where **52 Lowgate** would once have stood now forms part of *'Burstalls,'* *"Solicitors & Commissioners for Oaths,"* **(June 2000).**

Section 6: Victorian Shoplifting

Concerning two thefts from the shop of Thomas Hastings

Further insight into the business world of **Thomas Hastings** was gained via transcriptions of two court cases conducted in **1850.** An attempt has been made to reconstruct these untidily written documents. (The transcript of **Thomas Hindley's** testimony in the second case appears to have been written by two clerks, each with nearly indecipherable handwriting. Scratchy fountain pens were also a problem, as were ink blotches, especially around the magistrate's signatures.) **Thomas** had acted as a witness for the prosecution in both cases – the prosecutor being a certain **Andrew McManus.** In the first of these, **Thomas** testified against a man who was obviously a hardened thief. As court transcripts show, the alleged crime was the theft of three expensive silk handkerchiefs from the premises. (Please note; although some attempt has been made to preserve the structure of these documents some amount of re-ordering had to be done to provide a greater sense of coherence.)

Transcripts of the *First* Court Case Involving Thomas Hastings
(Friday, March 15th, 1850)

Transcript One

BOROUGH OF} The examination of **Thomas Hastings** of **Lowgate** Street in the parish of **Saint Mary** in the said Borough, **Draper**
Kingston-Upon-Hull: -

Taken on **Friday** the **fifteenth day**
Of **March 1850** at the **Town-Hall** in the Borough of **Kingston-Upon-Hull,** bore the
Undersigned two of Her Majesty's Justices of the Peace in and for the said Borough in the presence and hearing of **James Brande**
Who is now charged before us the said justices for what he did on the
Fourteenth day of **March 1850** at the said Borough

Three silk handkerchiefs   --

Of the Monies, Goods, and Chattels of the said **Thomas Hastings** then and There being found feloniously, to steal, take, and carry away, contrary to the form of Statute, in such case made and provided.
 And the informant upon his oath saith as follows:
"I missed three Silk handkerchiefs last night- ~ they were in apiece.
It was between seven and eight.
The handkerchiefs produced are my property.
The handkerchiefs were just within the shop door."

Taken upon oath} **Thomas Hastings**
Before us
Tho. Firbank
Robert Blyth"
                                   Transcript Two

BOROUGH OF} The examination of   **John May** of **Stewarts' County** Street in the parish of **Holy Trinity** in the said Borough, **Sailor**

Kingston-Upon-Hull: -

Taken on **Friday** the **fifteenth day**
Of **March 1850** at the **Town-Hall** in the Borough of **Kingston-Upon-Hull,**
bore the
Undersigned two of Her Majesty's Justices of the Peace in and for the said
Borough in the presence and hearing of **James Brande**
Who is now charged before us the said justices for what he did on the
Fourteenth day of **March 1850** at the said Borough

Three silk handkerchiefs   --

Of the Monies, Goods, and Chattels of **Thomas Hastings** then and
There being found feloniously, to steal, take, and carry away, contrary to the
form of Statute, in such case made and provided.
And the informant upon his oath saith as follows:
*"I heard a cry of "Stop thief" in **Chapel Lane** between **7** and **8** o clock last night.*
I saw the prisoner running with a bundle of handkerchiefs - he threw them away. I picked
*them up and gave them to **Craven.***
The Policeman stopped the prisoner.
*Prisoner was running from **Lowgate** towards **High Street.***
In answer to the prisoner - I did see prisoner throw handkerchief way."

John May

Taken upon oath
 Before us -------------}
Tho. Firbank
<u>**Robert Blyth**</u>

Transcript Three

BOROUGH OF} The examination of   **Henry Graven** of **Eastcheap
Street** in the parish of **Holy Trinity** in the said Borough, **Police Constable
Kingston-Upon-Hull: -**

Taken on **Friday**   the **fifteenth** day
Of **March 1850** at the Town-Hall in the **Borough of Kingston-Upon-Hull,**
bore the
Undersigned two of Her Majesty's Justices of the Peace in and for the said
Borough in the presence and hearing of **James Brande** ----------------------------
----
Who is now charged before us the said justices for what he did on the

Fourteenth day of **March 1850** at the said Borough

Three silk handkerchiefs --

Of the Monies, Goods, and Chattels, of **Thomas Hastings** then and
There being found feloniously, to steal, take, and carry away, contrary to the
form of Statute, in such case made and provided.
And the informant upon his oath saith as follows:
"I produce three Silk handkerchiefs, which I received from the witness **May.**
I saw the prisoner running out of **Lowgate** *into* **Chapel Lane.**
He was some distance before me – there was a crowd between the prisoner and me."
Henry Graven

Taken upon oath
Before us -----}
Tho. Firbank
Robert Blyth

Transcript Four

BOROUGH OF} The examination of   **Thomas Sanderson** of **Moxon
Square** Street in the parish of **Holy Trinity** in the said Borough, **Police
Constable
Kingston-Upon-Hull: -**

Taken on **Friday** the **fifteenth** day
Of **March 1850** at the **Town-Hall** in the Borough of **Kingston-Upon-Hull,**
bore the
Undersigned two of Her Majesty's Justices of the Peace in and for the said
Borough in the presence and hearing of **James Brande** ---------------------------
----
Who is now charged before us the said justices for what he did on the
Fourteenth day of **March 1850** at the said Borough

Three silk handkerchiefs -------------------- --------------------

Of the Monies, Goods, and Chattels, of **Thomas Hastings** then and
There being found feloniously, steal, take, and carry away, contrary to the form
of Statute, in such case made and provided.
And the informant upon his oath saith as follows:
"I was on duty last night and saw the prisoner running down **Chapel Lane.**

I stopped him and took him into custody.
That was a little past seven o'clock."
Thomas Sanderson
Taken upon oath
Before us}
Tho. Firbank
Robert Blyth

Transcript Five

BOROUGH OF **James Brande**
Kingston-Upon-Hull: -

Stands charged before the Undersigned two of Her Majesty's
TO WIT Justices of the Peace in and for the said Borough, this **fifteenth**
Day of **March** in the Year of our Lord **1850,** for that he the
      Said **James Brande**- did on the **14ᵗʰ Day of March** in and at the
Parish of **Hilton** in the said Borough,

    "Stole Silk Handkerchiefs"

      Of the Monies, Goods, and Chattels, of **Thomas Hastings**
Then and there being found feloniously, steal, take, and carry away, contrary
To the form of Statute, in such case made and provided, and the said charge
Being read to the said **James Brande** and the witnesses for the
Prosecution: -
Thomas Hastings, John May, Henry Craven and Thomas Sanderson

Being severally examined in his presence, the said **James Brande**

Is now addressed by me as follows: *"Having heard the Evidence, do you wish to say
anything in answer to the charge? You are not obliged to say anything unless you desire to do
so, but whatever you say will be taken down in writing and may be given in Evidence against
you upon your trial."* Whereupon the said **James Brande** saith as follows: -
"I know nothing at all about them."

Taken before us at the Said Borough, the day and year first above mentioned.
Tho. Firbank
Robert Blyth
In the second case, held almost nine months later, charges were brought against
what seems to have been a rather inadequate woman who allegedly stole a

bundle of *'married lace'* from his shop. The court transcripts portray her as being a rather sad character, one who could easily have walked out of the pages of a **Dickens** novel. Apparently, **Thomas Hastings,** faced by the demands of the pre-Christmas sales, had been reluctant to attend this second case. Evidence for this lies in the fact that he had to stand £10.00 surety for himself and another £10.00 for his apprentice **Thomas Hindley.** (This meant that £20.00 was deposited at the court and would be forfeited if either **Thomas** or his apprentice failed to appear as witnesses.)

Transcripts of the *Second* Court Case Involving Thomas Hastings (Wednesday, December 11th, 1850)

Transcript One

BOROUGH OF} The examination of **William Dresser** of No **4** Street in the parish of **Sculwates** in the said Borough, **Police Constable**
Kingston=upon=Hull: -

Taken on **Wednesday** the **eleventh** day
Of **December 1850** at the **Town-Hall** in the Borough of **Kingston-Upon-Hull,** bore the
Undersigned two of Her Majesty's Justices of the Peace in and for the said Borough in the presence and hearing of **Mary Nicholson**
Who is now charged before us the said justices for what she did on the
Third day of **December 1850** at the said Borough: -
"A quantity of lace."
Of the Monies, Goods, and Chattels, of **Thomas Hastings** then and
There being found feloniously, steal, take, and carry away, contrary to the form of Statute, in such case made and provided. And the informant upon his oath saith as follows:
"On Tuesday week, I took prisoner into custody for being drunk and incapable.
She had the basket produced with her.
In it, I found a large quantity of Lace, which I produce.
*She said she had brought some of it at **Newcastle** before she went to prison. She had been **8** months in prison and come out that same morning.*
She stated that she had it in fact with her, but I found the Lace and two small pieces there with her.
*On fresh examination, she told me after I had made enquiry at the Gaol that the Lace was in her basket at **Mr Tusseys** while she was in Gaol."*
William Dresser

Taken upon oath before us -
James Heywood
Geo Cookman

Transcript Two

BOROUGH OF} The examination of **Thomas Hindley** of No **52 Lowgate Street** in the parish of in the said Borough, **apprenticed to Mr Hastings Draper**
Kingston=upon=Hull: -

Taken on   **Wednesday** the **eleventh** day
Of **December 1850** at the **Town-Hall** in the Borough of **Kingston-Upon-Hull,** bore the
Undersigned two of Her Majesty's Justices of the Peace in and for the said Borough in the presence and hearing of **Mary Nicholson**
Who is now charged before us the said justices for what she did on the
Third day of **December 1850** at the said Borough: -
"A quantity of lace."

Of the Monies, Goods, and Chattels, of **Thomas Hastings** then and
There being found feloniously, steal, take, and carry away, contrary to the form of Statute, in such case made and provided.   And the informant upon his oath saith as follows:
The *"Prisoner came into my master's shop last* **Tuesday** *Week.*
She asked for some married Laces, I showed her some.
She brought three yards – no more.
I know three pieces of those produced; they belong to my master.
I showed them to the prisoner, she did not buy them.
On fresh recollection, she came into the shop at half-past 12 o'clock.
We did not notice that any Lace was missing until the Policeman came to make enquiries."

Thos Hindley
Taken upon oath
Before us
James Heywood
Geo Cookman

Transcript Three

BOROUGH OF} The examination of **Thomas Hastings** of **Lowgate Street**
in the parish of **Saint Mary** in the said Borough, **Draper**
Taken on   **Wednesday** the **eleventh** day
Of **December 1850** at the **Town-Hall** in the Borough of **Kingston-Upon-Hull,** bore the
Undersigned two of Her Majesty's Justices of the Peace in and for the said
Borough in the presence and hearing of **Mary Nicholson**
Who is now charged before us the said justices for what she did on the
Third day of **December 1850** at the said Borough: -
"A quantity of lace."

Of the Monies, Goods, and Chattels, of **Thomas Hastings** then and
There being found feloniously, steal, take, and carry away, contrary to the form
of Statute, in such case made and provided. And the informant upon his oath
saith as follows:
"I can distinctly swear to three pieces of the Lace produced. One piece I had sold myself on that
Tuesday at about half-past two in the afternoon and when we searched for it to send it off it
was gone.
I did not show the other two pieces.
I'd seen the two pieces a day or two before."
Thomas Hastings----
Taken upon oath
Before us   ------
James Heywood
Geo Cookman

Transcript Four

BOROUGH OF ---
         Kingston=upon=Hull
Mary Nicholson stands charged before the Undersigned **two** of Her Majesty's
TO WIT Justices of the Peace in and for the said Borough, this eleventh
Day of **December** in the Year of our Lord **1850,** for that she the said **Mary**
Nicholson did, on the **3rd Day of December 1850,** at the Parish of **Holy**
Trinity in the said Borough,

"A quantity of lace."

Of the Monies, Goods, and Chattels, of **Thomas Hastings**
Then and there being found feloniously, steal, take, and carry away, contrary
To the form of Statute, in such case made and provided, and the said charge
Being read to the said **Mary Nicholson** and the witnesses for the
Prosecution: -
William Dresser and **Thomas Hastings** and **Thomas Hindley**

Being severally examined in his presence, the said **Mary Nicholson**

is now addressed by me as follows: - *"Having heard the Evidence, do you wish to say anything in answer to the charge? You are not obliged to say anything unless you desire to do so; but whatever you say will be taken down in writing and may be given in Evidence against you upon your trial."* Whereupon the said **Mary Nicholson** saith as follows: -
*"What I have to say is all that property that was found in the basket I left in **Mr Tussey's** Shop."*
  Taken before us at the Said Borough, the day and year first above mentioned.
James Heywood
Geo Cookman

From reading the recorded words of **Thomas Hastings** it was very apparent
that he was a meticulous, somewhat fussy man with a very detailed knowledge
of his stock. He would have viewed anything of an underhand nature with great
distaste. One can easily imagine him having had very sharp words with **Thomas
Hindley** whose failure to notice that the lace had gone missing would have
been a source of great annoyance. Clearly, if my Great Grandfather had not
been very good at his own business then **Thomas Hastings** would have
quickly *'shown him the door!'* Despite the formality involved in such court
proceedings, a definite personality did emerge from the records. It was exciting
for me to read the words of a man who had been closely linked with my own
family.

Section 7: Meeting Edmund

Concerning how Edmund Smith met his first wife, Helen Hastings

Edmund would have entered upon this scene as a Commercial Traveller (for
no Trade Directory shows him ever having been based in **Hull**.) Near the
junction of **Lowgate** and **Market Place** were large stables, which may have
provided horse-drawn carriages to visit outward-lying areas. The presence of
this facility perhaps explained why three out of the eleven Commercial Hotels in
Hull were in **Market Place**, itself within an easy walking distance of **52**

Lowgate. Edmund would most probably have never stayed at the *"Kingston Hotel, 5 Market Place,"* because this establishment was nearer the Docks and would have had a *'rougher'* clientele, comprising mainly of sailors – hardly **Edmund's** type of people. The *1857 'Post Office Directory of Yorkshire'* revealed this hotel as *"a commercial and family house"* with **Henry Dean** as Proprietor. The word *'commercial'* suggested that it catered especially for visiting business people, though probably, in the main, with those connected with the shipping trade. Another lodging place may well have been *"The Cross-Keys Commercial, Posting and Family Hotel, 32 Market Place"* run by **Mrs Ann Varley.** A final alternative was *'The King William, family and commercial'* Hotel established in **1834** under the proprietorship of a **Charles Barnaby Walker** at **41 Market Place.** It was sited below **Lowgate** and the retailing heart of **Hull.** Its location suggested that this latter place was where **Edmund** would most likely have stayed in **1857.** Unlike the former two Hotels in **Market Place,** *'The King William'* still exists today as a Public House.

The previously mentioned grand buildings in the City Centre, (with their obvious display of wealth and opportunity) may well have attracted **Edmund.** One could easily imagine him wanting a share in some of this and grandeur. Another attraction was the considerable number of Drapery Shops located in **Hull City Centre** – it was positively teeming with them! Here **Edmund** could make the most of the vast array of business opportunities. It was also apparent that **Thomas Hastings** was, quite literally surrounded by very stiff competition. He will have needed to be good at his trade to have outshone his competitors.

A marvellous insight into **Edmund's** business world was provided by **Arnold Bennett's (1867-1931)** wonderful novel *'The Old Wives' Tale,'* initially published in **1908.** The first part of the story was set in the **1860s** – just when my Great Grandfather's career was beginning to make greater headway. Most of the main characters in the book worked in a Draper's shop in the Midlands (with one main exception – a Commercial Traveller, selling the same line of goods as **Edmund** would once have done). Whilst reading this book (in **November 2001**) it became clear that the author had conducted his research very well. I was transported back to the nineteenth-century Drapery Trade with all of its sights, sounds *'petty snobberies'* and *'jockeying for position.'*

Bennett's novel more than adequately portrayed the leisured classes of the landed gentry. They looked disdainfully down upon those who *'had to work for a living,'* all the while assuming they had a *'natural right'* to rule the country! Even amongst the gentry themselves, those with titles were shown to have had only little to do with those without! Professionals such as Doctors and Lawyers were only barely tolerated. This snobbery could be seen to cascade down through the social scale. Doctors, Vicars and Lawyers would look askance upon those who worked in *'trade,'* and they, in their turn, would look down upon those who worked in the *'dirty'* manufacturing industries. Even within these same industries a *'pecking order'* existed wherein an overseer would differentiate between skilled workers (who, within their own circle could be well respected) and those less skilled. Near the bottom of the heap were the *'feckless poor,'* considered as an underclass of labourers. Lastly, came the unemployed and the *'criminal elements'* of society. It was amongst this category that social problems such as drunkenness and wife beating were most noticeable. (As opposed to the *'feckless poor'* the *'respectable poor'* consisted mainly of hard-working people who had fallen on tough times through ill health or some other misfortune. There was even a rank of *'distressed gentlefolk'* – meaning financially poor members of the middle classes who, at one time, had been respected members of the trading community.)

Even the small world of the Draper's shop (akin to that described in *The Old Wives' Tale*) had its own hierarchy. The Manager-owner and his family were at the summit of their social pile. Just beneath them was the Senior Assistant who, if he had the right skills, could hope to marry the owner's daughter or sister and become a partner in the business. If the owner died and had no male heirs, the business would then be passed on to the partner (as possibly happened with **Samuel Heron** in real life and with the fictitious **Samuel Povey** in *The Old Wives' Tale.*) Being a partner (or Senior Assistant) would have had its own responsibilities and privileges – the latter of which was to have a private bedroom. Owners would have been keen to maintain the goodwill of such a skilled employee. Below the Senior Assistant in rank came the Apprentices who were learning their trade. Their prospects depended upon their ability to do such jobs as cutting cloth and dealing with customers. The newest apprentices would be expected to do the menial jobs *i.e.* sweeping the floor and moving heavy goods. Further below in the *'pecking order'* were the largely female Shop Assistants who would be expected to work until they married. (Gradually. over the passage of time, this segment would grow to greatly outnumber any male assistants.) The owner himself (or a trusted assistant) would deal personally with important customers. Both the Census Returns for **Hull** and the narrative in *The Old Wives' Tale'* suggest that the Draper's shop ran like an extended family. A special sense of closeness (but also bitchiness) often characterised such social units. Apparently, a Draper's daughter could be quite free with her comments about a female customer's attire – once that customer had left the shop! Practical jokes played on the more pompous employees were not unknown. Should the Senior Assistant be offended at such pranks he would perhaps retire to his *'den'* – *i.e.* the cutting room – to sulk over a cup of tea.

Throughout the **1860s** the advertising and promotion of goods took place through word of mouth, reputation and display. Shop signs would clearly name the owner, and window displays would always look neat and tidy. Only little in the way of aggressive advertising would be apparent – anything more being deemed as far too vulgar. On **page 73-77** of *'The Old Wives' Tale,'* the owner's wife rebukes **Samuel Povey** for placing the word *'EXQUISITE, 1s 11d'* on a price label pinned onto a broad tartan ribbon. She evidently felt its use was lowering the shop's reputation. More overt forms of advertising only became more acceptable in the later part of the nineteenth century. Even shop signs tended to be on a smaller scale; a reputable Draper's shop priding itself upon maintaining a *'genteel'* appearance. Any attempt to be too *'showy'* would receive much criticism from fellow shopkeepers. For those working in such places, the shop represented their whole life. It was their daily bread and butter. Any economic downturns were greatly feared, not least because they could tumble any respectable shop assistant into the labouring classes. Loss of social respectability in **Victorian England** was something dreaded. Given his background, I would suspect it was something also greatly dreaded by **Edmund** himself. Avoiding poverty and rising to respectability perhaps formed the main motivating factor in his life.

Breaking into this rather narrow world was the Commercial Traveller, who, if young, could cut *'a dashing figure'* with the ladies in the shop. Always smartly dressed (and usually of a distinguished appearance) his travels would give the impression of a knowledgeable fellow – someone very worldly-wise. He would carry with him the name of the Company he worked for and if that name enjoyed a *'sound'* reputation then he could expect to be guaranteed a sale – unless times were very bad. In good times, the *'Traveller'* would need only to beg for orders if he was opening a new round or working for a Firm which did not enjoy a trusted reputation. The Commercial Traveller would announce his presence in advance by sending an elaborately designed card or circular. It would read something like this: - *'Our **Mr Smith** will have the pleasure of waiting on you **Thursday next, the 4ᵗʰ inst.**'* Sometimes the circular would also announce a display of samples, which could be viewed at a local Hotel. Following his arrival at the railway station, the Commercial Traveller would often pay a boy to trundle his boxes of samples. These boxes would have ornate (brass coloured) handles to convey a feeling of quality. In mill towns like **Keighley,** some of these young porters were known to have had missing fingers – because of mill machine accidents. Working as a porter was probably one of the few remaining ways for them to earn a living. (If **Edmund** ever saw young lads in that condition he perhaps would have had an unhappy reminder of his father's own demise.) The *'Traveller'* himself would carry a Gladstone bag (or suitcase) containing any spare clothes and toiletries. Money and documents would be kept on his own person, with a pocket watch in his waistcoat to keep track of time.

Having left his personal belongings at a nearby hotel – one with a recommended menu – the *'Traveller'* would call into the shop with the air of a man who felt he was entitled to a sale. Nevertheless, whatever his grandiose feelings, he would always observe one rule. Should the owner (or even a humble assistant) be talking to a customer he would <u>never</u> interrupt. He would remain discreetly in the background until the customer had left the premises. This constituted one of the most basic rules of etiquette, in that the Commercial Traveller had no right to intrude upon the business dealings of his client. In the event of having a great deal of business to get through it was not unknown for cloth salesmen to arrange a gathering of local drapers in a large hotel room. Here, he would attempt to sell his products to the assembled clientele, all the while speaking in a dignified baritone voice. Once a sale had been successfully completed the elaborate process of filling in order forms would begin.

A long-serving Commercial Traveller would take immense pride in *'an old account,'* where cordial relationships had become firmly established with a client, often achieved over many years. If, like **Edmund,** the *'Traveller'* worked over a protracted period he could well be dealing with three generations of the same family. Near the end of his working life, he would have become something of a *'venerable'* and well-respected figure, known to be prim, punctual and stately. Having long since become a regular and welcome figure, he would now have less need to indulge in the petty haggling which may once have characterised his younger days. Experience, rather than dashing dynamism would now constitute his main selling point. Should the relationship with a shopkeeper be particularly friendly a Traveller could expect to enjoy good hospitality – sometimes over a silver tea set, or possibly invited in for supper. The example of **Edmund Smith** (and his fictitious contemporary **Gerald Scales** in *'The Old Wives' Tale'*) would suggest that it was not unknown for Commercial Travellers to marry the female relative of a Draper. Oddly enough, for **Edmund** specifically, his first of two such marriages would very lead to unhappy consequences and these would still be a talking point in the family until well into the twenty-first century.

A rather disreputable side to a Commercial Traveller's life was his reputation for being something of a womaniser. **Arnold Bennett** writes of this aspect, as did **Charles Dickens** in his Book entitled *'The Uncommercial Traveller'* (reviewed in the next chapter). He appeared to grasp the opportunity for *'loose living'* – a something not accessible to most other middle-class men. Wherever possible, the Commercial Traveller was also expected to socialise with influential figures in the local community to gain contacts and to enhance the prestige of the Firm. Undoubtedly, such pressure may, at times, have brought him into contact with the local, loose living *'fast set.'* By the standards of the time being a Commercial Traveller could be a good life and attached to it was a certain glamorous image. A proper Commercial Traveller was clearly distinguishable from a vulgar peddler (who would go from door to door trying to sell various wares.) For all its apparent freedom, a Commercial Traveller could not flout the constraints imposed upon him by the **Victorian** Class System. He was expected to *'play along'* with the snobberies of his day and to look every inch an elegant or (if older in years) venerable gentleman. He was also duty bound to maintain the reputation of the Company he worked for. Should he fail in this, he would be quickly out of a job. This meant that any *'womanising activities'* would have been done in a most discreet and clandestine manner.

To approach **Helen, Edmund** would have needed to impress her brother **Thomas** with his business acumen. (This would not have been an easy task.) In the initial stages, it would have lain with **Thomas** to decide whether to give **Edmund** access to his sister. Being *'the man on the spot'* he was, in effect, her guardian and protector. His decision to give **Edmund** a chance to woo his sister was to have powerful ramifications, spanning successive generations of **Smiths**. Many lives (including my own) would be affected by this pivotal decision. Only later would the approval of her father **James Hastings,** have been required. However, by that time, **Edmund** and **Helen** may well have made up their own minds to proceed anyway. For **Helen,** the attractions of the relationship were obvious – she could be guaranteed the protection of a rising businessman with good prospects. It was easy to imagine my Great Grandfather *'switching on the charm'* to get his own way. His line of work would require that he be fashionably and smartly dressed, making him something of an attraction to women like **Helen** who perhaps longed for the respectability and security provided by marriage.

Moreover, for **Helen** at the age of **33,** the only alternative to **Edmund's** proposal of marriage would have been a wretched existence as a spinster, caring for her elderly father in **Burton Pidsea.** (A spinster had low status and was viewed as something of a joke. The writings of the **Brontë** sisters would confirm that it was a social state to be dreaded – especially if no substantial legacy had been sustained.) Being a *'poor spinster'* was a social state to be avoided even at the risk of an unhappy marriage.

Given this alternative, **Helen** may well have been tempted to ignore any inner misgivings she may have had about her prospective husband. By **1857,** her brother **Thomas** (then aged **34**) may also have had his own future marriage in mind. For him, the chief attraction of any match between his sister and **Edmund** lay in the fact that her removal from the family home would make way for his own future wife. After all – it is difficult to imagine three **Victorian** housekeepers living together in harmony! It's likely that he would have been eager to find an honourable exit for an increasingly unmarriageable sister. For the **Hastings**, **Edmund** represented a *'last chance'* to provide **Helen** with some degree of respectability. They were perhaps desperate to see her married off; hence some degree of matchmaking may well have taken place. **Thomas** may also have encouraged my Great Grandfather to maintain links with the **Hastings** family by giving him large orders, so helping him to secure his position as a Commercial Traveller. As a change from the *'Commercial Traveller'* hotels of the time, **Edmund** may have stayed overnight at **52 Lowgate,** talking *'shop'* with **Thomas** as they relaxed by the coal fire. **Helen** would have flitted dutifully in and out with tea and sandwiches. Such hospitality would have elicited a sense of gratitude on my Great Grandfather's part.

However, an air of mystery remains concerning **Edmund's** motives. Being a widely travelled man, he would have had a broader range of prospective brides from which to choose. My own inclination is to believe that **Helen** constituted the first meaningful relationship he had with any woman. Before meeting **Helen** there may well have been surviving relatives, who knew one or two embarrassing things about his past. Also, he may (subconsciously) have viewed **Helen** as a substitute for his deceased mother. Marrying her would provide him with much-needed stability as well as useful family connections. Almost certainly, from a purely business point of view, the **Hastings,** with their own thriving business, offered **Edmund** the prospect of financial gain as well as enjoyable hospitality. They also gave the promise of a fresh start for an essentially *'rootless'* man, eager to break with certain elements of his past life. For such a person **Helen** would have seemed an ideal choice, especially if no questions were asked about his background. What **Edmund** did <u>not</u> appear to have asked himself was whether he could live with this woman. His motives may have been complex but shallow. He would have been a young man of about **25** at that time – possibly very adept in business but lacking in emotional maturity. He may have been unaware that **Helen** may only have given her consent out of a sense of duty. She may have walked down the aisle with severe misgivings in her mind. He for his part, may have been convinced that he was doing both her <u>and</u> the **Hastings** family a favour by consenting to this union. Something about this marriage seemed later to grievously disappoint him. Perhaps he'd made the fatal mistake of viewing his marriage as an extension of his business. (This is a common enough fault amongst those who are successful in this area.) He may have viewed **Helen** as a commodity, bought at a very good price, whilst totally failing to see that there was more to marriage than money. A strange epitaph (quoted in another chapter) on her tombstone reflected something of his disappointment – **Helen** had not been such a good bargain after all! One wonders whether (in that epitaph) my Great Grandfather was expressing a deep sense of anger towards **Helen** – or towards himself for having married her. The question remains – what could have gone wrong in their marriage and why did he seem so begrudging of her?

Section 8: A Wedding in Hull

Concerning a marriage in Victorian Hull

After his time spent in **Burnley, Edmund Smith** was to vanish (somewhat mysteriously from sight) until late **1857** when he married **Helen Hastings** in the **Saint Mary's** district of **Hull.** He seems to have been exceptionally well travelled – having moved as far away from his own locality as it was possible to do – whilst <u>just</u> remaining within the **Yorkshire** region. Unlike most of his contemporaries, for him, there'd been no question of settling down with a *'local lass.'* Already, by his mid-twenties, he was obviously breaking with convention. Evidence for this can be seen in his Marriage Certificate – the first documentary evidence we have of **Edmund** after his Draper's apprenticeship in **Burnley.**
1. When married? December 10th 1857
2. Name and Surname: Edmund Smith, Helen Hastings
3. Age: Full, Full
4. Condition: Bachelor, Spinster
5. Rank or profession: Commercial Traveller
6 Residence at the time of marriage: Pannal (Ripon), St Mary's, Hull, (Lowgate)

7. Father's name and surname: John Smith, James Hastings

8. Rank or profession of father: Corn Miller, Farmer

Married in the <u>Parish Church</u> according to the Rites and Ceremonies of the Established Church <u>by licence</u> by me W. Ward, Curate of St Mary's.

> **The marriage was solemnised between us**
> <u>**Edmund Smith**</u>
> <u>**Helen Hastings**</u>
> **In the presence of us**
> <u>**[Eunice G. Hiestrue']**</u>
> <u>**Thomas Hastings**</u>

N.B: The word *full'* in the age column was simply a quick way of saying that the couple was of sufficient years not to have required parental consent. Underlined words and the information in the lower two rows were all handwritten.

As was customary, their marriage was announced in a local newspaper, but a quick glimpse at its brief entry revealed no further details.

A visit made to **Hull** (on **Wednesday, April 19th, 2000**) confirmed that the location of their marriage (at **Saint Mary's Lowgate**) looked much as it had done in the **1850s.** The main difference was the *'Rood Screen'* and altar, both of which were installed during **1861-63** at the height of the *'Gothic Revival'* in Church architecture. A **Georgian** balcony would have been seen in **1857** – only to be torn down during the modifications made in the **1860s.** Nevertheless, it was easy to imagine **Helen** and **Edmund** exchanging vows on the grey flagstones immediately in front of a large, colourful, *'Perpendicular'* stained glass window. To have stood in the very place where my Great Grandfather had stood at a formative period of his life was a very moving experience. I was glad to have had my youngest son with me to share it.

The absence of **Edmund's** name from any of the Trade Directories for **Pannal** (or nearby **Ripon**) reinforced the idea that he was in **Pannal** for only a fleeting period. He certainly does not appear to have established any form of business in the area (although there were plenty of hotels where he could have been staying). Later evidence (provided by **Knaresborough** museum) showed that the textile industry in the **Pannal** to **Harrogate** area was declining. It was unable to compete with a large number of textiles produced by the coal-fired power looms of **Leeds.** Consequently, it was unable to offer any long-term financial security for my great Grandfather. He would go where the money was.

Edmund's signature on the document is rather interesting. It sweeps across the whole line, suggesting a bold and confident man who knew his own mind. **Helen's** signature is a little more cramped. Both signatures denote that the couples had been educated to at least a reasonable standard of literacy. Clearly, my Great Grandfather and his wife had received a tolerably good education. The same point also applies to **Helen's** brother's signature (that of **Thomas Hastings**). There was an enormous cross over the *'T'* extending from the first to the last letter of his surname. Was this evidence of a strong man who liked to get own his way? This tentative conclusion does not apply to the other faint signature, which is almost illegible. The writer's name (possibly *'Eunice'*) simply cannot be made out.

One unusual feature was the way **Edmund** broke with strong social convention by marrying a female who was six years his senior. In **Victorian** times, such a union would have been met with raised eyebrows. What was his motive for doing this? Being carried away by love does not seem to have been the answer. There appeared to be nothing in **Edmund's** constitution to account for this – he was a calculating businessman. He was not a giddy romantic who would impulsively fall for the charms of an older woman. The most likely reason was finance; **Edmund** needed capital to help make his way in the world and **Helen,** along with a generous dowry, provided just the right means. He would adhere to strict **Victorian** social etiquette only when it suited him. During this early part of his business life, my Great Grandfather was already displaying a vigorous independence of mind and a strong hankering for material success. It's very likely that these traits emerged as a response to the severe adversity he had endured in his early years as an orphan in **Skipton** and as an apprentice in **Burnley.** By the late **1850s,** he seemed to have been doggedly determined to compensate for the psychological and social deprivation over which he'd had endured. He was, in today's terms, a *'high achiever,'* wholly was determined to leave his mark. Little did he know that he would successfully achieve this in ways he could not have imagined.

Edmund was known to have possessed a gold ring with the monogram *'E'* etched upon it. He would have used this to stamp this monogram on warm sealing wax (after having first poured it out onto the open edges of an envelope). The ring is still in the family and has been dated to the **1850s.** It was passed down to my Grandfather who then left it to my Uncle **Stewart,** who in turn passed it on to his daughter **Pamela**. Its ownership conveys the impression of a man preoccupied with external appearances – of wanting to *'look good'* in front of other people.

CHAPTER 11: FLAWED PATRIARCH

Section 1: An Old Photograph

Concerning a photograph of Edmund Smith

On the first page of an old photograph album is the picture of a man with a long bulbous nose and severe expression. A dark suit jacket, necktie and winged shirt collar mark him out as a man determined to look his best. His clothing may have been slightly old-fashioned when the picture was taken for his seventy-ninth birthday on **Saturday, 21ˢᵗ January 1911.** It is almost as if he was thinking, *"This is how I would want my family to remember me!"* Prolonged exposure times would have meant he will have been seated for at least two and a half minutes in one position. (Photographers were not unknown to clamp the heads of their clients to keep them still!). Completely dominating the picture and set against a sombre background is this very imposing face; a near-white neatly trimmed beard – indicating a recent visit to the barbershop, possibly on the day the photograph was taken. A groomed, slightly bushy moustache obscures his thin, austere lips (whose thinness may well be attributed to the removal of his dentures!) A domed forehead and large ears serve to add to his patriarchal appearance. His expression is somewhat forbidding; modern observers (in the early months of **2000**) used words like *'scary' 'narrow' 'stubborn'* to describe it. At least two people thought he was a Mill Owner; which indeed may have been the impression he himself had wanted to convey. Of most interest were his eyes – which stared imperiously straight ahead. His skin was creased in ridges under each eye. From the right eye came a look of cruel and set determination, which seemed to challenge anyone, *"Don't dare interfere with me!"* However, from the left eye was a look of hurt, defensive timidity that seemed to convey the message, *"I am terrified that the disclosure of certain secrets about me will cause my whole respectable world to come tumbling down."* Revealed in the photograph was a complex person who had been deeply wounded by an event (or series of events) in his past; there perhaps was the shame of poverty from which he was determined to escape. Yet what sights those eyes must have seen; there would have been **Leeds** in its **Victorian** commercial heyday, perhaps even **Queen Victoria** herself when she visited the city in **September 1858. Edmund** would also have seen the belching factory chimneys and disease-ridden slums. Thankfully, rural areas remained, providing fresh air and mental relief for anyone who was not an agricultural labourer. During his life, those eyes would have beamed with satisfaction at the closing of a shrewd business deal or ignited with fury in the event of any misdemeanour by a family member. Tragically, they would have stared in sad incomprehension as they saw two wives and five children die prematurely from a range of diseases. In addition to the actual sight of death, there would have been the associated sounds of ill health leading inexorably to those deaths. His ears would have heard his beloved exhausted second wife coughing ceaselessly as the dreaded consumption took hold. Alongside these sights would have been the sounds and smells of his time; the noisy cries of street vendors desperate to sell their wares and the smell of soot emanating from the myriad factory chimneys and residential coal fires. During times of thick smog, a sickly taste of gritty dirt would have filled his mouth. Here then is **Edmund Smith,** flawed patriarch of a family who would later seek to build upon his own very real and personal achievements.

Section 2: The Move to Leeds

Concerning Victorian Leeds

By late **1858,** my Great Grandfather was living with **Helen** at **8 Blenheim Place, Leeds.** Confirming this location were details from the Birth Certificate for his first son, **James.**

1. When and where born: Seventeenth September 1858 8 Blenheim Place

2. Name if Any: James Hastings

3. Sex: Boy

4. Name and Surname of Father: Edmund Smith

5. Name and Surname of Mother: Helen Smith, Formerly Hastings

6. Occupation of Father: Commercial Traveller

7. Signature, description and residence of informant: Helen Smith, 8 Blenheim Place Leeds

8. When registered: Twenty-Sixth October 1858

9. Signature of registrar: G. Jackson

Details provided by the **census** held on **Sunday, 7th April 1861** revealed that the household consisted of:

Edward Smith aged **29,** *'a Commercial Traveller in woollen cloth'* **Sutton-in-Craven**

Helen Smith aged **35, Burton Pidsea** in **Holderness**

James aged **2**

Betsey aged **1**

Hannah Learoyd aged **28,** *'servant'* **Wakefield**

Joseph Hodgson aged **21,** *'a warehouseman'* from **Manchester** (He was listed as a visitor.)

By then, the population of **Leeds** stood at **207,165.** (This contrasted with a population of **172,270** in the **1851 Census** and **152,054** in the **1841 Census**. In **1831** (the year **Edmund** was conceived) the population of **Leeds** had stood at **123,548**. Despite such rapid expansion, the city was by no means the fastest growing urban area of the Industrial Revolution. **Middlesbrough,** for instance, grew from **4** houses with **25** inhabitants in **1801,** to a town of **91,302** one hundred years later! Incidentally, **April 1861** was the month the **American Civil War** broke out. This was to be the first war to have used industrial methods of mass production to produce military equipment.

Already for **Edmund** traces of dynastic ambitions may have begun to ripple to the surface. **James** was given the name of **Edmund's** father-in-law. Evident here was a close and obvious identification with the **Hastings** family. **Edmund** seemed keen to impress them.

Why **Edmund** was clearly recorded as *'Edward'* in the **1861 Census** is not known. Was it a simple transcription error or, alternatively, did he prefer to be known by the name of the then **Prince of Wales?** (The latter widely known to have been a well-dressed man.) The **1881 Census** was to show that **Edmund** was not above making his name sound rather grander than it really was. Was this name alteration evidence of an *'identity crisis'* or a desire to impress his business associates? In no other document was my Great Grandfather ever known as *'Edward.'* Given his tendency to grandiose exaggeration, this is not as far-fetched an explanation as one would initially suppose. Perhaps he'd also had important customers to impress. In those days, Commercial Travellers in textile or clothing related industries worked hard to convey a positive image to their wealthier clients. This was a trait my own father was to inherit when he entered the industry several decades later.

The name **Edwin** (which kept cropping up in family tradition) seems to have been a shortened version of **Edmund** and was perhaps used only in family circles. Family tradition held that *'he was married three times and was courting a fourth when he died.'* (It also held that he had nineteen children which turned out to be only a little exaggerated.) However, it was his second wife **Rosamond** who gave birth to my Grandfather **Fred Hesselwood** (born on **23 September 1869**). In the family, he seemed to have been known as *'Frank'* (which will be the designation now used throughout this account to distinguish him from my own father who was also called *'Fred.'*) Slight confusion also took place over the name **Rosamond** – with one variation spelling it as **Rosamund.** The former variation **Rosamond** will be used in relation to **Edmund's** second wife (my Great Grandmother,) whilst the latter will relate to an aunt of mine who possessed the same name. It is hoped these distinctions will help lessen any sense of confusion felt by the reader.

Of their five children, **James** would live to be ninety-three (dying in **1953**). Like his father, **James** also married a few times and was said to have been something of a character. Even though he was reputed to have married more than once, **James** had just two children – one of whom was a daughter called **May.** According to my cousin **Pamela,** she was reputed to have attended **Leeds Girls' High School.** The other – a son named **Edmund Hastings Smith** later became a Vicar. **James** was an active member (possibly an usher) of **Saint Margaret's Church** on **Cardigan Road, Leeds. Pamela** who met the family in the early **1950s** recalls *'Jim,'* than in his nineties, as being a very gentle and nice man, short of stature and with a trim white beard. In contrast, his son was rather aloof and academic. At that time, his spinster daughter was looking after **Jim.** It was **James** who had inherited the large family Bible after his father's death, subsequently passing it down to his own son. Apparently, it contained the names of **Edmund's** family and should it ever come to light it would be a priceless historical document.

Any references to an **Edmund** living in **Leeds** before **1858** are somewhat problematical. The Census Return of **1851** shows **8 Blenheim Place** to have been occupied by an **Edward Hasse** (aged **30**) and his two sisters. He was a *'governor of children, employing six men,'* whilst of the two sisters **Amelia** (aged **32**) was a teacher in drawing and **Elizabeth** (aged **27**) was a *'daily governess.'* At that time, **Blenheim Place** was only half built. Surrounding lodges and a dairy farm bore witness to a pre-industrial era. Census Returns also conveyed the impression that this street tended to attract young newly married couples wishing to set up their first home. A certain **Edmund Smith** (aged **28**) at **no. 4** turned out to be the wrong age and none of the names of his three young children fitted. He was a tailor who employed **12** men. His name also surfaced in the Trade Directory for **1851**. This revealed an **Edmund Smith and Co – Tailors and Woollen Drapers** at **4 Blenheim Place**. This **Smith** occupied further premises at **10 Briggate** – having been there since **1849**. Initially, the name, location and trade did suggest a tenuous family connection with the **Edmund Smith** who was my Great Grandfather. At the age of **19,** he would already have been in the clothing business. However, by the middle of the **1860s** this later **Edmund Smith** had moved from **Briggate,** being replaced by a photographer. He thus disappeared. A Trade Directory for **1857** confirms that **8**

Blenheim Place was now occupied by a **Charles Boocock,** *'carrier.'* Another Trade Directory for **1861** showed **8 Blenheim Place** as having a new occupier by the name of **Mrs Elizabeth Petch.** It appears the information used for these Directories was out of date – reflecting a situation as it had stood two to three years prior to publication. For instance, by the last quarter of **1858,** the more authoritative source of **James'** Birth Certificate shows both **Edmund** and **Helen** to have already been established at **8 Blenheim Place,** yet this fact does not register in any of the Directories until some years afterwards. Interestingly, at **9 Blenheim Place** *'Whites'* Trade Directory for **1861** shows an apparently respectable lodging house run by **Mrs H. Parkin.** Those staying there included:
E. D. Sampson – agent,
Samuel Stears,
Edmund Smith,
C. L. Mason – Clerk

My wife made the interesting suggestion that there may have been some temporary lodging going on whilst people were waiting for the building work to be completed. Although an interesting piece of speculation there exists no way to either confirm or falsify this suggestion. Instead, all that can be stated is that it is a possibility that need not be dismissed.

However, in the Census Return for **1861 Mrs Elizabeth Petch** is revealed as being a **73**-year-old *'fundholder'* (someone who lived off shares) living at **1 Blenheim Place,** whilst **Mrs H. Parkin** is shown to be a **54**-year-old lady living at **2 Blenheim Place.** Living with her (at that same address) were four children aged from **18** to **26.** For his part, **Samuel Stears** aged **57,** is shown to be an umbrella manufacturer residing at **6 Blenheim Place.** At **9 Blenheim Place,** the head of the house was **Mr Charles Mason** aged **22** and cited as a bank clerk. Living with him were his sister **Josephine,** aged **23,** a governess and his brother **George** aged **20,** a woollen merchant. The reason for such a marked discrepancy between the Census Return and Trade Directory data is not known. A very likely possibility is that the Directory was drawing upon information two or three years prior to **1861. Blenheim Place** consisted of a row of redbrick houses, with narrow passageways, small yards and outside toilets. It was typical accommodation for the lower middle and upper working classes. Dickensian poverty it was not, but conditions would still have been uncomfortable for a growing family.

Such data throws open the interesting possibility that, before his move into **8 Blenheim Place, Edmund** had taken up temporary lodgings at **9 Blenheim**

Place. If this was the case, then he would have been conforming to normal *'migrant'* behaviour. The male head of the family would move into a new area first to find accommodation before summoning his wife to join him. From Census Returns it has been possible to list the occupations of what was evidently a respectable middle-class neighbourhood. In the following list (drawn from the **1861** edition of **White's Trade Directory**) the numbers in the left-hand column denote the house numbers at **Blenheim Place.**

<u>House Number and Occupation</u>
1. Fundholder
2. None listed
3. Stock Broker
4. Manager of a flax and woollen business
5. Manager in Cotton Goods
6. Umbrella Manufacturer
7. Writing Master
8. *Commercial Traveller in Woollen Cloth*
9. Banking Clerk
10. Accountant
11. Commercial Traveller
12. Mechanical Engineer
13. Woollen Salesman
14. Solicitor
15. None listed (a lady aged **60**)

It is possible to conclude that, by the time of the **April 1861 Census, Edmund** would have been living at **8 Blenheim Place** since just before **September 1858.** He would have been setting up a family with **Helen,** establishing himself in business and being most anxious to avoid the **Victorian** curse of poverty. The house itself would have been red bricked and terraced but on a less grand scale than the larger houses in nearby **Blenheim Square.** It was sited about a quarter of a mile from the town centre (with its grand shops and filthy alleys). For **Helen,** smoky, noisy **Leeds** would have formed a marked contrast to her birthplace of **Burton Pidsea,** where she had been surrounded by countryside. The fact that his eldest son **James** was born in the city late in **1858** confirms that **Edmund** had already been there earlier in that year – having married **Helen** in the last month of the previous year **(1857).** A reasonably firm reconstruction of **Edmund's** movements (during the early part of his life) can now be made: -
Early 1832: Born and registered in **Sutton-in-Craven**
June 1834: Living at **Cullingworth** near **Bingley**

6ᵗʰ June 1841: Living in **Skipton** with his family

30ᵗʰ March 1851: Edmund serving his apprenticeship with the **Joseph Lee** Drapery Shop in **Burnley, Lancashire**

Late 1857: Now a Commercial Traveller, **Edmund** is consolidating his already existing business connections with **Hull** although he's staying at **Pannal**

10ᵗʰ December 1857: Marriage to **Helen** in **Hull.** Following a brief honeymoon, they settle **Pannal,** but **Edmund** faces work issues

Summer 1858: Edmund moves to **Leeds** (without **Helen** who is now pregnant with their first child). **Edmund** resides temporarily at **Mrs Parkin's** lodging house at **9 Blenheim Place** to look or wait for more permanent accommodation. Later **Helen** joins him in **Leeds,** and they move to **8 Blenheim Place**

10ᵗʰ September 1858: James is born at **8 Blenheim Place**

6ᵗʰ December 1858: Helen back in **Pannal**

31ˢᵗ December 1858: In compliance with the **1853** *'Compulsory Vaccination Act'* Doctor **Geo L. Knight** vaccinates **James** against smallpox in **Blenheim Place**

Early 1859: Helen is firmly based in **Leeds**

Some of the dates are only approximations, but the general sequence of events seems to be correct. His marriage to **Helen** and his preference for an early family prompted **Edmund's** permanent move to **Leeds**. He would also be attracted by the expansion of the worsted industry that had been stimulated by new methods of mass production. This would create plenty of opportunities to make money for anyone possessing a shrewd business mind. Given his deep involvement in this industry, it seems likely **Edmund** would have already forged strong connections with the city – possibly using the lodging house at **Blenheim Place** as a base of operations. He would have realised that **Leeds** was a good place in which to earn a living and to provide for a young family. Therefore, when **Edmund** had arranged for **Helen** to join him in **Leeds** he was making no rash gamble. The City would have been a *'known quantity'* to him. As a rising tradesman, he seemed to know where he wanted to go in life. All the evidence points to his trade connections in **Leeds** forming a key motive in the permanent move there. It was a booming city and would also have been advantageous as a central location for the woollen business, providing opportunities for commercial gain. In **Edmund's** mind, **Leeds** would have represented money. His desire to start up a young family would certainly have given him another incentive to make such a move.

It's shortly after that period we obtain our first memory. **James** was on record as recalling how, as a very young child, he used to climb on top of a dresser with a glass top. He would then spend a long time gazing at his own reflection.

Section 3: A Thriving Commercial City

Concerning the economy of Victorian Leeds

Old illustrations confirm that, during the late **1850s, Leeds** was a rapidly expanding City; its skyline dominated by church steeples and tall factory chimneys belching out thick acrid smoke. (One illustration, shown in **Holland P.197** can be dated to **1858**. It shows the Town Hall with an incomplete dome.) When combined with the smoke from domestic fires it has been estimated that, in the second half of the nineteenth century, this pollution reduced the annual average of sunlight received in the wealthy outer suburb of **Headingley** by one-third. In the City Centre and around the mills themselves conditions must have been far worse. Especially during hot summers, the smell of filth emanating from the slums lying to the South and East must have been appalling. By the time of my Great Grandfather's move to the City, the middle classes were already fleeing to the hilly northern areas where the air was more breathable. **Leeds** had its own canal (leading to **Liverpool**) and expanding rail links, with the **River Aire** also in use as the main transport route for the movement of heavy goods. This river was so badly polluted by the toxic mixture of chemicals flowing into it from the mills that those who accidentally (or deliberately) fell into it had little chance of survival. It was little better than an open sewer. Until well into the **1960s**, it used to be said, *"anyone falling into the **River Aire** didn't drown, they dissolved."* Figures provided by the **Abbey House Museum** at **Kirkstall** in **Leeds** revealed that **12,000,000** gallons of sewerage flowed into it annually. The **Aire's** connection with the **Leeds Liverpool Canal** (which began in the centre of **Leeds** and ran parallel to the river) brought a greater increase in the traffic along this important waterway. This great feat of engineering began in **1770**, but regular financial difficulties delayed its completion until **1816**. Barges and small boats could navigate easily from the river into the canal. In **1857**, **William Osburn** wrote the following poetic description of the City: -

"The AIRE below is doubly dyed and damned;
The AIR above with lurid smoke is crammed:
The ONE flows steaming foul as Charon's Styx
Its poisonous vapours in the other mix.
These sable twins the murky town invest –
By them the skin's begrimed, the lungs oppressed,
How dear the penalty thus paid for wealth.
Obtained through wasted life and broken health...."
(Quoted in **Brears P.11-12**)

Almost as a relief from the squalor stood the newly built and domed Town Hall – designed by **Broderick,** a well-known architect in his day. This building constituted the chief symbol of **Leeds's** growing civic pride, the foundation stone having been laid on **17ᵗʰ August 1853** by the then Lord Mayor **John Hope Shaw** *'Esq.'* Five years later, (on **7ᵗʰ September 1858**) when **Peter Fairburn** was Mayor, **Queen Victoria** officially opened the Town Hall herself. *'Well mannered'* crowds greeted her. Almost all the City Centre buildings were decorated with flags and very colourful bunting. Clearly, the Queen's visit was a major event in the City's history, with contemporary illustrations marking the occasion. Whether **Edmund** and **Helen** were there amongst the sea of faces is not known – although being in the later stage of pregnancy would possibly have made attendance on her part a little risky. But for **Edmund** – would he have missed such a grand occasion for the sake of his business? This royal visit and the new impressive Town Hall would have leant weight to the impression that **Leeds** was a city from which the able-bodied and strong-minded could derive much profitable benefit. **Edmund** possessed both attributes. It is also worth noting that in **Victorian** times about **75%** of all accommodation was rented. Good housing was in short supply during most of the nineteenth century. New building programmes were unable to keep up with the exploding population. The annual rent for middle-class houses would have lain in the £**20-40.00** range. The houses in **Blenheim Place** would have been at the lower end of this range whereas those at **Vernon Road** (where **Edmund** and his family were subsequently to live) would have been at the higher end. It is not known whether **Edmund** eventually privately purchased any of the houses in which he lived. What is clear is that he would have started off in rented accommodation. A review of the photographs on the **Leodis Website** at **Dewsbury Road Library** on **Wednesday, May 30ᵗʰ, 2012** confirmed that, for **Edmund** and **Helen,** the move to **Vernon Road** had represented a *'step up'* in the world. Many of these houses were spacious and had bow windows. They were obviously for people with some degree of substance. They highlighted the fact that, in many ways, **Leeds** was a thriving commercial city.

A contemporary account of **Queen Victoria's** visit was provided on **pp.55-56** of **Israel Roberts'** Autobiography, edited by his Great Grand Daughter **Ruth Strong** in the year **2000.** Whilst spending all his life in the **Leeds** suburb of **Stanningley, Israel Roberts (1827-1881)** was a near-contemporary of **Edmund** my Great Grandfather. **Israel** was a devout **Methodist** who became a successful *'fancy cloth'* manufacturer, employing three hundred people by the time of his death. His business activities may well have brought him into direct contact with **Edmund** who would go to any place where there was money to be made. **Israel Roberts'** Autobiography was a marvellous source of information about nineteenth-century **Leeds** life. In part, this was because it was based on his diaries which recorded events as they happened. It is to be hoped that one day this excellent autobiography will be placed on the Internet. Its author conveyed the impression of being a most engaging, attractive character, more than capable of making many shrewd observations. Compared to **Edmund,** **Israel's** personality was far more at peace with itself and less complex in nature.

The following chronology relied heavily upon information provided by **Kershan (1990), Thornton (1996)** and **Ward (1972).** It conveys something of the dynamism of the city to which **Edmund** had chosen to move.
1825: Opening of the **Stockton** to **Darlington** railway line marking the commencement of the railway age.
1830: Opening of the **Liverpool** to **Manchester** passenger railway line – thus beginning the great **Victorian** railway boom.
1834: Construction of the **Leeds** to **Liverpool** and **Leed**s to **Selby** railway lines.
1842: Following a series of cholera epidemics, the **Leeds Improvement Act** begins to slowly improve the health of the City's populace.
1845: James Smith, a local historian, mentions that some privies had not been cleaned for six months! Children from working-class areas labour in textile factories from **5.00AM** until **9.00PM.** In contrast, the children of wealthy parents attend *'Town Schools'* in outlying districts, *i.e.* **Headingley, Beeston, Holbeck** and **Wortley.** The social reformer **Richard Oastler** campaigns to improve conditions for the underprivileged.
1846: Construction of the **Leeds** to **Midland** and **Leeds** to **Bradford** railway lines.
1848: Construction of the **Leeds** to **Dewsbury** and **Leeds** to **Manchester, Great Northern** railway lines.
July-October: An outbreak of cholera kills **2,000** in the **Leyland** slum district of **Leeds.**
1851: The Census held this year shows that the Textile Trade employed **29,000** workers. The **Jewish** population numbers around **150.**
1855: John Barren uses **Isaac Merritt Singer's** newly developed sewing machine to produce ready-made clothes in a small family-run business based in **Alfred Street, Leeds.** This contributes to the growth of the textile industry.
1857: Approximately **75%** of the **Leeds** workforce is employed in textile mills and dye houses. Whilst initially following an axis around **Woodhouse Lane,** the wealthier classes begin to spread **northwest** into **Headingley.**

1858: **Edmund Smith's** permanent move into **Leeds. September** of this year marks **Queen Victoria's** first royal visit to **Leeds,** confirming the City's new-found respectability.

1914: Birth (on **February 6th**) of my father **Fred Gordon Smith.** The outbreak of the First World War in **August** of this year marks the effective end of the **Victorian** and **Edwardian** eras in **Leeds.**

1915: **AJTMP** membership of **1,500** represents **23%** of the **Jewish** Tailoring Workforce in **Leeds.** Death of **Edmund Smith** on **July 25th** at the age of **83.**

One interesting point highlighted by this chronology was the major contributor to the commercial prosperity of **Leeds** made by the rapidly growing **Jewish Community.** This was possible partly through the invention and successful marketing of the **Singer** sewing machine. Through his own connections to the clothing industry, it is highly probable that **Edmund** enjoyed a business association with the **Leeds Jewish Community** from an early stage in his career. It is also worth noting that, throughout his adult working life, **Edmund** was closely associated with places like **Hull, Pannal** and **Leeds,** all of which enjoyed good rail links. My Great Grandfather seemed to have derived many commercial benefits from the rapidly expanding **Victorian** rail network.

After studying the previous chronology, it became abundantly clear that **Edmund** appeared on the *'Leeds scene'* at just the right time. He had evidently made the right connections as the textile industry began its huge expansion. He had a very sharp eye for making the most of business opportunities that came his way. Consequently, his work prospered, and he acquired enough income to live in the better type of new housing then being built. The only disadvantages (albeit huge ones) were the toxic atmosphere and the rapidity by which disease could spread. These drawbacks perhaps contributed to the early deaths of some members of his family – although health conditions were not necessarily much better elsewhere. In the long term, the effect of **Edmund's** move to **Leeds** was to establish the **Smiths** firmly within the **Victorian** Middle Classes. The latter, in that period, represented just fewer than **20%** of the population. (Apart from a few thousand aristocratic families most of the remainder of the population belonged to the working classes who could either be respectable or exist in near destitution.) In terms of income, my Great Grandfather would be in the middle of the middle classes – earning less than a professional Doctor or major Factory Owner but a lot more than a humble clerk. This would place him in about the top **15%** of the population. **Edmund** must have worked very hard to have got to this position – his mind firmly fixed upon one objective – to *'get ahead'* in the world. He appears to have been a man of driving ambition.

Section 4: A Distinctive Public Image

Concerning Victorian Commercial Travellers

Commercial Travellers seemed to have possessed a very distinctive public image. That barometer of mid-**Victorian** public opinion **Charles Dickens** conveyed something of that image when writing the first page of the opening chapter of his book *The Uncommercial Traveller'* in **1860.** It is worth quoting in full to convey something of the reputation that **Edmund's** line of work enjoyed during his own day. In addition, it's hoped that this bit of **Dickensian** *'whimsy'* should provide an amusing break from the factual emphasis of this chapter.

"1: His General Line of Business

Allow me to introduce myself – first negatively.

No landlord is my friend and brother, no chambermaid my lover, no waiter worships me, and no boots [boot shining boys] *admires and envies me. No round of beef or tongue or ham is expressly cooked for me, no pigeon–pie is especially made for me. No hotel advertisement is personally addressed to me. No hotel-room tapestried with greatcoats and railway wrappers is set apart for me. No house of public entertainment in the United Kingdom greatly cares for my opinion or sherry. When I go upon my journeys, I am not usually rated at a low figure in the bill; when I come home from my journeys, I never get any commission. I know nothing about prices and should have no idea if I were put to it, how to wheedle a man into ordering something he does not want. As a town traveller, I am never to be seen driving a vehicle externally like a young and volatile piano forte van and internally like an oven in which a number of flat boxes are baking in layers. As a country traveller, I am rarely to be found in a gig, and never to be encountered by a pleasure train, waiting on a platform of a branch station – quite a David in the midst of a Stonehenge of samples.*

And – yet proceeding now to introduce myself positively – I am both a town traveller and a country traveller, and always on the road. Figuratively speaking, I travel for the great house of human-interest brothers and have rather a large connection in the fancy-goods way. Literally speaking, I am always wandering here and there from my rooms in Covent Garden's London – now about the City Streets, now about the country by roads – seeing many little things and some great things, which because they interest me may interest others.

These are my brief credentials as The Uncommercial Traveller. "

To some extent, the above picture could be simply dismissed as a caricature, but for a caricature to appeal it must contain a strong element of truth. (Here, it must be remembered that **Dickens'** caricatures were very appealing to the public of his time.) If the above quotation did describe the qualities expected of a successful Commercial Traveller, it is possible to deduce that those who made a success of that occupation (as **Edmund** did) tended to: -

1. Be hard workers with an eye to considerable financial reward
2. Aspire to some degree of personal success
3. Be outgoing by nature
4. Enjoy the physical trappings of success
5. Be admired and envied for their wealth
6. Be physically robust to carry a heavy weight of *'samples'*
7. Be well informed about the product and its prices
8. Be good at *'haggling'* and not above persuading a customer to purchase a product they really did not want
9. Be reckless horse and carriage drivers who were always in a hurry
10. Be heavily reliant on the existing rail network to travel any great distance
11. Be self-sufficient – able to enjoy a certain degree of freedom in their workaday life.

They also possessed a rather dubious reputation for dishonestly *'dunning'* (conning) people out of their money and of *'having a chambermaid in every hotel.'* Away from normal domestic constraints, Commercial Travellers faced temptations that would not have been available to those working in a more fixed location. This is a point that **Dickens** himself raised with a certain degree of delicacy, realising that his more *'knowing'* readers would have been able to read between the lines. Despite a tendency to grandiose exaggeration, there is no proof that my Great Grandfather ever succumbed to the sexual temptations of his job. Nevertheless, he certainly possessed all the characteristics in the above list; otherwise, it's hard to see how he would have lasted in such a competitive market. The status and physical trappings of success did appear to have been exceedingly important to him. Commercial Travelling was often demanding work and insecure but in **Victorian** times there were far worse occupations. It would have been infinitely preferable to working in a mill or down a mine. Perhaps my Great Grandfather appreciated this fact and was happy enough to stay with this occupation for many years. It seemed to satisfy deep psychological as well as financial needs.

Kershen pp.38-39 provided an economic explanation over why salesmen like **Edmund** were needed in the **Leeds** area. He stated that *"**Leeds** wholesale clothing* *manufacturers could not, as did merchants in* **London,** *wait for the trade to come to them. The man in the street, the drapery store owner and the overseas buyer did not go to* **Leeds** *looking for clothes but were encouraged to place orders by travelling salesmen, employed to seek out and open new markets. Accordingly, the future trade could be estimated, labour styles predetermined and the destructive effects of seasonality, to some degree, reduced; factors which encouraged the utilisation of large-scale production units both in factories and workshops."*

The information provided by **Kershen** and other sources put forward very strong circumstantial evidence that **Edmund** will have enjoyed such a link. In the main, **Edmund's Jewish** contacts would have been tailors and drapers.

This quote was valuable because it showed why **Edmund's** line of work was important, what was expected of him and the type of business people with whom he will have been in contact. Given their huge involvement in tailoring, it's difficult to see how my Great Grandfather could have avoided having links with the **Leeds Jewish Community**. Today, it would have been the equivalent of not seeing **Pakistanis** in **Bradford.** How far he would have socialised with them remains a matter of speculation, but if **Edmund** had seen an opportunity for commercial gain through socialising with **Jewish** customers, then he would have socialised. **Edmund** was essentially opportunistic; for him, socialising and business went hand in hand.

An ornate silver-plated cigar case with rounded corners was one of **Edmund's** special possessions the existence of which pointed toward a close convergence between the business and social worlds. (It survived within my own family until the **1970s** before being stolen in a burglary.) At its centre was a plain oval area with his name engraved upon it in fine script. Inside was a strap to hold down the cigars. It was easy to imagine him passing around cigars to customers after a successful sale. My father used to keep it on his desk amongst all his business documents. When I saw it, the silver was somewhat tarnished, but it was still possible to make out the pattern of curly lines wrapped around the centre. With hindsight, I realise that it was the property of a man much concerned with promoting a highly respectable upper-middle-class image. Like the **Jewish Community** in **Leeds, Edmund** was very much concerned with *"getting on in the world."* He and ambitious tradesmen from within that community would have shared many of the same business-orientated values.

Edmund may have contacted **Mr George Gelder** (Draper), shortly after his move to **Leeds.** An advert on **p. 195** of the **1926** Leeds Tercentenary Handbook showed a pen and ink drawing of **Mr Gelder's** shop as it appeared in about

1861. Standing outside a large window (divided into **36** panes) was a woman, parasol in hand and wearing a crinoline and bonnet, conversing with a man in a top hat and dark frock coat. Adjacent to the window an open doorway revealed a wall stacked full of rolls of material. Sited over the window and doorway and set within two wooden pillars was an oblong sign bearing the name *'GEORGE GELDER.'* Above the sign were two windows, the lower of which consisted of two main panes; the window above was identical in design but slightly smaller, with each of the two panes subdivided into **27** smaller ones. The stonework was evidently red brick. Presented below this drawing was the following statement:
*"This is a seed planted over 65 years
ago from which has sprung the present
thriving business – known alike to thrifty
men and women as their favourite shop for
DRESS, DRAPERY, FOOTWEAR, CHILDREN'S
OUTFITTING, LINO, CARPETS, AND ALL
HOUSEHOLD NEEDS.*

*THE shop where quality is enhanced by a
BONUS as well as good value*

**Gelder Bros.
(Leeds) Limited
99, 100, 101, 102 Kirkgate, Leeds."**

This advert revealed that **Gelder Brothers** was very proud of its history and willing to use it as a sales point – the assumption being that customers would feel at ease with an old established Firm. It also appealed to the **Victorian** virtue of thrift, which possibly implied that its customers were from either the lower middle or respectable working classes. Was **Edmund** ever any part of this Firm's history? The location, nature of the business and **Edmund's** own thoroughness would have made this supposition highly likely. In his eyes, **Gelder Brothers** was a rising Firm – one from which a lot of money could be made. His keen business sense would have drawn him to it.

Information from an **1866** Trade Directory recorded **Edmund** still as a Commercial Traveller, now living at **27 Blenheim Place**. Later that same year an announcement of the death of his wife **Helen** in the **Leeds Mercury** revealed that he had moved to a new house in **Vernon Road** (still in **West Leeds**) where he was to remain for the rest of his life. **Blenheim Place** itself sloped downward – away from **Blenheim Square** toward the centre of **Leeds**.

This square still contains some very impressive **mid-Victorian** housing – although by the **1960s** they were in a rather shabby state of repair. Clearly, **Edmund** had entered business as a young man and his line of work had proved prosperous, even at the outset. By his late twenties, he could afford to be married and keep a servant. He must have derived some benefit from the **Victorian** economic boom that lasted from **1851** until **1873**.

Blenheim Place was demolished in the **1960s** to make way for the new **Blenheim Primary School**. This would not be the only time an old family house would make way for the building of an educational establishment and given the evident value he placed upon education, perhaps **Edmund** would have been pleased.

Trade Directories also confirmed that, by **1864,** the first eight houses had been built on **Vernon Road**. The upper section of the Road was completed by **1866,** with **Number 16** occupied by a certain Draper named **T. Hardwick.** (It seems that this section must have been constructed in **1865**, the year that the **American Civil War** reached its bloody close.) Before **1864** this locality had hitherto been known as **Hebblethwaite Row**, suggesting that a row of cottages had once occupied the site.

Section 5: Death and Re-Marriage

Concerning Edmund's widowhood and re-marriage

The first piece of evidence for a move to **Vernon Road** came via a certain 'Death Notice' on the eighth page of the **Saturday 6th October 1866** edition of the **Leeds Mercury.** Tersely expressed (even by the standards of a **Victorian** death notice) it read as follows: - *"SMITH – OCTOBER 4th. Helen, wife of Mr Edmund Smith, Commercial Traveller, Vernon Road, Leeds."* The 'Death Notice' seems to have said more about **Edmund** and his work than about his wife **Helen**. He seemed to be using the occasion of her death to advertise his business – this was hardly the most sensitive of responses!

The insertion of this notice in a Newspaper having **Liberal** sympathies suggested that, like most in his class, **Edmund** would have been a **Liberal** rather than a **Tory** Party supporter. After his experience of the civil disturbances in **Skipton,** he was most unlikely to have been a Radical. A review of Electoral Registers and 'Burgess Rolls' for **Leeds** (on **Wednesday, April 11th, 2001**) confirmed that my Great Grandfather was qualified to vote in **1861.** This was despite the stringent property qualifications which existed before the **1867 Reform Act**. Such information confirmed that, by the early **1860s,** he was already wealthy. These same sources also showed him moving to a new house in **1862** (from **8** to **27 Blenheim Place**) and finally to **Vernon Road** in **1865**. (Over **1861** until **1865** his name was incorrectly recorded as being *'Edward Smith.'*)

Decisive confirmation of this belief that my Great Grandfather was a *'Gladstone man'* came when I referred to the **1865** and **1868 Leeds Poll Book** (in **Leeds Central Lending Library** on **Monday, 1ˢᵗ October 2007**). These revealed that he consistently voted for **Liberal** Candidates like **Edward Baines** (of **Headingley Lodge**) and **Viscount Amberley** in the **1865** election and **Edward Baines** (again) and **Robert Meek Carter** (of **Woodhouse Lane**) in the **1868** election. (**The 1865 Leeds Poll Book p.83** and the **1868 edition p.77**). The introduction of the secret ballot in **1872** prevented any further record of his party loyalties but it's unlikely that they would have changed. His active voting behaviour suggests someone willing to keep abreast with the *'burning issues'* of his day. The **1868** poll book threw in the extra detail that **Edmund** had voted in the **West Ward Division, Number 1.** (Now covered by **Leeds University** area.)

A reading of **Lewis Apjohn's 1884** highly favourable biography of **Gladstone** (in **June 2016**) provided reasons over why **Edmund** may have taken **Gladstone** as a role model. The following quotation (taken from **p31-32**) showed that they shared many of the same values. In other words, this statesman was a man with whom my Great Grandfather could identify. **Gladstone** *"had brothers and children in business, working for their living; and many of the best qualities of his own mind are those which are wont to be engendered and strengthened by business habits. Scrupulous accuracy, in thought, word and deed; probity and integrity beyond reproach; conscientious fidelity in all things, coupled with shrewdness, industry and simple economy and aptitude for hard work – these are the marks of a commercial man in the highest rank of commercial life, and they are virtues which always distinguished the greatest statesman of our age."* In passing, it was possible to speculate whether **Edmund** had read this biography. As later evidence will demonstrate it was certainly the type of book he would have read. Like **Apjohn** he may have regarded **Gladstone's** rival **Benjamin Disraeli** as a disreputable adventurer.

Previously cited evidence showed that **Edmund's** move to **Vernon Road** also represented a move into brand new housing, built with the rising middle classes in mind. This suggested that **Edmund** was beginning to make his way up in the world. Another indication of his rise in the social sphere was his marriage to his second wife, **Rosamond,** in the **Anglican** Church of **Saint George's** in the centre of **Leeds.** Like most of his middle-class contemporaries, **Edmund** appeared willing to identify with the established Church the further up the social ladder he progressed. The certificate of his marriage to **Rosamond** provided the following details: -

Registration District <u>Leeds</u>
<u>1867</u> Marriage solemnised at <u>the Church</u> in the <u>parish of St George Leeds</u> in the <u>County of York</u>
1. When married? December 17th, 1867
2. Name and Surname: Edmund Smith, Rosamond Stamford
3. Age: 36, 24
4. Condition: Widower, Spinster
5. Rank or profession: Commercial Traveller
6 Residence at the time of marriage: Vernon Road, Vernon Road
7. Father's name and surname: John Smith, John Hazlewood Stamford
8. Rank or profession of father: Corn Miller, Farmer

Married in the <u>Parish Church according to the Rites and Ceremonies of the Established Church</u> by <u>licence</u> by me John Bloomfield.
The marriage was solemnised between us
<u>Edmund Smith</u>
<u>Rosamond Stamford</u>
In the presence of us
<u>Peter Palmer</u>
<u>Mary Palmer</u>

From this document, it was possible to elicit some very telling points. To begin with, **Edmund** had not spent a great deal of time in mourning the loss of his first wife. With marked determination, he had fixed his mind upon finding a replacement. This second match showed that he could act decisively in a crisis. Furthermore, he seemed to be going out of his way to marry someone who was a great deal younger than **Helen.** It was almost as if he was determined <u>not</u> to marry someone who was anything like his first wife. He also appears to have *'tested the waters,'* with **Rosamond** having lived at **Vernon Road** before he married her. Her rank was not noted down at all. She was neither a servant nor a governess, either of which would have provided the only respectable reasons for living at **Vernon Road** prior to her marriage. For the sake of delicacy, **John Bloomfield** did not press for the number of the Road. Presumably, he hoped to pass them off as next-door neighbours. Why was **Rosamond** living at the same address as the man who had married her aunt? Here two explanations suggest themselves – the *'innocent'* and the *'not so innocent.'* The *'innocent'* explanation would be that **Rosamond** had been sent by her parents to look after **Edmund's** surviving four children. If so, **John Stamford** and his wife had perhaps hoped that, once over the death, **Edmund** would marry **Rosamond** and thus someone connected to the family would at least bring up his children. In favour of this explanation is **Rosamond's** record as a *'carer'* for elderly **James Hastings.** She seems to have displayed the various practical qualities that **Edmund** would have found appealing. The actual location of the marriage in **Leeds** would have been simply due to convenience. In the depths of winter, it would have been far easier for the **Stamfords** to have travelled to **Leeds** with their grown children than for **Edmund** to have travelled to **Hull** with his young family – some of whom may have been in poor health. By marrying in **Leeds,** he was simply showing the practical side of his nature. Even so, for the sake of his future wife's reputation, one would have thought that he would have put her down as a *'governess.'* A curious *'I don't care what people think'* attitude appears to have been displayed here. For someone as fastidious and scrupulous as **Edmund,** it seems somewhat out of character. Here he is staking a lot on this marriage – even his business reputation.

The *'not so innocent'* explanation suggests that the marriage did not have the blessing of **Rosamond's** parents whose signatures did <u>not</u> appear on the Certificate. What may have taken place was a hurried elopement in which the female partner fled to **Leeds** and was married to her prospective suitor to whom she may well have formed an attachment. (Exactly where and when remained unknown.) **Edmund** must have been very charming and persuasive to have induced her to take such a step. What objection her parents may have had to this prospective match to an already highly successful businessman remains unknown – but perhaps word had got back to them concerning his uncaring treatment of **Helen.** Although there is little doubt that **Edmund** possessed the ruthlessness to have taken the *'not so innocent'* approach the balance of probability favours the more innocent explanation. One would have thought that a dramatic elopement would have left its mark in **Smith** family tradition. It had not.

On a somewhat *'naughty'* note, one wonders whether my Great Grandfather had enjoyed a physical relationship with my Great Grandmother before their marriage. *'Not proven'* would be the fairest verdict here. There is no trace of **Edmund** having fathered any illegitimate children. Also, **Edmund** would have been working all hours to have kept his family fed. What does seem most probable is that he may have held **Rosamond** in mind as a *'standby'* in the event of losing **Helen.** He would also have been keen to see how well **Rosamond** related to his children before making any formal proposal. Even so, it is not hard to imagine **Edmund,** within a year of **Helen's** death, receiving a stern note from his prospective father-in-law demanding that he *'make an honourable woman out of his daughter.'* The mid-winter timing of the marriage suggests that he may have been under some form of pressure to *'tie the knot'.* **Rosamond's** motives for consenting to this union are easier to fathom. Marriage to a successful businessman would have brought her status, continued contact with **Helen's** children and a social circle wider than that which she would have enjoyed in her own home village. Besides, her only alternative was an ignominious return to **Burton Pidsea** as an embittered old maid with a tarnished reputation. Even marriage to a difficult man like **Edmund** would have been better than that!

One further question worth exploring is whether, in true **Victorian** fashion, **Helen,** when nearing her death, had *'bequeathed to'* **Rosamond** both **Edmund** and her children. Such a custom was by no means unknown, but any such bequest must have taken place at an earlier stage; **Helen's** *'Death Certificate'* having showed that her end had come very quickly. However, **Helen** may have felt that she was not going to survive this pregnancy, so a bequest does not lie beyond the bounds of possibility. In some ways, **Rosamond** was a natural successor who would acquire a reputation for keeping a *'good house.'* If such a request had been made, its effect was to leave his family in very capable hands. Perhaps the **Smiths** are what they are today because of a long-forgotten decision made by an unappreciated woman.

A particularly noteworthy feature was the way in which his marriage to **Rosamond** was as near as possible to the tenth anniversary of his marriage to **Helen.** One wonders whether he was trying to blot out the memory of that first event by superimposing this second, happier marriage. His action was that of a man wishing to make a *'clean break'* with an unhappy past. He may have felt the need for a completely fresh start. Alternatively, he may have delayed the wedding just after this anniversary out of a sense of respect for the memory of his first wife and out of consideration for the feelings of her children.

A final unusual feature was the claim (transmitted through usually reliable family tradition) that **Rosamond** had come from a home called **Stamford Manor.** Neither Census Returns nor large-scale Ordnance Survey Maps (kindly provided by **Hull Central Library** on **Wednesday, April 19th, 2000**) revealed any such Manor. Moreover, two living members of the **Stamford** family (one with an interest in his own family history) expressly denied the existence of any such dwelling. Significantly, there were large *'manor type'* dwellings near the Millwrights where **Rosamond** had once lived. Perhaps this is where **Edmund** had derived the idea of a **Stamford Manor.** If this was the case, he may have first visited the village when courting **Helen** during the **1850s.** (A likely motive for visiting such a remote place would have been a desire to settle the dowry arrangements with her father **James.** It remains unlikely that anything else would have attracted him here. **Edmund** was a man for the city, not the countryside.)

Section 6: A Man to be Feared

Concerning a patriarchal Middle-Class Victorian family

My Grandfather **Frank** was the second son of the marriage to **Rosamond.** The Register of Births, Deaths, and Marriages duly recorded details of his arrival. These are set out below: -
Registration District Leeds
1869 Birth in the district of West Leeds in the County of York
1. When and where born: Twenty-Third Sept. (1869)
2. Name if Any: Fred Heselwood
3. Sex: Male
4. Name and Surname of Father: Edmund Smith
5. Name and Surname of Mother: Rosamond Smith, formerly Stamford
6. Occupation of Father: Commercial Traveller
7. Signature, description and residence of informant: Edmund Smith, Father, Hastings Place, Vernon Road
8. When registered: First November 1869
9. Signature of registrar: Gilbert Jackson

The **Census** held on **Sunday, 2nd April 1871** revealed that **Edmund Smith's** occupation was that of a *'Commercial Traveller in Drapery.'* This meant that he would have sold colourful fashionable items to small shopkeepers. An ability to keep abreast of the latest market trends would have been required. The **Census** contained the following list of people living at **16 Vernon Road: -**
Edmund Smith aged **39**
Rosamund Smith aged **27 Burton Pidsea** in **Holderness**
James Smith aged **12**

Betsey aged **11**
Ann (or Annie) aged **9**
Arthur aged **8**
Ernest aged **2**
<u>**Fred Hesselwood**</u> (*'Frank'*) aged **1**
Annie Pease aged **18** – domestic servant
Elizabeth Ainsworth aged **18** – domestic servant
(By then, the population of **Leeds** had climbed to **259,212** Incidentally, one wonders whether his second son had been named after King **Arthur**; interest in this legendary king had been fashionable at the time of his birth in **1863**.)

Aged less than forty, **Edmund's** business dealings had prospered sufficiently for him to have been able to afford to either buy or rent a new house in a respectable area of **Leeds**. He was able to pay at least two full-time servants to help run it. He would also have had to pay for the funeral expenses of **Helen** (his first wife) who'd died in childbirth along with their stillborn child in **October 1866**. **Betsey** seems to have been named after the first wife of his first-father-in-law the farmer **James Hastings**. **Ann** may have been named after **James'** second wife or **Edmund's** own mother. The use of these names perhaps represented an attempt by **Edmund** to please the man who may have given a very generous wedding dowry. Following **Betsey** and **Ann,** the children's names begin to become more grandiose – as if **Edmund** was announcing his arrival into the middle classes. *'Hesselwood'* derived from the middle name of **Rosamund's** father **John Hesselwood Stamford.**

One strange feature was the failure by **Edmund** to have named any of his children after his own siblings. There were <u>no</u> **Samuels, Daniels** or **Susannahs.** It seems as if he didn't want those names to be preserved in his family. Much time could be wasted endlessly speculating as to why this was, but the strong implication remains that he had <u>not</u> parted from his siblings on amicable terms. There appear to be faint traces of an old grudge. **Edmund** is snubbing his own kinsfolk and choosing to identify with the families of his two wives. Could there have been some quarrelling over money and legacies? This could possibly explain why, later in life, **Edmund** was to become so determined to prevent a similar *'fall out'* amongst his own children.

On **Wednesday, January 18th, 1871,** following the defeat of **France** in the **Franco-Prussian War,** the **Prussian** Statesman **Otto von Bismarck (1815-1898)** had *'stage-managed'* the inauguration of the **German Empire** in the Hall of **Versailles.** This was to set in motion a whole train of events which would impact strongly upon a future generation of **Smiths**. It is not known to what degree **Edmund** was aware of the wider affairs of his time. Perhaps he was too involved in his work to have given much thought to anything else.

Vernon Road was a little distance from the **Blenheim** area of **Leeds** which, at that time, was quite affluent. This meant that my Grandfather **Frank** had (in material terms at least) a relatively comfortable childhood. However, at the emotional level, this may not have been the case – especially in relation to his father. He is said to have divulged to his eldest son **Stewart** that, as a parent, **Edmund** had been *"a martinet, a man to be feared."* In family legend **Edmund** had gained the reputation of being a **Victorian** despot – one who expected to be obeyed; he very much the *'head of the house,'* even to having his slippers warmed by the fire! Reputedly God-fearing, **Edmund** was said to have been actively involved in **Blenheim Baptist Church** that had been founded in **1848**. (It was a congregation that was highly influential in **Baptist** circles.) Family members were said to have taken their faith seriously and to have received full baptism as adults. In those days, church attendance almost always led to membership. It moved to its present location in **1870**. (The former church building had needed to make way for the construction of the **Leeds General Infirmary,** itself having moved from **Park Place** to this new site.) It was a Church known to attract middle-class shopkeepers and business people. Its move to the **Blenheim** area would suggest that the building was following its prospering congregation into the new suburbs of **Leeds**. Its new location was only several minutes' walk from **Vernon Road.** A photograph of a Church summer outing to an unknown destination in around **1900** confirmed the impression of propriety. Despite being a time of relative relaxation, both the men and the women wore the formal attire of the middle, rather than the working classes. Their careworn faces were full of that rather prim respectability common at that time and there were few, if any, smiles on that photograph. Indeed, their expressions seemed as bleak as the moors upon which they stood.

Section 7: A Mysterious Absence

Concerning Edmund's absence from the churches of Leeds

Surprisingly, a review of **Blenheim Baptist Church's** painstakingly thorough archives (on **Tuesday 30th November 1999**) <u>failed</u> to confirm any link with the **Smiths**. There was no trace of **Edmund Smith** – nor of his increasingly large and sprawling family – <u>on any membership roll or in any other type of document.</u> From these rolls, it was ascertained that a certain **James Smith** had become a member by a profession of faith in **October 1877,** but then he vanishes from the scene. He seemed to have been from outside the area. Moreover, an **Annie Smith** (later **Dawson**) was received into membership in **October 1878.** She was still there until her death on **15th July 1916.** However, her marriage and the date of her death ruled her out from being **Edmund's** daughter.

A **Maud Smith,** who came into membership from Sunday School in **1896,** was too young to have been the **Maud Smith** of **Edmund's** family. Furthermore, one would have expected **Edmund** – of all people – to have left a lasting impression (albeit even a negative one) if he had attended **Blenheim Church.** Of the alternative **Baptist** venues, **South Parade Baptist Church** was too far away for a household that included young children whilst **Burley Baptist** was mainly for the working classes – hardly congenial company for a man of **Edmund's** social aspirations. Present was a tantalizing mystery. Up to five factors pointed strongly to a nineteenth-century link with **Blenheim,** yet when a thorough search was made of the available records nothing whatsoever was found. If not **Blenheim Baptist Church,** then where else did the **Smiths** attend? Alternatively, if they did not attend Church what else would a crowded household have done on a **Victorian** Sunday and how would they have managed to receive interment at the **Baptist** Cemetery at **Sutton?** The most likely answer is that a connection did exist with the **Baptists** but that it was with the more sectarian **Strict Baptists** – whose Assemblies did not tend to be as long enduring as those of the mainline **Baptists.** Even so, their absence from **Blenheim** does remain something of a mystery. It was the dog that did not bark in the night.

An extremely thorough search of the Records (belonging to both **Anglican** and **Nonconformist** Churches) at **Leeds Archive Centre** on **Friday, April 28th, 2000** also drew a complete blank. Even the baptismal records of **Saint George's** (where he married **Rosamond**) did not reveal anything. There was no trace of either **Edmund** or his family. His absence from very detailed **Anglican** documentation infers that he had no regular involvement with the **Church of England** (except for marital reasons). By this stage, it became clear that a whole pack of dogs was not barking. On **Friday, October 27th, 2000** a review of **Anglican** Baptismal records at **Colne Library** confirmed that **Edmund** never had any of his children Christened in the **Church of England.** What religious sympathies he did possess seemed to have lain with the Dissenters. Also, having failed to reveal anything was a thorough review of the membership lists of the main **Masonic Lodges** in **Leeds.** (This last review took place at the **Yorkshire Archaeological Association** on **Wednesday, June 19th, 2002.**)

Section 8: Commercial Contacts

Concerning the Clothing Manufacturer *'Stewart and Macdonald'*

The Trade Directory of **1872** shed further light on **Edmund's** business activities. This time he was on record as having been *'an agent for **Stewart** and **Macdonald,** Warehousemen.'* His address was given as *'**Hastings Place'** 16* **Vernon Road.** Such *'agency work'* may explain the presence of the warehouseman **Joseph Hodgson** in the **1861 Census.** The name **Hastings** is also telling. Its use conveyed the (possibly false) impression of someone who was still deeply attached to the memory of his first wife. Moreover, *'**Hastings Place'*** did sound rather grander than plain *'16 Vernon Road.'* In **1876,** his occupation was again listed simply as that of *'Commercial Traveller.'* The name *'**Stewart and Macdonald'*** drops out of the picture only to resurface later in an unexpected context.

Trade Directories, newspaper notices and family tradition alike confirm that **Stewart and Macdonald** were a **Glasgow-based** clothing manufacturer. In **1872,** this company operated from **Springfield House, Wellington Street, Leeds.** By **1881** it had moved to **Quebec Street** and was known to have had another branch in **Manchester.** It was at **31 Saint Paul Street** in **1894** when a certain **William Lawson** was a manager. The last known **Leeds** address was at **Victoria House** on **40 Park Lane,** adjacent to the tramway running to and from the newly expanding suburbs. The final year in which it appeared in any Trade Directory was **1921** after which it vanished. Family tradition (relayed by my mother) indicates that this Company went bankrupt after the **1914-18** war. In some sources, the last name of the Company was spelt as *'**McDonald'*** with the *'and'* or *'&'* between the two names having been dropped. (The more common name of *'**Macdonald'*** is used throughout this research.)

Further light on **Stewart & MacDonald** was shed in a letter received from **Glasgow City Archives** on Saturday, **6th May 2000.** It provided the following details about the Company: *"...The above firm appears in the Post Office Directories for Glasgow from **1830** or earlier until **1922.** It appears in the directory for **1922,** but not **1923,** and it presumably ceased trading about then. In the early years, they are described as retail warehousemen, but with various addresses in the city centre. In **1893,** they are described as warehousemen and manufacturers. As well as several addresses in the city centre, they had* *an address on the south side of the city at 187 **Rutherglen Road,** which was probably a factory. They also had a factory in **Strabane,** and what is referred to as the Ready-made Factory in **Park Lane, Leeds.** "*

A telephone conversation with a representative from the Archive Department confirmed that **Stewart & MacDonald** had been a large Firm, having representatives operating over the whole of the country. Some of its offices in **Glasgow City Centre** appear to have been rather grand. Unfortunately, its records do not seem to have been preserved in either the **City Archive Department** or at **Glasgow University** (whose records of past businesses seemed to date back only to the early **1960s**). Attempts to use the Internet to find its records in other archives also proved unavailing.

Further details concerning this Company only came to light with the publication (on **September 20th, 2000**) of **Honeyman's** *'Well Suited: History of the **Leeds** Clothing industry from **1850** until **1890**.'* (I first noticed it during a visit to **Waterstones Bookshop, Albion Street, Leeds** on **Monday, 18th December 2000.**) From this source, it emerged that the Company was a Clothing Wholesaler, which had a factory built at **40 Park Lane** during **1888** or **1889.** **(Ward p.379** confirmed that it was housed in property purchased from a **William Emsley,** solicitors.) At the same time, it owned what seemed to have been office premises at **31 Paul Street.** This expansion meant that by **1890, Stewart & MacDonald** had employed over **2,000** people in **Leeds.** (Along with the clothing manufacturer **J. Hepworth, Stewart & MacDonald** was the largest employer in the city.) It was clearly a major undertaking. Using surveyor documents as a source, **Ward p.379** confirmed that, in **1914,** the buildings were valued at £**12,177,** machinery at £**2,497** and **1,129** square yards of land at £**1,080.** During the First World War, a flood of government orders for clothing for the armed services brought the Company even more prosperity. However, in **1921** troublesome times following the end of a post-war boom, forced the company to merge with **J.** and **W. Campbell** and close its **Park Lane Plant.** Production was concentrated at works located at **36** and **38 Ingrams Road** in the **Holbeck** area of **South Leeds.** As *'Campbells & Stewart & MacDonald'* the firm lasted until the **1960s.** In about **1945,** it had moved to a smaller manufacturing plant on **Burley Road, Leeds.** Like many textile firms a mixture of foreign competition and a managerial failure to invest – either in people or new machinery – led to its eventual decline in the early **1960s.** Failure to adapt to change meant that the clothing giants of the nineteenth and early twentieth centuries ended their days as industrial dinosaurs. This latest information also confirmed that no records of this merged Company appear to have survived, presumably having been destroyed following its closure in the **1960s.** It was striking to discover how the many documents once produced by a large and thriving business organization could so quickly vanish into the mists of History.

From the **Leeds** Clothing Directory of **1881,** an interesting sidelight is given on **Edmund's** social aspirations. On the **Census Return,** his occupation is described as that of *'a Commercial Traveller in woollen goods.'* However, in a Trade Directory, he described himself as *'a manager'* (possibly of other travellers). The picture conveyed here is of a man fiercely protective of his *'respectable'* position in the **Victorian** class system of the day. Family tradition (usually reliable) states that **Edmund** did have an office at **4 Briggate.** It was reputedly known as *"Edmund Smith, Wool Merchant."* However, a review of many Trade Directories failed to confirm the existence of such an office. If it ever existed, it must have been on **Briggate** for only a very brief period– something less than two years. Yet, as was often the case with **Edmund's** exaggerations, there appeared to be some basis in fact. An advert on **p. 164** of the **1926 Leeds Tercentenary Handbook** revealed the presence of a major Draper in **Briggate** (founded in **1886**) which was called **'Smith Brothers.'** It seemed likely that my Great Grandfather had had some involvement with it. If he was a shareholder, then this could have formed the basis of his claim to have had premises in **Briggate.** The advert will now be quoted in full to reveal some details about the nature of this business: -

SMITH BROS.

(DRAPERS) LTD.,

Noted for the past 40 Years for
Dependable Goods at Reasonable

♣   ♣   Prices   ♣   ♣

DRESS FABRICS & SILKS

HOUSEHOLD & LINENS

FURNISHING FABRICS

CARPETS & LINOLEUMS

LADIES & CHILDRENS
DRESSES & COSTUMES

GLOVES, HOSIERY & FANCY GOODS.

LIFT TO ALL FLOORS, CAFÉ, RESTAURANT.

**98 to 103 Briggate and
County Arcade, LEEDS.**

Telephone 20367 (2 lines)

Although factual in nature, this advert did try to convey the image of a well-established Company, offering a good service at a reasonable price. Its connection to my own family, if any, has remained a matter of speculation. However, it did represent the type of business to which both my Great Grandfather and Grandfather would have endeavoured to sell goods.

Also (dating from **1881**) was some visual information provided in a very striking painting of **Boar Lane** by the **Leeds** artist **John Atkinson Grimshaw (1836-1893)**. Entitled *"Boar Lane, Leeds"* it vividly portrayed the many shops in that thoroughfare. The sky is a smoggy fading yellow, dimly lit gas lamps show that night is already falling, and the pedestrians are depicted as silhouettes walking past brightly-lit shop interiors. Some appear to be idly window-shopping whilst others wait on street corners. Their severely distorted reflections can be seen stretched out across the muddy pavements and cobblestones of a wide roadway, up which one horse-drawn cab is travelling. On the left side of the street (in the middle distance) stands a four-storied building. In bold lettering, above the second floor, are the words *'MEN'S TWEED.'* This represents just the type of business with which **Edmund** will have done business. The picture was of sufficient quality to provide fresh insight into the Commercial World of my Great Grandfather – you could almost sense the atmosphere tills ringing, rolls of cloth unfolded for the perusal of the customer … a faraway world together.

Section 9: A Crowded Household

Concerning a middle-class Victorian household

From the **April 1881** Census Return, it was apparent that **Edmund** and **Rosamond** had come to preside over a very crowded household – one that would have encouraged the rapid spread of any infectious disease amongst the children. By then there were five sons and four daughters – the youngest being a baby of five months. The **Census Return** provided the following list for **Sunday, 3rd April 1881**: -

Edmond aged **49**
Rosamond aged **37**
James aged **22**
Betsey aged **21**
Annie aged **19**
Arthur aged **18**
Ernest aged **12**
Fred Heselwood (*'Frank'*) aged **11**
Maud aged **8**
Hedley aged **2**
Florence aged **5 months,**
Priscilla Martin aged **18** *'domestic servant'*
May Walker aged **16** – *domestic servant* **Rothwell**
(A mining village South of **Leeds**)
(By then, the population of **Leeds** had climbed to **309,119**)
Poor handwriting by the **Census** clerk led to some confusion in the spelling of the names. (In this account, any discrepancies are recorded rather than reconciled.) There is also the possibility that the spelling of names may have changed over time. Also emerging is a possible tendency to grandiosity. Both heads of the household preferred to use the more refined *"ond"* ending to their name.

Details (provided by the **1881 Census**) added further weight to the impression that this was <u>not</u> a household living at the sharp end of **Victorian** poverty. Fear of being *'carted off'* to the Workhouse would not have been present (except possibly in **Edmund's** mind). It is easy to imagine the domestic servants being rather buxom **Yorkshire** *'lasses'* with something of a sullen demeanour. They most probably would not have been *'taken on'* unless they'd been deemed to have been in reasonably good health. **Rosamond** would have had the duty of chivvying the servants when exhaustion would have made them somewhat slow in their daily tasks. The amount of work they would have had to cope with must have been vast. The washing and drying of the heavy clothes of the period would itself have involved a considerable amount of labour.

Confirming this impression of wealth, was a photograph of my Great Grandmother **Rosamond** from around this period. Taken in **June 1882** at the luxurious **Sarony Studios, Alfred Street, Scarborough** it beautifully portrayed her. The most striking feature was her motherly appearance. One can see why **Edmund** would have chosen **Rosamond** to look after the children. She had an air of no-nonsense, down-to-earth common sense about her. Underneath her cap lay a mane of fairish curly hair. Her face was plump as was her build. Noticeable was a resemblance to her Aunt **Helen.** Her dress was ornate, as was a lace *'wrapper'* that filled the cleavage between two very ample breasts. A whole array of buttons adorned the front of what appeared to have been an early bustle whose sleeves ended in a lace pattern. Clasped her hands, was what seems to have been a small fur-lined parasol, whose tip lay just above a locket – itself attached to her dress by a chain. Her right-hand rests against a studio pillar. The impression gained here was of **Edmund** trying to make a *'lady'* out of what was essentially an ordinary farm woman. In **Yorkshire, Rosamond** will have been known as a *'strapping lass'* most attractive for childbearing purposes.

Old maps of the area showed that **Vernon Road** ran straight up to **Hilary Place** (where the Department of Education at **Leeds University** is now sited.) Number **16 (**or **18)** was located on the left side of the road, four doorways up from the **Leeds Church Middle-Class Board School** (present in the **1870s** and **80s** its building now a **University Department**). It had both a front and a small back garden. Tea on the lawn would have been a possibility. At **2 Vernon Road** dwelt a certain **Dr Ernest Robson,** *'Surgeon'* whose house also doubled as the surgery which was run in partnership with a **Dr Hall.** They would have made convenient Doctors for the **Smith** household. Below, at **4 Vernon Road,** was **Mr Snell,** a Cloth Merchant, at **6 Vernon Road Mrs Hannah Pollard** – most likely a widow. At **8 Vernon Road** was **Mr John Fletcher,** occupation undisclosed. At **10 Vernon Road** was **Thomas F. Glover** a Yarn Buyer, at **12 Vernon Road Mrs May Wilcock** who had the interesting occupation of Waste Dealer. Above **20 Vernon Road,** was **Mr Dalton** a Draper and at **22 Vernon Road** there dwelt a certain **John Halford,** occupation unknown. Other representatives of the Clothing Trade also dwelt on the other side of the road. The area was solidly middle-class. It was perhaps a world away from the tumbledown slums of **Hunslet** or the **Leylands. Victorian Britain** was indeed two nations. By the middle of **1964,** most of **Vernon Road** had been demolished to make way for some modern buildings on the expanding campus of **Leeds University.** My brother remembered seeing red brick **Victorian** houses being pulled down as he'd walked home from a temporary summer job at **Leeds General Infirmary.** Confirming his story was a leaflet promoting *'The University Archive'* found on a table outside the **Brotherton Library** at **Leeds University** on **Monday, 1st November 1999.** It displayed a photograph showing that the area had indeed been demolished by **June 1964.** The old family house had stood for about **99** years. After the Second World War **Edmund's** old house had supposedly been used as a Domestic Science Library for a certain school (name unknown). Immediately prior to its demolition, it had been found to have been divided into six flats – one of them situated in the basement. Such a division provided final confirmation that the house had been three stories high. It must have been a somewhat grand establishment in its day. Its use as a library is quite probable as various Directories show no one in residence until the **1950s** – but its size suggests that if it was used as a library it most probably covered more subjects than Domestic Science alone.

Except for **Edmund's** residence, the most interesting household of the **1881 Census** was **2 Vernon Road.** Living there were: -
Doctor Arthur N. M. Robson aged **28,** Surgeon, born in **Filey**
Robert Robson (brother) aged **15,** articled to what seemed to have been an architect, also born in **Filey**
John Dacre aged **19,** Medical Student, born in **Bradford**
Mary Baines aged **33,** widow and cook from **Sheffield**
John [Cammenridge] Aged **18,** a groom from **Filey**
Name illegible aged **16**, house or nursemaid from **Leeds**
Despite atrocious legibility, the Census Return did not disguise the fact that **2 Vernon Road** was a highly affluent household. A record has been made of it because other records would later show that both a **Doctor Hall** and **Dr Robson** were to visit **16 Vernon Road** on a professional basis. Sadly, **Edmund** would have known their faces all too well.

Section 10: A Sprawling Victorian Family

Concerning a middle-class Victorian family

Records provided by **Leeds Grammar School (L.G.S.)** have made it possible to reconstruct something of **Fred Heselwood's** own boyhood. Known as **'Frank'** in **'The Leeds Grammar School Admission Book'** his address was given as **16 Vernon Road**. What little remains of the road is sited on the campus of **Leeds University**. On **Wednesday 15th September 1999,** whilst using some of the remaining old buildings as a reference point I ascertained that **Vernon Road** would have run straight under the **Edward Stoner** building which during the late **1990s** housed the *'Computer Cluster'* of the Education Department. I had worked in this very building myself whilst completing a Post Graduate teacher-training course during the **1997/98** academic year. Amazingly, it was also the location where my eldest son had undertaken his school work-placement in **July 1998.** Hence, we had been no more than a couple of minutes' walk from where **No. 16 Vernon Road** would once have stood. Indeed, it very probably the site I worked in was where the old house itself had once stood! To find that five generations of **Smiths** had been closely involved in just that one site was an uncanny experience. No wonder I had *'felt at home'* there, at times spending up to thirteen hours acquiring new computing skills or fine-tuning some academic work! It was there that I discovered something called the Internet (or the World Wide Web) which was to greatly aid in the publication of this material. So, even the site of the old family house had been greatly used in the cause of education.

At first, attempts to obtain photographs of **Vernon Road** were unavailing. A temporary move of premises by **Leeds Central Library** into the neighbouring **Town Hall** during much of the first half of **2000** ensured that no good photographs could be found in the Local History section. There also appeared to have been little chance of finding anyone who had lived in that street. However, in yet another of those amazing coincidences (such a marked feature of this study) my wife, at her local **United Reformed** church, met a lady who had once lived at **21 Vernon Road** during the late **1950s** and early **1960s.** She kindly provided me with three black and white photographs of the street – mainly depicting her home at that time. She also spoke of her memories of the interior of her house (relayed to me during a telephone conversation (held from **10.25** until **11.00PM** on **Monday** on **23rd October 2000**). This contact made it very clear that, during her stay in **Vernon Road,** both the interior and exterior of the house had been left largely unchanged from **Victorian** times. She also recalled that all the houses were of the same design; one of her photographs confirming this point. I used her photographs as a basis to describe the exterior of **Edmund's** house whilst accurately surmising that the furniture would have been that of a prosperous middle-class household. In the words of my informant, *"These houses were built for rich people."*

Around **1885,** anyone walking up the left-hand side of **Vernon Road,** away from **Leeds City Centre,** would have spotted the tall thin spire of a Congregational Church. Its pale stonework would, even then, have been rapidly turning into a sooty black. The road surface itself would have consisted of greying cobblestones made uneven by wear and tear from horse-drawn vehicles. (There cobblestones will have helped horses to be more sure-footed in icy weather.) During the **Victorian** era, the most common mode of transport would have been the horse and cart, used to carry sacks of coal or clumps of scrap metal (given to the *'rag and bone man.'*) It would have been quickly apparent that these red brick terraced houses belonged to rich people so that house calls by tradesmen (desperate to sell their services or their wares) would have been frequent. On Sundays, a deathly quiet will have characterised the street, the silence was broken only by the chiming of church bells or the muted movement of families on their way to Church, all dressed in their *'Sunday best.'* Perhaps the most striking feature of the house where **Edmund** lived were the large bay windows at both the basement and ground levels. Equally striking will have been the triangular stone mantel and ornate cornice stone pillars, each standing astride the large wood panelled front door, complete with its own brass knocker. A knee-high brick wall capped by curved and blackened sandstone slabs would have enclosed a tiny front garden. However, ornate iron railings pointing up from the wall will have given the house a fortress-like effect. Further reinforcing any privacy was the tall hedges dividing one garden from another. Once through the gate, it would have been necessary to walk along a paved path and then several well-worn steps to reach the front door. Beneath the steps lay the coal cellar – with its square iron hatch through which coal was poured. An inside cellar door would have allowed the servants to come in and gather the coal.

Should an honoured guest have arrived **Edmund** himself will have made a point of greeting such a person, politely placing their outdoor wear upon the hat stand. Dressed in his best attire he will have made a good impression. Here was a man to be reckoned with – someone of substance. After placing their outdoor clothing on the hat stand, the guest will have quickly noticed the long cornice hallway with its mosaic-tiled floor adding a pleasing red, blue and green splatter effect. Brightening up the walls of the hall were colourful pictures of country wildlife scenes interspersed with the occasional family portrait. Such artwork would have added to the impression that there was a family which had safely arrived in the middle classes. The guest will have been politely ushered into a large living room with its white marble fireplace and clutter of mahogany furniture. Thick curtains, when drawn, would have provided a degree of privacy from the road. On and above the mantelpiece were more family pictures – some of the children who were no longer alive. (It is unlikely that there would have been any pictures of any relations from **Sutton.**) Such keepsakes would stand between ornate vases and possibly the odd stuffed animal enclosed in a glass case, its snarling expression barely picked out by the dim lighting. Positioned at the centre of the mantelpiece would have been an ornate ticking clock whose ringing chimes would mark the passing of every hour. A maid, bringing in a pot of tea (in delicate chinaware) would have broken any silence and quietly added to the genteel appearance that **Edmund** would have wished to convey. A few quiet words from the maid to the *'master of the house'* – **Edmund** – would have signalled that the meal was ready. **Edmund** would then have ushered the visitor back across the hall and into the dining room opposite. Here would be another ornate fireplace – but this time of black marble. The most imposing feature would have been the mahogany table covered by a lace-fringed tablecloth and a neat array of silverware and trinkets – some of it homemade. From the nearby pantry, a maid would bring in the food, which, more likely than not, would have consisted of such traditional English fare as roast beef and Yorkshire pudding. A special treat would have been the homemade cakes baked by **Rosamond** and **Betsey,** which will have served as *'afters.'* Although the food will have been excellent the conversation may possibly have been stilted. **Edmund** will have talked at length about business matters, but three subjects may well have been *'taboo'* for him – namely religion, politics and anything to do with his own past life in **Sutton** or **Skipton.** The dissension brought about by such subjects would have seriously risked spoiling the genteel atmosphere that both **Edmund** and **Rosamond** were keen to cultivate. Both were reputed to like only *'nicely mannered people'* – taking care not to slurp their soup or chew too noisily over the meat. If a guest was a young (or even middle-aged) single man of respectable and wealthy pedigree, he would probably have found himself seated opposite one of their daughters whom they were keen to see married. Care would have been taken to ensure that she was dressed in her very best finery. Meanwhile, a governess or maid would keep the younger children safely away upstairs to avoid embarrassment. They would be neither seen nor heard. In contrast to her husband (and any other family members gathered around the table) **Rosamond** herself would already have been looking thin and drawn, the pallor of her complexion warning that she did not have much time left in this world. Also, it seemed to be **Betsey** who chivvied the maids as if she was already getting ready to stand in the place of her mother. Once the meal was over, the men may have retired to the drawing room to smoke those cigars that **Edmund** would offer from his silver-plated cigar case. The ladies joined them only after these cigars had been smoked, as during this time the men would have wished to enjoy, what in **Yorkshire** is called a good *'cow,'* (gossip).

Any guests would not be expected to roam around the house – a most impolite thing to do. Those personally shown around would have found it divided into neatly partitioned areas. Downstairs was the basement where **Rosamond** and her servants washed the clothes. Also, in this cellar were a substantial number of cupboards used for storage purposes. There would have also been a wooden door leading to a coal bunker underneath the outside steps. It was in the basement that most of the washing would be hung out to dry. Any attempt to try and accomplish this task outside in the garden would have incurred the risk of grime from the lung-choking smog that afflicted the area. Also, such a practice was most vulgar. Only the working classes hung out their washing for everyone to see. Especially in wet weather, the basement will have been a very damp environment in which to work. It would not have been a healthy place for a lady such as **Rosamond** whose body had already been weakened by a succession of pregnancies.

Upstairs on the first floor were three large bedrooms and a bathroom. Facing **Vernon Road** itself was the master bedroom where **Edmund** and **Rosamond** slept. The other two bedrooms were for the older sons and daughters. **Betsey,** the eldest daughter, shared one room with her sister **Anne.** At one point, **James** shared a room with his younger brother **Arthur,** although by **1885 James** had already married and left home. All the bedrooms contained a wardrobe, chest of drawers and a large mirror, with the addition of an ornate jewellery case in the girls' bedroom. The beds themselves each consisted of a metal bedstead frame on top of which lay a feather mattress and pillows, with brass-knobbed bed heads. The beds may well have made a creaking sound as one lay upon them.

On the very top floor were two attic bedrooms with sloping roofs and rectangular skylights containing four square panes of glass. These rooms were for the younger boys and girls. Their floors may well have been dotted about with lead toy soldiers in the boys' room and china dolls in the less untidy girls' room. It was possibly in these rooms that those little ones who did not survive infancy had died. A wet nurse would also have used these rooms to nurse any infants as **Edmund** would probably have been most unwilling to share his master bedroom with any crying baby – after all that would have prevented him from having a *'clear head'* to manage his business dealings! It simply wouldn't do!

Even though some of the above details may not be wholly correct, the general picture to emerge is one of **Victorian** affluence. **Edmund** had ensured that his family had gained a respectable position in society. Nevertheless, thought must be given to the woman in charge of this dwelling. Despite the presence of servants, it could not have been an easy household to manage and the considerable number of children would have ensured very little privacy. Hardly surprisingly, at least two wives failed to live into ripe old age. Placing **Edmund's** slippers by the coal fire would have been the least of their worries.

Other surviving buildings from the same period (as **Vernon Road**) reinforced the impression that the area in which my Grandfather **Frank** had lived once basked under the high noon of mid-to-late **Victorian** prosperity. Tracing the most likely route that **Frank** will have taken to the **Leeds Grammar School** was not difficult. He would have walked up **Vernon Road**, turned left in front of the old Coach House, just before **Hilary Place,** and walked up towards the **L.G.S.** To his right lay the neo-gothic buildings of the **Yorkshire College of Science** (now part of **Leeds University**) whose foundation can be dated to **1874.** On his left loomed the ornate gold-leafed dome of the wealthy Presbyterian Church at **Cavendish Road.** As he made his way to school he would have passed several streets like similar in design to **Vernon Road.** If hurrying, he could have found himself in the Cathedral-like building of L.G.S within several minutes. Standing opposite to **Woodhouse Moor,** this building had been established on that site since **1859,** probably with an obvious view to gaining the sons of the aspiring middle classes. Ironically, its move away from the site in **1997** to the outer suburb of **Alwoodly, Leeds,** appears to have been motivated by almost the same considerations. **L.G.S.** thus demonstrated that, over the course of decades, the fundamental motives governing the behaviour of such an institution remain largely unchanged, despite vast alterations in the society surrounding it. Headmasters may come and go, but the factors influencing their decision-making often remain the same. Likely as not they wearied successive generations of parents with appeals for money, as they still seem to do today.

Section 11: Links to the Leeds Jewish Community

Concerning the Jews of Leeds

Whilst young **Frank** was engrossed in his schoolboy routine, events in **Tsarist Russia** were taking place that was to influence his own life and that of his descendants until the third or fourth generation. They would also lead to an unexpected influx of new pupils for **L.G.S.** The assassination of **Tsar Alexander II** by **Russian** revolutionaries in **1881** triggered large-scale pogroms against the **Jewish Community.** In **Kiev,** the situation was especially bad. Soldiers wearing spiked helmets or **French** style caps looked on smiling, as members of the **Jewish Community** were dragged through the streets by a violent mob and horribly slaughtered. Hardly surprisingly many in that community fled to the *'golden land'* of **America** and the *'silver land'* of **England.** (Some refugees landed in **Hull** believing that they had reached **New York!**) From **Hull** and other **East Coast** Ports, it was only a short journey to **Leeds.** Up to that period, the **Jewish Community** in **Leeds** had been small but, *'well to do'* and sufficiently assimilated to have enjoyed Christmas pudding (but not Christmas trees) during the festive season, **(Douglas Charing, pp.130-131).** The arrival of their strictly **Orthodox,** non-English speaking (and usually penniless) compatriots from the **East** filled them with horror. Not only did they represent a financial drain, their presence threatened to stoke up the fires of **anti-Semitism** in this country too. Happily, such fears did not consider the enterprise and industry of twice new arrivals. Crowded into the fetid slum area of the **Leylands,** this pogrom-ravaged community began to work its way up the social ladder through a mixture of business enterprise and educational attainment. Contemporary maps showed that the **Leylands** consisted of a dense cluster of back-to-back houses, offering only one third to one half of the space enjoyed by families on **Vernon Road**. The **1891** Census Return revealed that the average amount of people per household stood at **4.77,** higher than the **East End of London**. Only **5.3%** of the community were aged **45+**. In contrast, **43%** were aged **15** or under – offering a picture of a young dynamic community. Such dynamism was urgently needed because the conditions must have been indescribably squalid and many a child will have died young. One man forging his way out of such terrible conditions was a certain entrepreneur called **Joseph Gillinson**. There is no trace of the name *'Gillinson'* in the list of **Jewish** names provided by **Freedman (1995)** from the **1891 Census**. This **Anglicisation** also indicated that **Joseph** had wished to integrate with his host community from an early stage. It is unclear whether **Joseph** himself was a first or second-generation migrant. He certainly displayed an immigrant's desire to *'blend into'* and *'move up'* society. In time, **Joseph Gillinson** was to exercise a hugely formative influence over my father's own life. A lot more will be said about this extraordinary man in late chapters.

The growth of the **Jewish Community** in **Leeds** is charted in the Census Returns tabulated by **Freedman**. In **1841** the number of Jewish people in **Leeds** was **56,** in **1851** it was **144,** in **1861** and in **1871** it was **988**. By **1881** there'd been a surge in numbers to **2,937** and by **1891** even larger growth took the figure to **7,856**. The number of **Jewish** immigrants (mainly from **Lithuania**) was **4,032** in the **1880s** as compared to **1,322** in the **1870s**. By **1891** 2.1% of the total **Leeds** population was **Jewish.** (In the **Leylands** it amounted to **55%** of the total population.) The most common surname was *'Cohen,'* accounting for **493** members of the community or just over **6%** of the total. In the **1901** Census, explanatory leaflets in **Yiddish** were required. The ways of this community would have seemed very strange to **Edmund Smith** – but he may well have subconsciously identified with the feeling of being a migrant whose roots lay elsewhere.

A shared area of business was the clothing trade. Tailoring was the key speciality in the **Leeds Jewish Community**, accounting for **72%** of listed occupations in the **1891 Census**. Others included *'hawking'* (street selling) jewellery and windows. It's easy to imagine **Edmund** taking full advantage of the prospects this growing market offered – especially at a time when the late **Victorian** trade cycle was proving very erratic. Thus, this new **Jewish Community**, which had taken root on his very doorstep, directly contributed to **Edmund's** business remaining viable and even to thrive. His exact dealings with the **Jewish Community** remain unknown but it is likely that, in any business transactions, **Edmund** would have driven a hard bargain. Close business alliances between the indigenous **Yorkshire** and aspiring **Jewish** communities were relatively common at that time, being united by a shared determination to succeed. In **1884**, the **Jewish** immigrant **Michael Marks** founded a *'penny bazaar'* in **Leeds Market** that was eventually to become the famous Department Store **Marks and Spencer.** (The *'Spencer'* represented the **Yorkshire** end of the business. In **1894**, *'a bluff Yorkshire man'* from **Skipton**, *'Tom Spencer'* had been taken into partnership by **Marks** after supplying a £300 half share in this enterprise.) Incidentally, if **Edmund** had once enjoyed a connection with a wool merchant's office in **Briggate** then he'd been at the best possible location to have served the main **Jewish Community** in **Leeds.** Given his trade or location, it's hard to see how he could have missed being in contact with this community.

Section 12: Another Loss

Concerning the *'white death'* of TB

By **1887**, Trade Directories recorded **Edmund's** family address as **18 Vernon Road.** Whether there had been an actual move or (as seems far more likely) a change of numbers is not at all clear. At **no. 16** was a certain **David Augustus Cruse B.A.** (private tutor). (This example highlighted **Edmund's** desire to only have *'respectable'* tenants.) Up to **no. 20** was a *'Wesleyan'* preacher. The **April 1891** Census showed that, sadly, yet another bereavement had stricken the **Smith** family. Baby **Florence** had died aged three and a half in **1884** and so also had **Rosamond,** less than a month before the Census was completed. Her death notice on the fourth page of the **Leeds Mercury** for **Wednesday, April 1st, 1891** was a little less terse than that of **Edmund's** first wife, **Helen.** It read **"SMITH – MARCH 30th** at 18 Vernon Road, *"Rosamond" wife of Edmund Smith."* Another revealing difference was that in this death notice it was very much the deceased wife who was the centre of attention. Unlike that first death notice for **Helen, Edmund** had made no attempt was made to publicise his own services as a Commercial Traveller. The impression gained is that, whilst **Helen's** death had been greeted with a sense of relief, that of **Rosamond** had produced a deep sense of sorrow. Later gathered evidence further reinforced this impression – that namely, **Edmund** had been fonder of his second wife than his first.

The recent death of what seems to have been a well-loved wife must have made the filling in of the **1891** Census Return on **Sunday, 5th April** a difficult experience. The house will have still been in mourning. Details of the household were then as follows:

Edmund Smith aged **59** Widow – Commercial Traveller,
Betsey aged **31**
Annie aged **29**
Fred Heselwood (*'Frank'*) aged **21** – warehouseman,
Maud aged **18**
Hedley aged **12**
Kathleen aged **5**
Anne Spencer aged **20** – servant.
(By this time, the population of **Leeds** had climbed to **367,505**.)

Rosamond possessed not inconsiderable financial resources; following her death a **Wakefield Probate Document** (dated 8th **February 1892**) revealed that she'd left her husband (who was recorded as being a *'Commercial Traveller'*) the not insignificant sum of £**203.16.10**. This amount (on a conservative estimate) would, in **2018**, be the equivalent of £**25,513.23**. Like the **Hastings**, the **Stamford's** were a prosperous family. For the second time, **Edmund** had married into money, he would follow the same approach toward his third wife – but with rather less happy consequences.

Family tradition mentioned that in his late twenties my Grandfather **Frank** had suffered a violent attack of rheumatic fever which had left him with a permanently weakened heart. However, an entry in his **James'** diary revealed that this illness occurred in **December 1887** when he was still in his late teens – a time earlier then that indicated by tradition. Nonetheless, the resulting weakness of his heart didn't prevent him from engaging in heavy warehouse work. It perhaps showed-up later in life. Yet this infirmity probably saved his life for he was rejected as being unfit for military service when he attempted to join the army at the outbreak of the **First World War** in **August 1914**. Another unusual feature was that, at the age of **28,** his hair suddenly turned snow white which served to give him a distinguished appearance. However, a genetic factor appeared to have been the cause, for exactly the same thing happened to other family members. Family Tradition had conflated two widely separated events.

One of my Great Grandfather's children (listed in the **1891** Census) ended up leading a rather tragic life. **Kathleen** married a Maths teacher named **Joe Burdon,** who was of senior rank in the Freemasons. Sadly, he hung himself in the late **1950s** – depression (rather than alcoholism) appearing to have been the cause. They had no children. My sister remembered him as being a very pleasant man who was somewhat dominated by his wife. My brother added the interesting detail that this unfortunate man believed his wife was having an affair with the milkman. An increasingly forlorn and eccentric figure, **Kathleen** lingered on until early **1964.** Behind the names listed on any official document lies many a happy (or tragic) story. Apparently, very close to her father **Edmund, Kathleen** had disclosed to a still living relation that **Edmund** *"had been very strict as a father."* She'd also divulged that one of **Betsey's** hobbies had been to make amateur silverware. A spoon made by her still exists as a family heirloom. My sister was astonished to hear of this fact when informed about it during a telephone call, made on **Sunday Evening, February 6th, 2000.** The reason was that she too had a great interest in silverware. A study of successive generations of **Smiths** has revealed re-occurring patterns of behaviour and inclinations.

Perhaps the suicide of **Kathleen's** husband influenced my father, **Fred,** against **Freemasonry.** Involvement with this group was one thing he deliberately avoided, even though doing this did cost him a certain amount of lost business. Although **Fred** (to my knowledge) never quarrelled with members of the **Smith** family who were **Free Masons,** his own attitude to this group was (for all the time I can remember) extremely suspicious. From my father's perspective, **Freemasonry** *"was psychologically damaging."* He said this with a fair amount of emphasis during the **1980s** following a discussion we had about a book he'd read on **Freemasonry,** entitled *'The Brotherhood.'* **Fred** had an especially strong dislike of its *"unhealthy rituals."* It was more this ritualistic aspect (than any possible scope for business corruption) which seemed to have bothered him most. His hostility toward it was second only to his hostility to the **Roman Catholic Church.** He would have been pleased that I dissuaded my younger son from joining the **Free Masons** in late **2013.** My own argument against the **Free Masons** lies in how the combination of secrecy, wealth and power inevitably produce corruption – as documented by writers like **Martin Short (1989).** I gave my son a copy of his book *'Inside the Brotherhood'* for Christmas of that year.

Section 13: A Third Marriage

Concerning death and re-marriage in Victorian England

My Great Grandfather **Edmund** continued to live at **Vernon Road** for the rest of his life. As family tradition would have us believe, he <u>again</u> remarried and, my father was known to remark that *"he was courting a fourth wife in his mid-eighties."* Written underneath **Edmund's** photograph are the words *"Edmund Hastings Smith; he had 4 wives, 17 children – died in his middle 80s."* My brother had assembled the photographs together during the **1970s** and it was he who had written these words next to them, my father supplied the information. The insertion of **Hastings** may have arisen from confusion with the **Reverend Edmund Hastings Smith** – a grandson of the original **Edmund**. In <u>none</u> of the records I encountered was my Great Grandfather ever known as **Edmund Hastings**. There was, however, the possibility that this was the designation he personally chose to be known by, for the name **Edmund Hastings** does have a certain *'grandiose'* ring to it!

This tradition – that my Great Grandfather had married for the third time was confirmed by a review (conducted in **January 2002**) of the **1901** Census (held on **Sunday, 31ˢᵗ March**) for **18 Vernon Road**: -
Edmund Smith aged **69** – Commercial Traveller, (Draper Worker) working on his own account, born in **Sutton, Kildwick**
Sarah Smith aged **62**, Sussex, **Brighton**
Kathleen aged **15** Leeds
Flora [Burnett or Barrett] – aged **24**, Cook Domestic, born in **Nottingham**
Anne J. Hewitson aged **22** – Nurse Domestic, born in **Leeds**
(By this time, the population of **Leeds** had climbed to **428,968**.)

Sarah's age implied that **Edmund** may have re-married for companionship rather than purely physical attraction alone – although this is speculative as **Sarah** could still well have been a very striking lady! It's a possibility that **Edmund** and **Sarah** may have known each other for a long time prior to their marriage. She appears to have had no previous connection to either the **Hastings** or **Stamford** families. The fact that she was not buried in the family grave at **Sutton** suggested that she was a widow who had wished, after her own death, to be interred with her first husband. Her birthplace in **Brighton** indicates a completely different background from that of **Edmund's** first two wives. He must still have remained a distinguished-looking man to have re-married in his sixties. Here again is the suggestion of him having *'a way'* with the ladies! One wonders how his last daughter **Kathleen**, (who'd lost her mother **Rosamond** when five and who was reputed to have been *'difficult'*) had got on with her new stepmother. **Kathleen** was probably quite a handful, and this would perhaps explain the presence of a Domestic Nurse in the house. However, it could just as readily be argued that the nurse had been there to help **Edmund** or **Sarah,** or both. After all, **Edmund** had apparently *'worn out'* his first two wives – was the same happening again?

Most of the above points found confirmation on **Saturday, July 19th, 2003,** when (after much searching) the relevant marriage certificate was received from the General Register Office, based in **Southport, Merseyside.**

Registration District of Marylebone

1892 Marriage solemnised at The Parish Church in the Parish of St Marylebone in the county of London

1. When married? December 27th, 1892

2. Name and Surname: Edmund Smith, Sarah Jane Thompson

3. Age: 60, 53

4. Condition: Widower, widow

5. Rank or profession: Commercial Traveller

6. Residence at the time of marriage: 18 Vernon Road, Leeds Yorks, 5 Beaumont Street

7. Father's name and surname: John Smith, Jacob Carden

8. Rank or profession of father: Corn Miller. Gentleman

Married in the Parish Church according to the Rites and Ceremonies of the Established Church by or after Banns by me E.W Raby - curate

The marriage was solemnised between us

Edmund Smith

Sarah Jane Thompson

In the presence of us

Fred Thompson

E.M Bonham

This important document showed that, by this point in time, my Great Grandfather was more than a provincial figure whose influence was confined only to the **North of England.** By **1892,** his social reach had extended to the metropolitan area of **London** where he'd been attractive enough to have been noticed by a widow from a privileged background. Family tradition suggests that she was a rich widow. In an era when most men of **Edmund's** years would have been content to accept their present lot in life he still had ambitions for social advancement. There always seemed to be a restlessness about him. In his heart, he was perhaps still *'a young man on the make.'* Maybe he viewed marriage into gentry as a pinnacle of his career. There was something clearly obsessive and unremitting in his ambition to *'get on.'* He also appeared not to have brooded over the death of **Rosamond** for too long. The interlude between the death of his second wife and his re-marriage was well under two years. This suggests that **Edmund** may have known **Sarah** for some time. Whether this lady had been my Great Grandfather's mistress before their marriage remains a matter of speculation. Finally, one wonders how **Edmund's** third wife would have taken to life in provincial **Leeds?** A few more details about this lady were provided by the following Birth Certificate, received from **Brighton and Hove** Register Office on **Monday, July 28th, 2003.**

1. When and where born: Twelfth of March 1839, 51 Frederick Street

2. Name if Any: Sarah Jane

3. Sex: Girl

4. Name and Surname of Father: Jacob Carden

5. Name and Surname of Mother: Maria Carden formerly Woodbridge

6. Occupation of Father: Gilder

7. Signature, description and residence of informant: Maria Carden, Mother 51 Frederick Street

8. When registered: Thirteenth of April 1839

9. Signature of registrar: T. R. Simmonds, Registrar

Her parents had married on **1st October 1834**. At **Saint Nicholas Church** in **Brighton.** From her Birth Certificate, it was established that her father, **Jacob Carden,** was a *'gentleman gilder'* who would have had access to local aristocracy and perhaps even to royal figures like **King George IV** who often visited **Brighton.** (**Jacob** was the fourth generation of **Carden's** to be given that forename.) The Society of Gilders Web Site helpfully revealed that *"Gilding is the application of thin sheets of metal (usually gold) as a means of surface decoration. Gilding is commonly seen on decorative items such as picture frames, mirrors and furniture; fine art such as illuminated manuscripts, sculpture and icons. Architectural uses include interior and exterior applications – in religious as well as secular settings, as well as signage. The gilding process requires a specialized set of tools and materials."* Sadly, he died aged only **26** – having only lived from **1st August 1813** until **6th May 1839**. He chose to be buried at **Brighton** in a **Non-Conformist** Graveyard belonging to an *'Independent Denomination.'* His death certificate of **4th May 1839** revealed that he'd died of *'consumption'* at **51 Frederick Street.** The informant was a certain **John Miall** of **Union Street.** His daughter **Sarah** was only several weeks at the time.

The **1841** Census simply revealed **Sarah** as being a daughter of twenty-five-year-old, **Maria Carden** – a schoolmistress. Other residents included **Eliza Pullinger** aged **11, Henry Pullinger** aged **9**, a servant **Jane Wilson** aged **25** and a **Cecilia Wilson** aged **4** months. Their address appeared to have been **Ladywalk Street, Brighthelmstone** in **Sussex. Brighthelmstone** had been a small fishing village and seems to have been an old name for **Brighton**. In **June 1847,** her mother married **Frederick John Reed (1815-1888).** She seemed to have had an extra-marital affair with him because **Sarah** had an older sister named **Martha Reed** who had been born in **1837**. There was also an **Ann Ellen Reed** born several years before her marriage in **1841**. (A legitimate **Maria** and **Amelia** would follow in **1848** and **1850.**) **Sarah's** background to use the language of the time was distinctly *'rackety.'*

Careful research uncovered the following details of **Sarah's** first marriage to **Alfred Thompson** (born around **1840**).
1861 Marriage solemnised at <u>the Parish Church</u> of <u>St John Southwark</u> in the <u>County of Surrey</u>
1. When married? October 22^{nd,} 1861
2. Name and Surname: Alfred Thompson, Sarah Jane Carden
3. Age: Full age, full age
4. Condition: Bachelor, Spinster
5. Rank or profession: Hosier
6 Residence at the time of marriage: St John's, St John's
7. Father's name and surname: John Thompson, Jacob Carden
8. Rank or profession of father: Gentleman, Commercial Gilder
Married in the <u>Parish</u> Church according to the Rites and Ceremonies of the Established Church by or after <u>Banns</u> by me <u>Samuel Abramson</u> – curate
The marriage was solemnised between us
<u>**Alfred Thompson**</u>
<u>**Sarah Jane Carden**</u>
In the presence of us
<u>**George Buck**</u>
<u>**Rebecca Thompson**</u> **left a mark**
This discovery made it easier to trace **Sarah** in various Census Documents.

<u>**1871 Census Return**</u>
(At 161 Stanhope Street, Marylebone, Parish of **Saint Matthew)**
Alfred Thompson aged **31** *'Hosier Shopman'* **Surrey Camberwell**

Sarah J. Thompson aged **32** Sussex, Brighton
Alfred J aged **9** *'Scholar'* Moberly, Marylebone
Francis J aged **7** *'At home'* Moberly, Marylebone
Emily M aged **5** *At home'* Moberly, Marylebone

<u>**1881 Census Return**</u>
(**At 5 Beaumont Street, Marylebone London** near **Cavendish Square**)
Alfred Thompson aged **41** *'Outfitter Manager'* **Surrey**
Sarah Jane Thompson aged **42** **Brighton, Sussex**
Francis J. Thompson aged **17** *'Apprentice to Hosier'* **Marylebone**
Emily M. Thompson aged **15** *'Apprentice to Millener'* **Marylebone**
Martha Weir aged **25** *'Cook'* **Marylebone**
Elizabeth Johnson aged **21** *'Housemaid'* **Marylebone**
Florence Weldon aged **42** *'Boarder'* **Pendleton Manchester, Lancashire**
Annie Dovaston aged **47** *'Nurse'* **Cockshott, Shropshire**

<u>**1891 Census Return**</u>
(Again at **5 Beaumont Street, Marylebone London**)
Sarah J. Thompson aged **53** widow *'Mistress of Invalids House'* – place of birth, **Sussex, Brighton**
Caroline Hamlett aged **22** *'Domestic servant'* – place of birth, **Norfolk, Harleston**
Janet Mason aged **21** *'Domestic Servant'* – place of birth, **Scotland**
Julia A. Meyrick aged **46** a visitor *'Medical Server'* – place of birth, **Staffs, Wolverhampton** (whether she had any lasting connection with Invalids House couldn't be established.)
Alice Hitchens aged **22** *'Domestic Servant'* – place of birth, **London, Marylebone**
George Simpson aged **14** *'Domestic Servant'* – place of birth, **London**
Despite doing well in his business something had happened to **Sarah's** first husband. A death certificate received on **Saturday, 21ˢᵗ July 2018,** disclosed the following information:
Registration District <u>Marylebone</u>
<u>**1888**</u> **Death in the** <u>**sub-district**</u> **of** <u>**Cavendish Square**</u> **in the** <u>**County of Middlesex**</u>
1. When and where died? Eighteenth September 1888 5 Beaumont Street
2. Name and Surname: Alfred Thompson
3. Sex: Male
4. Age: 48 years

5. Occupation: Gentleman

6. Cause of death: Paralysis of Brain 14 days, Exhaustion, certified by Thos Appleton MRCS

7. Signature, description and residence of informant: A. F. Thompson, Son, 49 Peterborough Lane, Parsons Green

8. When registered: Nineteenth September 1888

9. Signature of registrar: Wm Dawn, Registrar

A visit to **Beaumont Street** (made on **Thursday, 4ᵗʰ September 2008** when travelling to **The Hadrian Exhibition** being held at the **British Museum**) confirmed that it lay within an easy Hansom Cab ride (and even walking distance) from **King's Cross Station.** The original building no longer remains but its location and the presence of a *'Medical Server'* does suggest that it could have had some connection to a **London Hospital** – exactly which hospital and for what reasons remain a matter of speculation. Also, the business or personal reasons which must have drawn **Edmund** to **London** were equally a mystery. However, his contacts with the Capital do appear to have been well established.

One thing apparent from the entry is that **Sarah Thompson** was a most capable woman, able to supervise a diverse workforce. This quality would have appealed to **Edmund** – especially now that **Rosamond** was gone. He would also have quickly noticed her large *'portfolio'* of financial assets. (These included two neighbouring properties located in a good area of **London.**) If **Sarah** was a good socialiser who would impress business contacts by being a *'proper lady'* she would seem the ideal person to replace **Rosamond.** Given her age, there wouldn't have to be any pregnancies to worry about. For a man who was sixty, this would be another positive point. What **Sarah** had to gain from the relationship was less clear. Admittedly, to marry again would reduce the risk of being an unwanted *'dependent'* on resentful relatives. Yet **Sarah** had plenty of money inherited from her husband and she also held a responsible position that would have provided a reasonable income. Maybe she was just bored with being single. When he *'switched on the charm'* she may well have found my Great Grandfather to be a very attractive and witty – a man who could restore her lost youth. The union between them could have been a marriage of convenience, but a romantic element may well have intruded. **Edmund** could have felt he like a young man again. His powers were undiminished with age. One mysterious feature is; how did they first meet? In terms of trade common ground did exist but even as a possible manager of other *'Commercial Travellers'* would **Edmund's** reach have extended as far as **London?**

Section 14: A Marital Disaster

Concerning the breakdown in Edmund's third marriage

A full picture of **Edmund's** third marriage to **Sarah** only emerged during a most remarkable meeting. This took place in a modern private flat in **South London** on **Friday 13ᵗʰ July 2018.** Those attending this memorable occasion were the direct descendants of **Edmund's** eldest son, **James.** (The ever-efficient **Ann Dalton** was also present.) A copy of **Sarah's** Will (which I obtained as a result of this event) confirmed that their marriage had seriously broken down. They had got the nearest to a divorce as it was possible to get in those days. Given their mature ages, the main issue appeared to have been financial more than anything else. It boiled down to a matter of wills and legacies which **Edmund** may well have been casting his beady (and greedy) eye over. To see how things had reached such a head it was necessary to follow a chronological approach in relation to pertinent documents. What was revealed was a story that could have come straight from a **Victorian** novel (or melodrama) complete with its dramatic exits and unexpected entrances!

Sarah's original Will had been drawn-up at **18 Vernon Road** on **4ᵗʰ December 1900.** Except for one feature, the contents were not unusual. As would be expected, **Sarah's** children (by her first marriage) were the main beneficiaries. This source certainly revealed **Sarah** as a *'woman of substance'* who even owned a leasehold on the properties at **5** and **6 Beaumont Street, London.** (These may have been inherited.) There was clearly a large amount of money for **Edmund** to get his hands on. Once again he appeared to have been using marriage as a means to gain wealth and sustain a lavish lifestyle. However, this time the attempt would backfire on him in a spectacular manner.

The one unusual feature of this will of **1900** was the lack of even a nominal legacy to **Edmund** – leaving him <u>nothing</u> – not even trinkets or keepsakes at all. Instead, we find the statement, *"I give my watch and chain and trinkets attached and my emerald diamond ring to my grandchild* **Gertrude Irene Bonham.** *I give my other diamond ring with three stones to my granddaughter* **Violet Thompson.** *I give to my grandchild* **Alfred Sidney Thompson** *his grandfather's gold ring. I give my wardrobe and <u>all</u> my plate and plated articles and <u>all</u> the rest of my jewellery, also my furniture and effects which I brought from* **London** *to* **Leeds** *to my daughter* **Emily Marie Bonham."** The word *'all'* (which I underlined) confirmed that she'd fully intended a total *'clear out'* of all of her possessions. After ten years of marriage, all of **Sarah's** connections with **Leeds** were to be severed in what seemed to have been a deliberate attempt to snub her husband and wipe away all tangible evidence of him as best she could. All of her efforts (*i.e.* the will) by-passed him completely.

The *'residue'* of her estate was to be given to two executors, both designated as *'gentlemen.'* These were **John Thomas Campbell** of **17 Warwick Street, Regent Street, London** and **Frederick William Low** of **28 Foulser Road, London.** Very shrewdly, **Sarah** was ensuring she'd got two powerful, protective male figures to enforce the terms of the will and handle any potential legal problems created by her husband. The identity of these high-status males remains unknown – they may possibly have been former business associates (or customers) of her first husband. Generally, the third wife of **Edmund** came across as a very shrewd lady who knew <u>exactly</u> what she was doing. She seemed to have been following her own cunning and well-thought-out plan.

Sarah's Will contained two codicils or amendments:
The <u>first</u> of these (produced on **26th February 1902**) contained very detailed stipulations concerning how her children should handle her legacy. These need not concern this *'History.'* What is apparent is that **Sarah** had obtained some excellent legal advice when producing it – it's full of carefully constructed terms and conditions that only a highly competent legal team could produce. She seemed more than prepared for the possibility that **Edmund** would try and cause trouble, so she had taken care to get some good lawyers on board as well. The witnesses present at this codicil were *THOMAS HOGG of Great Wilson Street, Leeds, Medical Practitioner'* and *'F. G. HEPWORTH 18 Vernon Road, Leeds, Maid.'* The presence of a Doctor suggested health problems, as did the presence of a *'Nurse Domestic'* in the **1901** Census. One other detail worth noting was the reference **Sarah** had made concerning a son **Francis Joseph Thompson** who'd gone to **South Africa** *'some years ago'* and of whom *'nothing had been heard of or from him for a long period.'* In short, his mother didn't know whether he was alive or dead. This may or may not indicate some kind of estrangement. All we know about **Francis** is that he'd been born in **1864.** We also know that her eldest son, **Alfred John Thompson** lived from **1862** to **1935** and **Emily Marie Thompson** from **1866** to **1937.**

It was with the <u>second</u> codicil that things took a very curious turn. Dated **13th January 1903,** we find that the two attendee witnesses who attended (at **Sarah's** request) were an *'ANNIE BOOKER, Nelson Hotel, Littlehampton Barmaid'* and an *'ELIZA CLEAR, Nelson Hotel Littlehampton Servant.'* **Littlehampton** is in **West Sussex** and not far from **Brighton** where **Sarah** had originated and where she still may have had friendly contacts. (The **Nelson Hotel** closed in **July 2017**.) To say the least, these were rather unusual witnesses for a will made by a lady of her status, possibly suggesting this codicil had been made in a hurry. The location would also suggest that to have successfully inserted it **Sarah** decided to get away as far as possible from her husband. She appeared (in this instance) to have been a *'woman on the run.'* A *'dramatic exit'* had been made to escape his presence. This impression was reinforced by the following extract. *"Since the execution of my will I have borrowed from the **Temperance Permanent Building Society** of **4 Ludgate Hill E.C.** a sum on the security of N. 6 Beaumont Street, which sum I have lent to my daughter **Emily Marie Bonham** and she has agreed to repay the said sum of seven hundred pounds and interest to the said company by periodical instalments."* **5 Beaumont Street** (which had been left to **Emily**) would be held as security in the event of non-payment. **Sarah** ended this amendment by confirming the terms made in the original will of **1900** and the first Codicil.

What seemed apparent here was that through her daughter **Emily, Sarah** was gaining access to the funding needed to establish an independent existence away from **Edmund**. By passing it on to **Emily,** she lessened any legal claim her spouse may have had on it. **Sarah** was definitely a woman anticipating trouble. It was perhaps safer for her to do things indirectly rather than take the money herself. Her stance to my great-grandfather was one of profound mistrust – even fear! She had thought over very carefully how to break with him – although the final departure may have been a hurried affair. The full depth of her alienation was expressed in the probate document – dated, **23rd February 1905**.   Its preamble reads: *"Be it known that **Sarah Jane Smith** of **2 Surrey Street, Littlehampton** in the **County of Sussex**/wife of **Edmund Smith**/ formerly of **18 Vernon Road Leeds** died on the **20th** day of **December 1904** at 2 Surrey Street aforesaid."* The telling word here was *'formerly.'* It confirmed that, after ten years of living with him, **Sarah** had made a complete and well-organized break with her husband. Things seem to have soured badly with that marriage over a lengthy period. Perhaps she regretted having been *'taken in'* by his charm, and compared to her area of **London, Leeds** may well have proved a disappointment – drearily provincial around the edges. A laconic entry in the diary of **James** (dated **24th December 1904**) simply recorded, *"**Mrs Smith, S. Thompson** died at **Littlehampton**, buried at **Highgate**."* Her burial in a **North London** Cemetery suggested that in accord with the convention of her time, she'd had been interred with her first husband.

Frederick William Lowe, *'gentleman'* was on record as being *'the surviving executor.'* He was still based in **28 Foulser Road, Tooting**, which was a substantial red-brick property – now apparently divided into flats. The *'Gross value'* of **Sarah's** Estate amounted to £740.0.0, it's *'Net value'* was £478.9.0 (worth **£56,501.95** in **2018**). This was more than enough to live apart quite independently from her ex-husband who must have been deeply humiliated and enraged to have been outwitted by someone he would have dismissed as a *'mere'* woman. Both my excellent proof-reading wife and I wondered aloud whether he had *'received a taste of his own medicine.'* When, during the interwar period, a Great Granddaughter had broached the subject of **Sarah** with **May** (the daughter of **Edmund's** eldest son **James**) she'd snapped, *"we don't talk about her."* A long-lasting rancour had been the result of this marital shipwreck. It's very likely that **Edmund** would have thought, *'to be fooled by a woman, what an utter disgrace!"* In **Sarah,** my Great grandfather appeared to have met his match. She'd certainly had been no **Helen** or **Rosamond.**

After all that, a Death Certificate (received on **Saturday 28th, July 2018**) produced an astonishing piece of information. At the very end of his third wife's life, my Great Grandfather was to make the most dramatic and unexpected of entrances. The Certificate revealed that despite strong evidence of estrangement from **Edmund** it was he who was present at her death! This was an utterly unexpected twist. Details were as follows:

Registration District East Preston
1904 Death in the **sub-district** of **Littlehampton** in the **County of Sussex**
1. When and where died? Twentieth December 1904, 2 Surrey Street, Littlehampton U.D.
2. Name and Surname: Sarah Jane Smith
3. Sex: Female
4. Age: 65 years
5. Occupation: Wife of Edmund Smith, Commercial Traveller
6. Cause of death: Cerebral Hemorrhage, certified by Y. L. Richardson L.R.C.B.
7. Signature, description and residence of informant: Edmund Smith, widower of the deceased. Present at death 18 Vernon Road, Leeds
8. When registered: Twenty-first December 1904
9. Signature of registrar: William Gibbs, Registrar

When I first reviewed this piece of information, I wondered whether my Great Grandfather had pulled another *'surprise.'* He was the very last person I'd expected to see at the bedside of his estranged wife! Had **Edmund** been summoned to do this? Had he attempted a reconciliation? Did an attempt to pressurize her to return to him bring on a stroke? Who knows? All we do know is that in the depths of mid-winter the journey from **Leeds** to **Littlehampton** would have been a long and arduous one to have made – requiring at least one change of trains in **London.** My Great Grandfather must have possessed a strong personal motivation to have undertaken this journey.

Section 15: An Active Old Age

Concerning Edmund's old age

Edmund's old age was apparently an active one, free from any prolonged infirmity. He was to see many changes in his local environment. From his own doorstep, he could observe the modest **Yorkshire College of Science** amalgamating with other educational institutions to become **Leeds University.** (In **1904,** he might have read in the local newspaper about the College receiving a charter granting it *'full'* **University** status). **Edmund** would live on to become something of a **Victorian** anachronism in an age that was rapidly adopting very different values to the ones he had known. In this period, he may have taken pleasure in seeing his surviving sons making their way forward in the world of business. He may have felt he'd done a decent job as a father. It's very much an open question as to whether he had any inkling that he was to enter **Smith** legend as *'something of a character'* whose influence was to last up to five generations.

Trade Directories continued to feature **Edmund Smith's** name alongside the occupation of *'Manager'* or *'Commercial Traveller.'* This evidence indicates that he chose not to retire until toward the very end of his life. The last entry was made in **1915** when he was aged eighty-two. At that time of poor pension provision working to an advanced age was not uncommon. His working life overlapped (by ten years) that of a certain **Jewish** draper called **Joseph Gillinson** who was to exert a major influence on my father's life. Whether **Joseph** and **Edmund** ever met is not known but both alike were renowned for their business acumen. Those who lived to a great old age tended to be the most vigorous of the population and could well have wished to have continued their working lives. The **1911** Census (held on **Sunday, 2ⁿᵈ April**) contained further details about the last phase of **Edmund's** life. It instructed enumerators to *"Write below the number of rooms in this building (House, Tenant or Hostel) count the kitchen as a room but not scullery, landing, lobby, closet, bathroom. No warehouse, office shop"* before revealing: -

Edmund Smith *'Head'* born about **1832** aged **79**, *"Commercial traveller 'Retired' Wholesale Drapery"* widowed, birthplace **Kildwick Parish Church**
Kathleen Hastings Smith *'Daughter'* born about **1887** aged **25**, single **Leeds**
Lily Waite *"Servant"* born, **1884** aged **27**, birthplace **Barnbow**
(By then, the population of **Leeds** stood at **445,550.**)

Edmund gave a very strongly written and clear signature. It was not that of a senile or ill man. The implication here was that he was still vigorous but rather at a loose end, living in a largely empty house with eleven rooms and only a highly-strung daughter for company. This would have left him restless and open to the possibility of striking up another relationship with a lady should the opportunity arise. As a *'hard grafter'* all his life he would have found retirement extremely boring. Incidentally, I take a similar stance, I plan to go on working for as long as my health holds out. If that is until my eighties so be it! As for *'retirement,'* I've never heard of the word. I've seen too many mumbling old men in care situations for it to hold any attraction. The only ones who seem to make a success of it are elderly academics who possess an engrossing interest. In contrast, old women tend to form their own cliques where they complain about the food and care given to them.

Towards the end of his life, my Great Grandfather would possibly have seen my own father **Fred** (the son of **Frank**) as a baby and may even have cradled him in his arms. **Edmund** will have great satisfaction from seeing the **Smith** clan multiplying in the face of many premature deaths. By then, the Nineteenth Century World to which **Edmund** had belonged was over and the world of the Twentieth Century was being born amidst the carnage of the Great War. This New World would hold both opportunities and horrors far beyond the grasp of his provincial **Victorian** imagination. The fact that his story can be told at all owes much to the ICT *'revolution'* which took place toward the end of that century. I'd first acquired my own ICT skills in a computer laboratory on the lower floor of the utterly hideous **Edward Stoner Building** at **Leeds University.** It on the site where **Edmund's** house seemed to have stood. No wonder I felt at home in that computer work area. It was there in **October 1997,** that I first came across the Internet. (Computers back then were rather bulky, they didn't yet have flat screens and compact discs were still being used.)

Two events in **1914** perhaps increased **Edmund's** sense of isolation during the final period of his life. The first was the death of **Ernest,** his eldest son (by **Rosamond**) in early **1914.** The diary of **James** briefly noted, *"1ˢᵗ February*

1914, Ernest dies at Whitley Bay [worth] *£2,800."* A Death Certificate (received on **Saturday, 28th July 2018**) added further details:

Registration District Tynemouth

1914 Death in the **sub-district** of **Whitley Bay** in the **County of Northumberland**

1. When and where died? First February 1914, 49 Esplanade Whitley Bay and Monkseaton U D.

2. Name and Surname: Ernest Harward Smith

3. Sex: Male

4. Age: 46 years

5. Occupation: Commercial Traveller (Drapery)

6. Cause of death: (1) General paralysis (2) Cerebral Hemorrhage, cardiac failure, certified by W.A Dewhurst M.B.

7. Signature, description and residence of informant: Elizabeth Lambert, Present at the death, 49 Esplanade Whitley Bay

8. When registered: Third February 1914

9. Signature of registrar: Registrar J. W. Stokes

It must have grieved my Great Grandfather to have outlived yet another of his children. As a slight digression, it's worth mentioning that **June** and I used to stroll along the **Esplanade** at **Whitley Bay** during our courting days (that lasted from **Thursday 10th March 1978** until our wedding on **Saturday, 23rd June 1979**). Whilst holding hands, fun fighting and chatting away merrily, we must have passed the house where **Ernest** had died on more than one occasion. This was a very surprising and unexpected connection.

The second event was the marriage of his youngest daughter **Kathleen** to **Joseph Burden** at **Emmanuel Church** on **Tuesday, 14th April.** His last child was fleeing the nest.

Registration District Leeds

1914 Marriage solemnised at **the Church** in the **parish of Emmanuel Leeds** in the **County of York**

1. When married? April 14th, 1914

2. Name and Surname: Joseph Burden and Kathleen Hastings Smith

3. Age: 33, 28

4. Condition: Bachelor, Spinster

5. Rank or profession: School Master

6 Residence at the time of marriage: 18 Vernon Road, 18 Vernon Road

7. Father's name and surname: Thomas Burden, Edmund Smith

8. Rank or profession of father: Steel Worker, Traveller

Married in the <u>Parish Church according to the Rites and Ceremonies of</u>
<u>the Established Church</u> by <u>licence</u> by me J. F. Philips
The marriage was solemnised between us
<u>Joseph Burden</u>
<u>Kathleen H. Smith</u>
In the presence of us
<u>H. Francis</u>
<u>Rosamond V. Campbell</u>
<u>Edmund Smith</u>

Joseph had apparently worked his way up from humble beginnings, whilst **Kathleen** doesn't appear to have done any work at all. It could be argued that she was caring for his father, yet he still seemed to be vigorous enough to still working and write a clear signature. Also, if he had been that infirm **Kathleen** would have done a *'daughter's duty'* and postponed her marriage. Maybe her father was wanting his last child away so he could settle in with a fourth woman he was supposed to be courting. Worth noticing is an ongoing link with the **Campbell** family A photograph taken of **Joseph** in **1948/9** revealed a rather large man, with a thickset face and glasses. He looked every inch an old-fashioned maths teacher. His presence at **Vernon Road** can be explained if he's been taken in as a lodger. Less than four months after **Joseph** and **Kathleen's** marriage The First World War broke out.

It would have been interesting to know **Edmund's** reaction to this tragic event. Would he have considered it as a major catastrophe for all concerned? Did it affect himself or his family personal way? Was the world about him was crumbling under his feet? Perhaps he would have *'tutted'* at the growing amount of refuse being left in the street due to the considerable number of dustbin men having left their employment to join the armed services. Although **Edmund** died before the horrors of the **Somme** and **Passchendaele**, his last months did see the use of poison gas, unrestricted submarine warfare and the first Zeppelin raids over **London.** Further abroad was the disastrous **Gallipoli** expedition and a defeated **Russia** heading for a revolution. Surely, the twentieth century had arrived with a vengeance.

Section 16: Death of a Titan

Concerning the death of Edmund Smith of Leeds

Local newspapers confirmed that on the last day of **Edmund's** life (**July 25th, 1915**) the **Germans** were advancing on **Warsaw,** the **French** had made some gains in the **Vosges,** whilst the **British** had endured a bombing attack **East** of **Ypres.** At **Gallipoli** stalemate reigned. In **Otley,** the wife of an artillery officer (a certain **Mrs Duncan**) was selling flags for the **Serbian Relief Fund.** The picture reveals a smiling round-faced woman wearing a wide-brimmed floppy hat. Ironically, after another **84** years in **1999, Serbia** would again feature in the newspapers around the time of the death of **Fred** (my father and **Edmund's** grandson.) However, on this occasion, there would be no one in **Otley** selling flags for the **Serbian Relief Fund** and the **Germans** would be an ally rather than an enemy. Such are the twists and turns of International Politics. How aware **Edmund** was of such events at the very point of his own death is not known.

We find from **James** diary, that my Great Grandfather died at **8.00AM** on 25th **July 1915** and that (on the **28th** of that month) his body had been taken to **Crosshills** on a train from the (now long closed) **Midland Station,** once located on **Wellington Street.** His death notice reinforced the impression of a man whose life had centred upon his work. The fourth page of the **Monday, July 26th, 1915** edition of the **Yorkshire Post** read: - **"SMITH – JULY 25 at 18 Vernon Road Leeds, in his 84th year, Edmund Smith, a representative for Messrs Stewart and MacDonald Ltd, Glasgow for 42 years."**

Although loyalty to one's Employers was a common feature of the age in which he lived, **Edmund** must have had a profound respect for that Firm to have worked for it for so long. From **Stewart and Macdonald Ltd** he would have gained a respectable living, a certain position in society and the financial means to fulfil any wider aspirations. Both **Edmund's** economic needs and his deep-rooted yearning for personal esteem would have been fully met. In fairness to my Great Grandfather's memory, he must have been an excellent worker to have retained his position throughout the wild economic swings of the late **Victorian** period. He had obviously <u>not</u> been the first person laid off when times became hard. Simply to have survived and provided some material comfort for his family was a hugely creditable achievement. In contrast, to other male death notices (that often extolled the deceased for being a *'loving father'*) **Edmund** was being remembered for his dogged work record rather than family relationships. This suggested a certain coolness had grown between him and his eldest son **James** – the most likely author of this notice. It also wrongly recorded his death as being **84,** not **83.** However, this may have been due to a typographical error on the part of the **Yorkshire Post.**

Section 17: Leaving a Legacy

Concerning the will of Edmund Smith Leeds

Edmund's methodical nature can be clearly seen in his Will, drawn up on **January 25th, 1912,** four days after his eightieth birthday. Lying behind the legal jargon was his clear intention to ensure that every detail was covered to avoid future family disputes. My Great Grandfather seemed fully aware that his legacy could create ill-feeling amongst his children. This may explain his choice in asking an old friend **(James Barraclough)** to be one of the administrators. **James Barraclough** belonged to a well-known family of jewellers who remained in business in the **Leeds** area until the **1970s** or **80s.** Presumably, they had been one of **Edmund's** business associates. His close association with a jeweller (and with the solicitors who had helped him prepare his will) had brought him into contact with two professions where the **Jewish Community** was growing in prominence. However, the **Barraclough's** were not **Jewish.** They were known to be an old **Yorkshire** family.

Evidently written in the neat copperplate writing of a solicitor's clerk, the tone of this document shows a still vigorous personality, free from any evidence of senility. **Edmund** was determined to leave his affairs in the best possible order. Here was a man who knew exactly what he wanted. A mildly surprising feature was the obvious lack of any legacy to a Church. There was not even a token legacy to any of the congregations in his locality. My Great Grandfathers will read as follows: -

*This is the last will and Testament of me **Edmund Smith** of **Leeds** in the County of **York,** Commercial Traveller, made in my own name and form following that is to say I nominate and appoint my sons **James Hastings Smith** and **Ernest Alexander Harwood Smith** and my friend **James Barraclough** of **Leeds** (aforesaid jeweller) to be the Trustees and Executors of this my will and I give, devise and bequeath all and every of my land, buildings and real estate and also all and every [of my] personal estates and effects whatsoever and whensoever and of what nature or kind soever and whether in possession, reversion, remainder or expectancy [out of my own] which I may have at the time of my decease a power of appointment or disposition my said trustees, their being executive administrators and assigns according to the seven values and tenures thereof respectively upon* *and subject to the several trusts herein declared and contained of and concerning the same that is to say upon trust to sell and convert into money by public auction or private contract all my real and personal estates and effects and to stand possession of the proceeds paying all my just debts funeral and testamentary-expenses and the costs and expenses of proving and registering this will upon trust for eight of my children namely* **Betsey Hastings Smith, Arthur Edmund Smith, Ernest Alexander Harwood Smith, Fred Heselwood Smith, Maud Evelyn Campbell, Hedley Stamford Smith, Kathleen Hastings Smith** *and* **Anne Helen Smith** *in equal shares and properties absolutely, my eldest son having otherwise been provided for and I declare that in case any of my eight children shall die in my lifetime leaving issue such issue shall take their parents share under this my will and I also declare that in the case of my said eight children shall die in my lifetime without leaving issue the share of the child or children so dying shall go to the others or others of them my said eight children or their issues per [share] and I invoke all former wills by me at any time heretofore made and do declare this only to be my last will and Testament. In witness, whereof I have hereunto set my hand this twenty-fifth day of January one thousand nine hundred and twelve.*

Signed by the said Testator **Edmund Smith** *as his last*
Will in our joint presence and by us in his presence} **Edmund Smith**
    Joseph S. Lawson
      Solicitor Leeds
    John H. Dixon
      Clerk to **Bulmer, Lawson**
      & Ward, *Solicitors Leeds*

Until recently **Lawson** was a well-known firm of Solicitors. It seems that in financial matters **Edmund Smith** was unwilling to settle for anything less than the best although it was easy to imagine that he found all the legal jargon a trial to his patience. In his own patriarchal way, he seemed to want the best for his children. However, within a few months of his death, the arrangements he'd so carefully made would fall apart. The sad truth would emerge that **Edmund** had nothing to leave his family.

CHAPTER 12: THE SANDSTONE TIME CAPSULE

Section 1: A Decisive Discovery

Concerning Victorian graves

In death, **Edmund** did return to his home village. A photograph taken of the interior of **Sutton Baptist Church** (around **1900**) showed that his funeral service will have taken place surrounded by lavish fittings, with the organ occupying pride of place. Prior to the First World War, this church will have been at the pinnacle of its respectability. During my first visit to **Sutton** on **Monday, 22ⁿᵈ November 1999**, I discovered where both he and some of his family had been buried. **Edmund's** twelve-foot high obelisk-shaped monument was standing proudly there like a sandstone *'time capsule'* containing a message from the past. It was in a largely overgrown cemetery, sited **40** yards behind the **Baptist Church** (now in a modern new building.) To the **East** of this graveyard lay a grass field (dotted about with grazing sheep) which gently sloping down towards **Holme Beck,** flowing some **50** yards away underneath the **Crosshills Road.**

The earthly remains of **Edmund** and his **Victorian** family lay in a vaulted grave – on top of which stood the twelve-foot-high sandstone obelisk surrounded by an engraved plinth. A mossy path lay to one side whilst in front, the ground was sunken and uneven. Time, weather and wildlife had all taken their toll. A long thin stream of bird droppings ran down from the very tip of the obelisk whilst the sandstone itself had faded into a mildew green. The inscriptions on the plinth had also begun to erode and I felt that deciphering them in a few years' time would have been impossible. My visit seemed to have come in the *'nick of time'* – capturing all the information I needed before wind and rain would obliterate all evidence. (Thankfully, I was proved wrong on that score, these inscriptions proved to be far more robust than first anticipated and most were still legible in **September 2015.**)

In its day, this memorial would have represented a considerable outlay – proclaiming in no uncertain manner the prosperous status of the **Smiths.** Occupying a prominent position, near the front of the graveyard it was as if **Edmund** was proclaiming *"Look at me! I am the local boy who made good in **Leeds!**"* He seems to have wanted to make a point. A neighbouring tomb was that of the **Tetley's** – also known to be a family of some respectability. It was in reading the inscriptions on the plinth that I felt I came closest to **Edmund** himself.

The story of my discovery of that monument is fascinating. On **Sunday, 21st November 1999,** two **Advanced Level Economics** students I was due to teach rang to cancel their lessons (due the following day) because of bad head colds. Suffering from the miseries of this condition myself, I decided I might as well spend the next day **(Monday, 22nd November)** visiting the **Sutton** and **Crosshills** area to see whether I could find a family vault that had been mentioned by a relative. On arrival, I first visited the **Methodist** graveyard – but finding nothing decisive. I tried the **Anglican** graveyard – with the same result and finally the **Baptist** graveyard. Here too the result seemed to be negative. Having had quite enough of gingerly traversing around bramble bushes and almost tripping over broken headstones I had resigned myself to the fact that the monument (last seen in **1953** by my first cousin **Pamela** who'd been taken there by her father **Stewart)** was no longer present. Just as I was about to leave through a small wooden gate I happened to look behind me and saw the faded name of *'Helen'* on a sandstone obelisk. With impetuous haste, I dashed up to it and, sure enough, it was the memorial I had been looking for! I was so excited by this discovery that I jumped up and down, punching the air and kicking the headstone in delight until a sinking feeling beneath my feet warned me not to do it again. Then I realised that old **Edmund** would not have taken kindly to one of his Great Grandsons leaping about on his grave. For several minutes, I was lost in wonder, staring at the inscriptions. I was strongly moved by the pathos of the list of prematurely deceased children. I can only compare the moment of discovery to the former **BBC** archaeological programme *'Meet the Ancestors'* where the face of a long-dead person is reconstructed and made to look real again. A drop of rain warned me to quickly record the contents of the three inscriptions. I then took some photographs to provide proof of this discovery. Instantly, the resolution formed to show my own family this site. Out of respect for my deceased relatives, I closed my visit by reading *'the Mosaic blessing'* of **Numbers 6.24f.** Before I had undertaken this journey to **Sutton** I had prayed to be led to that tomb if it were still to exist. **Monday, November 22nd, 1999** had turned out to be an amazing day. Even at the time I instinctively realized that the discovery of this monument was hugely significant. The way it opened doors to further research would confirm that it represented one of the most important discoveries of my life. Certainly, it was a discovery that allowed this Family History to really get underway. Decades after his death, **Edmund** had finally got himself noticed. Given the size and location of his monument, I felt that this may have been just what he'd wanted.

A second visit made to the site on **Wednesday 29th December 1999** revealed further details. In contrast to the dull conditions of the first visit the weather this time was clear, sunny and frosty. Consequently, various new features stood out more clearly. The lighting was ideal for photographs to be taken. Behind the memorial and running parallel to the path was a shallow gully where a wall may once have stood. This would tie in with the description my cousin had given – she'd remembered the memorial being sited next to a wall. Surrounding the memorial itself was a barely perceptible indentation where an iron railing would once have encircled it. Even more noticeable was the fact that, in comparison with the other memorials in this Churchyard, the stonework was very good, with no gaping spaces between various parts of the structure – nor any horizontal *'scratch lines'* left visible beneath the lettering. (The stonemason would have put these lines in place to ensure he chipped each letter resting on a straight line. When his work was finished any trace of this line should have been removed.) Also, despite being in a far more exposed position than the **Tetley's** tombstone, the erosion rate on its inscriptions was only around **5%**. In contrast, three of the four inscriptions on the **Tetley** tombstone had eroded away and the fourth was beginning to wear at the edges. The erosion rate upon the **Tetley** inscriptions was **80%** even though it was obvious that a great deal more money had been spent upon this monument than upon **Edmund's.**

The need to connect my children with their roots was one reason why this second visit had been made. This time I went accompanied by my wife and two younger sons. A series of photographs emphasised the link between two of my sons and their forebears. Even old **Edmund** may have been moved by the sight of his great-great-grandsons visiting his place of rest after so many years. However, I'm sure he would have found much to disapprove of concerning their lively behaviour. **Rosamond,** for her part, would have been relieved that her own efforts to rear a family had not been in vain. Thanks to her own sacrifices the **Smith** dynasty has continued. Despite the heart-breaking losses of her children, the **Smith** story continues.

Even in death, the **Victorians** seemed to have wanted to *'keep up with their neighbour.'* One conclusion drawn from this finding was that **Edmund** had most probably exercised a very tight supervision over the construction of this obelisk. He was not going to allow the stonemasons to get away with a poorly done job. My feeling is that he would have been pleased to find that his memorial had survived in better shape than that of the **Tetley's**. Should the inscription erosion rate have been similar to that of the **Tetley's** memorial his own would never have been discovered! The severe neo-classical style of the monument was in keeping with **Edmund's** own character. It was a style preferred largely by non-conformists, as appeared to the **Anglicans** of that period who tended to choose Gothic headstones.

A comparison with other headstones in the graveyard confirmed that **Edmund's** obelisk was one of the longest surviving monuments; virtually all the others had been erected in the late nineteenth to mid-twentieth centuries. It was clear that my Great Grandfather had ensured his obelisk was built with a view to it lasting for a very long time. He seemed to have wanted something that would bring him recognition even after his death. This Family History amply confirms his wishes. It has become an important means whereby his achievements are amply recognised and given all due credit.

Reinforcing this point was an aerial photograph of the graveyard taken in **1975.** (This had been kindly provided by **Pastor Rob Harris,** the minister of **Sutton Chapel,** when we had visited there on **Friday, 4th September 2015).** Taken in colour, this photograph revealed what looked to have been gravel pathways bordering the rectangular plot in which **Edmund** and his family were buried. The obelisk itself was near the top right-hand corner of an oblong grassy area. The photograph suggested that the plot contained around **45** monuments – possibly more because some were so jam-packed together it was impossible to tell them apart. By my **1999** visit, many had gone due to the monument erosion that has continued apace. Compared to what it had been the plot was relatively empty. Even some of the old paths had vanished. A sign lay on the wooden gate warning *"DANGER, Gravestones are constantly liable to subsidence. Care should be taken when visiting a graveside. Church Secretary …"*

Given the passage of time, this development was hardly surprising. What was surprising was how **Edmund's** monument was the only one which could be clearly seen through the window of the Minister's office. The other graves were obscured by foliage whereas **Edmund's** obelisk stood out clearly in a gap amongst the trees. It was almost as if he was watching over proceedings!

Section 2: Revealing Inscriptions

Concerning grave inscriptions

The three inscriptions etched into the obelisk were also most of concerning **Edmund Smith's** character. Their words give some idea of the domestic tragedies which faced a middle-class **Victorian** family. An attempt has been made to reconstruct the lettering of these inscriptions. The inscriptions covered the period from **1866** to **1922** it was hardly surprising that there was some variation in punctuation, font style and size. At least three generations of stonemasons would have worked on this monument.

The first inscription read: -

IN MEMORY OF

HELEN,

WIFE OF EDMUND SMITH,

OF LEEDS,

WHO DIED OCTOBER 4TH1866,

"SHE DID WHAT SHE COULD,"

ALSO OF JOHN WILLIAM,

THIRD SON OF THE ABOVE WHO DIED APRIL 7TH 1867.

AGED ONE YEAR TEN MONTHS.

ALSO OF THE ABOVE EDMUND SMITH

BORN JAN Y 21ST 1832

DIED JULY 25TH 1915

The strangest feature of this inscription was the less than enthusiastic epitaph given to **Helen.** Perhaps for reasons of health she had been unable to keep up with the exacting domestic standards which **Edmund** had expected. One could easily imagine him shouting at her and calling her a useless woman when she'd failed to do something he'd wanted. I certainly gained the impression that the man who devised the epitaph had a very troubled conscience – the lavish nature of the memorial lending only more weight to this supposition. Perhaps it was the custom of domineering **Victorian** patriarchs to give their lately deceased wives an expensive headstone. Yet even at her death, **Edmund** appeared to be saying *'You did what you could, but it was never good enough.'* The words of the epitaph do not speak of a tranquil relationship, but one which was bleak, begrudging and occasionally volatile in nature. Oddly enough, in **1887** at **Sutton Baptist Church** a stained-glass window had been dedicated to a certain **Mrs Horsfall,** *"one of the Church's most earnest workers."* Her husband had also chosen the motto *"She hath done what she could,"* **(Pilling et al pp.13-14).** Was this an example of plagiarism from **Edmund's** grave or a reflection of a typical male **Victorian** attitude to women? Again, this is another puzzle which at present defies solution. However, as my wife remarked when proof-reading this second piece in **2016**, *'somehow, this sounds softer in tone – more forgiving, forbearing and loving.'*

Also, of interest was the name of **Edmund's** third son *'John William'* – a name commonly chosen amongst many families in the **Sutton-Kildwick** area, including the **Smiths.** Here **Edmund** had combined the names of his own father and grandfather. Part of him seemed to have wanted to identify with his early roots in **Sutton** to honour the memory of his immediate forbears

Possibly the origins of this inscription may have derived from **Christ's** words to the woman who had anointed Him with oil just before His death. In the (then widely used) **King James Version** of **Mark 14.8a** these words read, *"She hath done what she could."* Yet even if this <u>was</u> their origin, **Edmund** appears to have taken this phrase and sharpened it into a rebuke. Thus, what had originally been an expression of <u>commendation</u> had, through **Edmund's** paraphrasing, become a term of <u>condemnation.</u> One had the impression of a deeply angry man who, only very grudgingly had added a pious epitaph to **Helen's** name. The more I reflected upon this epitaph the odder it seemed. At the time of **Helen's** death, **Edmund** did not appear to have been altogether in his right mind. The emotional pressures caused by **Helen's** demise seemed to have unleashed a great deal of resentment. An **Asian** associate and future Private Tutoring Agent in **Manchester** (who visited the tomb with me on **Monday, May 28th, 2001**) wondered whether **Helen's** heart had lain with another man. If this was the case a possible rival in her affections may have been **Samuel Heron,** the able apprentice at **Lowgate.** To my **Asian** acquaintance, it was very clear that **Edmund** had borne a grudge against **Helen.**

The partly eroded second inscription read: -

IN SACRED

AND LOVING REMEMBRANCE OF

ALDYTH ROSAMOND

DAUGHTER OF ROSAMOND AND EDMUND SMITH

OF LEEDS,

BORN MAY 14TH 1874 AND DIED MARCH 1ST 1875.

Also **HILDA MARION,**

DAUGHTER OF THE ABOVE

BORN OCTOBER 5TH 1876, DIED APRIL 26TH 1879

Also **SYDNEY EDMUND,**

SON OF THE ABOVE.

BORN OCTOBER 16TH 1875 DIED APRIL 29TH 1879.

Also **FLORENCE MAY,**

DAUGHTER OF THE ABOVE.

BORN OCTOBER 28TH 1880, DIED APRIL 28TH 1884.

This moving inscription to long-forgotten dead children shows that, for all their middle-class standing, **Edmund** and **Rosamond** were not free from the heartaches afflicting many a **Victorian** family. Late **April 1879** was an especially dreadful time with two children being *'carried off'* in the space of three days! The proximity of each of these births strongly implies the possibility that **Rosamond** had employed the services of a wet nurse. In so doing **Rosamond** would have regained her fertility soon after each birth. Possibly these shared tragedies drew **Edmund** and **Rosamond** closer together as a married couple. One final interesting feature was that, unlike **Sydney,** there appeared not to be any death notice for **Hilda** in any of the local newspapers. Maybe this was because the loss of a son was felt more deeply than that of a daughter – a common **Victorian** attitude. The actual names of the children were conventional, middle class although *'Aldyth'* seemed to be a somewhat unusual designation. Like many a male **Victorian** dynast, **Edmund** had been keen that his own name (and those of his wives) be perpetuated down the bloodline. He must have been especially mortified when two children died within three days of one another. Further evidence showing greater respect for his second wife emerged on the third inscription. One telling absence from both the inscription and Census Returns was the name of any of his siblings. For someone possessing a strong concern to pass on family names, **Edmund** seemed to have been strangely unwilling to have preserved the names of any of his own brothers or sisters. It seems evident that he did not want to honour them in any sort of way – although **John William** was obviously named after **Edmund's** father and grandfather. This read: -

---

IN LOVING MEMORY OF

ROSAMOND

SECOND WIFE OF THE SAID

EDMUND SMITH

WHO DIED MARCH 30TH 1891 IN HER 48TH

YEAR.

ALSO OF

BETSEY HASTINGS SMITH,

ELDEST DAUGHTER OF

EDMUND *AND* HELEN SMITH,

BORN 27TH FEBRUARY 1860,

DIED 18TH JANUARY 1922

The relationship between **Rosamond** and **Edmund** does appear to have been more of a love match. Perhaps he had learnt something from his first marriage. **Betsey,** for her part, wished to be remembered as someone who had, even at death, wanted to identify with her parents. Perhaps she'd been something of a *'daddy's girl.'* Lending credence to this suggestion was her Death Notice (on the third page of the **19ᵗʰ January 1922** issue of the **Yorkshire Post**). The notice simply stated *"SMITH – January 18, at 44 Chapel Lane, Headingley, Leeds, Betsey Hastings Smith, eldest daughter of the late Edmund Smith."* The inscription suggested that she may have enjoyed an especially close relationship with her father.

On **Tuesday Evening 14ᵗʰ December 1999,** a telephone conversation was held with a very helpful representative from **Sutton Baptist Church.** This contract had ascertained that a train would have carried all the deceased as far as **Kildwick Station,** whereupon *"a wagon"* would have transported them the mile or so down to the cemetery. Unless exceptionally foul weather had intervened, such a mode of transport would have proved adequate for this arduous task. It says something of **Edmund's** determination and attention to detail that one of his Great Grandsons could stand in front of the grave and busily record these details with a view to placing them on the Internet and writing a book about them. Against all the odds the **Smiths** final ending had not been one of total defeat – enough of **Edmund's** offspring having survived to have made such an action possible. The many sacrifices **Edmund** and his wives had made to raise a family had not been in vain. Perhaps if they could have known this fact, they would have been comforted. In contrast, the state of the cemetery itself would have come as a shock. They would have been appalled at the disrespect shown to deceased loved ones. Sadly, such disrespect seems to be a symptom of today's *'throwaway'* society; the danger being that if little respect is shown to the dead, then only a little respect will be shown to the living. But that is not a theme to be explored in this book.

There was one interesting outcome to that visit. On **Monday, May 28ᵗʰ, 2001** I paid a third visit to **Edmund's** monument. This time I was accompanied by a then-twenty-two-year-old friend and former **Business Studies** student from **Pakistan.** After carefully scanning the headstone my **Asian** acquaintance patted it and exclaimed, *"You come from a very good family – you've got the job!"* He was referring to a Private Tutoring position he'd been considering me for in **Manchester.** The result was one of the most fruitful teaching periods of my life. Lasting from **September 2001** until **April 2007** it opened many doors including access to the **Orthodox Jewish Community** in that city. During our visit, we both noted how extraordinary it was that **Edmund** was still opening doors for members of his family decades following his death.

This same person (who didn't wish to be named) took a great deal of interest in my Family History and we would often discuss it during the long drives back from **Manchester** to **Leeds.** He used to love hearing of the latest discoveries and, in response, would make many useful observations. We did this when listening to Classic FM Radio which provided a very pleasant background. He said I was meant to write it. As will be narrated shortly, his friendship was to be the saving of me! Hence his inclusion in this book.

Section 3: The Burial Book

Concerning Victorian Burial Books

New light was thrown upon the monument inscriptions by details taken from *'The Burial Book'* kindly provided by **Sutton-in-Craven Baptist Church** on **Tuesday 14th December 1999.** The work undertaken in looking through these records is gratefully acknowledged, and their details are recorded below. To avoid confusion, it should be noted that the dates given are the dates of <u>burial</u> and not the dates of death. (*'Yr'* means *'year'* and *'m'* means *'months.'*)

NAMES RECORDED UNDER THE NAME OF *'EDMUND SMITH'*
[Graves numbered 11 - 16 in Section *'B'* of the Burial Ground]

<u>Burial Plots 11-12: Empty</u>

<u>No. 13</u>

Name:	Age:
Rosamond Smith	47
Betsey Hastings Smith	62
Ann Helen Smith	61

Place of Death:	Burial Date:
Leeds	2/4/1891
44 Chapel Lane, Headingley, Leeds	21/1/1922
The Madeline Joy Hostel, Headingley	20/9/1922

No. 14
Name:
Edmund Smith
Place of Death:
18 Vernon Road, Leeds

Age:
83
Burial Date:
28/7/1915

No. 15
Name:
Helen Smith
Place of Death:
Leeds

Age:
not recorded
Burial Date:
not recorded

No. 16
Name:
John William Smith
Aldyth Rosamond Smith
Hilda Marian Smith
Sydney Edmund Smith
Florence May Smith
Place of Death:
Leeds
Leeds
Leeds
Leeds
Leeds

Age:
1 yr 10m
9m
2 yr 6m
3 yr 6m
3 yr
Burial Date:
not recorded
not recorded
28/4/1879
30/4/1879
30/4/1884

The major discovery made from this list was the burial of **Ann Helen Smith**. Like **Betsey,** she seems to have viewed marriage as an unattractive prospect. One wonders whether the possibly strained relationship between **Helen,** her mother and her father **Edmund** (as well as the tragedy of so many children dying so very young) had deterred each of them from *'tying the knot.'* Her death in a hostel implies that she may have suffered from a prolonged period of illness. Her death notice (**page 6** of the **Tuesday 19ᵗʰ September 1922**) issue of the **Yorkshire Post** announced *"SMITH - September 17, at Broomfield Crescent, Headingley, Leeds, Ann Helen, second daughter of the late Edmund Smith, Vernon Road - interment at Sutton Chapel, Crosshills, tomorrow at 1 P.M."* However, **James** had failed to place her inscription on his father's monumentt even though there was space for it. Here again, was a strange reluctance to discharge a duty that would have been expected of him.

At the end of **April 1879,** the **Smiths** were faced with the prospect of hurrying back and forth from **Leeds** to **Sutton.** One's heart must especially go out to **Rosamond.** On **Monday 28th April 1879,** she appeared to have been faced with the awful choice of either staying at home to tend a sick child or of leaving him to attend another child's funeral. Instinct suggests that she would have taken the first option. Curiously, not much time seems to have been spent in placing **Sydney** in the family grave. This very quick interment suggests that arrangements had already been made beforehand. His condition must have been hopeless. In addition, fear of infection may have motivated a speedy burial. All this extra evidence lends weight to the view that late **April 1879** had been an especially dreadful period for the **Smith** family. Weather reports from the **Yorkshire Post** tell of a late spring with snow in **Northern Scotland** and plenty of chilly rain elsewhere. As likely as not the burial ground would have been sodden by rain and very muddy at the time of each funeral.

The idea of the suffering involved can be captured from a letter **James wrote to David Morton**. (It has been taken from in the **Morton Kin Book.**) In it, he described the *'decline'* of my Great Grandmother **Rosamond.**
"My father looks fairly well; my mother has been in bed for many months. She has shrunk to a very small woman and you will remember [in **1881**] *she was very stout."* The precise stages of her decline were revealed in the following journal entries: -
*"**1889 Nov:** About this time Mrs **Edmund Smith** my stepmother was down with a broken blood vessel.*
January 25th, 1890: *My mother taken seriously ill. No more of interest. But my mother at present very ill and cannot possibly live many days. She has been in bed since the above time. It is **Easter 1891**."*
What an immense amount of suffering lay behind these words. Like **Edmund's** mother **Ann** and many other women of her time, her body had been worn out by a succession of pregnancies. Beyond the children memorialised at **Sutton,** we find from the **Morton Kin Book** that an infant son had died soon after birth in **1871,** and a stillborn male who was in **1879,** buried in *'a pound'* (low priced) grave at the nearby **Woodhouse Cemetery.** My calculation is that during her marriage to **Edmund, Rosamond** must have endured twelve pregnancies over a period of roughly fifteen years. In those days, to be a mother was often tantamount to a death sentence.

Further correspondence with **Sutton Baptist Church** revealed no reference to **Edmund Smith** having had any direct link with this Church at all. However, this may have been due to the absence of useful records relating to this period. Nevertheless, when set alongside the absence of any involvement at **Blenheim**

Church either, there seems to have been something mysteriously lacking concerning **Edmund's** Church connections. He appeared to have held a greater attachment to the Church in death than in life. Evidence for this emerged from an old Burial Book showing that, in **October 1866,** he had paid a total of **£1.50** (equivalent to **£121.20 in 2014**) toward the cost of burial. This was the largest amount in a column of figures totalling **£4.10** – the next largest being **15** shillings. Such a figure speaks of the great amount of importance my Great Grandfather had given to investing in this burial site. His immediate family would have needed to have travelled a greater distance to attend any burial. Almost all the other interments came from the local area or if they did come from further afield, the distance covered was not as great as that from **Leeds.** The **Smith** burial site was not a typical local phenomenon; the deceased had been determinedly transported to their last resting-place. Indeed, the entire site appeared to have held a special significance for **Edmund.** He had chosen to be buried in the grounds of the Chapel in which his birth had been registered. His life had ended where it had begun.

No burial fees were paid for the other children. This was in keeping with custom as relatively few parents paid burial fees for young children. Perhaps as an act of charity, the Church did not have the heart to press grieving parents on this point. After the double blow of **April 1879, Edmund** was on record as paying **16s** for extra ground on **21st June** of that year. He was clearly anticipating further losses. The old Burial Book also revealed that the **Rev. William Archer** had performed the funeral services for **Hilda** and **Sydney** whilst the **Rev. John Aldiss** had officiated at **Florence's** interment. A **Rev. John Hopkins** had performed the service for **Rosamond** – apparently during the interregnum caused by the **Rev. Aldiss'** departure to another pastorate. Records for this later funeral showed that **Edmund** had paid for the ground but there was no payment of the common burial fee (normally charged for an adult interment.) Possibly due to his grief over **Rosamond's** death, his usual grasp of business affairs had temporarily left him. Perhaps out of charity the Church did not exact a fee.

One telling fact to emerge during the telephone conversation with a representative of **Sutton Baptist Church** was that **Edmund** himself had purchased the burial plots numbered **11 – 16.** They must have cost a small fortune. This again reinforced the impression that there was a man determined to make a statement. He was not returning to **Sutton** out of mere whim or fancy. Considerable planning and forethought had gone into the arrangement of this burial site. Having purchased the empty vaults, the question remains *'why* *two plots were left empty?'* Were they for later wives or for other adult children that he'd hoped would choose to be buried there? Alternatively, did he anticipate more children dying in infancy? Again, as has so often been the case with **Edmund,** the answer has remained elusive. Here was a man who did not easily relinquish his secrets.

A rather gruesome point raised by my then thirteen-year-old middle son (after the second visit) concerned the state of the bodies. He seemed rather fetched by the idea of having the remains dug up and the faces of his Great, Great Grandparents reconstructed by the team from the (then popular) **BBC** television archaeological programme entitled *'Meet the Ancestors.'* By so doing, one supposes that **Edmund** would have made his ultimate contribution to the cause of education. The remains would have amounted to very little. The soil seems to have been highly acidic in composition; minor subsidence had also taken place, which would have had the effect of crushing the bodies that were already piled one on top of the other. Of the original skeletons, only broken splinters would have remained. Also, any vaults would have long since been flooded. Nevertheless, such factors did not deter my son who wrote to the presenter of this programme requesting that the bodies of **Edmund** and his **Victorian** family be dug up. His idea was that having at least **Edmund's** face reconstructed would *'make my dad's millennium.'*

By way of light relief, I will include a slightly abbreviated transcript of my middle son's letter; dated **Monday, 24th January 2000.** It made for very amusing reading, not least because it conveyed his own thoughts concerning the writing of this Family History. (A copy of the previously quoted grave inscriptions was also enclosed with his letter.) In my defence, I would like to stress that this Family History was not as boring as he made it out to be!

*"Hello, my father has recently been looking up his family history. We have been able to trace back our family tree to **1784.** Near the end of **1999,** my father found the obelisk which stood over a vaulted grave containing the remains of my Great, Great Grandfather **Edmund Smith (1832-1915)** and his **Victorian** family. Although most of their lives were lived in **Leeds,** Edmund (who was born in **Sutton-in-Craven** near **Keighley** in **Yorkshire**) chose to be buried there. I wonder if you would like to dig him and his family up? Also, we have a photo of my Great, Great Grandfather and I would like to know how effective your face-remaking techniques are. I have also attached some information for you to read and my dad's family history can be sent if you want it. Honest, it's not too boring.*

Thank you for your attention, goodbye!

P.S. Please dig him up because I am bored with my dad repeating the same information over and over again and it would make his millennium. Also, an SAE is enclosed for your response."

A pleasant but definite *'no'* from the presenter of that programme was the result.

Section 4: Causes of Death

Concerning Victorian health and childhood diseases

Further information about the actual causes of death came in the form of copies of Death Certificates received on **Tuesday 1ˢᵗ February 2000.** To avoid needless repetition only unfamiliar information obtained from these Certificates will be recorded in the following Table: -

Name & Occupation: Rosamond Smith
Age: 47
Cause of Death: Phthisis Pulmonarias 18 months, exhaustion. Certified by A.W.M. Robson F.R.C.S.
When Registered: 3/4/1891
Name and residence of Informant: Edmund Smith 18 Vernon Road

Name & Occupation: Betsey Hastings Smith (Cookery Instructor)
Age: 62
Cause of Death:
(1) Carcinoma Breast (Right) 9 months
(2) Carcinoma Lung (Right) No P.M.
Certified by H. Bedingfield M.B
When Registered: 18/1/1922
Name and residence of Informant: Fred H. Smith – brother in attendance – 26 Hillcrest Avenue, Leeds

Name & Occupation: Ann Helen Smith (Dry Goods Traveller)
Age: 61
Cause of Death:
(1) Bronchitis
(2) Bronchitis, pneumonia 21 days
Cardiac failure 3 days
Certified by S. T. Rowling M.D
When Registered: 18/9/1922

Name and residence of Informant: Fred H. Smith – brother in attendance – 26 Hillcrest Avenue Leeds
(On a speculative note, it's possible to wonder whether these causes of death suggest that the two sisters had been heavy smokers.)

Name & Occupation: Edmund Smith (Retired Commercial Traveller)
Age: 83
Cause of Death:
(1) Chronic Bronchitis and Emphysema
(2) (Tricuspid Valvular Disease of the Heart.) Dropsy – 2 months.
Certified by S. I. Rowling M.B
When Registered: 26/7/1915
Name and residence of Informant:
Hastings Smith – son in attendance – 34 Chapel Lane, Headingley, Leeds

Name & Occupation: Helen Smith
Age: 40
Cause of Death: Rupture of the womb
When Registered: 5/10/1866
Name and residence of Informant: Edmund Smith 16 Vernon Road

Name & Occupation: John William Smith
Age: 1 yr 10m
Cause of Death: Mesenteric disease
When Registered: 5/10/1866
Name and residence of Informant: Edmund Smith 16 Vernon Road

Name & Occupation: Aldyth Rosamond Smith
Age: 0yr   9m
Cause of Death: Bronchitis, Convulsions, certified by Wm Hall M.R.C.S.
When Registered: 2/3/1875
Name and residence of Informant: Edmund Smith 16 Vernon Road

Name & Occupation: Hilda Marian Smith
Age: 2 yr 6m
Cause of Death: Scarlet Fever, Nephritis, Uraemia, certified by A.W.M. Robson M.R.C.S.
When Registered: 28/4/1879
Name and residence of Informant: Edmund Smith 16 Vernon Road

Name & Occupation: Sydney Edmund Smith
Age: 3 yr 6m
Cause of Death: Scarlet Fever 14 days, Nephritis, Uraemia Certified by A.W.M. Robson M.R.C.S.
When Registered: 29/4/1879
Name and residence of Informant: Edmund Smith 16 Vernon Road

Name & Occupation: Florence May Smith
Age: 3 yr
Cause of Death: Scarlatina Fever, Nephritis, certified by Wm Hall M.R.C.S.
When Registered: 30/4/1884
Name and residence of Informant: Edmund Smith 18 Vernon Road

'Phthisis Pulmonalis' was a type of tuberculosis of the lung, whilst mesenteric disease was a disease of the lining of the small intestine, often brought on by an initial *'primary'* stomach infection. **Betsey** and **Ann** were both of **44 Chapel Lane** (also **Betsey's** place of death). The family of **Edmund Smith** all died at one of the **Vernon Road** residences. Each informant attended the relevant death. *'Hastings Smith'* was an abbreviation for **James Hastings Smith** – **Edmund's** eldest son. The reason behind the non-use of his first name remains unknown, but he seemed to want to identify with his mother's family. Each of the five dead children (except for **John William Smith**) were by **Edmund's** second wife **Rosamond**. There was possibly an unnamed stillborn child by **Helen** when she had died in child labour. Hence, it was possible to estimate that six out of a total of fifteen children had died prematurely in infancy.

Behind these facts lay an immense amount of anguish. Insight into the suffering caused by these diseases was provided by the retired nurse and Family Historian **Joan E. Grundy** whom I met at the **York Family History Fair** held on **Saturday, 27th June 2015.** Concerning the highly infectious childhood disease **Scarlet Fever** (first given that name in **1675**) she stated that it *"is characterised by a sore throat, fever, vomiting and headache. A bright red rash appears around the neck and chest then spreads all over the body except the face. The rash blanches with pressure and fades after a week when the skin peels off in large shreds"* **Grundy, 2006 p.69).** As for tuberculosis that killed my Great Grandmother, **Rosamond,** its symptoms included *"fever, severe weight loss, cough with copious amounts of mucus, chest pain or coughing up of blood,"* **(Grundy, 2006 p.79).** This condition usually began with a throat infection with the result that its presence wasn't always immediately detected. However, it must have been utterly traumatic for **Edmund** to have stood helplessly watching as members of his family died. What must have been going through his mind at such a time? One suspects that he chose to cope with his grief by burying himself in his work. After all, there were funeral costs to pay for.

Nor would **Edmund's** end have been easy. **Grundy (2006) p.22** revealed that *"Chronic bronchitis is a condition of ageing and degeneration of the respiratory system. Caused by many years of irritation by pollutants in the atmosphere, smoking or inhaled disease-causing organisms; the bronchial glands secrete excess mucus and inflammation is caused by repeated infections and the airways gradually becoming narrowed. Resulting emphysema and pulmonary hypertension lead to right ventricular failure and the patients face becomes blue, breathing is shallow and profuse quantities of infected sputum are coughed up. Any acute infection on top of chronic bronchitis will cause respiratory failure leading to increased breathlessness, drowsiness, confusion, agitation, headache, a bounding and often irregular pulse, low blood pressure and eventual collapse of the circulatory system."* Having suffered from three or four bouts of chronic bronchitis I can partly identify with what **Edmund** must have gone through. You really do feel as if you're drowning. Twice in **September 2006** and **February 2013,** I was on the brink of hospitalization through this condition. Nevertheless, the fact that my Great Grandfather lived to such an advanced age indicated that he was of the typical hardy **Yorkshire** stock when it came to matters of health.

There are many things that could be said about the information given in the ten Death Certificates. One's immediate feeling is one of sorrow for the great suffering that even a prosperous family of the time will have undergone. (It was still a feeling I had when making final corrections to this section in **May 2018.**) Any religious faith possessed by **Edmund** and his wives must have been sorely tried. Their heartache and anguish can almost be tangibly felt, possibly their rage and anger too. Why would **God** allow their children to be taken at such an early age? How did they cope on a psychological level? Was simple acceptance of *'the* **Lord's** *will'* the best way to have come to terms with each death? **Helen's** own death would have been as a direct result of having endured a ruptured womb with its resultant massive blood loss. Death would have been very quick. Whether the rupture happened spontaneously before or during labour is unknown. Presumably, the child was still in the womb as there was no record of a birth. A stillbirth may not have been put on a Death Register. (My own wife had a similar problem at the birth of our fourth child on **27**th **July 1988.** Even with modern medicine, it required six pints of blood to get her out of danger and at one point I feared whether I would lose her.) With only **Victorian** medicine to rely upon (and blood transfusions not yet invented) **Helen** would have stood no chance of survival. She would most likely have begun her pregnancy in **February 1866.** Any weakness in her womb would have been worsened by the birth of **John William** in the previous **June.** Her body had simply not had time enough to recover following each of the four successive pregnancies.

Concerning the other members of the family, the most serious weakness was to surface in the lungs. The severe smog which often hovered over **Leeds** was in part to be blamed for this situation. Air quality must (for much of the time) have been abysmally poor. **Edmund** and his family were, to some extent, victims of industrial pollution. The technological developments which had helped give them success also helped shorten their lives. If this was the condition of health for a middle-class family what must overall health levels have been like for those living in the slum areas of **Leeds?** In our present age, we must surely be thankful for modern medicine and our greater awareness of (and determination to confront) environmental issues.

The Death Certificates also revealed some telling details about the social world of the **Smiths. Edmund** was very much in charge of such formalities, being the main witness cited on each of the children's and both of his wives' Death Certificates. Census Returns confirmed that he had called upon the services of the local Doctors to attend and certify each death. **Edmund's** children were to remain geographically close together in the same locality of **Leeds** following **Edmund's** own death. The presence of my Grandfather **Frank** at the death of both **Betsey** and **Ann** shows that some degree of closeness had been felt between them. However, **James** (who'd lived barely a street away) was once more mysteriously absent. He was their half-brother, having been born by **Rosamond. Betsey's** evident skill in cooking lends weight to the possibility that she had played the part of a surrogate mother to **Edmund's** other children (born to **Rosamond**) with some degree of effectiveness. It is most likely that she had picked up her culinary skills from her stepmother **Rosamond** rather than from her natural mother, **Helen,** who had died when she'd been a very young girl, aged six. Together **Betsey** and **Rosamond** seemed to have served a good table and if a time machine were available I would be tempted to travel back to the nineteenth century to taste some of their dishes! **Frank's** presence at the deathbed of both his half-sisters seems to have been a sign of care and respect. There appears to have been no division between the **Hastings** or **Stamford** children. The absence of any conflict bears mute testimony to **Rosamond's** diplomatic skills in running a crowded household, where bitter disputes could all too easily have festered. **Ann,** the other surviving daughter of **Helen,** had evidently inherited something of her father's flair for business. In today's world, she would most probably have done well as a very competent career woman. Her father's long involvement in the business realm may well suggest that the dry goods she sold were probably some form of clothing – something with links to the textile industry. However, this point is speculative as '*dry goods*' covered a wide range of products.

Yet even the most thoroughly researched documents simply fail to bring alive the raw feelings of the key participants as they faced all of life's tragedies. Perhaps for **Edmund,** the worst torment was to witness the slow decline of **Rosamond.** God alone knows what feelings of helplessness may have raged through his mind as the '*white death*' of tuberculosis took its toll. Yet his survival to the age of **83** told of a certain tough resilience. Grief did not destroy him. He came back from the brink, re-married and survived for almost another quarter of a century. My review of their Death Certificates renewed my respect for **Edmund,** for his two wives and his two eldest daughters who may all have played a vital part in holding the family together through very difficult times, not least of which were the childhood bereavements. They must have possessed the tremendous stamina to have pulled through it all. In this history, I can only pay tribute to their endurance amidst these highly distressing circumstances.

Section 5: Limited Medical Resources

Concerning Victorian medicine

Further insight into the medical resources available to **Edmund's** family was provided by **Jackson's** booklet on **Victorian Chemists.** (Oddly enough, this piece of literature was found by chance at a second-hand bookshop in **Scarborough** whilst enjoying a week's holiday there from **Saturday, 19th–26th August 2000.**) A photograph (on the inside sleeve of this book) showed a reconstructed interior of a chemist's shop. It had been run by a **Mr Castelow** of **Woodhouse Lane, Leeds.** Its location was on the main road, only some minutes' walk away from **Edmund's** family home. Like any other shop of the time, it had shelves and cabinets full of storage vessels containing liquids and powders which promised to alleviate (or cure) almost every sickness. For **Helen** or **Rosamond,** there were glass breast relievers and nipple shields. Of equal importance were the moulded flask-shaped glass baby feeding bottles. By today's standards, such aids look cumbersome and heavy, but they would have done their job. In contrast, little could have been done for those children who were terminally ill. Weighing scales would have been used to dole out appropriate amounts of Calomel and other similar powders. Sadly, the best that could have been hoped for would have been an alleviation of symptoms, if that. The same would also have applied to any prescribed syrups. The most any **Victorian Chemist** could have done for a dying person would have been the provision of those opiates capable of bringing about a relatively peaceful end.

With information gained from **Jackson,** it became possible to begin searching for a chemist's shop on **Woodhouse Lane,** which was sited nearest to **Vernon Road.** Trade Directories for **1876** revealed the following three chemists.
1) **F. Burnett** at no.**45,** a homoeopathic chemist
2) **J. Abbot** at no.**145,** a pharmaceutical chemist, able to provide the drugs that **Edmund's** family would have needed
3) **E. Brown** at no.**159,** another pharmaceutical chemist, also able to provide the drugs that **Edmund's** family would have needed.

Of these three chemists, **E. Brown** was the one located nearest to **Vernon Road.** His business operated from inside a narrow red brick house (now a Bistro restaurant). In **1876,** it adjoined the **Fenton Hotel** at **161 Woodhouse Lane,** run at that time by a publican called **John Midgley.** (This hotel is now **The Fenton Pub** and is much frequented by **Leeds University** students.) **E. Brown** was still running a Chemist's shop at **159 Woodhouse Lane** until the **1890s.** Sometime thereafter he moved into another shop well up the **Otley Road,** situated within the most respectable and genteel area of **Headingley.** His original premises were taken over by a chemist with the surname of **Bentley.** It was with **E. Brown** that **Edmund** would possibly have had the most contact, especially during the many times when serious illness had blighted his family.

One odd feature was that no Trade Directory showed a late **Victorian Chemist** of the name **Castelow** having been on **Woodhouse Lane.** The only conceivable explanation was that **Castelow** was a name somehow used in association with such a business. Exactly what association (if any) has remained a mystery. What could not be denied was the fact that the reconstructed interior of *"**Mr Castelow's** shop in **Woodhouse Lane, Leeds**"* was that of a pharmaceutical chemist of the kind my Great-grandparents would have used.

A Chemist shop continued to exist at **159 Woodhouse Lane** at least until the early **1960s.** An associate of my wife revealed that it had still preserved its **Victorian** ambience. At the front door and on the left, were three steps leading into the back of the building. The chemist will have worked here – leaving his daughter to serve any customers. In the main shop, she will have worn a black sleeved dress with a white lace collar, her hair tied in a bun or a knot. The chemist himself would have always been *'well turned out'* – wearing a coat and stiff-winged collar, and tie and white sleeves if working. Their demeanour would have been most serious; to smile would have been most unprofessional. (Teenage girls were known to enter the shop and loudly ask to buy contraceptives – cheekily done to provoke a reaction.) The inside cabinet will have held many drawers, each with glass or ceramic rounded handles. Atop the cabinet were ranged three large coloured jars, with another pointed jar taking-up the window space. Each jar contained different coloured water. Overall, the impression was of a small family shop has failed to keep abreast with modern times. Little appeared to have changed since **Edmund's** day.

A final look at the premises (made on **Tuesday, August 28th, 2001**) revealed another very interesting detail. Bright sunlight shone directly onto the glass panel sited above the entrance door. It beautifully silhouetted the following words: -

INCE'S
PULMONIC
CORDIAL

Whether this advert had existed in **Edmund's** day remains a matter of speculation, but somehow, I'd very much like to believe it did! It was clearly advertising a remedy for chest complaints.

Section 6: The Stonemasons

Concerning Victorian stonemasons

A final mystery to be resolved was the likely identity of the stonemasons who had constructed **Edmund's** monument. Unfortunately, a careful examination of the plinth (made on **Monday, February 5th, 2001**) revealed that no trade name had ever been engraved upon it. Consequently, recourse had to be made to the Census Returns which, in the second half of the nineteenth century, revealed three families of stonemasons in **Sutton.** These were:
1) The **Hargreaves** – the **1851** Census showed a **James Hargreaves** who specialised in quarry work. Nevertheless, the name **William Hargreaves** did appear on the plinth of the monument to the **Tetley** family; showing that quarry work was not their sole speciality. By **1881, Samuel Hargreaves** the son of **James Hargreaves** was, at the age of **21,** unemployed. He did not appear to have made a success of his (then late) father's business.

2) The **Heatons** – living at **16 'Bent,'** John Heaton (aged **56**) and **William Heaton** (aged **26**) only appear in the **1871** Census before vanishing again. Their business appears to have been too ephemeral for **Edmund** to have built up any regular contact. They also seemed to have lacked the resources to fashion his rather grand monument.

3) The **Smiths** – present in **Sutton** throughout the crucial period of **1841–1871.** In **1861,** various **Smiths** were living in the **Sutton** locality, including the *"rest of Main Street, head of* **Sutton Bridge** *including* **Sutton Chapel, Sutton Fields..."** Their proximity to the Chapel does indeed strongly suggest that they were the masons responsible for the construction of **Edmund's** memorial. A possible family connection would also explain why they took the trouble to produce a tombstone enjoying an unusually skilled level of craftsmanship. Extra trouble had been taken for someone who was a blood relation. If it wasn't the **Smiths,** then the **Hargreaves** were the next best candidates. Census Returns highlight the longstanding nature of the **Smiths'** business, portrayed in the Returns of **1841, 1851, 1861** and **1871.**

1841 Census
James Smith aged **60** – *'stone mason,'* living in the *'Ellers'* area of **Sutton**
Martha aged **55**
John aged **23** *'stone mason.'*
Jenny aged **20**
William aged **18** *'stone mason.'*
Eden aged **25** *'Bricklayer.'*
Mary Ann aged **2**

1851 Census
John Smith aged **33** *'stone mason,'* living around **Sutton Chapel**
William Smith aged **28** *'stone mason,'* the brother of **John**
Martha Smith aged **36** *'House Servant,'* the sister of **John** and **William**

1861 Census
William Smith aged **37** *'stone mason,'* living at **99 Sutton Fields**
Mary aged **31** *'the wife of* **William Smith***'*
Sarah aged **8** *'scholar.'*
James aged **6**
Maria Ann aged **4**
Elizabeth aged **1**
John Smith aged **42** – *'stone mason,'* living at **100 Sutton Fields**
Martha aged **45**

1871 Census
John Smith aged **52** *'stone mason,'* living at **44 Sutton Fields,** was born in **Sutton**
Martha aged **54** *'House duties.'*

1881 Census
Martha Smith aged **65** *'pauper - poor relief,'* living at **21 Sutton Fields**
William Smith aged **57** – *'stone mason,'* living at **22 Sutton Fields**
Mary aged **31**
James aged **26** *'stone mason.'*
Maria Ann aged **24** *'Twister (worsted).'*
Elizabeth aged **21** *'Rover (worsted).'*
William aged **16** *'Spinner (worsted).'*
Stephen aged **14** *'Spinner (worsted).'*
John aged **12** *'scholar.'*

It is just within the bounds of possibility that **Edmund** hired a stonemason outside **Sutton,** but the transport costs involved in moving heavy pieces of stonework would have been large. There would also have been the risk of damage on the way to the **Baptist** Cemetery. Having established that **William** and **John Smith** were the most likely candidates to have produced the monument in **Sutton Baptist graveyard,** a further question arose over **Edmund's** motive for employing them. After all, his previous relations with the **Smiths** of **Sutton** did not appear to have been very close. One reason was perhaps commercial; he could get a better headstone for a lower price if he employed relations to make it. His own business sense would have taught my Great Grandfather to look for a good bargain and he could easily have applied this skill in planning this memorial. Another motive may have been the desire to display his wealth to poorer relations who had perhaps offended him in the past. **Edmund** was emphasising the point that they were now dependent upon him for money and, unlike them, he would not have needed to send his children to work in a mill to make ends meet. Maybe my Great Grandfather had hoped that news of this expensive headstone would have been passed around to those members of the family with whom he may have *'fallen out'* in the past. Should this have been the case then **Edmund** showed a remarkable capacity to harbour a grudge. Unfortunately, this is a trait that appears to have been passed down successive generations of **Smiths.**

Section 7: An Opulent Household

Concerning the Household Effects of Edmund

One amazing discovery was made by my <u>second</u> cousin on **Monday, November 2015.** (**Ann Dalton** the Great Granddaughter of **Hedley,** <u>not</u> to be confused with my <u>first</u> cousin **Pamela Smith** the daughter of **Fred's** elder brother **Stewart** who told me of **Edmund's** tomb.) An e-mail I received from her on **9th November** of that year will take up the story and give a flavour of the excitement that can be generated when writing a Family History.

"Richard
Not knowing if you have already seen this article but my cousin (half-cousin of Mum) and I were trawling 'Find My Past' and found this under **Edmund.** *Reading it I had tears in my eyes – a man of taste, knowledge and my great-great-grandfather. Do you have an article registering his death and funeral at all – we tried looking but couldn't readily find"* [it]
Ann"

When I first scanned this article, I could only exclaim, *'What a man! What a man!'* Its contents will explain why I had this reaction.

*"**ROBERT LEVITT,***
AUCTIONEER and VALUER
1 and 2 VICTORIA CHAMBERS, SOUTH PARADE
Tel 2497 LEEDS
15, VERNON ROAD, LODGE STREET LEEDS.

*Items Mr **Edmund Smith,** deceased.*

***ROBERT LEVITT** – will be held by Auction at the above address,*
*On **MONDAY, November 1st, 1915** commencing at **11** o'clock*
T HE Very useful HOUSEHOLD FURNITURE

And Effects of the deceased comprising: –

The CAPITAL DINING ROOM FURNITURE, which presents a
7ft. Spanish mahogany enclosed sideboard, with marble top and
Plate-glass back; a mahogany suite of 6 apron-back chairs, gentle-
man's easy chair and couch upholstered in crimson velvet,

*mahogany telescope dining table, an American walnut secretaire
bookcase with glass upper doors. The APPOINTMENTS of the
DRAWING-ROOM embrace Italian chiffonier, en-
riched with plate-glass and marble; a carved walnut suite of 9
pieces of Genoa Velvet, and oblong walnut window table, large
chimney glasses in gilded frames. Wilton and Brussels CAR
PETS in the various rooms and on the stairs and landing,
Mahogany hat and umbrella stand, and a pair of hall chairs, a
Number of framed oil paintings, engravings and etchings, brass
And other fenders and hearth implements, a quality of glass
And china, some electro-plate clocks and mantel ornaments, including a fine oak bracelet clock striking on a gong. Mahogany
6ft winged wardrobe, with plate glass door; mahogany and painted
toilet tables and dressing chests, Ilkley couch, toilet glasses
and bedroom chairs, a very fine mahogany "Tall Boy" chest of
drawers, brass, iron and mahogany bedsteads, wire and hair
mattresses, feather beds, a quality of bed and table linen,
quilts and blankets, window curtains. The kitchen Furniture,
culinary and domestic requisites and other household effects
Also, at **2 o'clock***

*About 400 VOLUMES OF BOOKS
Amongst which will be found a subscription set of 25 Vols.
Historians History of the World in a set of oak shelves; **John
Leech's**, the works of **J. M. W. Turner,** Old England.
Picturesque America, and other illustrated works, **Collier's**
Shakespeare, **Morley's** Life of **Gladstone,** Annals of Yorkshire,
And a large selection of Miscellaneous Literature.
        To be open on the sales Morning after **9** o'clock"*

Beyond the crowded opulence of the house, several points emerged from this
advert and from the links on subsequent pages. It was reasonable to deduce that
my Great Grandfather was: -
1. A man of taste and refinement who aspired to be a gentleman
2. Still collecting books into his mid-70s when he was already established and
there was no need to impress customers
3. Had remarkably similar literary tastes to my own – even to those of two of
my children
4. In charge of a house that couldn't have been child-friendly

5. A man whose belongings included furniture brought in by his wives – the gilded items could well have come from his third wife, **Sarah.**

Most noticeable was how this late finding tended to confirm earlier judgements I'd made about my Great Grandfather's internal motivations. He appeared to have been compensating for his earlier deprivations by hoarding possessions and acquiring a great deal of self-taught book learning. (The latter trait was evident in my own late father.) This was a typical characteristic of a self-made man from a poor background. One wonders how he managed to pay for all of these items. Did he (like my late **Auntie Madge**) dabble in antiques and purchase them at knock down prices? Who knows? But it would have been like him to have done so.

On a far less happy note, his children (or at least **James** who was the executor of the will) appear to have been determined to get rid of everything associated with him as quickly as he could. Once again, an odd pattern of behaviour was being manifested by **James.** Although many of the items would have appeared old-fashioned by **1915** there would have been things like books, paintings and useful items of furniture which the family could have kept as heirlooms if, so they'd wished. But oddly enough the whole lot was got rid of in one go. Was it the case of a resentful son wishing to break all links with a once-feared father? The only things, known to have been passed down my own family line were **Edmund's** photograph and a silver gilded cigar case. A Family Bible that may have been in the family was passed down the line to his elder brother **Samuel** and appeared to have been lost around the time of his death in **1886.** However, a phone conversation with one of his descendants on **Wednesday 20th 2018** revealed no knowledge of any such heirloom. Perhaps **James** had that sold off as well. Again, he seems firmly determined to put an unhappy past behind him. But *'why the haste?'*

Section 8: Things Fall Apart

Concerning the hurried Sale of Edmund's Houses

One clue as to why **James** was apparently so keen to sell off his father's household assets with such apparently indecent haste was provided by the following notice (on the second page of the **Yorkshire Post**) dated **Saturday, 13th November 1915:** -

"ROBERT LEVITT,
AUCTIONEER and VALUER
1 and 2 VICTORIA CHAMBERS, SOUTH PARADE Tel 2497   LEEDS

Re **Edmund Smith,** *deceased.*

PEREMPTORY SALE BY ORDER OF MORTGAGES OF TWO EXCELLENT FREEHOLD DWELLING HOUSES in VERNON ROAD, off LODGE STREET WOODHOUSE LANE, LEEDS

Within a few minutes' walk of the Infirmary, University, and Grammar Schools and about ten minutes' walk from the centre of the City

*The two houses will be first offered in one lot, and if not sold Then separately; they are most substantially built of brick And blue slate. They were erected by the owner from the Designs of **Mr Wm Hill**, architect of **Leeds. Mr Smith** lived In **No. 18** from the time they were built until his death a few Months ago.*

If thrown together the houses would be very roomy, would make An excellent Nursing Institution, Boarding-House for students Or Education Establishment or for any of these purposes or For occupation as Dwelling houses. The position is most con- venient.

ROBERT LEVITT *instructed by Mortgagees will offer for Sale By Auction, at the **Packhorse Inn Woodhouse, Leeds** on* **MONDAY, December 6th, 1915,** *at 7 o'clock precisely, sub- ject to condition.*

THE TWO WELL-BUILT FREEHOLD DWELL- ING HOUSES
Nos 18 *and* **20 VERNON ROAD, LEEDS**
With early possession.
Further particular and arrangements for inspecting the pro- Perty will be announced next week; meantime inquiries may be Made of the Auctioneer **1** *and* **2, Victoria Chambers, South Parade;** *or*
Messrs **MIDDLETON** *and* **SONS** *Solicitors*
Calverley Chambers, Leeds."

A note of desperation pervaded this announcement. Revenue from the houses was needed to pay off the Mortgagees whilst family members would receive nothing. The clear implication is that these properties had not been fully paid for. It seemed that whilst in the process of administration this Will, **James** had opened the proverbial *'can of worms.'* Instead of dealing with legacies to be passed onto family members, he (possibly and very distressingly) uncovered only a pile of debts. He may also have found material of a scandalous nature. (*i.e.* letters from ladies perhaps?) If he came across **Helen's** letters for the first time, he perhaps felt that his father had shamefully neglected his mother. The resulting sense of disorientation at discovering that his father's wealth was only a façade must have been profound. Moreover, it would have been left to him to break the news to family members that in apparent contradiction to the will of **1912,** there were <u>no</u> shares to pass around. Whatever he did find, it was enough to provoke a sufficient to provoke a sufficiently large crisis of conscience for him to consult an **Anglican** Clergyman friend (the **Reverend Arthur** (or **Archibald**) **Hawthorne**) who advised him to destroy all personal references to his father in his diary. Interestingly, this clergyman was not on record as being a vicar of any church where **James** had any connection with which suggested he'd felt the need for assistance from a person somewhat removed from his embarrassing situation.

The first impression gained from the *'Probate Document'* of **14th December 1915,** was the speed at which the careful arrangements made in **Edmund's** will fell apart after his death. **James Hastings** and **James Barraclough** had resigned from their position as Trustees and were leaving the administration of the will to my Grandfather **Fred Hesslewood** – a man whose discretion they evidently trusted. The probate document revealed that, although the *'Gross Value'* of Edmund's estate was £2,131.18.8, (worth £212,845.09 in **2018** prices) once all liabilities had been deducted the *'Net Value'* was *'nil.'* **Edmund** <u>wasn't worth a penny.</u> There must have been a huge amount of debts to pay off. **Edmund** seemed to have subsidised his life with a series of loans. The Probate document mentioned that standing as sureties for my great Grandfather's debts were *"**Robertson Buchanan Stewart** and **Archibald [Terrill?]** both of **146 Argyle Street, Glasgow** in **Scotland**, merchants."* Both men appear to have been senior figures in the company he'd worked for. The man they'd trusted had not been all he'd seemed.

Edmund must have been very persuasive to have been able to keep up with this financial *'gerrymandering'* until his death in **1915.** On making this discovery, **James** may well have been overwhelmed by a sense of shame. Following such developments, it's hardly surprising that he and **Barraclough** would have wanted to abandon the responsibility of administrating the probate as quickly as possible. Very likely, there was nothing left for his brother **Fred Hesslewood** to administer when he took over the running of the Will. He perhaps did so to support his brother and keep peace in the family. The close relationship which **Frank** continued to enjoy with **James** suggested that he didn't resent having been given this task. My Grandfather **Frank** appeared to have been one of those sound, solid types who could be relied upon in a crisis. His children continued to visit their *'Uncle Jim'* long after his death which suggested that congenial relationships had only ever existed between the two men. Like my father **Fred** and my eldest son **Ben, Frank** appears to have naturally fitted in with the role of Family peacemaker.

The last question to remain is why did **Edmund** go to the trouble of producing a bogus will which would leave his children with the impression that they would have a generous legacy when in reality, there was none? Either my Great Grandfather thought he had the money when he didn't, or he'd written out a will to pacify family members and to stop them from pressurising him. Personally, I'm inclined to believe the last explanation.

Consultations with two psychologists confirmed that my Great Grandfather had displayed many of the personality traits associated with a child having been brought up in troubled circumstances. Like many victims of childhood deprivation, he possessed an all-encompassing obsession with personal achievement (which was to stay with him for the rest of his life). The effect of this obsession was to reverberate down the branches of the subsequent **Smith** line that **Edmund** himself was to produce. Furthermore, there were his restless wanderings as a Commercial Traveller (with **Leeds, Hull** and **Harrogate** being three proven locations), and his definite tendency to personal grandiosity. He seemed always to be compensating for some loss in his own childhood. One suspects that **Edmund** was not an easy man to get close to. Like my own father (and other members of the **Smith** family) he was, to some extent, *'a loner.'*. Behind the successful businessman, lay the twelve-year-old orphan desperately unsure of his future and knowing all too well what poverty do to people. The deprivation he had both endured and seen had left its mark. His line of work may have placed considerable pressure to constantly convey *'a positive social image.'* For much of this research into our Family History, I was left with the rather the disturbing picture of a very ambitious man willing to *'re-invent himself'* to acquire the status he so obviously craved

Furthermore, his sending of at least four of his sons to **Leeds Grammar School** showed a man willing to pay handsomely to fulfil his social aspirations. He may have wanted them to enjoy the *'respectability'* he felt he never had. The near marriage of **Betsey** to an *'up and coming'* medical student (who, in later life, would receive a peerage) pointed in the same direction. **Edmund Smith** was a parent wanting to realize his ambitions through his children This desire would inevitably create tensions.

On a much lighter note, a succession of photographs revealed that **Edmund** did have an eye for fashion in beards! During his lifetime what can be termed as his *'hair gear'* ranged from the **Abraham Lincoln** *'look'* of the late **1850s,** through to a **Charles Dickens,** then a resplendent **Charles Darwin** beard of later decades. By **1911**, he was sporting an **Edward VII** look. The only consistent feature was his desire to pass as a gentleman; for **Edmund,** image mattered.

Having now had **Edmund** on the Psychiatrist's couch, it must be stated that severe early childhood deprivation is only a plausible hypothesis rather than a proven fact; nevertheless, as a hypothesis, it would explain much that would remain otherwise unexplained. However, a word of caution must be sounded. If I have learnt one thing from this from almost two decades of producing a Family History, it is that all the available information may, at one stage be pointing in one specific direction only for proof to come along to disprove the whole thing entirely! In the end, despite my best efforts I could never quite wrap my head around **Edmund.** He remained in many ways an enigma who in his dealings with others could either be very constructive or very destructive, it was one way or the other with him.

Sadly, his flaws clouded very real and long-lasting achievements. These were of such magnitude that they helped set the tone for the succeeding branches of the **Smith** family. Without **Edmund** giving a high value to education many of the achievements of his descendants would not have been possible. Not only had this **Smith** patriarch brought up a large family in at least some degree of comfort – amidst the instability of the late **Victorian** economy, he also made *'key decisions'* which have reverberated down to this very day **(2018).** One of these was the erection of a prominent monument that almost seemed to invite discovery. Another was his establishment of a link with **Leeds Grammar School** and very possibly with the **Jewish Community** through his business work. My research into **Edmund's** life provoked tremendous feelings of ambivalence; sometimes, I hugely admired the man, whilst on other occasions, I was appalled by the implications of some of the things that were being uncovered – most notably the lack of consideration for his wives. In the end, I concluded that, although not necessarily a likeable character, **Edmund** could still be respected for his very real (rather than his imagined and sometimes exaggerated) achievements. The time really <u>has</u> arrived for him to be *'given him his due.'*

Section 8: An Enduring Influence

Two visits made to **Edmund's** grave (on **Saturday 26th July** and **Saturday 9th August 2003**) confirmed the insidious effect time was having on his monument. The stone facing surrounding **Helen's** inscription was beginning to flake off and elsewhere the stonework was becoming discoloured with a greenish black hue. This erosion confirmed that the discovery of **Edmund's** tomb had (like other discoveries in this Family History) come only just in time. During the first of these visits a conversation with the gardener confirmed that, other than the wind, the main corrosive agent had been layer upon layer of soot, steadily deposited over the course of a century. He also reassured me that, because of my keen interest in the monument, he would take care to cut the grass around it. Another visit made with my wife two weeks confirmed that he'd kept his word.

In **2010** further insights were also gained about the **Smith** line. During my fifty-fourth birthday (on **May 3rd, 2010**) I arranged a visit to previously described Family History Sites around **Cowling, Sutton and Crosshills.** Present was my wife, my middle son, his partner and our grandson **Arnold** (who'd been born on **Thursday, 23rd July 2009**). Photographs were taken around **Edmund's** grave and I couldn't help wondering what he would have thought of his monument being visited by his great, great, great grandson. He would also have been surprised that his great, great grandson's partner came from the same part of **Yorkshire** as his first two wives. The words *'chip off the old block'* may well have come to mind.

However, the greatest privilege of that day was being able to gain access to the upstairs room of *'The Old White Bear Inn.'* The **Kildwick Friendly Society** had met here in this very same room during the **1830s.** It was, by **May 2010,** a storage room (having also briefly been a former brewing area). Some of the old gas light fittings were still present – as was the fireplace, itself unchanged since that time. It was also possible to reconstruct where members of the society would have sat. To have been in the same room where one's great, great grandfather had socialised some **170** years previously was an amazing experience. We looked around in awe – feeling a deep connection with the past.

As an aside, I will mention that three days after this, (late on **May 6th** and into the early hours of **Friday 7th May 2010**) I along with my sons saw *'history in the making'* with my three sons. We were viewing (with each vociferously commenting upon) the results of The General Election on BBC television. This would see the formation of a new Coalition Government five days later. My middle son came in wearing a *'T'* shirt with a Liberal Democrat poster stuck to it. Meanwhile, my wife **June** had retired to bed after supplying a generous helping of food. With work the next day she'd felt it best to leave us *'to get on with it.'* Early on it became very apparent that a *'hung parliament'* was in the offing and that the wonderful **British** Public had made all three of the main political parties look like losers. I remember enjoying a feeling of paternal pride at the amount of political interest being shown by this younger generation of **Smiths.**

Edmund's influence was to linger on in another way. At the beginning of **2012,** my Private Tutoring Business almost collapsed. In part, this was due to the *'great recession'* of **2008,** but other factors had also come into play; including an increase in student tuition fees which made private tutoring appear far less affordable. On top of that, a sudden rush away from face-to-face and toward *'online'* tutoring had caught me somewhat unprepared (although I had considered this market only a couple of years earlier but had found nothing much was happening then). The severe weather of **2012** brought me no consolation either. In combination, these factors (amongst other) caused a sudden and prolonged collapse in demand and thus my opening bank balance for **March 2012** stood at a mere £**84.72.** Drastic steps needed to be taken to reduce outlays. For the first ten months of that *'horror'* year, I endured a grim struggle for survival. I battled to re-organize my business by gaining new online skills and contacting any agency that appeared even remotely capable of providing work. The worst thing was not knowing (at first) how this sudden reversal had come about. Things only began to improve towards the end of **October 2012,** when I gained four undergraduate **Saudi Arabian Business Studies** students. I knew then that I would survive – albeit by an uncomfortably narrow margin.

I had found that wavering so near to financial ruin throughout this ghastly period had been akin to pacing to and fro in a death cell; my mind had been thoroughly and acutely sharpened. I discovered anew where my priorities lay in this sort of situation. Furthermore, I'm of the opinion that you only ever really know you're a businessman when you've survived at least one major recession.

What proved hugely beneficial was my habit of going swimming twice a week which helped me cope with the inner stress. Many men in their mid-fifties couldn't have experienced what I'd gone through without having suffered a major breakdown in health. **2012** was certainly a year I was glad to see the back of. When my wife and I *'saw in'* the New Year of **2013** at my mother's flat we'd all sang *'Auld Lang Syne'* and I'd blurted out *"Thank God I've survived!"* My wife had responded by throwing me a reproachful look but that's exactly how I'd felt! By **March 2013** (after paying for half of our planned holiday to **Rome** in **August** of that year) my bank account stood at a far healthier £1411.18. Nevertheless, it had been a very close call – far too close for my liking.

During this dreadful period, the example of **Edmund's** own resilience in the face of hardship had proved an absolute inspiration. As one workless day succeeded another I'd thought, *"If my great-grandfather could survive six major recessions, I can survive one! This is not going to destroy me!"* My former **Asian** Agent from **Manchester** (who'd paid two visits – one in mid-**February** and the other in early **September** of **2012**) remarked that it seemed as if the genes of **Edmund Smith** were *'kicking in.'* His wise advice proved essential. His <u>first</u> visit had prevented me from taking a wrong decision whilst his <u>second</u> encouraged me to take a right decision! He shrewdly remarked that, whereas on his first chance visit I'd looked dreadful, on the second he could tell I was getting back on my feet again. His advice had perhaps been a life-saver and for that reason, I owe him much. Out of respect, I've included him in this history. When I bumped into him on **Sunday, March 11th, 2018**, outside his parent's home in **Headingley,** he still took a keen interest in it. He requested a copy which I promised he received as a well-deserved present on **Thursday, 31st January 2019.** Anyway, it's now fitting to begin tracing the mixed fortunes of **Edmund's** surviving children – beginning with those by his first wife **Helen.**

CHAPTER 13: IN EDMUND'S SHADOW

Section 1: A Pleasant Suburb

Concerning the Suburb of Headingley

The children of **Helen (James, Betsy** and **Ann)** lived in the respectable suburb of **Headingley** in **North West Leeds** from the **1880s** until **1953** The following is a *'Timeline'* of **Headingley's** history. The most significant period of growth took place during the nineteenth century. It was to transition from being a village (whose scattered buildings straddled around a heart-shaped green) to an outer suburb of **Leeds.** This accounts for the way the sub-sections of the following timeline are grouped, (all dates are A.D.).

<u>Pre-Industrial Period</u>
C650: **Anglo-Saxon** settlement, with an early Manor House. This was once situated on the present site of **Headingley Hall** – currently **(2018)** a Residential Care Home for the elderly, on **Shire Oak Road.** (Following a series of falls in her flat in **Alwoodley** my mother was there from **July 2014** until **July 2017**.)
C900: Period of Viking domination. Headingley – now the centre and meeting place of a wapentake named *'Skyrack.'*
1069-70: Headingley and other areas around **Leeds** (the latter allegedly spared because of the intercession of a priest) are *'laid waste'* by **William the Conqueror's** *'harrying of the North,'* launched in retaliation to an earlier rebellion. This campaign disgusted the **Anglo-Norman** Chronicler **Orderic Vitalis (1075-1142)** *"The King stopped at nothing to hunt his enemies. He cut down many people and destroyed homes and land. Nowhere else had he shown such cruelty! This made a real change. To his shame, **William** made no effort to control his fury, punishing the innocent with the guilty. He ordered that crops and herds; tools and food be burned to ashes. More than **100,000** people perished of starvation. I have often praised **William** in this book, but I can say nothing good about this brutal slaughter. God will punish him."*
1086: The Domesday Book provides the following details concerning **Headingley:** -
Hundred (an administrative sub-division of a county): Skyrack
Area: West Riding
County: Yorkshire
Total population: 2 households (very small).
Total tax assessed: 7 geld units (quite large)
Taxable units: Taxable value 7 geld units.
Value: Value to lord in 1066 £2. Value to lord in 1086 £0.2.

Households: 2 villagers.
Ploughland: 3.5 ploughlands for 1 man's plough team.
Lord in 1066: Thanes two,
Lord in 1086: Ilbert De lacy (based at Pontefract Castle).
Tenant-in-chief in 1086: Ilbert De lacy (The low population may well have been the result of the severe famine that followed **William the Conqueror's** *'harrowing of the North.'* **Headingley Manor** (the Manor House) was granted to **Ilbert's** sub-tenant, **Baron Walter de Poitevin,** who'd come over with **William the Conqueror** in **1066.**)

1152: Henry de Lacy persuades his sub-tenant **William de Poiteven** to grant land to aid the foundation of **Kirkstall Abbey.** The latter quickly becomes a local economic centre, based upon the woollen trade. Its prosperity meant that building on its site continued for most of its history.

c.1300: A bridge across **Meanwood Beck** (on the site of **Monkbridge Road**) links the **Headingley Estate** to other lands owned by the Abbey.

c.1310: Headingley Manor passes by marriage from the **Poitevens** to the wealthy land-owning **Calverley** family. The Manor House of **Headingley** recorded as having a barn and a Brewhouse beside it. Under its control is the Corn Mill at *'Bentley'* field on **Meanwood Beck.**

c.1324: John de Calverley grants the entire manor of **Headingley** (with all its dues and revenues) to **Kirkstall Abbey.** One of the **Poiteven** family contest this transfer in a bitterly fought legal case but is defeated. The **Abbey** subsequently rents off the **Manor House** to wealthy tenants.

1318: The Scots raid and devastate **Wharfedale.** They burn **Pannal Church.**

1341: John de Calverley gives the remainder of the township of **Headingley-cum-Burley** to **Kirkstall Abbey.** By this period the monks of **Kirkstall Abbey** have established a Grange in what is now **Beckett's Park.**

1349: The Black Death strikes; seven out of fourteen parish priests around the **Leeds** area die from that infection, as does the Prioress of **Arthington.** From that year until **1355 Kirkstall Abbey** has had four abbots in quick succession, with at least some of the incumbents dying of plague.

1509-1527: Abbot William Marshall heightens the central tower of **Kirkstall Abbey** and has his initials engraved on it.

1536: Two Commissioners (sent by **Henry VIII's** chief minister **Thomas Cromwell**) inspect **Kirkstall Abbey** with a view to dissolving it.

22 November 1539: Kirkstall Abbey – with its Abbott and remaining thirty-one community members peacefully surrender to **Henry VIII's** commissioners. During the subsequent dissolution, its bells are melted down and its roof removed. All its land is given to **Archbishop Thomas Cranmer** in **1542** but reverts to the Crown in **1556** following his disgrace and burning at the stake by **Queen Mary.**

1564: Sir Robert Saville purchases the Abbey estate (including **Headingley**) from the Crown – which is facing severe financial problems under **Queen Elizabeth 1.**

1583: The now ruined Abbey is added to **Robert Saville's** estate. The old buildings are used to store cattle and hay.

1619/20: A Chapel (with the capacity to hold **200** people and ministered by a curate) is built on **Headingley Green.** This is common land owned by **Sir John Saville (1555/6-1630).**

1627: Headingley Chapel is licensed as a place of worship.

1644: Cavaliers (fugitives from the **Royalist** defeat at **Marsden Moor**) are reputed to have hidden in the ruins of **Kirkstall Abbey.**

1649: Headingley Hall is built and replaces the old Manor House. **John Killingbeck** – future vicar of **Leeds (1690-1716)** and local benefactor is born in the Hall shortly after its construction. (The **Killingbeck** family hold the tenancy until the **1680s.**)

1661: Sir Thomas Brudenell is given the title **Earl of Cardigan**

1668: Marriage of **Francis Lord Brudenell (1654-98) and Francis Saville** (who died **1695**).

1671: The death of **James Saville (1647-71)** means that **Headingley** and the site of **Kirkstall Abbey** pass from the **Saville** to the **Brudenell** *('Earl of Cardigan')* family. Their son **George** becomes the third **Earl of Cardigan (1685-1732)** in **1703.** However, he pays only annual visits to **Headingley** to oversee the collection of rent and to visit his most important tenants. The family spend most of their time in **London,** enjoying fashionable society.

1711: A map reveals **Headingley** as a heart-shaped community with a chapel, labourer cottages and farmsteads scattered around a triangular village green. Enclosed fields are situated around the settlement with a large tract of common land, **Headingley Moor,** to the north. Each of the buildings is separated by smaller enclosed fields. A tannery and brewery are sited nearby, further down the **Otley Road** towards **Leeds.**

1724: The **Leeds**-based local historian **Ralph Thoresby (1658-1725)** describes **Headingley Hall** as *'a venerable fabric... near the Shire-ake'* (oak).

1745: Soldiers muster on **Woodhouse Moor** in response to the **Jacobite** rebellion (crushed in **1746**).

1752: A large country house *'The Grange'* is built on the site of a former **Kirkstall Abbey** farmstead in what is now **Beckett's Park.**

1755: The turnpike road (from **Skipton** and **Otley** to **Leeds**) is opened. A tollgate on **Woodhouse Moor** charges **2d.** Cattle Drovers stopping at *'The*

Original Oak' rest their cattle in the surrounding fields. (This continues until the early nineteenth century.)

1783: A Charity School is built. Its premises later become **The Skyrack Public House.**

1792: Benjamin Gott (1762-1840) uses £17,000 of capital to set-up the world's first woollen mill **(Park Mills)** on a **16**-acre site at **Bean Ing** by the **River Aire.** (Now the site of the **Yorkshire Post Building** in **Westgate**). This marks the beginning of the Industrial Revolution in **Leeds.** (The mill is demolished during the **1960s.**)

The Industrial Period

1801: The population of **Headingley** is **300**

1805: John Marshall (1765-1845) a flax entrepreneur, moves to **New Grange, Headingley** (formerly **The Grange**) as the upper middle classes begin to flee the noise and pollution of central **Leeds.** (He remains there with his family and twelve servants until **1818.**) Middle-class incomes range from £150 to £400 per year.

1811: Death of **James Brudenell (1715-1811)** the **Fifth Earl of Cardigan.** His estate begins to be divided up.

1819: John Marshall and **Benjamin Gott** are the wealthiest members of the Middle Class in **Leeds. John Marshall** purchases **Headingley House** for use in winter. (In **1825,** he would purchase a house in the exclusive **Grosvenor Square, London.**)

1820: Economic hardship means that owners of the former **Cardigan Estate;** to begin selling off their land for building plots. This directly paves the way for **Headingley's** development as a suburb of **Leeds.** Construction begins with the large sandstone villas specifically built for the wealthy merchants and industrialists along the **Otley Road,** near to **Saint Michael's Church.**

1827: Attempts (initiated by **Robert Brudenell** the **Sixth Earl of Cardigan, 1760-1837**) to find coal in **Headingley** fail, despite sinking bores down to **270** feet. This prevents it from becoming industrialised.

1829: An Act of Parliament encloses **Headingley Moor** (now under housing around **Moor Road**) and the land is placed for sale. Around thirty workers' cottages already encroach upon the fringes of the moor and upward along **North Lane.** (Land in this locality is generally cheaper than that of **Headingley Hill,** simply because it has failed to attract the building of affluent villas.)

1830: There are **100 Methodists** in **Headingley**

1831: The last plots in **Headingley** and the Moor are finely divided and enclosed, thus freeing it for future development. The population grows to around **2,000.**

1834: William Beckett purchases **The Grange** and in **1858** refurbishes the surrounding the estate.

1836: Headingley Hill House is built

1836-8: A new and larger **Saint Michael's Anglican Church** (with a seating capacity of **600**) is built on the side of the old chapel for a cost of £2,582 – in the old chapel people had been fighting over seats – it had simply become too small to accommodate everyone.

1839: Castle Grove and other villas are built **East** of **Moor Road**

1840: Headingley Castle (formerly known as *'The Elms'*) is built south of **Shire Oak Road.** Its grounds comprise around **25** acres of lakes and gardens and a Bear Pit (which in **2017** can still be seen on **Cardigan Road**). **The Zoological and Botanical Gardens** around **Cardigan Road** are opened to appeal to a middle-class clientele. **Buckingham House** (just back from the **Otley Road**) is also built and enclosed about with a large boundary wall. (By **2016,** it was being converted into apartment flats.)

1844: Saint Michael's National School opens near the Church.

1845: Headingley Methodist Church opens and, by **1851,** has **200** attending the morning service. Families pay the pew rent; the men wear starched collars and the lady's hats. There is little dialogue with other Denominations.

1846/7: The construction of **Headingley Terrace** and **Wesley Terrace** mark the arrival of the lower middle classes. **Meanwood Beck** continues to supply water for **Headingley.**

1849: Headingley Railway Station, situated on the **Leeds-Thirsk** branch of the **Leeds Northern Railway** is opened. It facilitates access to **The Zoological and Botanical Gardens** and further migration into **Headingley. The Rev William Williamson** becomes the first vicar when **Headingley** is allowed by the **Church of England** Authorities to become an independent Parish. He organizes a parish lending library and arranges for the re-building of **Saint Michael's Primary School** – bringing it closer to the Church. The school's small garden area is all that remains of the formerly large and heart-shaped village green. The remainder of it has been built over by the school.

25.10.1854: Lieutenant General **James Thomas** the **Seventh Earl of Cardigan (1797-1868)** leads the **Light Brigade** charge in the **Crimea**. Despite its near annihilation he is hailed as a popular hero, being honoured with a Grand Reception, held at **Leeds Stock Exchange** in **June 1856.**

1858: The Zoological and Botanical Gardens run into financial difficulties and close. By this period (and until **1870**) many professional and tradespeople move away from the centre of **Leeds** and further out into the newly forming suburb villas and semi-detached houses. These dwellings are constructed all along **Headingley Lane** and eastward toward **The Ridge** (overlooking

Meanwood Valley). Examples of the terraced housing (built in the **1850s**) include **Victoria Terrace, St George's Terrace, Balmoral Terrace,** and **Marlborough Terrace.**

7.9.1858: At a cost of **£122,000, Leeds Town Hall** is opened by **Queen Victoria** during a successful royal visit. **Dr Hook** leads the procession and presents the address. On the way to the opening, the Queen travels up **Victoria Road** and inspects **32,110** school children (with **60,000** adults) gathered on **Woodhouse Moor.** Up to **150,000** witness her arrival to the newly built Town Hall through triumphal arches and decorated streets. The **Leeds Mercury** boasts, *'for a portion of two days (through the condescension of Her Majesty) this old and busy seat of industry became the seat of the Empire.'* (The Town Hall subsequently becomes a new centre of Police and Court administration.)

1859/60: A pumping station is built on **Bennett Road** to supply **Headingley** with extra water.

1868: Saint Chad's Church is constructed in **Far Headingley** on land freely given by the **Beckett** Family – themselves now living in **Kirkstall Grange.** They contribute **£10,000** towards the building costs. The **Seventh Earl of Cardigan** dies following a fall from his horse. His extravagant lifestyle leaves his widow **Adeline** hundreds of thousands of pounds in debt.

1869: To begin paying off the late **Earl's** debts **Adeline** consents to the sale of land in **Headingley.**

1870: St Augustine's, Wrangthorne, facing **Woodhouse Moor** is built.

1873: The **Little Sisters of the Poor** nunnery in **Headingley** is completed and located near the **Otley Road.**

1874: The foundation stone of **Leeds University** is laid.

A Suburb of Leeds

1875: The extension of horse-drawn trams to a depot at **Far Headingley** ensure its transition from a village to a suburb of **Leeds** itself.

1876: The fee-paying **Leeds Girls High School** is opened. It caters to girls in the three to eighteen age range. (It would merge with **Leeds (Boys) Grammar School** in **2005.** In **2008** this educational facility vacated the **Headingley** site to join the **Grammar School** which had moved to **Alwoodley** in **1997.**)

1882: Bennett Road Primary School is opened

1883: Steam trams replace horse-drawn trams, further facilitating ease of access to **Leeds** Centre

1884-6: Following some local opposition a third **Saint Michael's Church** is built on the site of the second church at a cost of **£25,000.**

1888: The **Marshall family** sell the last of their land in **Headingley,** thus freeing it up to be used for house building. This development encourages a further increase in **Headingley's** population.

12.1888: The last of the **Cardigan Estate** (including **Kirkstall Abbey**) is sold off in a four-day auction. **Lot 17a** (comprising **17** acres of *'pasture and woodland, ripe for development'*) is sold to *'a company of gentlemen'* who plan to build a magnificent cricket and football ground.

1889: The ruins of **Kirkstall Abbey** are purchased by **Colonel John North** who hands it over to **Leeds City Council** who then begin to restore it.

1889/91: Headingley rugby and cricket grounds are built and opened on **Lot 17a.**

1891: A police station opens adjacent to the pumping station on **Bennett Road.** During the course of that decade, **Otley Road** develops into a major shopping site, with a large variety of retail premises.

1895: Kirkstall Abbey is opened to the public

1897: Rugby League's first Challenge Cup is held in **Headingley Stadium**

1899: The first *'Test Matches'* are held in **Headingley.** Electric trams are introduced

1901: The population of **Headingley** is **41,000,** (three times greater than in **1871**).

1903: Beckett's Park Teacher Training College is set up almost next door to **The Grange.** It had cost £**240,000** to purchase this **99**-acre site.

1909: South Parade Baptist Church opens

1911: The population of **Headingley** is **46,000.** By this period most of **Headingley** has been built and is now very much an important suburb of **Leeds. Saint Chad's Church** acquires a large new organ

1912: Opening of **The Cottage Road Cinema** – one of the first in **Britain**

1914: The **Hyde Park Picture House** opens, having been converted from a former hotel (itself having been built in **1908**).

8.1914: The First World War begins

12.1914: The **National Council of Women** initiate **Voluntary Women's Patrols** to *"define and assist in promoting a higher moral code among girls, and so to guide and encourage them that they will have every hope of becoming self-respecting citizens."* Their first patrols take place around **Headingley Football Ground, Woodhouse Moor** and **Chapeltown** – they are later extended to **Briggate** and the **Market** area.

1915: Mounting casualties force **Becketts Park Teacher Training College** to be converted into a military hospital – having a capacity of **3,200** beds by **1918.**

11.11.1918: News of the end of hostilities brings widespread rejoicing in **Leeds.**

1920-1: Leeds University has **1,600** full time, **450** part-time and **280** evening students.

1921: Headingley War Memorial – The Cenotaph (between **Saint Michael's Church** and **The Skyrack**) is unveiled to commemorate those who were killed during the First World War.

1923: Private estates (of semi-detached houses) begin being built at **Gipton Wood, Gledhow Wood, Oakwood, Weetwood Lane, Armley Grange,** and **North** of **Street Lane. Far Headingley** begins its spread further out from the centre of **Leeds** towards **Lawnswood.**

1926: The Clean Air Committee publishes a report which reveals that up to **50%** of natural daylight is lost through atmospheric pollution in central **Leeds.** (In **Headingley** it was **30%**).

9.1939: Outbreak of World War Two

5.1945: The war in Europe ends

29. 7.1956: The author of this work is christened in **Saint Michael's Church**

1959: Trams are replaced by buses

N.B: Information for this *'Timeline'* was provided by information from: -

- My own **History of Leeds** Teaching Notes **(2005-7)**
- **Eveleigh Bradford (2012)**
- **The Yorkshire Evening Post Website** on **Friday, 10th June 2016.** (This consisted of an article by **Dave Weldrake (2009)** which condensed a Historic Summary of the **Headingley Conservation Area** – originally written by **Kath Keith** at an unknown date.**)**
- The **Leodis Website**
- Town maps available in the **Family History Section** of **Leeds Central Library.** (These cover different time periods and are of variable quality.)

The place name **'Headingley'** is derived from the **Anglo-Saxon *'Heada'*** meaning *'headman'* or *'head'* of a war band. Its full meaning is *'The woodland of* ***Heada*** *and his followers'* This suggests that sometime during the seventh century (a period of great **Anglo-Saxon** advance in **Yorkshire**) a leader of a war band cleared some woodland to settle his followers into a village. It's unlikely that the band would have consisted of much more than a few dozen people. Later, in **Viking** times, it was to become the centre of a **Wapentake** (a largely self-governing administrative area, belonging to a wider County or Shire). The name of this **Wapentake** was ***'Skyrack'*** which, in the original *'Norse,'* meant **Shire Oak.** Tradition has it that the men of the **Viking** community would meet beside an old oak tree to settle disputes. **The Original Oak Pub** (which apparently began as a Drovers Inn during the seventeenth century) was built beside this very same tree which finally collapsed through natural decay in **May 1941. The Skyrack** lies nearly opposite the **Original Oak** across the **Otley Road.** Both Public Houses currently face the cenotaph war memorial (made of white Portland Stone). Towering above the cenotaph lies the blackened Gothic Revival Edifice of **Saint Michael's Church.** This church's large steeple is indeed an impressive landmark. Outside the old **Saint Michael's Primary School** (where I'd attended from **September 1961** until **July 1965**) is a triangular grassed area, enclosed by black iron railings. This is all that remains of the original village green. In **1980** the old primary school moved to new premises on **Wood Lane** behind the **Arndale Shopping Centre.** The old-school building is now a Parish Hall Community Centre, hosting a variety of community groups.

The rapid expansion of **Headingley** (throughout the nineteenth and first half of the twentieth century) left a crazy mixture of housing. On a typical **Headingley** road junction, it's possible to clearly view **Victorian** and **Edwardian** Terrace housing, Interwar semi-detached houses and **1960s** blocks of flats. During a twenty minute' walk, it's easy to pass-by early nineteenth century cottages; themselves next to large sandstone villas (now often converted into flats). Much of present-day **Headingley** certainly has an aura of faded gentility about it. Beyond **Shaw Lane** and out to **Lawnswood School** and the **Ring Road** lies **'Far Headingley,'** consisting, in the main, of Interwar suburban houses. The area is in **2018,** inhabited largely by the professional, upper middle classes, who have always tended to view themselves as being somewhat superior to the more mixed population of **inner Headingley.** This latter district begins approximately at the **Arndale Shopping Centre** and stretches to the borders of **Woodhouse Moor,** itself adjacent to the main campus of **Leeds University. Inner Headingley** is viewed as a major student area, where there's sometimes a *'town and gown'* tension between the rowdier students and the local inhabitants. This is especially the case on noisy **Friday** and **Saturday** nights when inebriated students (often in fancy dress) pour out of **The Original Oak** and **Skyrack Public Houses.** However, without the students, **Headingley** would now be a *'ghost'* suburb. Economically it's been kept alive by the two Universities of **Leeds** – one of which **(Leeds Metropolitan)** has a subsidiary campus in **Beckett's Park** (sited behind **Saint Chad's** Church in **Far Headingley**). Settled around the **Hyde Park Cinema** (also frequented by students) is a **Muslim, Kashmiri Asian** Community, whose homemade curries are most warmly recommended. (I've enjoyed them from the parents of certain former students.) There is also a sprinkling of **Chinese** who tend to run small takeaways. Both communities live in the older red brick terraced or unique *'back to back'* houses - which still dominate certain localities in **Headingley.**

Headingley is especially well known for its Cricket and Rugby grounds. However, as spectator sports are of absolutely no interest to me, I will only briefly mention that passing through crowds gathered around this venue can be a nuisance, especially when in a hurry. The rugby fans are especially lively. The only time I ever attended a cricket match was in **July 1971** with an **Indian** school friend. It was an **England** versus **Pakistan** match. My friend would cheer loudly every time **England** scored or a **Pakistani** was bowled out. (During that year, there'd been a great deal of tension between **India** and **Pakistan** over **Bangladesh's** struggle for independence. At **Leeds Grammar School, Indian** and **Pakistani** pupils were not speaking to one another.) As for me, I found that attendance at one cricket match was quite enough. I was glad to have brought a history book to read to relieve the boredom. School sports were never an interest for me – the only exception being swimming which I make a point of keeping up with twice a week.

The mix of population means that **Headingley** has and continues to enjoy, a rich cultural life. This is shown in its association with well-known literary figures *e.g.* **Arthur Ransome** – the author of the famous children's book *'Swallows and Amazons'* and **J. R. Tolkien** (author of *'Lord of the Rings'*). A major expression of this *'cultural mix'* is the **Headingley Literary Festival** which commenced in **2008** and lasted until **March 2018.** It has hosted a variety of literary events during **March** of each year, featuring both local and national talent. Most events are very lively and informative. **Inner Headingley** hosts a wonderful Community Centre named **Headingley Heart** (opened in **January 2010** and based in the converted **Bennett Road Primary School,** which itself closed in **2006**). It continues to host a wide range of music, poetry, theatrical and other cultural events.

Generally, there is now **(2018)** an air of fading glory about **Headingley.** Despite some new facilities, it gives the impression of having seen better days, especially during damp winter days when old houses loom out of the mist like unquiet spectres. The **2011** census revealed that the total population for **Headingley** stood at **20,533** consisting of approximately **51%** females and **49%** males. Students forming 14% of the total population, **(Miller 2015).**

Section 2: Kicking Over the Traces

Concerning the life of James's Smith

James Hastings Smith (the eldest son of my Great Grandfather **Edmund**) was married to **Annie Eliza Kilner** on **30th August 1882**. (Born in **Bradford** on the **2nd May 1858** she was a few months older than soon-to-be-husband.) The event took place at the **Anglican Emmanuel Church** which is now the chaplaincy building of **Leeds University**. It was only five-minutes-walk from **Vernon Road**. The signed witnesses were **Edmund Smith** (in his usual bold handwriting) and **William Kilner**. The lettering on **James'** signature was very narrow and cramped which suggested a rather suppressed personality. One can imagine his father hoping that marriage would *'make a man'* of his twenty-three-year-old son who was perhaps *'never good enough'* for him whilst **James** was trusting that marriage would get him out of his **Edmund's** shadow. In **1885**, he began writing his diary or *'Common Place Book.'* The first known entry read: *"1885: A little sister born at* **Vernon Road April 24th**. *She is named* **Kathleen.**" It was written in a terse *'matter of fact'* tone that would pervade this work.

The **1891** Census revealed that **Edmund's** son **James** was living with his family at **34 Chapel Lane, Headingley**. Staying with him at the time was his brother **Arthur**. The household consisted of:
James H. Smith aged **32** – Commercial Traveller,
Annie E. aged **32**
May H. Daughter aged **7**
Edmund H. Son aged **4**
Arthur E. married brother aged **27** – Commercial Traveller (presumably visiting **Leeds** for business reasons)
Arabelle Kilner Aged **27**– Sister-in-law visiting from **Bradford** – *'lived on her Grandmother.'*

Chapel Lane was a very genteel street, full of merchants, other associated traders and clerks who were sometimes able to afford domestic servants. At number **32** lived the **Johnsons** where the head of the house was a Machinery Merchant – with one son being a Chemist. At number **36** the head of the household was a cloth merchant. By the time he'd reached his early thirties, **James** had been able to put aside enough capital to live in a large corner terraced house at **34 Chapel Lane**, sited in the very pleasant **Headingley** area of **Leeds**. In an email I received on **Friday, 1st March 2019**, the granddaughter of **James** disclosed how the garden was large enough to play bowls in. She also recalled *"Possibly a basement kitchen, main living room, back room (which had a sink in the cupboard), either a parlour and three or four bedrooms."* She also noted a feather bed made from a visit made in about **1926** when seven years old.

The **1901** Census showed barely any change as **James** was still living with his family at **34 Chapel Lane, Headingley.** His household consisted of: -
James Hastings Smith aged **42** – Commercial Traveller, working on his own account, born in **Leeds**
Annie E. aged **42 Bradford**
May H. daughter aged **17 Headingley**
Edmund H. son aged **14 Headingley**
The emphasis on the name *'**Hastings**'* seems to have been motivated by a desire to honour his mother. Like his father, and **Frank** his half-brother, **James** worked *'on his own account,'* which meant he was self-employed.

Further insight into the life led by **James** and his wife at **34 Chapel Lane, Headingley,** was provided by the **1911** Census (which recorded the address as having **7** Rooms):
James Hastings Smith *'Head'* born about **1859** aged **52,** *"Commercial Traveller, Linen Doubles"* birthplace **Leeds**
Annie E. Smith *'Wife'* born about **1859** aged **52,** birthplace **Bradford**
May H Smith *'Daughter'* born about **1884** aged **27,** Single *"Teacher of Domestic Science,"* birthplace **Leeds**
This census revealed a typical middle-class family profile in which a single daughter lived with her parents. Interestingly, she'd followed the same occupation as her aunt *'**Betsey.**'*

Further details were provided by the Baptismal Register of **Saint Michael's Church** in Headingley: -
Saturday, 16th June 1883: Christening of **Helen May Smith** father a *'warehouseman'*
Saturday, 6th November 1886: Christening of **Edmund Hasting Smith** father a *'Commercial Traveller'*
Saturday, 3rd September 1898: Christening by an *'Assistant Curate'* **W. F. Swann** of **Francis Cyril Smith** at *'5 o'clock Evensong.'* At this early stage in his career, **James** was on record as being a *'warehouseman'* One person attending this event was **Fred Hesslewood Smith.** His presence suggested he had a friendly relationship with his half-brother. (Incidentally, **Francis** was referred to as *'**Cyril**'* by his brother **Edmund H. Smith** in later life.)

The **Catholic** sounding name of his last child and association with the still a highly traditional **Anglican Church** denoted a shift of spiritual allegiance away from the **Baptist Faith** of his forbears. Later, **James** gravitated to the overtly **Anglo-Catholic Saint Margaret's** of **Antioch** that began life as a **Church** around **1906**. (It closed in **1995** following a long period of decline and the building is now a cultural centre.) Apparently, **James** served as an active member for many years. An impression emerged of a man wanting to *'kick over the traces'* by assuming an identity that distinguished him from his father. His Granddaughter suggested that these two men shared the same basic Christian faith, but with **James,** *"the liturgical practice was more like pre-reformation."*

It was **Francis** who never made it into adulthood. A Death Certificate (received on **Tuesday, 21st July 2018**) revealed the following information: -
Registration District Leeds
1 Death in the sub-district of Kirkstal in the County of Leeds
1. When and where died? Fourth March 1899, 34 Chapel Lane, Headingley U.D.
2. Name and Surname: Francis Cyril Smith
3. Sex: Male
4. Age: 6 months
5. Occupation: Son of James Smith, Commercial Traveller
6. Cause of death: Teething, Infantile Convulsions
7. Signature, description and residence of informant: J. H. Smith, Father present at death, 34 Chapel Lane Headingley
8. When registered: Sixth March 1899
9. Signature of registrar: M. Smith Registrar
His mother **Annie** had been forty when she'd had **Francis** – and my guess is that their child had been a sickly boy from birth. Even so, the loss must have been difficult to endure.

An entry in **James'** diary provided a lead about his deceased child's burial place that was successfully followed up. Dated **14th March 1899** it stated, *"**Cyril** died and buried at **Headingley Churchyard** with his Great Grandparents."* The result of this lead was that (on **Sunday 15th July 2018**) **June** and I was stumbling around the graveyard of **Saint Michael's Church** on a hot summer evening looking for the relevant headstone. Eventually, I found it hidden under a large tree and surrounded by overgrown vegetation. Indeed, there was a small tree beginning to grow out of the burial plot itself. This lay in front of an expensive looking headstone of mottled, grey marble. The large overhanging tree appeared to have offered partial protection from the elements, allowing the inscription to be clearly legible. It read: -

"In Memory of
JOSHUA KILNER
Who Died **October 22nd 1864**
Aged **24** *years*
Also of **JOSHUA KILNER**
Father of the above
Who Died **May 5th 1882**
Aged **75** *Years*
Also of **SARAH KILNER**
His Wife
Who Died **Dec 17th 1891**
Aged **88** *Years*
Also of **FRANCIS CYRIL SMITH**
Their Great Grandson
Who Died **March 4th 1899**
Aged **6** *Months"*

James was known to have a love for history. During a phone call on **Wednesday, 20th June 2018** a female descendant of his revealed that around **1913** he had taken a party of **Americans** to all the sites mentioned in the first chapter of this book. Apparently, they were members the previously mentioned **Morton** family. It was astonishing to learn I wasn't the first or only **Smith** to conduct guided Family History Tours. It seemed to be part of a well-established tradition. This lady had been given my contact details by the very helpful Minister of **Sutton Baptist Church** following her visit to **Edmund's** early the previous **May** when accompanying her physically frail but still mentally alert **99**-year-old Grandmother – a daughter of **James'** surviving son, the **Reverend Edmund Hastings Smith.** They had even visited the remote village of **Burton Pidsea** together. From our conversation, I inferred that **James** father was a remote and distant figure who spent most of his time at work. Yet he still wanted to be noticed! The information was so detailed that at times, I felt as if parts of my Family History was being read back to me! It was uncanny.

James re-surfaced in the emergency census of **1939.** He was still living at **34 Chapel Lane** with his wife **Annie** and working as a *'Linen Commercial Traveler.'* **James** lived on until **16th October 1953** – a genial figure known affectionately as *'Uncle Jim'* by my father and cousin **Pam.** A **Wakefield Probate** document on **4th January 1954,** confirmed that he'd left his estate of £**7825** and nine shillings to the **Yorkshire Penny Bank Ltd.** This amount would be equivalent to £152,855.71 in 2018. He seems to have made a success of his trade although his working life began in far better circumstances than that of his father. Overall, **James** came across as an amiable, intelligent, methodical and hard-working man who greatly valued respectability. The more I found out about **James** the more I liked him.

James' meticulous and observant nature found expression in his *'Commonplace Book'* or diary which, as already stated was an invaluable source for this *'History,'* adding many precise details. For instance, we found that **Rosamond's** nephew, **Edward Stamford** had been killed aged **28** near **Ypres** in early **April 1918**. It's precise information like this which define a history and save a huge amount of research time. Even petty details weren't excluded. For example, we find that on **17th November 1890**, *"Arthur went to London 1.10."* presumably, the *'1.10.'* was the time of the train that took **James'** younger brother back to **London** which Family Tradition held to be his place of work at that time. As a Historian, I was extremely grateful to **James.** One feature that amused my eldest son was the way **James** liked to record a person's *'worth'* when they died. One associate (<u>not</u> a Family Member) was recorded as being worth £60,000 – a vast amount for the time.

From his entries, it's apparent that **James** and his wife were at the centre of a whole network of family relationships. Links with the **Stamford's** seemed to have continued for an entry dated **28th August 1928** read *"Rosamond's brother Edward Stamford dies, leaves £18,921 – had invented the Stamford Plow."* **James** clearly was a very well-informed man when it came to family matters. Overall, the contribution he made to this history was outstanding. He helped to clear-up many mysteries.

Section 3: A Curious Disengagement

Concerning the Reverend Hastings Smith

Family tradition claimed that **James'** son, **Edmund Hastings Smith,** became a vicar in the **Church of England.** Reference to the **Leeds Grammar School Registers** for **1820-1900** and to the **Crockford Directories** of **1947, 1967/68, 1977/79, 1980/82** and **1985/87** confirmed this. When information gained from different entries in the *'Who's who'* of **Anglican** Clergy was combined with details provided by **Queens College Cambridge** and his remarkable granddaughter it was possible to provide the following chronological framework for **Edmund's** career.

1897 (October 3rd): enters **Leeds Grammar School,** aged **11**

1902: *'Removed'* aged **16** *"to go to Apprentice College for Drapery – then decided he wanted to be ordained to, went back to school."* Assisting him in this decision was the curate of **Saint Michaels Church** a certain **Arthur W. Hawthorne** who believed **Edmund** had a vocation to the *'priesthood.'* A close friend of the family, he advised **James** to send *'Edmund to Cambridge.'*

1906 (October): Matriculated from **Leeds Grammar School**

1906: Enters **Queens College Cambridge** to study **Theology**

1909: BA Theology, **Queens College Cambridge**

1910: Ordained a Deacon

1912: Ordained a Priest

1913: MA

1910-1913: Curate at **Church of Emmanuel, Bolton**

1913-15: Curate at **Saint Martin's, Norris Bank, Stockport**

1916-17: Curate at **Holy Trinity, Habercham, Eaves**

1917-22: Curate at **Warmfield with Sharlston**

14.5.1917 Married **Constance Cross** in **St. Peter's, Burnley**

7.9.1918: Birth of **Margaret Winifred Hastings Smith**

30.11.1919: Birth of **Henry Hastings Smith**

1922-25: Curate at **Honley in Brockholes**

1925-32: Vicar of **Saint John Divine, Thorpe, Yorkshire**

1932-48: Harleywood Vicarage, Todmorden, Diocese of Wakefield

5.11.1947: Death of **Constance**

1948-55: Rector of **Kirk Smeaton**

1955: Retired

1957-1962: Resident in the Parish of **Great Massingham.** During this period, he got to know a man known as *'B'* who was *'Patron'* of the living of **Little Massingham.** He offered it to **Edmund** who took it.

1962-1974: Living at **4 Norton Road, Woolpit, Bury Saint Edmunds, Suffolk,** then **Great Massingham** followed by **Little Massingham.**

1975-1980: Living in a at **Ramsay Hall,** a home for *'clergy pensioners,'* **Byron Road, Worthing, Sussex**

27.9.1980: Died aged **94** at **Ramsay Hall,** (His daughter confirmed that in old age he became rather deaf and unable to see well enough to read.)

The **Reverend Edmund Hastings Smith** had followed the typical career path of the **Church of England** Clergyman. It should be noted that parish ministry in an industrial village could be extremely arduous. His remarkable one-hundred-year old-daughter emphasised this point in an email sent via her granddaughter on **Friday, 1st March 2019.** She made it clear that his ministry amounted to far more than *"snoozing in a country rectory."* Rather, *"he was a highly practical man who could turn his hand to coping with the demands of people's everyday lives."* However, he *"was not interested in his roots and didn't want to discuss them."*

Throwing a puzzling light on his career at **Cambridge** was the following correspondence received (from an extremely helpful source at **Queens College**) on **Thursday, June 29th, 2001.** It lucidly highlighted some of the enigmatic features in the background of **Edmund Hastings Smith.** It will now be quoted in full; *"Many thanks for all the details of the life of the **Revd Edmund Hastings Smith.** His career as a clergyman is not at all atypical of the time. There were plenty of clergy in the **Church of England** in those days and so it was not at all unusual to do several curacies. As to your enquiries about his career at **Cambridge,** I fear I have drawn almost a complete blank. We have no photographs of that era except a few group ones. Unfortunately, these are not dated nor are the people in them named, so we have no way of telling who he was. Rather surprisingly I can find no trace of **Edmund Hastings Smith** in the **Tripos lists** of the period. He must have obtained an Honours degree – otherwise, he would not have been an **M.A.** – but he does not seem to have sat any exams! I can only guess that he was allowed the exams through ill health. You might try the University Archivist at the University Library to see if she can throw any light on that subject. But we have no grades for him, therefore. In **Cambridge,** the **MA** comes automatically a little over three years after obtaining an Honours degree. There is, therefore, no thesis or exam. **Mr Smith** matriculated at **Queens'** from **Leeds Grammar School** in **October 1906.** He graduated **BA** on **16th December 1909.** This is a curious date – it would be much more usual to graduate in the summer, which lends some extra weight to my theory that he might have been ill. I have searched through all the magazines of the period, notably **The Dial,** a student publication at **Queens'. Edmund Hastings Smith** is not mentioned at all, which suggests he took little interest in College, especially sporting life. In conclusion, I can only say that few people have left so little an imprint on the College. I fear that I can add very little to your information on him. We have recorded, by the way, that he was born on **3 October 1886** and that he died **27 September 1980.** I can confirm that the last address for him that we have **(1977)** is indeed **Ramsay Hall, Byron Road, Worthing, Sussex."* Was some sort of chronic illness or nervous collapse behind this curious disengagement? Surely this was at a time and in an environment when one would expect a young man to be especially active?

Fortunately, in **July 2018** his daughter provided a plausible answer to these questions. She stated: *He and a friend failed their Church History Exams by a few marks. Rather than allow them to fail they re-sat the exam in **December** and were allowed to pass with a third. The problem was he didn't do **Greek** at school, only **Latin** and he had to learn **Greek** with a special tutor. This meant he had less time for Church History."* In

March 2019 she added, *"it seems as if they didn't do the exam at the same time, which could explain their missing record. He did take the exams, I have a postcard to prove it. Therefore,* **Dec 1909** *B.A (which would fit)".*

Incidentally, Church History is a favourite subject of mine. During the **1980s** and early **1990s,** I thoroughly enjoyed reading all of the **Ante-Nicene Fathers.** When visiting **Rome** with **June** from **(Saturday 17ᵗʰ** to **Friday, 23ʳᵈ August 2013)** I loved to regale her with *'naughty pope'* stories and tales of gruesome martyrdoms (all of which she found very interesting)! In one Church, a party of tourists began following me, having mistaken me for a guide! The **Christian** catacombs I found to be particularly fascinating and my good lady had to curb my over-excitement by tapping me on the wrist. She remarked that I was like a child in a toy shop.

Edmund's daughter further disclosed *"I suspect he was not involved in college life as he wanted to save his father money."* An especially fascinating insight into the college life led by **Edmund Hastings Smith** was provided by the following narrative. *"Once a year there was a tradition of 'town and gown' at the time of the may boating races, traditionally students damaged the town, the bill was then sent to the college. I remember being told that a round robin letter went around for all students to sign, to join in to pay for the damage.* **EHS** *refused to sign it, as* **JHS** *could not afford to pay as he was not personally responsible. He was the first to do this and other students then followed suit and thanked him for his moral conviction/bravery."* At the very least, this act suggested that **Edmund** had a very real respect for **James.** Like a typical **Smith** he also seemed to have a mind of his own. He wouldn't have found the snobbery prevailing in **Cambridge** College life easy to endure.

Section 4: Three Personalities

Concerning the personal character of Edmund, James and the Reverend Edmund Hastings Smith

A brief description of **Edmund's** personality was provided (by his then nearly one-hundred-year-old Great Grand Daughter) during an interview I conducted on **Friday, 13ᵗʰ July 2018.** This was the closest I ever got to my intriguing ancestor. I had just asked her what **Edmund** had been like as a person and this was the substance of her reply. (For editorial reasons it has been slightly paraphrased, and comments made at a later stage of our long conversation have also been included as have observations from the email received in **March 2019.)** *"He was a 'bon viveur,' who lived up to his income, ambitious, ruthless, probably* *selfish – not much opinion of women. Not very considerate to his wives although he could be very charming with the ladies. A clever man who would analyse what his employers wanted and give it to them. He wanted to be noticed."* She wasn't aware of any open dispute between **Edmund** and her Grandfather **James.**

Her interest had first been aroused in **Edmund** when, following her father's death in **September 1980,** she'd gone through family papers. Three years later (in **1983**) she visited the graveyard at **Sutton.** *"It was in a dreadful state with rubbish piled up against the back wall.* [An aerial photograph of the site in the mid-**1970s** verified this point.] *It has been cleaned up since then.* [This too I can confirm.] *We were about to turn away and then noticed the obelisk. We didn't think that **Edmund** would have had such a big monument. It was so well preserved. We looked-up to it as we were about to leave. He seemed to want to be remembered by his family."* [I too had experienced this same impression during my first visit to this graveyard in **November 1999.**]

I then asked her what **James** had been like. *"My father told me that my grandfather was of teetotaller drinking habits. **James** was very teetotaller because of his father's heavy drinking habits and debts caused by using up money on socialising and banquets. **James** was not a submissive person; he was determined not to copy his father, his debts or his drinking. He was a good sort and a man of principle. **James** was very methodical* [this was confirmed by the meticulous nature of his diary], *liked church architecture* [old photographs verified this point], *liked to visit bookshops for several hours and attend lectures at the Mechanics Institute. He was always writing, and he used to get into conversation at train stations. **James** met **Lord Woolton*** [**1883-1964** – the Minister of Food in **Churchill's** wartime government.] *at a railway station in the war and kept up a correspondence with him.* [At times, whilst listening to this then near one-hundred-year-old lady, I felt as if this source (whom I'd never seen before) was describing myself rather than **James** – as our interests and habit of *'striking up a conversation'* were so identical. Consequently, he rose greatly in my estimation.] It also turned out that *"He thought the Freemasons were a bunch of rogues who used to do business deals in secret. He used to stand back from them. My Father* [The Reverend **Edmund Hastings Smith**] *thought the same."*

James was a very intelligent, steady living and thrifty man who used to talk about the price of bacon at two and a half pence per pound. He did lots of writing in a diary. However, he tore out the all personal references [including those about his father] *following the advice of his friend the **Reverend Arthur Hawthorne.*** [A man whom return to in a time machine and cheerfully throttle for suggesting this act of gross historical vandalism!] *He was very polite and considerate. He taught my brother chess, but he never* *taught me, and we never discussed it! I can't play now and never have. Nowadays, he would get into* **London** *or* **Oxbridge.***"*

His near centenarian Grand Daughter disclosed that at the age of eighteen until well into her twenties, **James** took an interest in her. *"He was very kind, very witty and liked a good conversation. There was no boring conversation. He always asked a challenging question. He was of medium height well-turned out, wore a tweed suit winged collar and silk cravat. At mealtimes, he would 'wear' an impeccably starched napkin.* **Aunt May** *took the napkins 'to the girls' who starched them, to learn how to do it."*

In contrast to his father, *"***James** *was devoted to his wife* **Annie** *who'd enjoyed a good education and had been to 'finishing school' in* **Harrogate.** *They did everything together and had their diamond wedding together."* In his diary, he described the day he lost her in **20th June 1950** as *"the worst day of my life."* She was one of the last people to be buried in **Saint Michael's Churchyard.** (This happened only two days after her death.) **Annie** was remembered as being a *'plump'* lady which is borne out by the photographs taken of her in later life. In **March 2019,** her granddaughter mentioned that *"***Annie** *was good tempered, entertaining and my impression was that she was always the intellectual equal of* **James.** *She was always petite."* However, **James** had one bad habit – which husbands are advised not to emulate – he used to address his wife as *'mother.'* Oddly enough, my father **Fred** had the same habit – but whenever he jokingly called **Cynthia** *'Mom'* she would swiftly retort in a loud voice, *'I'm not your mother!'* As an experiment, I tried addressing my own wife in the same way; the response was a very deep growl and a firm *'don't you dare!!!'* This led to its prompt abandonment.

In the email of **March 2019,** she further disclosed *"***James** *was interested in political theory and history and wouldn't want to gossip. He complained that* **Edmund's** *money was drunk away. I think he lived life as a correction of his fathers! Quote self-confident and critical of his father. I don't think he felt inferior to his father in any way. He may have felt badly done to as he didn't get financial backing he sorely wanted to become a Doctor."* His interest in political theory and history is something that both I and two of children share.

Photographs taken of **James Hastings Smith** showed him to have been a fastidious-looking man with large ears (associated with the **Hastings** line) and a long nose. He consistently sported a King **Edward VII** beard. The only real changes as he grew older was his beard turning a silvery grey and, by his nineties, acquiring a slight stoop. His face was consistently expressionless, so the viewer never knew what he was thinking. Like most respectable middle-class men of his era, he wore a tweed suit and waistcoat from which there dangled a watch chain. My wife **June** (and a succession of female relatives) remarked how handsome he'd looked when a young man. Rather amusingly, ladies of a certain age were so enamoured with him that I thought some of them may fall into a swoon! The only vice which **James** appeared to have indulged in was pipe smoking – a common enough habit during his era. His spouse was a strikingly attractive fair-haired lady who'd obviously been well brought up. Tall and angular when young, she became rather stout when old. When photographed next to **James** she seemed always to look smiling and content. There was a dignity and quiet composure about this couple.

My source also provided a detailed character sketch of her father – the **Reverend Edmund Hastings Smith.** *"He was a very reserved man of very high principles and consistent behaviour. In those days the patronage system dominated the* **Church of England.** *You had to be known to get a 'Living.' It was a matter of luck. With endowments, you were never sure what it would be. A poor living was under £400 per year. My father never got a living offering that amount. Instead, he worked in mill villages. I remember seeing women with black shawls with flecks of cotton on them going to buy warm pies from the shop near the mill. His churchmanship was middling. He didn't have vestments – but wore his MA hood over his surplice to keep warm if the church was cold. He was 'normal.' There are no copies of sermons, However, my father was very methodical. His handwriting was extremely small. He kept skeletons of sermons. He was cold-blooded.* Nonetheless, *"my father could be quick, creative and plan very well. His main hobby was woodwork – he loved making furniture."* On viewing some samples of his woodwork (including a table) I could see that he possessed a genuine talent in this field and his work was of a very high standard.

However, he was liked by those who knew him. He wasn't a fashionable preacher like [**David Watson** at] *Saint Michael Le Belfrey. People then accepted what they got. During the First World War people in the mill village he ministered to, left cabbages and cauliflowers anonymously for his pregnant wife.* [This would be in **1918** – a period of severe rationing]. *They had considerable respect for him."* [The Reverend **Edmund Hastings Smith** must have been doing a lot right because mill families were a tough breed and often suspicious of outsiders. He wouldn't have lasted if, he'd been useless at his job.]

When my source mentioned that the Reverend **Edmund Hastings Smith** was *'embarrassed'* by the **Smiths,** I probed the reason for this, and the following answer arose; *"I think he found them pretentious. He didn't like Middle-Class pretentiousness and vulgarity. He preferred simple, honest people. His father James had* *saved hard to get him into* **Cambridge.** *Earlier a local Curate at* **Saint Michael's** *thought that it could be his son's vocation."* As a child *"he sometimes played in the house where all the children had died."* (Presumably, this was when his parents had visited the older **Edmund.**) A rather dour atmosphere seemed to have hung over the place. In **March 2019** she added. *"what* **James** *did find depressing were the funerals of his young siblings."*

With regard to the **Reverend Edmund Hastings Smith** to describe the father was to describe the son. There's the same well-trimmed beard, large ears, long nose and inscrutable expression. In the one photograph of his spouse **Constance (1879-1947)** – we seem to have the typical Vicar's wife. Large and welcoming she would surely see to it that the ladies in the **Mother's Union** would get along together. She was most probably an extremely capable organizer who got things done. A review of their photographs would suggest that **James** and his son were intelligent, honourable and dutifully hardworking men who had each led eminently respectable lives. What they didn't appear to possess was the creative drive of my Great Grandfather who, as a self-made man, pushed his way forward – regardless of the cost to himself or others. This was not a way of life **James** and his son *'found attractive or admirable.'* They were consolidators rather than pioneers – theirs was a *'respectable'* position in society – something that had been greatly sought after (and won) by **Edmund** himself. It was he who had secured them a place in the middle-classes. Consequently, I felt there was a whiff ungrateful hypocrisy in their disapproval.

My contact revealed some interesting insights into her **Aunt May** – the older sister of her father. It was disclosed that she *"was her own woman who'd married a man who was some ten years younger. Named* **Henry Eric** *but known as 'Eric' by family members. He taught* **History** *in evening classes and was in charge of the History Department at* **St Joseph's Catholic Grammar School, Bradford.** *He produced a Thesis on* **Thomas Aquinas.** *This was rejected at* **London University. Eric** *said it was because the panel consisted of people who didn't understand* **Catholic** *thought. To* **James** *the idea of a daughter marrying a* **Roman Catholic** *was disappointing. Her brother was very disapproving.* **May** *converted to* **Roman Catholicism** *although she wasn't a dogmatic one."* In a diary entry for **9th December 1922, James** mentioned that his daughter **May** was married in **Saint Anne's Cathedral** (sited **Leeds City Centre**). She would have been nearly forty at the time. **Aunt May** would live on until **23rd May 1954.** Her husband **Eric** (who'd been born on the **3rd October 1895**) would remarry in **June 1958.** He died in the **Totness** area of **Devon** on **27th August 1966.**

Section 5 An Abortive Engagement

Concerning an abortive engagement with Dr Berkeley Moynihan

By the time of the **1891 Census**, **Betsey's** heart was about to be broken. A proposed marriage to a medical student at **Leeds General Infirmary** had fallen through and she was never to go out with another man again. Apparently, wedding arrangements had already been made. The name of this medical student was **Berkeley George Andrew Moynihan (1865-1936)** who would later become an honorary surgeon at the hospital from **1896** until **1926**. **Berkeley** had been born in **Malta** on **2nd October 1865.** His father had been a junior army officer and **Victoria Cross** medal winner (from the **Crimean War**). His father continued to be based there until his death from *'Malta Fever'* in **1867.** During **1964,** (whilst engaged on a temporary summer job in the Hospital records office) my brother saw **written** records of **Moynihan's** work from 1878 until **1890.** The records consisted of thick bound volumes full of case histories, many of which my brother destroyed on a bonfire to make space for other more recent documents. **Doctor Moynihan** seemed to have handled the aftermath of a boiler explosion in a **Leeds** factory, which had made for gruesome reading. The bust of **Berkley Moynihan** still stands (encased in glass) in a large round alcove at the top of a flight of stairs, opposite to what once was the Hospital's main entrance on **Great George Street.** The **1891** Census described him as being a *'Resident Surgical Officer'* who was sleeping at **Leeds General Infirmary at that time.**

An insight into the world which **Berkeley Moynihan** entered as a young medical student was provided by his biographer **Dr David Bateman (1940)** who had been a close professional associate. (He had produced this work at the request of **Berkeley's** son **Patrick.**) On **p.89, Bateman** referred to **Moynihan's** superior **Doctor Jessop,** who always arrived at **Leeds General Infirmary** in the style of a monarch. *"The **Jessop** manner was in accordance with the man. Silk-hatted and with an orchid in the lapel of his coat, each day he drove up to the hospital in a carriage drawn by a pair of bay [horses]. Alighting, he was met by his R.S.O. and students; in a royal progress, the party marched through the corridors of the Infirmary. Having arrived at the theatre the great man stopped, and drawing from his buttonhole the orchid, handed it to the theatre-sister. Then after the usual preparation, on with the operation. With the steady speed of the inspired craftsman, the work went forward, no bombast and no fireworks. So secure was his learning that he did not hesitate to ask and where right, utilise the advice of his assistants. Like all the best of doctors, he lacked the grudging intellectual pride* *that in its arrogance is but the mask of ignorance. Small wonder that, for those who knew him, even while **Jessop** was still alive, something of mythology invested the master's name."*

From this account, it was very apparent that a successful surgeon had to have something of the actor about him. Given the relatively limited medical know-how of the time, there was some sense in wanting to convey an aura of confidence. Yet it is still reasonable to wonder whether all of this *'fawning over the surgeon'* was exactly healthy? At the very worst it could fuel a dangerous arrogance, against which there were no safeguards. As my late father used to say in relation to the medical profession, *"Consultants could always bury their mistakes."* Shocking – but one wonders – especially during this period in the history of medicine whether to be set on a pedestal was simply not advantageous to the patient. Where was the accountability?

When proof-reading this extract in late **2016** my wife couldn't help remarking in red ballpoint *"yuck, fawning toady hero-worship."* which summed up her view of it. I could only concur because his biography must rank as the most tendentious source used in this study. For **Bateman, Berkeley Moynihan** was the medical superman who could do no wrong and it was his clear intention to portray him in the most favourable of lights. The wording used by **Bateman** was hugely sentimental in tone even, at times resembling that of a romantic novel for teenage girls! A false flattering tone pervades the whole book. However, one point in its favour was the way it drew material from contacts inside the **Moynihan** family – therefore providing access to their highly-biased viewpoint. It turned out to be illuminating despite itself.

Despite his bias, **Bateman pp. 90-105** did cast some light on **Berkeley Moynihan's** affair with **Betsy**. This is highlighted by the following extract taken from **pp. 91-92**. My own insertions (in brackets) bring out any possible covert jibes which **Bateman** had chosen to make against **Betsey**.

*"He had always liked feminine company, preferred it in fact to that of men, but, up till now, had known few occasions to indulge his liking. Of his class, he had known few women, outside it none. Neither time, money, nor opportunity had allowed him to enjoy the society of ladies. But he 'had a way with them.' He had a remarkable, sympathetic understanding of their point of view; and this meant they **(Betsey?)** could get around him, could win him over. His susceptibility to them put pitfalls in his way. He readily believed in them, and when what they said ill-matched with later fact, was disconcerted. He was boyish, and his warm heart was too easily deceived (by **Betsey?**). But (unlike **Betsey**) there was no deception about **Isabel**. **Berkeley** was, from the day they met her hero. She had for him an awed admiration (unlike the more critical **Betsey**). In her eyes, everything he did was right. She was surprised, almost*

*amazed when she found him return this admiration. She was not an intellectual, could not follow the ranging of his learned, imaginative mind; but she did understand him; better perhaps than (**Betsey** and) any woman he had known. She saw his weaknesses and chinks in his armour. Young as she was, she knew in her heart that she possessed, as he might never do, a worldly knowledge that exceeded his. She saw how poor was his defence against sweet flattery and importuning (from women like **Betsey Hastings Smith**)."*

Apparent on any first reading of the extract was the contradiction between its portrayal of a man who had never had any experience of the opposite sex and one who was sufficiently experienced to have *'had a way with them.'* There were also the innuendoes against a woman who had *'deceived him'* and not provided him with the support he'd needed for his job. On **p. 97** the claim was made that *"**Isabel** gave **Berkeley** a faithful, loving loyalty"* and once again one can almost hear the words, *'unlike **Betsey Smith**.'* In this biography, what was left unsaid becomes ever more interesting. As a source, **Bateman** had a limited use in recording the attitudes of members of **Berkeley's** family wishing to *'cover up'* his less than chivalrous behaviour. Such behaviour, during the late **1930s** – when this biography was written – would still be viewed as poor in the extreme. The breaking of a marriage contract would not have shown **Berkeley** in a good light. It was as if my Great Aunt **Betsey** had been effectively *'airbrushed' out* of the **Moynihan** family history. However, in this history, she's back with a vengeance!

Further reading would possibly intimate the perceptions of a rather pampered, **late-Victorian** upper-middle-class teenage girl, furiously jealous of an older, more sophisticated rival. What seems to have been preserved in this account was **Isabel Jessop's** personal view of **Betsey** as relayed directly to **Bateman** (or indirectly through family members to **Bateman**.) It seems unlikely that **Berkeley** himself would have wanted to mention **Betsey** – even in an indirect, roundabout way. His main interest was firmly embedded in the medical profession. His future career prospects lay with **Isabel**.

Having broken off his engagement to **Betsey** at a date which can't be precisely ascertained, **Berkeley** decided to *'lie low.'* On **Monday, 14th March 1892,** he had obviously felt the need for spiritual encouragement from his brother-in-law, the **Reverend A. N. Claye.** Reading between the lines it's apparent that **Berkeley** was suffering from a crisis of conscience. Whatever the reason he delayed any marriage proposal until the following **June.** Finally, the marriage between **Berkeley** and *'Tiny'* took place in **1895** following a long engagement of three years. Something other than the need for **Berkeley** to get established into a medical practice seemed to be delaying matters. Here lies, perhaps, the distant echo of what may well have been a tremendous row between not only **Betsey** but her ferocious father **Edmund** (who may have felt that his daughter had been grievously wronged and that he himself had been made to look a fool). In **Edmund's** eyes, family honour would have been greatly affronted. He certainly would not take it lightly.

What did happen may well have gone something like this: around **1890,** whilst still a medical student, **Berkeley** had met **Betsey** – whose house was less than twenty minutes' walk away from the Infirmary. It's conceivable that he had been a tenant of my Great Grandfather who only allowed *'respectable'* people to stay in his property. How they met cannot (on present evidence) be known – but meet they did. **Edmund** will have had the shrewdness to quickly discern that **Berkeley Moynihan** had the potential to become an extremely successful doctor. Like many ambitious **Victorian** patriarchs, he would have pushed hard to make a good match for his daughter. But did **Edmund** *'overdo'* his grandiose personal claims, made on her behalf? He may have encouraged **Betsey** to exaggerate certain matters to do with her own background. Also, **Rosamond,** now terminally ill – will have been eager to see her life close on a happy note. For a young (and still emotionally naive) **Berkeley, Betsey** may well have *'come across'* as the very embodiment of worldly sophistication. In her late twenties, she herself would have been desperate to marry. However, tensions would soon have arisen over his long hours of work (which would simply have been expected of all medical students at that time). Should he have arrived late or tired for a social function, she may well have *'let fly'* with some cutting comments or, even worse a full-scale scene. The fastidious **Berkeley** would have hated such blatant emotional displays. As their courtship was around the time of **Rosamond's** final illness **Edmund's** attitude toward the medical profession may have been somewhat disparaging. One thing **Edmund** will have insisted upon was that any marriage would have needed to wait until **1890** when **Berkeley** will have passed his final Fellowship and received the **F.R.C.S,** (*'Fellowship of the Royal College of Surgeons'*). It was probably following that event that **Berkeley's** engagement to **Betsey** will have taken place. By early **1892,** after one *'scene'* too many, **Berkeley** will have been anxious to end the relationship. He knew he faced a choice between **Betsey's** emotional demands and the pursuit of his own medical career. He would also have known that, if he did break off this engagement to **Betsey,** he would then be liable to being sued for *'breach of marriage contract.'* (This remained the case until **1970.**) Under **Victorian** law, he would need to pay **Betsey** a great deal of financial compensation, which he could ill-afford. The result could easily be financial ruin. Hardly surprisingly, the appearance of **'Tiny'** was probably a cause of heartfelt relief; it would resolve both sets of problems. **Berkeley** would find a doting and pliable wife (who would accept his long working hours at the hospital), and his wealthy father-in-law could be relied upon to provide the money to pay off this irksome *'Breach of Contract'* to **Betsey.** In addition, he would gain the patronage to advance his own career. It was noteworthy that the woman he did marry was about ten years his younger and already familiar with the pressures faced by senior Doctors. In terms of age and character, she seemed to have been the direct opposite of **Betsey.**

When he did break off the engagement (in **March** or **April** of **1892**) both **Betsey** and **Edmund** would have been mortified. They would, as middle-class **Victorians,** have viewed it as an utter disgrace. **Edmund** would have been ruthless in his response – his personal pride having been bruised and battered by **Berkeley's** rejection of his daughter. **Edmund** will have threatened legal action – a threat that could only be averted by a generous financial settlement from **Richard Jessop** who would have been keen to prevent an embarrassing court case, which could have damaged his protégé's career prospects. Little wonder an undertone of acrimony was present in **Bateman's** account. The **Smiths** reaction to *'the breach of contract'* had threatened to stop **Berkeley's** brilliant medical career before it had even fully started. From this scenario, it now seems evident that the couple had never really been suited to one another. All available sources clearly show **Berkeley Moynihan** as a man firmly *'married'* to his career and any lady unwilling to accept a secondary role to this would have to go. Whether any element of deception came in was hard to discern, but **Edmund's** tendency toward grandiose exaggeration may possibly have been carried far too far. My Great Grandfather had correctly gauged **Berkley Moynihan's** brilliant prospects, but he had grievously underestimated the degree to which this man would ruthlessly place his career before any other consideration. As my own wife observed, *"with **Berkley Moynihan** Edmund had over-reached himself. It was one of his grandiose schemes that went wrong."* Certainly, it had backfired enough to become part of our family folk law as well as that of the **Moynihan's.** Neither **Edmund** nor **Berkeley Moynihan** came out of this affair particularly well.

A Photograph of the young **Berkeley Moynihan,** (date uncertain, but he was seated alongside other House Surgeons at **Leeds General Infirmary**) showed him to be of strong build and smart in appearance. In accord with late nineteenth-century fashion, he wore a three-piece suit, with his sleek straight hair neatly parted down the middle. However, the most striking feature was the look of fanatical intensity on his face. It conveyed the impression of a brilliant man, bursting with nervous energy and an exacting mind, wholly in pursuit of his vocation in medicine. I had the overwhelming feeling that for most of his time spent with **Betsey** his thoughts would have been elsewhere. This, of course, would have been a very ready source of tension. With hindsight, it seemed most probable that **Berkeley Moynihan** had never really been fully committed to **Betsey.** Whilst their relationship had lasted **Edmund** and **Betsey** will have been the ones who'd made *'most of the running.'* **Berkeley,** following **Victorian** etiquette, will have politely acceded until (and almost too late) he will have realised that his affections lay elsewhere. In one sense **Betsey** never lost **Berkeley Moynihan** – it seemed she never really *'had him'* in the first place – here was a man very much *'married'* to his vocation.

Another photograph this time of **Betsy** (received on **Wednesday 4ᵗʰ July 2018**) may offer some further clues as to why she was jilted by **Berkeley Moynihan.** Written next to the photo – in **James'** own hand, there is the caption *'Aunt Betsy.'* I'm afraid to say, that to put it charitably she wasn't exactly a beauty. Her clothing was respectable rather than lavish. She wore a dark bustle dress with puffed sleeves in the style of the late **1880s** (at approximately the time when she was becoming acquainted with **Berkeley.**) The top of her dress was braided – with white lace picked out on her sleeves and collar. Her hands were clasped around the top of an umbrella. Her curly fair hair was braided and plated but sadly, the effect was still not appealing. She has large **Hastings** *'jug-handle'* ears, a typical **Smith** nose and a prominent double chin; a beauty she was not! Her rather masculine face seemed only to express sour misery. My wife thought she seemed to look *'beaten down,'* whilst my mother had remarked that she'd *'looked bad-tempered.'* I myself (as a younger man) would have thought *'she looks like a **Yorkshire** sulky pot who could cause trouble; be polite but keep your distance.'* The picture suggests that she was the clingy type who, when crossed, could throw temper tantrums. Such behaviour – as far as the fastidious **Berkeley Moynihan** was concerned, would have been intolerable! As the relationship progressed the realization will have dawned on him that marriage to this woman could well become a social embarrassment. Her demeanour and behaviour could even jeopardise his medical career! Such a threat to his ambitions was not to be borne and its hardly surprising he wanted *'out.'* It was a telling sign (of desperation) that he was willing to risk being sued for *'Breach of Promise'* rather than follow-through from the engagement to the *'promise'* of a future marriage. His overall reaction, (once possible legal repercussions had been avoided) must have been one of heartfelt relief. Perhaps **Berkeley** had gone through his life thinking that he'd had a very lucky escape. For him, the whole affair had represented a regrettable *'first fling'* and was thereafter best forgotten.

One further feature to note about this photo is that **Betsy** doesn't look to have had the resolutely determined personality needed to have made *'the running'* in this affair. This would support the possibility that, from *'behind the scenes,'* **Edmund** was the one pushing **Berkeley** and **Betsey** together. After all – what could be more *'respectable'* than the prestige of having a daughter married to a promising young Doctor. One wonders – from **Edmund's** viewpoint – whether, in **Berkeley,** he saw the only man in his life who could be as successful as himself. His daughter's tragedy was to be caught between two exceptionally brilliant and forceful men. After the break-up, no other man was ever to be *'good enough'* for her. Given her upbringing, this outcome was sad but somehow inevitable. It was perhaps in the aftermath of this whole sorry business that **Betsey** began giving cookery classes in the basement room of **Vernon Road.** Her were thereafter channelled into becoming a Cookery Instructress and, quite wisely, she was beginning to *'start small.'*

Thus, **Betsey's** chance to escape the confines of her background had been thwarted – but then marriage to a career-obsessed Senior Surgeon – one who would have been treated as *'a mini-god'* in any hospital of that period, would have had trials of its own. In his own way, **Berkeley** would perhaps have been every bit as domineering as **Edmund.** Over time, he was to emerge as an extremely knowledgeable but coldly ambitious man. (This raises the question as to whether subconsciously. **Betsey** had wanted to marry a man like her father.) One could imagine **Berkeley** possessing the ruthlessness to *'dump'* **Betsey** if a better *'social catch'* came along which, of course, is exactly what happened. **Betsey** had been his *'first fling'* with an engagement to her having possibly been provoked by a temporary emotional infatuation rather than any deep sense of love. **Edmund** may well have *'talked him'* into making a premature commitment – about which **Berkeley** was subsequently to become increasingly uneasy. **Edmund** was trying to push his daughter into marrying someone who had great prospects of advancement; to be the father-in-law to a surgeon (who was later to become a Lord) would have been a major source of personal pride.

Although escaping the trap of what may well have been a loveless marriage, **Betsey** was heartbroken. She never courted again. Perhaps, after **Moynihan,** no man would have been *'good enough'* for either her. Could **Betsey** but see it now, she may well have derived great consolation from knowing that (even up to recent times) medical students fill up the glass case (enclosing **Moynihan's** bust) with water. Sometimes the odd goldfish goes in too – just to make it more interesting! (Modelled near the end of his career, this white stone bust of

Berkeley Moynihan reveals a thin-faced man with eyes raised upward in a frozen look of disdain.)

As a side note, it needs to be mentioned that the identity of this lady in the photograph has been disputed. However, the photo was taken in the late **1880s,** and any alternative *'Aunt Betsy'* such as **Helen Hasting's** sister **Elizabeth** or **Daniels** wife of the same name, would have been in their sixties and women in that period aged quickly. The one in the picture is in her late twenties or early thirties and still in the prime of life. It's hard to see that the *'Aunt Betsy'* referred to could be any other person than the eldest daughter of **Edmund** and **Helen Smith.** She was of the right age. In terms of looks, there's a resemblance to her younger sister **Ann Helen Smith.** On display are the same large prominent ears and double chin. However, **Ann** is slimmer, with an oval face, slightly more prominent eyes and darker curly hair. She has a look of studious intelligence about her. There's an attractiveness about **Ann** which, is absent from her (presumed) sister. Unlike **Betsy,** as a younger man, I could well have been attracted to.

Section 6: A Spinster's Existence

Concerning Victorian and Edwardian Spinsters

By the time of the **1901** Census, **Betsey** was living with her sister **Anne** at **13 Newport Mount** in **Headingley;** they had finally made a break with their father. The *'Return'* simply stated: -
Anne H. Smith aged **39, Yorkshire, Leeds**
Betsey H. Smith aged **41,** *'Cookery School Instructor,'* **Yorkshire, Leeds**
It seems that **Edmund's** third marriage was to mark the departure of **Betsey** and her younger sister **Anne** from the family home. This would allow their father's third wife to assume the role of *'mistress of the house.'* A household with three late **Victorian** women would certainly have had its tensions, particularly as both **Betsey** and **Anne** had a reputation for being very *'strong-minded.'* Intriguingly, they had chosen to live nearer to their brother **James** rather than to **Edmund,** which perhaps indicated some degree of alienation from their father. Their move into this address appears to have been recent; as they were not shown in any Trade Directory before **1899.** However, what Census Returns and Trade Directories did reveal was that **Betsey** had been working as a Cookery Instructress for the **Leeds Board of Education.** Her work will have entailed her moving from school to school. (Here again was a significant family link with education.)

The **1911** Census confirmed that both sisters were still living at **13 Newport Mount** (which had **7** rooms). Not much had changed in their lives as single spinsters.

Betsey Hastings Smith *'Head'* born about **1860,** aged **51,** Single *"Laundry or cookery instructress,"* **Leeds**

Anne Helen Smith *'Sister'* born about **1862** aged **52** single **Leeds**

The reason why **Anne** was not down as working in both this and the previous census can be attributed to ill health. Known as *'Nelly the Invalid'* family tradition asserted that it was her sister **Betsey** who looked after her. A laconic entry in the diary of her elder brother **James** lent credence to this story. Dated **29th January 1887,** it stated, *"Nelly (my sister) ill has been a sort of invalid since spending summer with **Ann Squire** at **Crosshills.**"* The cause of her indisposition remained a mystery, but her death certificate suggested that **Bronchitis** had may have been a significant factor. **Anne** appeared to be one of those delicate types who would get others to run after them. For **Betsey,** there was the compensation of feeling needed. A mutual dependence appeared to exist between the two sisters.

A slightly blurred photograph, taken around **1904,** gave some insight into the working environment in which **Betsey** had taught her culinary skills. The photograph showed a large cavernous basement, with white tiled walls, a fireplace and a double window through which railings could be seen. (Desks had been stacked to one side) A cookery class of eighteen girls, all wearing pinafore dresses, white aprons and working in small groups were gathered around four trestle tables. Some appeared of simple intelligence, others seemed deformed, possibly through rickets, whilst others looked relatively healthy and ladylike. They were preparing an assortment of recipes, each written on the blackboard in a neat column. Standing to the left of the fireplace was the instructress, wearing a long white apron and a cap. A mop of dark curly hair crowned her somewhat expressionless face and, like **Edmund,** she had a long aquiline nose. In terms of looks, she was dignified rather than strikingly beautiful. She was of the right age to have been **Betsey,** but sadly the photograph caption simply stated, *'A Cookery Room.'* Although it could not be proved whether the woman in the photograph was **Betsey,** it did show the kind of setting in which she would have worked.

One event, which may have brought some happiness to **Edmund** but was possibly tinged with sadness (and maybe even jealousy) for **Betsey** was the marriage of his daughter **Maud** to **Victor Campbell** at **All Souls, Blackman Lane, on October 9ᵗʰ, 1899.** The fact that she was already living away from home at the time of this occasion implied that **Maud** had also wanted to *'make room'* for a third wife of **Edmund's.**

Registration District <u>Leeds</u>

<u>1899</u> Marriage solemnised at <u>the Parish Church</u> in the <u>parish of All Souls Leeds</u> in the <u>county of Leeds</u>

1. When married? October 9ᵗʰ, 1899

2. Name and Surname: Victor Campbell, Maud Smith

3. Age: 27, 26

4. Condition: Bachelor, Spinster

5. Rank or profession: Traveller

6 Residence at the time of marriage: 19 St Peters Road Leicester, 5 Marlborough Grove Leeds

7. Father's name and surname: Alfred Campbell, Edmund Smith

8. Rank or profession of father: Traveller, Traveller

Married in the <u>Parish Church according to the Rites and Ceremonies of the Established Church</u> after [banns] by me [Name Illegible] Vicar.

The marriage was solemnised between us

<u>Victor Campbell</u>

<u>Maud Evelyn Smith</u>

In the presence of us

<u>Edmund Smith</u>

Alf Campbell

<u>R. Campbell</u>

From this documentation, it was apparent that **Maud** had married a man engaged in the same (or very similar) occupation as her father. This was unlikely to be purely coincidental. It seemed probable that the **Campbells** were Commercial Travellers, also employed by **Stewart Macdonald** – but with a base in a different geographical region. If this was the case, then **Edmund** would have known them for years, as the business world of that era was very tightly knit. The **Campbells** may even have been overnight visitors at **Vernon Road.** The marriage took place at the reasonably nearby **Anglo-Catholic** Parish Church. It's grand neo-gothic surroundings perhaps symbolised **Edmund's** determination to do the best for his daughter. As a passing thought, one wonders how **Betsey** felt attending her younger half-sister's marriage? Did she suffer from any pangs of jealousy (or sorrow) for her unmarried condition? Overall, it was very likely that she did. An entry in the diary of her brother

James noted that **Maud's** husband died in **July 1918.** Whether his death had any connection with the First World War remained a matter of speculation.

Section 7: A Glittering Career

Concerning the medical contributions of Dr Berkeley Moynihan

A glittering career lay ahead for **Berkeley Moynihan.** Further information (gathered from the Internet) revealed that he was to become a leading authority on abdominal surgery, attracting students from across the world. He co-authored well known academic articles on diseases of the stomach in the early **1900s**. In **1905,** he published his classic text *'Abdominal Operations,'* which was to remain an authoritative source for some two decades. During **1910,** his book on *The Duodenal Ulcer'* established his reputation in clinical science and was perhaps influential in gaining him a knighthood in **1912.** In accord with the practice of his time, he would have stressed the need to obtain evidence from living bodies. The following year he sponsored the introduction of *'The British Journal of Surgery.'* An inscription on a wall at **Leeds General Infirmary** revealed how, during the First World War, his efficiency became noticed. It read as follows *"The medical services, although initially overwhelmed, improved considerably as the war progressed.* **Berkeley Moynihan,** *a surgeon at the L.G.I, was responsible for many of the improvements. He took a surgical team from the Infirmary to* **France** *in* **1914** *and was to become a Major General in* **the Royal Army Medical Corps (RAMC)** *with key responsibilities for the organisation of medical services in* **France.** *These included two* **Leeds***-based Territorial Units, the first and second* **West Riding Field Ambulance RAMC***, who served with great distinction throughout all of the major battles on the Western Front."* A photograph alongside the text showed a rather plump **Berkeley Moynihan** who could nevertheless still cut a dashing figure when in military uniform. One could easily see why **Betsey** had been attracted to him all those years before.

Elevated to the peerage in **1929, Berkeley Moynihan** was, by **1931,** to become President of the Royal College of Surgeons. It was in this capacity that he officially opened **The Wellcome Institute of Medicine** on **Euston Road** in **London.** (I've visited it with my wife two or three times.) He died, five days after his seventy-first birthday on **September 7th, 1936** at **Carr Manor** in **Leeds.** His record of academic and professional work suggested that **Berkeley Moynihan** had been an obsessive high achiever, determined to make a reputation for himself regardless of the emotional cost to others. This facet of his personality perhaps in part explains why the relationship with my Great

Grandfather ended with what seems to have been a very sour note. In some ways, **Berkeley Moynihan** and **Edmund Smith** were too much alike to have ever really got on. Marrying **Edmund's** strong-minded daughter would not have been right for **Berkeley.** He had needed someone of a more placid and adoring nature like *'Tiny'* (who was obviously smitten by him). In addition, being a Doctor's daughter meant that Tiny would have been more than familiar with the pressures involved in being a Doctor's wife.

A further review of material concerning **Berkeley Moynihan** was conducted at the **Thackray Medical Museum** on **Friday, 5th, July 2002**. It reinforced my already existing impression that he was a very ambitious yet rather fastidious man who loved neatness and order. He would have hated any disorderly, emotional scenes. His book, entitled *'Abdominal Operations,'* provided evidence for this point. It was a masterpiece of detailed research, systematic thinking and lucid writing. The work that went into it must have been phenomenal, yet like all great teachers, he made it sound very easy. As a non-medical layperson, I could understand some of the technical points made – there could be no denying that **Berkeley Moynihan** had a very powerful mind. Here was a man utterly infatuated with his subject.

Also, more impartial sources (other than **Bateman**) confirmed that **Berkeley Moynihan** was a man of striking, not to say, charismatic appearance. This point was underlined by available photographs and by **Franklin's** statement on **p.5** of his introduction to the *'Selected Writings of Berkeley Moynihan'* where whilst in his twenties, he was described as, *"a big man, six feet tall, broad, muscular, neat for all his size, with bright red hair, which lasted into middle life. He excelled at swimming. He was a man who made his presence felt in any company. The force of his personality commanded attention, and his charm of manner, when he wished – and he usually did – was irresistible."* (In later years **Berkeley Moynihan** was to become a very accomplished after-dinner speaker.) It was easy to see how he had swept **Betsey** off her feet. Nevertheless, it must be said that he would most probably have heartily disliked a woman with a will of her own.

Yet there was also a dark side to his character. This included his personal arrogance and vanity which, in his later years, led to an obsession with procuring every honour available. When he didn't the result was often a childish rage. He also made impoverished medical students buy his books rather than lend them out. Even **Bateman,** somewhat ruefully, was unable to conceal that this was the case. Moreover, **Berkeley's** achievements tended to be gained at a very high cost to his family life. **Franklin** on **p.8** claimed that *"all this great activity exacted its* *price from* **Moynihan's** *domestic life. He had married in* **1895 Isabel Jessop,** *the daughter of his chief. They were, and they remained a devoted couple. But not for him the domestic peace and love* (of his medical predecessors like **Jessop**). *The busy life of the successful surgeon at the end of the nineteenth century and in the twilight period between the two world wars meant the sacrifice of domestic leisure and he did not get to know his children until they were already adults."* **Berkeley Moynihan's** son **Patrick** (in his introduction to **Bateman's** biography) admitted that he did not know his father until a serious illness had *'floored'* **Berkeley** in **1928.** His father had sent **Patrick** away to **Winchester Public School** when he was a boy. **Berkeley Moynihan's** many professional triumphs had been gained at the price of neglecting his own family.

However, it would do **Berkeley Moynihan** a huge injustice to portray him simply as a cold-hearted careerist. That he may well have been, but he certainly amounted to a whole lot more! In his profession, he came to see that he was not a lone genius but rather one member in a great medical tradition. His writings on other great surgeons, *i.e.* **William Hey** displayed a certain degree of humility. It seems that his vanity was aimed at solely gaining honours rather than affecting his everyday profession. Perhaps he had seen too much of death for it to be otherwise. Moreover, anyone reading his testimonial to his wife **Isabel,** written immediately after her death on **August 31ˢᵗ, 1936** could not entertain any doubt that his love for her was real. This point was underlined by the following extract, *"she was the daughter of* **Richard Jessop D. L. F.R.C.S** *of* **32 Park Square Leeds.** *He had the busiest and best surgical practice in* **Leeds.** *He was appointed surgeon to the* **Leeds General Infirmary in 1870** *and became Consulting Surgeon in* **1890.** *When I left the Infirmary in* **1893,** *I was already engaged to his daughter* **Isabella Wellesley.** *She was then* **20** *years of age, born in* **June 1873,** *was short and very slim. After her marriage and before we sailed from* **Liverpool** (to **Madeira**) *on our honeymoon, she weighed (with all her clothes on) six stone and three pounds. She was lively and accomplished. She played tennis well – her sister was* **Yorkshire Champion** *for years and she could occasionally beat her. She had had trouble with her ears owing to scarlet fever when young and was always a little deaf. She danced divinely, indeed everyone agreed that she was easily the most accomplished dancer in* **Leeds** *and in those days, one could judge, for it was considered almost improper to dance more than once with any girl."* (He then proceeded to praise his wife for her being a good housekeeper who treated the servants so wisely that they stayed with the family for years. One of these servants was a chauffeur.) *"She was a small yet great and lovely lady, worthy of all honour and remembrance."* These were perhaps the last words he wrote, for six days after the death of his wife **Berkeley Moynihan** was found dead in his study – having been felled by a stroke. For him, his marriage had been more than a simple career move. Incidentally, these last words also apply to my own wife although after *'remembrance'* I would add *'as an excellent proof-reader of inexhaustible patience.'*

The discovery of fresh information concerning **Berkeley Moynihan** made it possible to come to a final verdict concerning his relationship with **Betsey.** The main conclusion was that the initial scenario covering the break-up of the relationship was correct. On balance, it appears that **Berkeley** had taken what was for him, the right decision. He'd needed a wife who could understand and accept the burdens of being married to a successful surgeon. **Betsey,** largely due to her own single-mindedness had simply looked set to fail in fulfilling these conditions so she had to go. Once this decision had been made it was easy to imagine him being coldly logical about it. He would have taken the view that it had to be done and the sooner the better. One mystery remains over how he had needed first met **Betsey.** In his younger days, he was not a churchgoer, preferring the theatre instead. Was it at the theatre that he'd first encountered her? The answer to that question remains unknown.

However, there's one amusing epilogue to this story. During a tour (of **Lawnswood Cemetery, Leeds**) conducted by the **British Medical History Society** (on **Sunday, 19th August 2012**) I was shown **Berkeley Moynihan's** moss covered, cross-shaped headstone. I gleefully enjoyed *'spilling the beans'* about his broken engagement with **Betsey** to an assembled party of **29** people. Thankfully, I didn't hear any *'spinning sound'* emanating from within the grave! Regrettably, a torrential rainfall prevented the taking of any photographs. However, I did notice two very simple inscriptions which read: -
BERKELEY, GEORGE ANDREW
1ST BARON OF MOYNIHAN OF LEEDS
SEPTEMBER 7TH 1936.

ALSO ISABELLA WELLESLEY
HIS BELOVED WIFE
AUGUST 31ST 1936.
"In their death, they were not divided"

Section 8: A Grammar School Education

Concerning Leeds Grammar School (LGS) in the Victorian period

The **L.G.S**. Calendar confirmed that my Grandfather **Fred *'Heselwood'*** (better known as ***'Frank'***) had attended the school from the Easter term of **1879** until sometime in **1884/85**. (Relevant records for **1885** were missing – but by **1886** he had obviously left the school.) **Price (1910)** recorded that the school had **281** boys by **1878** and was still expanding. Annual tuition fees for that period remained at a steady **£10. 10s.** Most of **Frank's** form teachers had been graduates from **Oxford University**, although one, a certain **Mr Webb**, was a graduate of **Trinity College, Cambridge.** As was typical at the time there was a strong emphasis upon the *'Classics'* although the basic skills of maths and writing were not neglected. The sciences did not become an important subject area until the early twentieth century. Throughout this period, **Frank's** academic performance had been modest. His form positions were **12**th, **10**th equal, **11**th, **19**th **10**th and **14**th equal respectively. (These were out of a total of **12, 28, 16, 23, 20** and **15** pupils.) However, he did win a writing prize in the years **1883** and **1884**. The image conveyed from his school record was that of a boy who was not academic but who worked hard and was dogged in the pursuit of his aims. One of these prizes was a brown hard backed book entitled," *Half-hours in the far North – life amidst snow and ice*" published by **William Isbister** in **1881**. It still exists – its black and white drawings were a source of endless fascination for me as a child. The stories seem to have been a collection drawn from various popular magazines. Inside the front cover of the book were the following words, *"To F. H. Smith for proficiency in writing,* **W. E. Henderson.***"* Also written was the name ***"F. H. Smith, 51 Hillcrest Avenue, Chapeltown."*** The address indicates that his name had been written in the early **1900s** at which time **Frank** himself was raising a young family of his own. Even in adult life, my grandfather appeared to have derived a sense of personal pride from this prize.

Due to very definite influences from the clergy, the school was predominantly **Christian** in its outlook. Indeed, its purpose was to produce **Christian** gentlemen. This blend of financial pragmatism and moralistic idealism was to continue into the twentieth century – once again demonstrating that the priorities of an institution can remain largely unaltered, even within a rapidly changing world. There is little doubt that the quality of teaching was very high, though somewhat narrow in its range. Evidence for this point emerged in **Frank's** determination to send my own father to the **Leeds Grammar School**. Possibly exemplifying these trends was the then headmaster the **Rev. Dr W. G.**

Henderson whose tenure was to last from **1862** until **1884.** A somewhat formal portrait shows a **Gladstone**-type figure with bushy grey sideburns and the domed forehead of an academic. Despite the dog collar and official gown, his face displayed an open-hearted and kindly expression. He looked the sort of man who would have taken great pains to have done *'the right thing.'*

This **Christian** outlook surfaced in the **July 1882** edition of **The Leodensian Magazine** (of the **Leeds Grammar School**) in the form of an article entitled *'The two records of creation.'* It took a tilt at the theory of evolution whilst robustly defending the Mosaic record. Another article defended classical education against the charge that it was an impractical *'absurdity.'* Looking back from the viewpoint of **September 1999** both contributors were defending lost causes. But were they? They could not have imagined that, when applied in the social sphere, **Darwinism** would provide an important philosophical underpinning for an ideology **(Nazism)** whose chief effect was to ensure that many **L.G.S.** pupils (from a later generation) would end up having their names inscribed upon the school war memorial. Such an outcome could never have been imagined – even in their worst nightmares. Moreover, it is reasonable to argue that the near-total decline in classical education has contributed to that loss of historical memory which has become such a feature of modern society. Leaving aside such points, these two articles confirm that the school was not completely oblivious to the philosophical currents of the time. It was far less of an insular institution than one would have at first imagined. Some awareness of the outside world did exist. Thanks to the **Leeds Grammar School Admission Book** we have an idea of what most of **Edmund's** sons were doing by the year **1905.**

Admission no: 2526
Term Admitted: 1870, second term
Name at Birth: Smith, James Hastings, 11 yrs.
Date of Birth: Sept. 17, 1858
Details of Father: Edmund Smith, Hastings Place, Vernon Road
Later occupation: A Commercial Traveller at Orley Terrace, Chapel Lane, Headingley in 1905
Admission no: 2942
Term Admitted: 1877, first term
Name of Birth: Smith, Arthur Edmund, 13 years
Date of Birth: March 3, 1863
Details of Father: Edmund Smith, Hastings Place, Vernon Road
Later occupation: A Commercial Traveller at 705 St Louis Street, Montreal
Admission no: 3075
Term Admitted: 1878, second term

Name of Birth: Smith, Ernest Alexander Harward, 9 yrs.
Date of Birth: August 15, 1868
Details at Father: Edmund Smith, 16 Vernon Road
Later occupation: A Commercial Traveller at 39 Esplanade, Whitley Bay, S.O. Northumberland in 1905
<u>**Admission no:** 3161</u>
Term Admitted: Easter Term 1879
Name at Birth: Smith, Frank, 9 yrs.
Date of Birth: 23rd Sept. 1869
Details of Father: Edmund Smith, 16 Vernon Road
Later occupation: Fred Heselwood Smith, Commercial Traveller at 51 Hillcrest Avenue, Harehills, Leeds in 1905

The considerable outlay **Edmund** must have made in terms of school fees (and other expenses) bore ample testimony to the value he'd placed upon education. Giving his sons a good education was clearly an important priority of his life. Perhaps he'd wanted them to receive something that he felt had been missing from his own life. Certainly, the school would have provided an opportunity for upward social mobility, with **Edmund** fully aware that this was the case. His own life was something of a role model to his sons – at least in the business sphere, with them all becoming Commercial Travellers. Of notable interest was **Arthur Smith's** move to **Canada!**

A dark tale surrounds this event. On **Sunday 18th, December 2016,** a conversation with my first cousin revealed he'd been *'packed off'* to **Canada** for alleged *'kiddy fiddling'* (apparently with boys). She'd heard this story from a couple of aunts who'd said, *'It had all been kept very quiet.'* When **Edmund** had learnt of it his reaction had been wholly in keeping with his character – both ruthless and decisive. Intending to *'prevent scandal and preserve the good name of the family'* it was quickly arranged for **Arthur** to be *'packed off to Canada'* to join the **Stewart MacDonald** branch in **Montreal.** He had been working in the **Westminster** area of **London;** so, his transfer couldn't be taken as a promotion. The best that could be said for **Edmund's** reaction (and subsequent solution to prospective family disgrace) was typical of its time. Most of his Middle-Class peers would most probably have done the same. The story given out at the time was that **Arthur** wanted an *'adventure.'*

A review of passenger lists (from **1885** until **1905**) revealed one adult with the name **Mr A. E. Smith.** Unusually for such records no full name or year of birth was given, only that he was registered as an *'adult'* and a *'gent.'* He had sailed on the **S.S Labrador,** which had left **Liverpool, England** on **19ᵗʰ November 1896.** Although the ship's destination was for **Portland USA,** Mr **A. E. Smith** had disembarked at **Halifax, Nova-Scotia,** located on the **Atlantic Coast** of **Canada.** It was a normal disembarking point. From here, he will have boarded a train on a long journey bound for **Montreal,** viewing the **Saint Lawrence River** on the way.

The striking thing about the above information was the timing of his journey. Few in their right mind would have even considered travelling across the **Northern Atlantic** in late **November! Canada** at that time of the year would have been a bleak and coldly uninviting place. **A. E. Smith** must have had a very good reason for having travelled at this time. One can only hope that **Arthur** would not have continued his abusive behaviour in **Canada.** If he was a victim of a malicious allegation one can only feel very sorry for him. Thankfully, a quick search of available police records failed to uncover his name.

However, his work as a Commercial Traveller may well have provided *'adequate cover'* and an inroad to certain *'opportunities.'* Should he have availed himself of these *'opportunities'* he will no doubt have tried harder to have *'covered his tracks.'* After all, working as a Commercial traveller still carried with it an outward veneer of respectability. Yet, sadly, this may well have been all the cover he would have needed to pursue his abusive lifestyle. We can only hope that <u>this wasn't the case.</u> The fact that he was named in **Edmund's** will of **1912** suggests that it wasn't – or alternatively, that he'd avoided being caught.

One indicator of presumed innocence was a surprising entry in the diary of his elder brother **James.** Dated **Wednesday, 4ᵗʰ October 1899** it noted, *"**Arthur** and **Arabella** married at **Bradford** Parish."* A **34-**year-old spinster living in the respectable suburb of **Horton** in **Bradford. Arabella** was the sister of **James'** much-loved wife. It's unlikely that the highly principled **James** not challenge this marriage if he believed that there was something seriously *'amiss'* with his sibling. However, the couple were quickly out of the country because, on **Thursday, 12ᵗʰ October, James** noted that they were sailing back to **Montreal.** They had stayed in **Bradford** for as little time possible. Tellingly, **Edmund's** signature was not on the Wedding Certificate which may have been a sign of disapproval. (He was recorded as being a *'Draper's Manager.'*) Another odd feature lay in the way **Arthur's** *'Residence at the time of Marriage'* was given as **98 Horseferry Road, Westminster, London.** However, his ascribed Profession of *'Commercial Traveller, Drapery'* appeared to be accurate.

In late **1923, James** received word that *"**Arthur** had an operation in a hospital in Montreal, dead November 15th."* Over the period of **1st-7th August 1927** his widow **Arabella** *"had returned by ship"* to **Britain.** During her time here she and her daughter visited **James.** In **1938,** she passed away in **Montreal.** The best thing that can be done about **Arthur** is to presume innocence until proven guilty. Unlike the typical *'kiddy fiddler'* no pattern of offences ever came to light.

Hedley's absence from the Grammar School is unusual given the former attendance of his elder brothers. The exact location of his education remains unknown. Was fee payment a problem? Alternatively, did he lack the aptitude to be accepted? The balance of probability favours the second explanation. If that was the case, **Edmund** may well have voiced some very strong feelings of displeasure to **Rosamond's** youngest son, berating him for not achieving the desired goal. Despite this possible setback at least some of **Edmund's** sons would have pleased him by settling into the upper end of the middle classes.

Evidence for the marriage of **Hedley** emerged in the following Wedding Certificate, received from **Bridlington** Register Office on **Friday, July 25th, 2003.** This document confirmed that links with **East Yorkshire** still existed during the early **1900s.** The signature of my Grandfather's name suggested that he might have acted the part of Best Man for his younger brother. If this was the case, then it's reasonable to conclude that he was a valued member of the family – one who could be entrusted with such a responsibility.

Registration District of <u>Bridlington</u>

<u>1902</u> Marriage solemnised at <u>the Parish Church of Christchurch</u> <u>Bridlington</u> in the <u>county of York</u>

1. When married? 24th February 1902

2. Name and Surname: Hedley Stamford Smith, Annie Elizabeth Crofton

3. Age: 25, 24

4. Condition: Bachelor, Spinster,

5. Rank or profession: Draper

6 Residence at the time of marriage: Barnsley, 4 Belvedere

7. Father's name and surname: Edmund Smith, William Henry Crofton

8. Rank or profession of father: Commercial Traveller, Printer

Married in the <u>Parish Church according to the Rites and Ceremonies of</u> <u>the Established Church</u> by license by me <u>Robert Cross</u>

The marriage was solemnised between us

Hedley Stamford Smith [and] Annie Elizabeth Crofton

In the presence of us *Fred Hazelwood Smith and* Fanny Louise Hood

Much more would be discovered about **Hedley** in **April 2013** when one of his descendants **Ann Dalton** contacted me *'out of the blue'* by post. One odd feature about this contact was that this lady should never even have existed! Family tradition relayed by my usually reliable first cousin **Pamela** asserted that **Hedley** had indeed married but had <u>never</u> had any children! My mother who took a keen interest in **Fred's** Family never knew of any such child either. Yet this information was incorrect! A Birth Certificate dated **29th January 1904** records the birth of a **William Hedley Smith** at **161 Park Lane, Barnsley** whose father was on record as being a *'Draper's Manager.'* The date of registration was given as the **10th March 1904.** In the **1911** Census, **Hedley** appears to have suffered a drop-in status despite living in a house with **7** rooms. It revealed: -

Hedley Smith *'Head'* aged **33**, *'Drapers assistant'*
Annie Smith *'Wife'* aged **34**
William Smith *'Son'* aged **7**
Kathleen Smith *'Daughter'* aged **5**

On **7th March 1926, William Hedley Smith** married a **Mona Hilton Slater** aged **24** at **Manchester South Registry Office.** He was down as an *'electrical fitter'* and she a *'confectioner.'* Tellingly, his father **Hedley** was <u>not</u> a signatory and his occupation given as *'Draper, retired'* when he would only have been aged about **47** or **48!** On the **22nd May 1928, Mona** gave birth to a daughter **Nancie Hilton Smith** who would marry into the **Dalton** family and live on until **3rd May 2011** and become the mother of my *'source'* **Ann Dalton.** After occupying a succession of unskilled jobs **William** passed away on **25th, February 1965** at the **Jewish Hospital, Cheetham, Manchester.** Heavy drinking and self-neglect appeared to have been contributory factors to his death. A photograph confirmed that by his early sixties he looked a complete physical wreck. He s seemed to know he'd made a complete mess of his life. In relation to this couple (**William** and **Mona**) the **Smith's** perennial battle to *'maintain respectability'* was largely lost. Apparently, alcohol and a violently unhappy marriage were to blame. Both were reputed to have spent most of their evenings at the pub where **Mona** would play the piano. Perhaps this downward trajectory had begun with **Hedley** himself. He was to move from owning a prosperous Drapery business in the early **1920s** to becoming a publican in a poor area of **Manchester.** The example of this branch of the **Smiths** underlines the fragility of middle-class respectability during the interwar period. Thankfully, his great-granddaughter **Ann** had, by dint of *'hard graft'* regained a position of respectability which had once been lost. My wife and I would affectionately know her as ***'Lady Ann.'***

CHAPTER 14: A MIXED FAITH MARRIAGE

Section 1: The Rise of Joseph Gillinson

Concerning Joseph Gillinson and the Jewish Population of Leeds

No more Census Returns were available after **1911** because of the rule preventing their release to the public for a period of one hundred. From this time onward, family tradition becomes much more detailed and Trade Directories provide a reasonable account of the movements of my Grandfather **Frank.** They helped establish a chronological outline which listed his occupation as a *'Commercial Traveller.'* In **1900** his address was the inner-city location of **41 Sholebroke View Leeds,** but by **1903** he had moved to **51 Hillcrest Avenue,** in the inner suburb of **Harehills.** By **7 September 1911** (the day **Stewart** was born), he was at the larger home of **26 Hillcrest Avenue,** which stood on a street corner – his previous houses being terraced accommodation. He was still at that address when my father **Fred** was born in **February 1914,** remaining there until the **1927** to **1929** period. After this, his address was **36 Shaftesbury Avenue,** located on the edge of the wealthier outer suburb of **Roundhay.** All but the **Sholebroke View** address were mentioned in the family tradition. Modern technology was not something **Frank** quickly embraced, for his name failed to feature in the **1937 Leeds Telephone Directory.** The early years of business were hard, with him starting out by trailing (with a barrow in hand) from one business address to another, trying to sell cloth. Later events would suggest that at least he had made some sales at the premises of one **Joe Gillinson** whose family was said to have come to **Leeds** as refugees, having fled the poverty and continual threat of violence in **Tsarist Russia.** Although *"a rough diamond of a man"* **Joe** would grow to be an influential member of the **Leeds Jewish Community,** actively participating in a wide range of cultural activities. **Joe** and **Frank** became close business associates and seem to have struck up something of a friendship. This relationship bears testimony to **Frank's** business skills, for by more than one account **Joe** held a reputation for not suffering any sort of fool gladly – least of all if the *'fool'* concerned cost him time and money. Eventually, **Joe's** son **Bernard** (born **1911**) was to inherit both the family business <u>and</u> the link with the **Smith** family.

To reach **England Jewish** immigrants would have had to endure filthy conditions aboard old ships (which, in some cases, had been designed to carry animals rather than human cargo). Most of these people had never even seen

444

the sea before. A **Radio 4** documentary, entitled *'The Jewish Journey'* (broadcast on **Sunday 21st April 2002**) recorded how certain **Jewish** migrants travelled in cattle ships. When the stalls were hosed down at the start of the day, wet cow dung would drip into the holds inside which the migrants were crowded. During storms, they would have been rolling around in their own bodily waste as well as that from any cattle. It was hardly surprising that when they arrived in **England** many were in a foul-smelling and filthy condition. Most arrived utterly penniless and had to scrape a living together by either begging or peddling a variety of goods. Their **Yiddish** language and alien customs were a cause of acute embarrassment to the wealthier, more respectable members of the **Jewish Community** who had already settled in the **United Kingdom** for past generations. Not only were these migrants fleeing the reality (or threat) of persecution, they were also escaping the grinding poverty of *'The Pale of Settlement.'* This was an area in **Poland** and **West Russia** where they'd been restricted to live by the **Tsarist** authorities. (In **Vilnius, Lithuania** it was estimated that **17%** of the **Jewish** population went to bed at night not knowing where their next meal was coming from.) The feeling of insecurity in such areas had been so bad that one **Jewish** woman (possibly a contemporary of **Edmund**) was known to have thanked **God** every night that there had been no trouble with her **Gentile** neighbours. Her family had kept goats to provide them with their necessities.

Aris (1971) on **p.30** noted that in **1881** there were **15,000** Jews with **75%** being concentrated in **London, Manchester** and **Leeds**. After that, there was an influx of **4,000** per year. By the time of the **1901** Census, the Jews numbered **95,000** an increase of **600%**. This influx caused problems – not least for **Middle-Class Jews** who didn't welcome their co-religionists with their strange manners and exotic ways. They feared (with some justification) that it could create a revival in **anti-Semitism.**

There's an abundance of evidence to confirm that **Joseph Gillinson** did come from a very tough background – the sort which ambitious men would have done anything to escape from. **Gartner (1960) p.153** quoted a **Leeds** medical report which stated that the **Jewish** Quarter in the **Leyland's** (located near the centre of **Leeds**): *"consists of a number of small streets with red brick cottages. The sanitary accommodation is altogether inadequate. In one street where a great number of tailors live; we found only two closets for seven houses. These were placed back to back in a little passage between two houses ... The houses on this side of the street have no background or windows."* This source also disclosed that whilst the interior of some houses were dirty others were remarkably clean.

It was from such unpromising beginnings that the **Gillinson** family began their three-generation rise to wealth and influence. The following Death Certificate showed that **Joseph Gillinson's** entry into business had begun with a tragedy.

Registration District <u>Leeds</u>
<u>1901</u> Death in the <u>sub-district</u> of <u>North Leeds</u> in the <u>County of Leeds</u>
1. When and where died: Eleventh March 1901 Sheepscar Place U.D
2. Name and Surname: Barnet Gillinson
3. Sex: Male
4. Age: 44
5. Occupation: A Hawker
6. Causes of Death: Fracture of the spine from a fall, Accidental death
7. Signature, description, and residence of Informant: Certificate received from J. C. Malcolm, Coroner for Leeds, held 11th March 1901
8. When registered: Twelfth March 1901
9. Signature of Registrar: Isaac J. Bloomfield, Registrar

In Trade Directories **Barnet Gillinson** had been known as **Barnard** and then **Bernard Gillinson.** He'd been on record as working as a *'Commercial Traveller'* in **1899.** His death may well have happened after falling down the stairs of his house whilst carrying heavy material samples (or being drunk). Here was a tragic but telling parallel with **Edmund** who had begun his own rise to prosperity following the accidental death of his father in a mill accident. Both sons (**Joseph Gillinson** and **Edmund Smith**) alike would have felt strongly that poverty was something to be escaped from by every means possible. Shortly after **Barnet's** death, the **1901** Census provided the following information about the **Gillinson Household** at **9 Sheepscar Place:** -

Name: Jane Gillinson
Relation to Head of the Family: Widow
Age Last Birthday: 40
A Worker on Own Account: -
Occupation: -
Where Born? Russian Subject

Name: Joseph
Relation to Head of the Family: Son
Age Last Birthday: 21
Occupation: *'Peddler Hawker'*
A worker on Own Account: Yes
Where Born? Russian Subject

Name: Rachel
Relation to Head of the Family: Daughter
Age Last Birthday: 17
Occupation: *'Tailoress'*
A Worker on Own Account: Yes
Where Born? Russian Subject

Name: Dora
Relation to Head of the Family: Daughter
Age Last Birthday: 15
Occupation: *'Tailoress'*
A Worker on Own Account: Yes
Where Born? Russian Subject

Name: Archie
Relation to Head of the Family: Son
Age Last Birthday: 13
Occupation:
A Worker on Own Account:
Where Born? Russian Subject

Name: Louis
Relation to Head of the Family: Son
Age Last Birthday: 11
Occupation:
A Worker on Own Account:
Where Born? Russian Subject

Name: Solomon
Relation to Head of the Family: Son
Age Last Birthday: 5
Occupation: -
A Worker on Own Account: -
Where Born? Leeds

The information from the Census suggested that the **Gillinson's** had migrated to **England** during the period of **1891-1896.** At the time of this census, the premises of **Joseph Gillinson's** first shop at **76 Meanwood Street** were lying empty, ready for him to occupy later in the year. He would move into them within a few months at most. How he scraped together enough money to invest in this venture remains unknown, the most likely explanation being that he borrowed money from relatives.

Sheepscar was a very poor and overcrowded **Jewish** area, where tailoring (often done in appalling sweatshop conditions) was the most prevalent occupation. Like the **Leylands,** poor drainage and overcrowding would have ensured an utterly foul smell, particularly in sweltering summer weather. Most of the back-to-back, two-roomed terraced houses would have possessed only one cold-water tap. Consequently, personal hygiene could only have been maintained by using the local bathhouses. Hardly surprisingly, what few leisure activities did exist often took place outside the house or were mostly centred on the synagogue. Such entertainment may well have included things like a touring **Yiddish Theatre Company.** The address at **Sheepscar** indicated that the **Gillinson's** had started out near the very bottom of the social pile; it would take the major global economic disaster of the Great Depression (some three decades later) to finally secure **Joseph's** place in the middle classes.

Joseph may well have begun hawking items of clothing on both a street and door-to-door basis. Having encountered diverse types of people on his rounds he will have gained considerable experience concerning what factors had motivated their purchasing decisions. To have survived within such a concentrated and competitive environment will have needed pronounced and excellent sales skills on his part. The rebuffs must have been many and there would have been the constant realisation that he was now the chief provider for the family. At times, the local **anti-Semites** may well have taunted him as a *'vulgar'* or *'dirty'* **Jew.** However, such taunts would have only further driven **Joseph's** hunger to succeed and to have appreciated his cultural heritage even more. The **1901** Census showed **Joseph** on the eve of embarking upon what would prove to be a long and successful business career – which would play a major part in shaping my own family. (Incidentally, it is a fitting memorial for this talented and hardworking man, and he is cited as an example of far-sighted business acumen to some of my own private students).

Returning to the details provided by the **1901** Census, it could be seen that **Louis** had been born in **Russia** in **1890,** whereas his younger brother **Solomon** was born in **Leeds** during **1896.** This would suggest that the **Gillinson's** had come over from **Russia** at some time during the years **1891-1895.** The six-year gap between the two children implies that their father had migrated first – followed by the remainder of his family two or three years later. (This was and still is a very common migration pattern.) If this was what happened, then the main motivation will have been a very real need to escape from desperate poverty. If it had been to flee a pogrom, then the whole family would have come over at once. Nevertheless, the threat of a pogrom was always present, lurking in the background and ready to strike at any time.

The **Gillinson's** highlighted the absolute futility of **Russian anti-Semitism.** If they and thousands of **Jewish** families like them had been allowed to prosper without any major degree of molestation, **Russia** may well have acquired just enough economic edge to have won the First World War and have prevented the onset of any revolution. **Lenin** would have become a forgotten agitator and **Stalin** a gangster boss in **Georgia.** The folly of **anti-Semitism** was to cost millions of **Russian** lives as well as many **Jewish** ones too. With **Joe Gillinson, Russia's** loss was **Leeds's** gain. Later events would show that my own immediate family were also set to gain from him. They owe him a great debt.

Joe's own rise to business eminence is interesting because it reflects the rapid upward social mobility of the **Leeds's Jewish Community.** The following brief chronology, drawn from various Business Directories, is quite illuminating in the information it provides. All quoted addresses are in the **Leeds** area: -
1902/3: Gillinson Joseph, *"Draper and wallpaper dealer"* at **76 Meanwood Street** – in premises which had (in **1901**) been in previous use by an **Isaac Harris** – *"provisions dealer."*
1905: Gillinson Joseph, *"General Dealer"* at **54 Meanwood Road.**
1910: Gillinson Joseph, *"Draper"* at **58 Meanwood Road. Residing at 42 Leopold Street** near the **Chapeltown Road.**
1914: Gillinson Joseph, *"Draper"* at **58 Meanwood Road** and **267 Kirkstall Road. Resident at 35 Cowper Street**
1920: Gillinson Joseph, *"Draper"* at **1 & 3 New York Street** and at **267 Kirkstall Road. Resident at 35 Cowper Street**
1925: Gillinson Joseph, *"Draper"* at **1 & 3 New York Street. A resident at 35 Cowper Street**
1929: Gillinson Joseph, *"Draper"* at **1 New York Street. A resident at 35 Cowper Street**

What the above chronology conveyed was the picture of a very shrewd businessman, willing to trial a variety of product lines before finally settling for drapery. He chose to *'spread his risks'* until he knew what *'line'* was most profitable. Also displayed was his ruthless ability to control expansion by getting rid of loss-making branches. Quite wisely he followed a very gradual step-by-step expansion. Furthermore, his continued residence at **Cowper Street** implied a determination to keep a tight control over his personal expenditure. If he was unable to afford a house in an ostentatious area of **Leeds,** then he would not even contemplate it. (For much of the time he would have lived near to **Frank** and his family.) **Joseph Gillinson** did not appear to be in any sense *'flash,'* – rather he knew how to husband his resources. However, what he <u>did</u> appear to want badly was integration within **English** Society. His strictly Orthodox compatriots would perhaps have viewed him as being *'not quite'* fully loyal to his **Jewish** faith – although he would have argued this point with vigour. In the **1929** Economic Depression, **Joseph Gillinson** would have had to face the sternest possible test of his business skills. His incredible way of surmounting that ordeal will be described in another chapter.

Section 2: A Holiday Romance

Concerning the Isle of Man as a Victorian Holiday Resort

Over the years, **Frank** grew into a typically hard-working, taciturn **Yorkshire** man. Perhaps surprisingly, a romantic streak did surface whilst he was on holiday at **Douglas** in the **Isle of Man** during the **mid-1890s.** Staying at the same (apparently expensive) Hotel was a certain **Elizabeth Mary Foster** (born in **1872**). Family tradition holds that they were smitten with each other at first sight. The result was their marriage in **1899,** followed by the reception at a house in **Bromsgrove, Birmingham.** Apparently, it was a very lavish function. Their best man was a certain **Mr T. C. Walls** from **Carlton Hall.** A copy of their Marriage Certificate was kindly provided by the **Birmingham Register Office** in **May 2001.**

Registration District <u>Aston</u>
1899 Marriage solemnised at <u>St Anne's Church, Alcester Street</u> in the District of <u>Aston</u> in the County of <u>Birmingham</u>
1. When married? Twenty Seventh June 1899
2. Name and Surname: Fred Heselwood Smith, Elizabeth Foster
3. Age: 29, 27
4. Condition: Bachelor, Spinster
5. Rank or profession: Stuff Merchandise Traveller
6 Residence at the time of marriage: 25 Grange Terrace, Leeds, Victoria Villa, Strensham Road, Moseley
7. Father's name and surname: Edmund Smith, Daniel John Foster
8. Rank or profession of father: Commercial Traveller, Cattle Salesman

450

Married in the <u>Saint Ann's Church</u> according to the Rites and Ceremonies of the <u>Roman Catholic Church</u> by a <u>certificate</u> by me,
The marriage was solemnised between us
<u>Fred Heselwood Smith</u>
<u>Elizabeth Foster</u>
In the presence of us
<u>Edmund Smith</u>
<u>J. J. Foster</u>
<u>Daniel John Foster</u>
<u>Neville Foster</u>
<u>J. P. Dowling, Catholic Priest</u>
<u>E. H.</u>
 <u>Goodall, Registrar</u>

Whatever misgivings he may have entertained about the marriage **Edmund** made sure he was present at their wedding. It was also apparent that by this stage of his life **Frank** had left home and was already well established as a salesman in his own right. His address was in the **Chapeltown** district of **Leeds** – not far from **Cowper Street** (where my father was later to attend primary school). The address of **Elizabeth Foster** was of interest because her residence in a suburban villa suggested that she had come from a family possessing great wealth. Her father **Daniel** was connected to people who owned large landed estates. Although not aristocracy, his business would have brought him into contact with those who were of that class. One could easily imagine him using all his **Irish** charm to gain a good sale of cattle. Family tradition held that he had a mop of black curly hair. Whether **Edmund** would have taken to him is open to speculation. I suspect my Great Grandfather would have been more than a little envious of **Daniel's** apparent wealth. (By way of a brief digression, I observed that the name *'Dowling'* couldn't have been more stereotypical of a **Catholic** Priest. It was the sort of name expected to emerge in a period drama about the **Catholic Aristocracy** of **England** and showed that real-life history could, on occasion, contain more clichés than its fictitious counterpart.)

Elizabeth's own background was of special interest. Her family used to own and train racehorses in the **Waterford** area of **Ireland.** She may well have been born there because contacts with the **Birmingham Register Office** confirmed that she had not been born in the area in which she was living at the time of her marriage to **Frank.** The **Fosters** were allegedly very wealthy, with one of **Elizabeth's** sisters having almost married a Lord. The family were said to have possessed a large share in the *'Vono'* Bedding Company and certainly, a link <u>did</u>

emerge with that business. Moreover, **Daniel Foster** had sufficiently ingratiated himself with the local Bishop to have been made a **Knight of St. Gregory.** Tradition holds that some family members were buried beside a Senior **Roman Catholic** dignitary in **Birmingham.** This was possibly an award for them having paid for a new altar at **Birmingham Oratory.** Further reinforcing her **Catholicism** was the education she had received in a Convent near Paris. (In later life, she would give her **Grandchildren French** lessons.) The marked difference in social class, along with the strong **Roman Catholic** influences ensured that **Elizabeth's** marriage to **Frank** was to cause a major split within her family. She was the oldest of ten girls and five boys. (Two other siblings may have died in infancy, as some accounts hold that there had been seventeen in the family, others fifteen). Her mother was called **Julia.**

A photograph (dated around the **1890s**) revealed **Julia** to have been something of a late **Victorian** *'clothes horse'* of a woman, standing very erect with hands clasped firmly on the left corner of a chair partly covered by some drapery. The overwhelming impression was one of opulence. Her left hand sported at least three rings and adorning her right wrist was what looked like a diamond bracelet. An emerald neck broach lay centred upon her starched and stiffened lace collar. The upper part of her dress was decorated in elaborate lace with braided puffy sleeves. The dress tapered into the *'hourglass shape,'* common at the time. Half obscured by the chair the remainder of her dress was of a floral leaf design in a dark texture. Most interesting of all was her face. Her eyes, above a long Roman nose, radiated a serene inner strength – a woman very much at ease in her social position. **Julia's** dark coloured hair was all bunched up. A small round pearl or diamond earring dangled beneath a rather oversized ear. Here was a woman in the prime of her life. The photograph had been taken in the studio of **H. Whitlock, Birmingham. Julia's** maiden name had been **Neilus.**

The motives leading to this match are mysterious. Money does not appear to have been a major factor because (since the early **1890s**) **Frank** had prospered enough to have afforded an expensive holiday on the **Isle of Man.** Research conducted in **Douglas,** the **Isle of Man's** Capital on **Monday, 7th August 2011,** confirmed that this location had been a very popular tourist resort for the late **Victorian** Middle Classes. Regrettably, only the guest lists from some of the larger hotels where **Frank** and his future wife may have stayed still existed. (This research was conducted whilst staying there, on the way to **Belfast** with my youngest son on one of our adventure trips.) Perhaps **Frank** saw an opportunity for social (rather than economic) advancement. Here was someone far *'grander'* than any *'Leeds lass.'* However, Family Tradition has him down as saying, *"If my* *father could make his fortune by marrying a rich woman then so can I."* If true these are the words of an insecure man living in the shadow of his father and anxious to prove that he could do just as well as him. It need hardly be added that the desire to prove yourself as *'big'* a man as your father did not constitute the best sort of motive for a good marriage. The **Smith's** seemed to make a habit of Father-Son rivalry.

With **Elizabeth,** the motives are easier to fathom, she seemed to have been one of those highly-strung ladies in need of a strong, steady man, unlike many of the men she may have encountered. Another pressure was the fact that she was reaching an age when it was getting rather late for a lady of her era to marry. The *'biological time bomb'* was already ticking away. Perhaps she had been unduly influenced by the romantic novels of that time. These were known to have been popular amongst ladies of her good breeding. Especially telling was the fact that, like **Frank, Elizabeth** came from a highly restrictive background. She was a wealthy but devout **Roman Catholic,** imprisoned by a myriad of religious as well as social conventions. **Frank's** restrictions lay in the fact that he was the son of **Edmund Smith.** Perhaps both had reached the stage where they wanted to rebel and try something different. Moreover, love remains irrational – there must have been something alluring about **Elizabeth** for **Frank** to have fallen under her spell. It was most unlikely that he was calculating the prospects of upward social mobility when their eyes had first met. Whether it was at dinner or in the Hotel foyer is anyone's guess. What seems clear is that she had given only little (if any) thought at all to the likely consequences of marrying a man from such a different social background. One wonders how **Edmund** would have taken to her!

Given the religious attitudes of the age, it seems hardly surprising that from this union emerged a marked degree of religious conflict, the effects of which would reverberate down the generations. **Frank** had only been granted permission to marry **Elizabeth** if the marriage was performed at **St. Anne's Roman Catholic Church, Aston, Birmingham.** Also, all her subsequent children (including my father **Fred**) had to be baptised as **Catholics.** Apparently, **Elizabeth** attended **St. Anne's Cathedral** in **Leeds** whilst **Frank** was said to have maintained a link with **Blenheim Baptist** Church – however, his name cannot be found on any of its membership rolls. In **August 1972,** my Aunt **Julia** mentioned **Frank** as having had links with a **Methodist Church** by **1914** but even this point is uncertain. The fact that they married at all emphasises that both **Frank** and **Elizabeth** were sufficiently strong-willed to have broken with the religious and social conventions of their day. In their own individual ways, both were willing to defy the status quo for the sake of love. For **Elizabeth,** her great love for **Frank** led to a most bitter sacrifice. Most of her family ostracised her socially and financially for the mortal sin of having married a Protestant. It is also likely that trouble came from the **Smith** direction too. **Edmund,** of all people, would hardly have taken kindly to one of his sons marrying *'a papist'* whose family *'looked down'* on his own. Worsening any conflict would have been the fact that **Edmund** and **Frank** were both strong-minded men who liked having their own way. One can easily imagine hearing the former telling the latter that *'nothing good would come out of this match.'* Almost certainly **Edmund** would have resented the rejection of his parental authority. However, evidence of such a conflict remains lost to history. Of possible significance was the fact that, while **Frank** named his first daughter after his mother **Rosamond**, neither of his two sons was named after his father (at a time when it would have been customary to have done so). Also, the second name of his first son, **Stewart** was *'Foster'* and not **Edmund.** Was **Frank** making a rather telling point by this action? Was he showing his independence from a domineering father? It seems most probable.

For **Elizabeth,** the reality of married life at the turn of the century must have come as a considerable shock. Although *'becoming'* a good cook, she had never done any domestic chores up to the point of her marriage. Indeed, each one of the **Foster** girls reputedly had their own personal maid. Some five decades later she was to relate to my own mother how on first scrubbing the kitchen floor she had broken down in tears. Hitherto servants had done that sort of work for her. Marrying beneath one's class really was not a pleasant experience in late **Victorian England** – especially when having been repudiated by one's own family. According to my mother, **Elizabeth** spoke with a highly-refined voice, free from any trace of an **Irish** accent. This suggests that she would have viewed any regional accent as being thoroughly *'common.'* Neither were things all that easy for **Frank.** Not infrequently, those relatives of **Elizabeth** who still maintained some contact would send food hampers. Feeling thoroughly patronised **Frank** wrote them a stern letter, angrily pointing out that he was more than capable of providing for his own family. By taking this action, he had displayed a marked determination to keep interfering relatives well out of the way.

Probably adding deeply to **Elizabeth's** misery was the way her younger sisters married effortlessly upward into very high social circles. A letter I received on **Wednesday 3rd February 2000** (from my cousin **Pamela**) provided details of some of their illustrious connections. *"There were two of her younger sisters called* ***Celia (Vaughan)*** *and* ***Aileen (Scott-Owen).*** *I understand that the* ***Scott-Owens*** *were related to the* **Seymours, (Lord Henry Seymour).** *The* **Vaughans (Ernest Vaughan** *made* **Vono** *beds) were self-made. Amongst* **Celia's** *children was* **Molly Vaughan** *– one of the society beauties of her day. She married a society photographer but prior to that was friendly with* **Prince Ali Khan.** *For all her wealth, beauty and contacts,* **Molly** *committed suicide whilst still relatively young. I kept in touch with* **Aunt Amy Anslow,** *the youngest of the ten sisters who died… in about* **1969.**" Compared to such matches **Frank** must have seemed a very small fish and it appears that the **Foster's** let him know that they felt this was the case.

Although an element of mutual infatuation did exist the full motives leading to this union will forever remain a mystery. What family tradition does imply was that the habit of marrying into wealth was something that had been strongly encouraged by **Edmund.** He evidently viewed it as a means of improving the social standing of the **Smiths.** A photograph of the couple, taken at an East Coast Resort in **August 1931,** provided another clue. They were formally attired, walking down the promenade (with an unknown boy in baggy shorts standing by in the background). After over three decades of marriage **Elizabeth** is looking sideways toward her husband with the smiling adoration of a highly-strung teenage girl still freshly in love. She had maintained her emotional dependence upon this special man, whom she had perhaps come to view as her anchor in life. In contrast, **Frank** stared at the camera, a large bulldog of a man with waistcoat and bowler hat. It was as if he was thinking *'How much is this trip going to cost then?'* Their body language for this photo shot had been quite revealing.

Section 3: A Touch of Irish Blarney

Concerning mixed Catholic and Protestant marriages

A view of Census Returns during **May-August 2007** failed to confirm the picture of great wealth which had been created by the **Fosters.** This became apparent with the Return for **1871.**
30 Bradford Street (St Martin's Parish, Birmingham)
Daniel John Foster aged **24** *'Pig and Cattle Salesman'* **Ireland**
Julia aged **20 Warwickshire**
The details given in the Census imply that **Daniel** had come over from **Ireland** in response to the potato famine. By **1881** the Return shows a large and expanding family. Ten years later the family had ballooned to provide the following entry for the **1881** Census.

3 <u>Moat Lane</u> (St Martin's Parish Birmingham)
Daniel John Foster aged **34** *'Cattle, sheep and pig Salesman'* **Ireland**
Julia aged **30** *'Salesman's wife'* **Warwickshire, Birmingham**
<u>**Elizabeth**</u> aged **9** *'Scholar'* **Warwickshire, Birmingham**
Julia aged **8** *'Scholar'* **Warwickshire, Birmingham**
Thomas aged **3** *'Scholar'* **Warwickshire, Birmingham**
Marie K aged **2** – place of birth **Warwickshire, Birmingham**
Maria Temple aged **19** *'General Servant'* – place of birth… **Staffordshire**
Annie Smith aged **58** – *'Nurse S M'*
The cost of running this household of many girls must have been huge.
Elizabeth's education in a **French** or **Belgium** Convent appears to have taken
place from about **1883-1890**. In the next census of **1891**, notice how the family
is having to supplement its income from farming and even then, could employ
only one servant. Even in the following **1901** Census, only one servant is
employed and there's no evidence that **Daniel** sold horses – at least not on a
regular basis.
<u>Green Lane, *'Polless Farm'*</u> (St Oswald Parish near Bordesley,
Birmingham)
Daniel John Foster aged **44** *'Cattle, sheep and hog Salesman'* **Ireland**
Julia aged **40** *'A Farmer'* **Warwickshire, Birmingham**
<u>**Elizabeth**</u> aged **19** single **Warwickshire, Birmingham**
Julia aged **18** single **Warwickshire, Birmingham**
Marie aged **12** *'Scholar'* **Warwickshire, Birmingham**
Cecilia aged **8** *'Scholar'* **Warwickshire, Birmingham**
Regina aged **7** *'Scholar'* **Warwickshire, Birmingham**
Aileen aged **5** *'Scholar'* **Warwickshire, Birmingham**
Amelia aged **4** *'Scholar'* **Warwickshire, Birmingham**
Irene M. aged **2** **Warwickshire, Birmingham**
William aged **1** **Warwickshire, Birmingham**
Ellen Conway aged **22** – *'General Servant'* **Staffordshire, Wednesbury**
Julia Neilus' had daughter (also called **Julia**) who led a tragic life In **March
2019,** the granddaughter of **Irene M.** sent me emails revealing that following a
stillbirth, **Julia** stayed with her widowed mother at **Beechwood Drive,
Birmingham**. This proved too much for her ageing parent. Consequently,
Irene and her spouse arranged for her admittance to a lunatic asylum In **May
1918, Julia** wrote to her husband **Richard Hunter-Hicks** asking him to obtain
her release. The address given read *'The City of Birmingham Lunatic
Asylum, Winson Green.'* From **1921-1945** her brother-in-law, **Ernest
Vaughan** paid for her removal to *'Chichester Nursing Home'* where she

eventually died. Her son **Basil** was always told that his mother had died. (He was **14** at this time). Happily, he was reunited with his mother before her death.

The **1901** Census revealed that the once large **Foster** household had thinned out
Strensham Hill, Moseley, Birmingham
Daniel John Foster aged **54** *'Wine & Spirit Merchant & Livestock Salesman'* **Ireland**
Julia aged **50 Warwickshire, Birmingham**
Thomas aged **25** *'Livestock Salesman'* **Warwickshire, Birmingham**
Cecilia aged **18 Warwickshire, Birmingham**
Sarah Turner aged **51** *'General Servant & Domestic'* **Warwickshire, Coventry**
So where do the tales of fabulous wealth come from? Some daughters (like **Cecilia)** do appear to have married into wealth and this could have led to some confusion in transmission. However, given the previous reliability of family tradition, any confusion seems unlikely. One can only conclude that the tales of **Foster** wealth had been concocted by **Daniel** himself who didn't so much fabricate but rather exaggerate his social standing. His social status was no higher than that of **Edmund.** Perhaps the difficulties between **Frank** and **Elizabeth's** family arose from the fact that he'd felt he'd married into non-existent money. Religious differences were perhaps used as an excuse to justify a family division which had its real origins in financial issues. Who knows? But one thing which is apparent is the marked discrepancy between the information contained in Census Returns and the testimony of family tradition. When it came to the **Fosters** I didn't find what I'd been led to expect to find. **Daniel Foster** (the most likely author of these fabrications) died in **Chesham** during early **1911.** When I presented these details to my aged mother in **2011** she exclaimed, *"Well fancy finding all that out at my age!"* She remarked that **Fred's** own reaction to such discoveries would have been one of amusement.

Section 4: Settling In

Concerning the Smith Family of Chapeltown Leeds

In **1900** came **Frank** and **Elizabeth's** first child, a girl named **Rosamund.** Sadly, she was to grow up with a reputation for being a cantankerous mischief-maker, able to set people off against one another. She had a disconcerting habit of conveying her displeasure through third parties. Even my (usually long-suffering) father had, by the mid-**1960s,** decided to keep out of her way. Apparently, he had tried to make peace between her, and other family members and the attempt had backfired. Although **Fred** never said much about the nature of the exact trouble he did come to express a deep loathing for any form of family acrimony. My brother recalls him using exceptionally strong language about **Rosamund** some ten years after her death. From knowing one word that was supposed to have been used I can only conclude that he must have been driven to the last extremity of frustration by her behaviour. Hardly surprisingly, **Rosamund** was the one aunt I never did get to see. A very isolated figure, her death resulted from a brain tumour in **1969**. Almost every relative of her generation mentioned her name in a negative light. To some extent, her poor reputation may have been attributed to the rivalry felt by her younger sisters (**Julia** and **Madge**) who were strong and difficult personalities themselves. Far less easy to explain away was the fact that my father – known to be a first-class judge of character – on the few occasions he ever mentioned his eldest sister, always spoke of her in tones of rueful regret. It was with **Rosamund** that I felt closest to having stumbled across family secrets that were best left buried. Out of deference to still living relatives the decision was taken not to publish all the allegations held against her. I can only state that **Rosamund** displayed a rather disturbing but very consistent pattern of behaviour of being devious and divisive. Only **Madge** would visit **Rosamund** in her later years. Apparently, she did this out of a sense of pity. According to one family source, my father believed that many of **Rosamund's** problems lay in the fact that she'd never had enough to do. This source also stated that *"**Rosamund** was a drama queen and you never knew which way she was going to jump."* My normally very tolerant mother also echoed this sentiment by simply exclaiming *"she was horrible!"* Beyond causing trouble, her one hobby appeared to be that of painting – a hobby she shared with her sister **Julia**.

Whilst **Joe Gillinson** was poised to begin his climb out of poverty, my Grandfather **Frank** had settled into **41 Sholebroke Road, Chapeltown** with his wife (later more commonly known by her second name **Elizabeth**) and new daughter **Rosamund**. The **1901** Census offered the following information about my Grandfather's household: -
Fred H. Smith aged **30** *'Traveller, (Dress Foods), working on his own account'* **Yorkshire, Leeds**
Mary E. aged **27 Warwickshire, Birmingham**
Rosamond daughter aged **11 months, Yorkshire, Leeds**
Mary A. Neilus aged **33** (visitor) *'Buyer in Fancy Shoes, working on her own account,'* **Warwickshire, Birmingham**
(It seems that *'Frank'* was the name by which he was known by other family members.)

These findings were full of interesting implications. One surprising detail was the fact that my Grandfather was not working for **Stewart Macdonald**, but for **Dress Food**s. He had left Drapery, the occupation which his father **Edmund** had followed all his working life. It appears that like some of his siblings **Frank** had wanted to move out and away from **Edmund's** shadow. Somewhat strangely, Family Tradition – which is rich for this period – <u>never</u> mentioned **Frank** working in the food line. My own father (who was very close to **Frank**) said nothing about it either. Instead, what tradition speaks of is a time of great hardship, where his wife's family had felt obligated to send up food hampers until an outraged **Frank** put a stop to it by saying that he could provide for his wife himself. This seems to have been the angry reaction of a somewhat insecure man, engaged in a business venture which was not going according to plan. After **1901 Frank** had, possibly with his father's help, found work as a Commercial Traveller selling high-quality tweed material for the firm of **Stewart Macdonald**. Before the First World War **Frank's** relationship with that Firm had been happy enough for him to have named his first son after it. This action speaks of a man's gratitude to a Company which had provided a much-desired opportunity for social advancement. The balance of evidence would suggest that the **Dress Foods** interlude was not one **Frank** would have wished to recall with any degree of pride. It formed one of the more eloquent silences in this history.

Providing evidence of an early struggle against financial hardship was the absence of that key middle-class status symbol, a live-in maid. **Elizabeth** would have hired such assistance even if it had been barely affordable because having a maid was very important to her. It was easy to imagine my Grandmother continually nagging **Frank** about this issue. To her the lack of a maid would have been a social disgrace, reducing her to the rank of the common person. The fact that he couldn't afford to hire one (even though he had only a wife and baby daughter to look after) perhaps provided decisive evidence that the venture at **Dress Foods** had not been going at all well. **Frank** may have resented not being seen to do as well as his father at a similar stage of his life. Sadly, for him, it was not the destiny of every **Smith** to be a genius in business. **Frank** was a very good salesman but lacked the strategic genius of his father. In terms of advancing family respectability, he was a *'consolidator'* rather than *'developer.'*

One other interesting feature of the **1901** Census was the presence of a **Mary A. Neilus** (who was perhaps a cousin to my Grandmother). This would suggest that whatever difficulties there may have been with the **Fosters,** some contact had been maintained with the **Neilus's** of **Birmingham**. The most likely motive for **Mary's** visit had been to see the baby.

Section 5: A New and Respectable Suburb

Concerning the history of Chapeltown, Leeds

Having reviewed the Census Return for **Frank's household** the next step was to describe the area of **Chapeltown** where he'd once lived. Reference is made to **Gordon Stowell's** fictional representation of **Chapeltown** in his *'History of Button Hill,'* first published in **1929**. Also, to research conducted in **1999** by **Max Farrer,** a lecturer at the **School of Cultural Studies, Leeds Metropolitan University.** When used jointly both these sources shed much light on the development and ethos of **Chapeltown** throughout the period when my father's family had lived there. The **Smith** family connection with the area was to last for almost thirty years, from about **1899** until **1927**. This dovetailed neatly with **Stowell's** novel, which covered the years **1889-1929**. However, it was **Farrer pp.138-147** who provided the most useful historical details concerning the development of this **Leeds** suburb.

The modern history of **Chapeltown** began in **1875** with the establishment of the first horse-drawn tram (whose travelling time to **Leeds City Centre** was thirty minutes). **Farrer p.139** implied that one effect of this development was to connect what, at that time, was a large farming area with **Leeds City Centre.** This reduction in travel time made commuting a definite possibility. It, therefore, became worthwhile to build many houses in this area. Prior to **1875 Chapeltown** had consisted of estate land divided amongst three major landowners, who were: -
Lord Mexborough – owning most of the land **west** of the **Chapeltown Road**
Earl Cowper – owning most of the land **east** of the **Chapeltown Road**
Mr Brown – owning most of the remaining land.

Possibly stimulated by the agricultural depression (which began in **1873**) the above three distinguished gentlemen sought to disinvest from increasingly unprofitable farming by selling off large tracts of land. Very large plots so that only substantial homes for the respectable middle classes could be built. The intention was to ensure the locality's preservation as a *'nice'* neighbourhood. **Chapeltown** was to be a middle-class fortress. Even at this early stage, it was already viewed as a haven of respectability, where one could escape from the smoky, filthy City Centre and fend off the *'unwashed'* masses of **Sheepscar** and the other slum areas. From the very start, its attitude was one of snobbery.

By **1876,** the **South-East** Corner of **Chapeltown** had been built. This consisted of **Spencer Place, Louis Street** and **Leopold Street**. Most of the heads of these households followed *'respectable'* middle-class occupations, *i.e.* within the professions, manufacturing or in a skilled trade. (Their occupational profiles were akin to those of **Vernon Road.)** Throughout the last quarter of the nineteenth century, a prolonged building boom gave the suburb its present shape. By the **1901** Census, virtually all the buildings had been completed – although there were some late developments in the **1930s** around **Mexborough Street.** By the late **1890s,** my Grandparents will have taken up residence at **41 Sholbroke Road** in a highly-developed suburb. Apparently, **1901** was also the year in which the electric tram replaced the old horse-drawn and steam trams. This further reduced the travelling time to **Leeds City Centre** to fifteen minutes.

Stowell's *'History of Button Hill'* was rather better history than fiction. Although very good on the description, its narrative style was depressingly dreary, and the author was clearly in two minds as to whether he loved or loathed his subject. Interesting characters were left under-developed and the plot was rather tenuous. As for the main character, **Eric Ellersby,** he really was so irritating that one almost wished the author had *'killed him off'* in the first few pages! Nevertheless, the book had merit in brilliantly catching the middle-class ethos within **Chapeltown** itself. It depicted the somewhat pretentiously genteel world in which my Grandparents had lived and into which my own father was born. The book's similarities to **Chapeltown** were so striking that it was possible to locate individual streets. As well as drawing from his own experience of growing up in the area, the author had clearly made a thorough research of all the available facts.

In the following extract (from **Stowell pp.31–37**) I have replaced his fictional names with real-life characters from my own family, (any alterations will be shown by square brackets.) I have used his text to describe **Frank's** house, as it may have looked just before **Queen Victoria's** death in **January 1901.**

Number **41 Sholebroke Road** was a red brick terraced house, typical of **Chapeltown.** *"Downstairs [was] a passage or 'hall,' a sitting room, a drawing-room (full of [reproduction] - covered furniture and bamboo tables, used only when visitors came), and a kitchen and scullery pushing themselves out into the back [yard]. Upstairs you found a landing, the best bedroom, a small bedroom, and a spare bedroom for aunts and uncles; and over the kitchen was a bathroom which, like other bathrooms of the period, was not only a bathroom, [but had a toilet too]. Above these were attics – a servant's bedroom, a lumber [or* *storage] room, and a room with steel bars across its dormer-window, evidently intended as a nursery [for baby **Rosamund** as she grew older].*

Beneath the habitable part of the house were subterranean cellars. Even at midday, the cellars were as black as night, and one had to light a candle or taper before negotiating the steps.

*Of course, [in **January 1901**] Mr and Mrs **[Smith]** did not need so large a house. The attic remained disused because Mrs **Smith's** maidservant was a girl who came up daily from **[Sheepscar]**. But you could not have found a house at [**Chapeltown**] with fewer rooms. The builders of those days did all they could to encourage the birth-rate…*

*You must not imagine because **Queen Victoria** then sat on the throne as imperturbably as she now sits on a thousand memorials, that she was represented in the sitting rooms of **Chapeltown** by horsehair sofas and [wooden bowls of] wax fruit. The **[Smiths]** had at least progressed beyond that stage. [Dominated by two large urn-like **Dresden** vases, standing either side of the mantelpiece and a porcelain **Madonna** at the centre,] the room was not [otherwise] crowded with useless bric-a-brac. There were merely a few elegant and amusing knick-knacks here and there such as ornamental vases, china figures, dusty bunches of 'honesty' (a flower so named because it just avoids being artificial), an assorted collection of trinkets in **Goss** chinaware, decorated with the heraldry of thirty **English** towns, brassware suggestive of the gorgeous **East**. [Also, clay gaily painted horses] at either end of the mantelpiece [each one outflanked by the bluish-white swirl of the tall **Dresden** vases].*

*The walls were covered with **Moorish** wallpaper, its pattern of **blue roses** being broken by a number of pictures – three tiny photographs of **Scarborough** [and **Bridlington, Frank's** favourite holiday resorts]. In one silver frame [was] a circular plaque upon which pears and plums had been painted by hand, [another larger frame showed] mountainous landscapes complete with lochs and Highland cattle, and [the final picture was of] a large photogravure reproduction of the popular picture 'Good-morning papa.' On either side of [the **Madonna**] were enlarged photographs of **Mr** and **Mrs Smith** taken [when they had first courted on the **Isle** of **Man**]. Over the bookshelves, in the recess between chimney and window, a chromo-lithographic **Christ** reassured [**Elizabeth's** faith] by walking on a chromolithographic sea. In the corresponding recess on the opposite flank of the chimney, a young lady in the costume of the Regency period smiled at you from under an umbrella and called herself '**April** Showers.' From over the sofa you were frowned upon by **[Edmund]**, a severe old gentleman with a white beard and a clean-shaven upper lip, [who still cast a shadow over the whole family.]*

Curtains of lace, looped gracefully from the bay window, were supplemented by more sombre hangings of green guipure [velvet cloth] with a ball fringe, which matched the [mantelpiece]

462

cloth, the cloth on the dining table, and the curtain that hung across the door to keep out the draughts. Before the centre of the bay, a rampant aspidistra arose from a still more [rampant] stand. This, of course, was a long time before the aspidistra fell into disrepute and became a joke, like kippers or **Wigan.**

When **[Frank]** left home after breakfast, **[Elizabeth** could see him] through the window, as he waved her off at the gate. And then [she could spend] some time watching the other businessmen as they trotted along **[Sholebroke Road]** to the tram; always in a hurry, grasping umbrellas in one hand and [work cases] in the other. Soon they had all caught their trams, and [the row of terraced houses] became comparatively deserted until teatime.

Once **[Frank]** saw a pair of tram-horses take fright at the sound of a bicycle bell. The driver jumped clear with a shout, and, catching hold of the traces, twisted them round and round a lamp-post, and so pulled both horses with a jerk before any damage was done – except to the lamp-post, which was forced very so slightly from the perpendicular…

[In the small front garden] there was an immaculate bed of **tiger lilies** and **phlox** and **geraniums** and **shrubs** of **rhododendron.** [Around the back] there were drains and a square of concrete, and a shed and posts to which the clothes-line was hooked on washing days, and then a patch of rough grass where **[Rosamund** would later play whatever games she pleased. It was in this yard that she was to have the first of many quarrels with her younger sister **Julia**] At the foot of the garden [in front of the rear brick wall and green wooden gate] rose a square brick ash pit [filled with ashes from the coal fire] the presence of which made the smell of the back garden quite different from that of the front. It had a pungent jolly smell, whereas the front seemed to be flavoured always with **chestnut-blossom** and **rhododendron** and noonday sunshine.

From the flat roof of the ash pit [which contained the remains of many a coal fire], you looked at the backs of the houses of **Sholebroke Road,** [and at the backs of the houses opposite, which were only separated by a narrow-cobbled lane]. These back streets had a life of their own. You saw coal being delivered, a great black heap opposite somebody's gate, slowly shovelled away in barrow-loads. Itinerant greengrocers hawked their wares. Errand boys whistled **"Daisy, Daisy."** Occasionally a barrel organ or hurdy-gurdy came along and droned out the same tune. Servant girls in caps and aprons kept popping in and out of gates with mysterious buckets, or appeared perilously at upper windows, sitting out on the ledges to clean the windows. **[Elizabeth** would sometimes sigh thinking, 'If only **Frank** could afford just <u>one</u> live-in maid, rather than the unreliable daygirl from **Sheepscar.** She knew that the absence of such an accessory made her less respectable in the eyes of her neighbours.]

And on **Mondays,** *all the vista of back gardens as far as you could see was transformed as for some festival, with white, flapping garments and huge sheets and blankets pegged out to dry.*

Each [one of the local shops] had its own distinctive smell. At the chemists, where the round, affable face of the [proprietor] popped up at you over a glass counter between towers of soap-boxes and cards of corn-plaster or babies' soothers, against a background of jars and labels – the smell was the sweet pungent, tonic smell of medicine, with a hint of the sealing-wax with which the [proprietor] secured his parcels. At the grocer's, the dominating smell was always that of coffee, for between the great canisters in the window there was a coffee-grinder perennially at work. The stationer's shop was stuffy and smelt of gum. The milliners were even more stuffy and smelt of a gas stove. At the greengrocers, which was open to the street like a market-stall, there was a cash-register with numbers jerking up and down and you smelt wet earth and cold fish. The butcher's shop, of course, smelled like nothing but a butcher's shop."

On **p.40** is a brief description of the milkman: -.
"By virtue of his calling, Milkie was supposed to be weather-wise, and you usually called upon him to prophesy. Then he would cast a sagacious eye towards the heavens and tell you what he thought. "Ay, it's lookin' a bit watery-like this marnin," or, "Nay, I doubt if t' sun'll show hissen to-day," or, "Eh, it's bahn to be a reet 'ot spell this time," However, it would be misleading to portray **Chapeltown** as a static community. Major changes were afoot between the time of the death of **Queen Victoria** (in **January 1901**) and the birth of my father in **February 1914**. These changes were somewhat disapproved of by **Stowell,** as the following extracts (from **pp.202-205)** of his work show: -

"Others again trace a certain vague deterioration in quality back to the opening-up of the [new **Harehills]** *Estate, with its smaller houses and smaller gardens and slate roofs. It was all very fine they say, for the* **[Leeds]** *Education Committee to vow that* **[Cowper Street]** *was a model Council school, a paradigm among Council schools. A Council school's a Council school for all that.*

The new **[Chapeltown]** *Cinema was held by some to be partially responsible, at a time when the cinema was the scapegoat for every evil.*

In the two years preceding the war [and **Fred's** *birth], it became evident to an increasing number (when they bothered to think about it) that* **[Chapeltown]** *was no longer what it had been.*

Ironically enough, the very tramway which had first nurtured **[Chapeltown],** *and without which the suburb could never have been, was now in danger of overlying and smothering its own*

464

pet child. **[Chapeltown]**, *as I have said before, was essentially a horse-drawn suburb. Electricity [in the form of the electric tram, which was introduced in* **1901***] had brought the town nearer the terraces and the terraces nearer the town; while new suburbs at* **[Moortown]** *and* **[Oakwood]** *grew rapidly as more attractive places to live. No longer was* **[Chapeltown]** *on the edge of the countryside. It was fast becoming hemmed in.*

And it was chiefly because of the electric trams, with their noise and vulgarity, that the wealthy people who had lived in the big detached houses on **[Chapeltown Road]** *now moved out to the* **[Moortown]** *estate. To-let notices appeared in the windows – and remained there, the houses becoming shabby for want of paint and looking like discoloured teeth, the grass growing rank in the gardens. For no one whose means permitted them to live in such houses would wish to be so near the factories, within a stone's throw of an ugly Council School and buttressed by houses of the [new* **Harehills***] Estate.*

Where wealth and fashion led, many followed. The years **1912, 1913** *and* **1914** *saw a steady secession from the terraces of* **[Chapeltown]** *to the newer suburbs [which would be a pattern of settlement that the* **Smith** *family would follow later].*

*"**[Chapeltown]** is getting common" was a remark one frequently heard at this time. And it was clear that the* **[Harehills]** *Estate was mainly responsible. The people who lived [there] were no doubt all very well in their way, but they were not the stuff of which* **[Chapeltown]** *was made. For the most part, they were struggling tradesmen, foremen of works, shop workers, insurance agents, jobbing printers, tramway inspectors. Their respectability was just a shade too much emphasised. The men waxed their moustaches and wore creaky boots on Sundays. They grew nasturtiums in their gardens. Their wives took in lodgers and were agents for patent corsets.* <u>*They kept no maids.*</u>*" (The last four words were originally placed in italics by* **Stowell p.205***)*

"The sons and daughters of the **[Harehills]** *Estate went to the* **[Cowper Street]** *Council School and some of them won scholarships to the Modern [School at* **Lawnswood***].*

One had to go down to business with them on the same trams. They were, you understand, too much of a daily-bread class – with little time for butter or jam, little concern for the social arts and graces. One suspected that the menfolk breakfasted in their shirtsleeves and that the women slept in their combinations.

I do not hold any brief for those who called them "common." I do not say that they were better or worse than the original **[Chapeltown]** *settlers. No doubt as individuals they were mostly excellent people, full of the milk of human kindness, model husbands, wives and parents, patient, noble, self-sacrificing, the possessors of immortal souls, and all that sort of thing. But* *as a chronicler, I cannot be expected to sentimentalise over them. I merely record that, whatever they were, they were different; and that, though as individuals they were welcomed warmly enough into the fraternity, their presence as a class was vaguely resented. If there was any snobbery in this, it only shows how much the quality of the original* **[Chapeltown]** *had already deteriorated.*

One became thankful for the amenities of **[Potternewton] Park.** *But even this was not the rural place it had once been. It was overlooked by houses on all four sides, by the backs of houses indeed. They seemed to dwarf the park to the size of a pocket-handkerchief. The sheep had disappeared because the urchins who came upon the penny trams from* **[Sheepscar]** *had been fond of chasing them. New paths of gritty black asphalt had been cut, and in the centre of what had been one of the prettiest vistas, the Corporation had put up two ornamental shelters and a cheap refreshment bar. The front of the old* **[Potternewton]** *Mansion was lined with penny-in-the-slot machines, many of which did not even work.*

All these things were disturbing. But once again **[Chapeltown]** *was in tune with the age. The closing years of the Great Peace [from* **1815** *until* **1914***] marked a period of general bad temper. They were punctuated by a series of bitter strikes and lockouts. Doctors were in the sulks over the Insurance Acts [passed by the* **Liberal** *Government to provide some security to the poor].* **Ragtime** *was demoralising the ballrooms. In the House of Commons, ragtime manners and inflammatory speeches from* **Tories** *and* **Irishmen** *were the rules rather than the exception. Even a* **Derby** *winner was disqualified.*

It was no longer safe to post a letter in the pillar-box, for it might be burned or vitriolised [with acid] by green-and-purple **suffragettes.** *Perhaps this pillar-box business, as much as anything else, was responsible for the wide sense of insecurity. Whence were we drifting if the honest red mouth of a pillar-box could no longer be trusted?*

Looking back on those days of restless uncertainty [around the time of **Fred's** *birth], it seems as though everyone, everywhere was, as people say, "spoiling for a fight." They were like overtired, overfed, over-excited children who have reached a mood that is hysterical and snappy, the mood which makes a wise mother hasten to avert the imminent storm…"*

Clearly, it would be a mistake to assume that my father was born during a golden age of peaceful prosperity. As a baby, he entered a highly volatile society, one already poised to leap into the abyss even without the intervention of World War One. **Stowell** noted how there was a rebellious youth sub-culture in **Chapeltown,** with the men being known as *'Knuts'* and the girls as *'Flappers.'* The height of this youthful rebellion was for the young men to wear trilbies pulled down firmly over their foreheads and to do without the traditional winged collar, whilst the girls wore silk stockings and even showed their ankles! Many of the men joined the **Leeds Pals Volunteer Regiment** at the outbreak of the First World War and in so doing left nothing but a haunting memory to their former sweethearts. The First World War rapidly decimated a generation, which in many ways had already begun to slide into rebellion against the accepted norms.

Overall, it appears that the **1914-18** War had merely accelerated previous socio-economic trends rather than created new ones. This was the impression gained from **Stowell** in his description of **Chapeltown** in the post-war period. Unfortunately, a rather unpleasant **anti-Semitism** had now crept into his work, when (on **p.375**) he made a rather disparaging reference to *'slick **Semitic** experts'* who taught the **Fox Trot** and **One Step**. Even worse (on **p.421**) he criticised one character for adopting the pose *"of a successful **Jew**."* He also made it very clear that he disliked the *"stealthily"* insidious invasion of **Jewish** business. In one case (on **p. 373-4**) he described how three of the larger houses on **Chapeltown Road** had *"been converted into makeshift premises for firms of ready-made clothing manufacturers, wooden sheds being erected indiscriminately over lawns and flower-beds. Another house has become a new telephone exchange, and another a **Jewish** maternity home."* It was obvious that this author was not *'at home'* with the **Chapeltown** in which my father was to live out his childhood and build his first links with the **Leeds Jewish Community**.

My own independent research confirmed that **Chapeltown** had <u>always</u> been a place of migration. Firstly, for the indigenous middle classes from **1875–1920,** then for the **Leeds Jewish Community** from **1920–1960** and finally for the **West Indian** Community from about **1960** onwards – my own father having grown up when the second wave of **Jewish** migration was gathering momentum. The considerable number of **Jewish** boys attending **Cowper Street School** during the early **1920s** confirmed this point. For **Jewish** migrants like **Joe Gillinson, Chapeltown** represented a *'step up'* in the world – but what wouldn't be after the slums of the **Leylands** and **Sheepscar?** It was evident that, within one generation of their migration into **Leeds,** the **Jewish Community** was most eager to adopt middle-class values and lifestyles. Their chief desire was for integration. **Stowell** apparently viewed this influx of **Jewish** people as a threat to his **English** Middle-Class **Eden**. He misinterpreted their presence as being a sign of decline rather than of change and renewal. His prejudice, along with its unpleasant taint of **anti-Semitism,** betrayed a hopeless lack of vision. **Stowell** failed to see that the rising **Jewish Community** represented a triumph rather than a threat to the middle-class values of

Chapeltown. In general, **Stowell's** stance was one of snobbery, tinged by an insidiously covert form of **anti-Semitism** – an attitude very typical of the time in which his novel was written.

In contrast to **Stowell,** my Grandfather **Frank** appears to have willingly adopted much of the social snobbery of **Chapeltown** whilst rejecting its anti-Semitic element. Set against his appallingly rude treatment of a future daughter-in-law (who happened to come from the *'wrong social class'*) was his friendship with **Joe Gillinson** who appears to have left a very good impression. To a lesser extent, my own father displayed this same mixture of cultural broadmindedness and class-based snobbery. My family appear to have been a strange mixture of the **conservative** and the **radical.** In terms of class attitudes, my Grandparents rigorously upheld the snobberies of their day, yet when it came to racial matters they were decades ahead of their time (as was my own father). Representatives from both **Asian** and **Afro-Caribbean** ethnic communities have often asked me how my Grandparents would have felt if one of their sons had wished to marry a black woman. My reply was, *"Fine, as long as she was the daughter of Prince* **Mandela** *or the Maharajah of* **Faisalabad**, [in **Pakistan**] *but no chance at all if she was the daughter of a* **'Baldrick'** *(rough, common person) from* **Lagos** *or* **Calcutta**. *The same would also apply to any* **Baldrick** *in* **Sheepscar, Leeds.***"* As it turned out one of **Frank's** daughters **Irene** did marry into the **Jewish Community** – an act that many a middle-class **English** family would have viewed with horror during the **1930s.** The pattern of my family was always to be far more *'class-conscious'* than *'race-conscious.'* I suspect this trait will still exist in future generations. If it came to same-sex-marriage family members would be perfectly accepting of the same-sex partner so long as they were of the right background and weren't viewed in any way as being *'common.'* Having money would also help. As my wife once remarked, *'The* **Smiths** *have always been a pretty mercenary lot.'*

Section 6: Family Divisions

Concerning the rivalry between four sisters

After the birth of **Rosamund** other children followed. These were **Julia, Madeline** (or **'Madge'** as she was to become commonly known), **Irene, Stewart,** and finally my father **Fred Gordon Smith** who was born on the **6th February 1914**. Although **Frank** and **Elizabeth's** marriage had been very much a love match, it still had its own tensions. Until near the outbreak of the Second World War **Elizabeth** had always insisted on keeping a maid, even though she could barely afford to pay her. Furthermore, she was a rather meddlesome matchmaker who would loudly comment that a proposed spouse for one of her children did not meet the required social specifications. According to my cousin **Pamela**, *"she could be ultra charming or ultra-difficult."* She was also reputed to have kept a Madonna (statue of the **Virgin Mary**) on the mantelpiece of her living room. In contrast, **Frank** was known to be *"morose and dour"* at home. As the only breadwinner, he was evidently consumed by the financial worries of trying to run a large household, most of whom possessed extravagant tastes. From a discussion, I had with my father (in early **September 1976**) it was obvious that, in his own case, it was his mother who seemed to have inflicted a certain amount of emotional hurt. Only after attending a prayer meeting at a (now-closed) **Roman Catholic** Convent in **Fenham, Newcastle upon Tyne,** could **Fred** bring himself to forgive something his mother had done. The convent establishment had been run by the *'Teaching Order'* of the Sacred Heart. I was there at that meeting and rarely have I seen him so visibly moved – least of all by anything **Catholic.** He made quite a favourable impression on the nuns who were gathered there at that time. They thought him a most distinguished gentleman – and so he was! In our subsequent discussion, he divulged that this meeting had helped him to come to terms with some problem he'd with his mother. What it was he didn't specify, but it certainly seemed to have had a long-lasting impact.

In fairness to **Elizabeth,** the difficulties do not seem to have lain exclusively with her alone. Outside the domestic sphere, **Frank** was, as photographic evidence suggests, reputed to have been an extremely gregarious individual, not above having a tipple with his favourite customers at a nearby Public House. Sometimes, he would come home late at night, slightly tipsy, and in a somewhat noisome manner demand that all the children be got out of bed to see him. One could imagine his wife regarding these displays as being highly vulgar and embarrassing. Perhaps she spent much of her life regretting that she had married *'beneath her station.'* A photograph (taken in **1936**) did not suggest a happy woman.

A meeting with my mother (on the afternoon of **Sunday, February 6th, 2000**) gave added details about **Frank's** line of work. From the early hours of the morning to late at night he would be engaged in selling cloth. Before the age of the motorcar, he would collect a skip full of clothing samples (possibly material rather than a full set of clothes) from the **Leeds** warehouse of **Stewart MacDonald**. He would then trundle it to the Station before placing it in the Guards' van of the earliest available train. On arriving at his appointed destination, he would remove the skip and trundle it to a clothing shop, wholesaler or manufacturer. For **Frank,** the main attraction of this itinerant work would be the sense of freedom to *'be his own boss.'* He also seemed to thoroughly enjoy meeting people and building up good relationships with long-standing customers. He would make the most of every opportunity – following up any useful tips or seeking out new contacts. Over time the goodwill he built up would enable him to gain repeated custom and hopefully make links to other new businesses. Hard and precarious though the work must have been, it would have been preferable to slaving away in an office or warehouse. Moreover, a skilful salesman like **Frank** would most probably have enjoyed a certain degree of status within the circles in which he moved. In the commercial world of that time, good personal service was highly valued, with most sales representatives expected to socialise with their customers. My Grandfather also possessed a vivid way of speaking. My cousin **Pamela** disclosed that when wiping a young child's running nose, he would refer to the task as *"blowing out the candles."* His intention had been to inject some fun into this common chore.

Much personal rivalry existed amongst **Fred's** sisters. In **August 1972,** I remember my Aunt **Julia,** recalling in the most bitter of terms how, in **1914 Rosamund** had stolen her jewellery (and other girlish) items, locking them up in a metal chest under her bed. The resentment caused by this alleged misdemeanour had remained very fresh in **Julia's** mind. She also remarked that to lessen family tensions, **Frank** would take her on excursions to **Roundhay Park** on the omnibus on **Sunday** afternoons. Indeed, my aunt **Julia** could have passed for the *'Grande Dame'* of an exclusive girl's Boarding School, but for the fact that she didn't like children – especially me! In her younger days, she had served as a governess to the daughters of wealthy families. The main task seems to have been to teach them proper *'social deportment.'* Married to **Eric Moffat** (who worked in banking) her father-in-law was **James Moffatt (1870–1944)** the **Glasgow**-born Bible translator. **Julia** was the child said to most resemble **Fred's** mother, her ambition being to reclaim that parent's high social standing. Unlike any of her siblings, she had fair hair which seemed only to have added to her icy appearance. By **1966, Aunt Julia** lived alone in a large house near **Taunton** in **Somerset.** She never used to talk about her husband (who had died in about **1957**). **Fred** would regard his visits to her with a certain degree of trepidation. During our (thankfully rare) stays there I used to hide in her private library. It was full of novels from the interwar period. (Also, in an abandoned garage were stacks of old **Picture Post Magazines** dating from the war.) There was a frigid coldness about the house and the incessant yapping of two little dogs called **Henrietta** and **Shortie** (whose coat was moulting) served only to reinforce this sense of oppression! Whilst conducting research for this history, I discovered that I wasn't the only relative who had noticed the strange atmosphere in the house; it certainly seemed rather creepy and as cold as the unheated baked beans she would serve with her elaborate salads.

At Christmas, **Julia** would send up bottles of expensive Sherry; this continued until shortly before her death in the early **1980s.** In **1966,** she accused me of stealing a book from her library. My father wrote back a strongly worded letter saying that I would never do such a thing. The book was later found, and we received a very grudging apology. She had also accused me of tampering with the inside of a Grandfather clock. Recent correspondence with other relatives revealed that they too had experienced similar difficulties with her. Full of a haughty pride, my aunt seemed to have been one of those people who were quick to accuse and slow to apologise. As will be seen later a major tragedy involving her husband had almost completely blighted her life. It was perhaps this tragedy which had helped make her such a cold person. The only people who attended **Julia's** funeral in **1984** were her solicitor, her gardener and two relatives who had decided to turn up at the last minute. It was conducted in a large, almost empty crematorium. Her death seemed to have been as lonely as the life she had lived.

In part, this sad end arose from the fact that she had become constantly suspicious that people were always after her money. Ridiculous as it seemed, her suspicions extended to other <u>wealthy relatives</u> and even to my own father! It was in this area that, when aged twelve, I behaved somewhat tactlessly. At the reception for my sister's wedding (in **July 1968**) I had drunk a little too much wine. Whilst under its influence I had rather loudly announced to **Julia** (three or four times) *"Don't forget to leave me money in your will."* The curled-up lips and florid complexion on her face provided ample confirmation of the fact that she was not at all amused by my amateurish attempt at legacy-hunting. Incidentally, we never did get a penny. I would later get chivvied by my brother and sister for losing them an inheritance. Personally, I don't think she'd ever intended to leave us anything anyway. She had a habit of cutting relatives off.

Julia left a large amount of money (around £**500,000**) to the **Elizabeth Svendson Donkey Sanctuary** (located near **Sidmouth, Devon**) and other charities. (The money had really been her late husband's.) I was blamed for getting our family *'cut out'* of the will by having shuffled around on my potty as a toddler and doing a large *'poo'* in her presence. However, her track record of turning against family members suggests that she would have found some other excuse <u>not</u> to have considered us in her will. **Julia** was someone who was very easily offended. I don't believe my childish indiscretions will have made any difference at all! This point was amply confirmed by my cousin **Pamela** who disclosed that the only family member, for whom **Julia** had time for was **Tony** and **Pam's** (now sadly deceased) husband **Roger**. However, *"there was no question of any family member being left anything in the will!"* The fondness for **Roger** stemmed from the fact that he'd been to the same school as **Julia's** husband **Eric**. In **Julia's** own words *"he reminded her of **Eric** in so many ways."* **Julia** had once caused great trepidation by expressing a wish to move-up to **Guiseley,** near **Leeds.** There was a heartfelt relief when this came to nothing. The feeling by other family members was that she should very much remain in her part of the country! They would have found her snobbery unbearable.

Old photographs gave something of a hint as to the motives behind the sisters' bitter rivalry. Where **Rosamund** was dark haired and thick set in appearance (she became rather stout as she entered her fifties) **Julia** was fair-haired and angular deportment. Among the girls, she was the family beauty, and this could only have inflamed her elder sister's jealousy. She must have felt like an ugly duckling threatened by a beautiful swan. In terms of character, however, they could each be equally unpleasant.

A letter received from one of **Stewart's** children **Pamela** detailed one incident which had taken place between the two older girls. *"**Julia** and her mother did not get along and **Rosamund** and **Julia** had huge rows. **Rosamond** had a boyfriend – **Jack Kidd** – whom she eventually married. **Julia** couldn't stand him and where they lived was a bedroom window situated over the front door. **Jack** came to knock at the door; **Julia** opened the window and threw a bucket of water over him. My father said, 'that was the straw that broke the Camel's back' and **Julia** had to leave. Reinforcing this decision was an ultimatum by his wife who warned, 'either she goes, or I go!' **F.H.S. (Frank)** and **Joe Burdon (J.B.) (Kathleen's** husband) always took **Rosamund's** side. **J.B** used to tell me about my 'wonderful' Auntie **Rosamond**."* From this account, it was clear that tensions had been simmering for a long time. The outcome of this incident around **1920** was that **Julia** left home to live with one of **Elizabeth's** well-connected sisters in **Cheltenham**. Somehow, I suspect that this is what **Julia** had wanted all along. She had resented being squeezed out of her parent's affections by **Rosamund** and, once having made her break with **Leeds,** she could now enjoy the opportunity to rise into the social stratosphere. Like **Julia,** her way of climbing the social ladder was to marry into money and then cut off her family. **Edmund's** daughter **Kathleen** was said to have remarked that **Rosamund** was the only one of **Frank's** daughters she'd found *'intolerable.'* She'd been aggrieved at the way **Rosamund** had completely fooled her husband who wouldn't say a bad word about her. **Rosamund** also grew to be very jealous of **Stewart** who, as the firstborn son, received the attention that had once been hers. The long-sought-for birth of a boy had diminished her privileged position within the family and sewn the seeds for later strife. To maintain control **Rosamund** would follow a *'divide and conquer'* policy toward her immediate family. It was made easier to implement because her own mother thought she was *'wonderful'* and could do no wrong.

However, **Julia's** escapade didn't prevent **Rosamund** from marrying **Jack Kidd** in **1924.** Further details of their wedding are provided below: -
Registration District <u>Aston</u>
<u>1899</u> Marriage solemnised at <u>The Parish Church</u> in the Parish of <u>Saint Aiden's Leeds</u> in the County of <u>Yorkshire</u>
1. When married? July 3rd 1924
2. Name and Surname: John Thomas Kidd, Rosamund Marie Smith
3. Age: 25, 24
4. Condition: Bachelor, Spinster
5. Rank or profession: Dying Chemist
6 Residence at the time of marriage: 23 Airlie Avenue Leeds 26 Hillcrest Avenue
7. Father's name and surname: John Kidd, Fred Hesselwood Smith
8. Rank or profession of father: Electrical Engineer, Representative

Married in the <u>Parish Church</u> according to the Rites and Ceremonies of the <u>Church of England</u> by <u>certificate</u> by me,
The marriage was solemnised between us
<u>John Thomas Kidd</u>
<u>Rosamund Marie Smith</u>
In the presence of us
<u>William Kidd</u>
<u>Fred Hesselwood Smith</u>
<u>Irene Constance Smith</u>
<u>Daniel John Foster</u>
<u>John Kidd</u>
<u>Wilfred Handy, Assistant priest</u>

An Aunt possessing a more generous disposition was **Madge** who, in the early **1960's,** used to ply me with the princely sum of five pounds when visiting our house. There was something of the motherly eccentric about her. She was also an enterprising businesswoman in her own right. These had included an antique shop or a guesthouse for elderly ladies. During her final illness, my father and my sister visited her in hospital. On seeing them arrive her eyes twinkled as she exclaimed, *"Here comes little **Freddie** with his daughter!"* Like **Julia,** she too seemed to have had troubles with **Rosamund. Madge** only ever mentioned **Rosamund's** name in terms of irritated annoyance. I seem to remember her saying (whilst sitting in our old living room) *"she's been a fool unto herself."* My father's response had been to nod in sad agreement. In all her bustling eccentricity **Madge** would also regale us with anecdotes about her husband, **Edward Nixon (Ted).** These would concern his bladder problems when she would mutter loudly in a rather loud, squawking voice *"he can't hold his water!"* Playing the part of the downtrodden spouse, **Ted** used to respond with a shrug of the shoulders and a sheepish smile. Named *"Uncle Ted"* by the family he was a World War One veteran who liked to vividly recount descriptions of the **Gallipoli** landings of **1915.** With an old soldier's enthusiasm, he used to show me the scars of the wounds he had received on his arms whilst fighting there and regale me with tales of how the sea water had turned to red with the blood of dead and dying soldiers. He always described the **Dardanelles** campaign as being *'**Churchill's** blunder.'* For all his alleged bladder problems, he outlived **Madge** by about six years, dying in **1988.** (Much more will be said about this couple and their strange marriage in **Part 4, Chapter 3, Section 6,** which will also provide an account of **Madge's** business ventures.)

There's an intriguing footnote to this tale. On **Thursday, 5th February 2015** I managed to take a photograph of the **Gallipoli Peninsula** whilst on a visit to **Troy** with my youngest son. Earlier on in a restaurant, we briefly encountered a local historian named **Mustafa Askin** and purchased his book on the **Gallipoli Campaign.** It turned out that his grandfather had been manning the searchlights during the early stage of this campaign. It was interesting to swap notes with someone whose family had been on the other side. As with my uncle **Ted,** the **Gallipoli** Campaign appears to have made a significant long-term impact.

Except for **Julia,** I have no detailed recollections of my other Aunts, although **Irene** vaguely comes to mind as a somewhat sensitive, nervous woman who retained the after-glow of an alluring glamour about her. One family tradition holds that, in her youth, she had been a beauty queen. Old photographs confirm that she was of a beautifully striking appearance. After marrying **Edward Stern (1908-1960)** in **March 1933,** she was eventually to settle in **Bedford** after a time spent with her husband in **Northern Ireland.** Poor health (in part caused by inherited diabetes) ensured an early death around the same time as **Stewart,** (who died in **May 1962**). The story I heard was that she'd collapsed and died in a shop. A photograph (taken around **1960**) showed a woman who looked older than her years; absent was either the bustling vigour of a *'Madge'* or the iron-maiden strength of a *'Julia.'* Yet the body language in other old photographs showed that, along with **Madge, *'Rene'*** was the sister with whom my father had felt most relaxed.

My mother (who first met **Fred's** family during the **1940s**) mentioned that a gap in years had ensured that there were almost two families in one. The two older sisters **Rosamund** and **Julia** formed one unit whilst **Madge, Irene, Stewart** and **Fred** had formed the other. My mother had also noticed that both sets of sisters seemed to keep a certain distance from one another. Being an only child, my mother had eagerly looked for some *'sisterly'* sisters-in-law with warm and welcoming dispositions. However, she was to be sorely disappointed. Her overarching attitude toward **Fred's** sisters was that *'they were all 'bonkers!'* Three were *'nuts'* and one **(Rene)** was a *'bundle of nerves.'*

My mother wasn't alone in having that impression. In **July 2017** my sister **Valerie** remarked that she didn't know *"why the girls were so horrendous – after all they'd come from a good family."* (Around the same time, **Pamela** remarked that her deceased mother **Edith** had made an identical observation.) Any explanation for their behaviour remains speculative, but I do wonder whether it was a case of energetic, talented and ambitious girls being frustrated by the restrictive conventions of their time. What was clear was that they were all *'social climbers"* with a desire to *'get on in life'* through either *"marrying-up"* or pursuing a successful business enterprise. They wished to be admired or, at the very least, respected by others. Maybe their visits to **Edmund's** opulent house as children had made an impression. Perhaps in their young minds, they thought, *'why couldn't daddy be rich like that?'* If so, he would have provided them with an example to emulate. Possibly, they were trying to re-create for themselves the opulent lifestyle of their Grandfather.

Also, was there something in their background from which they'd wanted to escape? If so, what was it? Maybe, they'd felt that their mother had made a mistake in *'having married beneath her'* and was determined <u>not</u> to repeat this for themselves. Of all the four girls, it was **Irene** who seemed the most normal and even she reputedly suffered from *'nerves.'* My cousin **Pam** made the added point that hypertension (a common medical problem in the **Smiths**) may have been a major contributing factor. It may well have accounted for some of their cantankerous behaviours in their later years. What cannot be doubted is that my father's sisters left a lasting impression on the family folk law. They seemed to have been a collection of *'drama queens.'*

Sometimes major family events can trigger memories in an elderly person. This is exactly what happened with my mother – following the wedding of my middle son at **Scarborough** Register Office on **Saturday, 18th February 2012.** After the reception, my wife **June** and I (driven by **Kathryn,** an old family friend) had safely returned my mother to her flat in **Alwoodley, Leeds.** Over a much-needed cup of tea, my mother began chatting about **Fred's** sisters and it was apparent that a whole deluge of memories had come flooding back. For a good **45** minutes (from roughly **8.45-9.30pm**) she disclosed the following details about them which I then scribbled down as best as I could: -

1) They were always rivalling one another. If one got an additional item (or even a new house) the other would have to have a better or bigger one.

2) Jack Kidd was *"an innocuous academic, under **Rosamund's** thumb"* (My sister would later concur with that point by remarking *"he was a very nice man."*)

3) They were all *"horrible."* **Rosamund** was jealous of **Stewart** who, as his mother's favourite, had been *"spoilt,"*

4) Fred was *"an afterthought and regarded as an afterthought."*

5) Julia was *"a crashing snob who'd cut people off."* She'd been very close to her nephew **Tony** (**Irene's** son) but had *'cut him off'* when he had married **Sally,** whom she'd regarded as *"a common slut."* Her large and rather grandiose house had been located near **Taunton** in **Somerset.**

6) Irene (known as **'Rene'**) was *"a bundle of nerves and a bit mad."*

7) Madge *"could turn on people."* After being very generous she would expect her generosity to be repaid. *"She could be horrible."* In **1942,** her son (a future heart Doctor) **Peter** was given a wallet by **Fred** for his fourteenth birthday; for some unknown reason, they'd refused to allow him to have it. *"Her and **Ted** would lock him in his room to do his work."*

8) All the sisters mocked their mother's **Catholicism,** saying she was *"doing a knee bender"* whenever she prayed

9) Elizabeth disclosed to **Cynthia** how much she felt closer to her than to her own daughters. This was whilst **Cynthia** was staying with her mother-in-law from **1944** until moving to **Crossgates** with **Fred** in **1946.**

10) Each of the sisters would try to get **Cynthia** to take their side but *"I refused to be drawn into it all."* For herself, she admitted to having felt disappointed because, as an only child herself, she had looked forward to having some sisters.

11) Julia had *"cut **Fred** off after he'd sent her that naughty postcard,"* complaining that **Fred** had *"shamed her before the postman."*

(I could imagine my father responding to that one with a mischievous smile.)

My mother closed by remarking *"If I was younger I could write a novel about **Fred's** sisters."* At this point **Kathryn** nudged me in the side saying *"There – that's something you could write about!"* (**June** and I had known **Kathryn** since we'd attended the same church in **Newcastle-Upon-Tyne** during the late **1970s**. She lived in **Worksop, Derbyshire.** She was also to attend my mother's ninetieth birthday celebrations in **November 2013.**)

Recounting these memories appeared to have rejuvenated my mother. During the previous snowbound **Sunday,** (when **June** and I had spent over an hour and a half trudging to her flat) **Cynthia** disclosed that her mother had taught classes of up to sixty children. She had also stated that *'teachers got blamed for everything'* whenever the school had been inspected. (What changes in education one may ask?) As was the convention of the day her mother had had to leave her profession when she'd got married. At that time, middle-class men were expected to provide for their wives.

Further research (conducted in **May 2015**) threw some extra light on the lives of these sisters. **Madge** married **Edward Nixon** – early in **1924** whilst **Irene** didn't marry **Edward Sterne** until **March 1933**. This latter marriage had taken place in **Nantwich, Cheshire**. **Edward** came from a secular **Jewish** family, **Edward** and reputedly held a senior position in the planning department of **Bedford Council**. At his death, in **June 1960** the local bookmakers and publicans sent some very large wreaths, which suggests that he had been rather popular with that clientele. **Edward** had been born in **July 1908**. His death at the early age of **52** suggested he'd suffered from health problems.

Particularly intriguing were pictures of **Julia** and **Irene** obtained from a member of the **Sterne** family at Ancestry.co.uk. This showed **Julia** wearing a white cap and sunglasses standing next to a palm tree in the garden, with a white painted house in the background. Erect and clasping her hands in front of her she looked every bit the colonial grand dame. The picture was presumably taken in **Singapore**. Another picture shows her husband **Eric Moffat** in a garden chair also clasping his hands. Domed forehead, goggle type spectacles, long Roman nose and thin moustache showed him looking every inch the traditional banker. However, his demeanour was friendly and open. He looked the sort of man one could trust one's money with. Exactly how he'd managed to tolerate his wife's snobberies can only remain a matter of speculation. In the end, what was the point of all this snobbery? After all, **Julia** had only been but a mere governess herself from a family working in *'trade.'* She'd demonstrated all too well that the *'nouveau riche'* can be the worst of snobs.

In contrast, **Irene** (in a photograph taken in about **1940**) emerges as a friendlier if more emotionally brittle character. Under a mop of black curly hair (apparently inherited from **Daniel Foster**) she manages a rather fragile smile. Wearing a tartan style dress, she holds a young **Anthony** (always known as *'Tony'* by family members) by the arm. He too had possessed jet black hair. Overall, **Irene** gave the impression of being one of those women who needed to be married to a strong man. If this was the case, she certainly found him in **Edward Sterne** who was believed to have been in the meat trade. Thick set and with a heavily jowled face, receding hairline and wispy moustache he certainly gave the impression of strength. His somewhat rumpled three-piece suit only highlighted his boxer-like appearance. One would certainly not have liked to have argued with him when he was a younger man!

What appeared to emerge in the case of **Fred's** sisters was a disturbing **Smith** tendency to snobbery plus a willingness to begin and maintain family feuds over the course of decades. These were characterized by rather pointless rivalries and bitter *'cuttings off.'* No wonder my (normally highly tolerant) mother wanted to keep out of it all. Even my father, one of the most charitable men on this earth, referred to his sisters as *'the bitches'* when in private conversation with my brother towards the end of his life. Where this snobbishness emerged from is not completely clear. Was it due to the restricted position of middle-class women in those days or were these sisters simply reflecting a trait that had existed for generations? Perhaps both explanations apply.

Lying amongst photos of deceased **Stern's** was one of my father and mother. When I told my mother this when visiting her on the afternoon of **Friday, 29th May 2015,** she sighed before exclaiming, *"I'm not quite dead yet!"* Indeed, she was then very, very much alive!

Section 7: Birth of My Father

Concerning the birth of Fred G Smith in Chapeltown Leeds

The following birth notice (on **p.8** of the **Yorkshire Post,** dated 7th **February 1914**) announced my father's entry into the world. It simply announced, **"SMITH – FEBRUARY 6, at 26 Hillcrest Avenue, Leeds, to Mr& Mrs Fred Heselwood Smith, a son."** (Family tradition added the detail that he had been born in the large front bedroom.) A scan of its other pages revealed that little seemed to have been happening in the world at that time. Locally, parents were creating a fuss about a county headmistress in **Dronfield** wishing to provide sex education at her school. Nationally, there were violent industrial disputes in **High Wycombe** and **Londonderry** over the use of alleged *'scab'* labour. There was also a call for **Lloyd George** to give an account of himself after being embroiled in another financial scandal. In contrast, the **Tory** Politician **Mr Balfour** was giving his time and effort to more edifying pursuits. He was scheduled to give a public lecture on *"The Theistic Embodiment of Beliefs."* Abroad, there were rumours of an **anti-Bulgarian, Greco-Rumanian** alliance and news of frontier skirmishes with restless natives in **East Africa.** There was also a new High Commissioner for **Australia** and a cricket tour in **South Africa**. The general picture was that of a world marking time before the big cataclysm that was soon to come. My father had been born in a lull before a truly frightful storm. His birth came just six months before one of the major turning points in human history – the outbreak of the First World War.

Amazingly, on **Sunday** morning **January 28th 2001,** an opportunity arose to strike up a conversation with an elderly lady whose **ninety-ninth** birthday was due to take place on **March 1st**. She was the eldest of nine children. Still possessed with an incredibly alert mind, she provided me with a picture of what **Leeds** had been like around the time of my father's birth. The two distinct impressions she had were of the smog and the financial struggles which many people were enduring at the time. Her own father had been a qualified engineer who had trained at the **Yorkshire College of Technology** (later to become **Leeds University**). In later life, he was to teach at **Hunslet Mechanics Institute.** One of her Grandfathers had served in the **Crimean War.** With a rueful tone in her voice, she explained, *"Money was always short in them days. Life was hard. I remember seeing boys selling newspapers on street corners without any shoes or stockings on their feet. My mother had to struggle to bring us all up. There were always worries about money. I was sent off to start work as a Tailoress for **4s 6d** a week. This was just before the First World War in **1913** or **1914**."* When one of her brothers was taken ill with polio she remembered how, at **Leeds General Infirmary,** *"We had to sit for hours on hard wooden benches before a Doctor would see us."* She thought that today's medical facilities were *"absolutely marvellous!"* When asked about **Vernon Road** and the locality around **Leeds University** she exclaimed, *"It was a lovely area; Doctors, Teachers and Solicitors used to live there. It was like **Roundhay, Chapeltown** and **Beeston**. It's gone down since, mind."* A note of bitterness crept in when she recalled the two World Wars, *"We lost all our youth then, and between them (wars) times were very hard. My late husband was gassed in the First War and he would suffer terribly in* *the fogs we used to have – always gasping for breath and needing an inhaler. Bronchitis was so common."* My informant was convinced that clean air was one of *"the greatest blessings of today."* Finally, this truly remarkable lady attributed her longevity to *"the goodness of the Lord."* She was a devout **Anglican** Churchgoer. Her somewhat watery eyes beamed with delight when I informed her that her memories would be used for my Family History. They were indeed extremely useful in conveying something of the world into which my father had been born.

As the youngest child, my father was very much seen as the baby of the family. He was nicknamed *'Little* **Freddie***'* by his siblings, (a designation he came to dislike in later life). **Madge** especially doted on him. He was somewhat overshadowed by his older brother (the dynamic and charming **Stewart** who was to make a success of himself in the clothing business) and his four older sisters. Each one of **Fred's** sisters had extravagant tastes in clothes and jewellery which contributed to a certain amount of financial hardship within the family. Whenever the girls were out **Frank** would stand at the gatepost at **10.30 p.m.** awaiting their return. Another irritation came in the form of **Roman Catholic** priests and nuns who kept calling around and requesting money in a rather wheedling fashion. **Frank** was reputed to have thrown some of them out of the house.

My own father's ingrained distrust of organised religion seems to have dated from about this time. The **Roman Catholic Church** was not for him, nor for his brother **Stewart** – both adopting something of a hostile stance towards it. Even in my day, **Fred** would often mention (in a tone of quiet horror) *"the wicked things"* the **Spanish Inquisition** had done – not least to the **Jewish** people. In his own words, *"**Roman Catholicism** was a religion of fear."* He would frequently dismiss this Church as being *"a racket."* The child abuse scandals that came to beset this church from the **1980s** onwards would suggest that, on this matter, as in so many others **Fred's** judgement was sound.

On **Saturday, August 25th, 2001** I received copies of the Birth Certificates for my late father's siblings from **Leeds Registrar Office.** Information from these documents made possible the following table; in it, the initials *'U.D.'* stand for *'Urban District'*: -

1. When and where born?
12th April 1900, 41 Sholbroke View, Potternewton U.D

2. Name if any: Rosamond Marie

3. Sex: Girl

4. Name and surname of father: Fred Heselwood Smith

5. Name, surname and maiden name of mother: Elizabeth Smith, formerly FOSTER
6. Occupation of father: Commercial Traveller
7. Signature, description and residence of Informant: Fred Heselwood Smith, Father, 41 Sholbroke View, Leeds
8. When registered: 23rd May 1900
9. Signature of Registrar: Benjamin Wick, Registrar

1. When and where born?
12th June 1901, 41 Sholbroke View, Potternewton U.D
2. Name if any: Julia Neilus (named after her aunt Julia Foster who spent time in a lunatic asylum in Whitley Bay, Tyneside)
3. Sex: Girl
4. Name and surname of father: Fred Heselwood Smith
5. Name, surname and maiden name of mother: Elizabeth Smith, formerly FOSTER
6. Occupation of father: Commercial Traveller
7. Signature, description and residence of Informant: Fred Heselwood Smith, Father, 41 Sholbroke View, Leeds
8. When registered; 24th July 1901
9. Signature of Registrar: Benjamin Wick, Registrar

1. When and where born?
21st June 1903, 51 Hillcrest Avenue, Potternewton U.D
2. Name if any: Madeline Heselwood (known as *'Madge'* by family members)
3. Sex: Girl
4. Name and surname of father: Fred Heselwood Smith
5. Name, surname and maiden name of mother: Elizabeth Smith, formerly FOSTER
6. Occupation of father: Commercial Traveller
7. Signature, description and residence of Informant: Fred Heselwood Smith, Father, 51 Hillcrest Avenue, Leeds
8. When registered: 28th July 1903
9. Signature of Registrar: A. E. J. Wick, Deputy Registrar

1. When and where born?
17th October 1909, 51 Hillcrest Avenue, Potternewton U.D
2. Name if any: Irene Constance (known as *'Rene'* by family members)
3. Sex: Girl
4. Name and surname of father: Fred Heselwood Smith

5. Name, surname and maiden name of mother: Elizabeth Smith, formerly FOSTER

6. Occupation of father: Commercial Traveller

7. Signature, description and residence of Informant: Fred Heselwood Smith, Father, 51 Hillcrest Avenue, Leeds

8. When registered: 27th November 1909

9. Signature of Registrar: A. E. J. Wick, Deputy Registrar

1. When and where born?
7th September 1911, 26 Hillcrest Avenue, U.D

2. Name if any: Stewart Foster

3. Sex: Boy

4. Name and surname of father: Fred Heselwood Smith

5. Name, surname and maiden name of mother: Elizabeth Smith, formerly FOSTER

6. Occupation of father: Commercial Traveller

7. Signature, description and residence of Informant: Fred Heselwood Smith, Father, 26 Hillcrest Avenue, Leeds

8. When registered: 23rd October 1911

9. Signature of Registrar: Isaac J. Bloomfield, Registrar

1. When and where born?
6th February 1914, 26 Hillcrest Avenue, U.D

2. Name if any: Fred Gordon

3. Sex: Boy

4. Name and surname of father: Fred Heselwood Smith

5. Name, surname and maiden name of mother: Elizabeth Smith, formerly FOSTER

6. Occupation of father: Commercial Traveller

7. Signature, description and residence of Informant: Fred Heselwood Smith, Father, 26 Hillcrest Avenue, Leeds

8. When registered: 17th March 1914

9. Signature of Registrar: Isaac J. Bloomfield, Registrar

Many of the children's forenames appear to have derived from names already existing in the **Foster** or **Smith** families. For instance, my **Aunt Julia Neilus** was clearly named after her maternal Grandmother, whilst my Aunt **Madge's (Madeline)** second forename **(Hesselwood)** originated in the **Stamford** line before being passed down two generations of **Smiths**. Family Tradition held that between **Madge** and **Irene** their mother **Elizabeth** had suffered from one or two miscarriages. This would explain the lengthy gap between their births.

The **1911** Census added the following details about **Frank's** Household.

51 Hillcrest Avenue, Potternewton, 7 Rooms

Fred Heselwood Smith *'Head'* born about **1869** aged **42** Married, *"General Drapery, Commercial Traveller"*

Elizabeth Marie Smith *'Wife'* born about **1873** aged **38** Married

Rosamund Smith *'Daughter'* born about **1901** aged **10** School

Julia Neilus Smith *'Daughter'* born about **1902** aged **9**

Madeline Heselwood Smith *'Daughter'* born about **1904** aged **7** School

Irene Constance Smith *'Daughter'* born about **1910** aged **1**

All the birthplaces were recorded as being in **Leeds** – the only exception being **Elizabeth** whose birthplace was recorded as **Egham, Warwickshire**. A hurriedly written signature and a failure to complete part of the *'Return'* gave the impression of it having been completed in haste. The meticulous approach of **Frank's** father was wholly absent in his son.

Around this time **Rosamond** would pay **Madge** six pence from her pocket money to wash her underwear despite this being a chore the girls were expected to do for themselves. *'Eager for money even at that young age'* **Madge** would happily comply. **Rosamond** would leave her underwear under mattress of her bed for **Madge** to pick-up. Their parents didn't know about this arrangement. However, her brother **Stewart** claimed that at home she was *'bone idle.'* This story was related to me by **Stewart's** daughter (my cousin **Pam**) at my mother's funeral wake on **Tuesday, 4th December 2018.** When older **Rosamond** acquired a reputation *'for sowing dissension wherever she went.'* In response, **Irene, Stewart** and **Fred** formed a threesome who kept their distance from their volatile siblings. As my mother remarked, *"they were like a family within a family."*

Under the auspices of **Frank's** father **Edmund,** the **Smiths** had reached a pinnacle of **Victorian** and **Edwardian** respectability. This would be maintained during the carnage of the **First World War (1914-1918).** During that conflict, **Frank's** work as a Commercial Traveller prospered. This arose from the fact that many of his rival travellers had joined the armed services. Added security was provided by the way his firm **Stewart MacDonald** profited from large army orders. These more than compensated for any loss of civilian custom. He was reputed to *'have done well'* during this period. Nonetheless, it remained an open question as to whether subsequent **Smiths** could retain their respectable position in society? After all, they were to endure a global depression, another world war and other massive cultural and political changes. The decades following my father's birth would see the **Smiths** engaged in a protracted struggle to maintain their hard-won position in the middle classes.

CHAPTER 15: LONDON CALLING

Section 1: Mother's Orders

Concerning Family History Research in London

It was my mother who revived my Family History as it was beginning to flag, acquiring an interest in it in her eighties. She was perhaps anticipating shortly meeting some of her own ancestors. Over the weekend of **Saturday 23rd** to **Sunday, 24th September 2006** I was staying with her whilst recovering from a feverish chill and awful asthma. On a **Saturday** evening, I was conversing about Family History matters when she said, somewhat sharply, *"You've done quite enough of* **Fred's** *side of the family, now it's about time you did something on mine!"* Present was a request I couldn't refuse, and my mother showed an enormous willingness to provide a lot of what turned out to be an explosion of information. This I managed to follow up during two short visits to **London** (from **Wednesday 3rd September 2008** to **Saturday 6th September 2008** and from **Tuesday 15th September** to **Saturday 19th September 2009**). On both occasions, I stayed at my brother's home in **Rickmansworth** and he too made many helpful suggestions. However, trailing the streets of **London** to visit various sites and archive centres proved somewhat exhausting. During a visit made to **Vincent Square in Westminster** (on **Friday 5th September 2008**) the weather was so wet that I had to retreat to the National Gallery to get some shelter (where I observed some extremely unimpressive examples of modern art). The opposite applied during a visit to **Crouch End** (on **Friday 18th September 2009**) where I was so hot that heat exhaustion became a problem! An added menace to many of my ventures was the traffic and once, when standing in a narrow side alley taking a photo of an old **Myerson** residence, I nearly got knocked down by a dispatch rider! A few minutes later I was nearly struck down by a van outside **Hammersmith Market. London** certainly did pose its challenges! The photos taken during these visits were to bring back a flood of memories of my mother's early life and it was possible to reconstruct it in detail. The first of these visits was noteworthy because it almost immediately preceded *'The Financial Crash'* that began on **Monday, 15th September 2008** with the collapse of the large investment bank, **Lehman Brothers.** My poem *'Meltdown,'* conveys the mood of global panic which accompanied this event.

484

The first **London** visit was also noticeable for some misleading clues which led me down the all too familiar *'blind alleys.'* I'd taken many photos of a rather plush **'Vincent House'** that overlooked a **Vincent Square**. I remember (as a three-year toddler in **1959**) getting a *'piggyback'* from my sister so that I could touch the red pillar box that lay a few doors down. (My sister, wearing vividly striped shorts at the time, hadn't been very pleased.) Everything appeared to *'fit'* until (during my second visit) my brother informed me that it had been the <u>wrong</u> **Vincent House!** Our Grandparents had lived in another, rather less plush **Vincent House,** just around the corner at the top of **Regency Street,** facing the junction of **Rutherford Street.** Consequently, I had to visit the site again to take yet another set of photographs. It was during my second visit that my brother **David** disclosed an unexpected detail about our father. **Fred had** served as a gunner on a Minesweeper and had admitted to **David** that he'd brought down at least one **German** plane. (He'd disclosed this during a family visit to **Rickmansworth** in the mid-**1990s**.) The pilot had not bailed out. Over half a century had elapsed before my father could disclose this detail.

Perhaps the high point of the **London Family History** trips was the time I spent in the **Westminster Archive Centre** (on **Thursday 17th September 2009**) trying to get photos of the bombsite where the **V1** Rocket (which had so nearly killed my mother) was found. After much research, the picture was unearthed, and it showed just how close my mother had come to death. Skimming over **Vincent House** it had landed in a block of flats in **Rutherford Street,** demolishing them entirely. If it wasn't for the nearby **Royal Oak Public House** acting as a physical *'shield'* the damage to **Vincent House** would have been far greater. Fifty yards nearer and my mother would not have lived. It was very moving to look at those black and white photos showing bomb-blasted walls on which the only surviving features were mantelpiece ornaments (including an oval mirror) and a wall picture. Everything else had gone. Hanging around the scene were cloth-capped workers who appeared at a loss as to what they should do. Both as a family member and a historian, it was amazing to view the same street scene my mother would have seen as a twenty-year-old young woman sixty-five year previously! (A similar sense of amazement occurred the very next day when I visited **Crouch End** and examined photographs of public events celebrating the Coronation of **King George VI** on **Wednesday, 12th May 1937** My mother had let me know that both she and her parents had been part of a crowd of people cheering. There were also close-up photos of shopkeepers with whom her family would have done business.)

A review of **London City Council (LCC)** War Damage Maps confirmed that my mother had experienced a whole series of escapes, especially as (a **1935** map showed) there were two gas work plants nearby! One can only question the wisdom of her parents in deciding to move from the relatively quiet **Crouch End** to an area of **London** which they must have known would have been heavily targeted by **Hitler.** Admittedly they could obtain property at a very cheap price, but they did so at significant risk to their lives. My mother threw only limited light upon what was a seemingly irresponsible decision. It would be the equivalent of a **Russian** family moving to **Stalingrad** as the Panzers were advancing towards it. The fact that they didn't seem able to find relatives or friends to put them up in **Crouch End** possibly suggests there'd been some degree of friction there. If so, my mother wasn't aware of it. The impression gained was of a family simply hardened by war.

During both visits, I managed to combine substantial Family History research with some cultural activities. On **Thursday, 4th September 2008** I visited the splendid **Hadrian Exhibition** held at the **British Museum** and was in awe of the beauty of some of the artefacts on display. It also felt decidedly odd to see how the **Romans** seemed to have been the forebears of **1970's** hairstyles! Just over a year later (on **Friday, 18th September 2009**), I visited **Dr Johnson's House** in **Gough Square.** I got in free of charge because staff members were celebrating his three hundredth birthday – indeed they had stood outside and sung *'Happy Birthday'* to him which I thought was rather moving. I also enjoyed some discussions with interesting people I met, either on the tube or in the places I visited. As a poet, I'd that found **London** was getting my *'creative juices'* going. This is evidenced by my poem in the Prologue, entitled *'Click!'* which highlighted some of the frustrations to derive from Family History Research and is printed in my poetry book *'At 47: Poems on 'This' or 'That''* It recorded (in exaggerated form) some of my misadventures with my wife's digital camera. I was engaged in Family History research at various **London** locations from **Thursday 4th September** to **Friday 5th September 2008.** Another poem (entitled *'Metro-Class Scape'*) described the various views I could see from the tube window as I travelled from my brother's house in **Rickmansworth** to central **London.** It recorded the journey my brother used to take daily when working as an economic forecaster in the City District. It can be found in my poetry book *'At 47.'*

Section 2: An Interview with My Mother

Concerning the early years of my mother; Cynthia Mary Smith

On **Sunday, June 30th 2002** (after much persuasion) my mother was kind enough to provide the following account of her life from the time of her birth until the outbreak of the Second World War. I have tried to keep true to her spoken words, inserting only key dates and responses to questions, to further clarify certain points.

"*I was born in* **1923** *in* **Salonika, Greece.** *My father fought in the First World War on the* **Western Front** *and in the* **Balkans.** *He decided to stay on in* **Greece.** *For a while, he had a yacht and travelled between the* **Greek Islands** *selling all kinds of goods. But unfortunately, this didn't pay. After giving this up he got a job with the* **League of Nations** – *helping to settle the new* **Greek-Bulgarian** *frontier. At this time, there was a lot of trouble between* **Turkey** *and* **Greece** *over* **Smyrna** *and this resulted in many refugees coming to* **Salonika.** *My mother and father had been married twelve years and had no family. They had given up hope of having any family, as my mother was nearly forty. My mother took in one of the refugees and was kind to her. Before the old lady returned home she said to my mother 'You will have a daughter by this time next year' and, sure enough, I was born. We continued to live abroad in either* **Greece** *or* **Bulgaria** *until my father's work with the* **League of Nations** *finished. Although I was only seven years old when we returned to* **England,** *I can still remember a great deal about when we lived in* **Sofia** *[***Bulgaria's** *capital] and remember seeing a Zeppelin flying over and also sledging in the park in winter.*

Chickens were bought alive then so as to make sure they were fresh. One day I walked into the kitchen and saw a chicken tied to the kitchen table. It flew up at me and ever since I have had a phobia about birds.

My mother and I returned to **England** *in* **1930** *and we lived in* **North London** *where I went to school. The discipline was very strict and if we didn't do our work properly we got a hard smack over the knuckles. Except for this, we were all happy. I enjoyed school. After about two years my father got a job in* **Paris.** *It was for the Accountants* **Price and Waterhouse,** *and his job was to help a* **Jewish** *Businessman get back on his feet. It was only on a temporary contract. My mother and I went to join him. I went to a* **French** *school. At first, I could speak no* **French** *at all and the first words I learnt to say were 'shut up!' I got teased a bit but after a term or two I learnt to speak* **French** *fluently and by the time we left* **France** *in* **1936** *I could speak* **French** *as well as* **English.** *I also visited* **Vienna** *when I was aged about nine.*

The schools in **France** *were very strict. We only went to school in the mornings, but a great deal of homework was given. When we were at school it was all work and no games were played. We had a woman in the flat above who was a piano teacher and we heard a continual 'thump, thump' on the piano, which was often played out of tune! The maid who looked after the flats lived in an attic. She was a funny old woman.*

I enjoyed living in **Paris** *and was quite sorry to leave. It was very hard for me to return to* **England** *as in* **France** *everything was in decimals. I had never learnt weights and measures, or pounds, shillings and pence.*

We lived in **London** *until the war broke out and I remember everyone believed* **Chamberlain** *when he signed the* **Munich Agreement** *with* **Hitler.** *My father was sceptical and said it wouldn't last.* **Chamberlain** *was an old fool who was very gullible in believing that* **Hitler** *wanted to keep the peace. He was totally taken in.*

Before the last war, there was a lot of unemployment and there weren't the benefits there are now. My father was unemployed for two years and used to do lots of reading to pass the time. For a single person, the dole was only **10s** *a week although for a married man with a child it was more. We found it hard to manage. In* **1938** *with the war coming, he obtained a job in the* **Censorship Office,** *censoring letters from* **Europe.** On **September 2nd, 2001,** my mother divulged that *'just before the war'* they had acquired a day servant called **Betsey.** (Surely this was a sign of their desire to speedily regain a middle-class status, which had been under threat during her father's period of unemployment. Another sign of this status was apparently, that when the husband earned enough he could then prevent his wife from having to go out to work.)

"My aunt had a boarding house, so we had to live with her for a while, which wasn't good as she and my mother didn't get on, although my aunt was always kind to me.

My other aunt lived in **Birmingham** *and had a very hard time. She had three children who had to wear second-hand clothes and had to share an egg between the three of them. Things didn't improve until the outbreak of war when there were plenty of jobs available; (my father was quick to join the Home Guard) but the* **1930s** *were a bad time for many people."*

The long-term effect of being brought up overseas was to make my mother *'far broader minded'* then would have been the case if she'd been brought up in England. She would mature to develop liberal social attitudes and an interest in foreign cultures. She liked holidaying abroad – leaving my father to complain about the expense and mutter *"there's nothing like the* **East Coast** *of* **Yorkshire!***"*

He could never see why my mother wouldn't be content with **Filey, Scarborough** or **Bridlington**. In later life, he would leave her to travel abroad with friends. On this matter, I came to sympathise with my mother although from **1987** until **2003** my wife, myself and our four children holidayed every year in **Scarborough** – a wonderful place to bring a family of young children. During some of these years, my parents would stay at a nearby hotel and babysit for us. Overall, I have very happy memories of these holidays. I would make a point of taking each of our four children on a special *'night out'* to give them individual attention. Sometimes, this would just involve a walk along the beach, on other occasions a trip to the ballpark or some other fun fair type of attraction. When gathering them together in the morning, I would often say, *"assemble in the courtyard and no bickering!"*

Sometimes, information from my mother would come out in *'dribs and drabs'* rather than by any formal interview. For instance, whilst staying with my mother (on **Sunday, 16th June 2013**) she disclosed the origins of her forename *'Cynthia.'* It was a very rare name amongst her contemporaries. Apparently, her mother had come across it when reading a Socialite Magazine about *'Lady Cynthia Moseley.'* This lady had been the second daughter of **George Curzon**, the former viceroy of India and later **1st Marques Curzon of Kedleston (1859-1925)**. Despite parental misgivings, she'd married **Sir Oswald Moseley** (a then Tory MP) on **11th May 1920**. (**Oswald Moseley** would later become a Labour MP and then a notorious Fascist leader, interned during the war.) Throughout the **1930s Cynthia** and her mother would often have a laugh about her being *"named after a **Fascist.**"*

Documentary evidence supporting the early part of her account was provided by her Birth Certificate, details of which are recorded below.
1. When and where born: Salonika 26th Novr. 1923
2. Name if Any: Cynthia Mary
3. Sex: Female
4. Name and Surname of Father: William John Absalom
5. Name and Surname of Mother: Marguerite Eliza Myerson
6. Occupation of Father: Merchant
7. Signature, description and residence of informant: W. J. Absalom, Father, Salonika
8. When registered: 28th Novr. 1923
9. Signature of registrar: E. H. Mitchell, Acting Vice-Consul
N.B: On maps, **Salonika** has often been spelt *'Salonica,'* it is a port in **Macedonia, Northern Greece**.

November 1923 was also the month in which an unknown **Austrian**-born agitator, named **Adolf Hitler** had launched his abortive *'Beer hall Putsch'* in **Munich.** This first attempt to seize power had ended with his humiliating arrest and imprisonment. However, his next attempt (made in the early **1930s**) was to prove successful. More than once this man was to be responsible for the near-death experiences of my parents; he would bring them much grief.

Especially intriguing was the story surrounding the birth of my mother which I will elaborate here in more detail. Whilst living in **Salonika,** her parents had stayed with them a female **Armenian Christian** refugee who had fled the murderous **Turkish** persecution of that community in **1915.** At that time, **Marguerite** was approaching forty and had almost given up hope of ever having a child. Near the end of **1922,** their lodger had told my maternal parents, *"God will bless you for the great kindness you have shown me and in a year's time you will have a daughter."* Within the time period specified by the prediction, this was precisely what happened. My mother reiterated this story during a telephone conversation made in **July 2001.** Incidentally, she was the <u>only</u> child of **William** and **Marguerite Absalom.** Her parents had wanted a child for ages and had almost given up hope of this happening. The result was that, when they did have my mother, they spoiled her.

Section 3: Establishing a Chronology

Concerning a timeline of my mother's life in London

The particularly helpful follow-up to the **London** visits took place at a meeting with my mother over **Sunday** lunch at our home on **16th November 2009.** I showed her the photographs I'd taken or had obtained from certain archives. Seeing these had released a flood of memories and unexpected associations for her. It was possible (with her help and now well-established enthusiasm) to ascertain the following chronology of her early life: -
<u>1930-32/3</u>: Lived near **Priory Park** in the pleasant **North London suburb** of **Crouch End.** At the age of seven, she used to ride (by herself) on her Fairy Bicycle. When I remarked on her lone cycle rides she'd stated that *"You couldn't do that these days, but times were different then."* (She didn't remember the park memorial which had been constructed in **1900**)
<u>1932-36:</u> Lived in a **Paris** suburb where her father worked for **Price-Waterhouse Cooper** trying to help the Firm get back on its feet by auditing its books. Living in the flat below was a musician who was a major source of

annoyance due to him loudly practising his instruments. It was during this period she took a trip to **Vienna.**

1936: Returned to **London** and attended **Crouch End High School** which moved premises whilst she was there, (records in **Crouch End Library** confirmed that it had moved in **1936**). Her father was now unemployed.

1937: She attended a fair in **Priory Park** to celebrate **George VI's** coronation. She remembered the swings, prominent on one of the archive photos shown to her. However, she missed the floats but saw later photos of the parade in a local hall. My mother also remembered walking around the **Crouch End** clock tower (which I saw on my second visit to **London**) before her school moved in **1936.** There used to be a Department Store with a cafe sited at the **Broadway** where she would sometimes go with her parents. Whilst in **Crouch End** they lived with her father's sister **Elizabeth** in **Mount View Road.** She was a spinster who owned a Boarding House in **Cheltenham.** She would write *'Gentile'* after her name to clearly show customers that she wasn't **Jewish.**

1938: Fred Myerson my mother's *'very kind'* grand uncle, died **aged 89.** He'd been a local bowls champion and from all accounts had been a very kind man. (A review of the **London Gazette** confirmed that he'd left a will). The voters register for her mother shows the family to have been living in **Tottenham Green Lane.** Around that time (or a year earlier) she was given a volume of **Shakespeare's** works as a prize for her work in **English Literature.** (Published in **June 1937,** it's now in my possession.)

1939: Almost as soon as the war was declared, there was the expectation of being bombed immediately loomed large. **Cynthia** and her mother moved to **Hyde Heath** where her aunts **Emeline** and **Laurie** lived. (Her father stayed in **London** and joined the Home Guard.) However, boredom soon set in. *"We soon got fed up – it was dark and there was nothing to do. This cured me of ever wanting to live in the country. At night, the shadow of the cows scared me."* In frustration, her mother even exclaimed, *"I'd rather be bombed in **London** than stay here!"*

1940:

January: Cynthia and her mother returned to **London**

September: By this period the Blitz was on. At **Crouch End,** she would stay in the **Anderson Shelter** with her parents, playing cards. *"I found the Anderson Shelter very uncomfortable."* She had to get to work for the Civil Service at **Great Southern Street, Westminster;** firstly, travelling by bus to **Finsbury Park Station** then a train to **Charing Cross.** She then walked or got a bus to Westminster. The air raids became so bad that at work they used to sleep on mattresses on the floor and play cards. *"It was good fun."* She would see her parents only at the weekend.

Late 1940 or early 1941: Her parents moved to **Vincent House** because *"it was cheap and convenient."* They lived immediately above the entrance to a dairy and at **3.00 am** every morning would hear the milk churns being rolled down into it. This kept them awake until they got more accustomed to it. (In contradiction to map evidence my mother indignantly denied that there were a gas works nearby.) The flat was well furnished with a large room, a large table and a three-seater settee and chairs. (My brother recalled that in the **1950s,** the bathroom had a very large and noisy Ascot heater.) My mother noted how **Saint Matthew's Church** (which her father attended) had been hit by an incendiary bomb. When making purchases at **Westminster Market** (still going in **2009**) the cockney store holders would call her *'precious.'* **The Royal Oak Pub** (with its **1872** capstone) had something of a rough reputation – with children often hanging around outside waiting for their parents. In contrast *'The Barley Mow'* (where her father would go) was pleasant and had a restaurant – it still has. She expressed surprise that the **Victorian** toilets (which she remembered) were still there.

1941: She was evacuated to **Bournemouth** where she first met **Fred.** However, the **Germans** used to drop bombs during the **Baedeker Raids.** She and **Fred** were nearly killed when a bomb landed in the square from which they'd just left a moment or two before via a side slipway. Her father now joined the regular **British Army** following the **German** invasion of the **Balkans.**

1942: When **Fred** was on shore leave, they visited his sister **Madge** at **Whitley Bay** *"only to be caught in a terrible air raid. It was a case of going from the frying pan into the fire!"* (My wife, who's from **Newcastle-Upon-Tyne** remarked they'd possibly been aiming for the docks of **North** and **South Shields.**) This was shortly after their marriage.

17/6/1944: A **V1** Bomb skimmed over them during the early hours. They heard the engine cut out and it went over their roof to crash into the flat opposite killing six to eight people. *"It was close enough to blast our windows out."* (She couldn't identify any of the people in the photograph showing the incident.) Her mother rang relatives at **Crouch End** (they lived near the **Priory Park** mentioned earlier) to move in with them. However, about a fortnight later a bomb landed in (or near) their garden so they were bombed out again! **Fred** got compassionate leave and avoided a posting to **Malta.** The Military Police called around looking for **Fred** because they couldn't believe his wife had been bombed out a <u>second</u> time!

On the prompting of **Fred's** mother, **Cynthia** moved to **Leeds.** *"When I moved to **Leeds** I thought it was heavenly. There were no air raids. **Leeds** was very lucky."* Initially, she tried working as a bus conductress but, *"I was no good at that – I* *would keep falling over. Instead, I got a job working for* **Kershaw's in Harehills** *which then did optics."* (It was situated near to where **Fred's** mother lived.)

26/11/1944: Cynthia celebrated her twenty-first birthday in **Leeds** (she was still there seventy years later celebrating her ninety-first birthday at **Headingley Hall** Residential Home with my wife, myself and my oldest and youngest sons attending.)

8/5/1945: Cynthia celebrated VE day in **Leeds** by going to a pub with workmates. She said she only got *'merry'* – not *'drunk.'*

At the close of the conversation, she stated, *"When I look back we had some very narrow escapes. I don't know why I lived."* (She then mentioned acquaintances who, on moving to **Leeds,** had lodged all their furniture in a storage depot, only for it to be bombed out in one of the few air raids **Leeds** had!)

This meeting represented one of the most rewarding encounters with my mother. Somehow, I felt I'd got to know her better. She admitted to having found it all *"very interesting."* Thus, ended one of the most productive of any of my family History sessions. The above narrative added much detail to my mother's previous account of her early life. The pictures I'd shown her of **Crouch End** and the bomb damage at **Vincent Square** had unlocked a treasure trove of memories. She thought it *'wonderful'* how the Web could show pictures of **Priory Park** – the stomping ground of her childhood. I felt that it was a great privilege to have been able to share something of my mother's early life. It's now fitting to examine her connection with the **Balkans.**

Section 4: A Great Bunch of Chaps

Concerning the Salonika campaign of 1915-1918

The connection with the **Balkans** had become established because of my maternal grandfather's wartime service there. During a warm **Sunday** afternoon (on **September 2ⁿᵈ, 2001**) I had quizzed my mother (at my sister's house) when she'd disclosed a great deal of intriguing information about her father **William John Absalom (1886-1959)** and her mother **Marguerite Eliza Myerson (1883-1963).** (My mother recorded how she hated being called *'Eliza'* and never used the name.)

William Absalom's Grandfather was part of a family of seven **Hampshire** farmers, all brothers. **Absalom** was an old **English** name (and not a **Jewish** one). His own father (also called **William**) had first served in the Merchant

Navy (where he'd made a wooden storage box – is now in my sister's possession) and became a church verger. He'd married an **Irish** woman called **Irene Elizabeth** who'd had six children, three of whom had died young. One Grand Uncle, **George Absalom** (with the stage name **John Gillette – Gillette** being his mother's maiden name) was reputed to have been a well-known **Victorian** actor (although this seemed to have been an exaggeration). **William** himself had been born in **Felixstowe,** with one younger and one older sister. He'd attended **Ipswich Grammar School,** after which he'd begun work as a bank clerk in the same town – a job *'he absolutely hated.'* This was hardly surprising as he was apparently utterly hopeless with money. He much preferred an active, open-air kind of life.

Later **William** moved to **London** and continued the same work there until **1914.** (My mother couldn't recall the bank he'd worked for.) He'd also participated in amateur dramatics. In the First World War, he'd joined the **Lancashire Fusiliers** and was *'mentioned in dispatches.'* For him, the army would fulfil his aspirations to be a gentleman and joining it was his way of advancing up the social scale. After serving a brief time on the **Western Front,** he was moved to **Salonika** in late **1915** where he rose to the rank of Captain. During his service, he fell ill with malaria, which was probably fortuitous as it reduced the time he spent serving on the front line. Interestingly, my mother did <u>not</u> recall a family tradition (related by my brother **David**) which had stated that, whilst waiting for a train to take him back to the army (following a period of leave in **London**) he'd slipped on some ice and because of the heavy kit he was wearing couldn't get up again! It took the combined effort of two or three others to lift him from the ground!

My brother remembered him as *"a much laid-back old **Edwardian** Gentleman."* Regrettably, he had a reputation for not being good with money and he used to live *'above his means.'* A story exists that, when flat broke (at the end of the **1930s**) he purchased an expensive bottle of champagne (or wine) to cheer his wife up. Apparently, her reaction had been none too favourable! With his solid **Northern** values, **Fred** came to heartily dislike the way *"their social pretensions outmatched their income."* Perhaps influenced by the example of his in-laws **Fred** came to view *"**Londoners** as great escapists."* His relationship with my mother's parents was not without its tensions.

Other than the army the great love of **William's** life was old buildings. To the exasperation of anyone accompanying him **William Absalom** (nicknamed *'Nooky'* by the rest of the family) used to spend hours inside these buildings so that he could indulge his hobby of *'brick sniffing.'* (My brother **David** has the same interest and, to a far lesser extent, so do I.)

During a conversation held on **Sunday, 7th July 2002, Cynthia** revealed the surprising detail that her mother had been a good dancer and was once a dancing instructress. **William** had been one of her pupils. Their meeting had seemed to have been a case of romance on the dance floor (with the most likely period being around **1912**). Dark haired, **Marguerite** had had a reputation for being very intelligent, whilst in contrast, her future husband was more of a likeable *'charmer.'*

William and **Marguerite** married in **December 1914** almost exactly four months following the outbreak of the First World War. When this conflict arose, **Marguerite** was on holiday in **Switzerland** and had to travel back to **England** through **France** in what she called a *'sealed'* train. Part of her journey took her through the city of **Lyons** – she mentioned this story to my brother **David** after he'd returned from a school exchange visit to **Lyons** in **1961**. A photograph (taken during their week-long honeymoon in **Brighton**) which showed **William** proudly wearing his army uniform. Hosted by the devout **Baptist Myerson** family the wedding reception, held at a certain **North London** hotel, hadn't offered any alcoholic refreshments because they abstained from alcoholic drink. (My mother subsequently confirmed that her uncle – the family patriarch **Frederick Thomas Myerson (1848-1937)** had been a heavy drinker when young.) Consequently, **William** couldn't wait to leave to have a drink, which he did at a pub near **Victoria Railway Station!** With their *'Petit Bourgeois'* respectability, it seems the **Myersons** were a rather dour company.

During a phone conversation (on **Thursday, July 18th, 2002**) my mother divulged that her parents had met a year or two before the wedding. She had been a ballroom dancing instructress and he had attended her class, which was a bit incongruous as he was reputed to be rather clumsy just like myself. Further details of their wedding were provided by the Marriage Certificate received after much administrative delay on **Wednesday 12th September 2002.**

Registration District <u>Edmonton</u>
<u>**1914** Marriage solemnised at the church of S. George,</u> in the <u>Parish of S. George, Hornsey</u> in the <u>County of Middlesex</u>
1. When married? Dec.4th 1914
2. Name and Surname: William John Absalom, Marguerite Eliza Myerson
3. Age: 28, 32
4. Condition: Bachelor, Spinster

5. Rank or profession: Bank Clerk
6 Residence at the time of marriage: 17 Pusy Avenue
7. Father's name and surname: William Absalom, Henry Myerson
8. Rank or profession of father: Retired, Deceased

Married in the <u>Church of St. Peter</u> according to the Rites and Ceremonies of the <u>Church of England,</u> this marriage was solemnised between us,
<u>W. J. Absalom</u>
<u>M. E. Myerson</u>
In the Presence of us,
<u>F. T. Myerson</u>
<u>William V. Rose</u>
<u>Lydia Mary Absalom</u>
After <u>Banns</u> by me <u>F. P. Harton, Assistant Curate</u>
 A website search of the **Lancashire Fusiliers** revealed a few more details concerning my maternal Grandfather's war service. He'd been in the **Twenty-Second Division,** which had served in **Macedonia** (known to troops as *'Muckydonia.'*). On **September 5th, 1915,** they had embarked at **Boulogne** and, after serving briefly on the **Western Front,** had then left **France** (in **November 1915**) and shipped onward to the then newly forming **Macedonian** front. From early **1916** the **Twenty-Second Division** was engaged in various actions North of the Port City of **Salonika** in the **Doiran** region. Although **William** had been spared the horrors of the **Somme** and **Passchendaele,** the **Macedonian Front** was no *'soft option.'* The climate was inhospitable – with torrential rain in winter and baking heat in summer. A range of diseases was rife and as contemporary photographs showed, the terrain soldiers had to fight over was strewn with boulders and broken into deep gullies. Furthermore, the **Bulgarian** enemy was well *'dug in'* and occupied the high ground. A military history website showed that during the **Macedonian** campaign, **William's** Division **(The Twenty-Second)** had taken part in the following engagements (those with subsequent battle honours for the division are in block capitals): -
19th October 1915 - 30th September 1918: Official Duration of the Campaign
7th & 8th December 1915: KOTURINO
7th & 8th August 1916: Horseshoe Hill
30th September - 31st October 1916: STRUMP
24th & 25th April 1917: DOIRAN
8th & 9th May 1917: DOIRAN
1st & 2nd September 1918: Roche Noir
18th & 19th September 1918: DOIRAN

The discrepancy between the official duration and the **November** leaving date for leaving **France** mentioned previously is explained by the fact that some Units of the **22nd Division** had left for **Macedonia** ahead of the main force.

A visit to the **Kew Archive Centre, London** on **Tuesday, 22nd December 2015** unearthed the War Diary of the Twenty-Second Division of the Lancashire Fusiliers. This document showed that it was the **Twelfth Battalion** of the **65th Infantry Brigade** that was serving in **Macedonia.** From this source, it was possible to reconstruct some of the daily activities in which **William** will have been involved. After arriving at **Salonika** on **5th of November 1915,** his Battalion at **Dautli** was near the frontline by late **December.** It was located just **north** of a steep hill called **Matterhorn,** (approximately fifty miles **North East** of **Salonika.**) From **22nd-23rd December** the weather was fine and there was nothing to report. However, on Christmas Eve the Battalion moved from **Dautli** to occupy a camp on the slopes **north** of **Matterhorn** in the **Eastern** section of the Front Line. The weather continued to be fine and warm. On **Christmas Day 1915** there were only two hours of work in the morning. A voluntary **Church of England** Service was held in the camp at **3.00 pm.** A Christmas Message was received from His Majesty the King and read out by the General Divisional Commander (GDC). The weather continued to be fine and warm but was cold at night. The first parcels since arriving in **Greece** were received that day. Some distant firing was heard in the **North West.** Exactly a century later (around **3.00 pm Christmas Day 2015**) I read extracts from this diary to my mother in the lounge of her Residential Home. Her response was to sit bolt upright in her wheelchair and listen carefully to what was being read. She could barely believe that we'd obtained such a detailed account of her father's life.

Useful statistics concerning the rate of malaria on the **Salonika Front** was provided by watching a YouTube Edition of the Classic **1964 BBC Documentary; 'The Great War.'** It revealed that a mixture of an inept administration and harsh conditions (with a climate where temperatures could range from a summer high of **114** degrees Fahrenheit down to a winter low of minus **35** degrees) had ensured that in **1916,** there were **30,000** recorded cases of Malaria amongst British troops. In **1917, 63,000** and **1918, 67,000.** Therefore, it's fair to conclude that my grandfather's case was not untypical. The Director of Army Medical Services, based in **Egypt,** had failed to provide any mosquito nets or quinine! There appears to have been a staggering level of ineptitude even by the low standards of the First World War. (*'The Great War,'* Episode 25, viewed **Tuesday, 30/12/2014**).

However, a painstaking research of some very detailed hospital records did not confirm the family story of **William Absalom** being laid-up in his tent with malaria for days on end. This suggests that his case had been mild and treated nearer the front line.

Individual actions which **William's Division** undertook could be horribly vicious. The following account (from **Palmer p.121**) of an attack, made on **April 24th, 1917** makes this very clear; *"Meanwhile on the left of the front, the* **Twenty-Second Division** *had more success and fewer casualties because the* **Bulgarian** *artillery could not rake the gullies in this sector and it was, therefore, possible to find covered approaches to the outposts. The* **Twenty-Second Division** *reached the first objective and held it against five counter-attacks, but the costly failure on the right prohibited any further advance up the hills behind the* **Doiran** *as they would have come under strong enfilading fire from the strong* **Bulgarian** *positions."* An extract from the **Balkan News Monday**, **6th May 1918** retrieved from the **Kew Archive Centre,** confirmed that the **Lancashire Fusiliers** had been engaged in a major night raid against the **Bulgarian Lines** around **Lake Doiran.** Whether **William** was involved in what seems to have been a major trench raid cannot be proved. However, the scale of the operation suggests that this was a possibility. My mother claims that he had a good war record and had been mentioned in dispatches.

Oddly enough, **William** came out of these experiences with a real love for army life. A photograph (taken around **1917**) showed an upright figure wearing a monocle. He was very much posing as an *'officer and a gentleman'* – appearing to relish the status that this position gave. My mother remembered her father describing the **Lancashire Fusiliers** as being, *"a great bunch of chaps."*

One mystery needing explanation was how a **London** Bank Clerk had ended up becoming Captain in a **North of England** army Division? During a telephone conversation (held on **Tuesday, July 16th, 2002**) my mother suggested that he may well have been transferred to this Division when he was already in the army. This remained the most likely explanation; such transfers were not unknown in a conflict where officer casualties were very high.

One major event that would have attracted **William's** attention was *'The Great Fire of Salonika'* that broke out on **Saturday, 18th August 1917.** Although it seemed to have resulted from a domestic accident rather than deliberate sabotage, it destroyed a large amount of Allied Supplies. A vivid account of this event was provided by **Dr Emslie Hutton** on **pp. p.320-323 Lewis (2014).** Its effects upon the city were severe with large sections of it destroyed.

Section 5: Varied Backgrounds

Concerning William Absalom and Marguerite Myerson

To understand those formative influences which may have affected my mother it will be helpful to delve further into the background of her parents; **William Absalom** and **Marguerite Myerson**. A beginning will be made by referring to my maternal Grandfather's Birth Certificate:

Registration District <u>Holborn</u>

1886. Birth in the Sub-district of <u>Marylebone</u> the <u>County of Middlesex</u>

1. When and where born: 22nd October 1886, Queen Charlotte Hospital <u>Marylebone</u> Road

2. Name if Any: William John

3. Sex: Boy

4. Name and Surname of Father: William Absalom

5. Name and Surname of Mother: Lydia Mary Absalom, formerly Gill of Clonakilty

6. Occupation of Father: Coast Guardsman

7. Signature, description and residence of informant: L. M. Absalom Mother, Dunny Cove, Clonakilty, Co. Cork

8. When registered: 30th October 1886

9. Signature of registrar: E. Rossiter, Registrar

His Birth Certificate confirmed an old family tradition that he'd come from a sea-faring background and that **William** had worked as a Bank Clerk. His future wife's Birth Certificate showed that she was just over three years older than him.

Registration District <u>Holborn</u>

1883. Birth in the Sub-district of <u>Pentonville</u> in the <u>County of Middlesex</u>

1. When and where born: 14th July 1883, 6 Cumming Street

2. Name if Any: Marguerite Eliza

3. Sex: Girl

4. Name and Surname of Father: Henry Myerson

5. Name and Surname of Mother: Gertrude Eliza Myerson, Formerly Watson

6. Occupation of Father: Hosier

7. Signature, description and residence of informant: G. E. Myerson, Mother, 6 Cumming Street, Clerkenwell

8. When registered: 17th August 1883

9. Signature of registrar: Jasper William Parrott, Registrar

As the above document shows, my maternal Grandmother's maiden name had originally been **Marguerite Eliza Myerson,** but she hated the name *'Eliza'* and never used it. A rather vague family tradition claimed her Grandfather (or Great Grandfather) had been a **Polish Jewish Peddler** who'd come over to **England** to escape the pogroms. Only in **June 2014** (following much research) was the identity of this mysterious figure revealed. **Marguerite's** father had first worked in (and then subsequently owned) a *'pot and pan'* factory in **North London.** She had a brother **Harold** who was seven years younger than her. At the age of eleven or twelve, her parents died within a year of one another. Following their death two strict **Baptist** maiden aunts, **Emily** and **Laura** (who owned a Dame School in **Crouch End, London**) brought her up. They retired to **Hyde Heath.** These aunts were known to have been very snobbish and would walk miles to Church. They also forbade the playing of cards – a common pastime of the era in which they lived. (The effect of her strict **Baptist** upbringing was to turn **Marguerite** into a lifelong atheist. When staying with them they used to forbid her from sleeping with the light on, even though she was terrified of the dark.) As she approached adulthood **Marguerite** grew up into what was then known as *'the new woman' i.e.* one who held politically radical innovative ideas which challenged the traditional submissive female role expected of middle-class ladies. This stance demonstrated her firm willingness to defy the social conventions of her day. Her lifestyle, with its frequent travels abroad, was also unconventional. One has the impression of a lady in rebellion against **Victorian** values. At the time of the **1901** Census, she was working as a *'Board School Pupil-Teacher'* in **Islington, London.**

Meanwhile, her mother's side of the family (represented by two wealthy cousins, each with a private income) were said to have cared for and brought up her brother **Harold.** He eventually became a Dental Mechanic in **High Wycombe** – but was to become an optician later in life. He married a lady called **Stella** with whom he had three children (one a girl was called **Vera**). However, **Harold** was never close to his sister **Marguerite,** whom he had barely known since the age of five. She was often mistaken for being **Jewish** as she had a very dark complexion. Before she married she'd worked as a teacher (see above). From an early age, she'd suffered from bouts of asthma and this could have contributed to her volatile temperament. In later life, my maternal Grandmother was often heard to remark that one blessing of her old age was that it had cured her of her asthma. She had suffered from it quite badly. **Marguerite** also had a lifelong obsession with what she called the *'Yellow Peril.'* I remember her sitting upright in bed, declaiming fiercely on this subject shortly before her death. This tenacious anti-**Chinese** prejudice had apparently originated during the time of

The Boxer Uprising in 1900. One can only speculate what she would have made of China's growing power in the early twenty-first century.

Section 6: Exploring the Absalom Line

Concerning the Absalom's of Hampshire, Portsea and London

A beginning can be made with the Absalom's by referring to the 1841 Census which showed them living in very crowded accommodation at Drury Lane: -
John Timby aged 44 *'Licensed Vintner'*
Edna aged 40
Elizabeth Hirst age unknown *'Family Servant'*
Edward Kelly aged 30 *'Man Servant'* born in Middlesex
Robert Turner aged 25 *'Author'* born in Scotland
Abraham Absalom aged 45 *'Plasterer'*
Elizabeth aged 35
Henry aged 7 born in Middlesex
John aged 7 months born in Middlesex
In the 1851 census, we find: -

James Hobbs aged 37 *'Fishmonger'* born in Middlesex
Sarah aged 35 born in Middlesex
Abraham Absalom aged 56 *'Plasterer'* born in Putney, Surrey
Elizabeth aged 45 born in Reading, Berks
Henry aged 17 *''Labourer-moulder* born in St Mary Strand
George aged 14 *'Call boy'* born in St Mary the Strand
John aged 10 *'Errand boy'* born in St Mary the Strand
James aged 7 *'Scholar'* born in St Mary the Strand
William aged 4 *'Scholar'* born in St Mary the Strand

Confusion was created by the way some Census Returns spelt Absalom phonetically as **'Abjohnun,'** or **'Absalum.'** Other neighbours included shoemakers, a charwoman, printer and a boatman. A **Francis Robert Absalom** was born at **92 Doug Lane** and baptized on **11/9/1839** by the Rector **Joshua Renwick**. Abraham's occupation was listed as a *'Plasterer*. In the **1851** Census, their address was given as **1 George Yard (or Drury Yard) Drury Lane, St Mary Le Strand, Westminster, London.**

Officially a *'call boy'* was one who told actors when it was time to go on stage. Yet a librarian at **Leeds Central Library** (on **Monday 27/9/2004**) disclosed that a *'call boy'* was associated with male prostitution. Intriguingly the term was crossed out on the original form. This perhaps was possibly done out of a sense of shame. **George's** close association with the theatre suggested that he may have been sexually exploited in this *'high risk'* occupation. **John** appears to have been born on **2/11/1840** & baptized **13/1/1841** (by **J. T. Drahan**, Rector). **James** appears to have been born on **10/10/1843** & baptized by the rector **Joshua Renwick (Durham MA)** on **30/10/1843**.

1861 Census Return
(HMS Wellesley, Harbour, Medway River, Chatham Rest)
William Absalom aged **16** *'Boy Second Class'* **St Mary's**
William C. Barren aged **16** *'Registered at Anglesey, Haw Head'* **Middx**
John C. Bendal aged **16**
James Bird aged **15**

William was evidently on a training ship as it contained many boys in the **15-16** age group. In the same year, **George Absalom** was establishing a family at **42 Foster Street, Tower Hamlets** in **London**. This could be seen the following details.
George Absalom aged **24** *'Comedian'* **St Mary Le Strand, London**
Mary Ann aged **24** *'Dress Maker'* **Walworth**
George aged **4** *'Scholar'* **St Pauls, Covent Garden, Islington**
Mary Ann aged **1 St Pauls, Covent Garden, Islington**

George's neighbours included a tailor, labourer, farrier (who shoed horses) and sailor. The many addresses which **George** came to occupy were signs of an unsettled lifestyle – typical of those working in the theatre.

In the **1871** Census, we find that, at the age of **25**, **William Absalom** is based at **'HMS Juno, Victory Harbour, Hong Kong.'** He's a *'Second Class Stoker'* and his birthplace is given as **'St Mary's Middx, London.'** Meanwhile, **George Absalom** appeared to be staying with relatives who were connected to the **Church** of **St John the Baptist, Shoreditch, London.**
George Absalom aged **34** *'Actor'* the **City of London**
Mary Ann aged **31** the **City of London**
Mary Ann aged **14** the **City of London**
Mary aged **3** the **City of London**
Walter aged **2** the **City of London**
On **Sunday, 7/10/2007** my mother confirmed that **William** was reputed to have survived one shipwreck. (Being in the engine room would have specially

placed him in danger of drowning.) I discovered only a little about **George** in the **Victoria and Albert Theatre Archives.** He seemed to have served as a backing musician.

The **1881** Census revealed the following details about the families of **William** (whose address was given as *'Ireland'*) and **George Absalom.**
William Absalom aged **35** *'Coast Guardsman'* **London**
Lydia aged **31** *'Coast Guards Man'* **Stratford, Essex**
Mary Absalom aged **44 Stratford, Essex**

Sadly, **Irish** Census Returns were destroyed during the **Irish Civil War** that raged from **1922-1923** and this severely limited the amount of information which could be obtained about **William Absalom's Irish** connections. Still in the year **1881,** at **161 Downham Road, Islington London, George** appeared to have been *'resting'* as an actor and was eking out a *'hand-to-mouth'* existence which required his family to take on boarders.
George Absalom aged **44** *'Home Fashion Collar maker'* **London**
William aged **19** *'Home Fashion Collar maker'* **London**
Mary Ann aged **17** *'Tea Dealer'* **London**
Walter aged **12 London**
Bertie aged **7 London**
Chas Nichols aged **27** Boarder *'Farrier'*
Arthur Heron aged **18** Boarder *'Home Collar Maker'*

Moving forward a decade to the **1891** Census it was found that **William Absalom** was based at the **Coastguard Station** at **Dunwich.** Other details were as follows: -
William Absalom aged **45** *'Coast Guard'* **London, Strand**
Lydia aged **41 Stratford, Essex**
Elizabeth aged **9** *'Scholar'* **Cork, Ireland**
William John aged **4 Marylebone, London**
Lydia aged **6 mths Marylebone, London**

William John was my maternal grandfather. By the time of the **1901** Census (see below) he and his family appear to have achieved a modest respectability as Church Workers, living at **2 Princess Street, Walton.** The *'visitors'* mentioned in the Census Return may either have been daughters of missionaries or of British Army Officers or Colonial Officials.
William Absalom aged **54** *'Church Verger, St John the Baptist'* **London**
Lydia aged **51** *'Church Worker'* **Stratford, Essex**

William aged **14 London**
Lydia aged **10 London**
Annie Bigold aged **42** Visitor *'Living on own means'* **Rangoon** *'British Subject'*
Asa Mary Jones aged **37** Visitor *'Living on own means'* **Rangoon** *'British Subject'*
Maud J Jones aged **36** Visitor *'Living on own means'* **Soham, Tulse Hill**

The **1911** Census showed **William Absalom** to now be residing at **4 Queens Road, Woodbridge, Felixstowe, Suffolk.**
William Absalom aged **64** *'Church Verger'* **London**
Lydia Mary aged **61** *'Church Worker'* **Stratford, Essex**
Lydia Dorothy aged **20** *'Assistant schoolmistress, council school'* **London**
Thomas Percival Powell aged **29** *Church Organist, teaches music'* **Liverpool**
Dorothea Edith Clarkson aged **21** *'Milliner'* **Ipswich**

Absent from this household is my mother's future father; his name didn't feature anywhere in the **1911** Census. A serious misspelling of his surname is the most likely explanation for this absence. What the **1901 Return** <u>did</u> reveal was that he'd been one of five children, two of whom had died by **1911.**

At this juncture, it's possible to reconstruct a line of descent from the remotest known **Absalom** forebears to my mother. Here we find: -
1. **James Absalom (December 1753-1827)** of **Breamore, Hampshire** who, on **28th May 1776** at **Saint Mary's Portsea, Hampshire** married **Phoebe Clay (1754-1798)** of **Salisbury, Wiltshire** and had a son: -
2. **Abraham Absalom (2nd April 1796-January 1860)** who, on **15th September 1833** at **Saint Anne's Soho, Westminster, London** married **Elizabeth Sarah Gillett (1806-?)** and had a son: -
3. **William Absalom (1846-December 1917)** who, on **14th July 1873** at **Saint Anne's, Soho, Westminster, London,** married **Lydia Mary Gill (1850-September 1923)** and had a son
4. **William John Absalom (21st October 1886)** who, in **4th December 1914** at **Edmonton** married **Marguerite Eliza Myerson (July 1883-July 1963)** and had a daughter: -
5. **Cynthia Mary Absalom (26th November 1923-17th November 2018)** my mother who lived to celebrate the completion of this work in **September 2018.**

Thanks to this data we can also approximate the date of the **Absalom's** move to **London. Abraham** had an elder brother called **William,** who during **1788** was born in **Portsea Island, Hampshire.** However, **Abraham** was born in **1796.** His birthplace was **Putney** then a village beside the **River Thames** located approximately five miles **West** of **Central London.** We can, therefore, date the move (from **Hampshire** to **Putney**) between **1790-1795** where no children appear to have been born. The exact reason as to why a man in his forties, already with four children (**George 1781-1843, Sarah** born in **1783, Henry** born in **1785** and **William** born in **1788**) would uproot himself to live in **Putney** remains unknown but possibly a lack of money could well have been a major factor. (The only other explanation was that he was engaged in some form of government work and that the outbreak of war with Revolutionary **France** in **1793** had obliged a move to **London. Portsea Island** was adjacent to the major Royal Navy base of **Portsmouth.**) **GENUKI** revealed that **Portsea** was a parish and fortified town which included a Royal Navy Dockyard sited on a flat island of the same name that was known locally in **Portsdown.** This detail suggested that there could have been some association between the **Absalom** family and the **Royal Navy** in this period.

The move to **London** doesn't appear to have done his wife **Phoebe** much good because, within a couple of years, she had died (at only forty-four). She was subsequently buried on **16th August 1798** at **Portsea, Southampton.** When **James** died (in **1827**) he'd already chosen to be buried in the same place. Unlike his youngest son, **Abraham, London** was not a place with which **James** had wished to identify. Readers of the **Charles Dickens** novel *'Barnaby Rudge'* (with its graphic description of the casual lawlessness pervading late **Georgian London**) would readily understand why. I read this novel during **February 2017** and was amazed at the insight **Dickens** displayed on such matters as religiously-based violence and political corruption. Each of those social *'types'* remains highly topical in today's world. No writer could *'do'* murder, riots or public executions as well as **Dickens.** Undeservedly forgotten, **Barnaby Rudge** is a novel that could do with being rediscovered.

Around the time of the **Absalom's** move to **London,** another of my mother's ancestors was being born in **Saxony, Germany.** He too would make his way to **London;** he would also fall victim to the kind of violence narrated by **Dickens,** but that is the subject of another Chapter.

CHAPTER 16: THE WILDERNESS YEARS

Section 1: An Interview with my Father

Concerning changes in Chapeltown, Leeds

Much of my father's boyhood was spent playing cricket in **Potternewton Park** with playmates, many of whom were **Jewish** from the nearby terraced houses. Childhood for the middle classes in those days was far more of an outdoor affair. **Fred** seemed to have taken after both of his parents – mention being made at his funeral that there'd been something of the **Irish** storyteller about him. **Fred** could certainly switch on the *'blarney'* (**Irish** charm) whenever he'd wanted. When aged about ten, he remembered the first black **Ford** car chugging up what would have been the cobbled stones of his street. He also recalled disabled World War One veterans aimlessly hanging around local parks with nothing to do. Being in possession of several industries had saved **Leeds** from suffering the worst ravages of the **1930s** slump. Even so, times were hard and, although middle class, **Fred's** family were not spared the insecurities of that period. Some memories of the time in which he lived were preserved in an informal interview I had with him on the evening of **Saturday, 22ⁿᵈ October 1994.** Although slightly paraphrased, the following account reflects his words: -

"What was your area of Leeds like when you were young?"
*"In 1920 both **Harehills** and **Chapeltown** were typical middle-class areas with a good choice of schools, churches and shops of all descriptions. Most homes at this time were well built **Victorian** houses, constructed with a large family in mind, i.e. for families of 4, 6 and even 8 children."*

"What was the Jewish population like in Leeds?"
*"Both **Harehills** and **Chapeltown** were of equal distance from **Leeds City Centre** which was arrived at by old-fashioned tram car. Much nearer the centre of **Leeds** was a district entitled the **Leylands**, which was largely populated mainly by immigrant Jews from **Russia**. This was perhaps the poorest, cheapest area to live in the city of **Leeds** but was only one and a half miles from the City Centre. The **Jewish** people figured prominently in the tailoring trade and were ultimately responsible for making **Leeds** into a clothing manufacturing City. The **Jewish** people at this time aspired to move up to a better class district, away from the **Leylands.** They fulfilled that ambition to a large extent. Consequently, **Chapeltown** had its own Synagogues and a substantial population of **Jewish** people who themselves contributed to making **Leeds** a prosperous City."*

"How did these areas change?"

"After about forty years there was an influx of coloured immigrants into **Chapeltown** *which meant that the* **Jewish** *people again looked to move higher up. Consequently, they then moved up into* **Moortown** *into an even more residential area than* **Chapeltown.***"*

"What did people do with their leisure time?"

"At that time, most families had to work to make a modest living. There was no TV, but radio was being developed and the main source of leisure seemed to be a weekly visit to one of the six Picture Houses and the usual pursuits of reading, the local libraries and walking. There was apparently a change in religious and church life taking place. More people seemed to abandon Church – probably caused by the appalling suffering of the First World War."

"How was Leeds affected by the slump of the 1930s?"

"It wasn't particularly affected by the slump of the **1930s.** *It did not hit* **Leeds** *as badly as other Cities – probably because of lower 'cost efficiencies' particularly in the clothing trade and the wide variety of other industries associated with* **Leeds.** **Leeds** *was not solely dependent upon one industry like engineering. We had several trades.* **Bradford** *was worse hit because of its dependency on wool."*

"How high was the standard of education during your day?"

*"***Cowper Street School** *(which I attended) had about* **60** *to a class. The standard of teaching was high but strict."* (The **Cowper Street School Logbook** and two **Inspector Reports** confirmed this statement.)

"Were you ever caned as a boy?"

"I was canned two or three times."

"Did you ever know of anyone who belonged to the Black Shirts?"

"Shh! I don't want you to write this down! The **'Black Shirts,'** *were led by a demagogue called* **'Sir Oswald Moseley.'** *They were very* **anti-Semitic** *and would hold parades on* **Woodhouse Moor.** *Yes, I knew one man – he was a nice man, but he would always have to be in some kind of fight. It did not matter what the cause was he would have to be against something. He was a very unsettled kind of fellow who found it difficult to hold down a job."* (In a previous conversation, **Fred,** had stated that this individual had been a warehouseman in one of the textile firms **Fred** had worked for in the **1930s.** My father also described him as a storeman, which suggested that he may have been responsible for the release of stock.)

"When did you leave Harehills?"
"We moved to a place in **Roundhay** *when I was* **13** *(in* **1927***). I was going to the* **Grammar School** *then. To quote a few prices of those days - the average wage of a workingman was* **£4.00;** *a loaf of bread would be* **4d** *in old coinage, a dozen eggs* **1s,** *a pound of bacon* **1s 3d,** *a new car would cost* **£300.00.** *It's hard to understand how inflation grew over a long period.* **£1.00** *in those days (in about* **1920***) is now probably* **£20.00** *(in* **1994***). Fees at the* **L.G.S.** *were* **£250.00** *per annum. (When I last enquired, it was* **£2,300.00** *per annum.) If only increased wages would match the increase in the cost of living life would be bearable, but unfortunately, this is not the case and wages have stayed (in lots of cases) well below the cost of inflation."* (At this point my mother broke in and claimed that the average wage around **1930** was only **£1.50.** After some debate, I concluded that the higher figure was for skilled workers in **Leeds**, whilst the **£1.50** was for unskilled labourers in the areas where the great depression had hit hardest.)

"When did Chapeltown and Harehills begin to deteriorate as areas?"
*"***Spencer Place** [a road that runs approximately **North-South** between **Harehills** and **Chapeltown**] *– which was once a highly desirable residential road – deteriorated as a result of prostitutes. They, first of all, bought the properties and then used them for their own trade in the* **1930s.** *They were originally high-class prostitutes."*

"How would you sum up the changes over your lifetime?"
"It's a misleading thing to say the more things change the more they remain the same. Sometimes the change is so dramatic they can't *remain the same. For instance,* **Spencer Place** *is now recognised as a centre of prostitution and has lost its original highly residential status. There are two things to remember here, change is taking place all the time and if the change is for the better then change is very necessary because good comes out of evil. We all live in hope of living in a healthier and happier age than hitherto."*

"Why has the Church declined?"
"I think the Church has been the architect of its own decline. Because the Church claims to represent **Christ,** *and all it has done is to misrepresent Him because it's simply not lived up to the high standards and principles advocated by* **Christ** *Himself. I've always been aware of the danger of being so intoxicated by religion that it affects your better judgement."*

"What do you mean by that?"
"That's a double line under that. I am not going to tell you more tonight. It all started with **Harehills** *and* **Chapeltown** *and now you go onto philosophical ideas. But I think the philosophical side always fits in because you are talking about the environment and the nature of the districts in* **Leeds** *and then you go further onto something else."* (By these words my

father was showing his unwillingness to take the conversation further. He was not keen to philosophise. Our *'informal interview'* finished at this point)

Of interest was the way my father's account so closely mirrored that of **Stowell (1929).** Present was a strong element of mutual confirmation. However, a difference <u>did</u> emerge in their attitude toward the local **Jewish** population. My father and his brother **Stewart** were very happy to socialise with them in a way that would have deeply offended **Stowell's** narrow **anti-Semitic** prejudices.

One curiously interesting story survived from my father's boyhood. When aged about ten he and his brother **Stewart** were curious about where their father attended Church because, at the time, they were being brought up as **Roman Catholics**. (This seemed to be a source of their future prejudice against this religion). Under **Stewart's** instigation, they decided one **Sunday** morning to follow their father to Church. Taking care to keep their distance, they followed their father (who was dressed in his very best suit) for what seemed to be a very long way. Eventually, they saw him enter the Church, but they did not go in because *"they feared a tanning."* Apparently, the Church **Frank** had entered had been **Blenheim Baptist Chapel,** but this detail is rather uncertain. **Stewart** had related this story to his daughter **Pamela** sometime during the **1950s.** It was fascinating because it showed something of the relationship which then existed between the two brothers – with **Stewart** very much being the lead figure.

Section 2: Cowper Street School

Concerning the early education of Fred Smith

To understand the formative influences in my father's boyhood it would be helpful to look at the Headmaster's log for **Cowper Street School.** Records were found from the time of its foundation until my father's departure. All bracketed inserts are the author's own additions and are <u>not</u> part of the original **Cowper Street School** records. The records used here are with the kind permission of **The West Yorkshire Archive Service** which has custody of the originals. This source contains the names of some of the teachers my father knew. In it, **T.C** seems to mean *'Teaching Certificate.'*

THE LOG

27/11/1905:
This new school was opened for instruction at 9 'o' clock this morning and 69 boys and 95 girls were enrolled. The following is a list of the members of the staff with the classes to which they are attached: -
Mr Joseph Lang, Head Master
Mr James W. Shortridge (T.C.) Senior Assistant ST V.
Mr Fred H. Garner (T.C.) ST IV
Mr Herbert E. Chambers (T.C) ST VI
Miss Faith Pickard (C.) ST III
Miss Florence E. Lanele (C.) ST IV
Miss Nellie Ridge (T.C.) ST III

1/12/1905:
Attendance for the first week. The school has been open for the admission of scholars: -

> Number on roll – 77 Boys, 101 Girls – Total 178
> Average – 74.2 Boys, 98.5 Girls – Total 172.7

(Entries before my father's birth are omitted for reasons of space. On **4/8/1914** Britain declared war on **Germany** following her invasion of **Belgium.** This event marked the beginning of British involvement in the First World War.)

1/9/1914:
Mr Thomas Watkins (T.C.) commenced duties here this morning. He completed his training at Leeds City Training College last July.

25/10/1918:
The number on roll 381, average attendance 300.3. *"Today 90 children were absent on account of influenza."*

30/10/1918:
No. on roll 378, average attendance 281.6.

11/11/1918:
In view of the continuation of the influenza epidemic, the school will remain closed until Monday, the 18th November.
N.B: The date 11/11/1918 was Armistice Day – the day hostilities ceased against **Germany.**

18/11/1918:
The school was re-opened at the usual time. Miss Hewson resumed duties this morning.

13/12/1918:
Word has been received that Mr T. J. Watkins, a member of staff, has been killed in battle. He was Regimental Sergeant Major - Sanitary Section, 84 Royal Army Medical Corps.
Attendance of the past week: -
No. on Roll 372, Average Attendance 319
N.B: Mr Watkins' position would suggest that he was a little way behind the front lines at the time of his death. The cause of death would most likely have been due to a shell burst. The list of teachers showed that he had been born on **10/5/1892** and would have been **26** when he died. He had previously lived at **3 Avenue Crescent, Appareinlai? Duffrey Amysch, Mountain Ash, Cardiff, South Wales)**

28/7/1919:
School Bank – Year Results
15758 transactions with a balance of £110-14s-0d due to depositions

9/9/1919:
The school was re-opened this morning at the usual hour. Miss Latimer resumed duties.
N.B: This was a likely date for my father's own first attendance at the school.

12/9/1919:
Attendance for the past week
No. on roll 398, average 345.9
Nature study class arrangements were made for visiting Potternewton Park.
N.B: On the evening of this day **12/9/1919, Adolf Hitler** would attend a meeting of **The German Workers' Party** – thus commencing his political career.

13/10/1919:
It has been decided that classes of scholars may be taken to recreation grounds or open spaces to play football or other organized games at 2.45 o'clock on one afternoon each week.

12/12/1919:
School Concerts will be held this evening commencing at 6 'o' clock. Each class is responsible for at least one item – only scholars admitted. Admission 3d – proceeds to be devoted to the school library, sports etc.

22/1/1920:
26 University students led by Mr Wepton? The *'master of method'* spent the afternoon here in observation work.

31/3/1920:
Close of financial year:
Total Attendances for the year	134,984
Number of Openings	409
Average Attendance	330
Names on roll	369

1/4/1920:
Mr Joseph Lang (T.C) – Head Teacher
Mr Fred H. Garner (T.C) VI Boys
Mr Arthur Joy (T.C) V Boys
Miss Kate Elizabeth Hewson (T.C) IV Girls
Miss Elsie A. E. Fleming (T.C) VII Mixed
Miss Laura C. McGregor (T.C) IV Boys
Miss Minnie Beevers (T.C) V0 Mixed
Miss Faith Elizabeth Pickard (C) V Girls
Miss Emily J. Latimer (C) VI Girls
N.B: Fred would most likely have been in **Miss Beevers'** class.

12/4/1920:
Medical inspection, about 150 children will be examined – also there will be 50 re-inspections.

4/5/1920:
200 children accompanied by teachers visit the museum, subject *"the life of the plant"* – illustrated by lantern slides and cinema films.

10/5/1920:
Swimming instructions will commence today.

20/1/1922:

Attendance for the past week:
The number on roll 387. Average 326.3
The low average is due to the severe weather experienced recently. Many children suffering from colds and coughs.

23/1/1922:

Two female teachers absent, one with severe cold and cough - the other with an eye infection.

7/7/1922:

The university students complete their teaching practice this afternoon.

27/7/1920:

Mrs M. C. Crowther (T.C) being married, has been asked by the Education Committee to resign her appointment, terminating 28th August.
Attendance for the past week No. on roll 360 Average 320.2

2/10/1922:

All Jewish children are absent from school today. It is the Day of Atonement.

11/9/1923:

Jewish Holidays – Sept 11th, 12th, 20th, 25th 26th October 2nd, 3rd and December 3rd. Jewish boys will be absent from school on all these occasions. The attendance will be considerably affected, as there are 108 Jews on the roll.
N.B: The total number of pupils on the roll for that year was **404.**

7/2/1924:

Mr Lang (H.T.) is absent from school duties this morning from a severe cold.
N.B: He returned to duties on **11/2/1924.**

9/2/1926:

Mr Lang has delegated to Messrs. Joy, Hunter and Dunning and Misses Crossfield and Beevers to administer corporal punishment within the regulations of the Leeds Education Committee.

29/3/1926:

The Jewish Passover commences this evening. All Jewish boys will, therefore, be absent from school for the two following days.

31/3/1926:
Teachers employed in this department on 31/3/1926
Mr Joseph Lang (T.C.) – Head Teacher
Mr Arthur Joy (T.C.) Va Boys
Mr Henry F. M. Hunter (T.C.) VI
Mr Alfred Dunning (T.C) VII + VIII
Mr Arthur Gibson (T.C.) VIb
Miss Laura C. MacGregor (T.C.) III
Miss Faith E. Pickard (C.) IVa
Miss Marjory Crossfield (T.C.) II
Miss Minnie Beevers (T.C.) IVb
Miss Doris N. Moore (T.C.) 1
N.B: Fred would most likely have been in **Alfred Dunning's** class. A careful scan of relevant lists produced no evidence of my father ever having won any school prizes during his time at **Cowper Street School.**

A Summary of the Board of Education's Inspector's Report on 8th June 1923 – by Mr P. L. Gray

Cowper Street School:
1. Was *"thoroughly sound and efficient."*
2. Was attended by boys of an *"emphatically superior social class."*
3. Had many boys who left to attend Secondary Schools
4. Found that *"parents showed much interest in the school and supported the teachers."*
5. Enjoyed high-quality staff where *"the Head Teacher obtains loyal help from well-qualified staff ~ with excellent relations with the boys."*
6. Displayed a growing tendency to use literature.
7. Obtained excellent results in reading, recitation and drama.
8. Ensured that *"Arithmetic is well taught."*
9. Made sure that *"PE is very well done."*
10. Gave *"effective teaching, evident in singing and playing."*
11. Caused the older boys to attend *"the practical instruction centre – where the work is sound and educational."*

N.B: The absence of girls in this report was telling – they were evidently viewed as being less important than boys.

A Summary of the Board of Education's Inspector's Report on 4th February 1927 – by Mr P. L. Gray

514

This report repeated most of the points made in its predecessor, but also added that:

1. *"The school is situated in a 'well to do' residential district."*
2. *"A pleasant tone of quiet discipline pervaded the school."*
3. The Head Teacher's schemes of work *"are very carefully prepared with helpful summaries posted in the staff room. They provide a unity of aim."*
4. Progress was being made in natural science.
5. Speech-making was aided by excellent dramatic exercises.

N.B: Although a modern inspection report produced by OFSTED would not use the (now politically incorrect) term *"emphatically superior Social Class,"* many other phrases such as *"thoroughly sound and efficient"* would still be used. These reports appear to possess a certain timeless quality about them.

The historical sources used in relation to **Cowper Street School** were very informative. They played a vital part in reconstructing my own father's childhood. In addition, they confirmed that **Fred** enjoyed: -

1) An excellent education at a very good school, which engaged in many lively activities
2) A close association with the Leeds Jewish Community from **a very early age**
3) A relatively privileged middle-class background

Perhaps the main threat facing my father at this early stage in his life had been the Influenza Pandemic. This event could easily have shortened his life by **81** years.

N.B: The mention of a teacher who'd been *'killed in action'* at the age of 26 was particularly moving.

Section 3: A Crushing Disappointment

Concerning Leeds Grammar School during the interwar period

Prior to my father's attendance, **Leeds Grammar School (LGS)** had moved on (both academically and numerically) from what it had been in **Frank's** day. **The Rev. Canon Wynne-Edwards,** (headmaster from **1902** until **1922**) had equipped the school with new science laboratories, thus preparing it to engage in the twentieth century. Page six of the **Tuesday, 19th September 1922** issue of **The Yorkshire Post** announced his retirement to a country living. This source revealed that the number of pupils had increased from **168** to about **600** during his incumbency. The picture is one of a highly successful tenure by. Tragically, it had fallen upon his shoulders to take the school through the carnage of the **1914-18** war when **126** former pupils had given their lives *"for king* *and country."* A retirement photo (taken in **1922**) showed a round-faced gentleman with a large grey walrus moustache. The masters ranked around him were in gowns but, despite its formality, they were smiling and seemed relaxed. It appeared that this headmaster had been a well-liked man. Perhaps a common tragedy had established a certain bond of affection. In his later years, **Wynne-Edwards** had been known to have given the teaching staff a large amount of leeway. His far stricter successor **Dr Terry Thomas** may well have found it difficult to challenge this cosiness – but nevertheless, he did so with a determined ruthlessness that did not make him popular with the staff fraternity. One story had it that he'd endured a terrible time whilst fighting in the trenches on the Western Front. An old photograph revealed a determined man with a domed forehead and piercing ice-cold eyes. One source stated he later became a much-feared magistrate. He took up his appointment at the school in **1923.**

Some of the pitfalls awaiting the new headmaster **(Terry Thomas)** were described by one **Jewish** ex-pupil, (aged **91** in **1999**) who was to become my father's future accountant. Named **Joshua Barrett** this gentleman had first attended the LGS in **1920** and was to remain there until leaving to study higher education in the early **1930s.** When first interviewed on **Friday, 16th July 1999** he disclosed that: -
*"When **Terry Thomas** came he formerly had been 'Master of the Military' at **Halibury College.** He had military precision. He was a wonderful organiser. I was the first **Jewish** Prefect at the time. He introduced white lines along the length of the corridors to control the movement of pupils. I used to stand at the school entrance to control the movement of the boys. In addition, he introduced the school roll; here was every boy in the school. Every boy had a number. He had everybody taped. Most people feared him. The staff, in general, tended to be suspicious of him. **Terry Thomas** was not an academic although he had taught maths. They would make snide remarks about him because they did not view him as an academic. I found him to be extremely fair although he would say things quite tough to you. He took an interest in 'the first fifteen' rugby team. Rumours went around the **Jewish Community** that he was an anti-Semite. To me, this was a wrong judgement. He'd never met any **Jewish** boys until he came to **Leeds.***

*Other people in the **Jewish Community** thought I used to go to the school on a Saturday because I was a scholarship boy. I used to go down to his study and he would ask 'how would so and so leave (Saturday Morning School) and still be playing on the school ground?' They were getting time off and fooling around in the playground. His puzzlement gave him the reputation for being **anti-Semitic**. He asked a **Jewish** pupil "how one boy did not attend school on **Saturday** morning but could still play in the first fifteen on **Saturday** afternoon?" He was absolutely baffled. In asking these questions he gave the impression of being **anti-**

516

Semitic when what he was really doing was trying to learn. He introduced detention on a Saturday afternoon, but one Jewish boy said that he was not allowed to write on Saturday. Terry Thomas asked, "Why should he be allowed to upset the whole routine of the school?" To me, he was wondering what was going on.

There was not much anti-Semitism at Leeds Grammar School, (L.G.S.). There were (during the 1920s) 40 Jewish boys (out of a total of several hundred). The school was very good. When pupils used to go to the upper school for prayers Terry Thomas and the Rev. Dr Billam gave the Jewish boys a form room. I was in charge of them. They were given something to do to prevent them from wandering around the corridors. We would sit around and chat. Some of them were noisy and I would tell them to keep quiet."

In the second interview (on **Wednesday 15th September 1999**) Joshua Barrett also divulged *"I was in the 'First Fifteen' Rugby Team from 1924 until 1928. Your father used to watch me – he was my biggest fan. Fred used to say that I was the most popular lad in the school."*

A further account of this institution (the LGS) which my Father attended as a day scholar (from **13th September 1927 to 25th July 1930**) was provided by an older contemporary (who preferred to remain anonymous.) He had attended the school from **1922** until **1933** before going on to **Oxford** to study **Maths**). The following details were provided over the telephone (on **Thursday 16 September 1999**):

"From about 1926 the L.G.S. was divided into an 'upper stream' – geared for getting people into Oxbridge Matriculation; A 'middle stream,' for getting people a job with a school certificate and a 'lower stream' for those academically less able. The school had damned good masters although one or two I would have shot at birth. Terry Thomas was pretty stern and dare I say it ambitious. He tried to use the L.G.S. as a 'step-up' to getting a Public-School Headmastership, but in that, he was disappointed. He did a good job in pulling the L.G.S. away from being a Victorian School and into the twentieth century. The standard of teaching was excellent – 90% of the teachers were damned good! There was no bullying. I only remember one incident where a pair of loutish sixth formers pushed us children through a revolving door. Prefects put a stop to it immediately. There were 40 to 50 Jewish pupils who stayed in the gym whilst prayers were being said. They tended to be very brainy or were sons of rich parents. Only one went to Oxbridge – most tend to go into the family business. They had no need for education; they had their own empires. The Jewish boys did not tend to be very athletic. They kept themselves to themselves. One of the things I liked about the L.G.S was that there was damned little sectarianism. Other schools were appallingly run with bad masters. I would rank it very high. It was on the fringes of a Public School. We used to play

them at Rugby. But running a day school was different from running a residential Public School. In those days, Grammar Schools tried to compete with the Public Schools. Terry Thomas allowed the boys to dance with the girls. This was unheard of in the 1920s. At that time, there were 600 pupils. That should be the maximum size; otherwise, the school ceases to be like an extended family and becomes a business. The L.G.S. got too damned big. It was always on the fringe of Residential Public Schools."

These details were of interest because they complemented those given by **Joshua Barrett**. They also dovetailed with certain comments made by **Fred** himself. A coherent impression of life at the **L.G.S.** in the **1920s** did begin to emerge.

One further source of information was the **Leodensian Magazine** of **December 1927**. It contained information which helped me to discover some of the activities of **Bernard Gillinson,** the son of **Fred's** future boss **Joe Gillinson.** His active participation in *'the Literary and Debating Society'* was recorded on **pp.142-144.** *"On December 5th B. G. Gillinson proposed the motion that 'this house is afraid of ghosts' with fear in his voice and though he extended a challenge to the opposition to continue in the dark was obviously relieved when the lights were switched on at the president's request. (Perhaps he was afraid that the proposer would slink off in the dark.) Motion carried by eleven votes to ten."* It had been *'seconded'* by a certain **P. H. Kelsey** (who was to become Deputy Headmaster of the school during my own time as a pupil there from **September 1965** until **July 1975**).

On **p.76** of the **May 1928 issue** of the **Leodensian,** the dauntless **Bernard** featured again in the following notice concerning certain characters in the *'Literary and Debating Society.'* *"B. G. Gillinson is another keen supporter of the society who may be relied upon to have his own opinion on any subject and to express it in vigorous and intelligent language. Perhaps his eloquence would be improved, however, if it owed as much to art as it did to natural pugnacity of temperament. Of his political views, we say nothing."* I seem to recall my father echoing similar sentiments when he used to work for **Bernard,** only the language employed by **Fred** was a little less flowery and more to the point. Usually after a bad day at work **Fred's** language was more one of rueful regret than of anger. With hindsight, I believe that **Fred** perhaps *'bottled up'* his business worries too much for his own good. (**Bernard,** by the way, became a devoted supporter of the **Labour** Party and used to entertain its more senior members at his large house in **North Leeds.** Some of these members were reputed to be of ministerial rank – the name of a former Chancellor, **Dennis Healey,** being mentioned.)

On a far less frivolous note, **pp.110-113** of the same magazine also revealed a school still very much scarred by the memories of World War One. This was shown in the details about the opening ceremony for the School Baths and for the War Memorial positioned on the back wall of the Baths. It took place on the annual speech day, one of the high points on the school calendar. Unless illness intervened, my father would almost invariably have attended, as to miss speech day was a serious offence. His reaction would have been one of boredom as such occasions were guaranteed to try the patience of any schoolboy. Perhaps (as in my day) a few stink bombs would have been let off by way of forlorn protest. However, it's highly unlikely that **Fred** would have had the impertinence to have committed such a misdemeanour. **Viscount Lascelles,** Lord-Lieutenant of the **West Riding,** gave the speech on **May 21st, 1928.** Much of it amounted to a rather tedious defence of **Latin** teaching – a lost cause if ever there was one. *"The teaching of **Latin** he* [Lascelles] *considered far from reactionary, even though the boys might think it was. He was convinced that the learning of **Latin Grammar** was the only true and sound foundation for anyone who wished to think and speak well in any language in afterlife."* **Lascelles** ended by mentioning the need *"to perpetuate the memory of the old boys of the School who fell in the Great War. No matter how remote the war might seem to boys of today, they must never regard it lightly. A great lesson could be learnt from it."* His speech had historical interest because it revealed the current attitudes then governing the more elite sections of **English** education. Of more obvious interest was the photograph of a gowned **Terry Thomas** and (mainly ecclesiastical) dignitaries wearing top hats standing behind him. One of them was **Alderman Ratcliffe** the then Lord Mayor, wearing the gold chain of his office. Incidentally, **Fred** told me how a shrapnel wound (inflicted whilst in the trenches) had left one of his masters with a terrible scar running right down the side of his face. Another was supposed to have limped because he'd lost his leg in the war. Some of the masters themselves were living memorials to that conflict.

A still more poignant note was struck on **p.106** of the **June 1930** edition of the **Leodensian Magazine.** It contained an account of the first rugby team tour of **Germany.** In their spare time, they had managed to visit **Cologne Cathedral, Frankfurt, Heidelberg** and an assortment of Castles. Their performance on the playing field had attracted favourable notices in the local **German** newspapers. A **Leodensian** report stated that this sporting gathering *"was a cosmopolitan one, for not only were **Germany** and **Great Britain** represented, but also **Norway** and **Russia** and overall these reigned an atmosphere of perfect happiness and commonality."* Within just over a decade many of these protagonists would meet again but this time it would be on the battlefield rather than the playing field.

Also, by then, many of the sights viewed by The First Fifteen Team would lie in smouldering ruins. Perhaps it was best that all concerned were oblivious to what was to lie ahead.

My own father did not make a sufficient impact on the wider life of the school to merit any mention in this magazine. However, it was known that he loved attending some of the school's camps. Whilst there he would have worn long boy-scout shorts, slept in a bell tent and participated in gruelling walks in either the **Lake District** or **North Yorkshire.** He would also have joined in the meal queues and the nightly songs. It's easy to imagine him laughing at the public-school humour displayed in *'The Masters' Song'* where the teachers had to give a rendition for the boys. From that time, he developed a deep love for country outings. That love, along with an abiding interest in the school itself, was to remain with him for the rest of his life.

Less happily, the greatest disappointment in **Fred's** life took place at the **L.G.S.** From records kindly provided by that institution it was evident that my father's academic performance was modest. For the years in which he attended his form positions were **9th, 20th** and **16th** respectively. (These were out of a total of **32, 23** and **19** pupils.) By his last year, he was in the *'remove form'*, which was the lowest band of attainment. At that time, this meant that a pupil was unlikely to advance any further. However, like **Frank,** my father did excel in *'the three R's of Reading, Writing and Arithmetic.'* Regarding myself, my own untidy writing was a continual source of despair to him. The legacy of his **Grammar School** experience was to leave **Fred** with a tendency to markedly underestimate his own abilities. On a happier note, his (then future) accountant stated that my father had often actively involved himself in a range of sports, including rugby and cricket. When first interviewed (on **Friday, 16th July 1999**) this same man had remarked how **Fred** *"used to throw himself into everything."* However, finding it difficult to keep up with the educational requirements of the time he was (along with his mother) ushered into the Headmaster's study. There he was told that a difficulty in paying fees (due to the impact of the depression) coupled with his lack of academic performance meant that there was longer a future for him at the school. This must have been a crushing blow to someone who was perhaps already beginning to lose his self-confidence. It's easy to imagine that, if a pupil was not **Oxbridge** material, **Dr Terry Thomas'** interest in that pupil's educational progress would abruptly cease. He was well known to have had a cold, ruthless streak about him.

The long-term effect of **Fred's** great scholarly disappointment was that he very much wished his children to finish the education that he had never completed. Present was a *'compensation mechanism'* in which he tried to fulfil his thwarted aspirations through his own children. In **June 1998** (even though his health was failing) he still drew pleasure from the news that I had obtained postgraduate qualified teacher **(PGCE)** status at **Leeds University.** Almost daily I had prayed for him to live to see me gain that qualification. Earlier in his life, in **1967,** he had also been delighted when my brother had gained a **2.1 *'Hons,'* Economics** degree at **Trinity College, Cambridge** My brother had first gone up to **Cambridge** in **October 1964.** Whilst attending his graduation ceremony in **1967** two ex-public-school boys were overheard to have engaged in the following conversation: -
"What degree did you get?"
"A third."
"Oh, that's a gentleman's degree."

My father's reaction to such banality would not have been the least bit favourable; he never did like the *'ruling establishment'* of this country.

Section 4: At Rock Bottom

Concerning the effects of the Great Depression in Leeds

With aspirations for academic advancement crushed my father was, at the age of **16,** reduced to packing parcels and sweeping the floors of a warehouse for about **ten shillings** a week. This was a Clothing Wholesaler named **Wilkinson and Warburton, Leeds**. A pay rise to **ten shillings** and **sixpence** was viewed as being generous. The conditions were said to be *"Dickensian."* Placed under the heading of *"costume makers"* this firm had premises in **46-54 West Street** and **43-53 New Street, Leeds.** It also had a branch in **Manchester.** The *'West Street'* premises appear to have been the scene of my Father's sufferings as it handled the *'despatch'* of goods. Hardly surprisingly, **Fred** was so unhappy there that after six months of drudgery amidst uncongenial *'rough'* company, **Frank** requested a job for him through the good offices of **Joseph Gillinson. Fred** duly became a warehouseman (in early **1931**) at *'Gillinson and Dewhurst.'* Such an action strongly lends weight to the supposition that *'Joe'* **Gillinson** regarded **Frank** with a considerable degree of respect and perhaps even friendship. As was stated earlier, **Joe** had a reputation for not suffering fools gladly in any walk of life. If he had regarded either **Frank** or **Fred** as falling into that category, he would not have complied with that request – least of all at the height of the great depression! My father's former accountant divulged that **Joe Gillinson** *"was a very good psychologist. Before taking anyone on he would ask 'what would be his long-term contribution to the business?' He ran his affairs by intuition and never took things at face value."* Somewhat vaguely, the record provided by **L.G.S.** simply stated that **Fred's** *'occupation taken up after leaving' was in the 'wholesale trade.'* It would obviously not help the image of the school to admit that one of its pupils had been reduced to such a menial occupation. After all, **Wilkinson and Warburton** were hardly **Oxford** or **Cambridge!** Together, these events dealt a shattering blow to my father's confidence which, in some ways, never completely recovered – at least in the intellectual area. Yet the fact remains that, in the chill winds of the **1930s** depression, he was lucky enough to have been offered even a modest position. Around this time, he used to go out on *'commercial runs'* with his father even though much of it *'was dead.'* It seemed that **Frank** was trying to give some practical help to a thoroughly depressed son. However, **Fred's** real helper in the business area was **Joe Gillinson** himself. His first words to my father (when he worked as a textiles representative) were, *"**Fred**, I do not want to hear from you why you can't sell. I want to hear the reasons why you can sell some cloth to a reluctant customer whose first word is 'no.'"* Nagged and goaded by **Joe's** pushy demands, **Fred**, in the end, learnt that he could at least sell. In later years, with his former boss evidently in mind, he would often observe that *"**Jewish** people expect you to work very hard for them. But if you do make friends with them they are friends for life."* In a way, **Joseph Gillinson** had been an unexpected saviour to my father at a crucial phase in his life. So how did **Joe Gillinson,** this business maestro, survive the great depression? The answer will take a whole paragraph to explain.

Trade Directories for **1932** showed that **Joseph Gillinson** was the *'Managing Director'* of a Limited Company called *"**J Gillinson, Gibbon and Demaine Ltd, Wholesale Drapers, 1 New York Street, Leeds.'** He resided in the more affluent* *"'Roeburn Moor,' Allerton Gardens, Harrogate Road, Moortown."*

Amidst a major economic crash, **Joseph Gillinson** had not only survived – when many other firms in his industry had failed – he had also radically improved his position. This could be seen in his affording to purchase a better house. He also successfully discharged a leadership position, requiring rather different skills from those needed to run a couple of drapery stores – as he had done previously. (As a qualified teacher in **Business Studies** I can only admire his virtuoso performance in this area.) The question remains *'how he had managed to prosper amidst the greatest economic disaster in modern history?'* The most likely answer was that he followed a ruthless strategy of cost cutting, acquisition and merger to achieve *'economies of scale'* (the reduction in costs and other benefits that can occur as an organisation expands and gets larger). Any business contacts would have been thoroughly exploited with pronounced effect. The man must have had nerves of iron to have done all of this. Undeniably, **Joseph Gillinson** kept his head at a time when many in the business world were losing theirs. No wonder he became something of a legend. Yet amidst all this frantic battle for survival, he respected **Frank** enough to have taken on what probably looked like an unpromising younger son, whose talent for selling had been completely overlooked by a rival firm. *'Old **Joe**'* was certainly willing to take a risk if he judged the odds to be sufficiently in his favour. For his part, **Frank** must have been very good in his line of work to have even gained a hearing from this man. My guess is that **Joseph Gillinson** saw in **Fred** a potential that no one else had noticed. **Joe's** track record and proven ability in crisis management reveal a man who was a very shrewd judge of character. After several decades, one can still respect his entrepreneurial skills and abilities. He would have had little to go on but *'gut instinct'* and an ability to see opportunities where others saw disaster. Although not exactly generous with his wages, **Joseph Gillinson** did adopt a paternalistic style of management, which appears to have gained staff loyalty. From an early stage, there were Company *'outings'* where there were plenty of games and alcoholic refreshments. **Joe Gillinson** seems to have regarded his employees as something of an extended family.

Eventually, **Joe** was to have a warm respect for **Fred** himself – he liked hard workers – especially those who produced satisfactory results. **Fred** was to produce them in abundance. His more refined **Oxford**-educated son, **Bernard,** was also to inherit the same respect (for **Fred**) when the time came for him to take over the Firm. From a variety of sources, it seemed that **Joe Gillinson,** this self-made man, had been somewhat scathing of his son's *'high status'* education. He was reputed to have said to him *"Humph! The only thing **Oxford** ever taught you was how to drink!"* Surviving evidence would suggest that **Bernard** was one of those men who was always having to prove his worth before an over-exacting father. He too seems to have had a problem with his own self-confidence. One can only wonder whether **Joe** was secretly jealous of his son's academic and social connections. It's easy to imagine **Joe** thinking *'Now if only I had been given those same chances!'* One is left wondering what else **Joe** will have wished to achieve with his life.

A phone conversation with my late father's accountant **Joshua Barrett** (on **Thursday, June 6th, 2002**) revealed further details about **Joseph Gillinson**. It transpired that his father knew **Joe Gillinson** *"when he was starting out on his own.*

He expanded from running a warehouse when he took over **Fosters in Briggate.**" The accountant's father, (who would have known **Joe** in the pre-**1914** period) had also stated that *"***Joseph Gillinson** *was very, very straight. He had strong principles and belonged to the old school, a conservative type of businessman. He was honest and trustworthy. He would go steadily along, surviving all obstacles."*

The accountant knew **Joe** during the late **1920s** and early **1930s** whilst a student at **Leeds University.** At that time, **Joe** was President of **Saint Louis Street Synagogue** on **Byron Street** in **Leeds 7.** (Founded in **1891** or **1893** it closed in **1974**) In that capacity *"He used to let rooms to a student group called the 'thirteen' of which I was a member. It consisted of twelve to thirteen men. We had talks on* **Bernard Shaw's** *'Man and Superman,' the latest theories on* **Psychology** *and a detailed (page by page) study on the* **British Mandate.**" He also confirmed that **Joe Gillinson** *"took part in almost everything communal. (He belonged to the* **Orthodox,** *not the* **Reform** *community.)"* This included Presidency of the **Bnai-Brith** *"a religious Masonic Lodge"* and a role on **Leeds Jewish Representative Council**, which was a voluntary organisation. His son **Bernard** was also a **Free Mason** and *"had a brilliant intellect but was a bit of a socialite. He was very much in the shadow of his father."* (The accountant himself was never a Mason. Indeed, he expressed the robust view that the organisation *"was for careerists who wanted to parade their charity. One didn't need to join it to be charitable. Many did though. I was a lone ranger on that one."*)

At the end of what was, in many ways, a marvellous phone conversation the accountant made some pertinent observations about the present world. After referring both to my father and himself, he stated that he *"was pleased to see that I have achieved something of lasting spiritual and cultural value, which cannot be measured in financial terms. It is the best epitaph for* **Fred** *and me. We have been used to building up a tradition, which had been a dirty word among politicians. It has given me pleasure to see this development. All moral foundations have been destroyed and people are looking for what's missing. Business is all about profit these days. It has been encouraging to see that there is still an interest in the old-fashioned approach. I have been amused to see that people who have been greedy for money have lost it through* **Enron** *and* **Equitable Life.** *The world of lawyers who were too clever by half has come crashing down. Now I am only a bystander, but your father would smile at the irony of it all. We used to be a pair of moaners, never quite fitting into the commercial world of greed."* (He also added the following joke, which had been recounted to him by a businessman in **Bradford** during the Great Depression. *"Even the people who never pay have stopped buying!"* (Apparently, it was quite a common joke at the time.)

Section 5: An Active Social Life

Concerning an encounter with Anti-Semitism

Photographs of my father (taken in **1932**) show a strong resemblance to the young **King George VI.** The smartly parted hairstyles of the two men were identical. By then it was also evident that my father was a very neat dresser with a taste in sports jackets and wide ties that seemed to follow the fashions set in **America.** He obviously took a pride in his appearance. This showed that he belonged unmistakably to the middle classes. In none of the surviving photographs of family members were there any top hats at one end of the social scale or cloth caps at the other.

Before the Second World War **Fred's** favourite leisure pastimes had been rugby and drives in the country. From the rugby, he gained a broken nose and a damaged left knee that in later life would contribute to his osteoarthritis. (However, there may have been a genetic element because [in **July 2013**] my left knee began to suffer from this very painful condition and two of my children also endure a milder version of it.) He also used to attend *'The Institute'* at **Blenheim Baptist church** (which formed part of this Church's premises). An old Church member (whom I spoke to on the evening of **Sunday 19 September 1999**) revealed that *'The Institute'* had been founded in **1934.** It was located on the lower floor, (the upper was rented out to a local government department) and was a young person's social centre, complete with three billiard and table-tennis tables and other such amenities. A black and white photo of my father, taken in his twenties shows a thin, rather shy young man. He is standing beside his brother **Stewart** who is sporting a *'Clark Gable'* moustache. **Stewart** and who was always ready to *'cut a dash'* with the young ladies. Another photo of **Stewart** (taken in about **1931**) showed him sitting on a pebbly beach wearing a baggy set of *'plus four'* trousers. He died in **May 1962** aged **50** from the effects of high blood pressure. I have only dim memories of him as a large hearty black-suited **1950s** figure. By then my father too had *'filled out.'* In **1964,** his weight at sixteen stone had become such a problem that he suffered a severe attack of angina (which was to reoccur in my presence in **November 1970).** I remember that, on seaside weighing scales, he would weigh up to about **16** stones even though he was only about six feet in height. To his somewhat grumpy mortification, he had to cut back on his vast food intake. He also gave up smoking at about the same time. In his late seventies, he was to look far healthier than he had done in his early fifties. By then he had also obtained a certain degree of serenity that had not been fully present in his earlier years.

During the **1930s, Fred** learnt to socialise with a wide range of people; *i.e.*
Roman Catholics, Protestants and **Jews.** They both realized that *'networking'*
was the way to get ahead in business. Amongst his early **Jewish** associates were
two brothers, **Bernard** and **Jack Lyons.** Both my father's former **Jewish**
Accountant **Joshua Barrett** and my cousin **Pamela** concurred that in their
friendship with the **Jewish** Community both **Stewart** and **Fred** *"were way ahead
of their time."* They shared similar values and were extremely **Philo-Semitic.** Like
their **Jewish** contemporaries, they wanted to *'work their way up'* in the world.

On one occasion, this friendship brought **Stewart** into direct conflict with the
management of **The Mansion House Hotel** that overlooked **Roundhay Park**
in **North Leeds.** Along with another **Jewish** friend **Henry Hyams** (who later
became a solicitor), he entered the premises with a view to attending a Saturday
Evening Dinner Dance. (It's easy to imagine **Stewart** smartly attired in a formal
evening suit.) The entrance fee was five shillings. When **Stewart** had paid his
entrance fee admission was refused to his friend because *'no **Jews** were allowed.'*
Stewart responded by saying, *"If his five Bob isn't good enough, neither is mine. I'll have
my money back and we'll go elsewhere."* The two men then strode out. This incident
happened before **Stewart** met **Edith** and can be dated to the period of **1933-36**
when **Hitler** was chancellor of **Germany.** This *'lovely story'* was relayed to **Pam**
by an old **Jewish** friend of her father shortly after his death. Apparently, he'd
witnessed this confrontation and had strongly admired **Stewart's** stand.

An old (and now deceased) friend of my mother's whom I met (at my sister's
house on **Easter Sunday, 27ᵗʰ March 2005**) provided further testimony to the
prevalence of **anti-Semitism** in pre-war **Leeds.** As a young girl of sixteen this
lady had moved into **Leeds** from the country, just before the outbreak of war in
September 1939. She testified how *"I'd never seen anything like it. When a **Jewish**
man was near the head of a bus queue local people would mutter, 'B- **Jew** – always having to
be the first by pushing their way ahead of everyone else."* She also recorded how her own
father had walked out of a cinema when the first pictures of the concentration
camps were shown in **1945.** This lady had been born in the same year as my
mother **(1923)** and had felt it important that this sort of information should be
passed on. In **Leeds,** the term *'to be Jewed'* meant *'to be swindled.'* A detailed
account of the of **English-based anti-Semitism** of this period can be found in
chapters four and six of **Julius (2010).** It doesn't make light reading!

A computer-enhanced photograph (taken in a suburban garden during the
summer of **1936**) revealed much about **Smith** family relationships at the time.

On the right, sitting on the grass was my father wearing a sports jacket and wide spotted tie. He was evidently enjoying an animated conversation with his father **Frank** who was himself seated in a deckchair and wearing a white suit. **Frank's** snow-white hair gave him a very distinguished appearance but at only **67** he looked some fifteen years older. Since the photograph of **1931,** he had become an old man, with a considerable loss of weight. Yet he clearly beamed with pleasure, looking at **Fred** with a fond smile of regard. The body language between **Fred** and **Frank** was very relaxed – they were obviously the best of friends. One senses that **Frank's** closest family relationships were with his sons. Kneeling at the centre in a plain darkish dress and looking toward the right, away from the men, was **Rosamund.** Her hairstyle very much belonged to the **1930s** with a parting down the middle. Fixed on her face was a false toothy smile, evidently trying to convey the impression that all was *'sweetness and light.'* Eyes half closed, her glance swept upward toward **Elizabeth** who was staring straight into the camera. **Elizabeth's** hands were tightly clasped together as she leaned forward (wearing a floral summer dress) her expression the most disturbing of all. Beneath slightly dishevelled and curly greying hair were some beady eyes which seemed to radiate a mixture of cunning, disappointment and quietly seething anger. The woman was obviously not at ease with herself. (This too is indicated in another photograph taken in about **1937** which revealed a slight stoop, so ill health may well have been a problem.) Seated on the far left (with a look of bored detachment) was **Rosamund's** son **Malcolm,** then aged about eleven. Wearing a bright blazer and shorts, he obviously wanted the photo to be taken as quickly as possible. His straight black hair seemed to have been combed into a neat parting to give a good impression. **Rosamund's** husband **Jack** was the person most likely to have taken the picture.

Section 6: Marrying Beneath Himself

Concerning the relationship between Stewart Smith and Edith Bratton

The late **1930s** appear to have been clouded by a great deal of family tension between **Stewart** and his parents. They had been very keen for their favourite son to marry a well-bred county lady. Apparently, they'd favoured a match between him and a certain **Doris Heslop** (who came from a long established *'county'* family). However, **Stewart** had other things in mind. To the mortification of his parents, he broke off from **Doris** and started *'walking out'* with a very attractive blonde young lady called **Edith Bratton** whose father was only a humble police sergeant with a small holding. They had grand expectations for their favourite son and felt that he had thrown his life away on a *'common'* woman who had entrapped him. **Frank** and his wife **Elizabeth** were most displeased at this turn of events. When **Edith** had first been introduced to them **Frank** had pointedly made cups of coffee for **Elizabeth** and **Stewart** but <u>not</u> for **Edith.** Infuriated by this snub **Stewart** had passed his cup of coffee to **Edith** and stormed into the kitchen exclaiming, *"Well I shall go and make my own!"* **Elizabeth** would regularly make loud her view that her once favourite son was throwing himself away on that *"common woman."* This development must have troubled **Fred** as he always used to be close to **Stewart** and in old age would recall the happy times they had had together, going on *'drives in the country.'* **The Yorkshire Dales** was one of their favourite haunts. I could imagine them drinking happily at many a country pub and perhaps sharing troubles with each other.

Sadly, matters did not improve after that first introduction in about **1938**. To escape the disapproval of his parents **Stewart** and **Edith** moved to **Blackpool.** For a year, there was no contact between the estranged parties. **Edith** gave birth to a daughter, **Pamela,** which was registered in **Mansfield** during the last quarter of **1938**. When **Pamela** was still a small baby who should arrive unexpectedly in a car but my father (who was driving) and his parents. Caught unprepared **Stewart** had initially been unwilling to allow them into the house. However, after prolonged discussion at the door, **Fred** managed to persuade him to change his mind whilst his parents waited anxiously in the car. Even then, a still belligerent **Stewart** warned that if they caused any trouble, his parents would be asked to leave. Apparently, **Elizabeth's** response had been, *"I know son, I know son. I only want to see my new Granddaughter."* **Elizabeth** had then taken the granddaughter concerned in her pram for a walk along **Blackpool** promenade. This incident can be dated to late **1938** (or very early **1939**) when the growing physical frailty of **Frank** and the nearness of war were highlighting the need for reconciliation. Family members noted how **Fred** (in later years) would sometimes remark that **Edith** had *"always got a very raw deal from the rest of the family."* He genuinely felt that she had received unfair treatment from his parents <u>and</u> some of his sisters too – most notably **Rosamund.** I just about remember **Edith** as a rather nervous, diffident woman who had a rather hesitant way of speaking. As for my father, he little realised that his visit to **Blackpool** that day was to mark the beginning of a sixty-year vocation as the family *'peacemaker.'* He was still following it days before his own death. It's a role that now appears to have been inherited by my eldest son! **Fred's** mother had consistently resented **Edith** for *'entrapping'* her favourite son into a marriage which she'd perceived as being beneath his social status. In her eyes, **Edith** would never be good enough for him. But as my father often noted that when it comes to marriage and sexual intimacy *'it takes two to tango.'*

Official records suggested **Stewart** didn't marry **Edith** until **September 1942** when the **Germans** were threatening the **Suez Canal** where he was then based. Presumably, he'd wanted her to obtain a war widow's pension should he be killed in combat. That way he could provide for his wife and daughter of whom he was genuinely fond. However, during a telephone conversation on **Sunday, 18th December 2016,** this version of events was challenged by his daughter (my first cousin). Already aware of these records, she was quite adamant that her father had married **Edith** within a few months of her birth. It would be easy to dismiss this claim except this lady has consistently been an exceptionally reliable source of information. It was her lead that got me to **Edmund's** monument and made this whole Family History possible. All I can do is to record this discrepancy and leave it there.

A more definite witness to past events was my mother who made a life-long habit of keeping abreast with every family scandal. (even in her early nineties, it was noticeable that the news of some *'scandal'* has a curiously rejuvenating effect on her.) She recalls furious rows between **Fred** and **Stewart** over the latter's alleged *'womanising.'* Their relationship appears to have been like that of the dashing **Edward** and his disapproving younger brother **George** in the excellent film *'The King's Speech.'*

A visit to the **Kew Archive Centre** (made with my wife **June** on **Tuesday, 22nd December 2015**) provided access to the emergency wartime census of **29th September 1939**. It revealed the following details: -
10 Grange Road Fleetwood M.B. (Municipal Borough) Lancashire, England, Household three people
Stewart F. Smith born 18th October 1911 Clothier (Wholesale) Married
Edith M. R. Born 10th October 1910 Unpaid Domestic Duties
Scheduled sub-number Stewart 2, Edith 1

The most noticeable feature was the rather clumsy attempt to conceal the reality of his domestic situation. What was deemed in those days as *'living in sin'* was very much frowned upon in a society where the old moral standards still prevailed. There was also a strange discrepancy between the birthdate given to **Stewart** here and his actual birth date of **7th September 1911**. The impression given here is that of a household on the defensive.

Section 7: A Sudden Death

Concerning a family's reaction to the coming of war

One source of grief to **Fred** was the sudden death of his father **Frank** at the age of **69,** some months before the outbreak of war in **September 1939. Frank** had still been trying to earn a living even at that age and was still bogged down in financial worries. He'd been talking with **Stewart** when he'd suddenly exclaimed, *"I'm am ill son,"* collapsing into **Stewart's** arms and dying shortly after. Around the time of his death, there'd been a final house move to **34 Fearnville Grove,** (situated in a good area of **North Leeds**.) **Stewart** had been responsible for seeing to the purchase of the house but only **Fred** lived in it with his parents. A photo of **Frank** (taken not long before his death) showed him standing (folded umbrella in hand) next to a garden pond, near to a wooden greenhouse. Lying behind him was some shrubbery and a hedge. The most striking feature was the way in which he was *'very well turned out'* in a darkish three-piece suit and white shirt with a neatly folded handkerchief in his jacket breast pocket. **Frank** had obviously been the sort of man who took extraordinary pride in his appearance. Underneath a trilby hat, his face gave a smile, full of playful mirth and even some vanity. Even after several decades, one could easily imagine how he'd managed to impress **Joe Gillinson** when he'd walked into his office that day, determined to sell some cloth. He must have been quite an outstanding salesman. The photograph certainly showed **Frank** at his most natural and best. Consequently, it is with this benevolent image in mind that we take our final farewell to him. He may have made his mistakes but at the end of the day, he was essentially a good man. My father's relaxed body posture (in a previously described photograph) perhaps provided the best testimonial to the fundamental decency of **Frank's** character. With hindsight, one is tempted to wonder whether **Frank** would have had an easier time if he'd married *'a down to earth **Northern** lass'* with less grandiose social pretensions. He may have enjoyed greater peace of mind – but there again this Family History would have turned out rather differently! I appear to have inherited my poetical gift from the **Irish Fosters.** I certainly feel a strong affinity to the **Celtic** literary tradition.

Strongly confirming the above story was **Frank's** Death Certificate. This was obtained (after much searching) from **Leeds Registry Office** on a very warm and sunny **Wednesday, 24th May 2001.** It showed that he had died in the presence of his son just before the Second World War. Original family tradition had stated that **Stewart** had purchased **34 Fearnville Grove** for his <u>already</u>

530

widowed mother. Quite possibly, my Grandparents had been in the middle of this actual purchase when **Frank** had suddenly died. **Stewart** had simply finished the mortgage payments on behalf of his mother (or maybe he was just responsible for administrative matters). It's interesting to note that **Stewart** had been living (or just staying) next door to his parents at the time of his father's death. (Alternatively, there may just have been a transcription error by the clerk.) This appeared to indicate that my own father's attempt at engineering a family reconciliation at **Blackpool** had been relatively successful. **Fred's** actions over this matter appear to have been vindicated six decades after the original event.

Registration District <u>Leeds North</u>
<u>1939</u> **Death in the** <u>sub-district</u> **of** <u>Leeds East</u> **in the** <u>County Borough of Leeds and County of York (W.R)</u>
1. When and where died? Thirtieth March 1939 34 Fearnville Grove U.D (Urban District)
2. Name and Surname: Frederick Hesselwood Smith
3. Sex: Male
4. Age: 69 years
5. Occupation: Wholesale Draper's Representative
6. Cause of death: (a) Angina Pectoris Certified by B. Stewart M.B.
7. Signature, description and residence of informant: S. F. Smith, son. Present at death 36 Fearnville Grove, Leeds
8. When registered: Thirtieth March 1939
9. Signature of registrar: H. A. Roberts Registrar

Frank's death was the direct result of the usual **Smith** killer – heart disease. Previously described family photographs had shown him as a man somewhat aged before his time. Nevertheless, he still seemed to have kept up some form of a living, working as a **Wholesale Draper's Representative.** This may well have been for **Joe Gillinson** (who was engaged in the Drapery Wholesale Trade). However, no documentation has survived to confirm this point. Evidence for his sudden death was found in his memorial notice on **p.3** of the **Friday, 31/3/1939** issue of **The Yorkshire Evening Post.** Apparently drafted by his wife, it stated: *"SMITH – March 30ᵗʰ suddenly, at 34 Fearnville Grove, Oakwood, Leeds 8, Fred Heselwood Smith, the greatly loved husband of Elizabeth SMITH – cremated at Lawnswood on Saturday, April 1ˢᵗ at 12 noon."* For all their muted understatement, these words appear to convey a very deeply felt sense of loss. **Frank** had died just three months before their Fortieth Wedding Anniversary.

His death may have been advanced by worries about the imminent outbreak of war. Earlier in **March 1939, Hitler's** armies had marched into **Prague** and (as my own mother would later remark) it had become clear to the **British Public** that a full-scale conflict with **Germany** could no longer be avoided. The following headlines from the *'Foreign News Section'* of the very last **Yorkshire Evening Post Frank** could ever have read were heavy with foreboding of the terrible struggle that was to come. The following extracts are taken from **pp. 13-14** of the **Wednesday, 29/3/1939** issue.

*"Smash-and-grab new-world, **Mr Eden** calls for united defence."*
*"**Daladier** answers **Mussolini** tonight, broadcast speech by **French** Premier."*
*"**British** army to be increased"*
*"Consultations with **Russia**, request to '**Poland**' all rejected, **Poles** ready to resist."*
*"Territorial Army to be doubled, establishment of **340,000** men Premier explains to Commons."*

Someone keeping an eye on world events was **Frank's** elder half-brother **James**. On the **11th November 1938**, he noted *"Persecution of the **Jews** increases. Could lead to a dreadful destruction of **Jewish** property in **Germany**."* He was referring to the infamous *'Crystal Night'* Pogrom that marked the beginning of the Holocaust. What **James** as an eighty-year-old **Victorian** made of such events can only be imagined. He would also live to see the liberation of **Belsen** on **15th April 1945**. As a thoroughly decent and civilized man, he must have thought the whole world was plunging into a new dark age. Such barbarities would have been unimaginable in his youth.

Perhaps it was a mercy that my Grandfather's life had ended just over five months before the beginning of this titanic conflict. Not only was he spared the worry over the possible fate of his sons in the armed forces; but he also did not see the full revelations of the **Nazis'** genocide of the Jews. An already ill man, with **Late Victorian** values, **Frank** would have had great difficulty in coping with that scale of evil.

On **Monday, July 21st, 2003**, details of **Frank's** modest estate were uncovered in the relevant Index at **The West Yorkshire Archive Service, Wakefield**. The following statement was made: *"**SMITH FRED HESELWOOD** of 34 Fearnville Grove Leeds. Died **30 March 1939**. Administration **Wakefield 1 May**. To **Elizabeth Marie Smith** Widow – effects £348 11s 5d."* (The equivalent of £15,904 in May 2018.) The fact that a letter of administration was required confirmed that he had not made a will. A search through other information sources (held at **Wakefield**) showed that, except for **Edmund**, none of my other forbears had made wills either. Although small by the standards of his father, **Frank's** legacy showed that he still had something left, even after *'The Great Depression'* and the hugely extravagant demands of the female members of his family. He'd managed his limited financial resources to the best of his ability and to significant effect. *'Being careful with money'* has become something of a **Smith** tradition although there are some who mistake this for *'stinginess!'*

Further details about **Frank's** death were disclosed during my mother's eightieth birthday celebration, held on **Saturday, 29th November 2003** in **Leeds.** A cousin recounted them (the son of **Irene,** one of my late father's sisters). He informed me that, on the evening before his death, **Frank** had overeaten and soon after waking the following day he had collapsed and died in **Stewart's** arms. (Apparently, **Stewart** had been staying overnight because he had had some business in **Leeds** the following day). At the same birthday function, another cousin (who had previously divulged the location of **Edmund's** tomb) was wearing a silver pendant and chain with a small purple stone suspended from it. She revealed that **Anne Hastings Smith** had made it herself. She also showed me a small ornate handbag, once worn during the **1920s** by my father's mother. It had a very elegant multi-coloured lace-like design. Such artefacts made me feel much closer to a time I had hitherto only reached through documents and faded grave inscriptions. Both cousins were very interested in the photographs I had taken of the pavement tombs, sited in front of the tower of **Kildwick Church, West Yorkshire.** However, my mother felt obliged to make it clear that she was not yet ready to join the ancestors! She asked whether I was *'wishing her on her way!'* I must admit that the lively discussion (about previous family ancestors) at my mother's **80th** birthday celebration was possibly a little inopportune (but nevertheless thoroughly enjoyable.) She needn't have worried for she lived to enjoy her ninetieth birthday ten years later and in the intervening period was to provide a gold mine of Family History information. Incredibly, she was still providing nuggets of information until her ninety-third year.

On **Tuesday, 24th February 2004,** I received a letter from my cousin **Tony** (**Rene's** son). It was sent in response to a written enquiry I'd made on **Friday, 30th January.** Dated **20th February,** the following extracts provide further insight into the manner of **Frank's** death – and his wife's subsequent life as a widow at the beginning of the war.

*"So far as Grandfather **Smith's** demise is concerned my understanding was that he'd died unexpectedly during the night following a heavy, late, meaty supper. I am not sure who told me this, but it might have been my mother **Rene**.*

*You might be aware that **Rene** produced me at **Eastbourne** on the **31st January 1937** and that when the war started. Father arranged for both of us [**Rene** and **Tony**] to be 'shipped' up to **Banchory, Deeside (Scotland)** – the reason – to "get away from the prospect of war with **Germany**" might be obvious. After the initial panic following the start of the war, mother and I spent a large part of the time living with **Grandma Smith** at **34 Fearnville Grove** in **Leeds** and that is where we were when the announcement of the war with **Germany** was made.*

*After the war, my father took up the post of County Planning Officer for **County Down** in **Northern Ireland** and was joined by **Rene** and myself. In **1948,** we all moved to **Bedford** where occasionally your father, **Fred,** would visit. **Rene** died of a stroke in **1961.**"* (Apparently, she'd collapsed in a shop in **Bedford,** aged only **52.**)

Sadly, my informant **Tony** (born in **1937**) would himself would pass away in **2006.** He'd been an ardent enthusiast of jazz music.

From this correspondence, it was possible to achieve a clearer picture of what my Grandmother had been doing when the war had broken out in **September 1939.** During that time, my father was still living at home. It's very easy to imagine the whole family gathered around the wireless with anxious looks on their faces. Who knows what could have been whirling through their minds at that time? The Emergency War-Time Census revealed the following details about **Fred** and his mother: -

34 Fearnville Road, Leeds
Fred Smith born 6th February 1914, wholesale Drapery traveller, Single
Elizabeth Marie Smith, Female *'Incapacitated'* Married
This appears to clearly indicate that, six months after **Frank's** death, **Elizabeth** (at both the psychological and physical level) was still very much suffering from his loss. She must have been depressing to live with.

Coincidently, **Frank's** death happened only two weeks after that of his younger brother **Hedley.** The following details portray telling similarities between the two events.

District <u>Manchester South</u>
<u>1939</u> Death in the <u>sub-district</u> of <u>Withington</u> in the <u>County Borough of Manchester</u>
1. When and where died? Sixteenth March 1939, 20 Nell Lane, Withington U.D
2. Name and Surname: Hedley Stamford Smith

3. Sex: Male
4. Age: 59 years
5. Occupation: Of 371 Moss Lane, Moss Side U.D. Publican
6. Cause of death: (a) A Vesico-Colic Fistula Certified by H. B. Slater M.B.
7. Signature, description and residence of informant: A. C. Smith widow of the deceased present at death 371 Moss Lane, East Moss Side
8. When registered: Seventeenth March 1939
9. Signature of registrar: M. Mellor Registrar

The odd thing here is that **Frank's** death had <u>never</u> been associated with the death of his brother **Hedley.** Had there been one of the infamous **Smith** family rifts between the two? Who knows, but they seem to have gone their separate ways. In passing, it's worth mentioning that **20 Nell Lane** was (and still is) the site of **Withington Community Hospital.** It was a medical facility known to have served the poorer members of the local community.

James' diary cast some extra light on this period and the Family Relationships during it. We find, for instance, that he enjoyed a close relationship with my Grandfather **Frank** but was distant from **Hedley.** This can be shown in the entries concerning their respective deaths. On **30th March 1939,** he noted *"Fred H died suddenly this morning at **4.00 am**. Last here **24th February,** had met him in* [the] *town centre, after that cremated at **Lawnswood, 1st April."*** **James** had been instantaneously notified of this tragic development. He'd appeared rather shocked by it. This was in contrast to his more dismissive entry concerning **Hedley's** death. Dated **1st April 1939** it read, *"Heard **Hedley** died in some institution on **16th**. **Maud, Kathleen** (from whom she heard news of **Hedley** death) and our **Anne** went to the funeral. I didn't."* The last two words were very pointed and indicated some kind of rift. However, it must be remembered that the date given in his diary was the date of **Frank's** funeral and he perhaps had felt his first obligation was to **Frank's** family.

Further evidence of a closeness between the two half-brothers was provided in the way **Frank's** children kept visiting **James** and his wife long after his demise. An entry dated **30th September 1940** confirmed that my Father **Fred** had called on **James** whilst on shore leave. **James** also noted *"His mother with **Madge** at **Monkseaton. Stewart** married, no objection."* In **1944,** he believed that my Uncle **Stewart** was based in **Persia.** However, he didn't record the marriage of my parents. The link between **James** and the children and grandchildren of **Frank** continued until the death of his wife in **1951.** (My mother divulged that visits to *'uncle **Jim'*** were very much my father's affair. She saw him rarely.) After that, failing health and sight obliged him to move to **Bradford** to be with his daughter. The link between the **James** and **Fred Hesslewood** lines faded out until it was suddenly and dramatically revived in late **June 2018** after an interlude of **67** years. In early **May 2018,** the Pastor of **Sutton Baptist Church** had noticed an elderly lady and a younger woman (who turned out to be her granddaughter) visiting the obelisk in **Sutton.** He e-mailed me to ask whether he could provide contact details and (following my permission) the previously mentioned granddaughter contacted me, and the result was a deluge of information – so much that I could barely process it! Incredibly, the obelisk which my Great Grandfather had erected some one-hundred and fifty years previously had become a means of bringing together two branches of his family that had been separated for decades. If **Edmund's** aim had to be noticed by his descendants, he certainly had achieved it. He was still making an impact over a century after his death. My great-grandfather must have done something right.

Hedley's widow **Annie** lived on for another eleven years. Her death notice on **p. 11** of the **Tuesday, 13th September 1949** issue of the **Manchester Evening News** read: -

"SMITH – on Spt. 13. At 82 Seymour Grove Old Trafford Manchester, 16 ANNIE ELIZABETH, aged 73 years, the dearly beloved wife of the late Hedley Stamford SMITH and dear mother of William and Kathleen. Service and interment Southern Service Cemetery, Friday, Sept. 16, at 11 a.m. inquiries R. Pepperdine and Telephone Mos. 2865 and Cho 4650."

Sadly, the reality differed from that suggested by the notice. During her widowhood, **Annie** (who was reputed to be a *'very sweet lady'*) would wait for hours at the front living window for hours hoping her son **William** would visit. He never did. The local pub was by far his favourite haunt.

During two visits to **Manchester Cemeteries Wednesday 3rd** to **Thursday 4th August 2016,** (the first one being with **Ann Dalton**) it was noticed that neither **Hedley** nor his son **William** had any headstones. This was a clear sign of poverty. Tellingly, **Mona** (who went to live near her daughter in **Sussex**) wasn't buried with her husband. She died in **April 1991.**

Section 8: An Upwardly Mobile Community

Concerning the Leeds Jewish Community during the inter-war years

By the inter-war period, the **Leeds Jewish Community** had become upwardly mobile. The nightmare slums of the **Leylands** were a distant memory and now the leafy suburbs of **Chapeltown** and **Roundhay** beckoned. A photograph of the **Francis Street Choir** in **1935** (in **Charing p.138**) conveyed something of the active social (and spiritual) life which existed at that time. Smiling boys of varying ages surrounded a beaming Rabbi; all of them wearing prayer shawls. An insight into the workings of this community and its relationship to the world of business was provided in the second interview with **Fred's** former Accountant, **Joshua Barrett**. This took place on the morning of **Wednesday 15 September 1999.** Information provided by this lovely gentleman confirmed that, even for professionals, the working world of the **1930s** was a very hard one. Also highlighted was the degree to which **Fred's** own life had run in tandem with that of the **Leeds Jewish Community**. **Joshua Barrett** will again be quoted: -

*"I qualified as a Chartered Accountant in **1938**. I was articled for three years before that and had no pay during that time. I was with a firm that did very large audits. I thought of being a teacher, but the prospects were poor. I had to earn money for the family. The Trade Unions had been smashed and the prospects for employment were very bleak. I did a lot of audits for Collieries and for large Engineering Firms that made printing presses and railways. They were flourishing because the owners were in control of labour. Yes, it was very much a 'capital' versus 'labour' situation with capital gaining the upper hand. The Trade Unions had been flattened by the General Strike of **1926**. I had paid a 'premium' of £**250** (of borrowed money) to cover initial expenses – that was from a woman who had lent it 'interest-free.' I got the **30s** a week from the firm and that was to pay off the loan. It was a nominal salary but at least they paid travelling expenses. It was slave labour. I would work a full five-day week and **Saturday** morning. It was a five-and-a-half-day week. They were getting a free service and charging a full rate to the clients. The reasoning was that if we were a dead loss we cost nothing. They also had to spend money on training. I was very competent – all the senior chaps fought to take me on.*

*My dad and sisters and I worked as a family, pooling resources. In addition, I used to earn some money in coaching in **Maths** and **Latin.** I taught a (now retired) Solicitor to do **Law** where you had to pass in **Latin Matriculation.** I used to coach a few hours a week. The study was done at night. I had to do a correspondence course with a British College who sent printed books and printed stuff. I do not know how I found the time for this. I hardly slept. I used to get a month to study for the exams. It was a hard life.*

*After I qualified it was hard because it was difficult to get a post in the office. The labour market was very saturated and difficult at that time. I stayed with the firm where I was articled for £**2.50** a week. £**2.00** - £**3.00** per week was the salary for a professional at that time. I could spend £**2.50** just to get a suit. The **50s** (shilling) Tailors (who sold cheap suits) were just starting.*

You had to have contacts in order to succeed in a profession. Other people with wealthy parents could buy a partnership. Mine was untypical. I started from scratch. Then I got a few very minor clients among refugees from the war that had just started. I used to work from home at night. I began by personal recommendation. My first clients were two or three elderly people from abroad. They were already very cultured – they came from **Germany, Austria, Hungary** *and* **Czechoslovakia***. At that time, I knew the* **Moor Allerton** *Golf Club treasurer. I became their unpaid secretary and I did the books for them. A number of members became clients of mine. It was the first* **Jewish** *golf club. I did not get many there. I had no leisure at all. I used to work seven days a week, I used to see clients at all times of the day until ten or eleven at night."*

For **Fred,** the **1930s** especially had been *'the groping years'* in which he'd striven hard to find a suitable position in life. He also seemed to have been a young man unsure of his own identity. An impression is gained of a somewhat shy individual who'd stood in the shadow of his rather dominant mother and dynamic elder brother, **Stewart.** He was united with his contemporaries by a common struggle to earn a decent living. Meanwhile, events in **Germany** were set to take a tragic turn. The rise to power of the **Nazis** in **1933** made possible the application of **Social Darwinism** on a massive scale. The degree to which the **Nazis** drew upon evolutionary philosophy was highlighted by one of their propaganda films (shown on the **1997 BBC** award-winning documentary *'The Nazis, a Warning from History.'*) Whilst employing a scientific laboratory as its setting, the point of the film was to demonstrate that, just as in nature a constant struggle exists in which only the fittest survive, so it is in the world of human affairs. *'The strong'* had a right (and even a duty) to vanquish *'the weak'* and to exterminate them if it suited their interests. **Social Darwinism** provided the **Nazis** with the legitimacy to convince themselves to the belief that peaceful co-existence between different races was unnatural. To them, war and struggle was part of the natural order of things and killing one's inferiors were good because that would lead to social advancement. More than once my father nearly became one of the millions of servicemen to fall victim to this twisted line of reasoning. I have no doubt that if the **Nazis** had occupied **Britain** my father's **Jewish** contacts would have made him a desperately vulnerable target. My family can be thankful that (in **1940**) the **English Channel** stood in the way of **Hitler's** armies. All of this, however, is to anticipate the next chapter.

Section 9: Working Class Memories

Concerning working-class life in Leeds in the early Twentieth Century

One limitation of this history has been its bias toward the middle classes. However, to some extent, this has been unavoidable because my own father was middle class. So too were most of the surviving witnesses to his life. Yet always in the background were the far more numerous **English** working classes who had a far harder time of things. Unless some account is taken of what might be termed *'The Condition of the English Working Classes,'* this history would be incomplete. There would be no context to explain why my father was so careful with his money and why he set great store on education and respectability. However, no point would be served in re-iterating the kind of statistical information readily found in many books on **British Social History.** A lively and pertinent *'take'* on this issue arose from an interview conducted with a mentally alert **Baptist** lady on **Sunday, 16th June 2002.** She was born on **1st August 1906** and gave her very enthusiastic permission to publish these, her memories. Once again it appeared to be a case of someone in their nineties wishing to leave behind a useful legacy. (The name of the lady and place of the interview are withheld for reasons of confidentiality.)

After disclosing that her father, a printer, had moved from **Newton-In-Furniss** to **Wakefield** in **1911** (where she'd attended **Saint John's School**) and to **Otley,** in **1914** (where she'd attended **Cross Green Church of England School**) she began to reminisce about her education and home life.

"We had slates with scratchy slate pencils. On one side were lines, with pothooks, (straight lines or curves, which could be formed into letters) *which children made into letters. The other side consisted of squares where you could place numbers. We used to sit on benches with large numbers of pupils. At home, mother kept muslin bags with salt in. They were like beanbags and were put on sore teeth and throats. They always worked. Mother would warm an iron plate on the stove, wrap it in a blanket and use it to warm the bed. Clay hot water bottles, which we had later, were a luxury.*

We didn't have them push button things to do the washing. We had metal tubs; pegged boards with holes in like a cheese grater and a dolly stick to circulate the washing. Unlike today, it wasn't at all easy. Workmen used to clear the middens at night - do you know what they are? (These were used to store the waste from household toilets.)

During the First World War, the Territorial Army trained in **Wharfe Meadows** *in* **Otley.** *They used to dig trenches, which I hear can still be seen from the air. I can still see a line of bell tents on the horizon. I recall seeing soldiers in puttees. They used to invite friends and neighbours to look around. Do you know what puttees were?* (They were the material bandage-like material wrapped around the lower leg.)

At **Blackhorse Corner (Otley)** *the locals took over an empty shop and turned it into a National Kitchen, run by women volunteers. It had a hand-written menu for children. There was* **Mashed potato, mashed swede** *(I really used to love* **swede***),* **carrots** *and* **cabbage.** *There was only a little* **meat,** *a* **sausage** *or piece of* **bacon.** *Everything was* **2d,** *except* **swede***, which was* **3** *halfpennies. There was a bit of rice or sponge for pudding. We could have everything for* **6d** *or with* **swede 5** *pence h' penny."*

I had two friends and we bought **2lbs** *of lavender and made them into drawstring bags, into which we placed the lavender. We sold them for* **2d** *and with the proceeds, we got more lavender. When we got* **1s** *we gave it to the* **Red Cross.** *That was our contribution to the war effort. I saw a zeppelin come over; everyone had to put their cigarettes out because it was thought a zeppelin could see them. In my childhood imagination, I thought that soldiers would drop down with guns. My mother's brother* **Ellam Dutton** *went all the way through the war only to be killed one or two hours before the Armistice on* **November 11ᵗʰ [1918]"**

My informant expressed some sadness at the memories of the economic hardships during the interwar period: -
"Oh! Everyone was out of work. That was in **1926** *when the General Strike was on. Everyone started to get a wooden box, place it on pram wheels and we would push them around to get bits of coal and anything that could be recycled. We had to do to go on living. My parents and I had to do it. I can't remember how long it lasted, but it was bad. We went near the railway line in* **Irish Fields, Otley** *and used to walk along the siding — scavenging. I still have a photo of the box on wheels with a parrot on the handle."* (She hadn't seen people scavenging on rubbish dumps as I had first imagined.)

One week later, when I was checking some of the details of this original interview she disclosed that she had worked as a printer in an **Otley** printing shop from about the age of **17** until **26** when she'd got married and had had to stop work.

CHAPTER 17: WAR AND DEATH

Section 1: Entering the Conflict

Concerning Fred's training in the Royal Navy

It was to be World War Two which constituted the formative experience of my father's life. An outline of his wartime service (over **1939-1945**) can be easily recreated. My mother stated that **Fred** had volunteered for service in **1939** because he'd wanted to serve in the navy. He thought that if he waited to be conscripted he would not be able to follow this option. Why he preferred it remains unknown – but my father belonged to a generation when the horrendous army casualties of the First World War were still a living memory. When war was declared in **September 1939,** no one could have foreseen that the future battles of the **Somme** and **Passchendaele** would be fought on the Eastern Front, deep in **Russia.** There, the monthly casualty figures could sometimes exceed one million.

After induction on a training ship called **'The Ganges',** he spent his early war years on Motor Torpedo Boats. In **1942, Fred** received a posting to the heavily blitzed Island of **Malta;** but fortuitously for him, the proposed transfer was cancelled on compassionate grounds. His newly married wife had been *'bombed out'* of her home and had needed help with the moving of goods. This turn of events resulted in his posting to minesweeping duties on **'The Firefly.'** That transfer perhaps saved his life. After two arduous years on mine clearance duties, he then became a chauffeur for Senior Naval Officers in the **Peterhead** area of **Scotland.** The last six months of the war saw him on a far better equipped **American** Minesweeper. The Navy had thought sufficiently well of my father to have recommended him for a commission. However, he was to turn it down because he possessed a raw dislike of the snobbery then existing in that branch of the armed services. Nevertheless, his refusal did not prevent him from leaving with a very good character reference. Alongside many of his contemporaries *"**Fred** was something of a socialist"* although later he was to grow cynical of all politicians. He would scathingly dismiss them as *"a lot of rogues."* During many subsequent General Elections, he would vote **'Liberal'** as a *'protest vote'* against the two main parties whom he felt were ruining the country.

His induction into the war effort was hard. During his first night in barracks, he had his watch stolen (it may possibly have been a **21st** birthday present). This was an incident he would mention in a tone of rueful sorrow. Whilst aboard

'The Firefly' his main duty had been to sail down from **Scapa Flow** to the **South Coast** of **England,** clearing mines. Sometimes these duties took *'The Firefly'* towards the dangerous shoreline of **German**-occupied **Europe**. Once, when joining the ship as part of a relief crew, he saw that the bow had been blown in – and learnt that eight of the previous crew had been killed. He rarely spoke about his wartime experiences although he did mention that there was a dog called *'Pluto'* on board. Coming straight from a fastidious middle-class home, run by his mother, he would have found it hard being closeted with men from the toughest of social backgrounds. Some of them came from the fishing industry where alcoholism was rife. Adding to the tension was a division between the professional seamen and those (like my father) who had been *'press ganged'* into the war effort. One Petty Officer *"whose nerves were in shreds because of the war,"* was particularly abusive to the nautical neophytes, swearing and cursing them with impunity. The risk of a sudden sinking also made it necessary for all crew members to sleep fully clothed on shared bunks. Irritating skin infections such as impetigo and scabies were the result. However, the worst hardship seems to have been the broken sleep patterns. He would often be woken up anywhere between two and six for the early morning shift. Inevitably, the resulting sleeplessness would have only added to the stress. Yet perhaps these hardships gave **Fred** a necessary toughening.

One incident highlighted the sort of dangers which my father faced. One of his duties was to fly (as an observer) in an antiquated biplane used by the fleet air arm. His task was to spot mines with the aid of a pair of binoculars. He would have been seated near the front because the *'Walrus'* engine was situated at the rear. On one occasion, the pilot flying the biplane was a traumatised former Spitfire pilot who had been shot down and badly burnt during **The Battle of Britain.** Because of plastic surgery *"half of his face was red, the other half white."* Unfit for more challenging duties he had been transferred to Coastal Command. Possibly because of nerves, this casualty of war caused an already rickety aircraft to land on the sea at the wrong angle. Completely out of control it started to bounce along the sea – heading toward the harbour wall at **Poole** in **Dorset.** Frantically, the pilot pulled the joystick and, just in time, the aircraft started to climb, missing the wall by inches. It was only after another forty-five minutes, with fuel running short, that the trembling pilot attempted another landing. My father had escaped death by the narrowest of margins.

Another brush with death had also come whilst *'The Firefly'* had lain in the harbour. **Fred** was in what was known as the anchor locker which stored the anchor chain. (Apparently, sailors used to go in there for a quiet smoke – safely away from any explosives.) Suddenly, without any warning, the ship began to put down anchor. The chain started to swing all over the place. My father had hastily hidden behind a bulkhead to avoid a gory decapitation. Once again, his life had been mercifully spared.

Further information about **Fred's** war service only emerged during a visit to **The Kew Archive Centre** on **Tuesday 22nd December 2015.** My father had mentioned how eight men had been killed on *'The Firefly'* and he'd seen how part of it had been blown in when it was towed into harbour. (He was to form part of the relief crew.) Whether these two incidents were connected weren't known until my wife and I came across the Admiralty File for the minesweeper **(M/S)** *'Firefly.'* These revealed details of the sailor's names and ranks: -

H.M. M/S TRAWLER FIREFLY 2/2/40

KILLED
BALDWIN Charles M. Chief Petty officer
BARKER Benjamin N. Engineman
BEAVERS Henry E. Seaman R.N.R.
CLAY John R. Seaman R.N.R
COWIE John 2nd Hand
JOHNSTON Walter E. Seaman Cook
REID Peter Seaman R.N.R
STEWART Alexander Seaman R.N.R
STEWART James Seaman R.N.R

DIED OF WOUNDS
BARKER Edward 2nd Hand

WOUNDED
GEDDES Alexander Seaman R.N.R
MANSION George Engineer man
WHYTE William W. Leading Seaman

And six other walking wounded cases

It was an incredibly moving experience to put names and a date to what had hitherto been a vaguely described but obviously very traumatic memory. The Admiralty File had also revealed that the explosion had taken place at **16.50** hours on the **3rd February 1940** whilst a mine was being recovered half a mile

North of **West Gunnet Buoy,** off the **Forth of Firth** estuary on **the East Coast** of **Scotland**. Although damage had been confined to the Superstructure the crippled **Firefly** still needed to be towed back to **Leith Harbour** by tugs. (This is where my father appears to have joined the ship. The wounded were treated at **Leith Infirmary.**) Stamped in bold red lettering at the end of this part of the file was the word **'DESTROY.'** Fortunately for this Family History, this command appears to have been ignored. It had been reviewed by a certain **P. Leslie** *'Navy Reviewer.'*

What seems to have been very clear from this source was that in **February 1940** my father wasn't joining a happy ship. He would have been all too aware of the risks involved.

His brother **Stewart** entered the war at a later stage because of some essential work he'd needed to do. Perceiving an opportunity to stir up mischief, **Rosamund** had begun to send white feathers and abusive letters to his home and place of work. (Apparently, **Stewart's** employees thought she was mad.) In the end, **Stewart** took legal action and had her *'bound over'* to keep the peace. My father's response was to wish that it had been possible to keep the problem within the confines of the family. **Stewart** was to spend much of the war directing shipping traffic through the **Suez Canal;** a responsible position which apparently had a detrimental effect on his health. Meanwhile, back in **Leeds,** their already frail mother **Elizabeth** was consumed by worry. She had recently lost her husband; would she lose her sons also? The wartime marriage of **Fred** must have come as mixed news to her – especially as my mother was based in the heavily bombed **South East** of **England**.

Section 2: A War-Time Marriage

Concerning the marriage of my parents at Saint Peter's, Bournemouth

Haunted by the possibility that he may have only a little time left to live, **Fred** met my mother **Cynthia Absalom** at a wartime dancehall at **Bournemouth** in either **January** or **February 1941**. She was wearing a borrowed friend's dress. Meanwhile, her father **William** was a widely-travelled army officer who, after serving in the **Home Guard,** was to spend much of the Second World War smuggling guns to the partisans in **Greece.** By the summer of **1944,** he had risen to the rank of **Major.** If caught by the **Germans,** he would have been treated as a spy rather than as a prisoner of war. The treatment he would have received does not bear thinking about. A photograph (taken on **25th July 1944**) showed the ship used for this work. Named the *'Ketch Meander'* and possessing three main sails it's obvious that this vessel had been designed for speed. A black and white photograph of a **Greek** village that was overshadowed by a cloud-covered mountain range survived as a memento of **William's** service in the **Balkans.** Pencilled on the reverse was the following note, *"Thunderclouds over the* **Hyrenid Range** *and the first rain I've seen since the beginning of* **May. Buffa Vento** *almost hid on the left,* **23 Aug. 1944."** The words suggested that **William** had found army service in that climate rather taxing – as well he might have done, for he was a man in his late fifties. Other photographs showed him looking his age although he still liked to sport a monocle! His love for army life continued unabated. During the **1950s,** my brother **David** noticed that his flat in **Westminster** was full of old army mementoes. As a ten-year-old boy, **David** was permitted to don **William's** old uniform. Personally, I remember seeing all of **William's** campaign medals in an old brown storage box at our home in **Leeds.** There were lots of them.

Thanks to the **German Luftwaffe** (air force) **Fred** and **Cynthia** were nearly not married at all. Whilst walking in **Bournemouth** a bomb dropped about fifty yards away from them, exploding a nearby gas main. My mother remarked that *"It was a very frightening experience."* It was whilst my father was lying in the gutter shielding my mother that the decision to get married was perhaps made. At **Saint Peter's Church Bournemouth,** they duly *'tied the knot.'* The date of their wedding was **Saturday, 13th December 1941** – when **Japan** was attacking **America** and the proud armies of **Germany** were bogged down in the snows before **Moscow.** (My father would often remark that *"Hitler's biggest mistake was to have attacked* **Russia.***"*) For the Jews of **Europe,** the very worst period of their history was about to begin. Within just over a month **The Wannsee Conference** would set in motion the attempt to eradicate them from the face of the earth.

Throwing extra light upon their wedding was the Marriage Certificate itself. It provided several useful details, *i.e.* the identity of the curate who had officiated at the ceremony and the addresses where my parents had been living at that time. Here was definite objective information to balance the subjective impressions of memory and personal accounts.

Registration District
1941 Marriage solemnised at <u>St. Peter's, Bournemouth</u> in the <u>County Borough of Bournemouth</u>
1. When married? 13th December 1941

2. Name and Surname: Fred Gordon Smith, Cynthia Mary Absalom
3. Age: 27, 18
4. Condition: Bachelor, Spinster
5. Rank or profession: Seaman, Civil Servant
6 Residence at the time of marriage: R. Naval Air Station, Sandbanks Dorset, 63 Edmondsham House, Terrace Road, Bournemouth
7. Father's name and surname: Fred Heselwood Smith, William John Absalom
8. Rank or profession of father: Merchant, Civil Servant

Married in the <u>Church of St. Peter</u> according to the Rites and Ceremonies of the <u>Church of England</u> by license by me. The marriage was solemnised between us
<u>Fred Gordon Smith</u>
<u>Cynthia Mary Smith</u>
In the Presence of us,
<u>M. H. Nixon</u>
<u>M.E. Absalom</u>
<u>Nevil Francis Tucker</u> in the Register Book of the said Church of <u>St. Peter's Church</u> in the <u>County Borough of Bournemouth</u>

Witnessing to that event were **Fred's** sister *'Madge'* and my mother's mother **Marguerite Eliza Absalom**. Following the ceremony, celebrations were held at my mother's flat. Unfortunately, the **Rev. Tucker** found that one tot of Royal Navy Rum had gone straight to his head. When this young curate had had to leave in a hurry to conduct his next wedding he was seen to have staggered rather than walked!

Incidentally, **The Crockford Directory** showed that the **Reverend Francis Tucker** (a graduate of **Kings College London** in **1936**) had managed to survive the war. In **1944,** he'd left **Bournemouth** to take up a post as curate at **Stratford-on-Avon**. From **1947** onwards, he'd become vicar of a succession of mainly **English South Coast** Parishes – one of these being in **Ramsgate**. Later in his career, he was to live in **Canada**, serving as a Clerical Secretary for the **Quebec Diocesan Synod** from **1960** until **1963**. Whilst still living in **Canada** he retired in **1979** and had died by **1985**. The tot of Royal Navy Rum he had drunk at my parents' wedding had not inflicted any long-term harm to this *'gentleman of the cloth!'*

Their wedding photograph vividly portrayed the wartime atmosphere of the time. The greatest irony was that, whereas my father had another **57** years to live, his best man (standing next to him in Petty Officer's uniform) had only another six to eight weeks. (A close-up of the wedding photograph seemed to indicate he was suffering from decayed teeth.) His ship was torpedoed and all those aboard were lost. At my father's funeral, my mother dimly remembered him as *"a very nice man."* His mates knew him as *'Chippy.'* If not killed in the initial explosion his death would have ensued either through drowning or by freezing to death in the ice-cold water. Apparently *'Chippy'* was not the only fallen comrade my father knew. Towards the end of the war, a ship (with many of his pals on board) was also blown up when it struck a mine. Once again, there'd been no survivors. The wartime years of their marriage had been constantly governed by the realisation that my mother could have suffered from an early widowhood. Shortly after her marriage (when living *'in digs'* on the **South Coast of England**) my mother felt the necessity to sit-down on a chamber pot. However, it broke into jagged pieces and her posterior began to bleed profusely. *"A doddery old doctor was called"* and as he began to do the stitching the **German** air force struck once again! An incompetent stitching operation was performed amidst the wail of air raid sirens and the whistle of crashing bombs. Apparently, the scars from this operation still exist today. She'd also known what it was like to have been so close to her own demise.

In later years, **Fred** claimed he'd rescued **Cynthia** from the GIs (**American** servicemen). He would proudly remark, *"If it wasn't for me, she'd have been in trouble!"* I've not had any long-lost half brothers or sisters contacting me from **America,** at least not so far! In contrast, my mother asserted, *"If it wasn't for me, Fred would still have been with his mother!"* Both my parents seemed to think they had rescued one another, and they weren't afraid to re-state that belief on various occasions!

Section 3: Fleeing the Japanese

Concerning the Shanghai Bank and the fall of Singapore

Another relative who suffered greatly (shortly after my parent's marriage) was my father's elder sister **Julia.** At the beginning of **1942,** her husband **Eric Moffat** was working as a Senior Manager for the **Hong Kong-Shanghai Bank** in **Singapore.** (In the **1930s,** he had been based in **China.**) Although childless, **Julia** and **Eric** were known to have enjoyed a very privileged colonial lifestyle, living in a large suburban house with a veranda. **Julia** would spend her leisure time painting (mainly watercolour) scenes of **China.** In **February 1942,** this privileged lifestyle ended abruptly when the **Japanese** army swept down the **Malaysian Peninsula.** Without adequate navy or air support, the defence of **Singapore** simply became impossible. **Julia** escaped in the nick of time – fleeing **Singapore** on a boat bound for **Bombay.** (If it really was the very last boat then it has been recorded for posterity on old black and white newsreel pictures.) She had only the clothes she stood up in. The journey was both frightening and uncomfortable as she had to sleep on a crowded deck and the boat risked being sunk by the **Japanese.** Having alighted in **Bombay,** she then boarded another boat to **Melbourne** (or **Sydney**) in **Australia.** After borrowing some money from her husband's bank, she earned a living by selling further paintings of **China.** A sudden shower had sprinkled one painting after it had been left to dry. This caused the paints to run – thus creating an unusual surreal effect. Oddly enough it was this painting that won an award. (I remember seeing some of her paintings as a boy – they were indeed most impressive – consisting mainly of **Chinese** landscapes and children.) Through the money earned she was able to pay off any debts caused by her refugee status and earn her own passage to **England** where she was to spend the remainder of the war. Meanwhile, her husband would endure a terrible captivity in **Japan,** having presumably been deported there from **Singapore.**

Amazingly, an undated newspaper cutting (from **1942** or **1943**) survived to give some idea of **Julia's** artistic activity whilst a refugee in **Australia.** It was received on **Saturday, 19th October 2002** from a relative who had discovered it in an old photograph album.

Venture into Art

When **Dr C. Irving Benson** *opened the exhibition of paintings by* **Julia Neilus Moffatt,** *at* **Kozminsky's Gallery** *yesterday, both he and the artist were venturing onto new ground. For* **C. Benson,** *it was the first occasion on which he had performed such a ceremony, belonging (as he explained) to the school that knows what it likes but for* **Mrs Moffatt** *it was her first one-woman show since she came here on one of the last ships from* **Singapore** *where her husband is still in* **Japanese** *hands.* **Mrs Moffatt** *has had a job with the navy but has devoted her day off to exploring country and seaside for her delightful studies in watercolours and oils. She has also included in her collection some paintings of* **Malayan** *scenes, taken from the sketchbook she brought with her. A number of her friends from* **Malaya** *were among the visitors to the exhibition, which will remain open until* **July 20.**"

Julia would not have been amused by the way her name was wrongly spelt *'Moffatt'* instead of *'Moffat.'* The newspaper report conveyed the impression of a woman desperately trying to keep herself busy to alleviate the very real anxiety she felt for her husband. For all she knew **Japanese** soldiers could have been using him for bayonet practice or burying him alive; they'd done so with **Chinese** prisoners taken during *'the rape of Nanking'* in **December 1937.** (**Nanking** was near **Shanghai** where **Julia** and her husband were based. They would undoubtedly have heard of the atrocities associated with this event; as it had been well publicised at the time.)

It was perhaps fortunate for her that amidst horrendous adversity the *'good old'* **Smith** business streak had kicked in. She certainly displayed a great deal of enterprise and initiative when almost flat broke. Although utterly insufferable, **Julia** certainly was certainly a highly resilient and tough lady!

Section 4: The Battle of the Scheldt

Concerning the *'Battle of the Scheldt'*

A postcard photograph (taken of my father in **August 1942**) shows something of the strain he was under. Clad in the uniform of a Royal Navy Rating he gives a forced smile for the camera, but the face is slightly thin and gaunt. His ears stick out in a way they never did in later life. However, the most telling symptom of exhaustion were the bags of skin under his eyes, which had already seen too much suffering. It seems that this photograph was taken so that his new wife would have something to remember him by in case he met the same fate as his former Best Man. He could not have guessed that he had another **56** years and **8** months to live. The timing of the photograph was also significant. **August 1942** is now considered to have been a major turning point in the war. During that month, the German Sixth Army was driving forward to a then-obscure city called **Stalingrad.** The **Panzer Corps** was being checked in its advance in **North Africa** and the **Americans** were making their first landings in the **Pacific.** Nevertheless, millions more were still to die throughout the next three years before the war would be brought to its final, nuclear conclusion at **Hiroshima** and **Nagasaki.**

An Admiralty File (reviewed at the **Kew Archive** Centre on **Tuesday 22nd December 2015**) revealed further details about the operations in which **Fred** had been involved. This invaluable source confirmed that **Fred** had been operating under **The Nore Command** which meant being engaged in sweeping for mines on the **Essex** to **Kent Coastline.** Over the period of **19ᵗʰ May to the 2ⁿᵈ June 1944** *'The Firefly'* was involved in substantial mine clearing operations to help prepare for the **D Day** landing scheduled for **June 6ᵗʰ**. Also participating were other minesweeping trawlers with the names of *'Bunting,' 'Edward Walmsley,' 'Berberis'* and *'Wyoming'* and at least four ships of **The Royal Netherlands Navy Flotilla** (one of which was blown-up – leaving only one surviving crew member.) Four rewards were to result from this operation. One of these was the **Distinguished Service Medal** awarded to **Kenneth Vass** *'leading seaman'* on *'The Firefly'.* My father perhaps owed his life to this man.

After commending his *'efficient and praiseworthy manner'* the Admiralty File mentioned how **Leading Seaman Vass** had provided *'a cheerful and meritorious example of devotion to duty'* by continuing to organize the successful towing of *'The Firefly'* back to harbour when it had been damaged by a near mine explosion which had injured him. To do this he had had to disregard the resulting pain, injury to his ears and physical discomfort. His award was published in the **London Gazette Supplement** on the **5ᵗʰ September 1944.** This suggests he was a very experienced seaman. Also commended was the commander of *'The Firefly'* who persevered with the operation, despite being *'shaken'* by the blast.

The minutes of the Admiralty Secretary confirmed that this had been a highly dangerous operation because it had involved clearing a moored minefield. Even worse a shortage of ships meant it had to be swept by trawlers, deemed by the Admiralty not suitable for this type of work. Other difficulties had included shallow water, only twelve to fourteen fathoms deep, the presence of wrecks and new, inexperienced captains. Moreover, the mines were lightly moored and could drift easily. There were twelve known moored mines, plus sixteen *'ground'* and five *'acoustic'* mines. **German E. Boats** were another danger. Given such dangers, it was surprising that only two ships were lost – both on **20ᵗʰ May.** The central ship (which appeared to be crewed by the **Dutch**) was destroyed by a mine explosion. Later at **12.06** hours, **H.M. Wyoming** was sunk when one moored mine failed to respond to the sweeping gear. This was an incident that my father did see. He would sometimes describe how he saw a ship being blown up. Overall, a close convergence existed between my father's memories and the official records. It was extremely satisfying to place a precise date on events in which he'd been involved. A conversation with my mother about the sinking of *'The Wyoming'* took place on the evening of **Wednesday, 6ᵗʰ April 2016.** (This vessel had been a sister ship of *'The Firefly.'*) My mother repeated a

550

point made to her by my father that there'd been no known survivors. It seemed possible that some of the crew had been his friends.

Later, in **October 1944,** whilst helping to clear mines from the **Scheldt Estuary,** some months after the D Day landings, another ship sailing next to *'The Firefly'* struck a mine. As it erupted into flames all hands were lost. Whether this was the ship with many of his *'pals'* on board is not known. However, a full account of this action only came to light in an obituary of one of my father's former Commanders; **Hugh Boyce (1911-2004).** My brother had noticed it in the Obituary Section of the **Daily Telegraph, Monday, June 28th, 2004.** He subsequently posted me a copy and it contained the following informative extract: -

*"**COMMANDER HUGH BOYCE,** who has died aged **92,** was one of the first specialist electrical officers in the Navy and helped open **North Sea** ports to supply **Montgomery's** advancing armies.*

*In **1944** Boyce was senior staff electrical officer in a minesweeping flotilla of **120** ships when he received an insistent message from **General Montgomery** that his lines of supply were bonnet-to-tail from **Le Havre** to the front; he was getting only **9,000** tons of supplies daily and wanted the shipping channel to **Antwerp** opened at once.*

***Boyce,** after hastily dressing in khaki combat uniform with Royal Navy flashes, was sent to reconnoitre the damage inflicted by the retreating **Germans;** he went by motor torpedo boat to **Ostend** and then by jeep to the **South Bank** of the **Scheldt** estuary where the **Canadian** army was preparing to advance.*

*Whilst inspecting the port facilities at **Ostend,** Boyce recovered papers which revealed a controlled minefield at the mouth of the **Scheldt;** he made this safe, before returning to make his report and prepare a plan, He improvised experiments to destroy acoustic mines and the deadly multiple-fused Oyster-type, finding the simple hand grenade to be effective.*

*Despite fire from **German** positions on the north shore, the minesweepers cleared more than **400** mines from the **Scheldt** – although **eight** out of **50** ships were lost. Meanwhile, **Boyce** had to recover mines dropped by aircraft during the nights while this operation was going on.*

*Later, he was on the bridge of the headquarters ship **Prompt** when, despite his earlier efforts, she was blown up by an acoustic mine. **Boyce** managed to get the emergency power working, saving the ship from sinking until the many badly-injured engine room crew could be evacuated.*

For the next month, **Boyce** *worked from a shore base at* **Scheveningen,** *clearing the way to* **Rotterdam;** *he later recalled his joy at seeing defeated* **Germans** *dejectedly lining canal and river banks, as he steamed by. He was awarded the DSC."*

His obituary also revealed that: -
*"***Boyce** *developed a strong* **Christian** *faith as a teenager, choosing his church by the quality of its choir and strength of its preaching. Although he had been baptised at* **Street Baptist Church** *in the* **1980s** *he was churchwarden at* **Bath Abbey.**

He was a keen sportsman, playing a number of ball games to club standard; he played his last game of tennis aged **84,** *after which his doctor diagnosed osteoarthritis and he underwent two knee and hip replacement operations."*

Hugh Boyce's death came on the sixtieth anniversary of the D-day landings.

My brother **David** added one piece of information about this conflict. During the early **1990's**, my father admitted that, whilst manning an anti-aircraft gun he'd brought down a **German plane** which had been attacking his ship during the battle of the **Scheldt.** Apparently, the pilot had not bailed out. I found it hard to mentally accept that my normally peace-loving father had taken a human life, albeit during the heat of battle.

The war left **Fred** with a distrust of politicians. Around **1978,** I observed him almost foaming with rage and muttering *"damned liar"* as he watched a flickering old newsreel (part of a television documentary) of a long dead **1930's** politician defending the **1938 Munich Agreement** with **Hitler.** It was a rarity to see him come out with distinctly nautical language. Although the politician in question had long since been forgotten it was evident that my father still held him partly responsible for the loss of his comrades. Indeed, family and friends would pity any politician whom **Fred** happened to *'buttonhole'* after a public meeting. With a *'finger-wagging'* lecture, **Fred** would soon *'set them to rights.'* He would adopt much the same approach with various hapless clergy of the **Church of England**. I still remember the odd pained grimace of one black-robed curate who had been *'set to rights'* by my father. The unfortunate man had left our early **1960s** living room with a rather fixed expression on his face. However, when I met this clergyman again many years later (in early **1991**) he had only fond memories of **Fred**. It was obvious that my father was one of those very rare men who could argue without antagonism. A rare gift indeed! His nerves having been badly affected by his war experiences, my father went through a profound religious

552

crisis in the late **1940s.** The cruelty of the World War had shaken his compassionate view of humanity; newsreel of the **German** concentration camps had left a singularly distressing impression – one which remained with him for the rest of his life. Decades afterwards he still found it hard to accept that people could have been so evil as to have masterminded the destruction of **Europe's Jewish** population. With perhaps his **Jewish** friends in mind, he would refer to this crime as *'a monstrous evil.'* (In passing, I wonder what he would have made of my visit to the **Auschwitz-Birkenau** death camp with my eldest and youngest sons on **Friday, 7th October 2011.**)

With hindsight, my only wish was that **Fred** had written a memoir of his war years. Such a step could have been very therapeutic – possibly helping him to come to terms with his grief for his lost comrades. It would also have been a very interesting historical source to pass on to younger generations. **Fred's** own feelings about the war were summed up in something he said to my sister when he'd admitted: *"I've been very lucky, so many of my pals were blown up."*

He had indeed been lucky. On **Tuesday, 17th August 1999** (whilst staying on a certain **Scottish Isle** with my two eldest sons) I visited a Royal Navy Cemetery. There, laid to rest, were the dead of two World Wars. I lost count of the graves which read *"to unknown sailors"* – this meant that only bits of them had been found. The oldest victim was **67** and the youngest **16** – the age of my eldest son at the time. Some could well have been those with whom my father had rubbed shoulders when visiting these isles during his minesweeping duties. As a mournful wind blew along the ranks of the white headstones I said to my two sons, *"These are the men who did not live to be 85 or see their children or grandchildren grow up. It could so easily have been your Grandfather's name chiselled into one of these headstones. Then none of us would have been here."* Together we left the Cemetery in humbled silence.

Balancing this account of my father's wartime experiences were my own mother's memories of the events covering this period. In response to a request I made she recorded these memories in an account she herself wrote during the summer of **2000.** It now follows – quoted in its entirety, with only the minimum amount of editing. I wanted her account to be comprised almost entirely of her own words. Its chief point lay in how it accurately reflected the wider social attitudes of the time.

Sections 5: War-Time Memories

Concerning the Battle of Britain and the London Blitz

"*My memories of the War – as told by Cynthia Mary Smith, widow of Fred Smith (2000)*

When World War Two broke out (in **September 1939***), I was fifteen years old and the school I was at closed. It was in* **North London** *and, at the time, everybody expected that London would be heavily bombed straight away, so my father persuaded my mother and I to go to* **Buckinghamshire** *to stay with some relatives. We stayed in digs in the village. It was a very cold winter and we were frozen. We weren't at all happy and decided to return to join my father in* **London,** *who was not yet serving abroad. At the time, the 'phoney war' was on and there were no air raids. I have a particularly vivid memory of the barrage balloons hanging over* **London** *– not that they did much good!*

In **January 1940,** *I began work in the Civil Service and had to commute from* **Crouch End** *in* **North London** *to* **Westminster** *every day, which involved taking two buses and the tube. At the time, we worked from* **9.00AM** *until* **5.30PM** *and from* **9.00AM** *until* **1.00PM** *on a* **Saturday.** *There was no such thing as a five-day week! For this I earned the princely sum of thirty shillings (£1.50) a week, my fares and lunches cost twenty shillings (£1.00) so I was left with* **10s (50p)** *for myself. Everything was very quiet until* **June 1940** *when the* **Germans** *overran* **France** *and it was soon realised by everybody that it wasn't a 'phoney war' anymore!*

The Battle of Britain

Although the odds were very much against us nobody ever thought that we would lose the war. **Winston Churchill** *made a lot of rousing speeches, which kept up people's morale. The blitz against* **London** *then began in earnest. One of my most vivid memories (whilst visiting relations in* **North London***) was looking out of the attic room window and seeing the city ablaze. It was very spectacular although frightening.*

Getting to work was a real problem and I remember getting lifts on Lorries. The tubes were still working quite well, and many people took refuge in them and slept all night on the platforms. The air raids started about six in the evening and went on all night. It was impossible to get home before the raids started so most of us slept in the basement of whichever building we worked in. We were given mattresses and blankets.

554

When at home I slept in an **Anderson Shelter** in the back garden. These were made of corrugated iron and buried in the earth. We had a camp bed and deck chairs, but it was cold and uncomfortable. The noise of the raids was so loud it was impossible to sleep much. One night the house opposite us received a direct hit and our house was damaged but not too badly.

At work, my office was on the sixth floor and we spent more time going up and down to the air raid shelter than working. Despite everything, there was a great spirit of camaraderie and we had many laughs.

One morning my friend **Iris** and I were walking down **Whitehall** and had just turned into **Downing Street** when we heard some planes overhead. As there had been no air raid warning we thought the planes must be ours but when we looked up we saw they were **German** planes – they were flying so low we could even see the pilots. We began rushing down to **Saint James' Park** and threw ourselves onto the ground. When we looked around we saw that a few government buildings had been hit [by bombs.] We were lucky to escape with our lives. Our main worry was whether we had ruined our stockings – because clothes rationing had made stockings hard to come by!

Another incident during the blitz occurred when an incendiary bomb burned down the Church along the road where we lived. We were all afraid that the **German** bombers would see the blaze and drop more bombs. Luckily this didn't happen.

A Wartime Marriage

As we were getting no work done, the Government (in **September 1940**) decided to evacuate everyone to **Bournemouth.** A hotel was requisitioned to make offices and we were all put into digs. The digs were pretty 'grotty' and there were eight of us altogether – all young so we had a lot of fun and a good time. It was in the **Rink Ballroom** in **Bournemouth** that I met **Fred** (my future husband) – he was in the Navy serving on Motor Torpedo Boats in **Poole Harbour.** We met in **January** and got married in **December 1941.** We had a very quiet wedding in **St Peter's Church.** I just wore a blue dress and had a sprig of carnations. **Fred**, of course, was in uniform. I remember being very upset because I couldn't have a white wedding cake (as white icing had been prohibited) so I'd had to settle for chocolate. When I got married friends gave me some of their clothing coupons. There was a thriving black market in clothing – both in clothing coupons and food, which could be obtained if you knew (at a price) where to go! We went for lunch in a restaurant and then we got a coach to **Balcombe** for one week's honeymoon.

When we got back to **Bournemouth** we rented a furnished flat but after about three months **Fred** was moved to **Lowestoft. Bournemouth** was not free of air raids as the

*Luftwaffe used to jettison their bombs there on the way back to **Germany** after the so-called **Baedeker** raids. **Fred** and I had a lucky escape when a bomb dropped very near us.*

*I stayed in **Bournemouth** for a while after **Fred** left. My mother, who had come to **Bournemouth,** had returned to her flat in **London** and I decided to join her as the raids had subsided. I got a job at The War Office and used to see **Fred** in **Lowestoft** at weekends. He was then serving on minesweepers – a very dangerous job.*

*My father had gone back into the army. He [had now] served in two World Wars and was in **Greece** helping the Resistance – as he could speak **Greek.** We had some sad news as **'Chippy'** (our Best Man and a good friend) had been lost at sea. We were lucky as he was the only person close to us who was killed in the War. All was quiet for a while and life went back to normal. All the theatres and cinemas were open again and despite the 'blackout' I used to go out quite a bit with friends. It was a sign of the times that I could walk through the centre of **London** on my own and never come to any harm.*

*It's difficult to analyse the mood of the people. Everyone was cheerful and joked and laughed but there was a real hatred of the **Germans** and we used to cheer if any of them were killed and were really pleased when their towns were raided. We had no compassion at all. We were especially pleased when we heard that the **Germans** had been turned back from **Moscow** in **December 1941.***

The 'Doodle Bugs'

*The next raids were the worst, when the **Germans** used the so-called 'Doodle Bugs' – the **V1** rocket bombs (from **June 1944**). One could hear the 'chug, chug, chug' and then there was silence. We didn't know where it was going to land. A bomb skimmed the roof of our flats and landed in the block of flats opposite where quite a few people were killed. About an hour later we heard another loud explosion: a bomb had landed on **Saint James' Chapel** where many other people were killed. As we couldn't stay in our flat we got a taxi and went to stay with relatives in **North London,** but we had only been with them for a week when a 'Doodle-bug' landed in their garden. Luckily none of us was hurt but the house was badly damaged. **Fred's** mother then persuaded us to come to stay with her in **Leeds** and not wait to be bombed out for the third time!*

*There was a funny side to this. **Fred** had been granted compassionate leave when we'd first been bombed out – but when he told the authorities we'd been bombed out again [a second time] they didn't believe him and sent the police to check!*

*Luckily, I wasn't in **London** when the **'V2s'** were launched but from what friends told me this was even more frightening as there was no warning at all until they landed.*

***Leeds** seemed really peaceful after **London**. It was a very lucky city and had only one air raid during the war. I stayed in **Leeds** for the rest of the war and worked at a factory in the wage's office. We couldn't choose where we worked and were directed to our jobs. **Fred** was on minesweepers for the rest of the war. He was very fortunate as his sister ship hit a mine and all the crew were lost.*

*Looking back, I realise how lucky we were to have come through safely in spite of 'narrow shaves' and although it was a terrible time for many people, I have many happy memories – especially of course meeting **Fred**. We had over fifty years of happy marriage before he died – despite it being a war-time marriage!"*

Compounding their troubles was the way her parents had kept receiving threatening phone calls from a man, accusing them of holding a certain lady against her will. When they denied this, he'd become steadily more aggressive and threatening. In the end, the police were contacted, and the caller was found to be a man phoning from his office during the lunch hour. Apparently, he'd been menacing many of people. (My mother confirmed that this incident had occurred shortly before her move to **Leeds**.)

Subsequent research both confirmed and added further details to her account. The visit to the **Westminster Archive Centre** (on **Thursday, 17th September 2009**) revealed her close brush with death. This had occurred on **Saturday, 17th June 1944**. However, a fuller picture of the events of that day only emerged during a visit (with my wife) to **The Churchill's War Rooms** on **4th January 2014**. One of the Rooms displayed a notice (dated **17th June 1944**) pinned to the wall) which read: -
248 rockets had been launched
154 had crossed the coast
61 had reached London
19 had been destroyed by the FTRS (Full Time Reserve Service)
32 Destroyed by *'Ack Ack'*
0 Destroyed by balloons
77 Fatalities
314 Serious casualties
177 Slightly Injured
My mother had very nearly been one of those fatalities. Within the space of less than a month, both my parents had come close to losing their lives in a conflict

which killed tens of millions of people across the world. Yet **Cynthia** didn't altogether escape. One effect of this incident was to cause my mother to miscarry a baby boy. The fact that the sex was known suggests that my mother had been in an advanced stage of pregnancy. When I spoke to her about this loss on **Saturday 8th April 2017** she divulged that she *"had been three to four months pregnant – possibly more."* This may partly explain why she'd been so sympathetic when our own Granddaughter **Penelope Jemima** was stillborn in **March 2008.** On being told of the miscarriage my sister **Valerie** had remarked, *"I could have been outnumbered three to one!"* As this information hadn't been disclosed by **Cynthia** until **2016** (when my brother had paid her a visit) it could so easily have been lost to this *'History.'*

The second piece of information concerned the factory my mother had worked in when at **Leeds.** It turned out to be **Kershaw's Optics** in **Harehills.** On **Wednesday, April 22nd, 2015** my wife and I visited **Headingley Hall** Residential Care Home where **Cynthia** had lived since the previous **July** (and would be there until her health deteriorated in **July 2017**). After discussing the forthcoming election (my mother would vote **Conservative** by postal ballot) she disclosed what she'd done on **VE** day. *"My friends and I at **Kershaws** went to the pub to celebrate. We got rather merry but not drunk, mind you. I remember people waving flags on the streets."*

Further insight into my mother's time at **Kershaws** was provided by one of the most astonishing coincidences ever witnessed in this whole project. It involved my mother encountering a former workmate she'd not seen in over seventy years. What happened was this. Around **5.00 pm** on **Monday, 28th March 2016** my wife **June** was visiting my mum at the Care Home. **Cynthia** was seated with another lady (aged **91**) around a dining table. (Meals were due to begin at **5.30 p.m.**) Earlier that afternoon **June** and I had visited **Meanwood Valley Urban Farm** where we'd photographed an array of old glass bottles and lamp glasses, all neatly assembled on a shelf in the dining/classroom area. The name *'Kenyons'* could be seen on one of the glass objects. **June** now asked **Cynthia** whether she'd ever heard of the name of this company? My mother who was slightly deaf misheard the question and stated that she'd worked at **Kershaws** during the war. Immediately on hearing the name *'Kershaws'* her dining partner chimed in by saying that she too had worked for the same firm. The two old ladies then began speaking in a very animated way. The result was that both released a flood of memories in each other and for the first time ever, my mother's testimony of an early part of her life was receiving witness corroboration. Astonishingly, after an interlude of several decades, my mother now found herself dining next to an old workmate whose account of a situation would complement that of her own. Present here was a coincidence that most historians can only dream of. Anyway, from their conversation (with only the odd interruption from us to ask some clarifying questions) the following points emerged: -

- My mother's workmate (who had an **Italian** surname) had worked on the *'shop floor'* at **Kershaws** – dismantling and assembling binoculars. In contrast, my mother had worked in the upstairs wage's office.

- Her workmate seemed to have worked longer at this Firm because she remembered (when she'd first started there) an elderly gentleman standing and carefully watching the production process. She wondered what he was doing. (He'd apparently been one of the **Kershaw** brothers who owned the Business.) My mother admitted that there'd been two brothers and that *'they were held in awe.'*

- My mother's workmate admitted to having done *'something silly'* with the low heat ovens where the binoculars were placed. This had nearly caused a fire! However, her memory of the incident was rather hazy, so she was unable to provide any further details

- Like my mother this lady remembered VE Day, *'everyone was smiling and happy. People were dancing on the street.'* They went to a nearby pub (possibly the same one as my mother as it was frequented by **Kershaw** employees) but, like my mother, admitted to only getting *'merry, not tiddly.'*

- At work, they would have met face to face for my mother used to go down to the *'shop floor'* and hand out the wage packets. This jovial lady had then jokingly put her hand out to my mother requesting more wages!

Once dinner had been served my wife and I left these ladies to continue their very lively conversation. Thoroughly *'gobsmacked'* we sat in the lounge area – with me scribbling down notes of what had been discovered. A very pleasant **Polish** carer was especially interested in what had transpired. It was remarkable to see how aspects of my mother's early life were coming back to exercise a thoroughly benevolent influence in her extreme old age. As my wife remarked, *'she's been given a new interest.'* The discovery of my mother's old workmate had come just in time because in the **December** of that same year this lady sadly passed away.

Yet my mother's ordeal was not quite over. Shortly after the war had ended **Fred's** sister **Madge** had turned up at **Kershaws** making all sorts of groundless accusations against **Cynthia** in front of her employers. **Madge** was wanting to sabotage **Cynthia's** job. Thankfully, my mother's employers recognized that

Madge was so obviously *'barmy'* that they'd simply not taken her seriously. My mother attributed this bizarre action to **Madge's** resentment at her taking *'little Freddie'* away from her. But it must also be remembered that **Madge** herself was most probably a deeply unhappy woman with a husband apparently involved in a string of extra-marital affairs. The trauma of war may also have played a part. My mother had first related this event when I'd visited her flat on **Saturday, 18th January 2014. Cynthia** had been known to be wary of **Madge** who'd possessed a reputation for unjustly *'turning'* on people.

Most of my mother's account was in accord with official records and subsequent post-war accounts. Her vivid recall of female comradeship was echoed by that of the historian **Bruley** in her interviews (conducted in the **mid-1990s**) with former female wartime **South London** factory workers. In many ways, my mother's war experience was typical – regarding her vivid memories of both the horror <u>and</u> of the camaraderie of the war years. However, **Leeds** did have more than one air raid although, when compared to other cities, it still got off very lightly. One discrepancy between my father and my mother's account was in the actual number of mutual acquaintances killed in the war. This contradiction can be seen when my late father's words are placed alongside those of my mother.

"I've been very lucky, so many of my pals were blown up," **(Fred).**
"He (Chippy) was the only person close to us who was killed in the war," (my mother).

Present here is that kind of discrepancy that could easily puzzle historians who would not have known my parents. However, I think a credible explanation was that, out of his honourable desire to protect my mother, my father had never disclosed to her the full number of lost friends. Perhaps my mother had never known some of these friends because **Fred** was often away for extended periods of time. Moreover, **Fred** was never keen to speak much about his wartime experiences. As noted earlier, he displayed a marked contempt for those who *'went on'* about their war experiences. This was the age of the *'stiff upper lip.'* What **Fred** did divulge often came out only in snatches, separated by protracted periods of time. Without my mother's assistance, no coherent account of them would ever have been possible. In a note received on **Wednesday, 22nd November 2000,** my mother herself finally resolved this discrepancy. She did this through stating that, *"Although* **'Chippy'** *(our best man) was the only person I knew who was killed,* **Fred** *lost quite a few of his comrades when his sister ship struck a mine and all hands were lost."*

The first and surname of *'Chippy'* remain unknown, but I vaguely remember my father referring to a certain *'Chippy'* **Norton** whilst we were on holiday in **Llandudno, Wales** during a rain-soaked **August** in **1966**. This was in conversation with some friends who'd dropped in and were sharing wartime memories whilst playing cards. I was lying on the floor playing with some plastic **Daleks** at the time. (These were robotic monsters from the Science Fiction series called **Doctor Who**.)

In conversation, my mother would sometimes let slip the odd extra detail. For instance, she was of the decided view that **Britain's** Prime Minister (from **1937** until **1940**) **Neville Chamberlin,** had been *"a bit of a wimp."* Her first impression of **Leeds** was that *"it was very dirty."* I also found an old picture of her friend **Iris** enclosed in a photograph album. Taken around **1940,** it showed a rather buxom, jolly-looking lady. After the war, she had married a man called **John** but had remained close friends with my mother until her death in a village located in the **Southeast** of **England** during the summer of **2000**. Although this additional information provided an extra *'feel'* of the period it did not substantially alter my mother's written account.

Once the war was over my parents could think of settling down to a normal married life. For **Julia,** it was a different matter. In late **1945,** she travelled down to **Southampton** to collect her husband, newly released from **Japanese** captivity. Whilst looking for him she passed a hunchbacked old man. She heard a voice call *"Julia"* and on turning around she saw that the hunchbacked old man was her husband! According to my informant, **Julia** would later remark that *"that day in **Southampton** was one I remembered for the rest of my life."* Her husband died in about **1957,** his health never fully recovering from his captivity. I dimly remember a story that his digestion had been permanently affected by his captivity. he was an utterly broken man. His very sad story well illustrates the cost war could have on people's lives. Yet, as my mother often admitted, people in places like **Poland** *'got it'* far worse.

CHAPTER 18: PEACE AND LIFE

Section 1: Post-War Difficulties

Concerning post-war Britain

During the war years, the business of **Fred's** future accountant **Joshua Barrett** prospered. In his own words *"In 1942 I opened my first office opposite the Town Hall. I could do this because I had just won a big audit. During the war, a lot of young boys of 15 or 16 came in as refugees from Germany. They were housed in a big house in Potternewton, acquired from the Belgian Consul. 'The Polish Club' now occupies it. The 'Organisation for Rehabilitation and Training' was started there. At that time, some friends and professional associates used to come along and help them by teaching them various subjects. I taught them Maths and English.*

During that time, a lot of the boys became very successful. Most of them became my clients and made millions. I taught them maths. I wish they had taught me to make money. This is how my practice was built.

After the war, I just went on acquiring clients. In later years, I finished with 500 clients, large and small. Some of the small ones became much bigger. Fees grew from a few guineas to many thousands. Altogether, with my wife, there were ten of us in the firm." (His wife appears to have acted as secretary.)

Following the end of the war, **Fred's** first struggle was to regain his old job as a textile representative. His immediate need to support a young wife prevented him from following up the idea of entering the teaching profession. A cloud of post-war economic uncertainty also meant that his former employers were reluctant to re-engage old staff, especially when they believed that their products could *'sell themselves,'* because of a large, pent-up post-war demand. **Fred's** firm only relented when he threatened to use the law (which guaranteed former servicemen their old positions) on them. Once re-employed further haggles took place over his commission, with **Joseph Gillinson** arbitrarily changing the terms. My mother recalled, *"there was quite a furious row between Fred and Joe"* who perhaps secretly respected a man who would fight to be re-employed in <u>his</u> Firm. Nevertheless, this incident doesn't show **Joe Gillinson** in a good light.

A Trade Directory for **1947** showed that the Company **Fred** worked for still went under the name of *"Gillinson, J. Gibbons & Demaine Ltd, wholesale drapers 1 - 13 New York Street."* **Joseph Gillinson** was still at the helm as

'Managing Director,' having obviously taken steps to ensure business survival amidst war as well as economic depression. Concerning the years **1946-1949, Fred** would remark, *"The first year after the war you made nothing, the second year you made a little, the third year you made a little more and the fourth year you could start to make a decent living."* In that period, he also seems to have suffered from what today would be known as *'post-traumatic stress disorder.'* On at least one occasion he was said to have woken up and paced around the bedroom, thinking he was on *'watch duty'* in the navy. Around **1948,** whilst waiting on a platform at **Leeds Station** he suffered what was to be his first attack of angina. He recovered but the attack was a sure sign of the stress he was under. Whilst my sister was still a baby my father also suffered an attack of pneumonia. In his fever, he'd kept shouting, *"Get this man out of my bed!"* The late **1940s** were indeed challenging times for him; only in the early **1950s** did he begin to financially prosper.

Around the early post-war years, **Fred** used to go around giving *'sermons'* to members of his family, driving them mad in the process. As my brother said in **1991,** *"His was 'a do it yourself' kind of religion."* Yet it seemed to work. Throughout much of the **1950s,** he was to act as a sides-man in **Saint Michael's Church, Headingley.** This voluntary post involved escorting people to their seats before the service, collecting offerings during the service and putting away prayer books at the end. He subsequently left this church because of a disagreement over missionary fundraising. His disillusionment with the *'Established Church'* became as total as his disillusionment with politics. My father appeared *'to know where things were going'* with that Denomination. His disengagement from the Church echoed that of **John Smith** in the early **1840s** (and my own during the **Easter** of **2012**). Oddly enough, **Fred** began to sporadically re-attend **Saint Michaels** in the early **1970s** when it was under the incumbency of the **Reverend Luxmoore.** In **March 2000,** I came into possession of a small *'Book of Common Prayer'* owned by my father. It had been given to him on his thirty-second birthday (on **6th February 1946**). This artefact would suggest that, by then, his faith had become strong enough to have been noticeable.

Following the war, my parents lived with **Fred's** mother **Elizabeth,** until her death in **1947.** Throughout that conflict, she had worried greatly for her sons who had all been on active service. She'd still thought **Rosamund** was wonderful and didn't discover her true nature until it was far too late. (Later events will show that, when she did so, it was to cause her much grief.) Post-war conditions were harsh and even when she suffered from cancer of the womb **Elizabeth** still clung doggedly to *'old-time'* values. Reasons of pride prevented her from accepting the State Old Age Pension, despite family attempts to persuade her that doing so was <u>not</u> the equivalent of living off charity. In the end, she was only persuaded when **Stewart** promised to accept her pension as rent. Consequently, every week, she would make a point of meeting with **Stewart** with *'the rent'* hidden at the top of her stocking. To pay it she would loosen her garter, slowly remove her stocking, shake out the money and then hand it over. Apparently, this routine caused quite a lot of mirth. **Elizabeth's** concern with appearances never left her. Once, when my mother had called at a neighbour's house to check the time she had returned to the accusation of having *"lowered the tone of the neighbourhood"* by having gone out <u>not</u> wearing a hat and gloves! My mother recalled that **Elizabeth** was still very class-conscious. One of her favourite sayings was *"you can't make a silk purse out of a sow's ear."* The impression gained was that of a rather elderly lady who had lived beyond her time. Her middle-class **Victorian** values sat somewhat uneasily with the world of the Atom Bomb. During a private conversation (on **Sunday, 18th February 2001**) my mother remarked that *"**Fred's** mother was an autocrat."* Suffering badly from cancer, **Elizabeth** spent her last days of tortured infirmity being nursed by **Madge** who, at that time, was living in **Whitley Bay,** on the **North-East Coast,** about twelve miles East of **Newcastle upon Tyne.** She'd been running either an Old Person's Home (named **'Starcross'**) and therefore had had enough room to accommodate her mother. A recent photograph shoed **'Starcross'** as a very large, redbrick detached house with six spacious bedrooms, set in some grounds and located in a *'prestigious'* area of **Whitley Bay.** **'Starcross'** appeared to have been a Residential Care Home until well into this century. It was put up for sale in **2013** and was finally sold for **£995,000** in **2015.**

A cousin **Pam** (aged ten around the time of my Grandmother's death) disclosed that *"**Elizabeth** died at **Starcross, Whitley Bay.** **Stewart** and **Madge** were there. Your father brought me home a few days before she died. I was rather noisy! Cremated at **Whitley Bay** – ashes at **Lawnswood** with **Frank**. She didn't own her home so only left £200-£300 from the sale of her furniture. Funeral expenses were paid out of it."* This piece of information was written on a postcard, which I received on **Saturday, August 25th, 2001.**

Further details were provided by her Death Certificate, which I received on **Monday, September 3rd, 2001** from the Registrar Office at **Newcastle-upon-Tyne.** It said nothing about cancer, which if it had been present, was not the cause of death.

Registration District <u>Northumberland South</u>
<u>1947</u> Death in the <u>sub-district</u> of <u>Whitley Bay</u> in the <u>County Borough of</u>
<u>Northumberland</u>
1. When and where died? Fourth May 1947 *"Starcross"* [72] Marine Avenue,
Whitley Bay D. D.
2. Name and Surname: Elizabeth Mary SMITH
3. Sex: Female
4. Age: 75 years
5. Occupation: Widow of Fred Hesselwood SMITH (Draper)
6. Cause of death: I (a) Cardiac failure (b) Endocarditis. Certified by R.F. Kaye
Webster M.B.
7. Signature, description and residence of informant: Stewart Smith, son, 30
Moss Gardens, Alwoodley, Leeds
8. When registered: Fifth May 1947
9. Signature of registrar: Edwin H. B. Fletcher Registrar
N.B: Endocarditis was an inflammation of the lining around the heart.

The discomfort experienced by **Elizabeth** in her last days had been worsened
by the very harsh winter of **1947** which lingered on into **April.** It had also not
been helped by the behaviour of her daughter **Rosamund** who'd refused to
allow her mother to visit her in **Winslow, Cheshire** – claiming that *"she wasn't
good enough"* to mingle with her select company of friends! Her mother had been
used and dumped. This act of spite made it easy to explain why this aunt of
mine had come to acquire such an awful reputation in family folk law. Nor was
it enhanced by some rather peculiar events following **Elizabeth's** death.

Any sense of grief my father suffered from the loss of his mother was
compounded by what could well be termed *'the Dresden Vases affair.'* It was
one of the worst family disputes in which my father was ever embroiled. Details
of it only emerged some eighteen months after **Fred's** death. The following
account was based on the testimony of my mother and first cousin **Pam.**
Although each witness provided extra detail, their account largely concurred. It
may also be noted that the **Dresden Vases** involved in this strange business
were not that sort of dainty pottery which often adorns a mantelpiece. Rather,
they were large, heavy urn-like objects, which stood on the floor either side of a
fireplace. To move them would have required some strength and determination.
When my Uncle **Stewart** visited his mother's house at **34 Fearnville Road**
shortly after her death, he noticed that the **Madonna** (which used to stand on
top of the mantelpiece, beneath a large wedding photograph of **Frank** and
Elizabeth) was missing. Preoccupied with other matters he thought nothing of

it. However, on a second visit, made shortly afterwards, he saw (to his horror) that the **Dresden Vases** had also vanished. He quickly gathered together a family conference (which pointedly excluded **Rosamund** with whom **Stewart** was already on very bad terms). **Madge** (who had experience in the antique business) suggested that **Rosamund** may well have sold them to a nearby antique shop, as she could not have taken them very far. At **Stewart's** request **Madge** called into the nearby shop and, sure enough, found the vases in question. These she repurchased to keep the vases in the family. When **Stewart** was later to distribute **Elizabeth's** legacy he pointedly ensured that the cost of re-purchasing these objects was deducted from **Rosamund's** share. My second informant (my own mother) added that, concerning the legacy, *"**Fred** had always felt cheated in this matter. He'd got only £30.00, which wasn't much."* On being asked further about **Rosamund** my mother (who was normally an extremely tolerant person) had exclaimed, *"Oh, she was horrible!"* Sadly, this was still the image of my aunt just over three decades after her death. To say the least, **Rosamund** had managed to leave an abiding impression, albeit a most unfavourable one. She seemed to have been one of those people who *'stuck in one's mind'* for all the wrong reasons.

However, as usual, my father must have been very forgiving because a black and white photograph (taken in **1954**) showed **Rosamund** with her husband **Jack Kidd** and their son in **Roundhay Park,** along with members of my own family. **Rosamund** was by then a very stout, amply bosomed woman with sleek black hair. Her husband **Jack** looked the typical **1950s** academic in a tweed suit. The final rift between my father and his eldest sister **Rosamond** came about in the early **1960s** and had involved other matters entirely. (By every account her behaviour by then had become thoroughly impossible.) Incidentally, the Dresden Vases remained with **Stewart** and were subsequently passed on to his widow **Edith,** who, towards the end of her life, apparently suffered from dementia. During the **1980s** they were sold off to help defray the costs of a Nursing Home she'd had to enter. (Thankfully, by this time they had appreciated considerably in value). On hearing of their sale, **Fred** was alleged to have remarked, *"Its poetic justice. It's about time the **Smiths** did something after the way they'd treated **Edith**."* From what I knew of him, this was something he would have said; he was always a man with a marked sense of fair play about him.

With the birth of my eldest brother **David** (on **7th June 1946**) and my sister **Valerie** (on **16th May 1948**) **Fred's** life outside work centred on his family. The death of his mother reinforced this focus. In **1947,** my parents were buying a house of their own in the **Crossgates** area of **Leeds**. During the conversation (on **Sunday, 13ᵗʰ May 2012**) **Cynthia** disclosed that from **1947** to **1954,** she and **Fred** had lived at **56 Hawkshill Gardens, Crossgates, Leeds.** However, I didn't manage to visit this red brick semi-detached dwelling until **Saturday, 10ᵗʰ January 2015.** In early **1954 Fred** and **Cynthia** had then moved with their two children **David** and **Valerie,** to **2 Buckingham Grove, Headingley** where they were to live until **September 1985.** They then moved into the **Alwoodley** area of **Leeds.** I was born on **May 3ʳᵈ 1956** as *'an afterthought.'* When I was aged around three, my father had thrown me to the bottom of the bed because he'd been fed up with me disturbing his sleep. Like **Edmund** and **Frank** before him, **Fred** was always passionately keen for his children to gain a good education.

Outwardly, his life appeared uneventful. Looking very trim in a variety of neat suits, his career as a Textile's Representative became a success. Still very much alive at this period *'Old **Joe Gillinson'*** would have been pleased with **Fred's** contribution to business revenue. He would have viewed the gamble he took in **1931** as having been fully vindicated. Even at weekends, **Fred** would still look well-groomed, with checked sports jackets being his favourite attire. When measuring him for a suit in his premises, a very small **Jewish** tailor used to stand on a stool to gauge the length of **Fred's** arms. (This was during the **1950s** and early **1960s** when male clothing was a great deal more formal.) Numbering some **25,000** in **1955,** the **Leeds Jewish Community** was then at the peak of its influence. It represented **5.49%** of the total city population of **Leeds,** the highest percentage in any **UK** city. (By the **1960s** it had dropped back to **18,000** and had by **June 2017** it had stabilised at over **8,000** out of a total population of approximately **430,000** for **Leeds** itself and **730,000** for the whole metropolitan borough. However, the **Jewish** population in **Leeds** was still exceeded only by **Manchester** and **London.**)

My father was sufficiently well thought of by certain members of the **Jewish Community** to have been invited to Bar Mitzvahs and weddings. By the middle of the **1960s,** his salesmanship had enabled him to reach a fair degree of affluence. His technique of selling was highly individualistic. When a **Jewish** textiles businessman would shrug his shoulders in protest, exclaiming, *"Oy-oy-oy **Fred**, times are bad, I can't possibly buy anything. Au gevolt! Do you expect to ruin me?"* My father's response would be to go into action by giving a solemn lecture as to why such times represented the very <u>best</u> possible moment to buy cloth. After all, prices were low and there would be plenty of stock to satisfy customer needs for the good times. Following this verbal rap over the knuckles the party concerned would feel he had no choice but to comply. His was a kind of salesmanship which involved lecturing people into submission. Sometimes, to get his own way he would, whilst on the phone, adopt a loud and hearty *'I am your best friend'* manner which used to make my sister and I laugh. We called it **'Fred's** *telephone voice.'* Once, in the **1970s** he got an obscene caller on the line. By the time my father had finished with that person, it was the caller who was in tears! When it suited him, **Fred** was more than capable of what the **Victorians** would call *'a little humbugging,'* yet it was always harmless fun. There was never any conscious manipulation– it was the over-enthusiastic pitch of a good salesman. My father was a man without malice. Shortly after his funeral one of my wife's aunts had said: *"You could always disagree with him and still remain friends with him."* He was a man with a big smile and a warm heart.

Section 2: Some Departures

Concerning Jewish Cemeteries

'Old Joe' was still working (at least part-time) for some of the **1950s**. Apparently, he was, at times, rather free with his comments over how badly his son was running the business, (which he himself had both made and caused to prosper). My mother was of the firm view that *"**Bernard** was never cut out for business. His father had forced him into it; he was far more suited to be an academic. **Fred** always got on far better with **Bernard** than with **Joe**."* **Cynthia** recalled **Joe** as being a small man and something of *"a rough diamond."* The frustrations of being in the wrong occupation could explain why **Bernard** took to drink in the last ten years of his life. My mother only disclosed these extra details on **Wednesday, August 21st, 2002**, whilst visiting my wife and myself during a week-long family holiday at the **South Bay** in **Scarborough**.

One disappointment in **Joe's** life was that, through marriage to a (possibly divorced) woman (rather older than himself) his son **Bernard** had not produced any grandchildren. He had married this lady when in his forties. What grandchildren there were came from a daughter called **Rosie** who had married into the wealthy **Brill** family. Alongside **Edmund Smith and Berkeley Moynihan, Joseph Gillinson** was one of the three remarkable men to have featured in this Family History. As *'outsiders,'* these men had prospered in the highly competitive **Leeds** business or professional environment and both had been feared for their ruthlessness as well as respected for their abilities. In their own separate ways, they had played a leading role in shaping my family. Only now can their achievements be fully appreciated.

A visit to a certain **Jewish** Cemetery outside **Leeds** on **Wednesday, 3rd July 2002** revealed that **Joseph Gillinson** lay interred beneath a ridged black granite slab, the **Star of David** engraved on its base. At the opposite end of the slab stood a small black headstone with the following inscription: -

"IN REVERED MEMORY OF
A BELOVED HUSBAND AND FATHER
JOSEPH GILLINSON
DIED APRIL 11TH 1956,
AGE 75 YEARS"

Lying above these words was the same inscription, but this time in **Hebrew,** a **Star of David** crowning it all. Slightly further down and to the left was a similarly designed tomb, this time with a flat black granite slab. There was no **Star of David.** The small headstone contained the following inscription: -

"IN REVERED MEMORY OF
OUR BELOVED MOTHER
GERTRUDE GILLINSON
DIED MAY 6TH 1974,
AGE 89 YEARS"

To the right lay an overgrown patch of ground and a hole. The cemetery keeper informed me that this was where **Sir Montagu Burton** had been buried until his body had been removed to a more prestigious resting place in **Harrogate.** He also divulged that each of the **Gillinson** tombs would have cost several thousand pounds in today's prices. From the surrounding memorials, it was very clear that this was the area where the successful businessmen were buried. The memorials to various members of the **Lyons** family were particularly lavish, having tall headstones, flanked by ornate columns. All of them lay just to the left of a gravel path. As I toured the ground, I came across one or two names which sounded vaguely familiar. Their ages and dates of death suggested that they could have been former business associates of my father. I had the definite impression of having heard their names mentioned before.

By making this visit to **Joe Gillinson's** grave I was paying tribute to a man who had possessed the courage to employ my father during the height of the Great Depression. His influence had been such that it prevented any root of **anti-Semitism** from growing within my family at a time when this prejudice was prevalent. Although very exacting as an employer, **Joe Gillinson's** influence upon the **Smiths** was hugely benevolent. (It is one which continues to this day, each time I cite him as an example of business leadership and acumen with my students. Somehow, I think he would have appreciated his life being remembered and honoured in this way.) In the end, his memorial amounted to far more than an ostentatious tombstone.

Another exit around this time was my maternal grandfather, **William.** Until shortly before his death (from a stroke at the age of **72** in **March 1959**) he'd worked as a Tour Guide in central **London,** taking people around the Houses of Parliament. Apparently, on coach parties with **American** tourists, he was not above telling his rather credulous audience that some of the statues they drove past had been taken from Ancient Greek temples. A great admirer of **Winston Churchill,** he would often quote **Doctor Johnson,** saying, *"If a man is tired of London, he is tired of life."* Secure in his cheaply purchased **Westminster** flat he was very much in his element. In the basement flat below him, lived a couple of ladies. One (a cartoonist for national newspapers) wore a man's suit. *"It was obvious what they were, but in the **1950s** no one ever said anything. It was all 'brushed under the carpet' – things were different then."* My sister **Valerie** added that they were always very nice to her. My brother confirmed that, with hindsight, he could see they were a lesbian couple. *"The 'femme' was very kind to me, but the 'butch' looked angry – which is why I remember the event – perhaps because she feared her partner resented never having had children. I was around eight at the time and understood the situation only many years after of course."* My brother's disclosure of his age meant that this encounter could be dated to the **1954-5** period.

Sadly, following a series of minor strokes, a major stroke left him in bed half paralysed and speechless for three months before a merciful end took place. Sometimes tears would well up in his eyes; this seemed to indicate that he had some understanding of his condition. Located in **Tooting, Grove Hospital's** idea of treatment was to place a glass of beer by his bedside. (This was a custom still observed in the **mid-1970s** when I worked through the summer of **1974** and **1975** at the (now demolished) **Rothwell Geriatric Hospital**, in **South Leeds**. Sometimes patients would need help to drink it.) His Death Certificate provided a few more details:

Registration District Wandsworth
1959 Death in the sub-district of Tooting in the Metropolitan Borough of Wandsworth
1. When and where died? Tenth March 1959, Grove Hospital, Tooting
2. Name and Surname: William John ABSALOM
3. Sex: Male
4. Age: 72 years

5. Occupation: Of 4 Vincent House, Regency Street, Westminster, a Travel Agent's Guide and Lecturer
6. Cause of death: I (a) Broncho-Pneumonia (b) Cerebral Thrombosis. Certified by H. B. Raeburn
7. Signature, description and residence of informant: L.D. Wildbore, Sister, 15 Vera Road, Yardley, Birmingham 26
8. When registered: Tenth March 1959
9. Signature of registrar: C. H. Dalrymple, Registrar

From an early age, this sad story inspired in me a desire to safeguard my own health through healthy eating and twice weekly swims. I regard good health as an investment never to be squandered. My wife, a former nurse and midwife, thinks I'm something of a hypochondriac, which of course is mistaken!

After his death, his widow **Marguerite** moved up to **Leeds** and lived in a ground floor flat on **Clarendon Road** (on the outskirts of the City Centre). Asthma which had troubled her for much of her earlier life cleared up in old age. When I visited her she always used to ply me with generous portions of tomato soup. I have distinct memories of a small, silver-haired, crook-backed figure who used to speak in a light quavering voice. To my childish eyes, she appeared to be very old – her face was creased with many wrinkles. I used to pester her with questions about the war and she once told me about a shot down German Plane crashing into some burning ruins. She seemed rather gleeful about that event. **Marguerite** lived on into her eightieth year and died peacefully after a short two-week illness in **July 1963**. The end came quietly, my maternal grandmother passing away whilst the ward nurse looking after her had popped out to fetch her a cup of tea. Happily, my maternal grandmother died with her mind perfectly clear. In old age, she had greatly dreaded senility. A Death Certificate provided further details of **Marguerite's** demise:

Registration District <u>Leeds</u>
<u>1963</u> **Death in the <u>sub-district</u> of <u>St James North</u> in the <u>County Borough of Leeds</u>**
1. When and where died? Eighteenth July 1963 St James's Hospital, Burmantofts
2. Name and Surname: Marguerite Eliza Absalom
3. Sex: Female
4. Age: 80 years

5. Occupation: Of Flat B. 34 Clarendon Road, Leeds. Widow of William John Absalom, Travel Agent
6. Cause of death: I (a) Congestive Cardiac failure (b) Ischaemic heart disease Certified by N. F. Sahhar M.B.
7. Signature, description and residence of informant: C. M. Smith Daughter 2 Buckingham Grove, Leeds 6
8. When registered: Nineteenth July 1963
9. Signature of registrar: C. Maney, Registrar

My maternal grandmother had been a very intelligent woman with some extremely decided opinions. When I was very young she would warn darkly about *'the yellow peril.'* **Mao's** despotic rule in **China** seemed only to confirm her suspicions.

Cynthia's mother was well respected by **Pam** who knew her as *"Auntie Abby."* **Edith** noticed this and said, *"you always listen to **Auntie Abby**."* **Pam** further remarked, *"I really liked her – she was like a teacher and could talk at your level. I have warm, kind sentiments about your* [maternal] *grandmother. Your grandfather looked rather stern with a monocle in his eye. He struck me as a man's man."* My cousin fondly remembered how, during one of her trips to **Leeds** during the war, Auntie **Abby,** gave her the children's book **Polly Anna** as a gift. She *'loved'* its optimistic tone and treasured it for many years. *'Auntie Abby'* showed great patience in going through the story with her. This would have been in late **1944** or early **1945,** just before the war ended.

A far less happy departure was that of **Kathleen's** husband **Joe Burden.** Apparently, in the late **1950s,** he allegedly hung himself on the back of the bathroom door with his braces. This was because he'd come to believe that his wife was having an affair with the milkman. This may well have been a senile delusion or one borne out of depression. There was a big hook on the door and a blackout blind. My brother divulged how, as a child, he'd once got stuck in the blind. He admitted that *"I liked **Joe** – he was amicable. We never saw him with **Kathleen**. They didn't have children."*

Of **Auntie Kathleen, Valerie** remarked that *"she was very twisted. She was alright with me, but I found her rather frightening."* My brother added that *"she wasn't friendly to children."* **Pamela** concurred with this point by stating that *"she didn't understand children."* What stood out for **Pam** was *"her loud penetrating voice which was just like **Madge's**."* You could never ask her anything in a restaurant because if you did everyone would notice her. She lived in **Armley** in a house where the kitchen contained an old-fashioned coal-based cooking range. When, as a child, I was visiting her (along with **Valerie** and **Fred**) I'd put out my hand toward the electric bar of the living room fire. As I'd done so she'd said, (in a nasty tone of voice) *"Oh, let him put his hand on the bar – he won't do it again!"* **Fred** had been horrified – he'd simply swept me up and stormed out. In the end, **Kathleen** left all her money to **Pamela's** brother **Michael** (after firstly having intended to leave it to **Stewart** but who had passed away by the time this will was made). According to one source she *'used to wear a ginger wig and had a mean expression on her face.'* It seems **Kathleen** wasn't a happy woman. She lived on until about **1964** and appears to have been the last of **Edmund's** children.

Section 3: A Respected and Well-Loved Man

Concerning the business world of my father, Fred G. Smith

Fred was greatly respected in the business world – especially by members of the **Jewish Community**. From his former **Jewish** accountant words like *"honest,"* *"a man of integrity"* and *"an **English** gentleman in the finest sense of the term"* were expressed. Made during a very moving phone call (made on **Tuesday 4th May 1999**) these comments were given by a man all too familiar with some of the ruses that could be played in the business world. Until about a day previously I had never even known this man existed! He had last seen my father at a choral concert held at the **L.G.S.** in late **October 1998**. Here was an aspect of my father's life which I only vaguely knew existed. This same former accountant informed me that, *"**Fred** and I shared the same ironic sense of humour at how life had turned out. He was wonderful in conversation"* Once again, my father's quiet charisma had been in operation.

His former accountant provided further insight into my father's business life. They had first met in about **1949** when **Fred** had called in at his premises to request his services, which were to last until **Fred's** retirement in **1976**. From this elderly (but a still very lively man) I discovered that **Fred** would enjoy lengthy discussions with him on a variety of subjects. He granted his permission to publish extracts from my first interview with him (on **Friday, July 16th, 1999**) and to place them on a website. In his own words: -

*"My first memory of **Fred** was that he was a very tall handsome person. He was a 'toff'. This word is used as a mark of respect. He was good looking and had dignity. He had looks that made us envious. He was the perfect **English** Aristocrat. After the war, I met him when he became a client of mine. It was a very simple thing – I claimed expenses for him. He used to come into the office, and we used to have very long serious discussions. He never talked to me*

about the war. That was the thing – he was modest, prone to understate his experiences. We used to talk about the unfairness and corruption of life. Your dad and I thought in identical terms. We used to love discussion. Throughout the whole period, he never changed. We are both genuine; we never altered or changed for diplomatic reasons. I always felt that your father was badly done to by the firm he was loyal to. We felt we didn't fit into the commercial world because our values were different. We were both misfits in a commercial world where you were always trying to take the rise out of someone. It wasn't fair. We believed in justice and fairness. I have seen money make savages out of people. That's why I am so cynical. Yet he never complained, he did not moan or groan about it. I felt sorry for him because he should have earned considerably more. He was both loyal, consistent and hard-working."

Their friendship continued after retirement. *"We used to meet at **Sainsbury's.** My wife would go shopping. Your dad and I would be there, chatting. My wife used to go mad and try to drag me away. The main thing was that, when we met, we chatted forever. Our approach was different from the community around us. It was so genuine and sincere. I saw a lot of his paintings exhibited in the **Moor Allerton Centre.**"*

The firm **Fred** had worked for was very much a family affair. I remember one Company outing (possibly in **1961**) to **Pateley Bridge,** in **North Yorkshire** where they held all sorts of quizzes and competitions. Master of ceremonies was **Bernard Gillinson himself** who distributed raffle prizes with great gusto. Also present were rather formidable ladies who spoke in broad **Yorkshire** accents, their blonde peroxide hair was done up in the *'beehive'* fashion of the time. They were possibly the office staff. Like his Grandfather **Edmund, Fred** had benefited from a lengthy *'middle of the century'* boom. From the period of **1951** until **1967** he was, in material terms, at his most prosperous. He had come a long way from being the insecure youth of the **1930s.**

Fred's transparent interest in the **Jewish Community** showed itself in a variety of ways. At home, he would often use *'Yiddish'* phrases such as *"Gelt"* (meaning money) *"Mazeltov"* (meaning good fortune) and *"Toshka"* (meaning backside!). My father certainly had a gift for identifying with **Jewish culture.** In one sense, he belonged to a (now vanished) business world where personal service was all-important. By today's standards, this world looks amateurish and exclusive. Yet it produced sound and enduring life-long friendships. **Fred** managed to build up sufficient loyalty to last him for the rest of his life. Although (as his accountant readily testified) this world certainly had its *'sharp practices.'* perhaps something was lost when the salesman no longer acted as the customer's *'best friend.'* Modern business would gain a lot if it managed to recapture something of this *'personal touch.'* I try to do this with my own Private Tutoring Work.

574

Once, when I visited a synagogue with him on **Wednesday, 16th September 1992** my father struck up a conversation with a formidable **Jewish** lady who held some very decided opinions. With a mischievous twinkle in his eyes, **Fred** laid on the charm as if it was thick treacle being poured onto porridge. The *'telephone voice'* came on with all its loud *'bonhomie.'* From being a bristling **Zionist** warrior, this lady became just another middle-aged woman, flattered by the attention of a still fine-looking gentleman. Employing four decades worth of sales experience and using emphatic arm gestures he then began to haggle over the price of a proposed trip to **Israel** (which alas never took place). It was obvious that he was very much at ease in dealing with **Jewish** people in a **Jewish** environment. Somehow that meeting seemed to make him look years younger. He walked away from it with a spring in his step. Come to think of it my father always had a way of dealing with formidable women. If there was one *'battle axe'* on a coach or a train she would somehow always find herself sitting next to **Fred**. He would always pile on an extra *'dollop'* of charm to deal with such ladies. This trait was always a source of much mirth within our family.

Another feature of my father was his great care with money. **Fred** had a special dislike of those *"who gave themselves airs and graces and were as poor as church mice."* (This remark was perhaps directed against his former in-laws.) He hated pretence of any description – that was one characteristic guaranteed to annoy him. Those who grumbled about their war experiences he would dismiss as *'line-shooters'*. He adopted a stiff upper lip approach to such matters. In this, he was very typical of his generation. With furrowed forehead, I remember him *'doing his books'* (his business accounts) until late in the evening. Disaster once struck when the black cat we owned at the time suffered an attack of diarrhoea whilst sleeping beside the books on **Fred's** desk. The cat concerned was lucky to escape being skinned alive by both of us, as it had also soiled my book on The First World War. I was about twelve at the time. The cat concerned had the politically incorrect name of *'Blackie'* and was with us from the early **1960s** until his death in **1975** shortly before I left home. He had *'parked'* himself on us as a stray.

Yet such care with money did not stop **Fred** from being very generous to others. One of **Rene's** sons **Tony** was keen to raise **£300** so that his brother could stay on at a certain private school in **Bedford**. Two wealthy relatives (including **Julia**) were unwilling to help. In contrast, *"your father, when I made him aware of the situation, immediately wrote out a cheque for £100, being a one-third contribution with the promise of more as it became necessary."* Later he remarked, *"I will* *always be grateful for the compassion which your father showed at that time and it has been a lesson to me that if you wish to help anyone in a financial way it is far better to put forward your money than pontificate or give only a promise. As a tribute to* **Fred,** *I feel the above would be worthy of an inclusion in what you have written."* These remarks were made in a letter received on **Saturday, 5th February 2000.** It bore ample testimony to my father's generosity of spirit and his desire to see the best in people.

Another sign of this generosity was the way people who were experiencing business difficulties would be welcome to come to our house and share their worries. I remember one of these being an owner of a Driving Instructor business who'd been giving my sister driving lessons. In about **1968,** he'd got into trouble through over-expansion. Even today, I can recall the haunted look of depression in this man's eyes. My father acted as an informal business consultant and was often very wise in the advice he gave. To his credit, he may have prevented one or two people from committing suicide. I used to try and *'listen-in'* to some of these conversations from behind the living room door – sometimes with my ear pressed against it! In response, **Fred** would say that I was *"an earwig who loved to pry into other people's business."* He also called me a *'nosey parker!'* Perhaps this Family History has abundantly confirmed that judgement!

Before the advent of satellite technology in the **1960s,** political events (*i.e.* the Cold War) appear only to have made a limited impression upon my family. In **1956,** at the height of the **Suez Crisis,** my brother recalled **Fred** pacing around the Flat of his in-laws at **Westminster, London,** and exclaiming (in his usual loud and humorous way) *"Nuts to* **Nasser,** *Nuts to* **Nasser!"** During a private phone conversation in **May 2002,** my brother stated that there seemed to have been something of the **Marx** brothers in **Fred's** slapstick sense of humour. He'd apparently enjoyed seeing their films during the **1930s. Tommy Cooper** was another of his favourite comedians. At a more intellectual level, he was also an admirer of **Professor C. E. M. Joad (1891-1963)** who was on the **BBC Programme** *'The Brains Trust'* which ran first on radio and then on television during the **1940s** and **50s.** Another intellectual he admired was **Malcolm Muggeridge (1903-1990)** whom my mother detested for his pretentious mannerisms. She parodied his name by turning its first letter into a *'B.'* My father, in contrast, believed he was a *'brilliant man with an enquiring mind'* who saw where things were going in society. It was from **Fred** that I too appreciated **Muggeridge** whose writings were to contribute to my own intellectual development. **Muggeridge** provided me with a healthy scepticism concerning the direction in which our society was heading. However, this didn't prevent me from doing **Malcolm Muggeridge** *'voice-over'* impersonations to send my children to sleep when they were babies! In hindsight, I wonder whether my father's admiration for these two men acted as compensation for his own failure to have progressed educationally.

Section 4: Contrasting Brothers

Concerning Fred's Post War Relationship with Stewart

Gaining a handle on **Fred's** relationship with **Stewart** was a challenge – especially as **Stewart** appeared to have been a man of contradictions. Thankfully, a meeting with my sister **Valerie** (on **Wednesday, 17ᵗʰ August 2016** in her garden at **Huby**) threw some light upon this matter. She confirmed my mother's point of view that **Stewart** had been *'the family favourite."* He had black parted hair and bright blue eyes and was an obvious attraction to the ladies. He could also *'turn on the charm"* which greatly aided his success in business. Being the first son after four girls meant he was the *'darling"* of his parents with **'Little Freddie'** left mainly for **Madge** to bring up. Their close relationship in later years suggested that **Madge** managed this reasonably well. I do remember her being genuinely fond of my father.

My sister sensed that **Fred** had been *"slightly disapproving of* **Stewart,** *who had 'cut a dash.'"* *'They were very, very different people."* **Stewart** *"was a real showman. He liked the attention, whereas dad didn't as much."* Her most striking impression was that **Stewart** was *"incredibly smart,"* (meaning smartly-dressed – but so was **Fred.**) **Stewart** *'definitely had a presence. People would notice him. He had star quality.* **Fred** *was under his shadow but was a much kinder, tolerant and more pedestrian person.* **Fred** *was very much for the family."* Because **Stewart** *"was good looking and a bit of a charmer,* **Granny Smith** *thought he'd be for marrying into landed wealth."* She and **Frank** had *"very high expectations for him.* According to my cousin **Pamela** one major difference between the two men was that, where **Stewart** *"did things at 90 MPH,* **Fred** *would take things more slowly and methodically."* He also had a volatile temper.

In an e-mail, (dated **Monday, 8ᵗʰ May 2017**) my brother responded to this account by speculating whether his very stressful role in guiding shipping through the **Suez Canal** during the war had also been a contributory factor to his rages. In response to the heat, he would take salt tablets every day. When he later became ill the Doctor examining him had remarked that he'd taken so many salt tablets in **Egypt** it had seriously hardened his arteries.

Stewart and **Edith's** first child were their daughter **Pamela (Pam)** whom he favoured over his son **Michael. Pam** wasn't frightened of her father and always stood up to his rages when she was a teenager. My sister always held the impression that his wife **Edith** and son **Michael** were more *'under **Stewart's** thumb.'* She remembered **Stewart** shouting at **Michael** *"very nastily."* Temperamentally, *"**Stewart** was volatile,"* (a trait acknowledged by his daughter **Pam**). This trait may have been due to him suffering from severe hypertension. This condition can create the severe headaches that tend to provoke unpredictable outbursts of anger.

Despite his health problems, **Stewart** was always very nice to my sister **Valerie.** *"Uncle Stew Pot"* (as she called him) used to meet with her at **Shire Oak School** in **Headingley** during the middle of the **1950s.** Driving up in a luxurious **Silver Daimler,** he would take her for Tea at **Marshall and Snelgrove** *"a posh Department Store"* located at the junction of **Bond Street** and **Park Row** in **Leeds City Centre.** (It had been founded in **1837** and opened in **Central Leeds** in **1870.** It closed in **1971** when it was taken over by **Debenhams.**)

My sister also remembered how **Edith** had kept *"a very nice and clean house."* Once there *"you could either have bread with butter or bread and jam."* My sister admitted to feeling sorry for **Edith.** *'She was a very pretty and kind lady … she dressed nicely."* Her family used to keep **Great Danes** for show. **Edith** also had a **White Westie** that barked whenever strangers came. (I seem to have dim memories of it barking.) My brother provided the added detail that **Edith** often had her hair done up in a rather elaborate, plaited style. It was apparent that she'd been very beautiful when younger.

I just recall seeing a black and white photograph of an airman whilst visiting **Stewart's** house with my father as a young child. My sister believed it to have been a photo of **Edith's** brother who'd been killed in the war.

Stewart kept a couple of horses at stables in **Butcher Hill** and later **Cookridge,** each owned by a farmer called **Boothman,** who was well known in the racing world. One was an **Irish** pony called **Shamrock** whom **Stewart** looked after for eighteen months on behalf of a lady who was looking for other stables. It finally returned to its owner (who'd thankfully found a local stable) but only after having bitten **Edith** on the face. She'd required stitches but not plastic surgery. **Pam's** view was that her mother had *'got in the way'* and agreed with her father that the accident had been her own fault. The other horse belonged to the large *'Hunter Class'* and whose *'Roman'* nose which led to him being named **'*Emperor.*'** **Stewart** used to ride him up into **Headingley** where he'd trot up the drive at **2 Buckingham Grove.** He would nudge his head through the open kitchen window, looking for carrots. **Stewart,** as a special treat, would often pick **Valerie** up and place her on **'*Emperor's*'** back – they wouldn't go anywhere but she really enjoyed it. *"**Fred** used to think it was fun as he also liked horses."*

As part of this *'horsey'* interest **Stewart, Edith, Michael** and **Fred** would attend the **York Races.** My sister emphasised that *'dad could ride horses and he also loved motorcycles. He came off one when he was a young man."* He had wanted to be a motor mechanic but *"grandpa thought it was too common."* He used to attend dances at **Golden Acre Park.** *He loved it there."*

*"On **Boxing Day,** we went to watch the **Bramham Moor Hunt** in **North Yorkshire. Stewart** took me into a country pub to buy some orange juice. 'Dad was livid I'd been into a country pub! Dad "blew his stack" and said, 'don't take my daughter to a pub!" **Stewart** just took it."* When **Stewart** had returned home he admitted that **Fred** had gone *'absolutely ballistic'* but didn't know why. He wondered whether **Fred** had thought taking **Valerie** into the lounge would displease the nuns at **Clifford Convent School.** This was in **1960.** Both men were over-protective of their daughters and were uneasy about the cultural changes then beginning to take place. Both would take a lady into a lounge but <u>never</u> a bar – this being the custom of the era in which they lived.

My brother admitted to *"rather liking **Stewart**"* whom he'd regarded as *"a man's man."* He'd given **David** an old army officer's sword, with which he'd then taken great delight in chasing **Valerie** around the house! He used to tease her a lot and as a prank once placed wild rhubarb in her bed, which apparently provoked a loud screaming fit. Once whilst being driven to the **East Coast** for a holiday, their quarrelling was so distracting that **Fred** threatened to put them out of the car. Around **1960 David** began to suffer badly from acne, which was a cause for concern to **Fred.** In my brother's presence, **Stewart** had tried to re-assure **Fred** by saying, *"It's a sign of his manhood coming out in him."*

Along with **Madge** and **Irene, Stewart** was a sibling with whom **Fred** chose to remain in close contact. (With **Julia** contacts were far more infrequent and with **Rosamund** almost non-existent by the **1960s.**) **Fred** would often drive **David, Valerie, Michael** and **Pamela** out to such places as the open-air Swimming baths in **Ilkley** which my brother remembers as being *"cold and miserable."*

If **Stewart** had lived to my father's age he would have delighted in his daughter's **(Pam's)** achievements. These were many and various. Today, she'd be known *as 'a high flier.'* During a phone conversation (on **Sunday 9th July 2017**) my first cousin also disclosed that, in **1988,** she'd been awarded an OBE and in **1993** a CBE. Both were for Political and Public services rendered in **Leeds** and **Yorkshire.** My father (after the first award) declared that **Pam** should thereafter be known as, *"Old Big 'Ead"* for her OBE. In one of his sermonising lectures, he used to emphasise to **Pam** the need for humility. He once said to her, *"You've got humility. It's important that people keep that quality."* By her own admission, **Fred** had indeed exercised a very good influence upon her. She would later attribute her success as chairperson of *'Leeds Health Authority'* and of the more academic *'Leeds College of Health'* to having worked with *'a marvellous team.'* She was convinced in her own mind that *'a happy team works well.'* To foster such a team, she'd always kept an *'open-door policy,'* where pressurised team members could find an outlet and talk things over. She'd found it necessary to be a Prime Ministerial figure – *'with'* the people rather than a Presidential one – *'ruling'* from an elitist position. **Pam** commented that our current national leader **(Theresa May)** had failed to observe this distinction. The outcome of this was to lead directly to a lack of credibility in her own premiership and the loss of a government majority in the General Election held on **Thursday, 8th June 2017.** A top administrator in the **Irish** Government had paid my first cousin a backhanded compliment by remarking that only one leader had matched her **(Pam's)** effective style and that was **Martin McGuinness (1950-2017),** the former head of the IRA! Incidentally, **Pam** also served on *'The Bench'* as a Justice of the Peace. If there's anyone in our family who embodies the term *'Respectability'* it's, her! Indeed, she is *'Respectability'* personified. **Stewart** indeed would have been proud of her. Beyond providing *'the leads'* to begin and continue this *'History'* **Pam** also stressed the importance of integrating the lives of key characters like my father with some of their contemporaries. They were not to be seen in isolation. My cousin remembers my father as being very *'humane and kindly.'*

Thanks to the contributions made by my brother **David,** my sister **Valerie** and my **Cousin Pamela,** I discovered aspects of my father's life I had never previously known. Despite much research into it, I'd never learnt of **Fred's** passion for either horses or motorcycles. I felt I'd got to know him better as a man.

Section 5: Coping with Cultural Changes

Concerning post-war cultural changes and the *'swinging sixties'*

Strangely, neither my mother nor my siblings have any clear memories of the **Cuban Crisis** of **October 1962** when the entire world stood on the brink of nuclear destruction. My brother remarked that he was far more interested in listening to **The Shadows** and **Del Shannon** records than in hearing about Politics. However, on one occasion my brother heard a **Leeds Grammar School** master (a **Dr Black** who was giving him a lift home) exclaim that *"This whole business could get us all blown up!"* Apparently, government restrictions on information had been very effective in disguising just how serious the situation then was. Nevertheless, I do remember my mother attributing the **Kennedy** assassination *"to that **Cuban** business."* I also recall how our black and white television set seemed constantly to be repeatedly showing the same newsreel of **Kennedy's** death (which had taken place on **Friday, 22ⁿᵈ November 1963**) in **Dallas Texas, USA**. This was the day before the showing of the first episode of **Dr Who** *'An Unearthly Child'* – a science fiction show that continues to this day with the first female Doctor being introduced in **2018.**

Along with newspapers, our monochrome Television kept us informed of what was going on in the world. There was no internet or social media! My family, together with our neighbour, **Miss Melrose,** also watched the state funeral of **Winston Churchill** on **Saturday, 30ᵗʰ January 1965.** (**Miss Melrose** was a rather plump silver-haired music teacher who had distinctly **Victorian** mannerisms. She lived until her late nineties, possibly even her hundredth year.) I recall thinking, *'I wish I could have a funeral like that.'* We were all very excited over **England's** World Cup Victory on **Saturday, 30ᵗʰ July 1966,** when the **West German** football team was beaten by four goals to two. As **England** scored the final goal I jumped up and down on the sofa in boyish excitement. (I was then aged ten.) However, since then I've never been at all interested in viewing football or any other sport. Whenever it appears on the television I promptly press the off switch much to the annoyance of my wife who likes to follow it.

Other than the **Cuban Crisis,** my family did have some awareness of the cultural changes taking place during the **1960s.** When my older brother **David** quaffed his hair with *'Brill Cream'* and wore a garish green cord jacket over an equally garish check shirt my father's reaction to this act of youthful rebellion was to remark, *"You look like a seaside Pierrot."* When caught smoking in the toilet my mother said that if he had to do it he might as well do so outside the toilet. Thankfully, my brother's flirtation with this habit soon ended. Once he hid in a wardrobe from a girlfriend he wanted to drop. Unfortunately, the small dog she owned sniffed him out and the outraged young lady exclaimed, *"I do not know how such nice parents produced such a horrible son!"* Exercising with blue handled chest expanders and squeezing his many acne spots in front of our bedroom mirror were two other activities my brother indulged in during his teenage years. He was also used to throw stones through the glass of the old green pillared street gas lights we used to have.

David's biggest scrape as a teenager came a few months before he left to study an Economics Degree at **Trinity College, Cambridge** in **October 1964.** I was standing at the top of the stairs when suddenly my brother dashed passed me as a Policeman came to the door and spoke to our father. Taking my usual interest in other people's affairs, I overheard that he had been involved in some business to do with a female Student Hall of Residence. It was only during a telephone call I made on **Friday, 13th May 2016** that I received a full description of the incident from **David** himself. He had been a member of **Saint Michael's Youth Club** (as were some students from **Leeds University**). Apparently, they'd all been informed by some female students that there would be an all-night party at their Hall of Residence. The company of men was not allowed so they'd have to climb through a front floor window to get in. This is precisely what they proceeded to do in the evening in question. No sooner had they begun when the Police turned up! Everyone (including my brother) had made a mad dash for it – **David** remembers being chased down a nearby ginnel by a policeman. Although he escaped one person was caught and gave the names of all those who'd been involved. No charges were pressed or caution was given because the girls admitted that the whole incident had been a prank which they themselves had arranged – hence the prompt arrival of the Police. **Fred's** reaction to this incident had been one of amusement, although he would warn my brother not to be so naïve in the future.

David loved to *'talk politics,'* with my father. **Enoch Powell's** infamous *'Rivers of Blood'* speech (delivered in **Birmingham** on **20th April 1968**) was one topic of discussion, as was the outbreak of the **Northern Ireland** troubles in **August 1969.** My father dismissed the youth culture of the day as *"a load of nonsense."* He hated pretence in any form. He could never have imagined that songs produced by groups like **The Beatles** would ever become classics or that the **1960s** would be looked upon as a cultural *'golden age.'* My mother though thought that in their younger days the **Beatles** were *'rather nice.'* I remember watching on television the Beatles performance at the **Shea Stadium** on **Sunday, 15ᵗʰ August 1965.** My mother enjoyed viewing it, whilst **Fred** made dark comments about its *'mass hysteria'* reminding him of *'the **Nuremberg** rallies.'* He was always sceptical about the cultural changes then taking place.

David was to become a distinguished **Economist** in the **City of London** and be only one of ten men in this country (one apparently being an astrologer) who foresaw the financial crash of **2008.** On **31ˢᵗ December 2006, The Sunday Times Business Section** noted that he'd provided the most accurate economic forecast. When I congratulated him on this my brother replied by stating *"It was like winning the national lottery."* Publicising his success was the **Sunday Times Journalist** and **Economics** Correspondent (also called **David Smith**). Adding to any possible confusion was the fact that both men knew one another and sometimes met for business lunches. Sometimes this <u>other</u> **David Smith**) would refer to my brother as **David *'B'* (Brian) Smith**. Ah – such complexity! His full name was **David Henry Smith** and the two would jokingly refer to one another as *'Brian'* and *'Henry.'*

Sometimes being a Senior Economist could pose its own challenges. In early **2009** severe winter conditions meant that my brother was trapped in an **Oslo** Hotel along with other economists. They *'whiled away the time'* in the bar. Unfortunately for my brother, most of them could speak only **Norwegian.** This incident inspired a short poem *'Who Are those Men?'* which I first wrote down on **Wednesday, 12ᵗʰ February 2009**. (A copy can be found in *'At 47.'*)

This poem amused everyone whenever I read it in public. The only one who wasn't amused was my brother who, upon receiving it, sent me back a terse reply, *'I do not write my economic reports in blank verse!'* In fairness, he was very helpful in giving me *'leads'* and, with his wife **Carol,** in providing hospitality during two major Family History trips to **London** in **September 2008** and **2009.** The food was nice – but in portions, one would expect from the wife of an **Economist.**

When it came to their own children, my parents, to their credit, handled the cultural changes of that period in a wisely tolerant fashion. However, they were always firmly against the use of hard drugs. **Fred** realised that *'the swinging sixties'* marked the beginning of a steep moral decline. In his view, the rot started to become evident in about **1965.** Subsequent developments would prove his judgement right. Yet this analysis did not prevent **Fred** from driving around on a blue motor scooter called *'Tina.'* When he did this, he resembled what, in those days, was called a *'Mod.'* Clearly, there were some aspects of the **1960s** he enjoyed! Once or twice I suffered some hair-raising trips on the back seat – I was always glad to arrive back home safely!

At home, **Fred** had a wonderful gift for relating to children. During my own christening in **Saint Michael's Church, Headingley,** he had comforted and patted me as I lay on his shoulder to calm me down after I had drowned out the organ with my crying. This was on **Sunday, July 29th, 1956** and up to that point I had been held clearly by my cousin **Pam.** Young nephews and nieces would always eagerly look forward to seeing their *"Uncle **Fred**."* However, much to his regret, he was thwarted in his desire to see my brother or myself show any inclination for sport. Where, for him, the Rugby field had been a place of challenge – for my brother and I it was a place of torment, to be avoided at all costs. Many an excuse was used. The only sport I really came to like was swimming – which I do to this day two to three times a week. As a child and teenager, I was much more at home reading history books in the school library.

When I was a boy (in the late **1960s** to early **1970s**) **Fred** used to drive me to **Otley Chevin** for walks on the Moor. Sometimes the subject of **Israel** and the Jews would come up and he'd say, *"Even when I was a boy at **L.G.S.** I knew that **Jewish** boys were somehow different. The **Jews** are more intelligent than we are, they are very knowledgeable."* On our walks, we would frequently talk about the present significance and probable future destiny of the **Jewish** people. Once he divulged he had met a **Hebrew Christian** in the Cloth Trade who had told him, *"It will be one of the greatest events in history when the **Jews** recognise **Jesus** as the **Messiah**. However, they will only do so through great suffering."* His love for the **Jewish Community** (which had given him his first real break in life was very real. Some of the comments he used to make were profound. Without question, the influence my father had on my own thinking in this area was very deep. He suggested lines of enquiry that I have spent my whole adult life pursuing; one example being **Jewish** history (from the close of the second temple period in **70AD** until the foundation of **Israel** in **1948**). I still have vivid memories of him (at the time of the six-day war in **June 1967**) wandering around in rather absurd underwear, exclaiming that **Nassar** (the then president of **Egypt**) was *"a wily fox."* Present in our house was a large folio volume of **Josephus'** *'Jewish Antiquities'* that seems to have been obtained from **Madge** who was into antiques. I used to have a sneaky look at its yellowing musty pages, admiring the black and white print drawings. This created an ambition for me to read this history for myself – which I finally did in **November 2011**. This was from another edition as the original folio had long since been sold. Whether **Fred** had read this folio for himself I do not know. He did, however, have a good working knowledge of **Jewish** history.

Through sending me to **Leeds Grammar School (L.G.S.), Fred** brought me into contact with many **Jewish** boys, one who's Bar Mitzvah I attended in early **January 1971.** The boys were mostly from a secular background whose parents were newly rich members of the upper middle classes. By then the school had grown to around **1000** pupils. In what was perhaps the early summer of **1969** I remember trying to '*skive off*' school athletics with a **Jewish** boy. This was at the **Lawnswood Playing Fields,** not far from the running track. Although I did not know this boy well we started talking. If memory serves me correctly he intimated to me that many of his **European** relatives had perished in the **Nazi** concentration camps. I found this far more interesting than the running event we were supposed to be watching. True, his story was impossible to verify but it was clear that the near-complete destruction of **Europe's Jewish** population had left a hugely disturbing memory – even with the comfortably prosperous **Jewish Community** of **North Leeds.** It was always there as a sad background.

Another trait I picked up at an early age was the **Jewish** method of argumentation. I saw the livelier **Jewish** pupils try it out on a succession of schoolmasters. Once, when serving detention for belching during a history class in late **1967,** I saw one grey haired master, (nicknamed '*scruff*') being almost driven into a red-faced paroxysm by the argumentative antics of one older boy whose surname ended in '*berg.*' We all laughed at the time but with hindsight, I can see that there was something almost akin to the **Marx** brothers in the way '*berg*' had teased '*scruff.*' Poor '*scruff,*' all he'd wanted to do was to coast gently along into retirement. Instead, here he was facing the antics of a tall lanky clown, and there I was memorising it all. From my earliest years, I began to pick up an understanding of **Jewish** culture. Indeed, being at **L.G.S.** was the next best thing to being at **Yeshiva (Hebrew school).** This excellent grounding in **Jewish** affairs was only possible due to the considerable financial sacrifices my father made. When it came to members of his family he was utterly selfless in his giving.

It was through the **L.G.S.** that I became friendly with a small **Asian** boy who later became a dentist in **North London.** He was originally from near **Bombay, India.** During the **1968-1973** period, my best friends at the **L.G.S.** were this boy and a very rotund **Jewish** boy whose father used to sell shirts in the centre of **Leeds.** From an early age, I became deeply acquainted with both **Jewish** and **Asian** cultures. Particularly noticeable was the very great appreciation which members of these cultures had for **Business** and **Education.** I too shared this appreciation. There was some **anti-Semitism** in the school, especially from the school chaplain nicknamed *'Nod'* who should have known better. This was especially so as he had, so rumour stated, been a prisoner of war of the **Japanese.** The Second World War had indeed cast a long shadow on the schoolmasters. My early experience with **Jewish** and **Asian** schoolboys was marvellous preparation for my later work as a Private Tutor – for many of my future students were to come from these communities.

Except for swimming (where I eventually gained a bronze medal), I hated all sports and tried to bunk out of them as much as possible. Once I was supposed to be fielding during a cricket match. Instead, I crouched down and read a book all about the battle of the **Somme.** A cricket ball rolled by me and fell into a drainage ditch before being carried away by the water. The cricket captain soon had some very interesting words to say about that! What the **Grammar School** did develop was a love of History. This led me to win the *'Fifth form Project'* and *'Henderson Ancient History'* Prizes in **1973** and **1974.** The projects leading to these prizes explored such historical topics as the abortive **German** Invasion of the **Caucasus** in **1942** and the disastrous **Athenian** Expedition to **Syracuse** in **415-413BC**. Overall, about **40** out of the **55** masters who taught me ranged from the good to the excellent and their passionate sense of vocation greatly influenced my own approach to teaching. They were very positive role models. The remainder ranged from being utterly boring or a couple who seriously should have been *'detained at Her Majesty's' pleasure.'* (One, a classics master nicknamed *'Cissy'* was.) Nevertheless, my father's self-sacrifice gave me an excellent education which has benefited hundreds of students whom I've subsequently taught. In one teaching evaluation, I was informed that my teaching style was a cross between an *'Oxbridge Professor'* and a *'Night Club Comedian'* – very **'Leeds Grammar School'** in fact!

Sometimes, however, the considerable love my father had for his children did not prevent him from endangering their lives with a wide range of *'crude'* and *'often haphazard improvisations.'* If the gas cooker threatened to leak he would apply the black insulating tape; if there was a problem with the electricity he would again apply the black insulating tape. Once there was a bright flash, followed by a loud bang and then darkness. His attempts to repair a light had ended in the usual disaster. There was very much something of the late **Victorian** eccentric about **Fred**. Once, during a school play, he had embarrassed my sister by *'throwing'* his Trilby hat up and down into the air to attract her attention. He was also very reluctant to throw things away. For instance, right until my early twenties, we used to keep an old black **1930's** wireless in the dining room. With a look of deep concentration on his face, he used to fiddle around with it until it began to emit a whole array of squeaks, crackles and bleeps. Only rarely did it transmit a scratchy human voice. All this fiddling was done even though we had far more up to date radio sets in the house. His favourite hobby was painting. For hours at a time, he would closet himself in the small bedroom of our former semi-detached house in **2 Buckingham Grove** in **Headingley** with his artistic impedimenta. He produced a succession of sailing ships and flowers. His paintings were good enough to be exhibited in the local Community Art Exhibition. He would have been delighted in knowing that his oil paints were passed on to my eldest son (who also has an interest in art.)

On occasion, his sense of humour would the better of him. In late **August 1974,** he had sent **Julia** a naughty postcard whilst on holiday at **Ostend** in **Belgium.** On it was a statue of a naked boy flooding a pool with a fountain of water, which proceeded from his *'private member.'* Written on the back, in my father's neat script writing were the words *"This should keep you going. I think this fellow could hold his own in any society."* **Julia,** whose values were of a distinctly Upper Middle-Class **Victorian** nature, had been mortified. She was always highly snooty about *"people fitting in."* Two family members **Pam** and **Roger** were visiting her when she'd received the offending card. She'd exclaimed, *"I am not having that card in my house."* Anxious to safeguard her reputation in the village she'd also fumed *"Besides, the postman might have seen it!"* **Roger** had then pleaded to go to the toilet and once there had broken down into fits of laughter. *'Little Fred's'* boyish prank had produced the desired effect. Even now I can imagine my father's mischievous smile as he wrote that card. **Pam** and **Roger** had realised it had been **Fred's** way of saying, *"Don't be such a stuck-up old bat!"*

A review of the **1968** Telephone Directory showed that the Firm my father worked for had gone under the name of *"Gillinson, Dewhurst & Co Ltd, wholesale warehousemen, 20 Sweet Street."* In the **1970** Directory, the old name had gone and only **Gillinson, Dewhurst & Co Ltd** remained. In **1976,** (with the **Yorkshire** clothing trade being undermined by **Japanese** competition) **Fred** decided to take early retirement at the age of **62.** His old Firm (in **1972**) had been taken over by another company called **Baudmans.** As a Wholesaler, it specialised in buying and selling imported clothes. This was to be the case until **Fred's** retirement. The Firm was still there at **Sweet Street** in **1980** still operating as **Baudmans.** Overall, the picture was of a contracting business, unsuccessfully struggling to survive through specialisation. It was fortuitous that **Fred** had reached retirement age otherwise he would have faced redundancy.

This last period of his working life was rather sad, for instead of selling clothes much of his work had amounted to little more than trying to collect the debts of failing Textile Firms. The industry on which he had depended was dying a slow death. The prosperous times were now over as small shopkeepers could not compete when interest rates were high. The introduction of a bureaucratic *'Value Added Tax'* (VAT) in **1973** had served only to worsen the situation still further. Sadly, my father risked being dragged down by a dying industry.

On hearing that **Baudmans** had somewhat shabbily treated **Fred** by not giving him a proper pension, his old boss **Bernard Gillinson** had sent him a cheque for £500.00. This generous gesture had been much appreciated in our family – although **Joshua Barratt** suggested he was acting out of a sense of guilt for having exploited **Fred** in the past. Even if that was the case it was a good postscript to the business phase of **Fred's** life although he would often ruefully remark, *"there's no sentiment in business."*

Yet even his last years at work were not completely barren. During the late **1970s,** whilst walking with my brother in the **Canal Gardens** at **Roundhay Park,** a very small toothless, rather shabbily dressed **Asian** gentleman (sitting on a seat and haphazardly feeding the ducks) made a point of greeting **Fred.** A quick and jovial conversation followed about their former times in business. My brother stated that this man had said, with a twinkle in his eye, *"As you know Fred,* one Jew in business is worth ten **Christians,** but one **Asian** is worth ten **Jews."** Undoubtedly by today's standards a politically incorrect and perhaps even offensive comment but it did highlight the way in which **Fred** had had to juggle between different ethnic groups near the end of his working life. Whilst they walked away my brother had enquired as to the identity of that gentleman. My father then divulged that this man had been the first **Asian** businessman to have imported ladies' tights into the **UK** from **Asia,** sometime in the middle of the **1960s.** Despite his shabby appearance, he was a millionaire! What **Fred** (who had been reared under the *'Joe Gillinson'* School of *'Business Practice')* had exactly thought about that gentleman's wry comment, he kept quietly to himself.

Another **Asian** contact originally came from **Guyana** in **South America.** A **Hindu** by faith, he had met **Fred** whilst studying as a mature student for a Doctorate at **Leeds University** around the **1969–1972** period. As a family, we used to visit their family home in **Manchester** where I first acquired a taste for delicious homemade curries made by his lovely wife. **Fred** would associate with anyone so long as they were of the right social class. Once he had dragged me out of the house of an **Asian** school friend of mine whom he had judged not to have been of the right class. The action was not at all racially based; rather he viewed their house to have been *"a slum and a pigsty."* His reaction would have been the same if a white working-class family had been involved. Seeing what racial intolerance had led to during the war had only increased his toleration of people from a variety of cultures. He was, however, rather too class conscious. That was perhaps one of **Fred's** less endearing characteristics. Nevertheless, the honour of first establishing links with the **West Yorkshire Asian Community** belonged firmly to my father. In this area, it was he who was the pioneer. All I have done has been to continue this connection through my work in private tuition. My youngest son **Philip** twice did voluntary work in **Southern India** for the **Raleigh International Project** in the closing months of **2010** and **2012.** In establishing links with the **Asian** Community **Fred had** set a precedent for other family members to further develop. I've since come to enjoy close working relationships with many members of the **Asian** Community.

My father did tend to attract rather exotic people. In **1970,** I was confronted by the spectacle of a swarthy bearded figure, complete with caftan and hippy beads. He'd stopped by my father who'd been cutting the front garden hedge and on seeing **Blackie** had asked: *"Is that your cat?"* A conversation quickly followed, and he was invited in for a cup of tea. Related to a famous **Jewish** (but by then long deceased) **Austrian** Psychotherapist this man engaged in (what turned out to be) a deeply philosophical conversation with my father. His idea of solving the **Middle East** problem was to persuade hippies to drive along the **Israeli** border in colourfully decorated vans spraying both Arabs and Jews with LSD. Later (when I was out of the room) he'd offered **Fred** some LSD on a lump of sugar. My father had wisely declined. Sometime later, we read in a local newspaper that he had been arrested for drug pushing. **Fred's** view of this strange character was that he had been *"well-meaning but naive."* If memory serves me correctly I think he'd been a Postgraduate Psychology Student. My mother's reaction to this profession was to dismissively observe, *"they're all nuts."* **Cynthia** would sometimes complain about **Fred's** *'waifs and strays'* and *'the strange people he seemed to attract.'* She also noted that I seemed to have inherited his gift for attracting *'weird and exotic'* people.

One of the strangest of the *'waif and strays'* whom my father took under his wing was **Rosamund's** own son **Malcolm Kidd.** He was born on **16th September 1925** and was to leave an (often unfortunate) impression on different branches of the **Smith** family. *"A silliest creature"* was one of the more charitable comments made by one relative. He'd once annoyed **Julia** by having remarked: *"Oh you southerners must find it rather rough to be up North."* Represented here was a clumsy attempt to curry the favour of a woman who hated his mother. Unsurprisingly, **Julia's** response had been extremely icy.

Moreover, for every wedding, **Malcolm** attended he would always give the self-same present – always an alarm clock. There was speculation that he'd wanted to give away a whole stock of them. To my siblings and I he was known as *"creepy* **Malcolm** *– the man with the strangler gloves."* He was of stocky build with slick black hair and blotchy skin and to us children, he really did resemble a serial killer from a **1950s B Movie**! As an adult, my brother remarked that *"he gave the impression of having the bodies of primary school children buried in his back garden."* He would always wear those gloves which only added to the sinister effect conveyed by a general shiftiness in his everyday manner.

Poor **Malcolm** – did anyone have a good word to say about him? My father's reaction was to take pity on him. I remember seeing him in the living room of **2 Buckingham Grove.** Then aged in his forties, he would hover around my father with a furtive, lost look on his face, still wearing the *'strangler gloves'* as he shiftily moved around the room. I recall my father having many private conversations with him. Thoroughly downtrodden by his mother he held a succession of marginal jobs, *i.e.* selling **The Encyclopaedia Britannica** or working as a Laboratory Technician. The impression one had was of a man desperately trying to cling on to a vestige of middle-class respectability and not knowing how to do so. He was a profound disappointment to his parents who'd wanted him to be an academic, Doctor or a Vicar. He'd lacked both the intellectual equipment and personality needed for any of those professions.

In **1967,** he finally broke free from **Rosamund's** tyranny by running off with a nurse called **Francis Harris** who already had a child. He married her on **1st March 1968** in **Bucklow, Cheshire.** His mother was thoroughly outraged and bogged my father down in endless telephone calls. Secretly, **Fred** was cheering him on but didn't dare say otherwise. Whether this development was associated with **Rosamund** sending poison pen letters to **Edith** isn't known. But they were of such a *'vile nature'* that an injunction had to be taken out against her. By then a brain tumour was taking hold and this may have had a worsening effect upon her temperament. She died of it in **June 1969** – her life had indeed cast a dark cloud over much of the family. Not even the most patient members of my family had ever a good word to say about her. Overall, **Rosamund** appears to have been something of a sociopath.

For **Malcolm,** the end of the road with the **Smiths** came in **1982.** He had just attended **Madge's** funeral at **Lawnswood Crematorium** and was standing outside chatting to some **Smiths.** On seeing some smoke billowing from the chimney he'd clapped his hands before exclaiming *"There she blows!"* Apparently, this comment had been followed by a laugh which resembled the braying of a donkey. Outraged, the circle of **Smiths** had withdrawn further down the Drive, leaving him to himself. After that **Malcolm** vanished from the scene. My only hope is that **Malcolm** managed to find happiness in his later life. A search of records (in **May 2015**) on the internet confirmed that he'd died in **January 1996 Registration District <u>Macclesfield</u>**

1996 Death in the <u>sub-district</u> of <u>Macclesfield</u> in the <u>County Borough of Cheshire</u>

1. When and where died? Fourth January 1996, Macclesfield District General Hospital, Macclesfield

2. Name and Surname: Malcolm John Kidd

3. Sex: Male

4. Sate and place of Birth: 16th September 1925, East Wyne, Yorkshire

5. Occupation: Technician (Retired) 16 Deanway, Wilmslow

6. Cause of death:

I (a) Cerebrovascular Accident, certified by K. Ramsey M. B.

6. Signature, description and residence of informant:

Jacqueline Teresa Kidd daughter, Macclesfield

8. When registered: Fifth January 1996

9. Signature of registrar: Marjorie Abbott, Registrar

In retirement, **Fred** was a marvellous Grandfather – giving great happiness to my own children. The presence of some of his grandchildren in **Leeds** gave him a definite role that perhaps added years to his life. Frequently he would take them on outings to country areas or the Yorkshire East Coast. During the early **1980s,** he was quite happy to have my wife breastfeed our children in his living room. He often used to remark that, *"breastfeeding is a most beautiful thing."* Not for **Fred** a useless retirement, characterised by isolation and self-pity. Even after his first stroke in **November 1997,** he beamed with pleasure when his grandchildren visited him in hospital. Even though he would jumble his words; somehow it just didn't matter. His smile said it all.

Also, taking his leave from the business world was his former accountant **Joshua Barratt.** *"In about **1975** I merged with a larger firm who had about **60** staff in **Leeds** and **350** in **London.** It was a huge concern. After that, I became a consultant until **1980** to **81** when I retired from the firm."* Retirement, however, was not absolute.

This truly remarkable man (at the age of **91**) still had **4** clients at the time I spoke to him (in the summer of **1999** and in early **2002**) and I found his mind to be still as lively as ever. He did admit to specialising only in funerals and wills! My interviews with him provided persuasive testimony that **Fred** had indeed been very wise in his choice of friends. After reading an early draft of this Family History, a mutual associate (a former **North Leeds**-based **Tutoring Agent**) disclosed that **Joshua Barratt** had remarked, *"It was a work of a typical **Smith** – managing to get the best from both the **Jewish** and **Christian** Worlds."* He was also very keen that I would eventually release his name onto the Internet to preserve it for posterity. Rather movingly he stated, *"It would be the best kind of memorial for both **Fred** and I."* He has now received it

On **Friday 18th March 2011,** I rang a former Private Tutoring Agent (with links to the **North Leeds Jewish Community**) only to find that he'd retired. He disclosed that my father's old accountant had died in **2008** at the age of **99** and that his widow had died three to four months earlier (at the age of **90**) when her car had run into the back of a bus on **King Lane.** She'd suffered a fatal heart attack a few weeks later. The large house (in which I'd initially interviewed **Joshua Barratt**) had since been purchased by an **Asian** family who had then sold it on. Hearing of these deaths reminded me of just how close I had come to losing these vital sources of information. Outside of our family, **Joshua** had been the most enthusiastic contributor to this *'Family History.'* It seemed to have quite naturally become his way of securing immortality.

Another revelation concerned my mother's work at two Remand Homes for girls (from **1961** to **1967**). Over half of these girls had been victims of incestuous sexual abuse. They were mainly from the mining communities of **South Yorkshire** (which sadly had a notorious reputation in this matter). My mother always felt that these girls had been *'more sinned against than sinning."* She believed some had been associated with a (then unknown) manager of the **Mecca Locarno Ballroom** named **Jimmy Saville (1926-2011).** Even in the early **1960s, Saville** had had a *"very dodgy"* reputation in relation to under-age girls. However, the full extent of his depravity was not going to be revealed until after his death. With **589** known victims, he would go down in history as **Britain's** most prolific sex offender. When the scandal broke after his death it shook the media, many welfare agencies and the nation at large.

As if the first Remand Home wasn't difficult enough, in the second the manager was a schizophrenic lady who heard voices. I remember hearing quite a lot about her as a child. However, for my mother, perhaps the most dangerous incident at work took place shortly before her retirement in **1989,** *"just as computers were coming in."* By this time, she was a Home Help Organizer for **Leeds Social Services** and would visit potential *"clients"* (as they were then known) to assess their needs. The incident happened in the **Morley** area of **South Leeds.** It involved a *"hard man"* from **Glasgow** who had murdered his wife – apparently, she'd been unfaithful to him. **Cynthia** had been visiting him in his own home when he pulled out a gun on her. It had taken my mother's considerable social skills to dissuade him from using it. This last disclosure had been made by **Cynthia** on **Saturday 4ᵗʰ March 2017** when I'd visited her, accompanied by a professional associate who was also a close family friend. (She was a loud, *'larger than life'* **West Indian lady** in her early thirties whose private motto was *"always be nosey for a purpose."* Possessing a deep, throaty chuckle, she would not so much enter a room as to *'sweep'* into it.) We both responded to my mother's account with open-mouthed astonishment and were still talking about it a week later! This lady disclosed that my mother's memories had provided a greater understanding of how her own profession (as a Social Worker and Educational Practitioner) had developed. She could also compare her own work with that of someone from a previous generation.

Section 6: The Eccentricities of Auntie Madge

Concerning Auntie Madge's unusual Lifestyle

Adding a note of colour to this Family History was my Auntie **Madge.** Like my mother, **Valerie** noted how **Madge** had *'done an awful lot for* **Fred** *when he was growing up. She used to call him* ***'Little Freddie'*** *all the time."* **Fred** found his sister's bossy manner rather irritating. *"On a couple of occasions, I saw him storm out because of this."* Also, *'there was an 'atmosphere' between* **Madge** *and Mum who was very tolerant as she didn't want trouble."* In addition, *"**Madge** could be lethal if crossed. She was always very nice to me but horrible to* **Pamela**" [This was her daughter-in-law – <u>not</u> my cousin whom she affectionately called ***'Little Pam.'***] **Madge** tended to quickly and permanently turn against people. Like many **Smiths,** she could persist in maintaining a family feud for years. It's a trait that, sadly, continues to this day.

Madge's son **Peter Nixon** later divorced his first wife and remarried an **Iranian** lady and former nurse called **Suzie** who insisted that she was ***'Persian, and*** <u>*not*</u> ***Iranian.'*** She would attend his mother's funeral in **York.** He was to become a very successful Medical Consultant with a private practice in **Harley Street, London.** It should be noted he was Heart Doctor, <u>not</u> a surgeon who actually performed operations.

In terms of business acumen, **Madge** was a true granddaughter of **Edmund Smith.** She was by far the sharpest of **Fred's** sisters, having her hand in all sorts of successful enterprises. According to **Pam** *"Madge had the mind of a police detective and was very observant."* As her husband repeatedly found (often to his own personal cost) she could *'ferret things out.'* **Madge** had an enthusiastic interest in antiques and visited auctions whenever she could. She would buy fish for her guesthouse users from the **Quayside Market** in **Newcastle**. She also kept pigs – which sadly drowned in a flash flood.

Madge, it seemed, had led a rather nomadic lifestyle – which was the despair of her husband. He could never be sure which address he would be coming back to after a business trip! This point is highlighted by (a possibly incomplete) list of addresses with approximate dates of where they had once resided. It was provided by my first cousin **(Pam)** during an hour-long telephone call on **Sunday evening, 10th July 2017.**
1942: Holywell Avenue, Whitley Bay, Tyneside
1944: 120 Queens Drive, Whitley Bay, Tyneside
(later 119 on the opposite side of Queens Drive, purchased because it had a larger bedroom where her son **Peter** could study)
1948: *'Starcross,'* Marine Drive, Whitley Bay, Tyneside, Newcastle Upon Tyne
(A previous owner had named it *'Starcross'* after a winning horse)
1950: Newbiggin Hall, Blanchland, near Consett, County Durham. This was purchased from the sister of the then Conservative Prime Minister Sir Alec Douglas Hume. (It had a great deal of adjacent land surrounding it.).
1955: Morpeth, Converted Railway Cottage, Tyneside
1958: Links Avenue, Whitley Bay, Tyneside,
1959: Purchased a house for Peter on (or near) the Ring Road, Leeds. He was then an *'up and coming'* Doctor
1960: A large white clad house on Elmete Avenue, opposite Roundhay Park
1967: Goldsborough A converted village rail station in Goldsborough one-mile East of Knaresborough, and in the district of Harrogate district
1976: Rufforth – a village four miles West of York
Some of these addresses evoked memories. My cousin **Pam** remembered how she'd had to sleep in the pantry under the stair when staying at **Holywell Avenue (1942).** This was because **German** bombers were targeting the shipyards of **Tyneside.** She didn't hear any bombs falling – but recalled Air Raid Wardens in white hats rattling tins and shouting, *"turn off the lights!"* or *"close the blinds!"* As a four-year-old she thought to sleep in the pantry was a *"great adventure"* and she was happy to do it.

At **Newbiggin Hall** (in the early **1950s**) **Madge** was to discover that, in business terms, she had really overstretched herself. The accommodation was large – with thirty-eight bedrooms and a sizeable hall. The painting of the Madonna hung there as did a painting of some Renaissance Italian Gardens. The latter **Pam** attributed to **Daniel Foster's** father who'd reputedly been an artist. (Whenever she visited **Newbiggin Hall** both **Pam** and her brother **Michael** would stay in the Gamekeeper's Cottage.) For **Madge,** however, the premises proved to be a liability. Photographs of this exceedingly grand site suggested that maintenance would have been a severe problem. Neither was it easy to recruit and keep staff in such a remote location. The result was a hurried (and presumably rather embarrassing) *'sell out.'* My aunt was not the type of woman to take such a setback lightly, especially as she suffered from high blood pressure. The last owner known to **Pam** had been an Arab Oil Sheikh.

My sister noticed how **Madge's** house on **Elmete Avenue** *"was stuffed full of antiques."* There was also a large fireplace surrounded by an abundance of statues. (My own memory confirms these details.) She was married to **Teddy Nixon** from **Newcastle-upon-Tyne,** who was *"The Director of a Paint Firm."* **Ted** once chanced to ride on a friend's motorbike but fell off and broke his leg, infuriating **Madge** as he was **74** at the time! She evidently thought it was a case of an old man foolishly trying to be a young man. They had a small blue and white caravan (which I dimly recall being stationed in their drive) which they used to travel to **Italy** for weeks at a time. **Ted** loved the sun. In his late seventies, he travelled there alone because **Madge** disliked the long car journey.

Madge rented out the top two floors of one of her houses to theatrical people, including *"The 'Big Fry' Man."* (He was the **Australian** born actor **George Lazenby** whose role in advertising *'Big Fry'* Chocolates during the mid-**1960s** gained him the part of **James Bond** in the **1969** film *"On Her Majesty's Secret Service."*) **Madge** also owned some very grand flats. (I heard from **Fred** that the future Dictator of **Malawi,** a **Doctor Hastings Banda** had briefly been one of her tenants when he'd run a medical practice in this country. This would have been in the early **1940s**.) When **Valerie** stayed at **Madge's** with her friend **Caroline** she would invite each of them to venture their hand deep down into a white **Chinese** vase. At the bottom would be £**30.00** to pay for a trip to town. She was very insistent that they took it. She would also leave fudge, piles of jelly babies and chocolate around the house for my sister and her friend to find. **Madge** would also ply her young guests with *'Matthias Robinson'* gift vouchers. (**Matthias Robinson** was a Department Store, founded in **1875** with a branch opening in **Leeds** in **1914**. It was taken over by **Debenhams** in **1962**.)

In **1961, Madge** had obtained a good second-hand red and white bicycle for **Valerie** who had admitted to being *"absolutely thrilled with it. In fact, I loved it."* The handlebars had needed to be changed, but that was all. **Madge** had spotted an advert for it on **Victoria Road** in **Headingley** and had purchased it for a reasonable price. When it came to *'spoiling'* her relatives, it was the nieces she seemed to favour; although she would also give **Michael** presents.

Madge was very eccentric. She had a very loud voice with a curious rasping quality, (which I dimly remember). **Pam** noted how she seemed to *'draw in'* her breath before shouting something loudly. My Aunt **Madge** often used to dangle a lighted cigarette from the side of her mouth and my sister was surprised that she never caught fire. **Madge** would buy dresses from C&A maternity section to avoid paying Purchase Tax. However, this frugality didn't prevent her from treating herself to a lot of smart headscarves.

At one time, **Valerie** recalled how **Fred** had arranged to meet with **Ted** and **Madge** near **Roundhay Park. Fred** had parked on one side of the road and **Valerie** noticed that **Ted** had parked *'diagonally opposite."* (**Madge** didn't drive.) *"Out of a shocking-pink winged Cadillac, popped this head-scarved figure – wearing winged glasses. We were astonished because in the **1950s** this car was a really 'loud' colour. Rumour had it that she'd bought it incredibly cheaply precisely because of its colour. Once out of the car she squawked 'Hello, **Little Freddie!'"*** to my father's evident annoyance. (Incidentally, my cousin **Pam** also had vivid memories of that car.)

Ted and **Madge** didn't get on; there seemed to have been some sort of resentment. She dabbled in **Phrenology** – a pseudoscience popular in the nineteenth century. Its adherents thought they could tell a person's character and mental state from the shape of their head. When they moved to the old Railway Station in **Goldsborough Valerie** described how *"I went over with my husband **Ross** shortly after our engagement. **Madge** was very proud because she had positioned the lounge in the old Ticket Office. There was plenty of slab cake."* **Madge** had felt **Ross's** head before leaving the room to make a pot of tea and had later remarked to **Valerie,** *"He's got the right kind of head."* My sister speculated whether **Madge** would have tried to prevent the marriage (which occurred in **July 1968**) had the bumps been *"faulty!"*

During a two-hour phone call (on **Tuesday 6th June 2017**) **Pam** disclosed the reason for their mutual resentment. **Ted** had been serially unfaithful. During the **1950s** he and **Madge** had just returned from a holiday in **Italy** to be confronted by an array of bills. When looking through them **Madge** had noticed **Ted** was refusing to pay for a wastepaper bin. The bin hadn't been sent to their address. Puzzled by this, she rang the firm posing as someone working for her husband and so obtained the address of a **Miss Double** who was **Ted's** secretary. With great boldness **Madge** called round to **Miss Double** and (after confirming the details provided on the phone) the conversation between the two ladies went something like this: -

Madge: Are you going to pay for this bin?

Miss Double: No, I am certainly not – besides who are you?

Madge: I am Teddy Nixon's wife.

Cue for **Miss Double's** face to go as white as a sheet!!

Cue for the formidable **Madelaine Smith** granddaughter of **Edmund Smith, Victorian** Patriarch and Business genius to give the hapless **Miss Double** a large piece of her mind in that loud voice of hers!

Nor was that the end of **Ted's** alleged misdemeanours. **Pam's** mother **Edith** once accompanied them both to **Italy**. As they passed a field near their destination **Madge** had remarked to her husband, *"You remember that field don't you Ted?"* **Edith** subsequently learned from **Madge** that during the previous year, **Madge** had discovered a lady's earring in the back of the car that wasn't hers; the result had been a furious row. In response, **Ted** had stopped the car, flung the camping gear onto the ground and told her to look after herself. He'd then driven off saying he'd be back in a week. Somehow, (possibly with the help of locals) she'd got the tent-up and holidayed in that field. Apparently, when he'd returned **Ted** had been rather surprised by her pluck. **Madge** was *'about sixty'* or in her late fifties when this incident had happened. Yet through it all there was, in **Pam's** own words *"a strange bond that soldered them together. They could neither live with nor without each other."* Both were very strong personalities, who could never have tolerated marriage to a weaker or boring person. Such an individual would have been ruthlessly discarded. The male **Nixon's** had a reputation for being philanderers. **Ted's** father **George** was the same.

By **1977, Madge** was living in a small house at **Rufforth** – a village near **York**. By then, she was approaching her mid-seventies. She was friendly with the local grocer who admired her. He and his wife would later visit her in hospital. **Pam** noted that *"By then her diabetes was very bad and **Ted** was trying his best to look after her* *at home. She had sores on her legs which weren't aided by an unkempt dog that used to lie on her. She finally ended-up in* **York Hospital** *where she refused to have her leg amputated. Once there,* **Ted** *would always greet and speak to her in very affectionate terms. Sadly, she subsequently died in that hospital."* Her funeral was held in **York Crematorium** and, original to the last, she'd previously stipulated that her *'Wake'* was to be like a wedding reception. It was held at **The Station Hotel, York** which overlooked some lovely gardens. *"It was a very nice occasion, there were lovely food and enough drink to drown a battleship of sailors."* **Valerie** added that *"***Madge** *had been a strong presence in the family – most of the* **Smiths** *are quite strong characters."*

Following the funeral, the horizontal parking bar (which allowed vehicles to exit the crematoria car park) wouldn't rise. A couple of phone calls to the office produced no response. Seeing drivers getting more and more frustrated, my father grabbed a toolbox from the back of his car and then with *"slow, methodical deliberation,"* unscrewed the four bolts holding the bar in place. He then, *"again very methodically"* placed the bar to one side, standing the bolts neatly on top of it. He then returned to his car and, along with the other drivers, made his escape without having to pay any charge. According to my cousin **Pam** (who'd relayed this story), quite a queue had built-up, so my father had been the hero of the hour!

Fred got left about £17,000 by **Madge** – which was reduced £14,000 after lawyers had deducted their expenses. A large painting of the **Madonna** which had been passed onto **Madge** from the **Fosters** in **Ireland** and allegedly sold at **Sotheby's** along with **Madge's** other possessions. **Fred's** view was that the **Madonna** was a family heirloom that should <u>never</u> have been sold. Allegedly, **Fred** had been shocked to have seen everything being removed from her house – it was totally cleared. **Fred** had had a row with **Ted,** accusing him of *'acting with indecent haste.'* He tried to save some of **Madge's** fur coats for my sister **Valerie,** who didn't want them. There were also unproven allegations that **Ted** had destroyed a more recent will of his wife's. **Fred** took the view that **Ted** *"was greedy for money"* although he already enjoyed a generous pension. He viewed him as being a devious *'Tricky Dicky."* In the aftermath of this dispute, **Ted** had quickly moved to **London** to join his son **Peter.**

This version of events (provided by my sister) contrasted with that of my cousin **Pam** who, (on **6th June 2017**) remarked that the Madonna hadn't been of a particularly high quality and that it had belonged to one of **Fred's** aunts. She really couldn't see what all the fuss had been about – especially as there'd been better paintings in the house. Her husband **Roger (1938-2013)** had assisted in the house clearing and would have noticed if anything had been untoward. He was a gentleman of the utmost integrity.

Ted eventually moved into a small flat just off the **Marylebone Road.** He wanted to be near to **Peter** who was, by then, an apparently very successful Doctor in **Harley Street.** He used to visit his son once a week and dine with him every **Thursday Evening.** Once in **London,** he used to enjoy receiving visits from my cousin **Pamela** as they reminded him of family. She sometimes bought tins of food for him. Together they would go for walks in **Hyde Park** where he would disclose that he missed **Madge.** He'd viewed her as *"unique"* and *"remarkably self-sufficient for a woman."* **Pam** found that he spoke of **Madge** in very respectful terms. After **Pam** disclosed these details she agreed with my own comment *"I don't think he would have stayed with her if he had not respected her. He needed a strong woman in his life."* When **Ted** died only **Pam** and the **Nixon's** attended his funeral.

However, acrimony over financial matters continued until at least **1977** when I heard **Fred** having a furious row with **Peter** over the phone. At one point, matters threatened to get very nasty and legal but thankfully things didn't escalate further. The dislike my father had for him was visceral. This was strange, as in the normal course of things he found it extremely difficult to dislike anyone.

Section 7: Disgrace

Concerning the Public Disgrace of Doctor Peter Nixon

Both **Ted** and **Madge** were spared the embarrassment and upset of seeing their son's medical career end in a complete disgrace. As court action had been involved it's wise to leave the respective sources to speak for themselves. However, it's significant that one of these sources was the legal correspondent of the **British Medical Journal (BMJ)** – a publication known to be very careful with its facts. The sources relating to Doctor **Peter Nixon** were retrieved on **Thursday, 8th March 2018** from: -
http://www.duncancampbell.org/content/preying-hope
http://forums.phoenixrising.me/index.php?threads/a-few-questions-from-the-phd-student.22274/page-4.

Doctor loses C4 libel case

Channel 4 has won a £2m libel battle with a Harley Street doctor who the channel claimed rigged tests and misdiagnosed a terminally ill Aids patient. Dr Peter Nixon halted his case against the channel's 1994 program, 'Preying on Hope,' after five weeks at the Royal Courts of Justice in London. Dr Nixon has gained a high profile for his theory that a list of diseases including Aids, Gulf War Syndrome, ME and premenstrual tension are attributable to hyperventilation. [I watched a video of the program and **Peter Nixon** came across as coldly arrogant when being consulted by an AIDS patient.]

However, Channel 4 found that Dr Nixon rigged his patients' breathing tests by asking them to "breathe as if they were angry". He told Ian Hughes, an Aids patient who died last summer, that his fatigue was caused by over breathing. Dr Nixon who had a turnover of more than £100,000 a year, recommends a course of Valium or diazepam and "two weeks of sleeping" as a cure for hyperventilation. Paul McCann. [He charged **£275** for this particular consultation.]

Independent (UK), 16 May 1997, page 2

Cardiologist admits research misconduct
Clare Dyer, legal correspondent, BMJ

A £2 million libel action brought against Channel Four by a former consultant cardiologist at one of London's leading teaching hospitals collapsed last week after he admitted that errors in scientific papers co-authored by him appeared to be "more than an honest slip of the pen." Dr Peter Nixon, a consultant in cardiology at Charing Cross Hospital until his retirement six years ago, withdrew his action and agreed to pay £765,520 in costs to Channel Four, which he claimed had branded him a charlatan, unfit to practice medicine.

In a comprehensive climbdown, he also agreed to the disclosure of all documents in the case to the General Medical Council – unless he voluntarily retires from practice in the meantime – and agreed not to take legal action if the allegations are repeated by Channel Four, the producer and journalist Duncan Campbell, or his production company.

Dr Nixon, who claimed that hyperventilation could cause a range of illnesses, including many heart attacks, Gulf War syndrome, post-traumatic stress disorder and pre-menstrual tension, sued Channel Four, Mr Campbell and his company Investigation and Production (TV) limited over the programme "Preying on Hope", broadcast in February 1994. The programme secretly filmed and recorded a consultation with an AIDS patient, Ian Hughes, who died in 1996. Dr Nixon told Mr Hughes that his debility was caused by hyperventilation, not AIDS, and prescribed an antihistamine and diazepam. The programme alleged that he had "rigged" the results of a breathing test by telling Mr Hughes to get "hugely angry, frustrated, trapped" while on the capnograph.

Dr Nixon aged 71, who practised from private consulting rooms in Weymouth Street, outlined his theories in a series of articles in medical journals. His views were promoted in the Sunday Times by the then medical correspondent, Neville Hodgkinson, who wrote a front-page article in 1988 claiming that Dr Nixon had found a 100 per cent effective treatment for chronic fatigue syndrome. Patients diagnosed as suffering from hyperventilation syndrome were treated by a course of diazepam to induce sleep, followed by physiotherapy and breathing training.

Admitted errors

Dr Nixon pulled out of the libel action after he was cross-examined by Channel Four's QC, Desmond Browne, over a series of papers published in the Journal of the Royal Society of Medicine. He admitted that the articles contained a number of errors and said he had not written or in some cases even read all the papers which bore his name. The papers had not been peer-reviewed to his knowledge, Dr Nixon said. He conceded under cross-examination that he had "no honest grounds" for claims that a "hypnotic challenge" test for diagnosing hyperventilation syndrome was a reliable test. He also agreed that he reached a false conclusion in claiming that the "think test" he devised, in which patients were told to think about anger or other negative emotions, was more effective than the standard forced hyperventilation provocation test (FHPT). He did not know how the errors had come about.

In a paper reporting on two groups, patients and controls, who were given the FHPT, Dr Nixon appeared to apply different percentage criteria to controls and patients, Mr Browne suggested. Dr Nixon agreed: "At the moment I cannot think of another explanation." Asked whether the errors were not "so extensive that they could not simply be an honest slip of the pen", he answered: "It appears to be more than an honest slip of the pen". Mr Browne suggested it was dishonest because applying different criteria to the patients and controls would make the difference between the two groups appear greater. "Is there any other explanation for that other than scientific fraud?" he asked. Dr Nixon replied: "Carelessness". He acknowledged that it "looked rather suspicious" that three patients of 27 reported on in a Journal of the Royal Society of Medicine paper had been removed when he later reported the same study in the American Journal of Clinical Hypnosis. He conceded that this invalidated the results published in the latter journal, which had not been told about the earlier paper. Dr Nixon wrote a series of letters in the BMJ, the Lancet and other journals claiming to have found "effort syndrome" in all or virtually all of the patients who consulted him with diagnoses of chronic fatigue syndrome. But he failed to mention that there was a 55 per cent false positive rate in asymptomatic controls.

No informed consent

He also admitted that at Charing Cross and in private practice, he had carried out exercise tests and other diagnostic tests, which could in some circumstances be fatal, without explaining the risks and getting patients' informed consent, and had not sought the approval of Charing Cross ethics committee. Part way through his cross-examination, Dr Nixon's lawyers told the judge, Mr Justice Morland, that he was not fit to continue giving evidence and produced a neurologist's report and later two psychiatrists' reports. The settlement leaves the Medical Defence Union, which backed Dr Nixon, facing a bill estimated at nearly £2 million, including its own costs.

British Medical Journal VOLUME 314 24 MAY 1997 page 1501

Writ large: Marcel Berlins

I've never seen anything quite like the libel action settlement that was made recently. I say "settlement" but the words "humiliating and comprehensive climbdown" are more appropriate. The case, which attracted surprisingly little media attention, was brought by Dr Peter Nixon against Channel 4, the investigative journalist Duncan Campbell and his TV production company, over a programme which claimed that the doctor had rigged medical tests and published scientific papers riddled with errors.

After four weeks of trial in which the programme's allegations were confirmed, some even admitted by Nixon, he caved in. He has to pay the defendants a £765,000 contribution to their legal costs. He is not allowed to claim that he discontinued the case mainly on health grounds. He has agreed not to take action if Channel 4 or Duncan Campbell repeat their accusations. Finally, he is expected to retire from medical practice within weeks - if he does not all the documents in the libel case will be sent to the General Medical Council for action. I understand, however, that he is being allowed to continue breathing.

Guardian (UK), 27 May 1997, G2 supplement

On **Thursday. 9th May 2013** one of **Peter Nixon's** potential victims placed the following account in a certain medical forum in response to a question by another contributor about quack Doctors. *"One particular one stands out. His name is Dr Peter Nixon and he was a Cardiologist at Charing Cross Hospital in London. He also operated a private "deep sleep" clinic using his NHS patient practice to feed into this. Dr Nixon thought that ME was due to Hyperventilation and could be cured by drugging patients into a coma-like condition for a week or two. That's what he wanted to do to me. During my appointment with at his NHS clinic he put pressure on me to go into his private clinic to be drugged even though he could not induce hyperventilation (had a huge amount of equipment testing this) Here's a paper which includes the publicity he managed to get for his quack ideas"* *http://www.medicalsociologyonline.org/oldsite/archives/issue41/pdwolfe.html*

This characterisation of ME personality and lifestyle is also apparent in the theory that ME is an effect of hyperventilation or over-breathing. In this version of the 'yuppie flu' construction, sympathy for the sufferer morphs into contempt. The theory, based on the claim that a change in breathing lowers the level of carbon dioxide in the blood, inducing malfunction in muscles and other organs, was publicised in an article on the front page of the Sunday Times (Hodgkinson, 1988); the title, predictably maddening to sufferers, was ' 'Yuppie flu' is all in the mind, say, doctors,'. The doctors concerned were cardiologists Peter Nixon and Stuart Rosen, who expounded their views in the same issue of the Sunday Times, and whose proposed method of treatment was a period of sleep induced by heavy sedation, followed by breathing retraining and how he was eventually exposed here
http://www.duncancampbell.org/content/preying-hope

In an email (dated **Friday, 9th March 2018**) my brother **David** revealed the possible reasons for **Fred's** aversion to **Peter Nixon**. It reads as follows and describes events occurring around **1954**. *"I can just about remember visiting **Peter Nixon** before you were born when he was living with his first wife and children in **Sheffield**. **Valerie** and I, and some of the **Nixon** kids had fun running up and down some slag heaps which is why I remember it – I must have been eight or so at the time. **Peter Nixon** left his wife and offspring to shack up with an **Iranian** nurse, that I do recall. I also was aware that he had been accused of some sort of malpractice. However, I never knew any details. I think Dad never forgave him for abandoning his original family. I am not sure how much he knew about the malpractice libel action in **1994** as Dad was not so fit by then."* My father held firmly to traditional views of marriage and had no respect at all for those parents he perceived as deserting their children. By his first marriage, **Peter Nixon** had three girls and a boy, by his second at least one girl.

After reading these accounts, I concluded that **Ted** and **Madge** had made a terrible error in forcing their son to enter a profession for which he was not temperamentally suited. One can only wonder what moral values they had instilled in him other than pure materialism. What is clear is that the ultimate result of his upbringing was devastation. It seemed that **Peter Nixon** had lost the battle to maintain *'respectability.'* He'd seemed better suited for the world of business rather than that of medicine though he could well have taken ethical shortcuts here too. His whole career seems to have been the result of a misguided pushiness by his parents. Represented here is one of the darkest tragedies in this whole history. Future generations of **Smiths** would be wise to ensure that they <u>don't allow a misplaced desire for respectability to cause them to pressurise their children into following a wrong career path.</u> Instead, it's far wiser to encourage their offspring to find their own way in life.

CHAPTER 19: A QUIET TRIUMPH

Section 1: Coming to Terms

Concerning the Final Phase of Fred's life

It was perhaps in this warm autumn period of his life that **Fred** finally came to terms with his war experiences. During the Christmas of **1991,** I bought him the book *'Parallel Lives'* by **Alan Bullock.** (It recounts the lives of both **Hitler** and **Stalin.**) Inside the front cover, I wrote: *"Given to **Fred** from **Richard,** Christmas 1991 so that he can understand the times he lived through."* Over that Christmas, he became so wrapped up in that book that, for once, his behaviour was rather unsocial. Whilst staying at my brother's home (just north of **London)** my mother had had to drag him away from that book to join other family members for the Christmas meal. Having finally read it he somehow seemed far less troubled by what had happened in the war. **Fred** and I subsequently engaged in many a good discussion on that book; I gained the impression that he was deciding that his pals had not died in vain after all. In contrast to my mother, he did not think that the film *'Schindler's List'* was in good taste when he saw it in **1995.** His view had been *"Why rake it all up again?"* In contrast, my mother's response was *"It had to be made if only to show the younger generation what had gone on."* On this issue, I was more inclined to agree with my mother, my own thinking being, *'Why give these murderous tyrants a posthumous victory by forgetting their victims?'*

During my penultimate visit to **Fred,** made on **Sunday, 14th February 1999,** I took along a close friend and my middle son. At the time **Fred** was being cared for in a temporary Nursing Home whilst my mother was away on a well-earned break. Healthily grumpy about us being late, he took the trouble to pour us out a pot of tea, which had been prepared beforehand by the staff in the rather luxurious downstairs lounge. Despite being unshaven there was still something of the courteous gentleman about him. He confirmed that his mother had taught him excellent table manners. He took an especially keen interest in my middle son's **Spanish Armada Project.** His mind was still willing to assimilate additional information. After about forty minutes we departed, with me leaving a copy of *'The Sunday Times'* on his bed-table to provide further mental stimulation. My sister confirmed that he had been pleased by the visit. During this time, I prayed day in and day out that he would be spared the final indignity of senility. I also appealed to **God** that the **Holy Spirit** would be present in a unique and comforting way during this final lap of his life.

Section 2: The Last Visit

Concerning my last visit to my father

My last visit took place on **Wednesday, 31ˢᵗ March 1999. Fred** had been returned to the same Nursing Home whilst my mother was away on another much-needed break. This time I went with my ten-year-old youngest son who had already prepared some words to say to *'make Grandad happy.'* We got there just after **8.00 p.m.** and stayed for **35** minutes. My father was in his bedroom in a smart burgundy **1930's** type dressing gown. His silver hair was standing up which gave him a slightly *'mad professor'* look. I left my youngest ten-year-old son to do most of the talking – which he did eagerly as he always loved his *'grandad.'* We left a *'Yorkie Bar'* on his chest of drawers – his favourite chocolate bar. My father's speaking voice was clearer than it had been for ages even though he still slipped up on the odd word. His memory also seemed to be largely intact. He was pleased with my middle son getting an **A+** for his **Spanish Armada Project. Fred's** main complaint was of a loss of energy and of the food at the Nursing Home. He confirmed that he was getting carers from Social Services to help him get up in the mornings when he was at home. This was done to alleviate the burden on my mother. Despite a springtime rally, I could sense that my father was a lot nearer to being called home. Poor circulation ensured that his skin was a deathly pale colour. In his infirmity, I decided to reach out to him. *"**Fred**, you know that you were always interested in **Jewish** things? Well, I have decided to name an idea after you. It will be called '**The Fred Effect**' and refers to the blessings that result from a God-given love for the **Jewish** people. I will do my utmost to make sure that your name shall live on and be honoured in history. It will travel the world on the 'Internet.' You shall not lack a name in **Israel**."* I then briefly explained the concept of the *'Internet'* so that he could understand the implications of what I was saying. He sat up, and for a minute looked very thoughtful as I said, *"Your influence has not been in vain."* A pause followed and appreciating (if perhaps not fully understanding) the gesture he said, *"Well, that is very nice."* More gossip followed about **Leeds Grammar School.** His view of a recently publicised controversy concerning a former Headmaster's alleged *'homophobia'* was that the fuss *"It brought the school into disrepute."* He gave a chuckle as I said that our youngest son was taking after him in terms of his sociability. At one point his mind wandered slightly as he thought it was <u>our boys</u> (his grandsons) who were attending the **Grammar School.** This was something he'd always wanted to continue – in keeping with family tradition. Even in the final stage of his life my father still harboured thoroughly middle-class aspirations. It was then his turn to reach out to me. *"It would be nice if we could all have a drive in the country."* These few words revealed something of the gracious simplicity of my father – not for him the world of high theology and websites. He was content with just a simple drive in the country. The pathos of this gesture moved me to tears. More conversation followed. He then got onto the subject of my mother whom he obviously missed even though she was taking only a few days break. My youngest son and I looked at each other. It was time to leave.

"It's time for us to go. We have buses to catch."

"We'll take care not to leave anything behind."

*"I won't. The only thing I have left is a copy of today's **Daily Mail**. It will keep your brain cells going."*

"Please turn off the light."

"God bless you! And don't worry, I will ensure that your name will live on in history!"

As he waved goodbye, I switched off the bedroom light, leaving my father to his thoughts and memories. There was no need for any further words. Tears flooded my eyes as I strolled down the **Wetherby Road** with my youngest son. Desolated by grief I functioned like a robot to find a bus stop that would take us straight back home. The only consolation was provided by certain words from **Isaiah 53.4a** which sprang to mind. These were *"Surely He has borne our griefs and carried our sorrows."* Coming to a close was one of the most moving moments in my whole life; I don't think I will ever forget that last meeting with my father. Even writing about it has made me cry. (I could never have foreseen that it would take a further nineteen years to fulfil my promise to him.) Full credit must be given to **Fred** for inspiring this work. He has been honoured with a recognition usually reserved for top-ranking history makers. As I look back on this Family History I can only exclaim, *'what a legacy he helped to create!'* Almost two decades after his passing, my father's life continues to be vindicated. What honour he has received!

Section 3: A Quiet and Peaceful Ending

Concerning the death of my father, Fred G Smith

It was my older brother who telephoned at **8.30 p.m. on Friday, 9th April 1999** to break the news of my father's death. Whilst **Fred** was breathing his last, my brother had suddenly come down with an awful virus that was to lay him up for the next few days – just at the time his presence was needed to sort out the funeral arrangements. Despite my brother's advice to allow my wife to break the news to the boys, I felt that this was a responsibility that I could not abdicate. I gathered them together on the upstairs landing. My wife was present as I gave

606

the first sketchy details provided by my brother. The youngest broke down in tears (he was to sleep in our bedroom that night); the middle son looked pensive whilst the eldest looked thoughtful before going back to his Computer. My wife gave a big *'ah!'* and looked sad. Although not unexpected I still found it hard to believe the news. **Fred** was gone, and, in this world, I would see him no more.

The rest of the weekend was spent in a whirlwind of phone calls and Emails. Prayer support was asked for – especially for the funeral. Gradually, further details of my father's last moments emerged, although the full picture was only completed when I spoke to my mother at the funeral. It was very much a *'Fred kind of death.'* My mother had been shopping and had bought his favourite *'Yorkie chocolate bar.'* At about **4.15 p.m.** he had eaten it whilst having a cup of coffee in his favourite armchair. Before having his usual afternoon nap, he had called out to my mother who was in the dining room:
"What are you doing?" he'd enquired.
"I'm doing the ironing" was the reply.
After that brief dialogue, he'd closed his eyes for his usual nap and that was the last he saw of this world. My mother could hear that his breathing sounded strange. She telephoned for an ambulance and then called my sister. By the time my sister arrived (about twelve minutes later) he was already being lifted onto a stretcher and into the ambulance. The medical team was attempting to resuscitate him, and my sister begged them to stop. In fact, *'technically'* he had already died. In a private letter (dated **Tuesday, 15th June 1999**) my sister had disclosed that, whilst in the ambulance *"When I took dad's arm and said, 'It's all right dad, don't worry, I'm here,' I felt a 'whoosh' and felt that he was waiting for me before his spirit lifted. I instantly felt he was 'alright and at peace.' This brought me great happiness."* It would have been like my father to wait for my sister. Even after death, his concern for his family would have been present. His end was very peaceful, and, in a place, he had wanted it to be in – for he had felt a dread of dying alone in a Hospital or Nursing Home.

One difficulty following **Fred's** death came from the coroner who *'very officiously insisted'* upon a post-mortem. It was conducted on **Wednesday, 14th April** and showed that my father's death had been brought about by sudden heart failure rather than through the stroke we had all expected. Apparently, his circulation was in a terrible condition so that his end had come as a merciful release from any further disability. Previous attacks of angina had left some scarring on the heart itself. The death certificate revealed that my father's demise had been due to: -

"(a) Myocardial Fibrosis
(b) Coronary Occlusion
(c) Coronary Atheroma."

Apart from not having bronchitis, my father's death was in many ways like that of his Grandfather **Edmund Smith.** There was the same relatively good health until the early eighties, followed by a rapid physical decline and death through a combination of heart and circulatory problems. If it had not been for the life-prolonging effect of modern medicine my father, like **Edmund,** would most probably have died in his eighty-third rather than his eighty-fifth year. Incidentally, **Fred's** death was *"certified by **David Hinchcliff,** Coroner for the County of West Yorkshire (Eastern) after post-mortem without an inquest."* The date of registration was *"Fifteenth April 1999."*

Another trial was the making of transport arrangements for those wishing to attend the funeral. It was not clear until the last moment that all three of my own sons would be able to attend. Thankfully, the practicalities did finally fell into place.

The funeral was held at **Lawnswood Crematorium** at **2.00 PM** on **Friday, 16ᵗʰ April 1999**. During that week I had been comforted by some passages from the Psalms, one of which was **Psalm 116.15** which had read *"Precious in the sight of the Lord is the death of his saints."* The morning of my father's cremation saw a heavy flurry of springtime snow. As large flakes dropped to the ground, I wondered whether we would be able to get to the reception, which was to be at my sister's house in the country, just outside **Leeds**. Family friends kindly drove my youngest son and I to the Crematorium, whilst my wife and the other boys travelled there by bus. A small huddle of people quietly awaited the funeral service in an adjacent building. The **Jewish** connection held up to the end – I could see a former **Jewish** neighbour and another two **Jewish** friends amongst the congregation. We quietly filed inside the Crematorium and my sister ushered me onto the front row with my brother and mother. The vicar (chosen by my sister) preached a simple but moving sermon. It was entitled **"Down, Round and Up."** The vicar kindly sent me his sermon notes, which read as follows: -

"I would imagine that all of us if asked, would express the desire to be anywhere else but here today. The death of a loved one, a friend, a neighbour, causes pain inside which is difficult to describe, but which all of us would rather be without."

But to deny the pain is to deny the reality of the situation.

*Fred has died, suddenly and yet so peacefully, so we have gathered to say farewell to **Fred,** to celebrate a long and happy life, to support one another, and if wished, to seek **God's** support and help at this time. Someone once asked what it is we do at a funeral service.*

The reply is that we look down, then we look round, and then we look up.

<u>*Firstly,*</u> *we* **LOOK DOWN,**

*First, we look down at the coffin and the flowers and think of the loved one we have lost. It would not be right for me to talk of **Fred** as if I knew him well, for I never met him.*

*Each of you is here because of the memories of **Fred** which you have, memories that are personal and individual. I invite you to recall those aspects of **Fred** and his life for which you would like to thank God.*

*Firstly, it is right to say that **Fred** was very much a family man. Married to **Cynthia** for 57 years, a loving father and Grandfather, and a much-loved Uncle. But his love and care did not just stop at the boundaries of his family, but spilt over into other relationships, as **Caroline** and **Jean** discovered, and many others of you as well, perhaps.*

*I have been hearing that **Fred** met **Cynthia** whilst serving in the Navy during the Second World War, and following the war was, for many years, a sales representative for a clothing firm. Understandable then that **Fred** was always very smartly turned out – he took care of his personal appearance.*

*And yet, you may recall, he was far from being materialistic – **Fred** considered people much more important than possessions; relationships more meaningful than belongings.*

*And yet, there was perhaps a fair degree of self-sufficiency in **Fred's** nature, which I understand nearly led to disaster not just for him, but for the whole street, as he tried to repair a faulty gas appliance with insulating tape, rather than call out the Gas Board. **Valerie** commented that black insulating tape was an important part of **Fred's** armoury in dealing with many of life's troubles!*

*What else might you remember of **Fred**?*

*His enjoyment of good food and drink, his gentle sense of humour, his generous nature and strong **Christian** belief, his love of animals, his interest in painting and his involvement in the Art Club at the Community Association.*

Yes, there is much to celebrate and applaud in **Fred's** life and indeed his character. That is not to say that **Fred** was perfect, for I'm sure that, like each one of us, **Fred** had his fair share of problems and difficulties with life and people.

But, today, as you pay tribute to one who played a part in your life, I invite you to give thanks to God for all that he was, and for your unique memories of a unique person.

Secondly, we **LOOK AROUND** at ourselves,

The death of one who was close to us is a painful business. We come today to remind **God** of the pain that we feel. Pain and emptiness and numbness we would rather be without. Death is a part of life, just as much as our birth into this world. The pain we bear is the price we pay for loving and caring.

The loss also reminds us, perhaps, or our own mortality, a reminder which we are tempted to push to the back of our minds.

There will be a big hole in your lives because of the death of **Fred** – a bigger hole for some than for others. It is good at times like this to have the support of friends – support that comes through the understanding of a shared sense of loss.

Thirdly, we **LOOK UP,**

Figuratively, at least, we look towards **God** who is the one behind, or above all that we experience. Tempting to think that God is so far above that He has no understanding of what it is to face death and loss. In the sending of his son **Jesus Christ,** we see a **God** who loves the world, and who identifies with it in more ways than we can imagine. In His short life of **33** years or so, He experienced pain and grief, hunger and weariness and, as an innocent man, died a horrible death on a cross.

A death which his heavenly Father watched, able to rescue his Son, but willing to hold back, knowing that his death would bring the opportunity for salvation and life for the whole of humanity.

Yes, **Jesus** is more than one who just shares our troubles "I am the way the truth and the life, no one comes to the Father except by me."

Jesus is the way to **God,** through His death on the cross; He died in the place of you and me. His death was not the end – if it was we would be without hope. His Father raised him from death to new life. **Jesus** has gone before us, to set the pattern, to prepare the way.

*Through **Jesus**, we have the hope and the promise of resurrection to new life. In these days of grief, when your hearts are troubled, I invite you to remember the words of Jesus and to seek to draw near to Him. To **Jesus** who said, "Do not let your hearts be troubled, trust in **God,** trust also in me."*

As the conveyor hummed in readiness to take my father's flower-bedecked coffin to the incinerator, I looked at it whilst thinking *'Farewell **Fred** – you were the most compassionate man I ever knew. Your influence will live on; you shall not lack a name in **Israel**, I promise you that.'* A steely resolution had become firmly embedded in my own mind to honour my father's name on the World Wide Web. It was this precise moment that this Family History was born. I was glad that **Fred** had heard my proposal about this, made during my last visit to him. Apparently, he had already been given some notion about *'Information Technology'* whilst visiting my brother's home. It was there he had been shown the rudiments of **David's** Computer.

Overall, it was pleasing to see that there had been a peaceful dignity about the funeral. I shook hands with the vicar as we parted, thanking him for his *'excellent'* sermon. No one else could have done it better. However, my daughter **Hannah** was so distressed she had to be taking back to her place of residence by a friend.

Thankfully, the drive through the snow to my sister's house was straightforward enough and, as an old family friend remarked, the reception turned out to be *'a rather jolly affair.'* It was here, even more than at the Chapel Service, that the various aspects of my father's life came together. The tributes paid to him were fulsome – they confirmed that he had borne the kind of fruit that only a truly regenerate **Christian** could bear. Along with a marvellous buffet spread (including a plate full of **'Yorkie Bars'**) prepared by my sister and some friends, the room was full of photographs of my father at different periods of his life. After some socialising and chatting, some speeches were made. My brother made an especially moving speech. He had asked that my father's fallen comrades of the Second World War, who had died without issue, also be remembered. An old family friend (who had known my father since the **1950s**) also gave a moving speech, recounting how **Fred's** very presence was enough to stop uncharitable *"bitching"* about other people. He also praised him for being *'a gentle giant'* and *'a true gentleman.'* He was clearly moved by my father's departure. My sister amused everyone by reading out some of my father's proverbial sayings. Recalled with special affection were **Fred's** disastrous *'do it yourself jobs.'* In turn, my cousin **Pamela** beamed with pleasure as she recounted how, only two weeks before his death, **Fred** had attended a large wedding held by another branch of our wider family. There he had seen nine out of his ten grand-nieces. She also remembered *'his marvellous way of telling stories to children.'* One remarkable sign of divine blessing was the way my sister's best friend **Caroline** (whom my father had viewed as a second daughter) had travelled from **America** to see her sick mother and had just *'happened'* to be in the country on one of her twice-yearly visits. Her presence was an enormous comfort to my sister. She was due to fly back to the States on the following **Sunday,** two days after **Fred's** cremation. As the occasion was felt to be coming to its natural conclusion, I closed the heartfelt eulogies by summing up my father's character in one sentence; *"**Fred** was the most compassionate man I ever knew – His influence will live on."* Everyone applauded those sentiments and even my (normally critical) eldest teenage son gave a quietly enthusiastic *'thumbs up'* sign, exclaiming, *"Eh, what you said was kinda good."* Such general eulogies made it clear that **Friday, 16th April 1999** was not just the day of my father's funeral, but rather it was the day of his triumph. It was very much a *'**Fred** occasion'*, complete with convivial company and a well-prepared spread of food. Both his death and funeral were very individualistic.

During the reception, whilst talking and listening to those present, I learnt much more about my father. My brother informed me that **Fred** had been *"very pleased"* when my youngest son and myself had visited him. (Apparently, **Philip** had reminded him of what he'd been like at that age). Despite his tender years, my youngest son had also shown a dogged loyalty to his own *'grandad'* over the last two difficult years of his life. In fairness to all my sons, they had been adamant about wishing to attend my father's funeral. At the reception, they all sat together in a noticeable semblance of unity. **Fred** indeed had been one of those good, unpretentious men, capable of attracting the loyalty of all sorts of people. He was a man with a quiet charisma. In the kitchen of my sister's house, my brother remarked that *"we had been exceptionally lucky"* to have had him as a father. All I could do was to concur with that sentiment. Having him as my father has been one of the greatest blessings of my life. Yet it was to be only three months after beginning this Family History (in **April 1999**) that I felt I only really began to more fully know and appreciate him as my father (and as a person in his own right).

Section 4: The Thoughts of Chairman Fred

Concerning the wisdom of my Father

For about three weeks following his death, I thought much about **Fred**. My reminiscences were nearly always of him neatly turned out playing with my children. Such a picture says much for the calibre of the man. As my wife said he left a lovely image in my mind. It was only after drafting this piece that those thoughts began to fade a little. In this world, **Fred** is dead, but his influence will live on – and may increase over time. He was a fine gentleman in every sense of the word. On **Tuesday, 13ᵗʰ April 1999** I wrote down the following tribute. Entitled *'Farewell my Father'* it reads: -

"What I only analyse you now see,
What I only contemplate you now enjoy,
What I only study you now experience,
What to me is a hope is to you a glorious reality.
Farewell, my father,
Thank you for your compassion and
For the marvellous example, you provided.
Relish your life in eternity and
*May your name be honoured forever among the people of **Israel**."*

Weaving together the various strands of **Fred's** life was difficult. Although in many ways a graciously simple man he was, to some degree, a person of various parts. **Fred's** life demonstrated the blessing of Godly living – he amply illustrated the point that one's faith did not have to be *'showy'* to be real. The last ten years of his life saw my father develop a gentle peacefulness that had not been there before. He continued to grow in depth of character until the end.

In the intellectual area, **Fred's** major contribution was to show that the only way to fully understand **Christianity** was through **Judaism**. By sheer instinct, he explored the **Jewish** roots of the **Christian** faith decades before it became respectable to do so in the Church. Over this matter, he was very much an unassuming pioneer – one who led people in the right direction through personal example rather than by charismatic leadership skills. The lasting impression is that he was indeed a compassionate man who, in some ways, belonged to a past era. However, he was very much aware of current affairs and the wider world – with an acute apprehension of future developments. For instance, he foresaw the collapse of the indigenous **English Churches.** May his legacy continue to live on and enrich others – as much as it has enriched my own life and that of many family members. (As this history entered its last phase in **March 2018,** I could still marvel at the many times his judgements about people and circumstances have been vindicated.)

Having **Fred** as my father was one of the greatest privileges of my life. One especially fond memory was the recollection of his uniquely expressive sayings. Some were conventional, but others were more individualistic. Covering a wide subject area, they vividly conveyed something of the nature of the man and the values he held dear. They also highlighted his philosophical turn of mind and his dislike of pretence or *'humbug'* as he would often call it.

"Don't worry, we have bags of time" – invariably said (to my considerable irritation) when he was late in taking me to school in the **1967-1970** period.

"I'll pull you through" – said to agitated family members.

"Play it cool" – his advice on how to handle a crisis or setback.

"It is hard to ponder the imponderable" – said in repeated discussions.

"The hardest thing in life is to admit that 'I do not know," – said in repeated discussions.

"There are always two involved" – **Fred's** explanation for unhappy marriages.

"If you've got enough, you've got plenty."

"Richness is the fewness of your wants"

"If you've got your health, you've got your wealth."

*"Why go abroad when you have the **Yorkshire Dales** and **Bridlington?"*** – said after he had had his wallet stolen in **Palma, Majorca** in **September 1970.** (This was an event that put him in a foul mood.)

"Why pay an electrician when you've got yards of black insulating tape?"

"Don't sniff roses from the garden – I had a customer once and his daughter had her nose eaten away by green-fly!"

"Always wear your best jacket on bonfire night and claim on the insurance."

"If it ain't broke don't fix it."

"My mother kept a beautiful table – an excellent cook."

"There's no sentiment in the business world."

"This mad and crazy age" – his view of the **1990s.**

"Christmas is the most stressful time of the year" – an observation he would repeatedly make during the month of **December.**

"The country is morally and spiritually bankrupt" – a frequent observation made from the **1960s** onwards. Sometimes he would say the same about the Church in general or the **Church of England.**

"Never live in a fool's paradise regarding money" – a frequent observation based on his experience of the business world

"There are no leaders today, only misleaders" – a frequent observation, made in relation to the Church and to Government Politicians.

*"Of course, I believe that **Jesus Christ** was the propitiation for my sins"* – said in **1977** and again in **1996** when he had heard a taped sermon of mine, entitled *'The blood of **Jesus.**'*

*"If **Jesus** wasn't born of a virgin then how could He have been the Saviour of the world?"*

"Religious people can be an endless waste of time" – said in **June 1979** in the back garden of our old house.

"The Church is a racket" – said frequently in discussions, not only with me but also to various hapless members of the clergy who used to visit our house in the **1960s.**

"The most terrible kind of deception is self-deception" – said in **1981.**

"The Churches are latching onto this nonsense out of sheer desperation. They are like businesses in a failing industry" – his view of the *'Toronto Experience'* during the **1994-95** period.

(**The Toronto Experience** was a Movement that swept through several thousand churches in **Britain** and was characterised by hysterical laughter, uncontrolled shaking and other extreme phenomena. I was denounced from four pulpits for opposing it.)

The above-quoted sayings confirm that **Fred** had managed to combine a healthy sense of humour with sound judgement. He cared about the nature of society in general. Indeed, shrewdness was one of his most prominent attributes. Even today, many of his judgements continue to be vindicated. In about **June 1981,** he suggested that I should attend a *'Creative Writing'* class held in a certain Adult Education Centre. (Whilst making this suggestion he showed me an advert for it in the local paper whilst we talked together in the back bedroom of the old house at **Buckingham Grove.**) One result of that suggestion has been this present work. Also (from the time I was aged fifteen) he often said that he could always imagine me being a **History Teacher** and here I am teaching history to a succession of students. This now includes the history of **Fred** himself who, alongside **Edmund's,** has proved a fertile source of classroom discussion, his war experiences especially provoking much comment.

Maybe the most appropriate epilogue to **Fred's** life took place on **Friday, 13th August 1999.** I was enjoying a brilliantly cooked Sabbath meal with a certain **Jewish** couple (who then lived at **Kirkwall** in the **Isles of Orkney**). My two oldest sons (aged **16** and **13** at the time) were present too. Just before we drank the Sabbath wine I seized the opportunity to continue **Fred's** work by saying *"What your Grandfather taught me over the years I now pass onto you. That the best way to understand **Christianity** is to see its **Jewish** roots; you will not properly understand the faith without seeing this."* I elaborated this point a little further before I finished, feeling relieved at having discharged an awesome responsibility. My sons responded by looking very thoughtful. I felt greatly satisfied with seeing *'The Fred Effect'* continuing its work into the next generation. (By the term *The Fred Effect'* I mean my father's gentle influence, his integrity and his interest in the **Jewish** people.) During that meal, I felt that a great honour was paid to my father's memory. I was determined to pass on what had, after all, been a very good influence. Through this history, I've kept my promise, my father's influence will live on and be a blessing to others. He has received an honour that is usually reserved only for top history makers.

CHAPTER 20: A MAZE OF MYERSONS

Section 1: A Rabbinic Line?

Concerning Lewis Myerson and His Family

A final question to be raised about the **Smiths** was *'How typical were they of other English upwardly Socially mobile families of the late seventeenth to eighteenth centuries?'* To answer this question, it would be helpful to compare them with another family (in a different part of the country to sift out regional influences). One such family were the **Myerson's** of **London** – the maternal ancestors of my mother. Much of the information presented here was provided by herself and on two visits I made to **London** in **September 2008** and **2009**. The Internet was another vital help as were the contributions made by **Myerson** family members on **Ancestry.com**. Confusedly, in some documents, my Great, Great, Great Grandfather *'Lewis'* **Myerson** is referred to as *'Louis.'* I will keep the first version of his name unless a particular source uses the second. On two baptismal registers in **1828**, his full name was given as *'Lewis Adolphus Lois Myerson.'* He lived from about **1784** until **January 1860** and had come from the **German** state of **Saxony Anhalt**. Family tradition suggests links with nearby **Poland**. In **1813**, **Land Tax Records** for the **Parish** of **Saint Giles, Cripplegate Without** in the **Barbican** district of **London** recorded a *'Lewis, Louis'* (or *'Lois'*) being required to pay £3.0.9. If this was my direct ancestor, he was owning property that had presumably been inherited from his parents.

He definitely was not the *'Louy Adolphe'* (son of *'Cerf Louy Markovo'* and *'Adelaide Jacob'* whose birth was registered in **Paris** on 1st **June** of 1798 (or **1793**). A quick check of the **Genuki** website on a blazing hot **Tuesday, 26th June 2018** revealed that this **Louy** married a certain **Sarah (Charlotte) Cleves** to have two sons **Isidore** and **Alexandre**. He also had a brother named **Maurice (Moise Simon)**. The family were clearly **Jewish,** but any connection with my own family was very remote even if it existed, which is doubtful. In family history, it's easy to confuse ancestors with the same or similar forenames. Even the best-presented family history sites can give misleading information.

Lewis's eagerness to discard his **Jewish** roots was shown by his own baptism on 21st **March 1815**. On record as a *'Basket Maker'* in **Bethnal Green,** a supplementary note added that he was baptised *"According to the certificate of Rev C. J. Hawtry of the Episcopal Jews Chapel transmitted to me by Rev'd J King in the month of March."* **Lewis Myerson** seemed to have been in a hurry to escape from his **Jewish** roots. Later cited evidence will suggest he doesn't come across as a likeable man. At least three of his children seemed to have come to the same conclusion.

Lewis's baptism facilitated his marriage to **Elizabeth Mary Launder (c.1793-March 1851)** on 24th **April 1815** at **Saint Matthews Church, Bethnal Green**). A certain **Ancestery.com** site suggested she had been baptized at **Alfold Saint Nicholas, in Surrey** on 5th **May 1793** and that her parents were called **Richard** and **Martha Launder.** However, a close examination of the original parish records on **Tuesday, 26**[th] **June 2018** revealed that the girl baptised was called *'Marcy'* and she had no siblings. Her connection to my ancestor was highly doubtful. Intriguingly, the name *'Launder'* may denote **Huguenot** ancestry. An entry on the wikitree site stated, *"Based on the family stories handed down the line, the LAUNDON family were said to have been **French Huguenots**, their name originally believed to be **de Laundon** ... There is a known **French Huguenot** name of **De Landre** which could be another variation."* This connection is not as fanciful as it first appears for **Lewis Myerson** was living in the same area of **London** where the **Huguenots** were known to have settled in significant numbers. The **Launder** family appeared to have entered **Britain** during the early eighteenth century with **John Launder** being the first known representative. *"The surname of LAUNDER was derived from the Old French 'lauender' and was a nickname for a washerwoman or launderer."*

Louis and **Elizabeth Myerson** were known to have had the following children some of whom were baptized at **Saint Matthew's.** (The names of direct ancestors will, on this and other lists will either be underlined or be presented in bold capitals, depending on the nature of the list.)

<u>1</u>. **Louis Charles (1816-1875)** baptized in **1816** a *'Printer'* married on **6.8.1837** to **Phoebe Matilda King (1813-1880).** His sixth son **Edward Henry** also a *'printer'* migrated to **Australia** with his wife **Alice** and daughter **Maud Beatrice Reid (1875-1965)** on the ship *'Treveleyan'* that landed in **Western Australia** on **31.12.1877.** Once settled he became the first **Baptist Minister** in **Kalamundra Western Australia** and was still actively preaching in **1898.** Apparently, **Myerson Crescent** in **Maida Vale Perth WA 6057** is named after him. It runs through a featureless suburb in the foothills lying around **Perth.**

2. **Edward (1818-?)** a *'Painter Decorator'* married on **26.8.1835** to **Mary Ann Elliot (1816-25.2.1845)** and married again on **14.6.1846** to **Elizabeth A. Burrell Howard (1820-?).** By his first wife, he had a son *Thomas Lewis Myerson* who died young **(1842-1855).**

3. **Elizabeth (1819-?)** baptized in **1819** a *'Basket Maker'* married in **1843** to a person unknown

4. **Thomas (1821-1893)** an *'Iron Plate Worker'* married on **21.5.1846** to *Eliza Harley (or Hailey)* **(1822-1893)**

5. **Elizabeth Mary (1822-?.10.1869)** a *'Seamstress'* married in **26.12.1843** to **James Parison (1816-1855)**

5. **Sarah Ann (1.5.1825-?)** baptized in **1825**

7. **Eliza (1826-?.9.1852)** a *'Seamstress and perfumer'* married in **1849** to **Frederick Levins**. Whether he was the *'printer'* of the same name recorded as living in **Ward 10** of **New York City** by its **1855** census remained speculative. (His place of origin was **Poland** whilst his wife **Eliza J** was from **England**. Both were aged **28** – but had no children.)

8. **Henry (1827-1902)** baptized in **1828** a *'Clock Cabinetmaker'* and later a *'Baptist Minister'* married on **10.2.1848** to **Ann Higgins (1826-1905)**

9. **Ann (1828-?)** baptized in **1828**

10. **James Conway (1829-1865)** a *'Salesman'* and later a *Railway Messenger'* married on **14.10.1849** to **Caroline Johnson (1826-1867)**

One can only pity **Elizabeth** who had to endure at least ten pregnancies! Incidentally, my great, great Grandfather **Thomas Myerson** must not be confused with his nephew **Thomas Lewis Myerson**. One site on **ancestry.com** did just that. Consequently, on **Tuesday, 26th June 2018** I had to spend almost two hours in a sweltering library working out how an ancestor who apparently died in **1855** could still have children and engage in business dealing long after that date. During that search, I was covered with perspiration!

Three years earlier on **Tuesday, 16th June 2015** (whilst looking at the www.ancestry.co.uk website) I had ascertained that he'd only put a mark for his name on his original wedding certificate. (In contrast, his wife **Elizabeth** had written in an uneven sort of way.) His signature wasn't on any of the wedding certificates for his children either. He never appeared to have overcome his illiteracy. This site also showed that **Lewis** worked variously as a *'Basket Maker'* living at *'The Green'* and *'The Jews Chapel'* **(1816 & 1819)**, a *'Labourer'* living at *'Cambridge Heath'* and *'Sugar Load Court/Yard'* **(1825 & 1828)**, a *'Beadle at the Jews Chapel'* living at *'Cambridge Heath'* and *'Sugar Loaf Walk'* **(1826 & 1830)** a *'Gent'* **(1837)** a *'Dealer'* **(1843)** and a *'Perfumer'* **(1846-1860)** who in the early **1850s,** was living at *'Caroline Gardens, Sedburgh Street, Hackney,'* The picture is of a man clinging desperately onto the coat-tails of respectability. Why he described himself as a *'Gent'* at one point isn't known. However, it was indicative of rather an insecure man aspiring to a status he didn't possess.

The origin of the name *'Myerson'* is interesting. On **Monday 14th May 2018,** I retrieved the following information from the **Beit Hatfutsot Data Base** at: - https://dbs.bh.org.il/familyname/myerson

*"**Myerson,** in which the **Yiddish/German** suffix "-son" means "son of" means "son of **Myer".** **Myer** is a spelling variant of the **German Mayer,** literally "farmer" in **German,** however as a **Jewish** family name, it is a form of the **Hebrew** male personal name **Meir.** In **Talmudic** times, people credited with bringing light or intellectual clarity to their subject were given the name **Meir** (**Hebrew** for "illuminates or radiates" or "one who sheds light"). A **2nd**-century disciple of **Rabbi Akiva,** believed to have been named **Mesha** or **Nehorai** (the **Aramaic** forms), was known as **Rabbi Meir** because of his keenness in shedding light on the **Halacha** (the **Jewish** code of law). Associated **Jewish** family names are **Yair** ("will illuminate") and the **Aramaic Nehorai** ("light") or their variants and patronymics. Similarly, the names **Uri** and **Shraga** (literally "fire"). **Meir** is documented as a **Jewish** family name in **Arles, France,** in the **13th** century. It appears as **Meiger** and **Meyger** in the **14th** century in **Strassbourg,** as **Meyr** in **15th** century **France,** as **Maier** in **Germany** in the **18th** century. Other variants include **May** in **Germany** and **Poland, Major** in **Turkey,** both in the **16th** century, **Mayer** in **France** and **Germany,** and **M'riro** and **Merito** in **Morocco."***

This source suggests that **Lewis Myerson** could have been descended from a long line of Rabbis. The strong interest in Teaching and Bible Exposition that has often re-surfaced in different branches of the **Myerson** family lend support to this theory. In his desire to assimilate and gain social respectability, my ancestor may have turned his back on a distinguished lineage which could have encompassed such figures as the poetry writing **Rabbi Meir (c.1220-1293)** of **Rothenburg, Saxony** (now on the **German-Polish** border) and the quarrelsome **Rabbi Maharem (1558-1616)** of **Lublin, Poland** who engaged in endless feuds with other **Talmudic** Scholars. (He seemed to have a high opinion of his abilities.) Anyway, we shall now hear from **Lewis Myerson** in his own words.

Section 2: An Ancestor Speaks

Concerning the Old Bailey court appearance of Lewis Myerson

On the evening of **Saturday 28th June 2014** (the one-hundredth anniversary of the assassination of the **Austrian** Archduke, **Franz Ferdinand,** which triggered the outbreak of the First World War) an amazing discovery was made. It was one in which I could *'hear'* an ancestor in his own words. My eldest son was

620

visiting to help on the computer whilst my youngest son had two friends staying overnight. Consequently, we all came to share the excitement of this discovery which was very much a *'team effort'* by my eldest son and myself. It was one which would enthral my increasingly frail mother. Apart from some **bolding** and *italicizing* (done for reasons of clarity) I've retained the original format of the following transcript as much as possible:

ROBERT KING, JOHN ROBINSON, Violent Theft highway robbery, **14th September 1826.** (Cross Reference *'The Morning Chronicle'* edition of that date devoted two columns on its front page to that trial, which took place before **Mr Justice Gaselee.**)

1385. ROBERT KING and JOHN ROBINSON were indicted for feloniously assaulting Lewis Myerson, on the King's highway, on the 14th of July, at St. Matthew, Bethnal-Green, putting him in fear, and taking from his person, and against his will, 3 half-crowns, his property.

Mr ANDREWS conducted the prosecution.

LEWIS MYERSON. I am beadle of the Episcopal-chapel, Bethnal-green, and am constable of Bethnal-Green - I have been so nearly eleven years, and am well known in the parish, as Beadle and constable - I live in the parish. On the 14th of July, between six and seven o'clock in the evening, I was going to Whitechapel-market, and had to pass through Fleet-street-hill - I am quite sure I saw the prisoners there, with several others; when I first went to a corner of a street leading into a brick field, about twenty of them were there - some playing at cards, and others tossing halfpence; I looked at them, but did not speak. When I had passed them ten or twelve yards I heard a voice say, *"Here goes the bl -y beadle;"* I then thought I was in danger, and walked on quickly, but presently I felt a quantity of stones, dirt, and mud, coming from behind me; they were thrown at me. I turned around a corner, where I was obliged to turn, and turned shortly round to see if I knew any of the men who were throwing the stones, and saw the prisoner Robinson very active in throwing stones - I staid for a little while and six persons came from the rest - both the prisoners were among those six; King came and said to me, *"I say they say you legged some of our chaps;"* I understand legging means transporting, or convicting for different crimes; I am not certain whether they said chaps or pals - I made no answer; King then came and tapped me on the shoulder, looked quite close at me, and said, *"Have you got any money for us?"* I said, *"None for you;"* Robinson was close at his elbow; King said, *"We shall soon have it all you b - r"* — a soon as the words were out of his mouth he knocked me down with something which he held in his hand (it is a thing called a dumb-bell - a lump of lead with a nob at each end); an effusion of blood came running down the front of my face; I have the mark across my nose, and shall carry it to the grave; I did not fall from the blow, but stooped down, being in extreme pain, but sensible. I stooped down to let the blood run from me, and the pain was so great I put my hand to my face - I immediately felt King with his hand in my right-hand waistcoat pocket, where I had three half-crowns; this was while I was stooping – some of the half-crowns were out of my pocket directly; a kind of tussle took place between Robinson and King, and some of the money fell on the stones – I heard it jingle, and saw Robinson with some silver in his hand, but whether that was mine or not I cannot say - he said, *"Look at this, you b - r?"* he opened his hand, and I saw some half-crowns in it; I said, *"What have I done to deserve this punishment?"* they said, *"That is the chap that has legged some of our coves"* – both the prisoners said so - they left me and dispersed. The whole six were round while this took place; I know the other four but have not seen them since – I should know them again; I knew both the prisoners as well as I know myself – I had seen them several times. When they left me, several inhabitants came around – I spoke to a woman, who is not here, first; I described their persons. King was taken next day, and Robinson the day after, but I did not see him until several days – as sure as I stand here they are the men.

Cross-examined by **MR. BRODRICK**

Q. *Did you see a person named Wood after this happened?*
A. Yes – I applied to him for some vinegar a few minutes after - I did not know him before; I pointed out to him, and other two persons who were running - they were not a great distance from me. I am not a Jew. I mentioned to Wood about losing money – I swear that I complained about being both robbed and ill-used. I was rather afraid, having no one to assist me; I was in a state of fear, but not so much as to make a mistake in their persons. Robinson threw stones at me – King gave me the blows; his hand was in my pocket – I generally keep silver in my waistcoat pocket.

Q. *How long after his hand was in your pocket did you see Robinson?*
A. Not a minute; it was between six and seven o'clock, for when I was crossing Hare-street-fields I heard the clock strike six. I know Robinson's brother, but cannot say whether I saw him there, or spoke to him; I saw several persons, and spoke to them - I noticed particularly who the persons were who I spoke to; I should know the persons I spoke to if I saw them.

Q. *Did you say to any person that you had not been robbed, only ill-used?*
A. I did not – I said to several "*What I have lost is of no value, but I do not like to be ill-used*" – 7s. 6d. is of value to me, but I would rather lose three times that than be ill-used. I was asked if I was robbed while Wood was gone for the vinegar but did not say I had not been robbed; I told some of them I had only lost three-half-crowns - I do not know Denower, an undertaker, not by name; nor Tow or Low; these persons might have met me in the street after I was robbed. I told everybody I had been robbed – I always said I was robbed of three half-crowns.

Mr ANDREWS. Q. *Are you a foreigner?*
A. A native of Saxony; I always spoke of being robbed; Norris was the first person I desired to assist me in apprehending them; it was about twenty minutes or a quarter of an hour after I left Hare-street-fields – it was about twenty minutes past six o'clock.

JOHN NORRIS. I am inspector of the dismounted patrol. My district is about Bethnal-green. I saw Myerson about nine o'clock on this night - I was on duty with a party of men, to prevent bullock hunting; Myerson had a cut across the nose and the cheekbone, and his eye greatly swollen, in a shocking state; I could hardly see whether he had an eye - it had been washed with vinegar - he described the persons to me; I apprehended both the prisoners from his description. I took King the next night in Brick-lane, coming up Spicer-street, about twelve o'clock I took Robinson on a Thursday morning following, out of bed at his mother's house. I knew them from Myerson's account - he saw King in the watch-house the same night as I took him.

Cross-examined. Q. *Did you go to Robinson's mothers before?*
A. No – he was in bed; I had a difficulty to get in, being pelted with bricks and stones by a mob.

Mr ANDREWS. Q. *Were you before the Magistrate when these men were examined?*
A. Yes – they called no witnesses to my knowledge.

ROBERT DAINTRY. I am a patrol. I heard of this robbery the same night - I was with Norris when he took the prisoners; I heard Myerson describe their persons before they were taken, and by his description we took them.

RICHARD MEADOWCROFT. I am a patrol. I heard of this affair the same night but did not hear Myerson describe the parties.

KING'S Defence. I was looking after work all day.

ROBINSON'S Defence. At the time of the robbery, I was talking to Burdett, at his own door in Fleet-street-hill. I saw a mob at the corner of Wheeler-street - I looked down and saw them round the gentleman – I turned around and went to the door again.

JEREMIAH WOOD. I live in Ram-alley, Fleet-street, Bethnal-Green. I am a weaver, but at the time this happened I kept a coal-shed in Weaver-street. After the prosecutor was robbed he came up to me – I went to the public-house close by, got a halfpenny-worth of vinegar and brought it to him in a basin - the side of his face was cut – it did not appear swollen then – I was standing at my gate when he came up to me; just before he came up I saw two young men run by – he pointed them out to me- just after he got off the ground he said, "See how I have been ill-used by them young rascals, or them young villains;" I will not be certain which.

Q. *When he said that did he point to anybody?*
A. He put his arms out. I have known Robinson for nearly two years and used to see him frequently – I know both the prisoners; I am positive the men he pointed out were neither of them. I never heard him say a word of being robbed, nor did he inquire for an officer or anybody, to assist in apprehending them - he said he had been ill-used by them villains or rascals, and that he had done nothing to them.

Mr ANDREWS. Q. *Were you the only person by at the time?*
A. Another young man stood talking to me in the yard at the time they ran by - that was Abraham Robinson, the prisoner's brother; we both went out after these young men, to see what they were running after. Robinson is not related to me – I have known his family two years, and he has worked for a master whom I worked for; I had not seen John Robinson that evening.

Q. *Mind what you are about?*
A. I saw him that afternoon come home to his mother's house, just after this happened, about ten minutes after the affair happened - that was as near five o'clock as could be, I stood at my gate at that time - his mother lives close to the spot where it happened, not a dozen yards from where the beadle was ill-used - it was near five o'clock, to the best of my recollection; I had not seen King that afternoon, I am certain I was in Weaver-street that day, backwards and forwards about my business – I saw nobody gambling there.

Q. *When did Robinson send to you to come to the Old Bailey?*
A. About a fortnight ago – his brother Tom came to me, not Abraham; he did not send to me before that. I did not go before the Magistrate – I was never before one in my life.

Q. *Did you go to Myerson, in company with either of the prisoner's brothers, to offer him 10l (Sovereigns) to throw out this bill before the Grand Jury?*

A. No, I did not; I went to him before the prisoners' second hearing - the mother asked me to be kind enough to go down – Thomas Robinson went with me; I went to tell him I thought him under wrong notions - he had taken up the wrong parties; I told him so, and that is all. I did not offer him 10l. To get the bill thrown out - no such thing was mentioned – I will swear the offer was not made by either me or the prisoner's brother; I never heard it made by anybody. I merely went out of friendship to the old woman, she is a neighbour.

MR. BRODRICK. Q. *Do you speak of time to the best of your recollection?*
A. Yes.

ABRAHAM ROBINSON. I am the prisoner Robinson's eldest brother. I am a weaver, but now keep a greengrocer's shop. I was with Wood in his coal-shed when this happened; we went out to the end of the yard, to the gate, together, and saw two persons running, and then saw Myerson picking his hat up; I did not hear him say anything; he was twenty or thirty yards from me - neither of the prisoners are either of the two persons who were running - I did not see them on the street. Myerson made up to Wood, and while Wood was gone for the vinegar I asked him what they had been doing to him; he said he had been terribly ill-used; I asked if he knew either of them - he said No - he said he knew one who was in his shirt sleeves. I asked if he had been robbed; he said No, he was not robbed, but terribly ill-used, and he asked no one to assist to take them.

Mr ANDREWS. Q. *Where is your brother Tom?*
A. Outside.

Q. *What day was this?*
A. What day? it was about five o'clock in the afternoon - I think it was on Thursday, between four and five o'clock; I had come from my home to Mr Wood's - I lived in King-street, Spitalfields then; I have moved since; I was going to see my mother, but, Wood being an acquaintance, I called in to see him

first. I saw nobody about gambling in the way I came - I came into Weaver-street; I did not come over Fleet-street-hill - I was not holyday-making - I had but little work and my wife looks after that. When I left Woods, I went home to my own house; I stopped at Wood's three quarters of an hour, and it might be seven o'clock when I got home - I was not in Wood's company all that time; I sometimes chop wood for him; I was in the yard, but he was not with me; his wife and children might be there for what I know. I had seen nobody gambling that afternoon, nor had been with any – I never keep such company - I swear I had not; I did not know Myerson, the beadle, then; I did not know he was a beadle for six or seven days after. I went with my brother Tom to Myerson's, to ask him about the case – it might be six or seven days after, but I cannot say exactly.

Q. *Who desired you to go?*
A. I went of my own free will, to ask him how he meant to manage the case and acquaint him he had got the wrong person; I never mentioned a word about bribing him to throw out the bill, nor did my brother – I swear that.

Q. *As you did not see Myerson robbed, why did you go to tell him he had got the wrong men?*
A. Because I knew it was not the two people he had taken whom I saw run away.

Mr BRODRICK. Q. *Do you speak of time as far as you recollect?*
A. Yes.

LEWIS MYERSON re-examined. Wood is the person who brought me the vinegar, but I did not see this man there.

Q. *When the prisoners were in custody did anybody come to make you an offer?*
A. Yes, Wood, Abraham Robinson, and a third man; they came and asked if I was Myerson, and if I was beadle of the Episcopal-chapel; they asked if I would go and take anything to drink, I thanked them, and said I would rather not; Wood said, *"Now, you know me?"* I said *"Yes, I know you are the person who brought me the vinegar;"* he said *"Yes, now you know the proverb, 'If one hand washes the other, they will both be clean;"* "Yes,"* said I, *"but give me an explanation thereof;"* he said, *"Now, it is a serious case of this young man - you have got a family, and so have I, and I am an acquaintance of this person's, and you don't know what your children may come to."* –

Q. *Without stating all this did they offer you any bribe of 10 (sovereigns), by any means you could, to throw out the bill?*

A. They did – ten sovereigns. I mentioned nothing about shirt sleeves when I was robbed.

Mr BRODRICK. Q. *Who was present when anything was said about ten sovereigns?*
A. My wife was at the door but did not hear it; they came three times – Wood and a person not here came the first time, Abraham Robinson came the second, with Wood, and the third time they came to the chapel on a Wednesday – Wood came then with another person; it was only the second time that Wood and Abraham Robinson came together; there was another man standing a dozen yards or so off.

Q. *Now where was this?*
A. At my house, one evening - I think about three weeks after the prisoners were apprehended – ten sovereigns were mentioned when they were both present. I have heard them both deny this.

COURT. Q. *Was any offer made to you the first time?*
A. Ten sovereigns, if I would make a flaw in the indictment, and throw it out - they said the second time 10 sovereigns. was at my service – they had before said sovereigns, and at the chapel, they offered me ten sovereigns, and something handsome besides. I knew the prisoners by name before the robbery, and I mentioned their names to the officers when I described them.

JOHN DENOWER. I am an undertaker and live at No. 18, Princes-street, Mile-end New-town. I was passing at the time the prosecutor was ill-used and saw the persons who ill-used him – I was about one hundred yards off and could see perfectly the persons who did – I am confident neither of the prisoners was present – I have known them from their cradles.

Mr ANDREWS. Q. *As they did not do it, perhaps you can tell who did?*
A. No – I do not know the two, but can safely say it was not the prisoners, although the two men who did it ran by me; I should know them if I saw them; I was afraid they would serve me the same if I stopped them; I was going up to help Myerson, but before I could reach him they came running by me – I only saw two – I know Robinson's mother; I did not see her that evening. I happened to call on her two or three days after he was taken; I heard they were taken, and of course, thought it my duty to right them as well as I could; I did not ask when they were to be examined, being an undertaker I am so much engaged; they had been examined when I was at Robinson's mother's; I do not know what day they were taken up, but think it was Saturday; I cannot say

whether they had had their last examination. I told her I would come here with the greatest pleasure; I did not go before the Justice. I was going, on the 14th of July, to my brother's, about a bill he was answerable for - he lives in Fox-street, Pott-street, Bethnal-green-road – his name is Elias Denower - it is above half a mile from Fleet-street-hill, but that is the nearest way to it; I was endeavouring to get to my brother's about five o'clock; I went through Weaver-street - I saw nobody playing at cards or tossing; there were a few people at the top, but only two were near Myerson – I only saw two near him – they both had long coats on - neither of them was in his shirt sleeves. I saw Wood give Myerson some vinegar – I saw nobody go into Mrs Robinson's house – if Robinson had turned into his mother's house while I was there, I must have seen him.

MR. BRODRICK. Q. *Did you go on to your brother's?*
A. Yes. As I went along I saw Robinson talking with a young man at his own house – that, of course, convinced me that it was not him.

Q. *Did you know who that young man was?*
A. Yes, Robert Wilkinson – it was at Wilkinson's uncle's house.

Q. *Two persons were ill-using Myerson – how far off were any other persons?*
A. Sixty and seventy yards – at the top of the street; only these two were about him - there was no other person within sixty or seventy yards of him at the time.

COURT. Q. *How far was Wood's house from him?*
A. As near as I can guess sixty or seventy yards; it was done opposite Mrs Robinson's door – they were both taken when I heard of it – they had had their hearing; I did not notice the date – it was the second or third day after they were taken that I heard of it; I cannot say how long it was after it happened – I cannot say whether it was a week or ten days after.

ROBERT WILKINSON. My uncle lives on Fleet-street-hill – his name is Burdett. I was inside my uncle's room on this day; I heard a great noise, and came out to ask what it was – I did not see it begin, but I saw a mob at the corner of Weaver-street, and while I stood there Robinson came up to me from quite a different way – he was coming towards the crowd; he came to me as I stood at the door; I asked how he was, and if he had any work, and then he asked me what was the matter at the corner of the street – I advised him to stop with me till the crowd was gone away; he did so, and then went home.

Mr ANDREWS. Q. *Did you see the man ill-used?*
A. No. I know Denower, and saw him pass my uncle's door, going towards where Mrs Robinson lived – he was near the house, but had to turn a corner before he could get to her door.

Q. *Then if the man was robbed opposite Mrs Robinson's door he could not see it?*
A. He might see it after he turned the corner; he could not see her door when I saw him – but could directly he turn the corner. I am a weaver, and work for Mr Huxtable – I live in Church-street; I was holyday-making that afternoon; nobody was with me - I had just come from home. After seeing Denower I went into my uncle's; I left Robinson to go home – it was on Friday, the 14th of July. I do not know when the prisoners were examined; I did not attend as a witness – I said I would attend here; I should have gone if I had been asked. I never saw Myerson before to my knowledge.

COURT. Q. *When did you say, you would come here?*
A. About three weeks ago - it was after the examination; I do not know where Wood lives.

Q. *Did you see Wood when the prosecutor was there?*
A. Yes – he asked for a little vinegar, and Wood got it – the vinegar was there when I first went up; the prosecutor was asked if he had been robbed, and replied, no; he complained of being ill-used; I have known Robinson from his cradle, and always heard a good character of him; king was a carpenter and has a good character.

Mr ANDREWS. Q. *In what employ was Robinson when he was apprehended?*
A. A weaver; he manufactured lusterings for his brother, at his brother's house, which is a quarter of a mile from his mother's; I have seen King working at his father's; the prosecutor was ten or twelve yards from Mrs Robinson's door, on the opposite side.

Q. *And you saw it going on?*
 A. I was going by at the time.

Q. *Do not you know Robinson was taken up on a charge of robbery, six months ago?*
A. I know nothing of it – it was not for robbery; I did hear he was taken up, but what for I did not hear, whether it was for interrupting anybody in the street, or what – I never asked.

Mr BRODRICK. Q. *Did you see him at large afterwards?*
A. Yes.

ROBINSON. I was taken for assaulting Wood, and officer.

COURT to NORRIS. Q. *What time on Friday evening did the prosecutor describe the persons to you?*
A. As near nine o'clock as possible - he gave me both their names; I did not know where they lived – I found out where Robinson's mother lived on Tuesday, but understood he never lived at home, and did not go to disturb his mother till Thursday, at half-past six o'clock in the morning, when I took him; King had been taken before the Magistrates on Monday, when I took him, and both were finally committed on the following Monday.

Three witnesses gave King a good character.

KING – GUILTY – DEATH. Aged 21.
ROBINSON – GUILTY – DEATH. Aged 19.

Both of these men were hung next to **Newgate Prison** on **Wednesday, 29th November 1826** for *'Highway Robbery.'* Executed alongside them were **George Nicholls** (for Highway Robbery), **James Gouley** (for Highway Robbery), **John Hayes** (for Housebreaking) and **James Boyce** (for Robbery). All these men were from the **London and Middlesex** area. These details were provided by **David Mossop** who compiled a list of those executed during the period of **1800-1827**. According to the website hosting this list, it was found that over this period *"2,340 people were hanged, comprising 2245 men and 95 women. The average number of executions was 80 per year with a peak of 219 in 1801. Crimes against property still featured heavily in these lists, with burglary being the crime in 438 cases and housebreaking in a further 70. The move towards abolition of the so-called "Bloody Code" during the latter part of the period had begun and was reducing the number of executions. Spellings of names are taken from newspaper accounts and hand-written court records."* Highway robbery was the third most common crime (accounting for **288** executions). It was only exceeded by murder (accounting for **388** executions) and Burglary (accounting for **442** executions). All this information was retrieved on **Thursday, 26th March 2015** from
http://www.capitalpunishmentuk.org/1800.html

So much for the statistics of public hangings! What of the spectacle? Such events had a strong ritualistic element; they were also a source of mass

entertainment. Apparently, meat pie sellers often made a brisk trade. Executions were viewed as offering a moral lesson. Thousands would attend a *'good'* hanging and parents would often bring their children along with them. These points are highlighted in the following extract, taken from a website article, entitled *"The Ending of Public Executions in the Nineteenth Century."* It had been extracted on **Wednesday 20th May 2015** from
http://www.capitalpunishmentuk.org/endpublic.html

*"Where the criminal was unusual, the execution could be guaranteed to draw huge crowds. Such was the case with **39-year-old Henry Fauntleroy** who was the managing partner at **Marsh, Sibbald & Co,** a failing **Marylebone** bank, who had been convicted at the **Old Bailey** on the **30th of October 1824** of large-scale forgery. **Fauntleroy** was convicted of trying to defraud the **Bank of England** of £5000 in 3% annuities, belonging to a **Mr Francis Young.** His case got wide coverage in the newspapers of the day due to his social status and his alleged immoral behaviour. **Fauntleroy** confessed to the crime and claimed his motive was to try to prop up the bank. It was claimed by others that the motive was to support his lavish lifestyle and many girlfriends. It is thought that the crime for which he suffered was just one of many similar offences that had netted him a huge sum of money over several years.*

*"There was a considerable effort made to secure a reprieve and unusually further legal argument prior to his execution, but to no avail. This hanging of a "gentleman" at **Newgate,** just after **8** o'clock on **Tuesday, the 30th of November 1824,** was a major event to be watched by an estimated **100,000** people. It was reported that just three minutes elapsed between **Fauntleroy** leaving his cell and being suspended. He writhed on the rope for a moment before **James Foxen,** the hangman, pulled down on his legs, so ending his suffering. A broadside was produced giving an "Account of the Execution & Dying Behaviour" of **Fauntleroy,** whilst another purported to be his "Sorrowful Lamentation" and a third was an account of his trial. Two more gave details of the execution, such was the interest in the case.*

*Ordinary people would walk for miles to watch an execution and by the **1850's,** special trains were laid on to take them to the county town, as happened at **Stafford** on **Saturday, the 14th of June 1856** for the hanging of **William Palmer.** In many counties, executions were held on market days to enable the largest number of people to see them and school parties would be made to attend as a moral lesson, something which is certainly recorded as happening at **Lancaster Castle.** Public houses and gin shops always did a very brisk trade on a hanging day. In many counties, executions were carried out around noon to give the local people time to get there. Such was the case at **Bury St. Edmunds** when **William*

Corder was executed. Thus, many were more or less inebriated before the proceedings began, still a recipe for rowdiness and bad behaviour.

*By the **19th** century, newspapers had become more widely available and would carry detailed accounts of trials and executions. There was also a flourishing trade in execution broadsides which were normally single sheets of paper with the details of the crime, trial and punishment of the criminal, often including the "last true confession" and lament of the condemned person. They generally had a stylised woodcut picture of the execution scene, modified as required to suit the sex and number of prisoners. The only problem with them is that as they were usually printed before the execution, they could not accurately describe an event that hadn't yet happened and indeed may not actually happen at all, as it was not unknown for the criminal to be reprieved after the broadside had gone to print."*

It's unlikely that two relative nobodies like **King** and **Robinson** would have attracted such a crowd – especially on a cold winter's day. The numbers attending would likely have been relatively small. Whether **Lewis Myerson** was among them remains a matter of speculation. Incidentally, public hanging wasn't abolished in **Britain** until **1868.**

As the evidence used in the previous section showed, **Lewis Myerson** went on to become an itinerant perfumer. He lived with his damaged nose until his death in **January 1860** at a workhouse in **Yeovil, Somerset.** Possibly he was attempting to purchase materials for his perfumery business in the surrounding locality. In rural areas workhouses often dovetailed as hospitals and the one at **Yeovil** did have a cottage hospital for **60** patients attached to it and this presumably was where **Lewis Myerson** died. His death seemed rather lonely. I was left with the impression that he was a rather unhappy man.

Section 3: A Criminal Church Warden

Concerning Saint Matthew's Church

Imagine a church where the warden was a leading member of the **Kray** or **Richardson** criminal gangs. This was exactly the sort of situation facing the **Myerson's** in the early nineteenth century. It was a time of great disorder and violence, not least at **Saint Matthews** Church Bethnal Green. The **Saint Matthew's** website (accessed on **Thursday 25th June 2015**) takes up the story: *"Up to the 18th century **Bethnal Green** was a small rural hamlet within the parish of **Stepney,** outside the eastern gates of the city of **London's** walls. Its few houses centred* *around the Green, which open space survives in the park near the Underground station. With the breaking up of* **Lolesworth Field** *in* **Spitalfields** *for brick making* **(Brick Lane)** *in* **1576** *and the building of the* **Black Eagle Brewery** *in* **1669** *(which became* **Truman's** *in* **1694**)*, the village was slowly becoming more of a residential area. Then in* **1685,** *the revocation of the* **Edict of Nantes** *meant that it was no longer legal to be a* **Protestant** *in* **France.** *Huge numbers of* **Huguenots** *fled to* **England,** *many of the more prosperous settling around* **Spitalfields** *and* **Shoreditch** *and the poorer around* **Bethnal Green.** *The need for a church in the area became pressing.*

History of the Church

"As early as **1690** *negotiations were commenced for the creation of a separate parish of* **Bethnal Green. Nicholas Hawksmoor,** *then a pupil of* **Christopher Wren,** *drew up plans for a large, basilica-type church, which was to be built by the "Fifty Church Commissioners". There was opposition to this, however, from both the local population, who feared the increase in costs to themselves in maintaining a church building and its Rector, and from the* **Rector of Stepney,** *whose income from tithes in the area would be lost if it became a separate parish. Negotiations were drawn out and it was not until* **13 October 1725** *that a portion of Hare Fields (its last remnants are seen in the* **15** *metres of* **Hare Marsh** *remaining off* **Cheshire St**) *was purchased for the church at the cost of £200. The reason that the site for the new church was to be so detached from the old village green was that there had grown up, with the* **Huguenot weavers'** *community, a sizeable new commercial hub in west* **Bethnal Green** *around* **Hare St** *(now known as* **Cheshire St**)*. But by now the Commissioners scheme was in financial difficulties and the plans for the church building were abandoned. In* **1742** *the parish of* **Bethnal Green** *was finally authorised, and* **George Dance** *was commissioned to design a smaller (and more reasonable) church than that which* **Hawksmoor** *had done. No detailed description of Dance's designs survives but his drawings in the* **Sloane Museum** *show simple and spacious ideas. In* **1743** *the foundation stone was laid by* **Ebenezer Mussell,** *but* **St Matthew's** *troubles were not over. The following year work on the half-built church was halted as; once again, funds were insufficient. A petition was made to Parliament and in* **1745** *an Act was passed to pay all debts and complete the work. The Act began:*
'The want of a place for public worship of Almighty God hath been a great cause of the increase of dissoluteness of morals and a disregard for religion, too apparent in the younger and poorer sort.' The church was finally completed and dedicated on **15 July 1746.**

Characters and Quirks of St Matthew's Parish

The problems of a poorer community and a cultural distrust and disinterest in religion have been as much a part of the priest's work at **St Matthew's** *historically as they are today. Very soon after the church's consecration Vestry Records show that several hundreds of the local people were holding their Sunday pastimes of bull-baiting and dog-fighting in the field* *adjacent to the churchyard. There was particular outrage on the day the terrified bull ran into the church during the morning service!*

*With the burgeoning of scientific discovery in **18th century England,** it became necessary to protect the buried corpses in the churchyard from desecration by "resurrectionists". Medical schools at **Guy's** and the New **London Hospitals** were not overly-fussy where the bodies for their research and teaching actually came from. In **1754** the **Watch House** was built (now on the corner of **St Matthew's Row** and **Wood Close**) and by **1792** a person was paid **10s 6d** per week to be on guard. A reward of **2** guineas was granted for the apprehension of any body snatchers and the watchmen were provided with a blunderbuss and permission to fire it but only after sounding a rattle. This right is still held by the churchwardens to this day.*

*In **1809 Joshua King** became Rector and, at first, took a close personal interest in the post he was appointed to. This was contrary to the usual practice where the Rector installed a "perpetual curate" to do the parish work and proceeded to live off the stipend in a more pleasant part of the world, (There is no record of his predecessor, **William Loxham,** who was Rector from **1766,** ever having set foot in the parish!) What **King** uncovered was a great web of corruption and fraud among the Parish Officials, led by the **Churchwarden Joseph Merceron.** This "mafia"- type character ran brothels in many of the local Public Houses, which he'd also licensed, **[Merceron]** manipulated the "poor funds" and ran protection rackets in the area. **King** struggled for some years to bring him to justice, but he was a very canny operator. Finally, **Merceron** was sent to prison in **1818.** Shortly after this **King** inherited the right to a rich parish in **Cheshire** and so he left **Bethnal Green** and never returned though [until **1861**] he retained the position as Rector and the stipend. On his release from prison, **Merceron,** finding his adversary gone, promptly reinstalled himself in all of his old positions and continued his nefarious business 'as usual' until his death in **1861.** Ironically, his grand memorial tomb, stating that he "lived to an honourable old age", is one of only two to survive the World War 2 bombings.*

It seems that this church was continuing a time-honoured tradition when it conducted the funerals of **Ronnie Kray (1995), Reggie Kray (2000)** and **Tony Lambrianou (2004)** on its premises.

It's difficult to imagine someone as fastidious as **Lewis Myerson** fitting into this kind of scene – especially as he himself had been a victim of crime. His policy appears to have been one of keeping a distance. The excesses connected with **Saint Matthew's** may also partly explain why many of the **Myerson's** decamped to the **Baptists.** They were, perhaps, a safer option. Some insight into the world in which **Lewis Myerson** lived is provided by **John Oldland**

(1989) in his booklet on the history of this church. Available on the **Saint Matthew's website** at http://www.st-matthews.co.uk/ it noted the following:

From the writings, which survive it seemed that the clergy of this period did not have too high an opinion of their parishes. This is what the **Revd. J Colbourne** *of* **St Matthew's** *told a Select Committee of the House of Commons in* **1857.**
Q: *"What is the general moral character of your population?"*
A: *"Very low indeed."*

Q: *"Could you mention any vice as more prevalent than any other?"*
A: *"I am afraid that fornication prevails to an enormous degree."*

Q: *"Does drunkenness prevail?"*
A: *"We have several gin palaces and a great deal of gin drinking."*

He went on to say, however, that "you can walk the streets in safety and comfort at any hour of the night" but that he did not like either himself or his family to live in the neighbourhood of the church because of "the fair like appearance of the streets on a Sunday." In **1862** *the Rector said that "the greater part of the population consists of Radicals, Infidels and of persons who are to all good works reprobate."*

Exposed is a crucial weakness that has always blighted the **Church of England's** mission to the people of the **United Kingdom.** It is the divide between an **Oxbridg**e educated middle-class clergyman and his (often) ill-educated working-class parishioners. The latter viewed him as a complete outsider – someone who had been imposed upon them. The result was mutual incomprehension and alienation. This divide remains one major factor behind this Institution's present decline. In the case of the **Revd, J Colbourne** (who appears to have been a perpetual curate) one wonders why he continued trying to minister in an area the inhabitants of whom he so coldly disapproved? Was it out of a misplaced sense of duty or because it was *'the done thing?'* Who knows? But the sad impression emerges of a clergyman completely out of his depth amongst a people with whom he couldn't possibly relate. In fairness to him, even the most charismatic saint on earth would have found the inhabitants of **Bethnal Green** a major challenge. **Colbourne** was certainly not such a figure. However, he did provide further insight into the world in which the **Myerson's** lived. No wonder they'd wanted to *'get on'* and *'get out'.* Like the **Smiths** in **Yorkshire,** they knew all too well what a loss of respectability could mean, *i.e.* drunkenness, destitution and a squalid death. One branch of **Lewis Myerson's** family would prove that point all too well.

Section 4: An Elopement to Gretna Green?

Concerning an old Family Legend

Another meeting with my mother (on **Sunday 14ᵗʰ February 2010**) suddenly revealed a mystery. She'd disclosed how one of her ancestors' (in the **Myerson** family) had eloped to **Gretna Green** because his prospective *'in-laws'* had disapproved of the match. The lady in question was aged sixteen or seventeen and had apparently, the girl had climbed out of her bedroom window (presumably with the help of a ladder). She'd then got into a Hansom Cab to meet a stagecoach to **Scotland.** The girl's father had chased after them in hot pursuit (also in a Hansom Cab) but it was all too late. Intriguingly, I too have memories of my maternal grandmother recounting the very same tale during the early **1960's.** She'd viewed it as an outcome of the deception which can happen when families are too strict. She herself must have heard it from her adoptive aunts. My mother was very definite that a Great Grandfather had been involved but knew no further details.

On the evening of **Tuesday 16ᵗʰ June 2015,** I re-investigated this story with my mother in her room at a nearby Care Home. I found that she'd heard it from her own mother and that, as a child herself, she'd heard her mother's spinster Aunts **Loretta (1860-1946)** and **Emeline (1863-1946)** mention the very same story. Apparently, this had been a major scandal and the erring daughter had been entirely *'cut off'* by her family who'd become very strict **Baptists.**

An examination of relevant marriage certificates revealed that my mother's great-grandfather **Thomas Myerson (1821-1893)** had married his wife **Elizabeth (1828-1893)** in **June 1846.** The marriage had taken place in the **East London** area where they lived. If this story has any basis in fact, then it must have been **Thomas Myerson's** parents who'd been the original couples involved in this story. Consultation of the incomplete records from **Gretna Green** on the internet revealed nothing decisive. The records themselves were often so badly misspelt that **Myerson** could have been mistakenly recorded as **Morrison, Marrison** or even **Myers.** Tellingly, only a bare few couples appeared to have come from as far **South** as **London.** On the other hand, **Gretna Green** had been a major stagecoach centre during the first half of the nineteenth century and so would tie in with the family story. Set out below are some background details taken from original sources: -

Gretna Green, Scotland and Marriage Registers, 1794-1895

"Historical Background:

*Under the Marriage Act of **1753** (also known as **Lord Hardwicke's Marriage Act**), clandestine or common-law marriages in England were made illegal. All marriages were required to have an official ceremony performed by a Church of England priest unless the couple was **Jewish** or **Quaker.** The Act also required parental consent for parties under **21** years old and enforced the publication of Banns. This Act also applied in **Wales** and **Ireland.** However, it did not apply to **Scotland** as **Scotland** was under its own legal system.*

*Couples wanting to get around these laws (for example because of no parental consent or personal objections to marrying in a church) often fled to **Scottish** border villages in order to get married where the English laws did not apply. **Gretna Green, Scotland** was one such destination. Located just over the border, it was one of the first villages encountered by elopers heading north. To this day, **Gretna Green** is still a very popular wedding destination.*

About this Collection:

*This data collection contains what has become known as the **Lang Collection of Gretna Green Marriage Registers,** being named after **David** and **Simon Lang,** a father and son duo who were "priests" and performed many marriages in **Gretna Green** between 1794 and 1828.*

*The entire collection covers the years **1794** to **1895**, with a few earlier references. Since **Gretna Green** marriages were not exactly formal, the record keeping was not regulated, nor was it centralized. The **Lang Registers** make up approximately **50%** of all **Gretna Green** marriages performed during the specified time period. The **Lang Registers** is the largest single collection of **Gretna Green** marriage registers and includes over **10,000** records.*

Sometimes marriages were recorded on pieces of scrap paper. Other times they were kept more formally and recorded in a book. The amount of information recorded could vary as well. However, you'll generally be able to find the following information:

- *Names of bride and groom*
- *Their counties of residence*
- *Marriage date*
- *Witnesses' names"*

Source: http://search.ancestry.co.uk/search/db.aspx?dbid=1636   (retrieved **Tuesday, 2nd September 2014**)

Original data: *"The Lang Collection of Gretna Green Marriages Records,"* The Institute of Heraldic and Genealogical Studies, Canterbury.

Initially, I had reluctantly consigned the **Gretna Green** story to the realm of *'family fable.'* If there had been any basis in the story it certainly hadn't involved any direct ancestors (or their siblings). All the latter had married in **London** at the age one would have expected. However, careful research <u>did</u> reveal a possible *'suspect.'* The genealogy revealed a certain **Ann Myerson,** the youngest daughter of **Lewis** and **Elizabeth.** Born on **25th June 1828** and baptised on **17th December 1828** at **Saint Matthews, Bethnal Green, London.** She then vanishes from the scene so completely in fact that there's something mysterious about it. There's no record of her death, burial or marriage. If she'd died in childhood, her parent's names would certainly have been recorded. Instead, there was nothing – just a complete cut-off. Significantly, the **mid-1840s** was the last era in which stage coaches were used before being supplanted by the railways.

The link with **Gretna Green** is mysterious. It could be an exaggeration, but my Grandmother's exceedingly prim maiden Aunts were not the kind of people to exaggerate. It's possible that **Louis** (or the other father involved in this matter) thought they were heading for **Gretna Green** when they were not, or he may have been encouraged in that belief by his daughter who may have left a note to put him *'off the scent.'* Previously quoted court records <u>do</u> suggest a man with the temperament of a domestic tyrant. He was certainly willing to cast off anything and anyone that threatened his respectability. The disowning of his daughter would have been very much in keeping with both his character and the values of the time.

Another telling indicator is that this incident occurred around **1845** – very near to the marriage of **Loretta** and **Emeline's** father **Thomas Myerson (1823-1893)** to **Eliza Harley (or Hailey) (1828-1893)** on the **21st May 1846** at **Saint Giles, Cripplegate, London.** It's not beyond the bounds of possibility that this marriage may have encouraged **Ann's** decision to elope. Whatever the case, this marriage appears to have been closely linked in time to a major scandal which was to cast shame upon the family. Hence, it's possible to reconstruct a line of transmission from **Thomas Myerson** and his wife, down to their daughters **Loretta** and **Emeline,** then on to their niece **Marguerite** (my Grandmother) and finally on to **Cynthia** whose help (at the age of **91**) proved to be crucial. (Photographic evidence confirmed that, as a child, my mother made repeated visits to her Aunt's house at **Hyde Heath** and so could have heard this story. This is exactly what my mother claimed had happened. She was certainly in the right place at the right time to have heard its details.)

So, what happened to **Ann** (assuming it was her) and her unknown lover? The lack of subsequent records would suggest that they'd got a cheap boat out of the country – with both **London** and **Liverpool** being possible exit points. If **Louis** (or the other father involved) had taken a stagecoach up to **Gretna Green,** he would have been on a wild goose chase. What is clear is that there appeared to have been enough deception involved in this business to have wholly embarrassed the family. No wonder they'd been keen *'to have swept it all under the carpet.'* A teenage girl had perhaps made a fool of her father.

A careful review of the available evidence suggests that some form of elopement had taken place – with **Ann** being the only available *'suspect.'* However, the **Gretna Green** side of things appears to have been a myth – but whether hat myth stemmed from faulty transmission of the story or was embedded in the original event remained impossible to prove. My own instinct as a Family Historian leans toward the latter explanation. Never in this history have I come across such a well testified family story with so little supporting evidence.

My mother's sudden interest in the Family History project had been unexpected but hugely welcome. The information she provided was invaluable and opened a whole new area to explore. Some insight was gained into the more exotic influences in our family background. In terms of direct contribution, she must rank as one of the *'stars'* of this Family History. It was through her prodding that I could obtain a vast amount of information about the **Absalom** and **Myerson** families. She also gave me a lead which, in **2014,** was to lead to one of her **Jewish** ancestors – **Lewis Myerson.** This discovery must rank as one of the most astonishing made during this research – possibly as important as the discovery of **Edmund's** tomb itself. **Cynthia's** contribution to the formation of this History has been outstanding, despite the growing infirmities of old age.

I was especially moved to see my mother (in her early nineties) fumble through an earlier draft of this book on **Sunday, 5ᵗʰ July 2015.** I quipped *"You may never have made it as a film star in* **Hollywood** *in the* **1930s,** *but you've certainly made it into this Family History. Your life story can be told to future generations – fame at last* **Cynthia!***"* In reply, she'd exclaimed *"Well – it's a bit late now!"* before giving a hearty chuckle, her eyes beaming with pleasure.

Section 5: Mission to the Jews

Concerning the Myerson's of London and Christian Mission Work

During the **1841** Census, a branch of the **Myerson** family was living at **Barbican, St Giles without Cripplegate, Middlesex.** All (except **Martha**) were born in the county of **Middlesex.** Their neighbours were a tailor, artist, porter and cabinet maker. The nearby **Hebrew School** consisted of **Jewish** boys in the **7-14** age range

Another branch of the **Myerson's** was present at **Gloucester Place.** Their neighbours consisted of cooks, clerks, agents and a Laundress. A *'Pew Opener'* was a woman paid a small amount to look after the cleaning of the church and would be on duty at services to open pews upon the arrival of their renting occupants, **(The Yorkshire Family Historian Vol. 34, No 4, Dec 2008 p.35).** For ease of reference, the names of my direct forbears are placed in capital letters. The **1841** census revealed: -

<u>Elizabeth Myerson</u> aged **48** *'Pew Opener'*
Elizabeth Mary aged **20** *'Seamstress'*
Eliza aged **15** *'Seamstress'*
Fanny Martin aged **38** *'Nurse'*
Her son **Thomas** was based at the nearby **Barbican** and this Census revealed the following details about him.
Francis Lancelot aged **25** *'Iron plate worker'*
Martha aged **45**
Maria aged **20**
Ann aged **20**
Matilda aged **13**
<u>**Thomas Myerson**</u> aged **20** *'Smith's apprentice'*
James Scares aged **15** *'Smith's apprentice'*
These were very humble beginnings. The **Myerson's** very much belonged to the early **Victorian** working classes. They were *'getting by'* but no more. As it happened **Elizabeth** was married to **Lewis Myerson** although this wasn't known when I first came across this information. At the time, he was the mysterious **Jewish Pedlar** who lurked in the background of family mythology. In the **1841** Census, **Lewis** and **Elizabeth's** youngest son **James Conway Myerson** (aged **10**) was *'a scholar'* at the *'School for Hebrew Boys. Palestine Place, Parish of Saint Matthias, Bethnal Green.'* This institution was located at *'Palestine Hall.'* It had taken in **50** pupils. Precise details will now be given, but due

allowance must be made for the fact that the enumerator obviously found the spelling of these outlandish-sounding names rather difficult: -

Name	Age	Name	Age	Name	Age
Oliver Green *'School Master'*	46	James Goldsmith	11	Alfred Tartarkover	11
Sylvester Green	45	Frederick Hulbert	12	Henry Lyons	12
Matilda Green	17	Elijah Meshullan	11	Abraham Moses	9
Frederick Marius	14	Flory Lazarus	12	William Fliss	8
Edward Delwante	13	William Lyon	11	Edward Cohen	10
James Lyon	13	Samuel Solomon	9	Charles Meyer	8
Thomas Cohen	13	Roland Cohen	12	Robert Menden	9
John Mayer	13	James Lyon	11	John Engelmann	10
Philip Davis	12	Frederick Empery	10	Jacob Meshullan	8
Henry Joiner	13	John Jackson	11	David Delevante	7
Charles Cowen	13	John Lavvy	10	Thomas Myers	6
William Mayer	12	William Elkin	10	George Flaubert	7
John Alvarez	13	Alfred Feistal	10	John Netts	8
Solomon Wolff	11	Henry Krohn	10	Moss Moses	8
Joseph Myers	11	Alfred Cohen	8	William Keine	7
James Myerson	**10**	Maria Bargerman	8	Flenny Pruder	12
Abraham Krohan	11	James Goldsmith	11	David Alvarez	6
William Cohen	12	Samuel Tachson	11	Julius Fliss	6

Unfortunately, this education didn't prevent **James** from enduring considerable hardship later in his life. However, with this Census Return, we are well within the world of Church missions to the **Jewish** people.

Details of the mission impacting upon the **Myersons** was provided by the following website link, found at: -
http://familysearch.org/learn/wiki/en/Bethnal_Green_Jews%27_Episcopal_C hapel (**Retrieved, Monday, 30/6/2014**).
*'Bethnal Green Jews' Episcopal Chapel, located on **Old Nichol Street**, was the first Episcopal chapel to be built within the boundaries of **Saint Matthews, Bethnal Green Parish**, in the year **1814**. An **Episcopal** chapel built in **1814** by the Society for Promoting Christianity among the Jews. It was closed in **1895** and later became **Holy Trinity**. … **BETHNAL GREEN**, a part of **Tower-Hamlets** borough, **London**; it is 2 miles NE by E of **St. Paul's**. The **Jews' Episcopal Chapel** is attached to the **London Society for promoting Christianity among the Jews**."*

Further details of the Church's Mission to the **Jews** was provided by the site at
http://www.stgite.org.uk/media/jewishconverts.html
(**Retrieved, Monday, 30/6/2014**)
*"Seven of the clergy who served in three of our churches – **St Mark Whitechapel, Christ Church Watney Street** and **St John the Evangelist Grove Street** – in the mid to late **19th** and early **20th** century were converts from **Judaism**. Not surprisingly most took a special interest in ministry among the Jews, both here in what had become the heartland of **British Jewry**, and overseas. Some also became involved in the mission to those of other Faiths*

*The story of the **Christian-Jewish** mission is complex and, in some respects, controversial and has been extensively researched. This is merely a brief factual outline of some features of the 19th-century scene, to set their ministries in context. There were many agencies working among the **Jews,** each with different theological emphases, but the oldest, largest and best-resourced was the **London Society for Promoting Christianity among the Jews**, also known as the **London Jews Society (LJS)**. Founded in **1809**, and supported by many of the well-known **evangelical Anglicans,** [like the Rev **Charles Simeon (1759-1836)**] its original object was visiting and relieving the sick and distressed, and instructing the ignorant, especially such as are of the **Jewish** nation; this was later modified to relieving the temporal distress of the **Jews,** as well as to promoting their spiritual welfare.*

*Its first home was **59 Brick Lane Spitalfields** – an emblematic building which has been by turns a **Huguenot** chapel, **La Neuve Église (1743)**; they then leased it to **LJS** as* *the **Jews' Chapel (1809)**; then to a community of **Methodists (1819),** becoming **Spitalfields** Chapel **(Wesleyan)** in 1843; then to the **London Hebrew Talmud Torah** who sub-let it to the strictly Orthodox **Machzike Hadath** (Ashkenazi's, mainly from Lithuania) and it became **Spitalfields Great Synagogue 1897** (in the time when **10,000** of the **14,000** inhabitants of the parish were **Jewish**). It closed in **1952** (when a new synagogue was opened in **Golders Green**), it was sold to **Bangladeshi Muslims** and became a mosque, **London Jamme Masjid (1976).** 'Umbra sumus,' reads the appropriate inscription above its sundial: 'we are shadows' **(Psalm 144:4).***

*In **1813 LJS** activities transferred to **Cambridge Heath** in **Bethnal Green,** where the **Episcopal Jews' Chapel** (for **Christian** worship) and schools for **Jewish** children were established. A printing press to provide employment for converts had been set up in **1811,** and later they were taught bookbinding at the separately-run 'Operative **Jewish** Converts' Institution'.* The site was named **'Palestine Place'** in **1836."**

*After the end of the **Napoleonic Wars** in **1815, Lewis Way** began to advocate the causes of **Jewish Nationalism,** giving a fourfold mission objective: -*
***1)** Declaring the Messiahship of **Jesus;** to the **Jew** first and also to the non-Jew*
***2)** Endeavouring to teach the Church its **Jewish** roots*
3)** Encouraging the physical restoration of the **Jewish** people to the Land of **Israel
4)** Encouraging the **Hebrew Christian/Messianic Jewish Movement.

*In **1817, Way** induced **Czar Alexander I** to issue two edicts assuring all baptized Jews of imperial protection and promising them land for farming. In **Mémoires sur l'Etat des Israélites Dédiés et Présentés à Leurs Majestés Impériales et Royales, Réunies au Congrès d' Aix-la-Chapelle (Paris 1819)** he emphasized the Messianic importance of the **Jews,** considered their relation to the Biblical promises and their ultimate fulfilment, and pleaded for their emancipation in **Europe.***

*Critics, therefore, claim, ahistorically, that the Society was the first **Christian Zionist** association in **Britain.** In time, the cause became bound up with 'restorationism' – beliefs about the imminent return of **Christ** – which is why it mattered so much to some kinds of evangelical. The Society asserted that its aim was not to baptize **Jews** but to introduce them to the claims of **Christianity,** though about **5,000 Jews** were in fact baptized during its first century of work. The fact that there were not more has been put down to the fact that, as **O.J. Simon,** who corresponded with **Suffrin,** explained to a missionary, emancipation had removed the most practical argument formerly used in favour of baptism: the most pious, the most learned, the most cultivated and the most enlightened [**Jews**] remain honourably by the covenant (cited in **Geoffrey Alderman Modern British Jewry (1998),** who wrote* *that civil and political emancipation, because it was unconditional and preceded by social and economic emancipation, acted as a powerful breakwater).*

*In **1818** the Society sent its first foreign missionary to **Poland.** Realising the need for training, a missionary unit was opened, and scriptures in **Hebrew, Polish** and **Syriac** were produced. In **1840** the **Hebrew College** was established for the instruction of converts as missionaries – a facility which other societies used. Many were sent over the years: in **1914,** the Society employed **199** workers (**82** of them **Jewish** converts) at **52** stations. But 'home mission', serving the material and spiritual needs of poor **Jews** in the **East End,** remained important. In **1909 W. T. Gidney** wrote a history of the first **100** years of the society. Its name changed several times over the 20th century, reflecting shifting perceptions: 'Church Missions to Jews', **'The Church's Mission to the Jews', 'The Church's Ministry Among the Jews',** and in **1995** 'The Church's Ministry Among Jewish People.'*

This account was useful in providing details of the social and religious environment in which **Lewis** lived. Whilst it was impossible to trace where he was in **1841,** further research helped me to discover that in **1826** (whilst living in **Cambridge Heath**) and in **1830** (whilst living in **Sugar Loaf Walk**) he'd served as **Beadle** of *'The Jews Chapel.'* (In between those years, he'd worked as a labourer.) This meant he was ideally placed to witness the rise of **Hebrew Christianity** which has now metamorphosed into **Messianic Judaism.** My ancestor was truly a man among missionaries. Their (still controversial) beliefs will be explored in the next section.

Section 6: The Hopes of Prophecy

Concerning the rise of Christian Zionism and its resultant offshoots, namely Hebrew Christianity and Messianic Judaism

In this section, it's necessary to take the reader into a (still) largely controversial belief system – namely that of **Christian Zionism. Lewis** and **Elizabeth Myerson** were very aware of it in their day and age – and it was also something of interest to my father **Fred** (although he was somewhat ambivalent about it). He'd occasionally discuss the subject with me whenever we went for walks together on **Otley Chevin** (when I was twelve to sixteen years old). I personally encountered **Christian Zionism** when involved in a variety of church activities (from the **mid-1970s** to the late **1990s**). These have enabled me to compare secondary accounts with my own primary experiences. My intention is descriptive in nature, allowing readers to come to their own conclusions regarding this belief system.

Briefly, **Christian Zionism** consists of that interdenominational movement which believes that, following a period of global and national suffering (sometimes known as *'The Great Tribulation,'* brought about by a false world messiah commonly known as *'the **anti-Christ,***) a surviving remnant of **Jewish** people will recognize **Jesus** as their true Messiah. (This is a development I've explored in my book *'**Facing the Unthinkable.'**) This recognition will fulfil Bible prophecy and lead to the second coming of **Christ.** He will then restore **Israel** to a position of blessing where it can enlighten the **Gentile** Nations with true, **God**-centred teaching. **Jesus** will be **Israel's** head – in both a kingly and priestly capacity. Having studied the issue for decades, there's much in scripture to support this controversial set of beliefs. It's a natural *'follow-on'* from the traditional **Protestant** belief that scripture is the inerrant *'Word of **God'*** containing prophecies that will be literally fulfilled at some point in human experience. To some extent, this belief has been a reaction to the appalling history of **Christian anti-Semitism** (which provided scope for an **Auschwitz** to develop). It is not the role of this Family History to deliver a value judgement on this set of beliefs. However, it's worth mentioning that they're open to verification. The restoration of **Israel** in **1948** and it's taking of **Jerusalem** (during the six-day war in **1967**) created a keen sense of vindication in **Christian Zionist** circles and excited my father. During the **mid-1990s** the growing influence of the Internet began to make the way easier for the inception (and then growing development) of a *'One World System.'* Also, the growing amount of socio-economic, political and environmental disruption within the world are making it easier for an **anti-Christ** figure to emerge (and to be taken seriously) for when times get desperate. People tend to look for a saviour – someone influential to get them out of the mess they're in

However bizarre the beliefs associated with **Christian Zionism** (and its offshoots of **Hebrew Christianity** and **Messianic Judaism**) are eminently testable. Should the scenario they suggest begin to come to pass then greater consideration needs to be given to their claims (especially that which affirms that the Bible is the *'Word of God'*). Should a charismatic global Messianic figure suddenly come to the fore and seduce the remaining mass of the world's people (and churches) into recognizing him as a godlike world leader then prophetic claims pointing to this very event need to be accepted as correct and legitimate. Should this **anti-Christ** then proceed to establish a one-world government (based in **Jerusalem**) before turning on the **Jewish** people and ferociously persecuting them; then once again, there may be something in the claims of **Christian Zionism.** Moreover, if a substantial number of **Jewish** people (through horrendous suffering) recognize **Jesus** as their true Messiah and subsequently proclaim that belief to all the nations then that event too should be considered as validation (as would a final attempt to destroy the people of **Israel**). Should such a scenario begin to take place, my advice to any **Smith** descendants (and other interested parties) reading this history is to carefully study the **New Testament.** (Begin with the gospels, **Paul's** letter to the **Romans** and the Book of **Revelation**). They should also consider asking for divine assistance. If the **Christian Zionist** prediction (of a global holocaust) be even half correct, they're going to need all the assistance they can get. Overall, it's very easy to dismiss the leading proponents in **Christian Zionism** as religious cranks, foolishly allowing their zeal to outrun their judgement – but sometimes these supposed cranks might just be right after all!

From a historical perspective, **Christian Zionism** is best considered as an outcome of the religious *'Reformation'* that began with **Martin Luther's** *'protest'* against Papal-based corruption in **October 1517.** Beyond a welter of blood, one result of this development was a fresh interest in the teaching of scripture. This was especially noticeable amongst the **English Puritans** of the seventeenth century – where a growing political crisis culminated in **Britain's Civil Wars** of **1639-1660.** These events led to a renewed interest in Bible Prophecy. In its modern form, **Christian Zionism** can be dated to **1608** – the year when the **Puritan** Theologian **Thomas Draxe** published his *'The World's Resurrection or General Calling of the Jews,'* (dedicated to **Lady Lucie** the Countess of **Bedford**). In it, he fretted about whether **God** kept His **Word.** His line of argument was as follows; *'Is not **God** changeable in his promises and covenant seeing that he cut off the Jews whom formerly he chose and loved?'* In a later work, he would suggest that the Jews would be converted and *'temporarily restored into their own country, rebuild **Jerusalem** and have a most informed and flourishing commonwealth,'* (**Draxe,** quoted in **Victoria Clarke, 2007 p.35.**) Undoubtedly, **Draxe** would have viewed the restoration of **Israel** in **1948** as a fulfilment of Bible Prophecy. Consequently, this same belief system of **Christian Zionism** had already been laid down by **Draxe** (and other like-minded thinkers) in the seventeenth century.

Still more radical than **Draxe** was the **Puritan** Gentleman and Knight **Henry Finch (1558-1625)** who, in **1621,** published *'The World's Great Restauration'* – a book that apparently both amused and angered **King James 1 (1603-1625).** **King James** disliked having any rivals in the field of Theology, which he considered to be his own personal intellectual domain. Like **Draxe, Finch** followed the assumptions of the influential **Geneva-based Protestant** Theologian **John Calvin (1509-1564).** These stated that once **God** had made a promise it was unbreakable. This meant that if **God** had indeed chosen the **Jews** as his promised people then that's <u>exactly</u> who they were, and as such, would remain **(Jeremiah 31: 35-37)** with no *'ifs,' but's or maybe's.'* To assume otherwise would be to dishonour the **Lord** by strongly intimating that He was someone who broke His promises, like a newly elected politician. His faithfulness will have been impugned. **Finch** took things further than **Draxe** when vividly describing a **Jewish** homeland – in what is now the State of **Israel.** His main contribution to **Christian Zionism** was to equate a restoration of the Jews to a return to their original homeland. Like **Draxe** he would have felt vindicated by key events in the twentieth century.

However, the reaction to such assertions from a politically insecure ruling establishment was harsh. Denounced by the **Bishop of London,** had it an **Oxford Theologian** and by MPs. **Finch** was imprisoned for his views without trial before being released following an abject apology in what was yet another Stalinist touch. Given a sinecure as assistant to a bishop he died of the plague in the same year as **James 1ˢᵗ (1625). Bishop William Laud,** (later an utterly disastrous Archbishop under **Charles 1ˢᵗ**) at about this time, was sufficiently outraged by **Christian Zionists** to exclaim, *'Good God what a fine people have we here? Men in the moon!'* Not to be outdone in his contempt for **Christian Zionists** was **Bishop Hall of Norwich** who viewed **Finch's** work as being sufficiently *'deadly and pernicious … as to make shipwreck of their own or others faith.'* (**Laud** and **Hall** quoted in **Victoria Clarke, 2007 p34.**) Behind these comments was a real fear that **England** could be plunged into the same kind of religious strife that was tearing **Europe** apart. With the Thirty Years War, well under way, **1621** wasn't a good year to publish a controversial work of theology. Not for the first (or last) time events in **Europe** were to have a <u>destabilising</u> influence upon **Britain.**

Like **Draxe** in his later writings, **Finch** had apparently been heavily influenced by **Thomas Brightman's** near thousand pages long *'Revelation of the Revelation.'* In **1609, Brightman** had had the good sense to have published in **Latin** from the comparative safety of the **Dutch Netherlands.** By **1615** an English edition was being steadily smuggled into **Britain** and beginning to exercise an influence in **Puritan** circles. Utterly certain that the **Jews** would return to **Jerusalem, Brightman** predicted *'a most long and doleful tragedy which shall overflow with scourges, slaughters and destruction'* (**Brightman,** quoted in **Victoria Clarke, 2007 p.36**). The only problem with this prediction was that it was almost three hundred years premature – **Brightman** had predicted that these catastrophes would begin in **1650** – Whoops! Such premature predictions would be something of a feature of **Christian Zionism** right up to and including the twenty-first century. As a bible scholar **Brightman** should have known that **Jesus** Himself forbade any rash *'date fixing,'* **(Mark 13:32 & Acts 1:7).** In setting dates **Brightman** was somewhat arrogantly claiming to know more than the **Lord** Himself! This was a classic case of allowing zeal to outrun wisdom. However, for a nation about to be plunged into the horrors of Civil War, it must have seemed that *'the end was indeed nigh.'*

The period of **Puritan** predominance in **Britain** (throughout the **1640s** and **'50s**) provoked many emulators of **Draxe, Finch** and **Brightman,** but little in the way of constructive development in **Christian Zionist** thought. Their belief in a seamless unity between **Ancient** and **Modern Jewish History** remained, as did their specific Bible-based beliefs. However, their more *'silly ideas'* still held sway – simply being *'added on'* to their core beliefs. This unhelpful mixture, (closely entwined with an associated political extremism) helped to discredit **Christian Zionism,** ensuring its eclipse following the restoration of King **Charles II** in **1688.** Nevertheless, **Christian Zionism** continued to linger in **America** – under the influence of the **Puritan** minister and theologian **Increase Mather (1639-1723).** His book *'The Mystery of Israel's Salvation'* highlighted his heartfelt desire to see *'the conversion of the Jews,'* **(Increase Mather** quoted in **Victoria Clarke, 2007 p.48).** What **Mather** reinforced was an already existing evangelistic emphasis inside **Christian Zionism** itself. In contrast, the teaching of his son **Cotton Mather (1663-1728)** reflected a decline in **Christian Zionist** influence. Having foolishly predicted that the **Jewish Restoration** would begin in **1697** (to be followed by the millennial reign of **Christ** in **1716**) **Cotton** became bitterly disillusioned by the Jews *'damnable rebellion against God.'* By **1727**, he'd had a complete change of heart – publishing his *'Triparadisus'* which <u>denied</u> that **God** had any special purpose for the **Jews.** He went so far as to state that belief in the **Jews** having any special purpose was *'very derogatory to the glory of our God, very contradictory to the language of the Gospel,'* **(Cotton Mather,** quoted in **Victoria Clarke, 2007 p.49).** Somewhat unconvincingly he argued that **Paul's** scenario of a mass **Jewish** conversion had already been fulfilled before **AD70!** **Cotton Mather** appears to have been embittered by the fact that the **Jews** wouldn't follow <u>his</u> prophetic programme. A resentful, hurt pride appears to have lain at the root of his antagonism to **Christian Zionism.** Possibly this was an act of belated rebellion against a very domineering father. Also, the eighteenth-century enlightenment with its profound distrust of religious *'enthusiasm'* (a reaction to the previous century's religious wars) were other *'dampeners'* upon **Christian Zionism.** By about **1740,** it seemed set to fade and become just one of the many religious curiosities awaiting discovery in the annals of church history.

Its rescue came about because of the **Evangelical Revivals** which began with the itinerant ministries of the **Wesley** brothers and **George Whitfield** (during the late **1730s**). One result was a renewed interest in Bible prophecy and the role of the Jews in that prophecy. The upheavals associated with the **Industrial** and **French Revolutions** (each commencing in the **1780s**) appeared to be signs that *'the end was nigh.'* **Napoleon Bonaparte** was often identified with the **anti-Christ.** It was into this febrile religious atmosphere that **Lewis Myerson** was born. A concerted attempt was made to reach **London's Jewish** population with the **Christian Gospel.** Evidence for this can be seen in a sermon delivered on *'Sunday, August 28th, 1796'* by a **Mr William Cooper (1776-1848)** *'Minister of the Gospel and Preacher to the Jews.'* A copy of the sermon was made available by the very helpful staff of **Tower Hamlets Local History Library & Archives Centre** and read, *'CHRIST THE TRUE MESSIAH, SERMON PREACHED SION-CHAPEL, WHITECHAPEL, TO GOD'S ANCIENT ISRAEL THE JEWS … With PRAYERS before and after the sermon … Accurately taken in Short-Hand by E. HODGSON, Eleven Years Short-Hand Writer at The Old Bailey."* Clearly, this sermon was meant to have an impact. The fact that by **September 8th, 1796,** it was already being published by **John Fairburn** could be found in *"most of the booksellers in **London** and throughout **England"*** suggested that it had done just that. This was confirmed by a quick reference to the Internet on **Tuesday, 14th June 2016.** This revealed that, by **1823,** this sermon had run to **55** editions. It would have been quoted here except that other sermon material was deemed more relevant to this history. Moreover, its use of language was rather archaic in style, rendering it difficult to follow in places.

The zeal **Cooper** represented stimulated the formation of **Beni Avraham** (*'Children of **Abraham***') the first **Hebrew Christian Fellowship in Britain.** It was set up on **9th September 1813** under the patronage of **The London Society** and the direct leadership of **Joseph Frey.** (There was a total of **41 Jewish-Christian** members, but **Lewis Myerson** was not listed amongst them.) The following *'fellowship'* met for prayers every **Sunday Morning** and **Friday Evening** as well as for divine worship in the Chapel. They were also to visit daily (on a two-by-two basis) any sick member and read the Bible to them. Further reviews of the membership list confirmed an absence of **Myerson's** which would suggest that **Lewis** only ever had a limited commitment to **Jewish**

Mission – if any at all. It met at the **Jews Chapel** in **Palestine Place,** so he would assuredly have been aware of its presence. Fellowships like this one paved the way for the formation of **The London Hebrew Christian Alliance** of **Great Britain** founded by **Dr Carl Schwartz** in **1866.**

A major figure connected to **Jewish Missions** (with whom my ancestor may have enjoyed a more direct connection) was an influential, **Cambridge** based, **Evangelical Anglican** Clergyman **Charles Simon (1759-1836).** Educated at **Eton** and **Cambridge** he was wholly dedicated to supporting **The London Society** and its belief in a future restoration of **Israel.** (His ministry had a particularly strong impact amongst university students.) Drawing from **Revelation 7,** he believed that, once the **Jewish** people had been <u>successfully</u> evangelised then (the just as successful) evangelisation of the earth would follow as a matter of course. He argued (with extreme naivety) that *"**God** will shortly interpose to bring all nations to such a unity in religious faith and practice as has never been seen before on the earth."* **(Simon** – quoted in **Cohn-Sherbok 2006, p.23).** He seemed disposed to ignore the inconvenient fact that, in traditional evangelical theology, the one person who will attempt to accomplish this very thing is the **anti-Christ** himself! I don't think for one moment that this was **Simon's** desired scenario. Once again it was a case of zeal wandering far beyond sound Biblical teaching.

When **Lewis Myerson** became connected to the **Episcopal Jews' Chapel** in his role as Beadle, **Charles Simon** was a revered *'elder statesman'* figure who often preached there. His passing (in **1836**) was greatly mourned and provoked a lengthy eulogy by the **Reverend J. B. Cartwright** (the then minister of this Chapel and almost certainly known by my ancestor). The transcript of this eulogy (housed at **Tower Hamlets Local History Library & Archives Centre** came to thirty pages.) In flowery language, **Simon** was celebrated for both his love of the **Jewish** nation and his services to the wider Church. It was stressed that *'his love for the **Jewish** nation was founded on the Word of God'* and was *'expressed in earnest and persevering labours,'* **(Cartwright p.6 & 12).** More informative for this Family History were *the 'NOTICES OF THE LABOURS OF THE REV C. SIMON ON BEHALF OF THE JEWS,'* **(Cartwright p.31).** From this source, it could be ascertained that **Simon** had been one of the founding trustees of the **Episcopal Jews' Chapel** and had witnessed the laying of its foundation stone on **7th April 1813**. He'd also attended meetings of **The London Society** and had delivered a variety of lectures at various venues throughout **Britain's** capital. It's difficult to see how **The Episcopal Jews Chapel** could have escaped his attention, given that he was extremely diligent in the cause he served. **Lewis Myerson** (and his wife **Elizabeth**) may well have seen or spoken to this man who, by all accounts, was an arresting preacher. Any failure to have attended **Cartwright's** eulogy service would have been frowned upon – unless there'd been a good reason not to have done so. After all, my forbear lived in an age where proprieties such as attendance at this kind of eulogy were expected to be thoroughly observed. Hence, it's most likely that the words of the **Reverend Cartwright** (the very same words which I'd read in the Archive Centre) would have been heard by my ancestor **Lewis Myerson.** I felt a very strong sense of connection – one that sent tingles down my spine. For this reason, three extracts from *'Cartwrights'* eulogy are found below – each conveying something of the teaching my ancestor will have heard himself.

"My brethren! What is your hope? Have you fled for refuge to the only hope set before you in the Gospel? Have you found peace with God through our Lord Jesus Christ? Are you walking humbly with God? Are you living in the fear [reverent awe] *of God? Are you seeking the enjoyment of God's favour as your highest happiness? Is it your desire and your aim to glorify your heavenly Father before men in all your words and works? These are important personal inquiries which it becomes us to make."* **(Cartwright p.28-9)**

"Let us remember that it's by faith alone that we either attain to this holy character of being like Christ or realize this blessed hope of being forever with Him." **(Cartwright p.29)**

"We can do none of these things of ourselves, neither on our own strength nor on our own righteousness can offer us a gleam of hope. Jesus Christ must be to us wisdom and righteousness and sanctification and redemption." **(Cartwright p.30;** quotations from **Romans 8:34** and **Philippians 4:13** then followed.)

The third sermon by **Charles James, Lord Bishop** of **London** (preached at the **Episcopal Chapel** on **Thursday, May 4th, 1843**) consisted of an exposition of **Romans 11:1**. Although rather verbose, there can be no mistaking the passion and attention given in a sermon of **27** pages. On **p.21** he delivered a warning, which sadly was to anticipate the spiritual trajectory of the **Myerson** family. In what must have been solemn tones he warned, *"There is one danger, from which we pray that they may be preserved by that Holy Spirit who has given them the written Word and who alone can guide them to hold fast to the truth. It is to be feared that in casting off the trammels of Rabbinism, they may at the same time lose somewhat of their reverence for the Word of God itself. The transition from superstition to infidelity is neither unnatural nor uncommon."* Within three generations there would be **Atheist Myerson's** alongside those whose **Christianity** had shrivelled to become dry, legalistic and nominal.

Perhaps the rot had started with **Lewis.** Given his position as beadle, he would have seen (or at least known about) some of the key figures in the **London**-based mission work to the **Jews.** To assume he didn't would be the equivalent of visiting **Bradford** and not expecting to see any **Asians.** He and his family were in the right place at the right time to have witnessed the formation of **Hebrew Christianity.** The **Old Bailey** transcript revealed **Lewis** as possessing an observant and enquiring mind. His workplace would enable him to receive Bible-based teaching which, in terms of content and wording, would still be found today in **Christian Zionist** circles. In that sense, very little has changed. From my own observation of elderly members of the **Hebrew Christian Alliance** during the late **1970s,** I'm able to make an intelligent guess as to what kind of man my ancestor was. He could well have been one of those insecure, prickly types, desperately keen to preserve a facade of respectability. He would be both proud <u>and</u> ashamed of his **Jewish** roots. Here was a man who would be knowledgeable and diligent, but hardly likeable. An officious defensiveness would make it difficult for **Lewis** to work alongside others. He would only ever be *'his own boss'* and this could perhaps explain why he set himself up as a perfumer from the **mid-1840s**. From that point onward, he perhaps began to drift away from the world of **Jewish Missions.** As an illiterate man, able only to leave a mark, his interest in Bible Interpretation would be somewhat limited. However, the latter skill was a quality almost certainly displayed by his son **Henry** – who was later to become a **Baptist Minister.** (He will have needed this skill to discharge his role as a Minister and to hold down a post in one church for three and a half decades.) Maybe it was **Henry** who kept the flame glowing for a second generation.

With the likely exception of **Henry,** most of **Lewis'** family appear to have quickly abandoned their **Jewish** roots. Their ambition had been to *'get on'* and gain middle-class respectability. Certainly, as evidence in the next section will show, **Lewis'** unfortunate son **James** was to feel very antagonistic to those roots. The more successful **Myerson's** appear to have shifted from **Judaism** to complete assimilation via **Baptist Christianity** within three generations. My own maternal grandmother was a convinced **atheist** and **rationalist** who disliked religion intensely. It was only in **2014** that this lost heritage would be rediscovered. Up to this point, I'd assumed that the interest in **Jewish** affairs had come down exclusively from my father's line. The discoveries I'd made about **Lewis Myerson** were to lead to a major shift in my own personal perspective. My lifelong fascination with Bible interpretation and the **Jewish** people themselves had emanated from the paternal <u>and</u> maternal branches of my family. Indeed, my mother (as was her mother before her) had sometimes been mistaken for being **Jewish.** Rediscovering these **Hebrew Christian** roots (down my maternal line) had been a breakthrough, ranking second only in importance to the discovery of **Edmund's** monument in **November 1999.** I feel saddened that these roots lay neglected and undiscovered for so long, but hugely privileged to more fully claim them as an integral part of this Family History. Full credit must be given to my mother for preserving the memory of a **Jewish** Ancestor. Yet again, her contribution to this History has been decisive.

Section 7: The Price of Failure

Concerning the degradation of James Myerson and his family

Not all branches of the **Myerson's** won the struggle to claw their way up into *'middle-class respectability.'* One branch lost it with disastrous consequences. Evidence for this was provided by one of the most haunting sources ever uncovered by this History. Dated **6th January 1861** it divulged the following information about **Lewis Myerson** and his youngest son **James Conway Myerson.**

"James Myerson salesman, **Chapel House, Oval Hackney Road East** *and come from* **Stepney.** *Married at* **St Philip's Church, Bethnal Green** *on* **14th October 1849.** *To present wife* **Caroline 32** *and 7 children* **Geo 11, Caroline 11, Anne 9, James 7, Fleury 5, Walter 1 and Selmia 8 hours**

Son of **Louis** *and* **Eliz Myerson** *who was married. Believes father still living but not seen him for the last 7 years. He lived in* **Caroline Gardens, Sedburgh Street, Hackney Road** *but not there now. He believes he was a perfumer but in his younger days Beadle to the* **Episcopal Chapel, Cambridge Heath Road.** *Also went to school there. Never heard of father renting a house. Nor what parish he belongs to. Believes he was* **German.**"

This source represented part of an *'Order of Removal'* from **Stepney Union Workhouse.** Such orders were used when wishing to remove one of their inmates to a workhouse located in the parish in which they had been born. It was only discovered during the late evening of **Thursday 16th July 2015.** (This was just two days after the **New Horizons** satellite flyby of the planet **Pluto.** I was left gaping at both the ice mountains of this frozen world and at the document before me on the computer screen. To be honest I really don't know which of these discoveries excited me the more. My mother was to display a keen interest in both although she was in her early nineties.)

What was clear (in the first reading) was that **James Myerson** and his family had really fallen on desperate times. Their case demonstrated just how precarious a respectable social position was at that time. People could fall down the social ladder a very long way and at a very fast rate – especially so where the *'demon drink'* was involved. Exactly where he was located remains unknown. However, **East End** Workhouses had a very nasty reputation. What misery must have existed in such a grim place with **James** and **Caroline Myerson** and their children being very a much part of that misery. They must have wondered whether they would ever get out.

It's painfully apparent from this record that **James Myerson** had, in around **1853,** endured a rift with his father **Lewis** (or **Louis**). Whatever their difficulties they'd been so severe that **James** hadn't even known of his father's death in the previous year. When things are that bad something has gone very wrong in the relationship. Despite having numerous relatives in **London** to fall back upon, not one of them appeared to have been around to offer any support. A picture of complete alienation appears to have emerged. Strongly reinforced is the impression that **James'** father was a very prickly, difficult and puritanical character who'd had a gift for antagonising people to the point where, in one case, they'd physically assaulted him. Then there was the mysterious elopement and now this – a dispute so bitter that it had prevented **Lewis** from seeing his own grandchildren for several years (and this at a period when it suited families on the edge of survival to *'stick together'* to prevent the disgrace of being *'carted off'* to the Workhouse). A talent for *'cutting off'* awkward family members appears to have predominated **Lewis's** life. He seems also to have been extremely secretive about his background because **James** could provide only the sketchiest account of his father's origins.

The reasons for **James'** descent into the workhouse can only remain a matter of speculation. Born on **1st December 1829** and baptized at **Saint Matthew, Bethnal Green, London** on **14th March 1830** a clue as to why this descent took place is found on his Wedding Certificate.
1849 Marriage solemnized at Saint Philips the <u>Parish Church</u> of Bethnal Green in the county of Middlesex
1. When married? October 14th, 1849
2. Name and Surname: James Conway Myerson, Caroline Johnson
3. Age: 20, 22
4. Condition: Bachelor, Spinster
5. Rank or profession: Labourer
6 Residence at the time of marriage: Hackney Road, Alex Street

7. Father's name and surname: Lewis Myerson, Thomas Johnson
8. Rank or profession of father: Perfumer, Labourer

Married in the District Church of Saint Giles according to the Rites and Ceremonies of the Established Church, married by me Geo [William Buck] Incumbent of St Mary's.

> **The marriage was solemnised between us**
> <u>James Conway Myerson</u>
> <u>Caroline Johnson</u>
> **In the presence of us**
> <u>Gwendolyn Bedstall</u>
> <u>Frederick Gineback</u>

Being a labourer in early **Victorian England** was unwelcome news as it would have consigned **James** and his family to a very hard, precarious hand-to-mouth existence. Unlike his brothers, **James** appears to have undertaken no apprenticeship, neither had he learnt a skilled trade that could have advanced him further. **James** could not have hoped for support from his wife's family either because her father too was a labourer. If anything, **James Myerson** was marrying *'down the social scale'* and at a relatively immature age where he simply wouldn't have invested sufficient time to better establish his finances. Yet unlike other newly married couples both **James** and **Caroline** could sign their names in a reasonably neat fashion. A lack of literacy wasn't an issue. The **Hebrew School** had taught **James** to write.

The considerable number of children in their family would have placed a great deal of pressure on the household budget. Yet effective contraception wasn't freely available and having a lot of children was considered a form of *'social'* insurance. Ideally, enough children would survive to provide care in old age and lessen the risk of being *'carted off'* to the dreaded workhouse.

Whether the *'demon drink'* was the main factor or that **James Myerson** was one of those foolishly proud self-destructive types who wouldn't accept family help when it was offered, simply cannot be proven. All that is apparent is that, in contrast to the **Smiths** in **Skipton,** <u>no one</u> from his family appears to have rallied around to provide support during his lifetime. Their response may have been to *'cut off and cover up,'* which seemed to be their usual approach to dealing with embarrassments.

However, this branch of the **Myerson** family appears to have quickly struggled back to its feet for within three months it was out of the workhouse. The Census conducted on **7ᵗʰ April 1861** Census revealed that they were living at **14 Mapps Row** in **Mile End East.**
James Myerson aged **30** *'Messenger'* **Bethnal Green**
Caroline Myerson aged **33 Dartford Kent**
George Myerson aged **10 London Middx**
Caroline Myerson aged **10 London Middx**
Anne Myerson aged **8 Stepney Middx**
James Myerson aged **6 Stepney Middx**
Henry Myerson aged **4 Stepney Middx**
Walter Myerson aged **9 months Stepney Middx**
Missing in the census entry were the youngest children **Fleury, Walter** and **Selmia** who don't surface in any other records. The implication is that within the previous months they had all died. Such a mortality rate was not uncommon in poor **Victorian** families.

In **November 1865, James Myerson** died (aged **35**) and his wife **Caroline** followed just over two years later at the age of **41** – the place of death in both cases being **Mile End Old Town** in **London.** Only later research would show what became of some of the children who had outlived them. Evidence from their Death Certificates provided the following details: -
Registration District Mile End Old Town
1865 Death in the sub-district of Mile End Old Town Eastern in the County of Middlesex
1. When and where died? Second November 1865 – 19 Mapps Row
2. Name and Surname: James Conway Myerson
3. Sex: Male
4. Age: 35 years
5. Occupation: Railway Messenger
6. Cause of death: Phthisis Certified
6. Signature, description and residence of informant:
C. Myerson at death 19 Mapps Row Mile End
8. When registered: Fourth November 1865
9. Signature of registrar: Samuel Castleden Registrar

Cruelly highlighting his failure to prosper, was the **City of London Tower Hamlets Cemetery Daybook** entry for **Thursday, 9ᵗʰ November 1865.** Underneath his name and address were an entry for **George Thomas Myerson** aged **15** also of **19 Mapps Row.** For **Caroline,** it must have excruciating to have <u>both her husband and eldest son buried on the same day!</u> God knows what despair she felt. Even **Charles Dickens** couldn't do justice to such a scene. It seems highly likely that her already fragile health was further undermined by this double tragedy for just over years later we find: -

Registration District

<u>1865</u> **Death in the <u>sub-district</u> of in the <u>County Borough of</u>**

1. When and where died? Twenty-Ninth December 1867 – 109 Stepney Green

2. Name and Surname: Caroline Myerson

3. Sex: Female

4. Age: 41 years

5. Occupation: Widow of James Myerson Railway Porter

6. Cause of death: Phthisis Certified

6. Signature, description and residence of informant:

X The mark of Elizabeth Johnston present at death 99 Stepney Green Mile End

8. When registered: Thirty First December 1867

9. Signature of registrar: Samuel Castleden Registrar

Both **James** and **Caroline Myerson** had died of a form of Tuberculosis that was closely associated with poverty. After possibly catching **Phthisis** from her husband **Caroline** appears to have slowly wasted away and died in a squalid **East End** Lodging House. Mercifully, the unfortunate fate of this couple proved very different from that of members of my own branch of the **Myerson** family. As the next section will show they were on a steady climb to middle-class respectability. However, one haunting question emerged from this study. It was *'how did the surviving children fare after the untimely death of their parents?'* It was a question that would prompt further investigation.

Section 8: An Upwardly Mobile Family

Concerning Census Information and the Myerson Family

In this review of Census Information, I will place the **Myerson's** (my direct forbears) at (or near) the beginning of each section. I will then look at the Census results of other branches. These will show that a general upward trend prevailed in terms of social mobility. They were gaining the respectability needed to enter the middle classes. This made the failure of **James** to do the same all the less explicable.

8.1 The Myersons in 1851

In the **1851** Census, the **Myerson's** were based at **31 Gloucester Street, Bethnal Green, Tower Hamlets, near Hackney Road**. All had been born in the County of **Middlesex**. Their neighbours consisted of a laundress, an *'agent,'* a governess and a nurse.

Thomas Myerson aged **30** *'Iron Plate Worker'*
Elizabeth aged **30**
Frederick aged **3**
Rowland aged **1**

In the **1851** Census, another branch of the **Myerson's** was living at **11 Ada Street, South Hackney, Tower Hamlets**. All had been born in **Bethnal Green**. Their Neighbours consisted of labourers and bricklayers.

Henry Myerson aged 24 *'Clock Case Maker'*
Ann E aged **25** *'Hand Loom weaver – Silk'*
Anne E aged **2**

Details of **Henry Myerson's** marriage were provided by a search made on **Ancestry.com** at **Leeds Central Library** on **Wednesday, 1ˢᵗ June 2016**.

<u>**1848**</u> **Marriage solemnized at the** <u>**Parish Church**</u> **of Saint James, Clerkenwell**

1. When married? February 10ᵗʰ, 1848
2. Name and Surname: Henry Myerson, Ann Higgens
3. Age: 21, 22
4. Condition: Bachelor, Spinster
5. Rank or profession: Clock Case Maker
6 Residence at the time of marriage: 11 Pear Tree Court
7. Father's name and surname: Lewis Myerson, Robert Tarrant Higgens
8. Rank or profession of father: Perfumer, Thread Silk Weaver

Married in the District Church of Saint Giles according to the Rites and Ceremonies of the Established Church. Married by me [Name Indecipherable] Curate of St James.

The marriage was solemnised between us
<u>Henry Myerson</u>
<u>Ann Higgens</u>
In the presence of us
<u>Robert Tarrant Higgens</u>
<u>Elizabeth Myerson</u>

In **1857, Henry Myerson** began his career as a **Baptist** Minister. Information provided on the website of **The Strict Baptist Historical Society** revealed a very typical pattern of advancement. Firstly, he appears to have served in two smaller Chapels for limited periods. (Concurrently over the years **1859-61**) before moving to a more challenging post which required someone with proven ministerial experience. (**Henry** appears to have retained links with his first church for a couple of years until he was firmly embedded into the **Oval.**) Precise details of **Henry Myerson's** service record as a minister are as follows, (Retrieved on **Sunday, 3rd July 2016**).

Date	Place
1857-1864:	Bridge Street, Staines
1859-1861:	Egham
1862-1897:	The Oval, Bethnal Green
1897-1899:	Romford
1900-1902:	Ebenezer (as a *'Hearer'*)

Details provided by this source confirmed, that, following his death, **Henry Myerson** had left behind no *'writings.'* However, an Obituary and two memoirs had been written (both by him and by a third party who knew him well). His predecessor at **The Oval; William Thorp Haslop (1809-1860)** had commenced his ministry in **1859.** His successors **Joseph Mayhew (1843-1906)** and **George H. R. Higgens** commenced theirs in **1898** and **1907** respectively. The fact that **Henry Myerson** could spend thirty-five years ministering at **Bethnal Green** would suggest that he was a resilient and good pastor, respected by his congregation. Although not an intellectual he would have been able to impart sound Bible Teaching in a way that related well to his audience. If this wasn't the case, he would never have survived **Bethnal Green** for nearly so long as he did. Information in subsequent Census Returns gave a strong impression that he was a very caring and honourable man. His two successors appear to have lacked his *'staying power.'*

Further information about **Shalom Chapel, The Oval, Bethnal Green**, was provided by a series of brief references on the **British Online History Website** (also retrieved on **Sunday, 3rd July 2016**). From this source, it was possible to establish that **Shalom Chapel** was: -

- Built by **Calvinistic Independents** (or **Congregationalists**) in **1836**
- Able to accommodate **350** people
- Able (in **1851**) to enjoy an average attendance of **150** in the morning and **200** in the evening
- Still known as a Congregational Chapel in **1855**

- Taken over by **Baptists** (originally from **Squirries Street** in **1856**
- Registered to conduct weddings in **1872,** the recorded membership now **100** in number
- Able (in **1886**) to enjoy an average attendance of **77** in the morning and **86** in the evening
- In decline by **1903** – with an average attendance of **23** in the morning and **54** in the evening
- Closed in **1908.** The building was later to house **The Industrial Mission** in **1909** and (at an unknown date) **The Lithuanian Roman Catholic Church**

From this data, it's apparent that **Henry Myerson** was no **Charles Spurgeon (1834-1892)** – the popular **Baptist** preacher of the day – with a capacity to attract thousands. Throughout **Henry's** pastorate, (in what was a very difficult area) membership appears to have shown only a modest increase. Yet it's equally apparent that **Shalom Chapel** declined rapidly following **Henry's** retirement. Within just over ten years it had closed. This would suggest that it had been *'a one-man band.'* A cloud hung over the ministry of **George Higgens** who'd lasted barely a year. Beyond his name and starting date, no further details are provided by **The Strict Baptist Historical Society.** Along with his very short tenure, this lack of information may possibly imply that his association with them had not ended well.

8.2 The Myersons in 1861

By the time of the **1861** Census, one **Myerson** was living in very crowded accommodation at **Clerkenwell, St James, Middsx.**
126 Saint John Street
Edward Vincent (Head) aged **29** *'Water Gilder'* birthplace **Marylebone**
Elizabeth aged **22 Middx**
Louisa aged **2 Clerkenwell**
Thomas Myerson aged **40** *'Iron Plate Worker & Smith'* **Bethnal Green**
Eliza aged **33 Harleston**
Frederick aged **13 Hackney**
Eliza aged **2 Clerkenwell**
Loretta aged **11mths Clerkenwell**
Thomas Collins aged **20** *'Iron Worker Apprentice,'* **St Pancras**
Robert Josling aged **24** *'Hosier''* **Turling, Essex**
126 Saint John Street
John Goodman aged **70** *'Pauper – Former Coachman'* **Waltham Abbey**
Rebecca aged **73 Middlesex**

However, the **1861** Census provided evidence of the beginning of fulfilling the desire for upward mobility for one branch of the **Myerson** Family who had moved further out to **1 and 2 Field Cottages**, in **Park Place, Finchley.** Present was an early example of a move to the suburbs. The **Myersons** were already beginning to invest in the education of their children as a means of gaining respectability. The following Census Return showed where four of **Thomas'** children were. It was apparent that they'd been moved well away from the grime and dirt of central **London.**

Caroline E. Lockward aged **41** *'Mistress, Boarding School* **Wetlingness, Middlesex**

Catherine E. Woodruff aged **21** *'Teacher of Music'* **Poplar Middlesex**

Rowland Myerson aged **10** *'Board scholar'* **Hackney**

HENRY aged **8** *'Board scholar'* **Hackney**

Frank aged **6** *'Board scholar'* **Hackney**

Alfred aged **4** *'Board scholar'* **Hackney**

The overall movement of the **Myersons** from the **East End** to **Crouch End** provided further evidence suggesting that they were an upwardly mobile family, aspiring to become a respectable part of **London's** burgeoning middle classes. Their movement from the centre to the suburbs was very typical of the time. Equally typical was the connection with the **Baptist Church** – as shown by the address **Shalom Church, Baptist House, Tower Hamlets, Bethnal Green.** A review of other **Myerson** lines on **Ancestry.com** confirmed that they tended to produce a substantial number of **Baptist** teachers and preachers. Those occupations appeared to be *'in their blood.'* Living at **26 Oval Cottages** next to **Shalom, Baptist Chapel** was: -

Henry Myerson aged **30** *'Baptist Minister,'* **Bethnal Green**

Anne E aged **26 Bethnal Green**

Amy Elizabeth aged **12 Bethnal Green**

Harriet aged **3 Bethnal Green**

Thomas William aged **1 Bethnal Green**

This **Henry Myerson** appears to have been the uncle of my direct forebear with the same name. Very likely his chapel would have been involved in Jewish Mission Work. It was clear that the **Myerson's** were using a mixture of business, education and the **Baptist** Ministry to rise in the world. They seemed ambitious to put any history of poverty behind them. This point is reinforced by a quick review of another branch of the **Myersons** whose links to my own ancestors was uncertain. They lived at **Enfield, Edmonton** and appeared to be very affluent.

Ryder T. Myerson aged **42** *'Abalin Works'* **Stoke Newington**
Fred H aged **75 Thetford, Norfolk**
Eliza Reynolds aged **24** *'Servant'* **Chelmsford, Essex**
Mary A Gibbons aged **23** *'Cook'* **Chelmsford, Essex**
Fred White aged **14** *'Groom'* **Saint George's, Middlesex**

8.3 A Property involving Thomas Myerson

Further evidence of upward social mobility was to be found in details of a property deal connected with **Thomas Myerson.** (At this same time, his brother **James'** family was sinking ever deeper into the abject misery of **Victorian** poverty). **Thomas** was active as a trustee (a responsible position) for the 7th **Starr Bowkett Benefit Building Society.** According to **Wikipedia,** this was a co-operative, non-profit financial institution providing interest-free loans to its members whilst operating on the principle of mutual self-help as espoused by **Dr T. E. Bowkett** in **1843** (who apparently was a surgeon.) It was geared to assist those more respectable members of the working classes committed to thrift, sober living and self-improvement. However, *"In **1862 Richard B. Starr** made some changes to **Dr Bowkett's** scheme, including a slightly increased subscription fee and shorter subscription time, among others. The changes made the scheme more palatable to potential subscribers and **Starr** promoted his now copyrighted system aggressively. The **Starr** changes also made running a **Starr-Bowkett** Society profitable for management."*

Its method of working was as follows: *"A registered society is formed with a limited number of memberships available. New members are assigned a number and select the amount of loan they wish to apply for. Members then pay a monthly subscription for a set time period - e.g. **200** months. The amount paid each month is based on the amount of the proposed loan, generally **0.25%** of the loan. Once the society has accumulated sufficient funds from subscriptions, ballot meetings are begun and held on a monthly basis afterwards. Loan recipients are chosen by random lottery. Once a member has received a loan, they then pay back that loan and any amount still owing on their original subscription commitment. Once all members have had the opportunity to take out a loan, the society is closed, and the original capital returned to its members."*

However, they did enjoy a rather chequered history. *"Concerns over the "lottery" system used, as well as the actions of unscrupulous managers, led governments in the **United Kingdom** to outlaw **Starr-Bowkett Societies** there. However, they had spread to the **Australian** colonies and became a popular option for a burgeoning middle class to afford their own homes"* Eventually most would be closed or turn into mainstream banks.

*"The last known traditional **Starr-Bowkett Society,** in **Newtown, New South Wales, Australia,** sold its building in **2014.**"*

Indentures (a legal contract reflecting a debt or purchase transaction) and other related documents obtained from the very helpful **Tower Hamlets Local History Library** (on **Wednesday, 23ʳᵈ December 2015**) confirmed that **Thomas** had been involved in at least one property deal. He had obtained a mortgage on **32 Latimer Street, Stepney Green** on the **19ᵗʰ** and **29ᵗʰ December 1866.** (The difference in dates may have been attributed to the time needed to collect all the relevant signatures.) The borrower appears to have been a certain **John Gray,** *'Cigar Manufacturer'* of **6 Lesley Street, Mile End Road, Middlesex.** In contrast, the lenders appear to have been the trustees who consisted of: -

Thomas Henry Ellis of 57 Jewin Street, City of London, *'Engraver'*
Robert Blundell, 66 Tore Street, City of London, *'Bookmaker'*
Thomas Jones, 25 Silver Street, City of London, *'Tailor'*
Henry Martin, 25 Somerset Street, Aldgate, City of London, *'Pork Butcher'*
Thomas Myerson, 126 St John Street, Clerkenwell, Middlesex *'Iron Plate Worker'*

The trustees met together to endorse the surrender of the mortgage on **19ᵗʰ August 1875.** Of interest was the signature of **Thomas Myerson,** present on a later document confirming the receipt of all monies concerned with this transaction (on **28ᵗʰ August 1877**); placed next to a bright red wax seal. It confirms that (unlike his father **Lewis**) he was literate, although his writing was very much a scrawl and of poorer quality than the other signatories.

8.4 The Myersons in 1871

Proceeding to the **1871** Census finds the **Thomas** branch of the **Myersons** moving to a yet more middle-class location. Such a move was typical of those past migrant families – now in their third generation, and now able to take advantage of the booming mid-Victorian economy.
Thomas Myerson Aged **50** *'Iron Plate Worker, Crouch End'* **Bethnal Green**
Elizabeth aged **42** Hackney
Alfred aged **14** *'Scholar'* **Clerkenwell, Middx**
Elizabeth aged **12** *'Scholar'* **Clerkenwell, Middx**
Loretta aged **10** *'Scholar'* **Clerkenwell, Middx**
Emeline aged **8** *'Scholar'* **Clerkenwell, Middx**

Loretta and **Emeline** would be the paternal aunts of my maternal grandmother and would play a decisive role in her early life. They would become very prim and proper genteel ladies, having been brought up in the **Strict Baptist** Tradition.

By this time, **Thomas** and **Elizabeth's** son **Frederick** had struck out on his own. Aged twenty-three he had married a **Sarah Louisa Harris (c.1845-1925)** on **July 14th, 1869** at **Epsom, Surrey** – the banns of which had been read out at **Saint Mary's Church, Islington** three days previously.

An old photograph of **Sarah** (perhaps the oldest one my family has) shows a rather plump woman with a ruff collar and a broach. Her hair is divided into a **Queen Victoria** parting. She also has a large nose. Not a beauty perhaps but a practical, sensible-looking woman whose plump build would suggest to a **Victorian** man an ability to successfully bear children. In a later photograph (taken in old age) she has a rather sweet expression and a look of determination and wisdom in her eyes. Her husband was very much a **mid-Victorian** – possessed of a drooping moustache and side whiskers. He had very strong hands. A photograph of him (in about **1930**) shows him on a garden deckchair with my mother and large teddy bear on his knee. Wearing a trilby hat, suit and waistcoat **Frederick** looks a thoroughly benign old gentleman although he doesn't appear to be quite sure about having my mother on his knee. However, for a man in his early eighties, he looked extremely vigorous. He must have been rather good looking when young.

Whilst showing him living at **16 St John Street, Islington West,** the **1871** Census confirmed his growing independence.
Frederick Thomas aged **23** *'Iron Plate Worker'* **Hackney**
Luiza aged **25, Kentish Town**
Gertrude L aged **7 Months, Islington**
Their neighbours consisted of a teacher, carpenter and post office worker. **Gertrude** would later migrate to **Seattle,** in **Washington State, America.** My mother **Cynthia** remembers her coming over to visit **London** when she was a young girl.

Another of **Thomas'** sons were still based in **Hackney** at **Saint Dionysius, Backchurch, 165 Fenchurch Street** working in hosiery.
Catherine Jones (Head) aged **82** *'Housekeeper'* **London**
Sarah M aged **39** *'Draper & Hosier'* **London**
William Benbow aged **18** *'Hosier's Asst'*

Henry Myerson aged **18** *'Hosier's Asst'* **Hackney**
Mary A Skidmore aged **35** *'Housekeeper'* **Margate**

A review of **1871** Census Returns in **Leeds Central Library** on **Tuesday, 24ᵗʰ May 2016** partly answered the question *'what had happened to the orphaned children of* ***James*** *and* ***Caroline Myerson?'*** This source revealed the following details concerning **Thomas's** younger brother **Henry Myerson. Henry** was a **Baptist Minister** with a chapel based in **Bethnal Green.** (My wife and I paid a visit to the site on **Monday, 21ˢᵗ December 2015** only to find it was now a grassed area adjacent to some blocks of flats.) Living in **33 Poole Road** in **Bethnal Green** his household had consisted of: -
Henry Myerson aged **44** *'Baptist Minister, Shalom Chapel'* **Bethnal Green**
Ann aged **45 Bethnal Green**
Ann aged **22 Bethnal Green**
Thomas aged **11** *'Scholar'* **Bethnal Green**
Robert Higgens aged **68** (wife's father) *'Hosiery Silk Weaver'* **Hampstead**
Caroline Myerson aged **28** (Niece) *'Machine Fitter'* **Stepney**
Walter Myerson aged **10** (nephew), **Stepney**
Caroline Mears aged **28** *'Boot Machinist'* **Bethnal Green**

What the Census Return showed was that, possibly out of *'Christian charity'* and a sense of family obligation, **Henry** and his wife had acted as *'rescuers'* for the surviving members of **James Myerson's** family. To his credit, **Henry** had prevented them from being *'carted off'* to the workhouse for a second time – giving them a chance to get their lives back together. He may also have ensured that his nephew (also called ***'Henry,'*** and aged **14**) had been placed in a *'Boys' Refuge School'* with **128** other pupils in the village of **Bisley** in **Surrey.** It was a **Shaftsbury Orphanage** which, in this historical period, enjoyed a good reputation. The clean air of the countryside would have proved very beneficial to boys known to suffer from a *'delicate'* constitution.

One mystery is the discrepancy in age between the **Caroline Myerson** recorded here and the **Caroline Myerson** recorded in the **1861** Census. The latter records her as being the daughter of **James Myerson.** The former's date of birth was recorded as *'about 1843'* with a birthplace in ***'South Hackney,'*** whilst the latter was *'about 1851'* with a birthplace in ***'Limehouse, Middlesex.'*** The discrepancy between these two birth places can easily be explained because they were alternative descriptions of the same place. More puzzling was the discrepancy in ages. This could be due to a transcription error in which ***'20'*** was set down as ***'28,'*** or was there another niece named ***'Caroline'*** who just happened to be living in the same household as the orphaned son of **James Myerson**? Of these two explanations, the first appears more plausible, simply because serious transcription errors were not unknown in **Victorian** Census Returns.

Further information concerning **Shalom Chapel** was provided by the following notice, appearing on **p.2458** of **The London Gazette** 8th **May 1874**. *"NOTICE is hereby given, that a separate building, named **Shalom Chapel,** situated at the **Oval, Hackney-road,** in the parish of **Bethnal Green,** in the county of **Middlesex,** in the district of **Bethnal Green,** being a building certified according to law as a place of religious worship, was, on the **2nd** day of **May 1874,** duly registered for solemnizing marriages therein, pursuant to the **Act of 6th** and **7th Wm. IV., cap. 85.** Witness my hand this **4th of May 1874.***
***W. P. Howard,** Superintendent Registrar"*
This source indicated that **Henry Myerson's** Chapel was moving towards respectability in terms of social and legal standing.

Another survivor of **James Myerson's** family was his son, also called **James.** The **1871** Census revealed that he was living at **Bath Grove, Hackney.** Members of this household consisted of: -
James Davis aged **36** *'Chair Maker'* **Bethnal Green**
Rachel aged **35** Heppenston, London
Elizabeth aged **5** and a half **Hackney**
Anne aged **3** years **Hackney**
Frederick Byford aged **25** (Lodger) *'Warehouseman'* **London**
James aged **1** Bethnal Green
Matilda Smith aged **12** (Lodger) **Saint Luke's, London**
Joseph Byford aged **24** *'Smelter'* **Wolverhampton**
James Myerson aged **17** (Lodger) *'Warehouseman'* **Hackney**
However, no information could be found about **James Myerson's** eldest son **George** nor about his daughter **Anne.** The most likely explanation is that they had died before the **1871** Census Return. Poverty appears to have taken a terrible toll on this family.

8.5 The Myersons in 1881

Still living at **Hornsea** (but now at the new address of **7 Palace Road**) for the **1881** census. This revealed: - **THOMAS MYERSON** was living at **7 Palace Road** in the suburb of **Hornsey**
Thomas Myerson aged **60** *'Iron Plate Worker, employing two men and four boys'* **Bethnal Green**

Elizabeth aged **52** Hackney
Alfred aged **24** *'Iron Plate Worker'* **Clerkenwell, Middx**
Elizabeth aged **22** *'Governess at home teacher'* **Clerkenwell, Middx**
Loretta aged **20** *'Pupil teacher, school board'* **Clerkenwell, Middx**
Emeline aged **18** *'Board School Service'* **Clerkenwell, Middx**
Mary Ann Harley aged **48** *'Visiting sister in law'* **Clapton, Middx**

Through the **1881** Census, it also became possible to trace how my mother's grandfather the younger **Henry Myerson** met his future wife **Gertrude Watson.** Evident was a very typical case of an able shop assistant marrying the boss's sister to get on! Both would be the parents of my maternal grandmother and both were living at **7 Woolston Place, Old Christchurch Road, Christchurch, Hackney.**
Mary Watson aged **28** *'Hosier & Draper,'* **Bristol**
Gertrude **(Sister)** aged **23** *'Hosier & Draper,'* **Elsham**
Florence (Sister) aged **21** *'Hosier & Draper,* **Elsham**
Rowland aged **20** *'Hosier & Draper,'* **Elsham**
Henry Myerson aged **28** *'Draper's Assistant,'* **Hackney**
Sarah Horlick aged **23** *'Servant,'* **Blandford, Dorset**

This **Gertrude** appears to have been born in **December 1858** and died in the first quarter of **1893,** possibly of **TB**. She married **Henry Myerson** in the last quarter of **1882** at **Christchurch, Hamps.** Meanwhile, **Henry's** elder brother **Frederick** and his family were dwelling at **24 Langdon Rd**: -
Frederic T. Myerson aged **33** *'Iron plate worker'* **Hackney Middlesex**
Sarah L aged **35 Kentish Town**
Gertrude L aged **10 Barnsbury**
Alfred Fred aged **8 Barnsbury**
Ethel aged 6 Islington
Reginald aged **3 Islington**
Lillian Myerson aged **1 Islington**
The first and last of these addresses suggested that the **Myerson's Iron Plate** business was bringing in enough income to subsidise a move to the suburbs for at least some of the family.

Frederick would become close to my mother in old age and would have her play on his knee when she was under five. His signature was on the wedding certificate of my maternal grandparents, **William** and **Marguerite**. The **1881** Census revealed that the elder **Henry Myerson** had moved to **96 Bonner Road.** His household consisted of: -

Henry Myerson aged **54** *'Baptist Minister'* **Bethnal Green**
Ann aged **55 Bethnal Green**
Thomas aged **21** *'Bootmaker'* **Bethnal Green**
Sarah aged **20** (unmarried) *'Machinist'* **Bethnal Green**
Alice aged **5 months Bethnal Green**
Mary Ann Higgens aged **68** (widow) **Bethnal Green**

The implication here was that **Sarah Myerson** had recently given birth to an illegitimate daughter. However, fresh evidence unexpectedly received on **Sunday 13ᵗʰ May 2018** (from a contact preferring to remain anonymous) revealed that this wasn't the case. It had arisen from an error in the Census Return where the word *'married'* was wrongly transcribed as *'unmarried.'* According to my source *"**Thomas Myerson** married **Sarah Murrells** on 27 November 1879 at Shalom Chapel. Her father **John Murrells** was dead. Their eldest daughter **Alice** was born in 1880. I have the original marriage certificate. The clerk who wrote the census for **96 Bonner Road** was in error. The certificate is on **Page 100 No 199 Register Book of District of Bethnal Green**."* A very simple transcription error had led me to draw entirely the wrong conclusion. Interestingly, this contact also disclosed that this **Thomas Myerson** was friends with a professional photographer.

It's worth noting that the **Myerson** Family followed an upward social trajectory that was typical of the **Jewish Community** at that time (approximately**1815-1880**). As **Lipman p.74** noted, *"The outstanding change however in the economic structure of the Community between **1815** and **1880** was that at the beginning the majority numbers were poor or very poor – just scraping a living or supported by relief and the middle class was a minority; at the end of the period, the middle class comprised about half the community, and the poor although numerous were a minority. The transition from a predominantly lower class to a predominantly middle-class community was due to improvement and variety in middle-class occupations."* A major factor in the **Myerson's** climb to a position of social respectability was their willingness to assimilate. To them, being middle class was to enter the Promised Land. Respectability was what they hankered after.

8.6 The Myersons in 1891

By **1891** my Great, Great Grandfather. **Thomas Myerson** was living at the grand-sounding **3 Oxford Villa** in the suburb of **Wood Green, Tottenham**
<u>Thomas Myerson</u> aged **70** *'Iron Plate Worker'* **London Bethnal Green**
<u>Elizabeth</u> aged **59, London, Hackney**

Mary Ann Harley aged **59,** sister in law, *'Lady Help'* **London, Hackney**

From this information, one wonders whether **Mary** was a poor relative who'd been taken in. In **1893, Thomas** died and consequently his name no longer featured in any Census Returns. He'd certainly been upwardly mobile as far as his position in the **Victorian Class System** was concerned. Like my Great-grandfather, (**Edmund** in **Leeds**) **Thomas Myerson** apparently won the battle for respectability through a mixture of arduous work, shrewd business deals and sober living.

During the **1891** Census, the younger **Henry Myerson** and his family were living at **43 High Street, Islington.** By then my maternal grandmother was a seven-year-old child.

<u>Henry Myerson</u> aged **38** *'Hosier,'* **Hackney**
Gertrude Eliza aged **32 Lee, Kent**
Harold Percival aged **2, Hornsea**
Marguerite Eliza aged **7, Islington**

Marguerite became an orphan at the age of **12** – her mother died first. Meanwhile, in the **1891** Census the children of **Thomas** and **Elizabeth Myerson** (see list below) were still living together at **49 Middle Lane, Hornsea.** Loretta (Laurie) and **Emeline** were the maiden aunts who looked after **Marguerite** following the death of her parents. They were **Strict Baptists.** Of note in this Census is how they appeared to be doing everything they possibly could to stay financially viable in **late Victorian London.** They had taken on a lodger and had a servant, so releasing other household members to work. **Alfred** had possibly found work at the ironmongers too arduous and had gone into the more genteel and creative craft of wood engraving.

Alfred aged **34** *'Wood Engraver,'* **Clerkenwell**
Elizabeth aged **32** *'Governess at home teacher,'* **Clerkenwell**
Loretta aged **30** *'School Teacher,'* **Clerkenwell**
Emmeline aged **28** *School Teacher,'* **Clerkenwell**
Alfred H. Tongue (Boarder) aged **44** *'Clerk,'* **Finsbury**
Louisa Willis aged **23** *'Servant',* **Finsbury**

Probate Documents revealed that both **Loretta** and **Emeline** would live until **1946** and would possess sufficient capital to enjoy a comfortable existence: -

- **Loretta Myerson,** death on the **26th April 1946** in **Amersham, Buckinghamshire.** Probate document **15th October 1946:** "*Loretta*

Myerson Queynton Hyde Heath, Amersham, Buckinghamshire, to *Emmeline Myerson 'Spinster' £1152 14s 8d* (worth *£81,912.30* in **2018**)

- **Emmeline Myerson,** death on the **19th November 1946** in **Amersham, Buckinghamshire.** Probate Document **14th March 1947:** *"Emmeline Myerson, Queyton, Hyde Heath Amersham to Herbert Baker* retired *bank official £1993 12s 8d"* (worth *£79,520.70* in **2018**)

These two ladies had ensured they had carefully ordered their affairs. In this Document *'Emmeline'* was spelt with two *M's'* but in others, it's just one and the latter being normally the preferred usage.

Regarding **Fredrick Myerson,** the **1891** Census revealed him to have moved to the suburbs, with his address now being **4 Grove House Road, Hornsea.** As a family, they were clearly *'on the up'* Very typically for the time **Frederick** also hoped that his sons would follow him into the business: -

Frederick S Myerson aged **43** *'Iron plate worker,'* **London, Hackney**
Sarah A Myerson aged **45** *'wife'* **London, Kentish Town**
Gertrude L Myerson aged **20** *'Governess,'* **London, Barnsbury**
Alfred F Myerson aged **18** *'Bookkeeper,'* **London, Barnsbury**
Ethel Myerson aged **16** *'Amanuensis,'* **London, Holloway**
Reginald Myerson aged **13** *'Iron plate worker (Assistant)'* **London, Holloway**
Lillian Myerson aged **11** *'Scholar,'* **London, Highgate**
Grace Myerson aged **9** *'Scholar,'* **London, Highgate**
Beatrice Myerson aged **7** *'Scholar,'* **London, Highgate**

N.B An *'Amanuensis'* was one who took down dictation, usually within an office situation.

The **1891** Census also revealed the elder **Henry Myerson** still at **96 Bonner Road.** His household consisted of: -

Henry Myerson aged **64** *'Minister* **Bethnal Green**
Ann aged **65 Bethnal Green**
Harriet aged **16** (Daughter)
Elizabeth aged **5** (Grand Daughter)

8.7 The Myersons in 1901

The **1901** Census Return confirmed that **Marguerite** had not stayed with her maiden aunts for very long. She was to teach classes of up to sixty pupils and would later remark that *'teachers would get blamed for everything.'* How **Harold** was to end up in an orphanage despite coming from a reasonably wealthy family remains something of a mystery. (The age-range at this orphanage was from **7-14**.) On **Sunday, 7ᵗʰ May 2009, Cynthia** said she'd been told that **Harold** had been looked after by another branch of the family. This proved to be factually incorrect. However, **Laurie** & **Emmeline** had taken care to have remained in correspondence with him when he became an optician in **Aylesbury** with a family of two (or possibly three) children to look after. **Cynthia** wondered whether they'd acted out of a guilty conscience. Who the **Besant's** were and what association my grandmother had with them (other than lodger) also remains unknown.

Thomas Besant aged **57** *'Solicitor's Clerk'* **Westminster**
Charlotte Besant aged **48 Pentonville**
__Marguerite Eliza Myerson__ aged **17** *'Board School Pupil Teacher,'* **Pentonville**
Harold Myerson aged **12** at **Stockwell Orphanage**

The aunts, with whom my Grandmother appeared to live circa **1893** to **1900** were continuing to follow the strategy of maintaining their social position through teaching and taking in respectable lodgers. Their address in the **1901** Census was **43 Dresden Road** in **Highgate, North London.**

George S. Smith aged **59** *'Living on own account'* **Stow on the Wold, Gloucestershire**
Mary aged **58 Gloucester, Cheltenham**
Wallace aged **15 Hornsey, London**
Percy aged **14 Hornsey, London,**
Loretta aged **40** *'Teacher Own Account'* **Clerkenwell**
Emeline aged **38** *'Teacher Own Account'* **Clerkenwell**
Charles Thomson aged **23** *'Clerk'* **Scotland**
Frank C. Scott aged **22** *"Clerk'* **Scotland**
George A. Hill aged **31** *'Telephone Engineer'* **Hull, Yorkshire**

By **1901, Frederick's** family were at **Brooklands, Hornsey.**
Frederick S Myerson aged **53** *'Iron plate worker'* **London, Hackney**
Sarah A Myerson aged **56 London, Kentish Town**
Gertrude L Myerson aged **30** *'Governess'* **London, Barnsbury**
Reginald Myerson aged **23** *'Iron plate worker'* **London, Holloway**
Lillian Myerson aged **21 London, Holloway**
Grace Myerson aged **19** *'Lady Clerk'* **London, Holloway**
Beatrice Myerson aged **17** *'Pupil Teacher'* **London, Holloway**
Lillian and **Beatrice** would become close to my mother's family. They lived in a large house in **Hyde Heath** and were known as *'Lilly'* and *'Tricie.'* They each would rather deaf in old age. They kept China Gnomes in their garden one of

which they gave to my sister when she was aged six. **Val** remembers them both to have been very genteel. An old photograph shows them with their elderly aunts **Emeline** (who's holding a black dog) and **Laurie**.

The **1901** Census revealed that **Henry Myerson** had moved to **51 Stonebridge Road, Tottenham, North London** and was living with relatives in what seemed to have been a rather busy, crowded household, consisting of: -
Thomas William Myerson aged **41** *'Packer'* **Bethnal Green**
Sarah Ann aged **40 Bethnal Green**
Henry aged **74** (Father) *'Retired Baptist Minister* **Bethnal Green**
Ann Elizabeth aged **76** (Mother) **Bethnal Green**
Alice Gertrude aged **20** *'Ladies Machinist Shirts'* **Bethnal Green**
Sarah Ann aged **16** *'Ladies Machinist Shirts'* **London, Bethnal Green**
Harriet aged **14 Walthamstow**
Thomas William aged **13** *'Errand Boy'* **Tottenham**
It's possible to wonder whether they managed to establish a new role as supportive Grand Parents. A review of the Death Registers confirmed that **Henry Myerson** died at the age of **75** during **December 1902**. (He was buried at **Waltham Forest** on the twenty-third of that month.) His wife **Ann** lived until aged **79,** dying in the **April 1905**. (She was buried at **Waltham Forest** on the twenty-ninth of that month.) Their relatively long-life spans suggest that **Henry** and **Ann Myerson** had been a *'clean living'* married couple, who had taken care to have teetotal. The information on the Census Returns suggests that **Henry** had been a good, capable man shown in his ability to pastor a chapel in a tough **East End** area of **London** for thirty-five years.

8.8 The Myersons in 1911

By the **1911** Census, **Marguerite** (wrongly recorded as **Margaret**) was living with someone who worked at the ironworks at **51 Park Avenue South, Crouch End.**
Sydney Smith aged **39** *'Manager, sheet iron works. Working mostly to the order of engineering firms,'* **Camden Town**
Gertrude Louisa aged **40 Barnsbury**
Lawrence Sydney aged **14 Stroud Green**
Marjorie Gertrude aged **12 Stroud Green**
Margaret Eliza Myerson aged **27** *'Teacher, Council School'* **Islington**
Louisa Hedges aged **20** *'Housemaid/Domestic,'* **Quainton, Buckinghamshire**

By **1911**, **Frederick Myerson's** family were at **Brooklands, Hornsey**.

Frederick Myerson aged 63 *'Iron plate and metal worker, employs two,'* London, Hackney
Sarah A Myerson aged 66 London, Kentish Town
Lillian Myerson aged 31 London, Holloway
Grace Myerson aged 29 *'Block Print Trade,'* London, Holloway
Beatrice Myerson aged 27 *'Teacher,'* London, Holloway
aged 21 *'Housemaid/Domestic,'* London, Walthamstow

Worth noting are the following details concerning Frederick's son Reginald (or 'Rex' Myerson)
Rex Myerson aged 33 *'Sheet metal worker,'* London, Islington
Maggie aged 27 London, Islington
Rex Dudley aged 1 London, Hornsey
Elizabeth Evans aged 28 *'General Servant, (Domestic)'* London
They lived at 17 Danvers Road, Hornsey North in the registration district of Edmonton.

A photograph of Sydney Smith reveals a man with glasses, a moustache and dark receding hair. Wearing a stiff white collar and the three-piece suit he looks every inch a late Victorian or Edwardian manager. He was the son-in-law of Fred Myerson. He'd followed the usual strategy of marrying the boss's daughter to *'get on.'* A quick glance at the photograph hardly suggests he'd married her for her looks! His wife (also wearing glasses) is portrayed with a skeletal figure and very sour facial expression on her face. She looks neither well nor happy. One wonders how she would have got on with other family members.

Interestingly, Rex's hairstyle and manner of dress were like that of Sydney only Rex was taller and far thinner in the face. He didn't look like a particularly robust man. In the original family group photograph, both men were wearing carnations in their jacket buttonholes. However, my mother Cynthia recounts a strange story about Rex who'd died very suddenly (during an appendicitis operation) in December 1936. On the day of his death, his wife had been working alone in the kitchen and had suddenly cried out *"Oh my God – Rex has gone!"* He had continued to live in Edmonton until the end of his life. My mother remembers Rex and his wife as a *'very devoted couple'* and that his death was unexpected as by then an operation for appendicitis was deemed to be straightforward. Their son Dudley would live on to his eightieth year – not expiring until January 1990 in Ashford, Kent.

Further details of **Rex's** demise were provided by the following death certificate which I received in **October 2016.**

Registration District <u>Edmonton</u>

<u>1936</u> Death in the <u>sub-district</u> of <u>Hornsey</u> in the <u>County of Middlesex</u>

1. When and where died? Thirteenth November 1936, Hornsey Central Hospital, Park Road, Hornsey

2. Name and Surname: Rex Myerson

3. Sex: Male

4. Age: 59

6. Occupation: Of 14 Danvers Road, Hornsey U.D. Sheet iron Worker (Master)

6. Cause of death: I. Acute Appendicitis II. Hypocarditus certified Hector D. Apergis in R.C.S (Royal College of Surgeons)

7. Signature, description and residence of informant: Sydney Smith Brother-in-law in attendance, 23 Elmfield Avenue, Crouch End

8. When registered: Fourteenth November 1936

9. Signature of registrar: B. Y. Parkin (The initials are unclear)

What was apparent was that **Rex** had died on an operating table and that an already weakened heart was perhaps the fatal complication. It was fascinating to place an exact date and location to an incident that hitherto had been confined to the misty realm of family legend. Once again, my mother had, in her early nineties, provided a crucial lead. Her memory and judgment of people appeared to be incredibly accurate. Her contribution to the later stages of this history was outstanding. This was an incredible achievement for someone of her age and physical frailty. Her memories will be her best legacy to the family.

8.9 The Myerson Iron Works

Further details of the Iron Works (mentioned in the Census Returns) were provided in Trade Journals: -

Entry from PO Directory 1914:

Part 3 Commercial & Professional Directory

Myerson Thomas Frederick

Iron Plate Worker

Specialises in Sheet Iron Work for Engineers

213 & 215 St John Street

Clerkenwell

Works Sekforde Street Ec – In 6218 Central

Kelly's Directory
1901: Myerson Thomas Frederick
Specialises in Sheet Iron Works
For Engineers 213 & 215
St John Street
Clerkenwell

1914: Myerson Thomas Frederick
24 Sekforde Street
(26a has a Sutton Book Cabinetmaker
27 has a Tom Partridge, at the corner of Woodbridge Street
34 Sekforde Street has the Sekforde Arms)

1919: Myerson Thomas Frederick
Specialises in Sheet Iron for Engineers
213 & 215 St John Street

1923: Myerson Thomas Frederick
24 Sekforde Street

8.10 Comparison with the Smiths

It's clear that, in terms of values, ambitions, and the strategies employed to advance socially many similarities existed between the **Myersons** of **London** and the **Smiths** of **Yorkshire.** Both families possessed a fierce work ethic and were sometimes quite ruthless in maintaining their *'respectability.'* For them, wealth and status were to be created and not inherited as a birthright. Pervading both families was a deep sense of insecurity, borne of the realization that even in economically prosperous times, respectability was a very fragile thing. A descent into the most degrading kinds of poverty was all too easy. In all of this, they were very many products of the age in which they lived. At the close of this investigation, it's possible to reconstruct a line of descent, from the remotest known **Myerson** forebears to my mother **Cynthia.** Here we find: -
1. **Louis (Lewis) Adolphus Myerson (c.1790-Jan 1860)** of Saxony who on **24th April 1815 at Bethnal Green St Matthew,** married **Elizabeth Launder (1793-January 1851)** and they had a son
2. **Thomas Myerson (1821-1893)** who, on **21 May 1846 at St Giles without Cripplegate** married **Elizabeth Harley (1828-1893)** and they had a son
3. **Henry Robert Myerson (1853-January 1898)** who during the last quarter of **1882** at **Christchurch Hampshire** married **Gertrude Eliza Watson (1858-**

1893) and had a son **Harold Percival Myerson (14th February 1889-March 1976)** and they had a daughter

4. Marguerite Eliza Myerson (July 1883-July 1963) who, in **October 1914** at **Edmonton** married **William John Absalom (21st October 1886-1959)** and they had a daughter

6. Cynthia Mary Absalom (26th November 1923-?) who is my mother.

By halving the percentages at each generation, I could ascertain the extent to which my family was **Ashkenazi Jewish**. The respective percentages were: **Louis Myerson 100%, Thomas 50%, Henry 25%, Marguerite 13.5%, Cynthia 6.75%, myself 3.38%,** my **children 1.69%** and my **grandchildren 0.84%.** (This estimate assumes there was no **Jewish** input from other family lines.)

Section 9: The Testimony of Henry Myerson

Concerning the Faith and Ministry of Henry Myerson

The life of the elder **Henry Myerson (1827-1903)** is well worth examining. His vocation as a **Baptist Minister** has already been outlined in previous sections as was his care given to orphaned relatives. The focus here is upon using original sources (like Obituaries) to provide a more detailed account of his life. His autobiographical narrative is also included – vividly portraying what it was like to have served as a **Baptist Minister** in the **East End** of **London** during the nineteenth century. (This material was kindly provided by **The Strict Baptist Historical Library** and was received on **Saturday, 9th, July 2016**.) Moreover, a beginning can be made by recounting the personal testimony of **Henry Myerson** himself, given when he was sixty-three years old and originally published in **Volume XLV** of the **July 1889** issue of *'The Earthen Vessel and Gospel Herald Magazine'* – a publication of the **Strict Baptist** Movement. (Apart from some *italicisation* and minor corrections in spelling and punctuation I have kept to the original format. My own insertions are placed in square brackets [ ]). All hymns mentioned in this (and other accounts) are available on *'YouTube.'* I played them whilst compiling this account (in **March 2018**) and they really helped in establishing a sense of connection with **Henry** – and others involved in his life. For reasons, soon to become apparent, I believe **Henry Myerson's** personal testimony to be of more relevance today than when it was first penned over a century ago.

OUR PORTRAIT GALLERY, – NO. VII.

MR. HENRY MYERSON, PASTOR OF SHALOM CHAPEL, *"THE OVAL,"* HACKNEY.

My DEAR BROTHER W. WINTERS, – I forward you as requested a short sketch of my life. I was born January 12th 1827, in the parish of Bethnal-Green in the county of Middlesex. At the age of six years I was placed in the Hebrew School, Palatine-Place, Cambridge Heath, which school belongs to the London Society for promoting Christianity among the Jews, my father being a Polish Jew, having embraced the Christian religion. After a lapse of eight years, I was apprenticed to the clock trade. My mother was a God-fearing woman and my first impressions were, under God, obtained from her dear lips. She taught me to lisp God's name in prayer and told me of a beautiful heaven and a dreadful hell, and that God would punish bad people in the burning lake. She taught me also to sing of Jesus's love. I can almost hear her now singing that much-loved hymn, [by **Charles Wesley 1707-1788**] – *"Jesu, lover of my soul, let me to Thy bosom fly."* And although only about four years old then, I can to this day remember how dear that hymn was to me.

OH, THE BLESSING OF HAVING A GODLY MOTHER

She has long since gone to heaven, and I hope through God's grace to meet her there. My impressions were greatly deepened at school, the religious training of the boys being carefully maintained. Thus, was the seed of divine grace sown in my heart at an early age, but alas! as is too often the case, at my leaving school and commencing the pursuits of life, I was surrounded by bad influences which (for a time) produced injurious results. My master, as well as the men he employed, were not only worldly men but blasphemous and most degraded; and encouraged sinning rather than the fear of God, the result being that the good seed sown in my soul, for a time appeared to wither and die, and the hidden evils of my heart were, to a very alarming extent, displayed. Yet, nevertheless, in spite of myself and the sad temptations with which I was beguiled, God mercifully kept the spark of divine life still smouldering in my heart to burst out into a blaze to His glory in the afterlife. Many and sharp were the gnawing of conscience; heavy was my heart, and the fear of death and judgment constantly haunted my soul.

At about the age of seventeen the Lord graciously interposed, and at once put a stop to my mad career; thanks to His blessed name or I must have gone on in this path of sin to this day. A dear brother in the flesh, a God-fearing young man, remonstrated with me on the course I was pursuing and the sad end it would terminate in, and urged me to attend the house of God. [Was this my ancestor **Thomas Myerson, Henry's** elder brother whose family were known to be strict Baptists?] His entreaties took effect and the next Lord's-day found the brothers seated side-by-side in the house of God in Crown-street, Long Acre, listening to an earnest preacher, a Mr Blake. And from that time the Lord was pleased to deliver me from the snare of Satan and constrained me to look to Him to be preserved in the future. For a long time, I was under the law, and could not feel my sins forgiven or my soul saved: but at length the Lord delivered my soul from bondage, applying to my soul the dying words of Jesus, *"IT IS FINISHED."* About the age of 28 I was strongly impressed with a desire to preach the Gospel and, after much prayer for the Lord's direction and help, I commenced preaching in the open-air, and on one of these occasions I made the acquaintance of Mr Thomas King, who is now a deacon of the Surrey Tabernacle and we have been close friends from that time. I did not continue to preach long in the open air before the Lord sent me to deliver His message of mercy to His people at Romford and I proclaimed the Gospel of Christ there for sixteen months and about the same length of time at Egham, near Staines and both these places of worship filled under my ministry. From Staines, THE LORD DIRECTED MY STEPS TO SHALOM CHAPEL, HACKNEY, in a most marvellous way. Mr John Bonney, who was led to see and embrace the truth through my instrumentality, was impressed to seek out a place for me to preach in London. He came specially to see me on this subject one Saturday night, some 30 years ago and told me that he had felt uneasy and anxious about me all-the-day, and God had sent him to be my *"Joseph"* and with these impressions on his mind he took me to see my predecessor and we found him [Pastor **Hislop**] very ill. My dear brother Bonney asked him if he would allow me to preach in his chapel once a month. *"Well,"* said he, *"I cannot decide that now, but if you will come to a tea-meeting on Tuesday* (which was to be convened for his benefit), *he would let us know."* On the morrow being Sunday, we decided to go to Shalom Chapel and hear our brother Hislop preach. [spelt **'Haslop'** elsewhere] When we arrived at the chapel, no minister was in the pulpit, and the congregation was in a state of consternation. After some time, the dear man of God entered the chapel from the vestry looking like a dying man and managed to get to the singer's pew, being too weak and ill to ascend the pulpit stairs. He cast his eyes on me and beckoned. I, of course, went to him. He gave me the Bible and asked me to preach to the people. This I consented to do, and afterwards, he spoke approvingly to his flock on what I advanced. On the following Tuesday, Brother Bonney and I went to the meeting, and you may imagine our surprise when we were informed that our dear brother had breathed his last on the previous evening! On that never-to-be-forgotten occasion, I was requested by the deacons to occupy the pulpit on the next Lord's day, and thank God, I have been sustained by Him until now.

"Here I raise my Ebenezer   and hope by Thy good pleasure,
*   Hither by Thy help, I've come   safely to arrive at home."*

[An extract from the second verse of the hymn *'Come, Thou Fount of Every Blessing'* by **Robert Robinson, 1735-90.**] All the old members have gone home but four; yet thank God we have a good Church of about 80 members, and I venture to say that there are not a more loving and peaceable people to be found anywhere. The Lord has greatly blessed and honoured me in the work of the ministry and has maintained me in the pastoral office over one Church nearly 30 years, and my one theme has been and now is and I trust it will be until my eyes are closed in death, *"THE TRUTH, THE WHOLE TRUTH, AND NOTHING BUT THE TRUTH."*

I am thankful to tell you, my dear brother, that our gracious Lord still owns and blesses my ministry, as many can testify, and I pray God that you may be long spared to be a blessing to the cause of God and truth.

Yours in Christ Jesus   HENRY MYERSON

Pastor, Shalom Baptist Chapel, "Oval," Hackney-road, E.

A photo of **Henry** (in the magazine) showed his receding wavy hair atop his domed and furrowed forehead, bushy eyebrows, long aquiline nose and a rather unkempt beard – suggesting a visit to the barbers would have been in order! Although an unbuttoned waistcoat gave a slightly casual air, he looked every inch a **Jewish Rabbi.** His expression is kindly, yet curiously knowing. It's easy to imagine him chuckling at the thought of his personal testimony being distributed to the descendants of his brother, **Thomas,** and then across the world via the Internet! Quite justifiably, he may well feel rather vindicated and, like **Edmund,** his life will have been honoured many years following his death.

However, a note in *'The Earthen Vessel'* revealed that *"Our brother has left an aged widow totally unprovided for. We expect some further particulars to be supplied in next month's issue."* Like many Pastors, **Henry Myerson** appeared to have had *a 'blind spot'* as far as providing for his own family was concerned. Here was a man *'married to his vocation'* and one can only speculate as to what his wife will have felt about this! (As an aside, I wonder whether she proof-read his sermons?)

An account by a **J. P. G**. (in what appears to have been an early **1903** edition of *'The Earthen Vessel'*) largely repeated the information provided in **Henry Myerson's** original testimony. However, this latest account added some further detail, *e.g.* **'Brother Bonney'** having offered to pay for all of **Henry's** expenses whilst he preached once a month at **Shalom.** We also find that he's heard **Henry** preach before and that **Bonney's** first name was **'John.'** He was still alive and was *"now of Stevenage"* when this article was published. The following extract highlighted the struggles **Henry** faced during the early days of his work. *"He had not spoken long in the open air before a door was opened for him at **Romford,** and here I have heard it said that such was his zeal that the little pulpit which was of a temporary character, often had to be held by one of the friends while he was preaching; he preached there about sixteen months. **Egham** and **Staines,** he supplied about the same length of time, and in each of these places abundant blessing rested on his labours, and even in his last day, he shared some of the rewards of this early ministry in the kindness of friends towards him. In these early days, he was much tried in Providence. On one occasion such were his circumstances that, like the late **W. Huntington** he was obliged to part with his coat* [to the pawnbrokers?], *at another time he was compelled to walk from **Staines** to **London.** These were great trials and a conflict arose in his own soul as to whether he could preach at all. On one of these occasions, he cried, "**Lord** if You have nothing for me to do, stop my mouth. Why should I force myself on thee? **Lord,** Thou canst make this plain."* [An account of the meeting with **Mr John Bonney** then followed.]

On **August 6th 1861,** *he was recognized as the pastor. Nearly all who took part in that service, like himself, have gone home – brethren **Webster, S. Cousins, Dixon** and **C.W. Banks.** For many years our brother sustained this position with great acceptance and was in great request among the Churches and it is no uncommon thing today to hear, "I was called under **H. Myerson.**"*

*Owing to declining health he was compelled to resign after thirty-nine years and seven months labour. For a short time, he was **Nonconformist** chaplain at a **London** Cemetery, but this did not suit him. He came to **Stoke Newington** to live with his only son, and while here his health was greatly improved, and he again began to proclaim the truths he loved.*

*About two years ago he came to **Ebenezer*** [Baptist Church] ***Tottenham,** as a hearer (the writer only heard him twice before): but he soon became a constant hearer, and many a time has he given a word of encouragement.*

*At the end of **1901** he desired to join us in Church fellowship and though he had occupied the pulpit came before the Church and we shall long treasure his rich experience of the **Lord's** dealing with him. He was with us in spirit and love and though of such short duration, his loss is felt very much.*

On **Sunday, December 14**^{th,} **1902,** *though he was far from well, he preached at* **East Ham** *with great power and acceptance. In the evening his last message was from* **Psa lxxxiv. 11[84:11].** *On his return home, he was full of praise to his* **Lord** *for the help he had experienced. Through the day he was in great pain and weakness, and on* **Wednesday** *night became unconscious in which state he continued on till* **Friday Afternoon** *when, with a smile on his face, his spirit fled to be with the* **Lord.**

His mortal remains were brought to **Ebenezer Tottenham** *where a good few friends, old and new, had gathered, and a short service was held, myself offering a few suitable remarks from* **Josh. 1:2,** *first clause,* **Brother Hewitt** *closed with prayer. The body was then conveyed to* **Chingford Cemetery,** *where several friends had gathered, and there in the darkening* **December** *evening, we laid to rest all that was mortal, with a few words over the grave.* **Brother Kingston** *offered prayer. On* **Lord's-day** *following we referred to this event from* **Rev xiv.13 [14:13]."**

Further information was provided by a former member of **Shalom** – a certain **M. A. C.** from **Galleywood** [a village in **Essex,** about **30** miles from **London.**] on **December 28**^{th,} **1902.** The chief value of this source lay in the insight it gave into the congregational life at **Shalom.** *"I speak the truth when I say the Church was like a family; one helped the other in any case of need or trouble; and many of us who are scattered, look in vain for that honest and unsuspecting friendship which existed at the* **Oval.** [A description of **Myerson's** call to **Shalom** then followed.] *I was at* **Mr. Myerson's** *recognition meeting; I also went to his last meeting at* **Shalom,** *when his growing infirmities compelled him to relinquish his position; and I do not think there had ever been a thought of changing the pastor until his weakness called for it. We heard him preach not very long before then, and he really was most graciously led that night; his text was, "It is finished," and in the course of his sermon he gave us a vivid description of the way the application of that text delivered him from his slavish fears, when first brought to know his danger.*

He was generous to a fault, as his family have proved. He once owned a few houses (or collected the rents for someone else, I forget which), and one who knew him at that time told me that when he called for rents, if the tenants pleaded poverty, he would not only forbear to press for the rent but would give them money out of his own pocket. Forty years ago, he used to go with **C. W. Banks** *to* **Victoria Park** *and preach; in fact, he was a born open-air preacher and used to gather a good congregation at the corner of the* **Oval, Hackney-road.** *Then again, his* **Monday** *evening prayer meetings were unique in the* **London Churches;** *there were five or six whom he used to call his "curates."* **Mr Henry Mobbs, Matthew Branch, W. Morgan, Mr Ryder** *and others, most dropping in one after the other during the meeting, some from their* **Sabbath** *preaching, some from their work in the city: and oh, they* *did love each other. I was in* **London** *one* **Monday** *Evening and went; and two brethren had given out a verse or two of "Dear refuge of a weary soul." when another later comer said, "we'll sing a verse of "Dear refuge of a weary soul." And* **Mr Myerson** *said with such a gratified expression "We've had that hymn twice tonight brother." Well, these memories may be nothing to strangers, or to the present generation; but if any of the old folk remain who knew* **Shalom** *forty years ago, who remember when the four Johns met in the table pew –* **John Foreman, John Webster, John Bloomfield** *and* **John Pells** *(dear* **John Pells***) and who knew old* **Mr Blackshaw** *and* **Francis** *of the bass viol* [violin]. *And* **Mr Pierpoint;** *and good* **Mr Durman** *and* **Mr King***, they will, in their hearts, admit that there were ties formed in those days which have few parallels in these more flighty times. I am glad that for his sake he was spared a lingering illness, though his family must mourn that there was no farewell word. The churches will do well to see that his widow lacks nothing the little while she may yet stay behind.* [This would be no more than two-and-a-half years.] *One thing is certain, there are no regrets – no blindness, no decay, no sin. We know heaven best by its negatives. "And what must it be to be there?" What majesty and force too are in the apostle's words. "Now, he that hath wrought us for this self-same thing is* **God;** *who also hath given unto us the earnest of His Spirit."*

One thing that **Shalom Chapel** evidently provided was a sense of community. People supported one another and provided practical help in times of need. Very typically for the time, it was an extremely male-orientated Community. Women were almost completely omitted from the accounts provided here. The Chapel gave ordinary working people (who endured unspeakably hard lives) a sense of dignity, purpose and hope. Music (in this instance chapel hymns) was obviously very important in helping them to express their faith.

The information gathered about **Henry Myerson** was unanimous in its portrayal of him as a warm individual who was a good Pastor and a thoroughly decent human being. He was one of the most sympathetic individuals to have been recorded in this *'History'* and my heart really warmed to him. I especially liked his humour. Clearly, he was a *'people's pastor.'* However, some other less positive features emerged from his testimony. One was the relative silence concerning his own father, **Lewis Myerson.** The little mention afforded him by **Henry** was noteworthy, possibly indicated that he hadn't been exactly well-regarded. The silence of a warm and charitable person like **Henry** is even more telling than the openly expressed antagonism of his younger brother **James** (who took a very different path in life). Possibly it was **Lewis** who'd forced **Henry** into an apprenticeship which could have led him down the same destructive route as **James.**

In contrast, their mother **Elizabeth** appears to have been one of those Godly women who had much to endure from certain family members. To hear her words in a domestic setting was a very moving experience – connecting me to the lady who was my maternal Great, Great, Great Grandmother. I got to like her as I did her son **Henry.** Through her prayers and witness, she'd planted seeds that were to directly influence the lives of some of her own children and successive generations of **Myersons.** Even now, having been *'blasted'* for decades by the chill wind of **atheism** these seeds have once more been revived (through **Henry's** testimony) to provide a clear witness to the truths of the **Gospel.** The underpinning resilience of the **Gospel** has shone throughout this *'History'* again and again. It can be seen in the many and varied characters who faithfully held to *'its truths.'* The whole **Smith** family are now, once more, being reminded of these precious truths which had long lain forgotten. Maybe in this *'mad and crazy age'* we should quietly, yet wholeheartedly, return to them.

Both **Elizabeth** and **Henry Myerson** made a refreshing change from a glut of sociopathic **Smiths,** feckless **Absaloms** and mean **Myersons,** hitherto featuring in this work. They added a breath of fresh air. This isn't to say that **Henry Myerson** wasn't without his faults. His failure to make good provision for his wife (in a harsh age) was irresponsible and he didn't seem to be above a little personal vanity. Undeniably, the sentimentality of his language would jar on modern ears; sometimes he gave the impression of being so heavenly minded as to be of only limited earthly use. However, he was essentially a good man, willing to take in orphans and rescue (from certain destitution) some of the children of **James Myerson.** This act alone gives a true measure of his character. When I listened to various renditions of the beautiful hymn *"Dear refuge of the weary soul"* on *'YouTube'* I couldn't help feeling a connection with **Henry.** He's certainly one forbear I would make a bee-line for in the afterlife. What fellowship we would enjoy and what stories to share! Between us, there would be many a long and lively conversation! Perhaps though he'd be glad that **Heaven** is a huge place – enabling him to give me a wide berth should he so wish! Nevertheless, he would be delighted to know that amidst a time of great crisis for **Western Civilization** his witness to **Christ** has been renewed and able to reach both descendants and an audience he couldn't have dreamt of. Maybe that's his reward for his year's faithful service in the **East End** of **London.**

Now – in the early twenty-first century it's all too easy to sneer at or shrug one's shoulders in boredom at the simple **Christian** faith of **Elizabeth** and **Henry Myerson.** Yet did the *'clever'* intellectuals of his time – like **Friedrich Nietzsche (1844-1900)** and **Karl Marx (1818-1883)** produce any better alternative? My visits to **Auschwitz** (in **October 2011**) and **Budapest's *'House of Terror'*** (in **August 2015**) convinced me that they did not. Indeed, those places of death reinforced my conviction that **Christianity** is the worst of all faiths to follow until one considers the alternatives! The sights I saw at those hellish places made me *'dig my heels in'* as far as my own **Christian** faith was concerned. Neither the **Neo-Paganism** of **Nazism** nor the **Atheistic Materialism** of **Communism** has succeeded in making the world a better place.

Moreover, it's unlikely that today's variants of these so-called *'alternatives'* (like **Post Modern Political Correctness**) are faring any better. In our rapidly degrading civilization, a whole array of cultural developments appears to be producing a dangerously *'subjective way of thinking,'* so facilitating the kind of horrors I witnessed at **Auschwitz** and **Budapest**. We could easily be entering another period of *'social catastrophe'* of the kind explored by **Gellately (2007)**. The appalling **2016 American Presidential Election** highlighted just how far things have gone in this *'Post Truth, Fake News age.'* Usually, when societies have reached this level of decadence the result is a holocaust or collapse into tyranny and/or conquest by barbarians. I have explored these dark themes in my creative pieces; ***'The Exit Machine,' 'Hoofbeats of the Apocalypse'*** and ***'U.S. Redux.'*** (All these works are produced under the pen name **Leo Arland** and are available on **Amazon**.)

In response to the chilling prospect outlined above, all I can say is that the **Gospel Henry Myerson** preached with such fervour is the **Gospel** I follow. Over matters of basic belief, there's not one iota of difference between the two of us. His witness is my witness, his faith is my faith and his **Jesus** <u>IS</u> my **Jesus**. Together we testify that eternal life can be found in Him who is the true Messiah for all who turn away from their sins and believe in Him as their **Lord** and **Saviour**. This is our joint legacy to the family. If any of my descendants (or other readers of this History) wish to explore these things further, I would strongly urge them to read a copy of the **New** Testament – especially the Gospels of **Matthew, Luke and John and Paul's** letter to the **Romans**. Here they will find truths to revolutionize and change their lives for the better.

CHAPTER 21: IN THEIR OWN WORDS

Introduction: In this chapter, the decision was taken to allow key historical personages [like **Edmund's** first wife **Helen (1824-1866)** and her father – **James Hastings (1784-1872)** the farmer] to speak for themselves through their writing – with only the minimum amount of commentary from myself. I have retained any idiosyncratic use of capital letters but have updated a few spellings and provided punctuation where needed. Paragraphing was also my own.

The **province** of a document refers to the identity of its author (or authors) and the time and place where it was produced. It has been included so that readers can understand the context in which the document originated. However, such textual sources can be *'brought to life'* if they are complemented by visual evidence such as old photographs or some other physical artefact. This should enable readers to picture the faces and clothing of those who produced key documents or are mentioned in them. In the case of the **Helen-James** correspondence, we have photographs from around the time they were produced. Present here is the kind of material that would provoke the envy of most Family Historians.

Section 1: A Photographic Record

The earliest photographic evidence in the possession of family members consisted of three separate pictures of **Edmund's** father-in-law **James Hastings,** his wife **Mary Ann** and their married younger daughter **Betsy Heron.** (They'd been taken in the studio of **Richard Harvey** at **Kingston Square, Jarratt Street, Hull**). can be dated to **1856** – the year the **Crimean War (1854-56)** ended. The first of these photographs show **James Hastings (1784-1872),** Helen's father (and farmer) at **Burton Pidsea.** Despite being in his early seventies the impression he gives is one of great physical strength – he was not a man in his dotage. This was exemplified both by his massive hands and weather-beaten face which looked full of character. With his spotted neckerchief and thick overcoat, looked every bit the yeoman farmer. Present were bushy eyebrows, a beard (without a moustache – very much the fashion of the time), thick lips and noticeable cheeks. His forehead which is topped by a darkish hair. The photo conveyed the impression of a man who was twenty years younger than he actually was. His face showed a man of compassion – having endured much personal loss through family bereavement, *i.e.* his father **James the Elder (1752-1819)** his first wife **Jane** (formerly **Halliday 1790-1820** whom he'd married on the **28th June 1810**) and baby **James Richard (1818-1820)** Nevertheless, there was kindness and a sturdy rectitude about this man.

He does, however, look a little uncomfortable in the chair in which he's seated. Although his left-hand is resting on a table, he looks like a man who wanted to be *'out and about.'* The city was not his natural environment.

In contrast, **James'** second wife **Mary Ann (1792-1861**) known as *'Nancy'* was already an old-looking woman despite being about a decade younger than her husband. Wearing a white shawl and bonnet she sits there as if poised and ready to make a complaint. Of thin build, her clasped hands and face are wrinkled. The way her hair is tied adds to the severity of her look. Akin to her husband she had a long, aquiline nose, but unlike her husband, she looked thoroughly worn out. A notice at the back of the picture by her grandson **James** showed that she had been born in a settlement near **Leeds.** Other information suggested she had family connections in **Manchester.** Her first surname had been **Featherston**e and but on **11**th **January 1813,** she'd married a **George** *'Palframan'* a *'husbandman.'* The relevant entry had their ages down as **22.** Her first marriage couldn't have lasted long for she was married to **James** at **Holy Trinity** at **Hull** on the **21**st **August 1820.** They would be together for over four decades.

The third and final picture shows **Betsy Heron** (formerly **Hastings**) the younger sister of **Edmund's** first wife, **Helen Hastings.** Seated on a chair, she is clasping an open book on her lap. Her left arm rests on a studio table upon which there appears to be an ornamental vase. The photographer has gently positioned her hand against her cheek – giving the impression of intelligence. She seems to be wearing a crinoline with a lace top. Her face is long and rather masculine with something of her father in it. On display is what may be known as the **Hastings** *'horsehair'* – still existing in that part of the family. Attempts to convert the ends of her naturally straight hair into ringlets haven't really succeeded. There's the domed forehead (apparent in both parents). The impression conveyed is of a rather strong-minded and thrifty lady who knew what she wanted. She looked rather older than her eighteen years. Unlike her elder sister **Helen,** she would live into the twentieth century. (An entry in **James's** diary confirmed that she died on **1**st **October 1902** at the age of **74** in **Liverpool.**) All three of these members of the **Hastings** family could easily have stepped out of the pages of a **Dickens** novel.

The same *'Dickensian'* observation is equally applied to a photograph taken in early **1859** (the year of the publication of **Darwin's** *'Origin of the Species'* amidst great controversy). This time the location was the studio of **Winstanley, Myers & Thompson, 26 King Street, Manchester.** A young **Edmund** is seated, his right hand clasping a piece of paper. As expected, he is formally attired in a waistcoat, (from which dangles a watch chain) jacket and necktie. He has an *'Abraham Lincoln beard'* with no moustache. This made him appear as if he was trying to prove **Darwin's** theory of evolution! His hair is dark and curly with a bit of it sticking out. His expression is rather supercilious as if he's continually eying the main chance. It seems to have a sense of playful irony about it too. **Edmund** was still a young *'man on the make'* and not yet disillusioned with life. My ancestor was well-built rather than fat – absent was that paunch that would feature in later photographs. One could imagine him being a very good conversationalist – although I wouldn't be inclined to entrust either my money or my wife to him! There is an air of **Seth Pecksnith** about him. (He was the social climbing hypocrite in **Charles Dicken's** novel, **Martin Chuzzlewit.**)

In the centre, with his hands clasped is the rotund frame of **Samuel Heron.** Born in the **East-Yorkshire** village of **Garton-with-Grimston** and baptized there on **30th May 1826,** he's dressed formally and with the same type of beard and hair colouring as **Edmund,** he struck a far more benevolent pose. Beneath his receding hairline, his lively eyes looked foursquare at the camera whilst smiling all the while. His whole face was suggestive of a genuine warmth. A large bow tie added to the air of jollity. There was indeed a **Mr Pickwick** look about him – suggesting he would make *'merry company.'* Consequently, it was easy to imagine **Samuel** being an excellent salesman – one who was always charming to female customers in his drapery shop. **Thomas Hastings** seemed to have chosen wisely when he'd made him a partner. He would live and work as a draper and sadly die in his early forties on **13th April 1869.** He would leave to his widow **Elizabeth** an estate of just under £800 which suggested he'd made a success of his business. They had married on **26th November 1851** – the year of the *'Great Exhibition'* in **London.**

Of a less happy disposition in this photograph is **Helen,** who resembles one of these mature women in a **Dickens** novel who was born simply to suffer. This is suggested by her tense body language. She was holding **Baby James** on her lap. The blurred photograph of **James** would suggest he was struggling and not being well behaved. **Helen** was wearing a conventional **mid-Victorian** dress with a lace collar. Her naturally straight hair was curled into ringlets as was the fashion of the time. They dangled to her shoulders. A look of raw unhappiness crosses her face. Sadly evident is the haunted look of a woman trapped in a loveless marriage. (A point also implied in her letters.) Admittedly baby **James** appeared to have been a handful during the taking of the photograph, but there seemed to be more in her look than the tiredness of managing a difficult child. It's only in the letters to her father that we find the real cause of her despair. **Edmund,** it seemed, was rather indifferent to her. His work was his life. At present, he's got what he'd wanted; money, a position, a good friend in the form of **Samuel Heron** and a wife who'd borne him a male heir. Her personal happiness appeared to have been of little concern to him. He would perhaps have found her *'womanly'* emotions rather tedious. **Edmund** was the sort of man who appeared to thrive amidst an endless amount of social stimulation. He would become celebrated for his sociability in later life. An ailing wife simply held little interest for him.

A photograph of **Helen** (taken several years later in either **1865** or **1866**) showed that she'd filled-out into a classic **Victorian** *'frump'* – the type of woman **Dickens** liked to make fun of in his novels. Her double chin served only to heighten her masculine features. She displayed the wary look of a woman wondering what her husband got up to during his many nights away. Although putting on an appearance for the photographer **Helen** didn't look healthy. One rather podgy hand clasped on open book atop a round studio table. Her other hand rested on her a lap, partly covering a pendant. She was lavishly dressed in a crinoline. It's apparent that **Edmund** had taken care to ensure that she was well dressed – looking the part of the respectable middle-class **Victorian** matron. He wanted it to be obvious that she was well provided for by her husband. (This was perhaps done with a view to impressing business associates when entertaining them at his home.) The most worrying thing is that she doesn't look in any condition to bear children. As a prospective mother, she looked old and not in good health. This was perhaps the last photograph taken of her before childbirth was to kill her at **Vernon Road** in **October 1866.**

Evidence of **Helen's** taste in clothes was provided by some surviving dress patterns from the firm of **Stewart McDonalds.** They showed a taste for blue and purple with a non-floral abstract design. The quality of the cloth was good. Clearly, these were clothes for a lady. The most likely source of these patterns was the draper's shop in **Hull.** If **Edmund** had obtained them from that source (or from **Samuel Heron**) we can be sure he will have negotiated a discount. He was always a man who liked a good deal.

Section 2: Helen Vindicated!

Helen To James 1

Province: The most likely year is **1857,** (whilst **Helen** was on honeymoon nine days after her marriage). This year is the most likely one as there's no mention of a pregnancy and **Helen** appeared new to her surroundings. Already, she appeared highly uncertain about her marriage and distressed by **Edmund's** nights away. **Edmund's** first wife clearly disliked social pretence and this could well have been a source of friction between them. He was a high-spirited *'man of the world'* married to a pious lady whose religious faith may have *'grated'* on him. My Great Grandfather may have felt it depressing to be around her for too long. She appeared rather doubtful about their marriage from the very beginning. In terms of age, interests and personality, they come across as a rather mismatched couple.

Nevertheless, in this letter, she is a highly articulate and observant – if rather insecure lady. **Edmund's** first wife was certainly <u>not</u> a *'country bumkin.'* Like myself, **Edmund** seemed to have had an interest in historical buildings and I wondered whether he'd lectured **Helen** about them as I do with **June!**

When **Helen** made the comment about **Harrogate** seeming to be made for *'Promenade and Pleasure Seekers,'* I thought *'what's changed?'* There's the old **Yorkshire** saying which reads, *"in **Leeds** people only look down on those living in **Barnsley,** in **Harrogate** they look down on everyone else!"* Many of the sights **Helen** saw, my wife and I also have observed during the second week of our honeymoon in early **July 1979.** We were staying in a **Harrogate** guesthouse at the time. Even then we seemed to be following my ancestors. The view from **Castle Hill, Knaresborough** is indeed *'splendid.'* We gazed over it whilst holding hands.

Rose Mount

Pannal: Dec. 19ᵗʰ1857?

1857? My Dear Mother Father

Mother complains that my letters are short, but I think they are much longer than here or anybody elses. I like the House very much for everything but one it is all upstairs the kitchen and pantry are hewn out of stone the latter would make a good Dairy for cream if we had a cow; a thing we are not likely to have.

I have told you the House stands on an eminence. The sitting room window is higher than the Church steeple, consequently there is an excellent view of the vale below this is the first day since we came to Panal; the scenery is very good a few trees scattered here and there does not appear to be much wood clustered together as you have in Holderness. The land looks lighter than yours does, if I may judge from our garden – I cannot say much about the people, Mrs, Robinson being the only person I see excepting a lot of children who come to a school near our house. They seem as wild as an untaught Judean Brood and all have fair hair and fat faces what I have seen. I went to Church last Sunday – heard a man talk nonsense poor man he is a Blind Leader of the Blind.

When in York we went to the Minster – what a huge Pile of Building and yet it must pass away like the baseless fabric of a vision and leave not a stone behind. We went into the Ecclesiastical Court and heard a will case tried, but we could not stay for want of time to hear it out from there we went to the Castle, to the Assize and heard a Trial for forgery the Judge looks a perfect Guy in his scarlet and Ermines. I thought I like York.

On Tuesday went to Knaresborough and Harrogate. We had a splendid view from the Castle Hill at Knaresborough. Harrogate seems made for Promenade and Pleasure Seekers, we are two miles ahead. I am afraid we shall not oft go to Chapel this winter. Mother says how do I spend my days – very well the nights are the worst. I have been alone three nights already, not very pleasant, but they are past. I miss faces so much that I used to see, everything is strange. The old familiar faces, and the young laughing ones, that don't know a thought or care with their tiny hands and feet running into all kinds of mischief. It seems so strange to leave all for one but still, I don't regret, I think. I fancy Edmund will make a good husband. But time will prove.

I should like to see you here will you ever come. I am sure Ed will give you a hearty welcome. If you complain about this, it will be because of its length and now my dear Father and Mother. Farewell. May the blessing of the Lord Jehovah rest upon you and may you both abide in fine strength until the last sign is given is the sincere prayer of yours ever affectionately

Helen.

James to Helen 1

Province: This letter (apparently sent from **Burton Pidsea**) came at a decisive turning point in the lives of **Edmund** and **Helen.** They are soon to be moving from **Pannal** to *'the other place'* of **Leeds** which, for a restless **Edmund** represented a place of opportunity. His decision to move there was to have ramifications which would last to this day. He would find it easier (then his wife, **Helen**) to adapt to urban life than his wife. The reference to vegetables suggests that the then heavily pregnant **Helen** was still, at heart, a farming girl. Homesickness was a real issue. **James** was aged seventy-four when he wrote his daughter this letter. His letters reveal him to be a very kind and pious man who had a simple but dogged faith. He seemed to know his Bible. However, a faulty pen ensured that the last lines of his letter were very disjointed and unclear.

Aug 30/58

Dear Helen.

we received your kind letter Saturday with much pleasure and was very glad to hear you had formed a resolution to leave Pannal. I so think that the other place will be most convenient, and you know that it is a great matter that Mr. Smith will be much more at home. I know you feel rather timid in going to a strange place. You are not a child. You should try to master such feelings. You no doubt will find friends at Leeds as well as elsewhere. As for my part, I never went nowhere, but I soon found friends and you must be aware that you may get very many acquaintants, but a strong friend is few and far between. I read of a friend that is only a friend in name as for my past I always was rather shy at forming acquaintances over soon. You say you have turnips, and carrots, potatoes and apples and the [like]. I cannot say what you must do with the turnips and carrot. I fancy they are not ready. Should you find anyone that goes to the market they might give you something for them, but as to potatoes, you can take them with you. Potatoes is always ready when their skins is fast, and the apples is ready when they're ripening. Give my very best love to Mr. Smith and accept the same yourself and believe me your faithful and affectionate Father and Mother Ann and James Hastings

I have nothing but
A very bad steel
Pen and I cannot
Write to my measure
That is not all my
hand trembles I can
When [I] write it [I] try
Better [but] express worse

James to Helen 2

Province: Shortly following **Helen's** move to **Leeds** and three days after the birth of her first Child **James.**

Sept 20, 1858

My Dear Children,

Your much-esteemed letter we received the other day and I had to work under duress, or a gospel must have emerged between us which was to open the Epistle, it, having fallen into my hands by the postman. It was the Leeds postmark which did it. Well, we were exceeding glad when we read the contents. You say he is a big lad, In the country, they say *'he'd soon be fit for the plough.'* Everyone seems to boast of their fine and big ones. But oh, ask a mother another name is dearly brought. May the Lord bless the Lad and as he grows may he grow in peace with his Father and Mother and may their example be worthy of imitation in the earnest prayer of his Grandfather. I think I have nothing much to tell you that would be fresh. Death seems very thorough. We had three funerals the other week. Thomas Graysby is Sunday between Sunday before last and a little one and a young woman of the brain fever, so you see death had not forgotten Burton. I was asking John Brown and we have had [in] some way about 30 deaths this year. They have some of them died of old age. It speaks *'be ye always be ready.'* Your mother is only middlin, was in bed all yesterday, but is much better today. As for my part, I am among the middling ones. We had a note from Mary saying they are all well. How badly have I wrote, but you must remember that I am at the best nothing but an old man. Mother sends her love and to make all right I have set it down first, so I must be last with my love and believe me, I remain your affectionate father, Jas. Hastings

Helen To James 2

Province: By this stage, **Helen** was enduring the full force of a **North Yorkshire** Winter. **Pannal** is sited in a slightly higher elevation meaning that the cold would be more intense than in a lower lying, a place like **Leeds.** The presence of Baby **James** suggested that the most likely date was **6th December 1858.** If so, **Helen** appeared to be moving between houses in **Leeds** and **Pannal.** Possibly, she was in **Pannal** clearing up things in the old house. An interesting reference is made to **Mary Ann, Helen's** elder sister, who was married to **John Stamford** and who was the mother of my Great Grandmother **Rosamond.**

Edmund's first wife clearly felt isolated and had misgivings about her husband's many nights away. Even at this early stage in their marriage, **Edmund** appeared to be a remote and distant figure. Perhaps he'd viewed his marriage as an inconvenience. Yet in his defence, he perhaps felt the need to work every possible hour to avoid sinking into the kind of poverty he'd witnessed in places like **Burnley.** His work situation at the time was extremely precarious. Having dangled over the sharp edge of ruin in **2012,** my sympathies lie with my Great Grandfather regarding this matter. Being in that situation does leave its scars. You may have thousands in the bank, but still feel you have nothing! Even worse, when one honestly attempts to be thrifty, family members mistake you for being *'mean'* or *'stingy.'* In **Yorkshire,** we call it *'being careful with money!'*

Pannal 6th 1858

My Dear Mother and Father

I hope this time you both are better than you were, although I am afraid the cold weather will starve you very much. The cold here is intense – much colder than I felt in my life. We stand so bleak that we catch every gust of wind. If the hole up the chimney was wide enough, we should be blown up before this I oft think and talk about you and would wish I could see you will be a treat. I was very pleased to receive a letter from Father, it was so like Him in every word. I should have considered it before this, but I have not been well. I don't know what I should have done without E. Featherstone for the people here are not troubled with too much humanity. Mr. Smith has only been Home twice for the past fortnight. So, you may be rather sure it is rather dull. He will be in Hull next week I shall not come yet.

You have so many deaths lately – old faces passing way and fresh ones taking their places and it will be the event after we are gone to the hour appointed for all living but if our names are written in the Lamb's Book of Life it need not trouble us who takes our place. All will be well at last. Jim has sent his love and kiss for you father. I am to tell you he is a good Boy sometimes and sometimes naughty. I hope Mary Ann is better and the children loved. I give my love to them. Edmund joins me in love to you both.

Helen To James 3

Province: The most likely date of this letter was early **1859** around the time the photograph in **Manchester** was taken. **James** was still a baby, but there's no mention of a second pregnancy or of **Betsey** (who was born in **February 1860**). Worth noting was the continuing contact with her younger sister **Elizabeth Heron** and her willingness to keep her father in touch with outside events. **Helen** also displayed some knowledge of the religious controversies of her time. The **Dr Cummings** she mentioned appeared to have been influenced by **Adventist** teaching. With reckless foolishness, this *'lecturer'* had casually ignored the strong warnings **Christ** had made against *'date-fixing'* in such passages as **Mark 13: 22** and **Acts 1:7. Dr Cummings** seemed to think he knew better! I can easily imagine him being bombastic and very long-winded in his delivery.

8 Blenheim Place
Woodhouse Lane
Leeds

My Dear Father, Mother

The weather keeps very cold we had another downfall of snow this last night I am afraid you will feel it you will feel it severely so near the sea. Betsy has sent word that R Hastings was dead. I would like to see him again, but he's gone I trust to a better service that is the land where there's no night.

Dr Cummings has been giving two lectures in which he predicted the end of this dispersion in 1869. If so, those who live the longest have not long to live if he's correct. Be things as they may let us be ready.

I was glad to hear from you. I thought you had forgotten me. It is pleasant to know you have not forgotten. I shall be very thankful for the news. Have you a cat to spare for we swarm with mice. We cannot get a cat. Ed will be in Hull, perhaps next week if you have one. Is Mary Anne's last a boy or a girl? My Lad can run all over and can say a word or two but lacks a temper. We fight two or three times a day and he will emulate me in his words.

I had a nasty fall and sprained my ankle. I was a fortnight and could not get a stocking on. I am happy to say it is improving nicely under cold-water. Write as soon as you can. In the meantime, accept my best love and believe me your affectionate daughter.

Will send you another newspaper.

James to Helen 3

Province: The most likely date is the spring or summer of **1859,** but this is uncertain. **James'** wife still appeared to be alive at the time of writing. The letter seemed hurried and may only be fragmentary. The deep affection **James Hastings** felt for his daughter **Helen** was extremely apparent.

I cannot explain myself. We should be very much pleased to see Mr. Smith at Burton if he comes. I think I have given all the news I can the first time he is over at Hull. If he cannot I will send a horse to meet him. Only let me know when at Hull. Mr. Dickinson of Roos has 9 cows dead this week. So much for the disease going away. I think I have given all the news I can think of. I am very thankful to say we are all in good health. Have you been enjoying the sun? My kind love to every one of you.

You see I cannot conclude. I feel lost in a mist. Excuse all my blundering. I cannot think of anything. My Eyes are full and my Heart as well.

No more from your Father. May the Lord bless you all.

Believe me, to remain your most affectionate Father

Helen To James 4

Province: The most likely date of this letter was the spring of **1860.** Her second child had been born in late **February,** but summer had not yet arrived. **Helen** was feeling a strong nostalgia for her rural childhood. The marriage had not cured her homesickness. Her husband's situation was precarious – although he seemed to be an onlooker rather than a participant of the dispute described in this letter. Despite initially high hopes, the move to **Leeds** had not yet provided **Edmund** with the economic security needed to raise a family. He would be grateful to any Company which gave him scope to do this. At the time this letter was written his job prospects were extremely uncertain. He perhaps dreaded falling into the kind of dire poverty he'd seen in his early years.

8 Blenheim Place
Woodhouse Lane
Leeds

My Dear Father and Mother,

I am afraid you will think me negligent for me not writing sooner. I have thought daily about you and have intended writing now the days are so long. I am reminded of the old house at Home and the many changes since we used to play in front and back. What labour of heart have you known since our little feet pressed in playful glee their games. I would my memory is busy contrasting past and present, but we must look forward and upward when we shall all be brought to our Father's House above, we shall know why things have been permitted.

My two *"Bairns"* are very well, Betsy's hair is red. Jim has got such a temper. I oft wonder if his Grandfather would frighten him. We intend to stay a day or two or now with you this summer all being well.

Ed will want a situation soon. The firm is dissolving. They cannot agree. They know what trouble is now – they did not dream of this last year at this time. Roberts has behaved badly to Newton, I will tell you the particulars when I see you.

You will get a letter with this. I will send you one every week. I feel afraid you don't get them, as you, did not mention it in your last letter. Kind love and a paper kiss believe me your affectionate daughter Helen

3 Postage stamps a piece

James to Helen 4

Province: This letter was written on 28th **April 1861,** when **James Hastings** was being nursed by **Helen's** niece **Rosamond Stamford** – my Great Grandmother who was then aged seventeen. On 12th **February 1861,** he'd lost his wife **Ann** who appeared to have been infirm for some time. (Sixteen days earlier on 12th **April,** the bombardment of **Fort Sumter** had marked the beginning of the **American Civil War.)**

Graphically described are the hardships of nineteenth-century rural life in **East Yorkshire.** At times there were so many deaths that **Burton Pidesa** resembled a war zone! This strongly suggested that most of **James'** children migrated to

Hull for economic rather than family reasons. There were simply more prospects and a better chance of survival in the city. Ironically, the so-called agricultural expert and **Conservative** politician **Rowland Prothero (1851-1937)** – who later became **Lord Ernie** – described the period in which **James** wrote his letter as representing *'a golden age'* of **English Agriculture. James** would have disagreed.

Dear Helen,

I will not try to answer your request by endeavouring to write an answer, but like Mr. Baxter, I have lost my mother. I verily find you are like Paul of old, you verily proposed many things before you set about doing any of them. It is true I feel lonely and worn out, but I have one of the best of nurses Rosamond which is never weary of doing her best at all times and is so agreeable.

Mary Ann is often near, and they are all first rate. You talk of bad times. I understood by Mr. E. Smith that this spring and summer the times would revive, and things would become new and old things done away.

As to farming, things bear a bad aspect. We have had frosts every night and the weather is so cold that the onions and other small seeds cannot get out for want of moisture. As to the last harvest, the oats in a very many fields never got ripe and was given to cattle unthreshed and the beans very little better. The year before scores of fields were never so much reaped. The wheat last harvest was so much injured with rain and sprout instead of weighing at 18 ½ Was unable to make 16. As to the present wheat, it was very much according to the aspect it lies in.

My kind love to all. I am very glad to hear all of you is in good health. It is a great blessing and we ought to be ever grateful to the Father of all Mercies for the favours we receive at His hands. I have been very poorly last week and the week before. But I am thankful I am now much better.

Mrs Tavinder has lost a daughter the [same] age as Rosamond, Edward Hastings was buried yesterday age 79 and Sarah Middleton this day the same age 79. Mrs Spencer is coming to live in Mrs Pickups new House in the Street, Mrs Nilson has gotten in her new cottage and in much want of a male companion.

Believe me your affectionate Father James Hastings.

James to Helen 5

Province: by the time this letter was written **James** was in his early eighties but still taking an interest in his surroundings. There was no evidence of senility. In contrast, **Helen** had only two weeks to live before dying of a ruptured womb. An old photograph showed that she had assumed an unhealthy, dropsical appearance. When she died, her stillborn boy was buried beside her.

This was perhaps the last letter she received from her father who seemed completely unaware of the danger she was in with her sixth pregnancy. Instead, he seemed to have been pre-occupied with what seemed to be a *'foot and mouth'* contagion amongst the local cattle. My own visits to **Burton Pidsea** confirmed that the land flooded very easily.

The bad harvest of **1816** (referred to in this letter) was caused, or at least greatly worsened by the **Tambora Volcano Eruption** in **Indonesia.** Occurring **5th April 1815,** it was the biggest eruption in recorded history. The cloud of dust and ash that it shot into the atmosphere greatly reduced sunlight – causing widespread crop failure and famine across much of the world.

It is unclear whether the **William** mentioned in this post was **Helen's** third son who would die the following year. **James** would also outlive his eldest daughter **Mary Stamford** who would pass away in **1871**. He was truly a man of many sorrows.

Burton Pidsea Sep 20/66

You will be much surprised to hear from me so soon. I have been going to write every week since I last wrote, but one reason was I did not know that I could. You wonder what I am doing this rainy weather. I thought anyone would have known I have been looking at it. All our low land has been dreadful to look at. You will find out once you have had the new wheat you will find it very much sprouted as it had in 1816. The time I remember very well, wheat was 7 and 2 ounces that year. Mother was in Manchester when Jane Kemp made her own butter. It was a very hard time.

We began to (need) wheat this morning. You say your milk cost 7½. Since Wednesday we've had none for love or money. Mrs Clapham was scolding her girls about 3 weeks since. She thought they had not so much butter as they ought. As they have only 50 pounds this week. Often, they [the cattle] got distemper and lost 7 cows and a bull. William Ford [the] Grocer lost his cow – he only had one cow which took the distemper and died. We had 7 dead at our farm. Clapham's 6 cows got out of the North Close at night and came to our field and they got the complaint. We had 4 dead in 3 or 4 days. 3 of them was worth 20 pounds each. In all we lost 18, Mr. Baxter 54, Mr. Robinson 34, I Tavinder 2, Mr. Harland I know not what amount. His was a very valuable bull.

The paper feature is that the distemper is much afield. The matter is we have not so many to lose. My own opinion is that had the Government left things alone we should not have lost so many. The Doctor (vet) was very busy and rode from one place to another. I never hold that they did any good. And believed that they caused the disease to move from one place to another. They sail about. Douthwaite one of the Doctors told Mr. Stamford that he had a bill against the government of more than £300. When the Doctor heard of the complaint they came and sent for him.

Mr. Freeman came to Mr. Robinson. They had 13 ill and Freeman took 5 under his care to ensure Mr. Robinson would not have anything done to the other 8. Freeman's all died. Robinson lost only one.

Our crop is very raw. We grow wheat in general, but you will find the sprout very much worse. I fear you will think of William in Leeds was only very poorly when he first came over. I myself am sorry too Mary is very poorly at times. Please give my very best love to Mr. Smith and if he cannot yet come over, let me know, I will send a horse to Hull.

Conclusion: James too emerged from this correspondence with credit. He came across as a very humble and caring man. Over one hundred and fifty years after her death, **Helen's** reputation has been vindicated. She now speaks not only to family members but now to the whole world through the modern media. When it came to her children and contributing to this history *'she did what she could'* and it was marvellous.

Section 3: Celebrating Edmund

An Ode to Edmund 1

Province: The location and date of this document were fairly easy to establish. It seemed to be the stock department at the warehouse of **Stewart McDonald's** at **146 Argyle Street Glasgow** at the time of **Edmund's** retirement at the age of **78**. It was an elaborate six-storey building which had been rebuilt in **1903** – the architect being **Horatio Bromhead**. In terms of style and language, the poem echoed that of the famous **Scottish** Poet **Robert Burns (1759-1796).** The author was shrewd and had a playful way with language, but apparently from a rough working-class background where heavy drinking was the norm. It clearly reflected a hard-living masculine culture in which **Edmund** was a very well-liked member. His taste in cigars and wine were heartily celebrated. Ominously for his wives, he appeared to have had a reputation for being a womaniser, but that too seemed (in the poem) to be a cause of celebration. One can only wonder whether he had other children outside of his marriage. As my wife remarked, ***"Edmund** seemed to be one thing at work and another at home."* As a very successful Commercial Traveller, **Edmund** would have earned in the vicinity of £400 per year. As a manager of salesmen, his income could have doubled to £800 – a substantial amount that could have supported a comfortable middle-class lifestyle and leave scope for speculative investments. Rental income from the house he owned next door to his own would have cushioned him again any recession in his trade. Very shrewdly, my Great Grandfather appeared to have taken great care to spread his financial risks. He was not the type of man to invest in one project.

To Edmund.

The eve of thy departure's come,
Twas ever thus.
That all things to an end must run
So thou leave us.
Edmund! Thou portly frame
For well-nigh half a century
We've hailed at Stock
But ne'er again –
Such is destiny.

Thou'st frightful been
Nigh a score I ween
Thy offspring number
That night or day
They did encumber.

But yet, thou still art young.
For, after all, one is as young's one feels.
A 'witching' glance,
A skirt perchance

Just too high from the heels
And thou art young again.

Can it be, we ne'er again
Shall see thee in thy element?
With good red wine
Favourite of thine
A choice cigar
And thou by far
Than most men wert content.

And now, to shake the hand,
Thy good right hand and just
And should thy shadow, ne'er grow less,
Then Lord! 'Twill surely burst! Glasgow,

[Thursday] September 22nd, 1910

Conclusion: We're on murky ground when exploring **Edmund's** possible faithlessness. The only hint of him having been a philanderer was in this poem. It could be a case of their being, *'no smoke without a fire,'* alternatively it could just be a case of male posturing. Yet the fact remained that my Great Grandfather worked in a *'high risk'* occupation – requiring many nights away from home (which worried **Helen**). Commercial Travellers did have a reputation for being womanisers – there was always the available chambermaid or lonely female shop worker to possibly take advantage of. If this was the case, then **Edmund's** approach would have been both strategic and calculating. **Edmund** certainly possessed the charm needed to initiate such affairs and it's he may have spent large sums on keeping women quiet. However, he didn't suffer from any form of venereal disease, so it's unlikely he would have visited prostitutes on a regular basis. For him, there were better alternatives. The uneasy tone in **Helen's** letters and the disaster of his third marriage would suggest that at least two of his wives may have had their suspicions. A woman's intuition in such matters is not to be lightly dismissed. In the end, it's perhaps best to give a *'not proven'* verdict on **Edmund's** possible adultery on the grounds that decisive evidence was lacking.

An Ode to Edmund 2

Province: Once again, the date and location appear to be the warehouse of **Stewart McDonald** at **146 Argyle Street, Glasgow**. **Edmund's** retirement (mentioned in the last poem) seemed to have been temporary for he was still around as a respected and well-liked figure. My Great Grandfather did appear to have substantial charm and charisma. His intelligence and capacity for hard work were recognized as being exceptional. At the very least, he was well known as a *'character.'* Aged eighty, he was still extremely active, (without any trace of the decay most often associated with serious alcohol abuse). **Stewart MacDonald** appeared to be **Edmund's** real home; It was where his heart really lay. The staff there loved him.

Whoever **RC** was, he appeared to be well educated – possessing knowledge of the times **Edmund** had lived through and the *'cruel blows'* he had endured in terms of family losses. There was even some allusion to **Lloyd George's** pension reforms. Whether **RC** was the father of the **Victor Campbell** who married **Edmund's** daughter **Maud** remained a matter of conjecture. However, he seemed to have known my forebear for a very long time. Some knowledge of Scripture was also displayed. He was clearly an intelligent and well-informed man, but rather overconfident about the progress humanity was making, just before the outbreak of the First World War. A few weeks after this poem was composed the **Titanic** struck an iceberg and sank. This tragedy appeared to be the harbinger of a new and ominous age.

To Edmund Smith, on His Eightieth Birthday

21ˢᵗ January 1912

"Thy lease of life, Oh! Man shall be
But three score years and ten,"
It were thy fortune, Edmund
Thou wert not living then,
We dread the thought of what might be
Had we to "shuffle off this mortal coil"
On reaching seventy.
Where could a worried chancellor go
To spend a nation's money?
No aged poor to pension –
Poor, yes – aged, not any.

No venerable men of state
To guide our laws,
Nor hoary veterans who had fought
For us when we had cause.
But more than these, Oh! Edmund,
'T would not be our pleasure now
To greet thee on thy Natal day,
And hearty, too, we vow.
Eighty years! In life's history
'Tis but a day. One short, brief spell.
But yet a day which each hour
Has been spent well.
Thou'st seen men come and go
And nations rise,
The advancement of art
And Science enterprise.
Three monarchs of these Isles
Have passed and gone
Since that fair day
(And bright the sun had shone)
When first thou saw the light
But more than Regal Crown
And kingly wealth,
Are good deeds vigour
And manly health.

Eighty years! Not lived in [a] lap of luxury
Nor sheltered from the cruel blows
Fate holds in store.
But spent in Business
And we wonder at thy Eighty years the more
Eighty years! Go! Thou who chant
"Too old at forty"
Like sluggard to the ant.
Two-fold the time and yet still find a youth
Whole, hale and hearty.
Confess to eighty years the body may.
The mind is like a sunbeam
On a summer day
That flits about and out and in.

Although the parent sun
Counts its life from when
The world began

We miss thee, Edmund
Miss thy portly frame,
Thy comings and thy goings here
Will cause us to remember thee
While we have breath.
And when we think of thee
Shall we then say:
"He was a man 'among men,
A man of truest worth."

And so we greet thee
By our humble muse.
Inadequate and cold may seem,
But thou knowest us
And what we mean.
We wish thee every joy
And every goodly thing.
(And whisper it but softly):
We may see thee in the Spring.
R.C. [Monday] 19/1/12. 146 Argyle Street, Glasgow

Conclusion: It's difficult to reconcile the reports of **Edmund's** *'heavy drinking'* from his eldest son's Granddaughter with the fact that he lived to be an extremely *'hale and hearty'* octogenarian. Moreover, it's unlikely that his employers would have tolerated a drunkard. However, a possible answer emerges when considering his controlling personality whilst entertaining his business clients **Edmund** may well have encouraged others to imbibe more freely than he did. This way, he could encourage the *'bonhomie'* needed to clinch a business deal whilst not embarrassing himself. His son **James** would have overheard the noise of such events whenever they took place at **Vernon Road**. Perhaps he'd even seen some of his father's *'contacts'* stagger out of the front door, whilst being wholly unaware that **Edmund** himself had retained perfect control of the situation. On social occasions, **Edmund** certainly could make a very favourable impression – this would not have been the case if he'd been a drunkard. Generally, He seemed to have been an excellent actor knowing how to play the part of a genial host very well.

CHAPTER 22: HOW TO PRODUCE A FAMILY HISTORY

Section 1: Many Lessons

Concerning the Lessons Learnt from this Project

One word aptly sums up the whole of this research – *'Surprise!' 'Surprise'* at just how far back I could go in time; *'surprised'* at giving a coherent account and *'surprise'* at discerning the most likely human reactions to recorded events. A frequent problem was coping with the huge quantity of information. Sometimes I would come to a settled conclusion only for fresh evidence to come and refute it. My policy was *'if the facts change, I change.'* Admittedly, individuals like **Edmund Smith** appeared to go out of their way to leave clues for their descendants to find – his own headstone being one major example. At the time of discovery, I sensed that he'd been utterly determined to have his achievements recognised by future generations of his family. If that was the intention he has succeeded! In contrast, other **Smiths** appeared more reticent. My own father, for instance, was never keen to speak about the war or about his own parents. His attitude to the former was always; *"Why rake up all that business again?"*

Whilst engaged in this project I learnt many lessons about the intricacies of historical research. During this lengthy nineteen-year-long project any existing skills I had were stretched to the limit. I also discovered just how equally rewarding <u>and</u> frustrating historical research can be. It was not simply a matter of reading books and pertinent articles, but also of visiting relevant places to seek things out Sometimes this was the only way to resolve a questionable point concerning the location of a historical site. Every opportunity to discover a new fact or to obtain some fresh insight had to be seized upon. Often the same material would be sifted repeatedly to ensure I hadn't missed out a vital piece of information. This was particularly so with ambiguous or badly written documents, where occasionally something important would emerge only after I'd examined the same material half a dozen times. Yet, in many ways I was exceptionally *'lucky'* – my wife was a dedicated proof-reader – sometimes going through drafts eight or nine times. Without her assistance, the completion of this work would not have been possible. If my wife will be remembered for anything it will be for her proofreading. At the end of one draft, she wrote, *'Finished – Yeh! Can I have my life back now?'* I've often joked that on her headstone would be written the epitaph *"She was an excellent proof-reader and the best of wives."* It's most certainly something she deserves to be remembered for. I've also remarked that if there was a patron saint for proof-readers it would be her!

Section 2 Dealing with Ambiguity and Contradiction

Concerning the Strange Death of Edward Sterne

In a Family History, it is often necessary to deal with ambiguous, contradictory and sensitive information. One such case came to light during a telephone conversation on **Saturday, 9th December 2017.** It concerned the strange death (in **April 1960**) of **Teddy Sterne** – the husband of **Fred's** sister **Irene** (shortened to **Rene**). The following details were provided by **Sally Sterne** (the widow of his son **Tony**). She was to meet **Teddy** only once (in about **February 1960**) whilst he was staying at his sister's house. At that time, **Sally** was still courting her *'soon to be'* future husband.

Quoting **Sally's** own words; *"he looked very thoughtful and kept staring into the fire. He made no conversation."* This was obviously unusual behaviour for someone meeting their son's prospective wife for the first time. **Sally** further disclosed that **Teddy** been head of Town Planning and that drank at the **Embankment Pub** in the heart of **Bedford.** (It had been built in **1891** and a photograph taken in **June 2017** revealed that it possessed a mock **Tudor** Front.) According to **Sally,** *"was a hard-drinking man."* A habit of his was to sit at the kitchen table reading the newspaper. Ominously, the door of the kitchen had no inside handle and **Rene** (who had already suffered her first stroke around the age of **47** or **48**) was known to absentmindedly leave the milk boiling and spilling over on her gas stove. From **Sally's** account, the kitchen appears and to have been a Health and Safety Officer's nightmare.

Sally was staying in **Somerset** visiting her future husband **Tony** (whom she would marry in **1961**) when she'd heard news of **Teddy's** death. (This had taken place around **Good Friday – April 15th** of that year). He'd been found slumped behind the kitchen door – with gas freely escaping from the gas stove which had been left on (but presumably not lit). Even worse upset was caused when a verdict of suicide was given. Apparently, this is still a sensitive issue to this day.

So, if it was suicide what could have been the motive? A possible answer lies behind the *'story'* that **Teddy** had made a farm girl pregnant and subsequently had feared the damage that any resulting scandal would have done to his reputation. During our telephone conversation, **Sally** did mention that *"there were rumours of a shadowy half-sister."* Moreover, my brother had also heard (from **Fred**) the self-same story. In favour of this scenario was the fact that **Teddy** had much to lose and there was his strangely uncommunicative behaviour towards his prospective daughter-in-law. There was the equally telling fact that the kitchen <u>was</u> a gas trap (in those days Town Gas didn't leave any odour). Hence the following three scenarios are equally possible: -

1. He committed suicide but lay against the door to make it look like an accident for insurance purposes and/or to spare the feelings of his wife

2. He attempted suicide but panicked and headed for the door only to find he couldn't get out

3. He left the gas taps on while in a drunken stupor then fell asleep

4. His wife had left the gas on, but he'd been too inebriated to notice

These scenarios needn't be conflicting. Perhaps in a state of maudlin inebriation, he'd made an impulsive, but a half-hearted attempt at suicide. Alcohol can have a depressing effect. But who really knows? There are occasions when all the historian can do is to let the reader decide which scenario is the more plausible. Personally, mine would be an *'open verdict'* but then I don't have access to enough information to be other than very tentative. Such are the dilemmas of a Family Historian; it doesn't pay to be too dogmatic.

On a lighter note **Sally** divulged that, with her usual tactful sensitivity, **Julia** had vehemently voiced the opinion that their address at **197 High Street, Bedford** was *"like the name of a shop."* In preparation for a visit and to placate her **Edward** and **Rene** had mooted the idea that their address should be re-named *'Riverside!'* This time, the **Smith** obsession with respectability had emerged in a rather amusing way.

Section 3: *A Strategy for Researching a Family History*

Concerning the Production of a Family History

To produce the very best in any Family History. *'PALS'* must be used to its fullest extent. The acronym **PALS** stands for: -

Purpose – *'Why am I conducting this research? What is its aim?'*

Audience – *'Who would find it interesting? Who will constitute its readership?'*

Language – *'At what educational level am I writing? Which writing style would most suit the audience?'*

Structure – *'How may I plan and organize the available resources?'*

When researching, I found it best to follow the *'E-H'* or *'Easy to Hard'* approach. Common sense would wisely suggest that any research is best begun with the memories of a relative (or relatives). Also reading more straightforward texts to read around a given historical period would prove beneficial. Only after this should more specialised articles be tackled. Remember – go from *'easy'* to *'hard'* (**E-H**).

Section 4: The Perils and Joys of Researching a Family History

Concerning the Experience of Writing a Family History

1) The **perils** include: -
- Physical hazards – tripping over gravestones
- Psychological/emotional frustration – when not finding much sought-after information!
- Misleading clues – wasting time and energy
- Information *'overload'* – often leading to the mislaying of important documentation
- Loss of information – vital documents go missing or key contacts are no longer available
- Unexpected financial costs – these can quickly grow
- Technical hitches – the computer may crash
- Social disruption – being the *'Family History bore!'*
- Ethical & legal considerations – need for self-censorship about an abusive family member whose misdeeds relative don't want to be recorded
- A lack of purpose – is the main intention to *'tell a story'* or just *'recount facts?'*… or a mixture of both.

2) The **joys** include: -
- Seeing unfamiliar places – exciting because of their connection to the *'Family History'*
- Self-discovery – finding one's personal *'roots'*
- A sense of adventure – unravelling a mystery
- Learning new facts – often stirring the imagination
- Gaining new skills – *i.e.* using microfiche or the Internet
- Unexpected financial gains – monetary help given by interested parties
- Easier contacts via the Internet – thus saving on postage
- Meeting a variety of interesting people
- Being emotionally and mentally stretched

- Gaining a new sense of purpose in life
- Meeting new and interesting people – including long-lost relatives!

Section 5: Practical Tips for Historical Research Work

Concerning the writing of a Family History

To counter the **perils** mentioned in **Section 3** it would prove helpful to: -
1) Take personal health and safety seriously – wear appropriate clothing and footwear – to suit the prevailing weather.
2) Place an area of frustration firmly to one side for a brief time and turn your attention to a new topic. Then, after a pre-ordained time, return to the original challenge with a fresh mind.
3) Be honest if you're wrong, admit it and start again – if the facts change, you change.
4) Ensure administration is well organised and accessible – if you lose control of the paperwork you lose control of everything.
5) Ensure all information is safely stored and recorded so that it can be easily recovered should the need arise.
6) Monitor how you are faring financially. Should expenses begin to run out of control (or other serious unconnected financial problems arise) STOP until matters improve! Financial worries are too high a price to pay for even the best Family History.
7) Keep duplicates of all information in four *'storage areas'* – *i.e.* at home, on one's own person and another separate location *i.e.* via memory sticks. This may well be classified as *'information storage paranoia,'* but is well worth cultivating.
8) Don't be a bore – check that your audience has a genuine interest in your research <u>before</u> describing the latest developments.
9) <u>Respect confidentiality.</u> Should you consider publishing any of your research then find out about the legal guidelines on Data Protection, Libel, Copyright and Plagiarism – refer to *'The Artist and Writer's Year Handbook'* (available in most Public Libraries).
10) Summarize (in two or three sentences) the purpose of your research. From the onset, <u>have a reasonably clear idea of what you hope to achieve and why.</u> Do remember that researching Family History can easily take on a life of its own. In my own case, a work which began as a small-scale tribute to my father, following his death (at the age of **85**) in **April 1999** eventually became something of an epic. It was a case where the answer to one question tended to produce hundreds of other questions!

Finally, ENJOY the adventure and romance of researching your own Family History. Take care to reflect upon your research and learn from it. Grow as an individual. You may well be pleasantly surprised in finding that the production of a Family History can be one of the most rewarding experiences of your life. So long as due diligence is taken, the *'joys'* should far outweigh the *'perils.'*

Section 6: Lessons Learnt from This Project

Concerning the Practice of Family History

The following list has been drawn up to benefit those wishing to study their Family History. It comprises the lessons learnt over a nineteen-year period when compiling **'A Saga of Smiths.'** Any prospective Family History should: -

1) Adopt clear aims – listed in order of importance. The central purpose of any research should be summarised in <u>one core sentence.</u> *e.g. "I am writing this Family History to honour my late father, discover my personal roots and leave a worthwhile legacy to my descendants so they will know something of their own origins."*

2) Acknowledge that research is a dynamic process, requiring a great deal of mental flexibility. Allow newly acquired information to challenge previously held conclusions. E.g. Census Returns may have shown that the **Robert** and **John Clough** of Valley Farm were <u>not</u> the same **Robert** and **John Clough** who were Manufacturers even though both pairs of **Cloughs** lived in **Sutton.** Whenever necessary ask for help from the experts, *e.g.* professional archivists.

3) Acquire as clear a grasp as possible of the wider social, political and economic context in which historical personages lived and worked. (The rise of **Nazism** was something that nearly caused both my parents to be killed during the Second World War.)

4) Actively aid those readers unfamiliar with a given historical period. This is best achieved by using a *'timeline'* or chronology of events. A *'whose who'* of major characters of the day would also prove useful.

5)Take encouragement from the example provided by key historical personalities. In my own case, **Edmund's** capacity to survive multiple family losses helped me to come to terms with the stillbirth of my first Grandchild **Penelope** in **March 2008.** His dogged perseverance also inspired me to continue with this research even when it seemed as if no additional information would be forthcoming.

6) Allow the process of research to: -

6.1 Enable the reader to relate the past to the present and possibly even to the future

6.2 Provide a deeper understanding of a given historical period and of any key personalities within it

6.3 Provoke thought concerning a whole variety of areas – especially about the prevailing culture and the most likely motivations of key historical personages

6.4 Sharpen the researcher's own practical skills, *e.g.* fixing micro-fiche onto a reel

7) Always acknowledge the sources related to the research. Confidentiality may not allow for the mention of specific names. If so the following statement may well need to suffice; *"I wish to thank all members of my family who contributed to this project."*

8) Anticipate unexpected findings or results. Without exception, the researcher will come across a *'family skeleton'* quietly lurking somewhere. In this event, the decision must be taken over whether to *'exhume'* this skeleton or to leave it at rest. (Usually the more recent the skeleton the less likely it should be *'dug up'* unless it was already in the public domain as was the case of **Doctor Peter Nixon.**) As a rule, I chose not to disclose any events that could be hurtful to living relations if they had occurred within the previous fifty years.

9) Appreciate the technical constraints confronting those people who lived in the past. In **Victorian** times having a photograph taken could be a lengthy process, lasting several minutes. This fact explains, in part, why so few in those days smiled for the camera.

10) Avoid expecting to solve every mystery or answer every question. Some puzzles simply defy a solution, *e.g.* the reason behind **Edmund Smith's** apparent lack of any Church connection. Three thorough searches in an Archive Centre found nothing, yet (the usually accurate) family tradition had portrayed him as a *'God-fearing man'* who kept a large family Bible that recorded the names of his children.

11) Unless it's in a quote, avoid using slang terms like *'Aunt X were a right 'un'* or *'Cousin Y was cool'* when presenting a complex analysis. Slang words and phrases can become wholly meaningless very quickly.

12) Balance official sources (*e.g.* Census Returns) with informal sources (*e.g.* an old family story going back many years) to construct a coherent picture of historical personages and the society in which they lived.

13) Bear in mind the human factor behind any statistics. Remember these *'statistics'* were real people who lived, suffered and died. One moving case of *'a human being existing behind a statistic'* was that of *'Chippy'* my father's best man who'd sadly added to the statistics of the **British** war dead.

14) Begin with an account of what people said and did. However, such *'narrative history'* is best viewed as a *'first step'* toward what may become a very thorough analysis and evaluation.

15) Begin the research by firstly referring to more straightforward, easy to understand documents, *i.e.* Maps, Trade Directories or even school textbooks to obtain the basic facts. Then scrutinise more difficult material to gain more specialised information, *i.e.* academic research papers, archive material for churches and businesses or detailed statistical records. Always follow the **'EH'** *('easy-to-hard')* rule when referring to sources.

16) Bring the characters *'alive'* to understand them more fully. This could be done through the writing of short stories based on known events, *e.g.* my father's first visit (when a baby) made to his Grandfather, which shed light upon some of the family tensions that were later to shape his early life. So long as it doesn't stray from known facts, the imagination can be very helpful in creating an understanding of the likely motives and attitudes of key personalities.

17) Budget costs realistically. Administrative costs, travel expenses, payment for Registration Certificates, phone charges and other outlays can all too quickly add up. If resources are limited the wisest policy is to alternate high budget activities (*e.g.* travelling) with low budget ones (*e.g.* word processing). This approach means that the heaviest outlays do not all come at once. Should the research cease to be affordable then it is best to stop until it does. This was the case with me in the *'horrible'* year **2012** when I almost thought I was finished. Should it continue to be a financial burden after a year or two then consider whether it should continue. No research is worth continued financial stress.

18) Examine the underlying cultural influences of a source. *E.g.* the author of *'Self-Help,'* **Samuel Smiles** was heavily influenced by the values of *'laissez-faire'* Capitalism The latter strongly advocated the role of *'free enterprise'* in helping to create a robust industrial economy. His values were most pertinent in the middle of the nineteenth century.

19) Check and recheck the facts, particularly if they are drawn from badly written documents where the names of relevant people are unclear. For instance, it took half a dozen attempts to decide that a certain **Margaret Overend** was **Mary Anne Overend,** written in a poor script with a runny fountain pen. (I finally deduced this by pretending to write over the name with a pencil; as I followed the letters it became clear what the original name was.)

20) Convey something of the world in which people of the past lived. Let the reader feel as if they have taken a *'step back in time.'* My own wish was to transport the reader back to **mid-Victorian Leeds,** with all its noise and smells. I wanted them to feel as if they had dined with **Edmund** and his family and had been inside each one of the rooms in his house at **Vernon Road.**

21) Ponder various viewpoints when considering the underlying factors of a person's life. Wait until decisive evidence establishes a case one way or the other. For much of the research into my family, there was initially strong circumstantial evidence to suggest that **Edmund** displayed the behaviour pattern of someone having either been born illegitimate or left as an orphan. Later, I discovered certain facts which confirmed that although he was not illegitimate, he had indeed lost both parents at an early age.

22) Critically employ any relevant insights gained from such disciplines as **Psychology**, **Sociology** or **Theology.** Although Social Science and Theologically-based theories <u>should never be used arbitrarily</u> they <u>can</u> throw light upon past behaviour. (They were useful to me when scrutinizing **Edmund's** obsession with personal achievement. To some extent, this could be explained by the emotional deprivation he had suffered as a child.) However, great care must be taken to ensure that every piece of evidence is not made to *'fit-in'* with a given social or psychological theory. In historical research, such theories make good servants but terrible masters.

23) Cultivate a healthy form of *'information storage paranoia'* by duplicating the research onto at least four computer storage areas. Two should be kept at home and the other two on one's person or on *'The Cloud.'* Also, two empty storage devices should be readily available in case of a technical problem with the current computer. All small electronic information storage devices should be protected in plastic cases. When a manuscript is completed it should be recorded onto two more such devices and then stored either in a commercial bank (requiring a small fee each year) and/or some Internet facility like *'The Cloud'* or other storage areas provided by the Internet. (Without my own sense of *'disc paranoia'* I would have lost my entire Family History on at least three separate occasions!)

24) Decide the extent to which people followed (or deviated from) the social values of their time. By marrying my **Roman Catholic** Grandmother **(Marie Elizabeth Foster)** my **Grandfather Frank** (who was a Protestant) must have shown an incredible willingness to defy a strongly-held convention against *'mixed religious'* marriages. Probe for the reasons behind any marked deviation from the social norms of the time, *e.g.* rebellion by **Frank** and **Marie** against a restrictive social background.

25) Define any specialised words, either in footnotes or by having a separate *'Definitions'* list. (Avoid disheartening the reader by using impenetrable jargon, meaningful only to those with expert knowledge.)

26) Draw upon the insight and comments of interested third parties. Such people are often a little detached from the research itself and are therefore well placed to provide objective feedback. In my case, these people were often my teaching colleagues and current students.

27) Employ the latest facilities in modern Information and Communication Technology. However, the researcher must always be aware that such

Technology can sometimes fail badly. In my own case, e-mail correspondence with a member of the **Stamford** family was interrupted by prolonged problems with my personal computer. These lasted from late **July** until the end of **October 2000.**

28) Encourage people (especially the elderly) to record their memories. If this is not possible then try to have two or three interviews with them. Often the elderly will feel highly valued if they know that something of their experience is going to be recorded. One advantage of this approach is that the reader *'hears'* a fresh voice – someone other than the writer him or herself. Any risk of monotony is thereby reduced. Quotes from letters and other documents may offer the same benefit – however, care must be taken to ensure that such descriptions are relevant and are not used simply for *'padding.'* Adding the *'voices'* of my mother and my late father's accountant incomparably enriched my own Family History.

29) Enjoy the mystery in history. Treat it as a *'who done it?'* One unresolved mystery was *"Were the two men who allegedly had assaulted* **Lewis Myerson** *and were subsequently hung really guilty?"* (Narrowly, I think they were.)

30) Examine the *'body language'* in photographs very carefully to gain clues about possible relationships. For instance, the relaxed body posture between my father and his father in an old family photograph appeared to indicate a very close, nurturing relationship.

31) Expect historical research to involve much demanding work and tedium. Do not be discouraged by setbacks, *e.g.* an inability to find a key piece of information despite hours wading through tedious documents. Each piece of research will have its own problems.

32) Exploit every legitimate opportunity to gain fresh information. A chance conversation with a person in a library may throw new light upon a point. During my first visit to **Sutton,** I met an elderly man walking to **Cross-Hills** to do some shopping. After striking up a conversation with him I managed to find out useful background details about the community in which he'd lived all his life.

33) Feel free to draw upon family legend (or tradition) to establish new lines of enquiry. Although such information should not be accepted wholly uncritically it can provide substantial clues as to the location of a person or a historical artefact. For me, one of the most surprising features of this research was the way even extremely vague family stories led to crucial finds – one of these being the tombstone at **Sutton.** Where distortions did exist, their origin appears to have lain with the person who first began this oral tradition. Sometimes traditions can survive for a very long time, *e.g.* my family's **Baptist** background preserved intact for **160** years in a culture with a weak oral tradition.

34) Follow a thoroughly ethical stance throughout the research which <u>almost inevitably</u> will create some moral dilemmas. In practice, this means that the researcher will not:
34.1 Break any confidences
34.2 Claim other people's ideas as his/her own
34.3 Employ misleading words or information
34.4 Indulge in any personal vendettas
34.5 Publish any information known to be false (or damaging) to third parties
34.6 Use deception or undue pressure to elicit information
34.7 Violate a contributor's right to remain anonymous
34.8 Place informants in any position of danger
35) Follow intuition – and <u>never</u> rush ahead or accept things at face value. On about four separate occasions, I had a marked sense – a confident feeling or *'hunch'* that a previous generation of **Smiths** had been closely involved with a certain geographical location. Three of these locations have since been confirmed by hard documentary evidence (the fourth remains unproven.) In such cases, it was simply *'gut instinct'* which had provoked me to follow a given line of enquiry. Sometimes this instinct warned that I would be wasting my time in pursuing a certain area and, sure enough, this turned out to be the case.
36) Form clear opinions about the attitudes and actions of long-deceased people. However, such opinions must be based upon the available evidence and <u>not</u> from personal bias or prejudice. Emotion must never cloud judgement or lead to rash conclusions even if the person being scrutinised appears to be thoroughly obnoxious. The researcher must be personally aware of any bias in favour of or against a person. This is particularly the case with family histories where subjective opinions are likely to be particularly strong.
37) Glean information from surviving artefacts (*e.g.* a book or a building). These may well give clues about a person, group or the style of life that was lived. **Frank's** move from a terraced to a corner-terraced house on **Hillcrest Avenue** may have been due to a rise in living standards brought about by success in his work as a Commercial Traveller.
38) Bravely handle conflicting evidence. This can be a nightmare if the evidential sources have both proved reliable in the past. In relating to the **Smith Family History,** there was often a severe discrepancy between Trade Directories and Census Returns over the date a business was functioning. The only possible resolution was to assume that the information provided in Trade Directories was accurate but always outdated (by approximately two or three years). Sometimes, as in the case of **Stewart's** marriage, the best policy was to record both versions of the same event and leave readers to decide which one they believed to be the most credible.

39) Have fun whilst conducting research or drafting out the history. Personally, one of the highlights for me was the time spent with my youngest son in libraries engaged in archive work. I have especially happy memories of the whispered discussions we held together.

40) Keep careful control of any paperwork. Ideally, a Lever Arch (or Box) File should be used to store information, all arranged in relevant sections using file dividers. Rough work should be kept separately but not thrown away until the project is fully completed. Any key names and addresses should be logged in alphabetical order and stored in one unit. Important documents should be preserved in plastic wallets. Almost always each piece of research will end with far more paperwork than had first been envisaged!

41) Keep on asking questions to open new lines of enquiry, *e.g.* *"Who were the stonemasons who built* **Edmund Smith's** *expensive tomb?"*

42) Learn from the telling *'non-events'* of this history. These are the life-events which should have happened – but didn't. In the case of my family, one telling *'non-event'* was the *'non-marriage'* of **Edmund's** two elder daughters **Betsey** and **Anne.** Another was my Grandfather's non-participation in military duty during the First World War. The things that did <u>not</u> happen to people may tell us as much about them as the things that did. The same applies to those things that were left largely unsaid; *e.g.* my father's marked silence about his war experiences.

43) Look for clear and continuous patterns of behaviour (or character traits) within either a person (or group). Regarding my own family, I was amazed to see how almost identical patterns of behaviour could *'jump across'* the generations. My own sister (for example) had been unaware that she shared the same interest in silverware that her Grand Aunt **Betsey Smith** had once enjoyed. (**Betsey** had been dead for over a quarter of a century before my sister was born.)

44) Observe how past *'key decisions'* may still influence present behaviour. In my own family, the almost obsessive preoccupation with *'social respectability'* and *'education'* can be traced back centuries. The influence that my Great Grandfather **Edmund**, exercised in that regard is still very active today **(2018).**

45) Obtain help in proof-reading and checking over the recorded work, particularly if lacking in editing skills. Ideally, such a person should be familiar with the researcher's way of doing things. Never take such valuable help for granted and always acknowledge them unless there's a desire for confidentiality.

46) Provide an attractive, eye-catching format to assist reading and reference. Without resorting to expensive colour printing, it is possible to create an attractive layout, *i.e.* via the skilful use of **'bold'** and *'italicised'* wording. The appropriate use of <u>*'underlining'*</u> and *'bullet points'* may also prove helpful in the improvement of the layout. What should be avoided is any dull monochrome format.

47) Realise that the availability of sources may vary from one geographical region to another. For instance, **Hull** had court records dating back from the **1850's** but **Leeds** did not.

48) Retain a willingness to correct any major mistakes, no matter how much further time and trouble it takes. Always be willing to amend firmly held opinions <u>when new facts emerge.</u> When (in the middle of **2001**) it was discovered that the **Edmund Smith** of **Colne** (who featured in the **1841** Census) was <u>not</u> my Great Grandfather I was horrified! I'd been studying the wrong **Edmund Smith** for about six months!

49) See how things did (or did not) change over time, *e.g.* the anti-elitist values of my Uncle **Stewart** appeared to differ markedly from those of his parents (who held to strong *'class'* distinctions.) Moreover, during the period covered by this history two major technological revolutions had taken place – these being the Industrial and Information Technology Revolutions. Nevertheless, unexpected continuities <u>still do exist with the past,</u> *e.g.* **mid-Victorians** would possibly view the **Internet** as being a *'magic telegraph,'* able to carry pretty pictures. At least the concept of the Internet would have been understandable to them, possibly by explaining that it was *'like the telegraph, only it does a lot more.'*

50) Spot any attempt to distort history in the sources used. Perhaps the most blatant example of such historical distortion was the way in which the biographer **Bateman** (or his informants) attempted to hide the relationship which had existed between **Betsey Hastings Smith** and a well-known **Leeds Doctor – Berkeley Moynihan.** The effect of this was to sharply reduce the credibility of his account.

51) Summarise findings (especially long documents) to make them readily understandable. Highly technical information (*e.g.* statistical tables) should be placed in **Appendices,** away from the main body of the work.

52) <u>Make *'quality time'* to reflect upon any findings,</u> *e.g.* lay a manuscript aside and come back to it a few weeks or months later with a fresh mind. In this way, things can often be spotted which may have been overlooked before. <u>Tiredness can be a great barrier to any success.</u>

53) Travel to any historical sites. There is no substitute for going and seeing something first-hand. Gaining a sense of the actual geographical environment adds a great deal to the research at hand. However, before making such visits it is advisable to prepare thoroughly beforehand, *e.g.* by looking at past Trade Directories to find those businesses with which one's ancestors may have been connected. Good footwear (and a packed lunch) are essential items on any visit.

54) Try to get the petty things – like the spelling of names and basic punctuation right. Nothing can undermine the credibility of a work more than silly little mistakes. (Remember to have the work proof-read.)

55) Utilize any and every skill and resource to aid in the understanding of a person or an event. (Of use to myself were certain methods of Biblical Interpretation, which had originated in about the fourth century BC. I used these same methods to interpret a wide range of documents.)

56) Vividly catch a sense of both the humour and tragedy existing in the personalities of key people. My own father often brimmed over with a mischievous sense of humour, even though emotionally he had been scarred by his rejection at **Leeds Grammar School** and the tragedy of the Second World War. Whenever I think of him I can still see him smiling with something of a twinkle in his eye.

57) Wisely know when to *'take a break'* and rest from the project. Also, know when to finally *'call it a day;'* when no more can be usefully discovered or said. Also, try to *'round off'* a piece of historical research in a well-written manner – leaving the reader a little sad at coming to the end of the work.

58) Be opportunistic – take advantage of any *'chance'* encounters or finds to elicit further information. Family History Fairs can be especially helpful venues for this kind of approach.

59) Avoid thinking one can do everything – be humble enough to draw upon the wisdom, knowledge and skills of third parties. In my case, the practical help given by both my first cousin and second cousin once removed came to mind.

60) Keep abreast with relevant technical developments. During the time this Family History was composed **(1999-2018)** major developments took place in Information Technology. These made it possible to obtain information that would have been unavailable only a few years previously. In future, the pace of technological change is most likely to continue to increase. Old-fashioned floppy discs have been replaced by memory sticks and bulky screens by flat, streamlined screens. There's also been the rise of a new Social Media like Facebook or Twitter. This Family History was produced in the context of a worldwide technological revolution. To maximise sales, I hope to publish it in an electronic as well as traditional printed form. As a typical **Smith** *'opportunist,'* I intend to take full advantage of all the benefits that technology can offer.

61) Always expect the unexpected. The last thing I expected was a Great Granddaughter of **Hedley Smith** contacting me by e-mail on **Wednesday, 3rd April 2013.** Our meeting in **Leeds** for the first time on **Saturday, 3rd August 2013** exercised a major influence over the subsequent development of this History. Surely long-lost relatives turning up *'out of the blue'* was the stuff of soap operas, not Family Histories! However, in my case, that's exactly what happened! With her brisk efficiency, my second cousin **Ann Dalton** was responsible for contributing to the making of several important discoveries. Amidst many *'creative disputes'* she gave fresh life to this project. Thanks to her I gained access into places I wouldn't have done otherwise.

62) Expect the writing of a Family History to take far longer than anticipated. In my own case, what was initially envisaged as a tribute to my father – taking three or four months to prepare – became a major epic taking almost two decades to complete! A Family History can easily take on a life of its own. Answering one question may provoke several others. Furthermore, it's arguable whether any Family History can ever really be completed. Always some gaps in knowledge remain – no matter how thorough the research.

63) Never say producing a Family History is over until it <u>is</u> over. I made that mistake during the middle of **June 2018** and by the end of that month, a totally unexpected lead had caused an avalanche of fresh data to come my way. This took nine months to process and led to some re-evaluation of past evidence and a major re-structuring of my book. I learned the hard way that a *'never ending'* quality does exist about this kind of work. Further information continued to come in until **March 2019.** These required further amendments to this work.

64) Always budget for signed book presentations and public engagements should one's work begin to be recognized. On **Saturday, 1ˢᵗ September 2018,** a copy of this history was presented to **Pastor Rob Harris** of **Sutton Baptist** during another visit to **Edmund's** obelisk. Also, on **Sunday, 23ʳᵈ September** I read some extracts on **Five Towns Local Radio Station** based in **Castleford.** (It attracted a small but favourable reaction.)

65) Don't be surprised if (mainly elderly) relatives or other associates wish to add their stories to a Family History as soon as it begins to get noticed. It's can be their way of securing immortality. If possible, the best response is to incorporate whatever relevant information they offer. If not, a polite *'thank you'* will have to do.

66) Know when to *'let go'* and say *'goodbye'* to a major project that has taken up decades of one's life. Doing this can feel like a bereavement – but any sense of grief is diminished if one has another large-scale project to go to. Accept that one's work on the ancestor's behalf has been completed and it's time to do something different. If possible hand over the task of compiling a Family History to other interested parties.

Overall, I found that researching the history of a family is akin to finding a treasure trove hidden in a deep cave – amidst the gold and silver may lie the bones of a skeleton. Therefore, Family Historians need to be prepared for shocks as well as pleasant surprises! May your own journey be a fruitful one.

AFTERWARD: HER FINAL BOW

Section 1: Vindication

The final days of **Cynthia,** my mother, can be quickly told. Around **July 2017** she entered what the Doctor's had then described as *'a decline,'* where she became increasingly sleepy and her *'rallies'* ever weaker. Following a period in hospital she was discharged to a different Nursing Home. Although thankfully spared the indignity of senility, watching this physical deterioration was so utterly distressing that I could only express my feelings in poetry. Sometimes, I would leave the premises muttering *'How long, oh Lord, how long?'* Yet on **Saturday, 8th September 2018** she was able to see (and appreciate) the launch of my book, *'A Saga of Smiths'* which took place in the dining area of her Nursing Home. (The contribution staff members made in arranging this event was much appreciated.) Around a dozen family members and friends were present. Regrettably, **Ann Dalton** couldn't make it.

During my presentation, I recounted how this project had first come into being and how it had subsequently taken on a life of its own. Special care was taken to praise my mother's *'towering'* contribution to substantial sections of the book. Photographic evidence would later confirm that my mother had been fully engaged. She hadn't *'nodded off'* whilst sitting in her wheelchair but had seemed alert and aware of what was going on. She was very much the central figure in this *'Book Launch.'* Especially moving was the reading (by a female **West Indian** friend) of one of **Helen's** letters and also, my wife's reading of some of **Cynthia's** war memoirs. As these pieces were being read aloud, I could see an extremely thoughtful look come over my mother's face. She was receiving public recognition of her achievements – something only a few people of her age and background could ever hope to experience. With hindsight, I could sense she was harnessing her last remaining energies during an event that provided an incredible vindication of her life. As I guessed at the time, the occasion was to represent **Cynthia's** *'passing out parade'* or *'validation ceremony.'* I was overjoyed to ascertain (just over a week later) that she was able to recall who had participated and what the event had all been about. When I informed her that she was becoming famous in her nineties she replied, *"Well it's a bit late at my age – but better late than never!"* On **Wednesday 3rd October 2018,** my book *'A Saga of Smiths'* was finally released for Global Distribution; I ensured my mother was fully aware of this development.

By early **November** death was stalking nearby. When I mentioned to **Cynthia** that she was soon to be **95** she retorted *"Big deal!"* She'd had enough. On **Sunday, 11ᵗʰ November** the media was full of broadcasts concerning the hundredth anniversary of the armistice that had marked the end of the First World War. During the afternoon of that same day, I undertook what was to be the most harrowing visit I was ever to make to my mother. She looked dreadful. Only twice did she wake from her stupor and each time she did, I gently said, *"It's time to let go."* There was a knowing look in her eyes as I said this. Tears filled my own eyes as I left her bedroom – with its teddy bears, painting by my father and *'knick-knacks'* from her past life. Thankfully, it wasn't to be my last visit.

The following **Friday** morning, I revisited her. This time my sister, my eldest son and my wife were present. We had been alerted by the Nursing Home that *'changes were taking place to her body.'* The previous night she had been rushed into **Saint James' Hospital** with *'dehydration.'* However, whilst there the decision was taken that nothing further could be done for her – so back to the Nursing Home she went. It would indeed be the dehydration that would end her life – for her failing body had lost the capacity to absorb fluid. However, at least she would pass away in the very pleasant surroundings of her bedroom. That morning we all gathered around her bedside, yet even amidst the bleak circumstances, our time spent with **Cynthia** somehow proved extremely pleasant. My eldest son set his mobile phone *'app'* to play some war time *'Big Band Music.'* This provided a lighter background to some family *'chit-chat'* and the usual discussion about politics. As far as we could, we included **Cynthia** in whatever we were talking about. My wife inadvertently added some drama by accidently scalding herself with boiling tea. (The resultant injury wasn't serious.) We joked to **Cynthia** about this being the last family drama she'd hear about. Before we left we spoke into her ear, offering her messages of thanks for being a wonderful parent and grandparent. After I told her how successful her life had been, I couldn't resist adding, *"Don't forget to pass on my regards to the ancestors. Soon you'll be knowing your Family History better than I do and you'll be hearing how badly wrong I got everything!"* My son and I needed to leave and before going I remarked to my wife, *"I've said to my mother everything I've wanted to say. There's nothing more to add."* My wife felt the same way. As I headed to the bus stop I reflected, *'It's ironic how the Family History has gone around in a full circle. A project that began with the death and funeral of my father is now ending with the death and funeral of my mother.'* With these thoughts in mind, I then boarded the bus.

Section 2: Slipping into History

At **1.40 pm** on **Saturday, 17ᵗʰ November 2018** my mother **Cynthia Mary Smith** slipped peacefully into history, nine days short of her ninety-fifth birthday. It was my brother who broke the news (via a mobile phone call whilst I was engaged in teaching an **Asian** student in **Shipley**). He shared that he and his wife had been in attendance during her last few moments and that her passing away had happened within the space of five minutes. There'd been no pain or suffering, just a gentle *'letting go'* of life. Cutting my lesson short, I was driven back to **Shipley Market Square** to catch a bus back home. Finding that there wasn't one due for another twenty minutes I wandered around the vicinity of the square in a numbed daze. (At one point I wandered into a nearby library where an **Asian** man was raising money for a charity, then I found myself in a large supermarket.) My main feeling was one of vague relief – that her sad decline was now finally over. The weather was cold but dry – the dead brown leaves swirling around on the pavement seemed to appear oddly symbolic. Time itself seemed to have frozen. Eventually, the bus came and after what seemed an interminably long journey I alighted and joined my good lady in **Morrisons Café** where she'd been doing some proof-reading with her usual tireless enthusiasm! We chatted in subdued terms before we returned home. Once there, I performed the necessary tasks of informing people via e-mail. I would remain in a fairly dazed state for over a week and wouldn't really emerge from it until after my mother's funeral. One odd feature of **November 17ᵗʰ** was that, in the morning, I'd received an e-mail from a certain central library asking me to give a lunchtime talk on how to write a Family History. (It's now scheduled for **September 2019.**) So, on the same day that my mother died a new door of opportunity was opening. This positive development would be the first in a whole series of personal consolations. At that time, I remember thinking; *"amidst death there is life."*

There was a dispute over the cause of my mother's death. Initially, the Doctor had attributed it to *'Dementia'* in order to forestall an inquest. Rightly, my brother and sister protested that she'd not been demented at all. So, the decision was taken to attribute the cause of death to a *'stroke,'* which again wasn't accurate. As stated before, what killed my mother was *'dehydration.'* Her body had lost the capacity to absorb fluid. This incident left me rather sceptical about the information provided by Death Certificates.

722

Section 3: Consolations

The time between my mother's death and her funeral was like being in limbo. Her life had come to a full stop, but it had not yet been underlined. Not aiding matters were the darkening nights and the way the weather was becoming increasingly cold, wet and downright miserable. At the same time my wife was laid low with a three-week viral infection that had robbed her of her voice; she could only croak her sympathy. In such circumstances it was all too easy for depression to take hold but fortuitously three events prevented this from happening. They acted as hugely helpful consolations – tiding me over what was a very difficult period.

The first of these events was to be found advertised on posters placed in local shops and on a certain cultural website. The announcement (which I'd devised myself) read: *"**Wednesday 21st November, 7.30 p.m.** ... THOSE WHO HAVE GONE BEFORE: RE-LIVING THE LIVES OF OUR ANCESTORS: **Richard Smith** is a qualified and experienced History Teacher whose poetry is known to cover a wide range of subjects. In this event, he and his wife **June** will be reading extracts from **'A Saga of Smiths: An Epic Family History'** – a work that took nineteen years to complete. These will include poetry, an account of a **Tudor Murder**, part of an **Old Baily Trial Transcript, Victorian Medical Records**, a first-hand account of what it was like to live through the **London Blitz** PLUS lots more! Prepare to meet some 'larger than life' characters. If you want to know how your ancestors lived, this is the event for you! Entrance £3.50/£3.00 (members & concessions), including refreshments."*

Present at the aforesaid *'event'* was a total of nine men and six women (most of whom were of a mature age). Happily, the three times my mother had attended this same Cultural Group (in early **2017**) were fondly remembered by most of those present. (My wife wasn't there due to illness – but she'd also felt that this should be an occasion *'just for me.'*) The reading of the extracts went well, and the organizer did a commendable job in reading two of **Helen's** letters. My own revised epitaph to **Helen,** entitled *'She did what she could, and it was marvellous'* drew a round of applause. There seemed to be an almost palpable sense, that regarding **Helen,** a wronged woman was being vindicated. The whole event comprised of two parts, divided by a short break for refreshments. The second part became a tribute to my mother. After my performance finished there was a double round of applause – which **Cynthia** would have loved as it was mainly for her. Later feedback (given to the organizer) was positive as were the comments made by a member of the group whom I later encountered in town – on the following **Friday.** Normally rather critical he remarked how the event had held everyone's attention from beginning to end. Only one thing had been amiss – I'd worn my green striped jumper the wrong way around! I was tempted to claim that I was only following a *'quaint'* **Yorkshire** mourning custom, ahem!

The second event was more serious and was sad in nature. An **Asian** family (whose two sons I'd taught in the past) had just lost their maternal grandmother. She'd died in **Pakistan** – just over a week before my mother's passing. (She'd been in her late seventies.) On the very wet evening of **Thursday, 22nd November** I visited their red brick terraced house to pay my respects. The atmosphere was subdued in tone, but it proved to be good for all of us to share our grief over a cup of tea. We were in a position to strengthen each other. I left that family feeling very comforted. I was especially relieved that I didn't have to share my emotional load with my wife who was still suffering from the same viral infection. I remember (in an attempt to be light-hearted) saying to a number of people, *"My mother has gone, my wife looks as if she's going, I'm not too good either and the cat's still grumpy!"* The time between my mother's death and her funeral was indeed extremely trying.

The third event arose out of the advice of my good lady. In a rather croaking voice, she suggested that I get out for the day *'to clear my head.'* On **Monday, 26th November 2018,** (on what would have been **Cynthia's** ninety-fifth birthday) I took her advice by catching a train to Harrogate. The plan was to have a *'remembrance walk'* from **Harrogate** rail station to the **Valley Gardens** and then up through the pine woods (divided by a busy main road) and onto the Garden Centre at **Harlow Carr.** I would then retrace my route, taking in a long break at **Waterstones Bookshop** before catching the train back home. Fortuitously, the day was dry (if rather dull and cold) – consequently, I was free to think without being drenched. It was whilst strolling through the pine woods that I began to summarise lessons learnt from my mother's life. These I jotted down as a makeshift list of advice – the kind normally to be found in *'self-help'* books. Here it is:

1. Stay inquisitive and stay connected
2. Maintain an interest in people (especially – but not exclusively the young)
3. Have a hobby – even if it's only family dramas!
4. Make friends in later life
5. Display a perky sense of humour
6. Be adaptable and avoid endless moaning
7. Be willing to redefine one's role in later life
8. Retain a healthy interest in current affairs
9. Preserve your leg muscles through regular exercise

10. At the first *'fall'* get to the gym and *'tune-up'* your legs
11. In short, accept the inevitable <u>only when it is inevitable!</u>

These are lessons I hope to apply to my own later life. When it came to old age – most notably in the social area **Cynthia** provided an excellent role model to follow. As far as her physical fitness was concerned it's possible to wonder whether a lack of exercise contributed to **Cynthia's** frequent falls. One thing the family <u>did so right</u> was to keep her mentally stimulated with such things as gossip, discussion on news items and taking her out to cultural events. This strategy (only in part) explains why her body went before her mind. It makes me more determined to keep my wife's mind going with endless proof-reading. I'll encourage her to view it as a *'senility blocker.'* Indeed, my most cherished memories of her will be of her proof-reading!

A <u>fourth</u> consolation was my poetry. Writing poems about my mother proved to be immensely therapeutic. By early **March 2019,** I'd amassed a collection of twenty poems, each one having helped me to feel calm as they were composed. The old philosophers weren't wrong in claiming that consolation can be found in literature. As my tributes were being penned I imagined her smiling at me with a knowing look on her face and raising a full wine glass. Indeed, all of my recurring memories of **Cynthia** were always of her in her eighties – the period of her life when I <u>really</u> got to know her. (Strangely I had no clear memories of her in her younger days.) The fruit she bore in old age was incredible; **Cynthia** had indeed been my muse. Her later years had been a major inspiration to me.

Section 4: A Remarkable Influence

My mother's funeral service took place at **Lawnswood Crematorium** at **11.40 am** on **Tuesday, 4th December 2018.** About thirty were in attendance**. Glenn Miller Music** was playing in the background as we entered the chapel and again when we left. Sandwiched between two hymns was my brother's eulogy to **Cynthia.** It formed the centrepiece of what was a rather short event. (Please find it quoted in its entirety below. However, to preserve confidentiality, some personal references have been omitted.)

Cynthia Mary Smith: An Appreciation

*Cynthia Mary Absalom, as she then was, was born in **Salonika (Greece)** on 26thNovember 1923 and passed away at **1.40pm on Saturday 17th November*** *in the **Elmwood Care Home** [in **Roundhay, Leeds**]. However, these bare facts do not reveal the extraordinary richness of her long life.*

***Cynthia's** parents were remarkable in their own right. Her mother **(1883-1963)** was the archetype of an Edwardian 'New Woman' – who was well educated, supported herself financially as a school teacher, was feistily independent-minded and courageous during the **London** blitz. **Cynthia's** father **(1886-1959)** fought with distinction in the **British** army in both World Wars. **Cynthia** was born in **Salonika** because her father had served there in the **Great War.** He had decided not to return home after the war, but instead had asked **Cynthia's** mother to join him there. The upshot is that **Cynthia** spent much of her formative years outside the **United Kingdom,** initially in **Greece** and **Bulgaria** and, following a two-year stint in the **UK,** in **Paris,** where she attended school. This childhood influenced **Cynthia** both physically – her robust constitution was a result of happy childhood hours spent playing on **Balkan** beaches – and also psychologically. **Cynthia** loved being in the sun, adored foreign travel, and enjoyed mixing with people from the widest possible range of backgrounds and cultures. She also maintained her interest in **French** throughout her life.*

*This halcyon childhood terminated when her parents re-located to **London** in **1936.** Still in her mid-teens, **Cynthia** joined the Civil Service early in **World War II.** Initially, she worked in **London** and experienced the **Battle of Britain** and the **Blitz,** when she and her parents were 'bombed out' on several occasions. The Civil Service then moved her to **Bournemouth.** Here, **Cynthia** was placed in over-crowded digs. She took to the communal life-style of her wartime postings like a duck to water. It may explain why she was so sociable. Even more important, it was in **Bournemouth** that **Cynthia** met the man who would be her husband for the next fifty-eight years – the Royal Navy seaman **Fred Gordon Smith.** Their marriage took place at **St Peter's Church, Bournemouth** on **13th December 1941,** making **Cynthia** '**Mrs Smith**' six days after the **Japanese** attack on **Pearl Harbour.***

*With her husband at sea, and her father serving in the **Mediterranean, Cynthia** and her mother spent the later war years in London. Here, she lost the baby boy she was expecting in **June 1944** when a **V1** flying bomb hit a building across the road. This caused her to move to her mother in law's house in **Leeds** – the city where she was to remain for the rest of her life. After **Fred** was demobilised in **February 1946,** there followed the hardships of the early post-war years, while **Fred** fought to re-establish his business career at the relatively mature age of thirty-two. Their first child, **David,** was born in **1946,** followed by **Valerie** in **1948,** and **Richard** in **1956.** During this period, **Cynthia** was a full-time housewife. Almost none of the conveniences of modern life were then available. Being a **1950s** housewife was hard physical graft.*

*Later, in the **1960s**, **Cynthia** took a number of jobs before doing a long stint in remand homes for girls. This work brought out her strongly protective maternal side. Thereafter, she worked as a home help co-ordinator in **South Leeds** until her sixty-fifth birthday, before volunteering (unpaid) in charity shops, including the **Peoples Dispensary for Sick Animals (PDSA).** Hence the collection boxes today.*

***Cynthia**'s husband, **Fred** was ten years older, and died in **April 1999** after some years of indifferent health, which **Cynthia** had had to cope with. After she became a widow, **Cynthia** took to international travelling with such enthusiasm that her eightieth and ninetieth birthday parties should have been sponsored by **ABTA!** Throughout her life **Cynthia** took an extremely active interest, not only in her three children, and later on their partners **Carol, June** and **Ross,** but also her six grandchildren and five great grandchildren. She also loved playing with **Valerie's** dogs. As their children matured, **Cynthia** and **Fred's** home became filled with boisterous teenagers, including **Valerie's** friends. Because of her wartime experiences, **Cynthia** was pretty un-shockable and was very sympathetic to teenage foibles in those 'awkward years'. She also valued and maintained her friendships – sometimes for decades, including with former colleagues, her fellow Bridge friends and the jolly ladies with whom she had holidayed. **Cynthia**'s friends were very special and kind to her and were loyal and faithful to the end.*

*Above all, **Cynthia** was an enthusiastic 'people person.' She revelled in meeting new people, even in her nineties. These included her close friends, former neighbours and the carers at **Elmwood,** who were **Cynthia**'s family at the end. Latterly, **Cynthia** also relished the strong fellowship evidenced at **Kearby Chapel** and took great pleasure in **Richard's** 'Family History Book Launch' in **September,** when she was delighted to see her beloved niece **Pamela** and **Sally** – her late nephew **Tony's** wife. **Cynthia** will be most sorely missed."*

The above source has proved most useful in providing an outline to **Cynthia's** life and in adding further details to this *'Family History.'* I can vouch for the fact that my brother took painstaking care to check all of the available facts. As I read it, memories of some of the cleaning ladies whom my mother had to help with the house chores came back. There was a **Mrs Hardy** an elderly lady with a headscarf whom I remember coming in through the back door during a heavy thunder storm. This would be in about **1960**. Later, in about **1966** there was **Mrs Marsden** who was a fussy, bustling little woman who I used to annoy by calling her *'Mrs Mars Bar.'* I drew many a disapproving look from her. Inevitably, these ladies never seemed to meet my mother's exacting standards. She would often complain that all they ever did was light dusting and hoovering. However, Cynthia reluctantly tolerated them because she hated housework.

As I left the chapel, I looked for one last time at my mother's coffin and quietly said, *"Goodbye* **Cynthia***, you're now part of The Saga."* She did indeed now belong to history. My main feeling wasn't one of grief but of profound respect for all of the inspiration and help she'd provided in her extreme old age. Her achievements (throughout her eighties and early nineties) had been truly outstanding. For all of us, her passing had meant the end of an era.

Section 5: Passing on the Torch

The *'Wake'* (funeral party) held at the former **Parkway Hotel** was attended by about **26** people – evenly divided between male and female. Quite a few were elderly – with one old male family friend being aged **98**. With my sister's full encouragement, I had covered a couple of tables with old photograph albums and other family history material. Taking pride of place were three hard cover (and one soft cover) editions of **'A Saga of Smiths.'** I was pleased to find that three copies were sold for a total of £**66.00**. As I remarked to my sister, *"You know whose great Grandson I am. After all, we've always been a commercial family."* I think that my mother will have smiled at the prospect of her funeral *'do'* being used as an opportunity to make money. Why not? My sister's response was a knowing wink. I jokingly remarked that she was so good at organizing funerals that she could organize my own if I went before her. In reply, she'd said, *"Oh, I don't know about that."*

Two eulogies were given at the Wake. The first of these was delivered by my eldest son. He pointed to **Cynthia's** role as a grandmother and *'matriarch'* of the **Smith** family. He especially praised her for her mischievousness, adaptability and *'pluck.'* Highlighted was the lighter side of my mother's nature. One illustration was the way she'd connived with other patients to have a bottle of wine smuggled into one of the hospital wards where she was a patient. (This had been against Doctor's orders.) His eulogy was very well received. My own short speech mentioned some of the encounters already described in this *'History.'* I thanked her for her *'towering'* contribution to this *'Family History'* and to my poetry. At the end I read out a couple of poems and closed by saying, *"My epitaph to her is 'she was an inspiration and she still IS!'"* That comment drew a loud round of applause.

Afterwards photographs were taken. Whilst in conversation with my cousin **Pamela,** we were pleased to notice our nephews and nieces looking at documents on the Family History Table and taking pictures of the old

728

photographs of the ancestors. We noted how the younger generation seemed to be catching *'the family history bug.'* There was a sense of *'passing on the torch'* to them. Towards the end of the Wake two branches of the **Smith** family expressed an interest in me taking them for summer tours in the **Cowling** and **Kildwick** areas. I'd thought *"If this happens, I will be continuing the work of* **James Hastings Smith** *– but I refuse to wear a tweed suit and plus four trousers or a trilby hat with a feather stuck in it!"* My nephew's **Vietnamese** wife (who couldn't attend because she was expecting their second child) had apparently had some idea of having her relatives visit **Edmund's** obelisk. In response, I couldn't help imagining whether there would be some rumblings in **Edmund's** vault if some pretty young **Vietnamese** girls were present in the visiting party. He would be delighted! All too quickly, it was time to carefully pack up my memorabilia and leave, but before doing so I took a final glance at the Family History Table and thought *'The Saga continues,'* … and so indeed it does!

BIBLIOGRAPHY

B1: Booklist

Ackroyd Peter (2001) *London: The Biography* Vintage
Adair John (1998) *Puritans: Religion and Politics in Seventeenth-Century England and America* Alan Sutton
Anning T. Stephen (1980) *The History of Medicine in Leeds* W. S. Manney & Son Ltd
ApJohn Lewis (1884) *William Ewart Gladstone: His Life and His Times* Walter Leigh
Aris Stephen (1971) *The Jews in Business* Johnathan Cape Ltd
Bateman David (1940) *Berkeley Moynihan, Surgeon* London Macmillan & Co Ltd
Bennett Arnold (1908) *The Old Wives' Tale* Wordsworth Classics – 1969 edition
Bennett W. (1948) *The History of Burnley Part III* Burnley Corporation
Bennett W. (1985) *The History of Burnley Part IV* Lancashire County Council
Binfield Clyde (1978) *So Down to Prayer: Studies in English Non-Conformity 1760-1920* J. M. Dent & Son
Brears C. D. Peter (1993) *Leeds Waterfront Heritage Trail: A Guide to The Historic Sites and Buildings Along the Eight Miles of The Aire Valley Through Leeds* The Leeds City Museum
Brontë Anne (1988; first published in 1847) *Agnes Grey* Penguin Classics
Brontë Charlotte (1994; first published in 1849) *Shirley* Penguin Popular Classics
Brown G. Callum (2001) *The Death of Christian Britain* Routledge

Bullock Alan (1991) *Hitler and Stalin, Parallel lives* Harper-Collins

Burt Steven & Grady Kevin (1994) *The Illustrated History of Leeds* The Breedon Book Company

Cesarini David – editor (1890) *The Making of Modern Anglo-Jewry* Oxford: Basil Blackwell

Clarke Mike (1990) *The Leeds & Liverpool Canal* Carnegie Press

Clark Victoria (2007) *Allies for Armageddon: The Rise of Christian Zionism* Yale University Press

Cole H. D. G. (1989 edition) *Chartist Portraits* Cassell Publishers Ltd

Cook Faith (1997) *William Grimshaw of Haworth* The Banner of Truth Trust

Crambie R. Geoff (2000) *Images of England: Colne* Tempus Publishing Ltd

Cudworth William (1968; first published in 1876) *Round About Bradford* Mountain Press, Queensbury

Dawson Harbutt (1882) *History of Skipton* Simpkin Marshall and Co

Dickens Charles (1841) *Barnaby Rudge* Penguin Classics

Dickens Charles (1860) *The Uncommercial Traveller* London Chapman & Hall Ltd

Elwood Christopher (2002) *Calvin for Armchair Theologians* Westminster John Knox Press

Erikson H. Erik (1958) *Young Man Luther: A Study in Psychoanalysis and History* Faber and Faber Ltd

Farrer Max (2002) *The Social and Political Construction of Space* School of Cultural Studies, Leeds Metropolitan University

Ferguson Niall (2018) *The Square and the Tower* Penguin Books

Flanders Judith (2003) *The Victorian House: Domestic Life from Childbirth to Deathbed* Harper-Collins

Foster James (1974) *Elementary Education in Skipton during the Nineteenth Century* Leeds University (Dept of Education)

Franklin White A. – editor (1967) *Selected Writings of Lord Moynihan* Pitman Medical Publishing Club

Fraser Derek – editor (1980) *A History of Modern Leeds* Manchester University Press

Freedman Murray – compiler (1995) *1891 Census Leeds: List of Jewish Residents* Privately Published

Gellately Robert (2007) *Lenin, Stalin and Hitler: The Age of Social Catastrophe* Jonathan Cape

Gartner P. Lloyd (1960) *The Jewish Immigrant in England 1870-1914* Simon Publications

Gascoigne Bamber (1977) *The Christians* Granada Publishing

Gaskin J. M. (2005) *Blitz: The Story of 29 December 1940* Faber and Faber

Gregory S. Brad (2012) *The Unintended Reformation: How a Religious Revolution Secularized Society* Belknap Press, Harvard University

Hatfield Ella (1991) *Skipton* Smith Settle Ltd

Haralambos Michael, Holborn Martin, Chapman Steve and Moore Stephen (2013) *Sociology: Themes and Perspectives: 8th Edition* Harper-Collins Publishers

Haynes Ian (1990) *Stalybridge Cotton Mills* Neil Richardson

Hingley Ronald (1973) *The Tsars* Corgi Books

Hodgson John (1999, first published in 1879) *Textile Manufacture in Keighley* Shaun Tyas, Stamford

Hoss Elijah Embree Bishop (1916) *David Morton: A Biography* Methodist Episcopal Church Pub. House

Holland J. A. (1977) *The Age of Industrial Expansion: British Economic and Social History since 1770* Nelson

Honeyman Katrina (2000) *Well Suited: A History of the Leeds Clothing Industry 1850-1990* Oxford University Press

Hudson Patricia (1975) *Textile Industry: A Catalogue of Business Records from the Sixteenth to the Twentieth Century* Pasold Research Fund Ltd

Hull Lise (2005) *Tracing Your Family Roots: The Complete Problem Solver* Collins & Brown

Jay Peter (2000) *Road to Riches or The Wealth of Man* Weidenfeld & Nicolson

Jones-Wilkins C. (1979) *Stalybridge In Old Photographs* Libraries and Arts Committee Tameside Metropolitan Borough

Julius Anthony (2010) *Trials of the Diaspora: A History of Anti-Semitism in England* Oxford University press

Lane Margaret (1992) *The Brontë Story* Smith Settle

Lewis E. Jon – Editor (2014) *A Brief History of The First World War: Eyewitness Accounts of the War to End All Wars, 1914-1918* Robinson

Livett C. G. Ronald – editor (1932) *Register of Kildwick-in-Craven IV* (Volumes VII and VIII in part, Baptisms March 1744-April 1789, Marriages March 1744 – March 1754 & Burials March 1744 – June 1771) York Parish Register Society

Lock Alice – editor (1989) *Looking Back at Stalybridge* Libraries and Arts Committee, Tameside Metropolitan Borough

Lowe John (1985) *Burnley* Phillimore & Co Ltd

Mason Alistair – editor (1994) *Religion in Leeds* Alan Sutton publishers

McCann Mick (2010) *How Leeds Changed the World: Encyclopaedia Leeds* Armley Press

Mercer Derrick – editor in Chief (1996) *Chronicle of the World: A Global View of History as it Happened* Dorling Kindersley

Miller Stuart (1997) *Mastering Modern European History* Macmillan

Miles J. T. Geo A (1911) *A History of Withernsea* A. Brown & Sons, Ltd

Mitchell W. R. (2000) *A History of Leeds* Phillimore & Co. Ltd

Moorhouse Geoffrey (2002) *The Pilgrimage of Grace: The Rebellion that Shook Henry VIII's Throne* Weidenfeld & Nicolson

Morley Neville (1999) *Writing Ancient History* Duckworth

Moynihan A. G. B. (1905) *Abdominal Operations* W. B. Saunders and Company

Muggeridge Malcom (1989) *The Thirties: 1930-1940 in Great Britain* Weidenfeld & Nicolson

Palmer Alan (1965) *The Gardeners of Salonika: The Macedonian Campaign 1915-1918* Andre Deutsch

Price C. A. (1919) *A History of Leeds Grammar School: From Its Foundation to The End of 1918* Richard Jackson publishers

Rees Laurence (1997) *The Nazis – a Warning from History* BBC Books

Riley Doris (1996) *A Homespun Yarn* Pioneer Press, Skipton

Robinson Wheeler H (1912) *The Baptists of Yorkshire* Wm. Byles & Sons Ltd

Rowley Geoffrey R. (1969) *Old Skipton* Dalesman Publishing Company Ltd

Rowley Geoffrey R. (1983) *The Book of Skipton* Barracuda Books Ltd

Sherbok-Cohn Dan Rabbi (2006) *The Politics of the Apocalypse: The History and Influence of Christian Zionism* Oneworld Publications

Short Martin (1989) *Inside the Brotherhood: Explosive Secrets of the Freemasons* HarperCollins Publishers

Smiles Samuel (1969; first published in 1859) *Self-Help* Butler & Tanner

Stowell Gordon (1929) *The History of Button Hill* Victor Gollancz Ltd

Stratmann Linda (2004) *Whiteley's Folly: The Life and Death of a Salesman* Sutton Publishing

Taylor P. J. A – editor (1975) *Karl Marx, Friederich Engels: The Communist Manifesto* Pelican

Taylor David (1988) *Mastering Economic and Social History* Macmillan

Thornton David (1996) *The Picture Story of Leeds* D & J Thornton

Townend Michael (1999) *Images of England: Burnley* Tempus Publishing

Turner Horsfall J. (1897) *Ancient Bingley or Bingley Her History and Scenery* Thomas Harrison & Sons, Bingley Yorkshire

Unattributed (1881) *Half Hours in the Far North: Life amid Snow and Ice with Numerous Illustrations* Wm Ibister Ltd

Unattributed (1865) *The Leeds Poll Book* in the care of Leeds Central Library

Unattributed (1868) *The Leeds Poll Book* in the care of Leeds Central Library

Walker E. Walter (1991) *Around Skipton-In-Craven in Old Photographs* Alan Sutton

Ward M. Francis (1972) *Industrial Development and Location North of the River Aire 1775-1914* PhD Thesis, cited with the kind permission of The School of Geography at Leeds University.

Ward T. J. (1989 – ed.) *Popular Movements 1830-1850: Problems in Focus* MacMillan

Weber Max (1956) *The Protestant Work Ethic and the Spirit of Capitalism* George Allen Unwin Ltd

Wheen Francis (1999) *Karl Marx* Fourth Estate Ltd

Whiston William – Translator (1995) *The Works of Josephus: Complete and Unabridged* Hendrickson Publishers

Wilkinson Richard Paul (2007) *For Zion's Sake: Christian Zionism and the Role of John Nelson Darby* Paternoster

Wilks Brian (1975) *The Brontës: An Illustrated Biography* Hamlyn Publishing Group Ltd

Whitaker Peter & Wood Alec (1992) *Sutton-In-Craven in Old Picture Postcards* European Library

Wilkinson Richard Paul (2007) *For Zion's Sake: Christian Zionism and the Role of John Nelson Darby* Paternoster

Wood Alec – editor (1973) *Sutton-In-Craven: The Old Community* Riding Publishing Company

B2: Articles, Booklets, Diaries and Magazines

Askin Mustafa (2015) *Gallipoli: A Turning Point* Keskin Color Kartpostacilik A. S

Asquith T. C. (1953) *The Burton Pidsea Story* Privately Published

Bradford Eveleigh (2012) *Headingley Hall: A Historic House* Westward Care Limited

Bruley Sue (1997) *'A Very Happy Crowd': Women in Industry in South London in World War Two* History Workshop Journal Issue 44

Charing Douglas (1994) *The Jewish Presence in Leeds* (See Chapter 8 of Mason Alistair)

Day H. Marjorie (1996) *Hall Green Story: A History of Haworth Strict Baptist Church (1824 – 1996)* Privately Published

Freedman Murray (2003) *Chapeltown and its Jews* Privately Published

Grundy E. Joan (2003) *History's Midwives: Including a C17th and C18th Yorkshire Midwife's Nominations Index* FFHS Publications Ltd

Grundy E. Joan (2006) *A Dictionary of Medical & Related Terms for the Family Historian* Swansong Publications

Hall Brian (2002) *Burnley: A Short History* Burnley & District Historical Society

Haykin Michael (2015) *'I wish I had prayed more': John Sutcliff and the Concert of Prayer for Revival* Reformation Today, January-February 2015 Issue 263

Hirst Stuart – editor (1926) *Leeds Tercentenary Official Handbook* Tercentenary Executive

Howard P. W. (1874) *'Notice'* The London Gazette, May 8, 1874

Jackson A. W. (1981) *The Victorian Chemist and Druggist* Shire Publications Ltd

Jones Ian (2001) *Is There Still a Place for Ritual in the 21ˢᵗ Century?* The Odd Fellow Magazine, spring 2001, Volume seven, Issue one

Joseph Anthony Dr (2008) *My Ancestors were …* Jewish Society of Genealogists Enterprises Ltd ISBN: 978-1-903462-63-8

Kelsey H. P. (1952) *Four Hundred Years 1552–1952: The Story of Leeds Grammar School*, Privately Published

Kershan J. Anne (1990) *Trade Unionism amongst the Jewish Tailoring Workers of London and Leeds* (see Cesarini)

Lipman D. V. (1961) *Three Centuries of Anglo-Jewish History* Jewish Historical Society

Morton David (1881) *The Morton Kin Book: Description of a Visit to Edmund and Rosamond Smith* retained by his descendants

Mount David – M.I Co-coordinator (1990) *Monumental Inscriptions in Burton Pidsea* East Yorkshire History Society

Myerson Henry (1889) *Our Portrait gallery – No. VII. Mr Henry Myerson of Shalom Chapel "The Oval" Hackney* The Earthen Vessel and The Gospel Herald Vol, XLV July 1889

Oldland John – Revisionist (1989) *The Church of Saint Matthew, the Mother Church of Bethnal Green* Privately Published

Ottaway Patrick (2015) *The Products of the Blacksmith in Mid-Late Anglo-Saxon England* www.pjoarchaeology.co.uk

Pilling Edmund et al (1961) *Sutton-In-Craven Baptist Church: 250ᵗʰ Church Anniversary 1711- 1961* Privately Published

Riley Doris (1991) *One of the Gems: The Park in Sutton-in-Craven* Privately Published

Riley Doris (1991) *'Owd' Settings Sutton-in-Craven* Privately Published

Rous Derek (2016) *The Development of the Messianic Movement: How We Got to the Present-Day* Prayer for Israel Spring Magazine 2016

Smith David (2006) *Economic Outlook: Motoring Along in a World of Growth* Sunday Times Business Section 3.4, 31.12.2006

Smith Helen and **Hastings** James (1857-1866) *Private Correspondence* retained by their descendants

Smith Hastings James (1885-1950) *Commonplace Book (or Diary)* retained by his descendants

Smith Hastings James (1891) *Letter to David Morton* The Morton Kin Book

Smith Hastings James (1936) *Transcription of a Memorial Inscription to James Hastings and His Wife* at Burton Pidsea

Smith John Richard (2001) *Family Album: Edmund Smith* Yorkshire Family Historian Volume 27 No 4 December 2001

Smith John Richard (2003) *The Perils and Joys of Researching Family History* Notes of a Lecture Given at The Family History Section of The Yorkshire Archaeological Society on Saturday, 12th July 2003

Stell Nellie (1927) *The History of Sutton-in-Craven* https://www.sutton-in-craven.org.uk/stellch21.asp

Strong Ruth – Editor (2000) *Israel Roberts (1827-1881) Autobiography* Pudsey Civic Society

Todd Andrew (2003) *Problem Solving Through Family Reconstitution Techniques* Yorkshire Family Historian Volume 29 No 3 September 2002

Unattributed (1903) *Gone Home: Mr H. Myerson* The Earthen Vessel and Gospel Herald January 1903

Unattributed (1903) *Gone Home: Henry Myerson: An Appreciation* Earthen Vessel and Gospel Herald January 1903

Unattributed (1903) *Henry Myerson* The Earthen Vessel and Gospel Herald January? 1903

Unknown Obituary Columnist (2004) *Commander Hugh Boyce* The Daily Telegraph, Monday, June 28th, 2004

Various Contributors (1911) *Handbook of Grand Bazaar: in Celebration of Sutton Baptist Chapel 1711-1911* Privately Published

Various Contributors *The Leodensian Magazine 1882-1884 and 1928-1930 issues* Privately Published

Various Contributors (May 1937) *Moynihan Memorial Edition, University of Leeds Medical Society Magazine* Leeds University

Various Contributors (April 2000) *'The South Holderness Deanery Magazine,' Volume 106 No 4* The Vicar's Press York

Various Contributors (December 2001) *'The Yorkshire Family Historian' Volume 27 No 4* Journal of the Family History & Population Studies Section, Yorkshire Archaeological Society, Leeds

Various Issues of *The Leeds Intelligencer, The Leeds Mercury, The Manchester Evening News, The Yorkshire Post, The Yorkshire Evening Post*

Warren Isabel (1999) *Parish Church School: 20 Years of Education* Warren Associates on behalf of the Parish Church School Skipton

Wood Alec (1996) *History and Description of the Parish Church of St Andrew Kildwick in Craven* – Privately Published

B3: Archive Material from the Bairstow Mill-Owning Family

Archives (1801-1839) *Account Book (Loose Paper to 1857 – including Two Papers concerning the Purchase by John Smith of New Close, Silsden from Henry Spencer in 1831)*

Archives (1834-1850) *Hand Combers' Book (Wages for Outworkers)*

Archives (1809) *Money Paid at Sutton Mill for Temporary Dam (Labourer Costs Mainly)*
Archives (1830-1835) *Purchase/Sales Day Book*
Archives (1830-1839) *Purchase/Sales Ledger (with about 28 Managed Accounts)*
Archives (1834-1835) *Small Book containing Purchase/Sales Notes*
Archives (1834-1843) *Wage Account Cash Book*

B4: Archive Material from Cullingworth Baptist Chapel

Brigg Anderton William – Editor (1913) *The Parish Register of Saint Andrews Kildwick in Craven: Volume 1 Baptisms Deaths and Marriages 1575-1622*, Privately Published for the Parish Registration Society. (Available online)
Cullingworth Baptist Chapel (1836-1864) *Accounts of the Baptist Church at Cullingworth from its commencement to 1864 (Loose Paper to 1836 – letter from Isaac Constantine Thanking His Fellow Workers for Readmitting Him to the Church dated 3rd December 1836)*
Cullingworth Baptist Chapel (1836-1882) *Chapel Register of Members of the Baptist Church at The Lodge, Cullingworth formed June 1st 1836*
Cullingworth Baptist Chapel (1837-1880) *Cullingworth Baptist School Minute Book*
Cullingworth Baptist Chapel (1838-1920) *Internments in the Burial Ground of the Baptist Church, Cullingworth*
Cullingworth Baptist Chapel (1836-1837) *Minutes Book of the Management for Conducting Divine Service in the New Lodge Cullingworth which was opened for this purpose on Tuesday, February 16th 1836, in connection with the Baptist Denomination*
Cullingworth Baptist Chapel (1836-1847) *Minutes Book of The Baptist Church at Cullingworth – founded June 15th 1836 (Includes a Short History of The Baptist Church at Cullingworth 1911)*

B5: Archive Material from Kildwick Parish

Kildwick Friendly Society (1826-1855) *Minutes and Committee Appointments Book*
Kildwick Friendly Society (1782-1853) *Sick Book*
Kildwick Friendly Society (1827-1836) *Weekly Payments Book covering the period 1/4/1827 - 4/10/1836*
Kildwick *Parish Monumental Inscriptions – Kildwick*

B6: Archive Material from the Skipton Parish of Holy Trinity

Skipton (1840-1858) *Burial Registers for Holy Trinity Parish Church, Raikes Road Cemetery and for various Dissenting Churches*

Skipton (1840-1858) *Notes on Property Ownership for New Market Street, Skipton*

B7: Archive Material from Sutton Baptist Church

Sutton Baptist Burial Book (C1830-1892) *Register of internments in Burial Grounds*
Sutton Baptist Church Book (1780-1875) *"The Book belonging to the Baptized Church of Jesus, Sutton"*
Sutton Baptist Notes: *On Baptisms of the Smith family 1809-1845*
Sutton Baptist (1811) *Register of subscribers from Sutton, Bradford, Scarborough, Leeds, Shipley and Baildon Baptist Churches 'to do' fund for alterations to the Church*
Sutton Baptist Sunday School (1837-1853) *Minutes of the meetings of the teachers and committee of the Baptist Sunday School, Sutton, with Register of teachers*
Sutton Baptist Sunday School (1845-1846) *Scholars' register, includes name, residence, age, denomination, parents' occupation*
Sutton Baptist Sunday School (1845-1846) *Scholars' register, reading and arithmetic classes*

B8: Archive Material from Sutton Township

Sutton Township (1795-1809) *Disbursements to the poor book*
Sutton Township Rate Book (1854) *Rates made in February 1854*
Sutton Township Rent Book (1836-1838) *Rent Collections from 1836 until 1838*
Sutton Water Company (1860-1915) *Cash Book*

B9: Sermon Material

Bean Thomas George (1865) *"The Signs of the Times"* a sermon preached in Blenheim Chapel, Woodhouse Lane, Leeds on Lord's-Day Morning, October 22nd 1865
Cartwright B. J. Reverend (1836) *Love to the Jewish Nation: A Sermon Preached at the Episcopal Jews Chapel, Bethnal Green London on Sunday Morning 27th November 1836 on Occasion of the Death of the Reverend Charles Simon A.M Senior Fellow of Kings College and Minister of Trinity Church Cambridge* London Society
Cooper William (1796) *Christ the True Messiah: Sermon Preached at Sion-Chapel, Whitechapel to God's Ancient Israel, The Jews, on Sunday 28th August 1796 with prayers before and after Sermon* John Fairburn
James Charles Reverend Right, Lord Bishop of London (1843) *A Sermon Preached at the Episcopal Jews Chapel Cambridge Heath on Thursday, May 4th 1843 Before the London Society for Promoting Christianity amongst the Jews* B. Fellowes
Unknown (1877) *"Giving to the work of God"* a sermon preached in Blenheim Chapel, Leeds, on June 10th 1877

B10: Web Site References

All the below listed websites were available on **Friday, 10th August 2018.**
http://www.a2a.org.uk/about/contributors/index.asp
www.Ancestry.co.uk
https://archive.org/stream/parishregisterso47kild#page/n11/mode/2up
https://sites.google.com/site/leedsandbradfordstudios/home/charles-henry-braithwaite
http://www.ba-education.com/for/food/pudschool.html
http://www.bac-lac.gc.ca/eng/Pages/home.aspx
http://www.bazzasoft.net/cowling.htm
http://www.british-history.ac.uk/vch/middx/vol11/pp228-240#fnn244
http://www.burnleystpeterheritage.co.uk/victorianpage2.htm
http://www.capitalpunishmentuk.org/1800.html
https://dbs.bh.org.il
http://www.duncancampbell.org/content/preying-hope
htp://en.wikipedia.org/wiki/Cowling,_Craven
http://www.eyewitnesstohistory.com/londonhanging.htm
http://familysearch.org/learn/wiki/en/Bethnal_Green_Jews%27_Episcopal_Chapel
http://forums.phoenixrising.me/index.php?threads/a-few-questions-from-the-phd-student.22274/page-4
www.genealogylinks.net/uk/england/yorkshire/index.html
http://www.genealogyintime.com/GenealogyResources/Articles/top_ten_most_popular_online_genealogy_magazines.html
www.genuki.org.uk/
www.genuki.org.uk/big/eng/YKS/ERY/Burtonpidsea/Burtonpidsea92.html
http://www.glasgowwestaddress.co.uk/1891_Book/Stewart_&_MacDonald.htm
http://www.housefraserarchive.ac.uk/company/?id=c1224
http://www.housefraserarchive.ac.uk/company/?id=c0720
https://www.jewishgen.org/jcr-uk/Leeds.htm
https://legacy.lib.utexas.edu/taro/smu/00258/smu-00258.html
http://www.leodis.net/
http://www.medicalsociologyonline.org/oldsite/archives/issue41/pdwolfe.html
http://opendomesday.org/name/208670/gamal-son-of-karli/
http://www.rootschat.com/forum/index.php
http://www.scarboroughcivicsociety.org.uk/documents/BaronyExhibitionPart1.pdf
www.sog.org.uk/
http://www.stgite.org.uk/media/jewishconverts.html

http://www.strictbaptisthistory.org.uk/
http://www.st-matthews.co.uk/history/
https://www.sutton-in-craven.org.uk/historyVavasour.asp
https://www.thoughtco.com/top-genealogy-magazines-for-family-history-1422150
www.timeanddate.com/
www.ukgenealogy.co.uk/
https://www.wikitree.com/wiki/Launder-48#Possible_origins
http://www.worldcat.org/identities/lccn-n85-99767/
http://www.workhouses.org.uk/Yeovil/
www.youtube.com/watch?v=lDkk4PAb5rA

B11: Other Information Sources

Grimshaw Atkinson John (1881) *Painting: Boar Lane,* Leeds Museums and Galleries (City Art Gallery)

Lewis, Louis (1813) *Land Tax Records for the Parish of Saint Giles, Cripplegate Without,* Barbican London

Mallinson A (2012) *Cowling Parish Council: Agenda for the Meeting to be Held on Monday 5th March 2012 at 7.00pm at Saint Andrews Church* Cowling Parish Council

Rogers Jane *Shirley* (2002) BBC Sunday, 13th July 2002 Radio 4

Routledge Patricia (2003 – Presenter) *In Search of the Brontës* (Sunday, 3rd & 10th August 2003) BBC1

The Great War, Episode 25: *The Iron Thrones Are Falling* (Published on YouTube Aug 31, 2012) first broadcast by the BBC (1964)

The Lang Collection *of Gretna Green Marriages Records* The Institute of Heraldic and Genealogical Studies, Canterbury

Unattributed (November 1865) *City of London Tower Hamlets Cemetery Daybook*

Unattributed (1861) *'Orders of Removal'* Bethnal Green Ref: BEBG/267/019

Unattributed (April 2002) *The Jewish Journey* BBC Radio 4

Various *Broadcasts* (2000) from the BBC History Zone on Family History

Various *Census Returns, Telephone Books, Trade Directories and maps of the Leeds area* kindly provided by the Local Studies Section of Leeds Central Library and Keighley Main Library

Various *Crockford Directories,* Published by Oxford University Publishers from 1947 until 1985,

Various *Leaflets, Guides and Short Histories,* provided by different local churches in the Headingley Locality

Various *Publicity Materials* provided by Leeds University.

Various *Unknown Informants* in Leeds, Sutton-in-Craven and Cross-Hills

Various (2004, 2006-2018) *Who Do You Think You Are? Series 1-15* Broadcast on BBC 1 (128 Episodes and 2 Specials)

B12: Acknowledgements

Special credit must be given to the following helpful <u>family</u> contacts: -

- My wife **June** for her tireless feedback, proofreading and editing.
- My late father **Fred Gordon Smith** who inspired this project.
- My late mother **Cynthia Mary Smith** who renewed this project
- My youngest son for his assistance in what was often tedious archive work.
- My brother and sister for the information and encouragement they gave.
- My first Cousin **Pamela Smith** whose faithful preservation of family tradition provided many decisive *'leads'*
- A long-lost female relative, **Ann Dalton** who whose brisk, no-nonsense, efficiency was an asset.
- The late **Tony Sterne** and his widow **Sally**
- The Granddaughter of **James Hastings Smith** and her family members
- A Granddaughter of **Irene Foster**
- My long-deceased Grand Parents **Fred Hesslewood** and **Marie Elizabeth Smith** for helping to make my father the man that he was.
- My long-deceased Great Grand Parents **Edmund** and **Rosamond Smith**.
- My long-deceased Great, Great Grand Parents **John** and **Ann Smith**
- **Edmunds** first wife **Helen** and her father **James Hastings**
- Three members of the **Stamford** family for providing useful information concerning **Edmund's** first two wives.
- Those members of **Myerson** family and their relatives who provided invaluable online information, especially on ancestry.com

Further credit must also be given to the following helpful <u>non-family</u> contacts: -

- **Pastor Rob Harris** of **South Craven Baptist Church** who was a model of helpful courtesy and ability to provide useful leads
- The late **Joshua Barratt** and his late wife for providing details of the business world in which my father worked
- A contact in **Leeds Parish Church**
- A contact in **Glusburn** who provided information about the old Corn Mill.
- A contact near **Keighley** who provided access to the old **Smith Mill.**
- A contact in **Cullingworth** who provided details about the local Chapel

- Diana Tottle of the **Cullingworth Family History Group**
- Peter Stamford, Canada
- Barbara Stamford-Plows
- Julie M. Skellern, New Zealand,
- Professor Michael Green
- The Vicar of Kildwick Saint Andrews
- The Proprietors of Selestial Limited, Skipton
- Miscellaneous contacts in **Todmorden**

The assistance of the following bodies in assisting to complete this work over the period of **1999-2019** is gratefully acknowledged: **Beverley** Library; **Bradford** City Archives; **Blenheim** Baptist Church, Leeds; **Burstall's** Solicitors & Commissioners for Oaths in Hull; **Chapeltown** Branch Library, Leeds; **City of Westminster Archive Centre,** Westminster London; **Colne** Library, Local History Section; **Cullingworth** Family History Group; **Dewsbury** Road Library, Leeds; **East Ridings** Records Office, Beverley; **East Yorkshire** Family History Society; **Elmwood** Care Home, Leeds; **Family** Records Centre, Islington, London; **General Register** Office, Southport, Merseyside; **Glasgow** City Archive; **Hornsea** Library, Harringay Park, London; **Hull City** Archives; **Hull City** Library, Local History Section; **Keighley** & District Family History Society; **Keighley** Library Local History Section; **Kew** Archive Centre; **Leeds** Archive Centre, for its permission to quote entries from the Cowper Street School Diary; **Leeds** Central Library Local and Family History Section; **Leeds** General Infirmary; **Leeds** Grammar School; **Leeds** Metropolitan University, School of Cultural Studies; **Leeds** Museums and Galleries – including The Abbey House Museum, Armley Industrial Museum, the Thackray Medical Museum and the City Art Gallery; **Leeds** University – The Brotherton, Laidlaw and Edmund Boyle Libraries and the School of Geography; **Manchester** Central Library,; **Manchester** Museum of Science and Industry, **Manx** Museum; **Mill** Archives; **Queens College,** Cambridge University Record Keeping Section; **Register** of *'Births, Marriages and Deaths'* at Beverley, Birmingham, Brighton & Hove, Burnley, Camden, Hull, Islington, Keighley, Leeds, Newcastle-upon-Tyne and Wandsworth; **Saint Mary's** Church, Lowgate, Hull; **Skipton** Library, Local History Section; **Skipton** Museum; **Strict** Baptist Historical Society; **South Craven** Baptist Church; **Tameside** Local Studies and Archives Unit; **The Barley Mow Pub** Westminster, London; **Tower Hamlets** Local History Library and Archive; **West Yorkshire** Archive Service Wakefield; **West Yorkshire** Baptist Association; **York** Probate Registry; **Yorkshire** Archaeological Society, Family History Section.

www.ingramcontent.com/pod-product-compliance
Lightning Source LLC
Chambersburg PA
CBHW060319100426

42812CB00003B/823